We live in troubled times. Since 2001, in the aftermath of Al Qaeda's attack on the Twin Towers and the Pentagon, the nation has spent years at war in far-away lands. At home, the collapse of a massive housing bubble has ignited a major financial crisis and threatened the security of millions of families. College students—even those who don't think much about America's past—have to ponder these events. How and why did they happen? Such questions are at the heart of historical inquiry. In *America: A Concise History,* we aspire to develop students' abilities to think historically and to explore the relationship between the past and the present. We try to ask the right questions—the big ones and the not-so-big ones—and then write history that illuminates the answers.

One of the intellectual pleasures of textbook writing is the opportunity, with each edition, to revisit our historical narrative and make it better. This time, we have embraced that task again with a particularly ambitious goal. We want to bring *America: A Concise History* into the twenty-first century. On the intellectual side, this goal has led us to give greater attention to cultural history, the subject of much exciting scholarship, and to rethink and recast our post-1945 chapters. On the pedagogical side, it has led us to a back-to-basics approach, by providing an array of learning tools that will engage and instruct today's students. But we have not departed from the core idea of previous editions: to write a concise narrative that retains the comprehensiveness and explanatory power of its parent textbook, *America's History,* and is immediately accessible to every student who enrolls in the U.S. survey course. The story, we hope, tells not only what happened, but also *how* and *why.*

In composing our narrative, we focus not only on the marvelous diversity of peoples who became American but also on the institutions—political, economic, cultural, and social—that forged a common national identity. And we present these experiences in an integrated way, using each historical perspective to make better sense of the others. In our discussion of government and politics, diplomacy and war, we show how they affected—and were affected by—ethnic groups and economic conditions, intellectual beliefs and social changes, and the religious and moral values of the times. Just as important, we place the American experience in a global context. We trace aspects of American society to their origins in European, African, and Asian cultures; consider American industrial and technological development within the framework of the world economy; and plot the foreign relations of the United States as part of an ever-shifting international system of imperial expansion, financial exchange, and diplomatic alliances. In emphasizing the global context, we want to remind students that other nations experienced developments similar to our own and that by a comparative analysis, students can discern what was distinctive and particular to the American experience.

Structure

To give shape and meaning to America's history, we have long divided our narrative into six parts, corresponding to what we understood to be the major phases of American development. Part Six, which carried the story from 1945 to the present, was distinctive in that it was, by definition, unfinished. However, as we move into the twenty-first century, it has become increasingly clear that we have entered a new phase of American history, and that the era that began in 1945 has ended. So now we include a fully realized Part Six, which we call "The Age of Cold War Liberalism, 1945–1980," and a new—an open-ended—Part Seven, which describes the advent of a conservative America in a post–Cold War world. Students who have grown up in this new age will find the times of their parents and grandparents treated as coherent narrative history in Part Six. In Part Seven, "A Divided Nation in a Disordered World, 1980–2008," they will discover an account of an era that is truly their own, carried to the present with a full chapter on the years since 2000.

Given the importance of the part structure in our account, we have taken pains to assist students to benefit fully from this organization. Each part begins with a four-page overview. First, a **thematic timeline** highlights the key developments in politics, the economy, society, culture, and foreign affairs that characterize the entire period; then we flesh out these themes in a corresponding **part essay**. Each part essay focuses on a crucial engine of historical change—primarily economic or cultural in some eras, political or diplomatic in others—that created new conditions of life and transformed social relations.

Within each chapter, we have appended *NEW* **focus questions** to each main section. And where students might stumble over unfamiliar or difficult terms, we provide a **glossary** that defines key concepts, which appear in bold type at their first mention. At the end of the chapter, we remind students of important events in a **chapter timeline** and reiterate the main themes in an **analytical summary**. We have also added a *NEW* feature, **Connections**, that enables students to take a longer view, to see how the chapter relates to prior and forthcoming chapters. Each chapter concludes with **For Further Exploration**, a brief bibliographical essay designed to encourage further reading in historical works and to use the World Wide Web to the best advantage. To assist instructors and advanced students, a **full bibliography** is available on the Web at **bedfordstmartins.com/henrettaconcise**.

Features: Back to Basics

We want to encourage students to experience the past through the words and perspective of those who lived it and, equally important, to learn how to extract meaning from historical evidence. Thus, each chapter contains two page-long primary sources— excerpts from letters, diaries, autobiographies, and public testimony—offering a

following these steps.

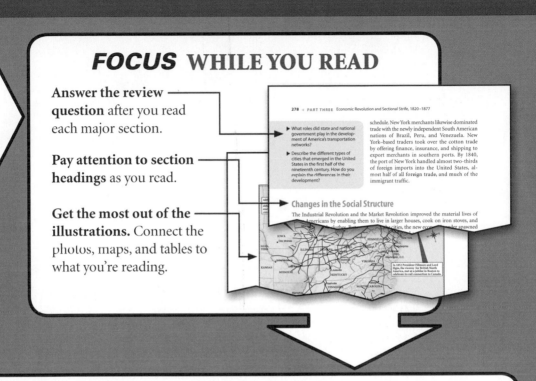

FOCUS WHILE YOU READ

Answer the review question after you read each major section.

Pay attention to section headings as you read.

Get the most out of the illustrations. Connect the photos, maps, and tables to what you're reading.

REVIEW AFTER YOU READ

Summarize and connect. Read the **Chapter Summary** to remind yourself of the major themes of the chapter, and review the **Connections** section to see the interrelationships among the chapters in the part.

Review the Timeline. Make sure you understand the relationships among events and their sequence.

America

A Concise History

FOURTH
EDITION

America

A Concise History

VOLUME 1: To 1877

James A. Henretta
University of Maryland

David Brody
University of California, Davis

Bedford / St. Martin's
Boston • New York

For Bedford / St. Martin's

Publisher for History: Mary Dougherty
Executive Editor for History: William J. Lombardo
Director of Development for History: Jane Knetzger
Developmental Editor: Danielle Slevens
Senior Production Editor: Lori Chong Roncka
Production Supervisor: Jennifer L. Peterson
Executive Marketing Manager: Jenna Bookin Barry
Editorial Assistants: Katherine Flynn and Robin Soule
Production Assistants: Lidia MacDonald-Carr and David Ayers
Text Design: Lisa Buckley
Copy Editor: Barbara Willette
Indexer: Leoni Z. McVey & Associates, Inc.
Photo Research: Pembroke Herbert and Sandi Rygiel / Picture Research Consultants & Archives
Cartography: Mapping Specialists, Ltd.
Cover Design: Billy Boardman
Cover Art: A group of escaped slaves that gathered on the former plantation of Confederate general
Thomas Drayton. After federal troops occupied the plantation, these former slaves began to
harvest and gin cotton for their own profit, c. 1862–1865, South Carolina, Confederate States of
America. © Corbis.
Composition: Aptara
Printing and Binding: RR Donnelley and Sons

President: Joan E. Feinberg
Editorial Director: Denise B. Wydra
Director of Marketing: Karen R. Soeltz
Director of Editing, Design, and Production: Marcia Cohen
Assistant Director of Editing, Design, and Production: Elise S. Kaiser
Managing Editor: Elizabeth M. Schaaf

Library of Congress Control Number: 2008925878

Manufactured in the United States of America.
4   3   2   1   0   9
f   e   d   c

For information, write: Bedford / St. Martin's, 75 Arlington Street, Boston, MA 02116 (617-399-4000)
ISBN-10: 0–312–48541–7 ISBN-13: 978–0–312–48541–2 (Combined Volume)
ISBN-10: 0–312–48542–5 ISBN-13: 978–0–312–48542–9 (Volume 1: To 1877)
ISBN-10: 0–312–48543–3 ISBN-13: 978–0–312–48543–6 (Volume 2: Since 1865)

firsthand view of an event or theme discussed in the chapter. Instructors will find these **American Voices** and **Voices from Abroad** to be a major resource for inducting beginning students into the processes of historical analysis. Each chapter now contains one American Voices and one Voices from Abroad, ensuring that students will understand how events were viewed both nationally and in a global context.

To enliven students' understanding of history, we have peppered the text with more than 150 **illustrations**, most of them in full-color and many new to this edition. We have also provided **informative captions** that set the illustrations in context. Keenly aware that today's students lack geographic literacy, we have included dozens of **maps** and cross-referenced them in the narrative text. Taken together, these documents, maps, and illustrations provide instructors with a trove of teaching materials and students with a chance to enter the life of the past.

Textual Changes

Of all the reasons for a new edition, of course, the most compelling is to improve the text itself. Good narrative history is primarily a product of good sentences and good paragraphs. So our labors have been mostly in the trenches, so to speak, in a line-by-line striving for the vividness and human presence that are the hallmarks of narrative history. We are also partisans of economical writing, believing that brevity is the best antidote to imprecise language and murky argument.

To enhance the narrative flow of our chapters, we have been especially attentive to chronology. That concern led us to reorder a significant amount of material. In Part Two (1776–1820), Chapters 6 and 7 now provide a continuous political narrative from the Declaration of Independence to the Era of Good Feelings. In Part Three (1820–1877), we have followed the suggestion of instructors and now discuss the pre–Civil War South in a single, integrated chapter. In Part Four (1877–1914), our chapter on Gilded Age politics has a better chronological flow and, because it now follows the chapter on the city, provides students with a seamless transition to the Progressive era.

Changes that are even more extensive appear in our treatment of the twentieth century. In Part Five (1914–1945), the three chapters on the 1920s, the Great Depression, and the New Deal have been melded into two crisper, more integrated chapters. All of the chapters in Part Six (1945–1980) and the new Part Seven (1980–2008) have been thoroughly reworked as part of our rethinking of the post-1945 era. In Chapters 26 and 27, we now offer thematic treatments of the 1950s, while Chapters 28 and 29 provide a coherent narrative account of liberalism's triumph under Kennedy and Johnson and its dramatic decline after 1968. Part Seven represents much-expanded coverage of the post-1980 years, with new chapters devoted to social and economic developments and America since 2000. Altogether, these organizational changes represent the biggest shake-up of *America: A Concise History* since its inception.

The revising process also affords us a welcome opportunity to incorporate fresh scholarship. In Part One, we have added new material on African life, the slave trade, and African American ethnicity and have boosted our discussion of the Scots-Irish and the Germans. In Chapter 11, we have added a new section on urban popular culture (masculinity, sexuality, minstrel shows, and racism) drawing on recent advances in cultural history. Inventive scholarship in cultural history also informs Chapter 18 (on the late-nineteenth-century city) and several twentieth-century chapters, including, in Chapter 27, our treatment of consumer culture in the 1950s. Chapter 16 contains fresh information about the impact of farming on the ecosystem of the Great Plains. Chapter 20 incorporates recent insights into the middle-class impulse behind progressivism and underlines the industrial strife that reoriented progressivism toward issues of labor relations. Of the many revisions in the post-1945 chapters, perhaps the most notable derive from the opening of Soviet archives, which allowed us to see the Cold War from the other side of the Iron Curtain and to amend our assessment of the impact of Communism on American life. In addition, Part Six contains fresh material on the civil rights movement, the Vietnam War, and the revival of American conservatism. Even richer are the additions to Part Seven, especially in the treatment of social movements and the information technology revolution in Chapter 31 and, in Chapter 32, an up-to-date and stimulating discussion of events since 2000.

Supplements

Readers of *America: A Concise History* often cite its ancillary package as a key to the book's success in the classroom. These ancillaries provide a flexible yet targeted collection of resources for instructors and a helpful set of study tools for students.

FOR STUDENTS
Print Resources

Documents to Accompany* America's History, *Sixth Edition. Edited by Melvin Yazawa (University of New Mexico) and Kevin Fernlund (University of Missouri, St. Louis) and easily assigned with the concise edition, this primary-source reader offers a chorus of voices from the past to enrich the study of U.S. history. Both celebrated figures and ordinary people, from Frederick Douglass to mill workers, demonstrate the diversity of America's history while putting a human face on historical experience. A wealth of speeches, petitions, advertisements, and posters paint a vivid picture of the social and political life of the time, lending depth and breadth to the textbook discussion. Brief introductions set each document in context, while questions for analysis help link the individual source to larger historical themes. Available free when packaged with the text and now available as an e-book (see next page).

Maps in Context: A Workbook for American History. Written by historical cartography expert Gerald A. Danzer (University of Illinois, Chicago), this skill-building workbook helps students comprehend essential connections between geographic literacy and historical understanding. Organized to correspond to the typical U.S. history survey course, *Maps in Context* presents a wealth of map-centered projects and convenient pop quizzes that give students hands-on experience working with maps. Available free when packaged with the text.

NEW Trade Books. Titles published by sister companies Farrar, Straus and Giroux; Henry Holt and Company; Hill and Wang; Picador; St. Martin's Press; and Palgrave Macmillan are available at a 50 percent discount when packaged with Bedford/St. Martin's textbooks. For more information, visit **bedfordstmartins.com/tradeup**.

NEW *The Bedford Glossary for U.S. History.* This handy supplement for the survey course gives students clear, concise definitions of the political, economic, social, and cultural terms used by historians and contemporary media alike. The terms are historically contextualized to aid comprehension. Available free when packaged with the text.

U.S. History Matters: A Student Guide to U.S. History Online, **Second Edition.** This resource, written by Alan Gevinson, Kelly Schrum, and Roy Rosenzweig (all of George Mason University), provides an illustrated and annotated guide to 250 of the most useful Web sites for student research in U.S. history as well as advice on evaluating and using Internet sources. This essential guide is based on the acclaimed "History Matters" Web site developed by the American Social History Project and the Center for History and New Media. Available free when packaged with the text.

Bedford Series in History and Culture. Over 100 titles in this highly praised series combine first-rate scholarship, historical narrative, and important primary documents for undergraduate courses. Each book is brief, inexpensive, and focused on a specific topic or period. Package discounts are available.

Historians at Work Series. Brief enough for a single assignment yet meaty enough to provoke thoughtful discussion, each volume in this series examines a single historical question by combining unabridged selections by distinguished historians, each with a different perspective on the issue, with helpful learning aids. Package discounts are available.

NEW *Rand McNally Atlas of American History.* This collection of over 80 full-color maps illustrates key events and eras, from early exploration and settlement, expansion and immigration, to U.S. involvement in wars abroad and on American soil. Introductory pages for each section include brief overviews, timelines, graphs, and photos to quickly establish a historical context. Available for $3 when packaged with the text.

New Media Resources

NEW *America: A Concise History e-Book.* This easy-to-use, dynamic, highly searchable e-book integrates the narrative, maps, and images from *America: A Concise History* with resources from the Online Study Guide, making it the ideal study tool. Instructors can easily add documents, images, and other materials to customize the text, making this e-book perfect for instructors who wish to use electronic texts and documents or build dynamic online courses. Can be packaged *FREE* with the print text or purchased as a stand-alone item at a discount.

NEW *E-Documents to Accompany* America's History, *Sixth Edition.* The most robust gathering of primary sources to accompany any U.S. history survey text is now available online. *E-Documents to Accompany* America's History, *Sixth Edition,* is easily assigned with the concise text and allows instructors to add an electronic dimension to their classes or integrate electronic documents into their online courses.

Online Study Guide at bedfordstmartins.com/henrettaconcise. The popular Online Study Guide for *America: A Concise History* is a free learning tool to help students master the themes and information presented in the textbook and improve their critical thinking skills. Assessment quizzes help students to evaluate their comprehension, and a wide range of further quizzing, map, and primary document analysis activities provide them with the opportunity for further study. Instructors can monitor students' progress through the online Quiz Gradebook or receive e-mail updates.

NEW Audio Reviews for *America: A Concise History,* Fourth Edition, at bedfordstmartins.com/henrettaconcise. Audio Reviews are a new tool that fits easily into students' lifestyles and provides a practical new way for them to study on the move. These 25- to 30-minute summaries of each chapter in *America: A Concise History* highlight the major themes of the text and help reinforce student learning.

Online Bibliography at bedfordstmartins.com/henrettaconcise. Organized by book chapter and topic, the online bibliography provides an authoritative and comprehensive list of references to jump-start student research.

Jules R. Benjamin's A Student's Online Guide to History Reference Sources at bedfordstmartins.com/henrettaconcise. This Web site provides links to history-related databases, indexes, and journals, plus contact information for state, provincial, local, and professional history organizations.

The Bedford Bibliographer at bedfordstmartins.com/henrettaconcise. *The Bedford Bibliographer,* a simple but powerful Web-based tool, assists students with the process of collecting sources and generates bibliographies in four commonly used documentation styles.

The Bedford Research Room at bedfordstmartins.com/henrettaconcise. The Research Room, drawn from Mike Palmquist's *The Bedford Researcher,* offers a wealth of resources—including interactive tutorials, research activities, student writing samples, and links to hundreds of other places online—to support students in courses across the disciplines. The site also offers instructors a library of helpful instructional tools.

Diana Hacker's Research and Documentation Online at bedfordstmartins.com/henrettaconcise. This Web site provides clear advice on how to integrate primary and secondary sources into research papers, how to cite sources correctly, and how to format in MLA, APA, *Chicago,* or CBE style.

The St. Martin's Tutorial on Avoiding Plagiarism at bedfordstmartins.com/ henrettaconcise. This online tutorial reviews the consequences of plagiarism and explains what sources to acknowledge, how to keep good notes, how to organize research, and how to integrate sources appropriately. The tutorial includes exercises to help students practice integrating sources and recognize acceptable summaries.

Critical Thinking Modules at bedfordstmartins.com/henrettaconcise. This Web site offers over two dozen online modules for interpreting maps, audio, visual, and textual sources, centered on events covered in the U.S. history survey.

FOR INSTRUCTORS
Print Resources
Instructor's Resource Manual. Written by Jason Newman (Cosumnes River College, Los Rios Community College District), this popular manual provides both first-time and experienced instructors with valuable teaching tools—annotated chapter outlines, lecture strategies, in-class activities, discussion questions, suggested writing assignments, and related readings and media—to structure and customize their American history course. The new edition includes new Classroom Activities and Oral History Exercises, lists of key terms, and model answers to both the questions in the book and the Chapter Writing Assignments. The manual also offers a convenient, chapter-by-chapter guide to the wealth of supplementary materials available to instructors teaching with *America: A Concise History.* Available on the Book Companion Site at **bedfordstmartins.com/henrettaconcise.**

Transparencies. This set of full-color acetate transparencies includes all full-size maps and many other images from the parent textbook, *America's History,* to help instructors present lectures and teach students vital map-reading skills. A guide correlating all of the maps and art to the concise edition is available on the book companion site.

New Media Resources
NEW HistoryClass. Bedford/St. Martin's online learning space for history gives you the right tools and the rich content to create your course, your way. An interactive e-book and e-reader enable you to easily assign relevant textbook sections and primary documents. Additional primary sources supplement the textbook and reader selections and provide more options for class discussion and assignments. Other resources include guidelines for analyzing primary materials, avoiding plagiarism, and citing sources. Access to the acclaimed content library, Make History, provides unlimited access to thousands of maps, images, documents, and Web links. The tried-and-true content of the Online Study Guide offers a range of activities to help students access their progress, study more effectively, and improve their critical thinking skills. Customize provided content and mix in your own with ease—everything in History-Class is integrated to work together in the same space.

Instructor's Resource CD-ROM. This disc provides instructors with ready-made and customizable PowerPoint multimedia presentations built around chapter outlines, maps, figures, and selected images from the textbook plus jpeg versions of all maps, figures, and selected images. Also included are chapter questions formatted in Power-Point for use with i>clicker, a classroom response system.

Computerized Test Bank. A fully updated test bank CD-ROM offers over 80 exercises for each chapter, allowing instructors to pick and choose from a collection of multiple-choice, fill-in, map, and short and long essay questions. Every question includes a textbook page number for easy reference. Correct answers and model essay responses are included for easy grading and the creation of answer keys. Both questions and answers can be easily edited by the instructor for maximum customizability.

Book Companion Site at bedfordstmartins.com/henrettaconcise. This companion Web site gathers all the electronic resources for the text, including the Online Study Guide and related Quiz Gradebook, at a single Web address. Convenient links to lecture, assignment, and research materials, such as PowerPoint chapter outlines and the digital libraries at Make History, are also available from this site.

NEW Make History at bedfordstmartins.com/henrettaconcise. Comprising the content of our five acclaimed online libraries—Map Central, the Bedford History Image Library, DocLinks, HistoryLinks, and PlaceLinks—Make History provides one-stop access to relevant digital content including maps, images, documents, and Web links. Students and instructors alike can search this free, easy-to-use database by key word, topic, date, or specific chapter of *America: A Concise History* and can download the content they find. Instructors can also create entire collections of content and store them online for later use or post their collections to the Web to share with students.

Content for Course Management Systems. A variety of student and instructor resources developed for this textbook are ready for use in course management systems such as WebCT, Blackboard, and other platforms. This e-content includes nearly all of the offerings from the book's Online Study Guide as well as the book's test bank.

Videos and Multimedia. A wide assortment of videos and multimedia CD-ROMs on various topics in American history is available to qualified adopters.

Acknowledgments

We are very grateful to the following scholars and teachers who reported on their thoughts about and experiences with the Third Edition. Their comments often challenged us to rethink or justify our interpretations and always provided a check on accuracy down to the smallest detail. Thanks are due to: Rod Andrew Jr., Clemson University; Miles L. Bradbury, University of Maryland; Paul Buelow, Indiana University–Purdue University Indianapolis; B. R. Burg, Arizona State University; James Carroll, Iona College; Sharon A. Roger Hepburn, Radford University; Pamela Hronek, Arkansas State University; Kara L. Lawson, Hillsborough Community College; Scott Lingenfelter, Roosevelt University; Delores McBroome, Humboldt State University;

Marianne F. McKnight, Salt Lake Community College; David M. Parker, California State University, Northridge; Jon E. Purmont, Southern Connecticut State University; David Rayson, Normandale Community College; Stephen Russell, Northern Essex Community College; Robert M. Sandow, Lock Haven University of Pennsylvania; Shawn Selby, Ohio University; Michael David Tegeder, Santa Fe Community College.

As the authors of *America: A Concise History,* we know better than anyone how much this Fourth Edition is the work of other hands and minds. In that regard, we are grateful to Lynn Dumenil, our fellow author through the first three editions, for laying the foundation for our treatment of the twentieth century. We also want to thank Mary Dougherty, William Lombardo, and Jane Knetzger, who oversaw the Fourth Edition, and Danielle Slevens, who used her critical skills to improve our text. As usual, Joan E. Feinberg has been generous in providing the resources needed to produce a handsome volume. Lori Chong Roncka expertly guided our book through the production process; Donna Dennison, Billy Boardman, and Rose Corbett Gordon provided the research and design for our covers; and Karen Soeltz and Jenna Bookin Barry used their superb marketing skills to help this book reach the classroom. We also thank the rest of our editorial and production team for their dedicated efforts: Katherine Flynn, Alix Roy, Adrianne Hiltz, Lidia MacDonald-Carr, and David Ayers; Pembroke Herbert and Sandi Rygiel at Picture Research Consultants and Archives; and Sandy Schechter. Finally, we want to express our appreciation for the invaluable assistance of Patricia Deveneau, whose work contributed in many ways to the intellectual vitality of this new edition of *America: A Concise History.*

James A. Henretta
David Brody

Brief Contents

Contents

CHAPTER 4
Growth and Crisis in Colonial Society, 1720–1765   96

CHAPTER 8

Creating a Republican Culture, 1790–1820   225

CHAPTER 11
Religion and Reform, 1820–1860   319

CHAPTER 14
Two Societies at War, 1861–1865 407

List of Maps

About the Authors

JAMES A. HENRETTA is Priscilla Alden Burke Professor of American History at the University of Maryland, College Park. Among other books, he has published *Evolution and Revolution: American Society, 1600–1820*; *The Origins of American Capitalism*; and an edited volume, *Republicanism and Liberalism in America and the German States, 1750–1850*. His most recent publications include "Charles Evans Hughes and the Strange Death of Liberal America" (*Law and History Review*, 2006), derived from his ongoing research on the liberal state in New York, 1820–1975, and "Magistrates, Lawyers, Legislators: The Three Legal Systems of Early America," in the *Cambridge History of American Law* (2008).

DAVID BRODY is Professor Emeritus of History at the University of California, Davis. He is the author, among other books, of *Steelworkers in America*; *Workers in Industrial America: Essays on the 20th Century Struggle*; *In Labor's Cause: Main Themes on the History of the American Worker*; and, most recently, *Labor Embattled: History, Power, Rights*. His current research is on labor law and workplace regimes during the Great Depression.

America
A Concise History

VOLUME 1: To 1877

The Creation of American Society

PART ONE

1450–1763

ECONOMY	SOCIETY	GOVERNMENT
From staple crops to internal growth	**Ethnic, racial, and class divisions**	**From monarchy to republic**
1450 ▸ Native American subsistence economy ▸ Europeans fish off North American coast	▸ Sporadic warfare among Indian peoples ▸ Spanish conquest of Mexico and Peru (1519–1535)	▸ Rise of monarchical nation-states in Europe
1600 ▸ First staple export crops: furs and tobacco	▸ English-Indian wars ▸ African servitude begins in Virginia (1619)	▸ James I claims divine right to rule England ▸ Virginia House of Burgesses (1619)
1640 ▸ South Atlantic System emerges: ▸ Mercantilist regulation: first Navigation Act (1651)	▸ White indentured servitude shapes Chesapeake society ▸ Indians retreat inland; Africans lose rights (1670s)	▸ English Puritan Revolution ▸ Stuart restoration (1660) ▸ Bacon's Rebellion in Virginia (1675)
1680 ▸ Tobacco trade stagnates ▸ Rice cultivation expands in South Carolina after 1700	▸ Indian slavery expands in the Carolinas ▸ Ethnic Dutch rebellion in New York (1689)	▸ Dominion of New England (1686–1689) ▸ Glorious Revolution ousts James II (1688–1689)
1720 ▸ Mature yeoman farm economy in North ▸ 1740s: Imports from Britain increase	▸ Major Scots-Irish and German migration ▸ Growing inequality in rural and urban areas	▸ Rise of the colonial representative assemblies ▸ Era of salutary neglect in colonial administration
1760 ▸ End of British military aid sparks postwar recession	▸ Uprisings by tenants and backcountry farmers	▸ Britain vanquishes France in "Great War for Empire" (1756–1763)

RELIGION	CULTURE
From hierarchy to pluralism	**The creation of American identity**
▶ Protestant Reformation begins (1517) and sparks century of religious warfare	▶ Diverse Native American cultures in eastern woodlands
▶ Persecuted English Puritans and Catholics migrate to America	▶ Puritans implant Calvinism, education, and freehold ideal
▶ Puritans in Massachusetts Bay quash "heresy" ▶ Religious liberty in Rhode Island	▶ Aristocratic aspirations in Chesapeake region
▶ Rise of tolerance among colonial Protestants ▶ Wars with Catholic France in Europe and America	▶ Emergence of African American language and culture
▶ German and Scots-Irish Pietists in Middle Atlantic region ▶ Great Awakening (1740s)	▶ Expansion of colleges, newspapers, and magazines ▶ Franklin and the American Enlightenment
▶ Rise of Evangelical Baptists in Virginia	▶ First signs of a distinct American identity within the Atlantic world

Historians know that societies evolve through decades, even centuries, of human endeavor and experience. Historians also know that the first Americans were hunters and gatherers who migrated to the Western Hemisphere from Asia. Over many generations, these migrants—the Native Americans—came to live in many different environments and cultures. In much of North America, they developed kinship-based societies that relied on farming and hunting. But in the lower Mississippi River Valley around A.D. 900, Native Americans fashioned a hierarchical social order similar to those of the great civilizations of the Aztecs, Mayas, and Incas.

In Part One, we describe how Europeans, with their steel weapons, attractive trade goods, and diseases, shredded the fabric of most Native American cultures. Throughout the Western Hemisphere, men and women of European origin—the Spanish in Mesoamerica and South America, the French in Canada, the English along the Atlantic coast—gradually achieved domination over the native peoples.

Our story focuses on the Europeans who settled in the English mainland colonies.

They expected to transplant their traditional societies, cultures, and religious beliefs in the soil of the New World. But things did not work out exactly as planned. In learning to live in the new land, English, Germans, and Scots-Irish created societies that differed from those of their homelands in their economies, social character, political systems, religions, and cultures. Here, in brief, is the story of that transformation as we explain it in Part One.

ECONOMY

Many European settlements were great economic successes. Europe at the time consisted of poor, overcrowded, and unequal societies that periodically suffered devastating famines. But with few people and a bountiful natural environment, the settlers in North America created a bustling economy. In the northern mainland colonies, communities of independent farm families in rural areas and merchants and artisans in port towns and cities prospered in what British and German migrants called "the best poor man's country."

SOCIETY

Simultaneously, some European settlements became places of oppressive captivity for Africans, with profound consequences for America's social development. As the supply of white indentured servants from Europe dwindled after 1680, planters in the Chesapeake region imported enslaved African workers to grow tobacco. Wealthy British and French planters in the West Indies bought hundreds of thousands of slaves from African traders and rulers and forced them to labor on sugar plantations. Slowly and with great effort, the slaves and their descendants created a variety of African American cultures within the European-dominated societies in which they lived.

GOVERNMENT

The first English migrants transplanted authoritarian institutions to America, and the home government intervened frequently in their affairs. But after the Glorious Revolution of 1688, white settlers in the English mainland colonies devised an increasingly free and competitive political system. Thereafter, local governments and representative assemblies became more powerful and created a tradition of self-rule that would spark demands for political independence from Britain after the Great War for Empire ended in 1763.

RELIGION

The American experience profoundly changed religious institutions and values. Many migrants fled from Europe because of conflicts among rival Christian churches and persecution by government officials. For the most part, they practiced their religions in America without interference. Religion became more prominent in colonial life after the evangelical revivals of the 1740s, and the churches became less dogmatic. Americans increasingly rejected the harshest tenets of Calvinism (a strict version of Protestantism), and a significant minority of educated colonists embraced the rationalism of the European Enlightenment. As a result, American Protestant Christianity became increasingly tolerant, democratic, and optimistic.

CULTURE

New forms of family and community life arose in the new American society. The first English settlers lived in patriarchal families ruled by dominant fathers and in communities controlled by men of high status. However, by 1750, many American fathers no longer strictly managed their children's lives, and because of widespread property ownership, many men and some women enjoyed personal independence. American society was increasingly pluralistic, composed of migrants from many European ethnic groups—English, Scots, Scots-Irish, Dutch, and Germans—as well as enslaved Africans and Native American peoples. Distinct regional cultures developed in New England, the Middle Atlantic colonies, the Chesapeake, and the Carolinas. Consequently, an overarching American identity based on the English language, English legal and political institutions, and shared experiences emerged very slowly.

The story of the colonial experience is both depressing and uplifting. Europeans and their diseases destroyed many Native American peoples, and European planters held tens of thousands of Africans in bondage. However, white migrants enjoyed unprecedented opportunities for economic security, political freedom, and spiritual fulfillment. This dual experience—of black bondage and white freedom—would continue far into the American future.

The Emergence of an Atlantic World: Europe, Africa, and America

1450–1620

Soon there will come from the rising sun a different kind of man from any you have yet seen. . . . [After that,] the world will fall to pieces.

— A Spokane Indian prophet

"**B**efore the French came among us," an elder of the Natchez people of Mississippi explained, "we were men . . . and we walked with boldness every road, but now we walk like slaves, which we shall soon be, since the French already treat us . . . as they do their black slaves." Before the 1490s, the Natchez and the other native peoples of the Western Hemisphere knew nothing about the light-skinned inhabitants of Europe and the dark-complexioned peoples of Africa. But when Christopher Columbus, a European searching for a sea route to Asia, encountered the peoples of the Western Hemisphere in 1492, the destinies of four continents quickly became intertwined. In 1502, Spanish settlers brought enslaved Africans to the Caribbean, initiating the centuries-long trade that would produce an African diaspora and many triracial societies in the Americas.

As the Natchez elder knew well, the resulting assemblage of peoples was based on exploitation, not equality. By the time he urged resistance against the alien intruders, the French were too numerous and strong. With the help of Indian allies, they savagely killed hundreds of Natchez and sold the survivors into slavery on the sugar plantations of the West Indies. The fate of the Natchez was not unique. In the three centuries following Columbus's voyage, many Native American peoples came under the domination of the Spanish, Portuguese, French, English, and Dutch, who seized their lands and often worked them with enslaved Africans.

How did this happen? How did Europeans become leaders in world trade and create an economically integrated Atlantic World? What made Native Americans vulnerable to conquest by European adventurers? And what led to the transatlantic trade in African slaves? In the answers to these questions lie the origins of the United States.

Native American Societies

When the Europeans arrived, most Native Americans—about forty million—lived in Mesoamerica (present-day Mexico and Guatemala) and along the western coast of South America (present-day Peru); another seven million resided in lands to the north, in what is now the United States and Canada. Native peoples in the north mostly lived in simple hunter-gatherer or agricultural communities governed by kin ties. But those in Mesoamerica and Peru resided in societies ruled by warrior-kings and priests, creating civilizations whose art, religion, society, and economy were as complex as those of Europe and the Mediterranean.

The First Americans

According to the Navajos, history began when their ancestors emerged from under the earth. For the Iroquois, the story of their Five Nations started when people fell from the sky. Most twenty-first-century anthropologists and historians believe that the first inhabitants of the Western Hemisphere were migrants from Asia. Strong archeological and genetic evidence suggests that in the last Ice Age, which began about 20,000 years ago, small bands of tribal hunters followed herds of game across a 100-mile-wide land bridge between Siberia and Alaska. An oral history of the Tuscarora Indians, who settled in present-day North Carolina, tells of a famine in the old world and a journey over ice toward where "the sun rises," a trek that brought their ancestors to a lush forest with abundant food and game.

Most anthropologists believe that the main migratory stream from Asia lasted from about 15,000 to 9,000 years ago. Then the glaciers melted, and the rising ocean waters submerged the land bridge and created the Bering Strait (Map 1.1). Around 8,000 years ago, a second movement of peoples, now traveling by water across the narrow strait, brought the ancestors of the Navajos and the Apaches to North America. The forebears of the Aleut and Inuit peoples, the "Eskimos," came in a third migration around 5,000 years ago. Then, for 300 generations, the peoples of the Western Hemisphere were largely cut off from the rest of the world.

For centuries, the first Americans lived as hunter-gatherers, subsisting on the abundant wildlife and vegetation. As the larger species of animals—mammoths, giant beavers, and horses—died out because of overhunting and climate change, hunters became adept at killing more elusive game: rabbits, deer, and elk. By about 6000 B.C., some Native American peoples in present-day Mexico and Peru were raising domesticated crops. They gradually bred maize into an extremely nutritious plant that had a higher yield per acre than did wheat, barley, or rye, the staple cereals of Europe. They also learned to plant beans and squash with the maize, a mix of crops that provided a nourishing diet and kept the soil fertile. The resulting agricultural surplus encouraged population growth and eventually laid the economic foundation for wealthy, urban societies in Mexico, Peru, and the Mississippi River Valley.

The Mayas and the Aztecs

The flowering of civilization in Mesoamerica began around 700 B.C. among the Olmec people, who lived along the Gulf of Mexico. Subsequently, the Mayas of the Yucatán Peninsula of Mexico and the neighboring rain forests of Guatemala built large urban

Using a global projection, the cartographer has placed North America in the center of the map, but parts of four other continents appear.

Evidence indicates that peoples came from Asia to the Americas during the Ice Age, when the sea level was much lower than today and a large land bridge—labeled Beringia on the map—connected the continents.

As scholars learn more about the advances and retreats of the ice sheets, the camping sites of the migrating peoples, and changes in vegetation zones, a more complete picture of the peopling of the Americas will emerge.

Current scholarship holds that the migrating peoples initially traveled on a narrow strip of ice-free land along the Pacific coast. As the area between the Cordilleran and Laurentide ice sheets lost its cover of ice, probably between 14,000 and 12,000 B.C., migrants may also have used the inland routes from present-day Alaska to the American interior.

Many groups, accustomed to living at the ocean's edge, probably continued along this route, pushing ever southward into South America.

25,000–12,000 B.C. Land bridge open

Migration Routes into America, c. 16,000–10,000 B.C.

☐ Ice sheets, c. 16,000 B.C.
☐ Ice sheets, c. 12,000 B.C.

Vegetation zones:

▪ Tundra
▪ Conifer forest
☐ Deciduous forest
▪ Prairie
▪ Desert
◀— Migration route

(after Tanner)

0   500   1,000 miles
0   500   1,000 kilometers

MAP 1.1 The Ice Age and the Settling of the Americas

Some 16,000 years ago, a sheet of ice covered much of Europe and North America. Using a broad bridge of land connecting Siberia and Alaska, hunting peoples from Asia migrated to North America in search of woolly mammoths and other large game animals and ice-free habitats. By 10,000 B.C., the descendants of these migrant peoples had moved south to present-day Florida and central Mexico. In time, these peoples would settle the entire vast continents of South and North America.

centers that relied on elaborate systems of water storage and irrigation. By A.D. 300, more than 20,000 people were living in the Mayan city of Tikal [*TEE-kall*]. Most were farmers, whose labor built the city's huge stone temples. An elite class claiming descent from the gods ruled Mayan society and lived in splendor on goods and taxes extracted from peasant families. Drawing on the religious and artistic traditions of the Olmecs,

Mayan artisans decorated temples and palaces with depictions of jaguars, warrior-gods, and religious images. Mayan astronomers created a calendar that recorded historical events and accurately predicted eclipses of the sun and the moon. Mayan scholars developed hieroglyphic writing to record royal lineages and wars. These skills in calculation and writing enhanced the authority of the ruling class of warriors and priests and provided the Mayans with a sense of history and identity. By facilitating the movement of goods and ideas, they also increased the prosperity of Mayan society and the complexity of its culture.

Beginning around 800, Mayan civilization went into decline. Evidence suggests that a two-century-long drought led to an economic crisis and prompted overtaxed peasants to desert the temple cities and retreat to the countryside. By 900, many religious centers had been abandoned. The few intact Mayan city-states would vigorously resist the Spanish invaders in the 1520s.

A second major Mesoamerican civilization developed in the highlands of Mexico around the city of Teotihuacán [*tee-o-ti-hue-KON*], with its magnificent Pyramid of the Sun. At its zenith, about A.D. 500, Teotihuacán had more than one hundred temples, some 4,000 apartment buildings, and a population of at least 100,000. By 800, the city was in decline, the victim of long-term drought and recurrent invasions by seminomadic warrior peoples. Eventually, one of these invading peoples, the Aztecs, established an even more extensive empire.

The Aztecs settled on an island in Lake Texcoco in the great central valley of Mexico. There, in 1325, they began to build a new city, Tenochtitlán [*ten-och-tit-LAN*], Mexico City today. The Aztecs mastered the complex irrigation systems and written language of the resident peoples and established an elaborate culture with a hierarchical social order. Priests and warrior-nobles ruled over twenty **clans** of free Aztec commoners who farmed communal land. The nobles also used huge numbers of non-Aztec slaves and serfs to labor on their private estates.

An aggressive people, the Aztecs soon subjugated most of central Mexico. Their rulers demanded both economic and human tribute from scores of subject peoples, and their priests brutally sacrificed untold thousands of men and women to ensure fertile fields and the daily return of the sun.

Aztec merchants forged trading routes that crisscrossed the empire and imported furs, gold, textiles, food, and obsidian from as far north as the Rio Grande and as far south as present-day Panama. By 1500, Tenochtitlán was a metropolis, with magnificent palaces and temples and more than 200,000 inhabitants—making it far larger than most European cities. The splendor of the city and its elaborate crafts dazzled Spanish soldiers. "These great towns and pyramids and buildings arising from the water, all made of stone, seemed like an enchanted vision," marveled one Spaniard. The Aztecs' strong institutions, military power, and wealth posed a formidable challenge to any adversary, at home or from afar.

The Indians of the North

The Indian societies north of the Rio Grande were less complex and less coercive than those to the south. They lacked occupational diversity, social hierarchy, and strong state institutions. Most northern peoples lived in self-governing tribes made up of clans, groups of related families that traced their lineage to a real or legendary common ancestor. These tribal communities were self-centered; anyone outside the narrow boundaries of kin was alien. Tellingly, their names for themselves—Innu, Lenape, and dozens of others—mean "human beings" or "real people." Clan elders and village chiefs set war policy, conducted ceremonies, and resolved personal feuds. They also enforced customs such as a ban on marriage between clan members. But elders and chiefs did not form a distinct and powerful ruling class; instead, they used personal authority within the kinship system to win acceptance of their policies.

The culture of these lineage-based societies did not encourage the accumulation of material goods. Individual ownership of land was virtually unknown. As a French missionary among the Iroquois noted, they "possess hardly anything except in common." The elders would urge members to share food and other scarce goods, fostering an ethic of reciprocity rather than one of accumulation. "You are covetous, and neither generous nor kind," the Micmac Indians of Nova Scotia told acquisitive French fur traders in the late 1600s. "As for us, if we have a morsel of bread, we share it with our neighbor."

Over the centuries, some Indian peoples became adept in trade or conquest. By A.D. 100, the vigorous Hopewell people of present-day Ohio had increased their food supply by domesticating plants, organized themselves in large villages, and set up a trading network that stretched from present-day Louisiana to Wisconsin. They imported obsidian from the Yellowstone region of the Rocky Mountains, copper from the Great Lakes, and pottery and marine shells from the Gulf of Mexico. The Hopewells built large burial mounds with extensive earthworks that still survive, and skilled Hopewell artisans fashioned striking ornaments to bury with the dead. For unknown reasons, the Hopewells' elaborate trading network collapsed around 400.

Another complex culture developed among the Pueblo peoples of the Southwest: the Hohokams, Mogollons, and Anasazis. By A.D. 600, Hohokam [ho-HO-kam] people in the high country of present-day Arizona and New Mexico were using irrigation to grow two crops a year, fashioning fine pottery with red-on-buff designs, and worshipping their gods on platform mounds; by 1000, they were living in elaborate multiroom stone or mud-brick structures called **pueblos**. To the east, in the Mimbres Valley of present-day New Mexico, the Mogollon [mo-gee-YON] people developed a distinctive black-on-white pottery. And by A.D. 900, to the north, the Anasazi people had become master architects. They built residential-ceremonial villages in steep cliffs, a pueblo in Chaco Canyon that housed 1,000 people, and 400 miles of straight roads. But the culture of the Pueblo peoples gradually collapsed after 1150 as soil exhaustion and extended droughts disrupted maize production, and they abandoned Chaco Canyon and other communities. The descendants of these peoples—including the Acomas, Zunis, and Hopis—later built strong but smaller village societies better suited to the dry and unpredictable climate of the American Southwest.

The last large-scale culture to emerge north of the Rio Grande was the Mississippian. By about A.D. 800, the farming technology of Mesoamerica had reached the

Mississippi River Valley, perhaps carried by Mayan refugees from the war-torn Yucatán Peninsula. By planting new strains of maize and beans, the Mississippian peoples produced an agricultural surplus. They then built small, fortified temple cities, where a robust culture developed. By 1150, the largest city, Cahokia [*ka-HO-kee-ah*], near present-day St. Louis, boasted a population of 15,000 to 20,000 and more than one hundred temple mounds, one of them as large as the great Egyptian pyramids. As in Mesoamerica, the tribute paid by peasant farmers supported a privileged class of nobles and priests who waged war against neighboring chiefdoms, patronized artisans, and claimed descent from the Sun God.

By 1350, the Mississippian civilization was in rapid decline. The large population had overburdened the environment, depleting nearby forests and herds of deer. The Indians died from tuberculosis and other urban diseases. Still, Mississippian institutions and practices endured for centuries. When Spanish conquistador Hernán de Soto invaded the region in the 1540s, he found the Apalachee [*ap-a-LA-chee*] and Timucua [*TEE-moo-KOO-wa*] Indians living in permanent settlements under the command of powerful chiefs. "If you desire to see me, come where I am," a chief told de Soto, "neither for you, nor for any man, will I set back one foot." A century and a half later, French traders and priests found the Natchez people rigidly divided among hereditary chiefs, nobles and honored people, and a bottom class of peasants. "Their chiefs possess all authority and distribute their favors and presents at will," a Frenchman noted. Undoubtedly influenced by Mesoamerican rituals, the Natchez marked the death of a chief by sacrificing his wives and burying their remains in a ceremonial mound (see Voices from Abroad, p. 13).

The cultures of the native peoples of eastern North America were diverse. Like the Natchez, the Creeks, Choctaws, and Chickasaws who lived in present-day Alabama and Mississippi had once been organized in powerful chiefdoms. However, the European epidemic diseases introduced by de Soto's expedition in the 1540s killed thousands of Indians and destroyed their traditional institutions. The survivors of the various chiefdoms intermarried and settled in smaller, less powerful agricultural communities.

In these Muskogean-speaking societies—and among the Algonquian-speaking and Iroquoian peoples who lived to the north and east—farming became the work of women. While the men hunted and fished, the women used flint hoes and raised corn, squash, and beans. Because of the importance of farming, a **matrilineal** system of kinship and inheritance developed among some eastern Indian peoples, including the Five Nations of the Iroquois, who resided in present-day New York State. Women cultivated the fields around semipermanent villages and passed the use rights to these fields to their daughters. In these matrilineal societies, the father stood outside the main lines of descent and authority; the principal responsibility for child rearing fell on the mother and her brothers, and men often lived with their sisters rather than with their wives. Among these peoples, religious rituals centered on the agricultural cycle. The Iroquois, for example, celebrated green corn and strawberry festivals. Although the eastern Indian peoples of 1500 enjoyed an adequate diet, their lives were hard and their populations grew slowly.

When Europeans intruded into North America, the strong Indian city-states that had once flourished in the Southwest and in the Mississippi River Valley had vanished.

Iroquois Women at Work, 1724
As this European engraving suggests, Iroquois women took responsibility for growing food crops.
Several of the women at the top are hoeing the soil into small hillocks, while others are planting corn and
beans. The lower section shows other women tapping sugar maples and boiling the sap to make maple
syrup. The woman at the left is probably grinding corn into flour; later she would add water to make flat
patties for baking. Newberry Library, Chicago.

The Customs of the Natchez, 1730   FATHER LE PETITE

The beliefs and institutions of the Mississippian culture (A.D. 1000–1450) survived for centuries among the Natchez people, who lived in present-day Mississippi. Around 1730, Father Le Petite, one of the hundreds of French Jesuit priests who lived among the Indians, wrote a fine description of Natchez society in a letter to his religious superiors in France. However, he misunderstood the reasons why the chief is succeeded by his sister's son: In a matrilineal society, lines of descent and inheritance pass through women, not men.

MY REVEREND FATHER, *The peace of Our Lord.*

This Nation of Savages inhabits one of the most beautiful and fertile countries in the World, and is the only one on this continent which appears to have any regular worship. Their Religion in certain points is very similar to that of the ancient Romans. They have a Temple filled with Idols, which are different figures of men and of animals, and for which they have the most profound veneration. Their Temple in shape resembles an earthen oven, a hundred feet in circumference. They enter it by a little door about four feet high, and not more than three in breadth. Above on the outside are three figures of eagles made of wood, and painted red, yellow, and white. Before the door is a kind of shed with folding-doors, where the Guardian of the Temple is lodged. . . .

The Sun is the principal object of veneration to these people; as they cannot conceive of anything which can be above this heavenly body, nothing else appears to them more worthy of their homage. It is for the same reason that the great Chief of this Nation, who knows nothing on the earth more dignified than himself, takes the title of brother of the Sun, and the credulity of the people maintains him in the despotic authority which he claims. To enable them better to converse together, they raise a mound of artificial soil, on which they build his cabin, which is of the same construction as the Temple. When a great Chief dies, his many wives are killed and are buried with him and personal goods in a great ceremonial mound. . . .

. . . [O]ne of their principles is . . . the immortality of the soul, and when they leave this world they go, they say, to live in another, there to be recompensed or punished.

In former times the Nation of the *Natchez* was very large. It counted sixty Villages and eight hundred Suns or Princes; now it is reduced to six little Villages and eleven Suns. [Its] Government is hereditary; it is not, however, the son of the reigning Chief who succeeds his father, but the son of his sister, or the first Princess of the blood. This policy is founded on the knowledge they have of the licentiousness of their women. They are not sure, they say, that the children of the chief's wife may be of the blood Royal, whereas the son of the sister of the great Chief must be, at least on the side of the mother.

SOURCE: Reuben Gold Thwaites, ed., *The Jesuit Relations and Allied Documents* (Cleveland: Murrow Brothers, 1900), 68: 121–135.

There were no great Indian empires or religious centers, as there were in Mesoamerica, that could sustain a campaign of military and spiritual resistance to European invaders. "When you command, all the French obey and go to war," the Chippewa chief Chigabe [*chi-GAH-bee*] remarked to a French general, but "I shall not be heeded and obeyed by my nation." Because households and lineages were the basis of his society, Chigabe explained, "I cannot answer except for myself and for those immediately allied to me."

▶ What were the main characteristics of the Indian civilizations of Mesoamerica?

▶ How were eastern woodland Indian societies organized and governed?

Europe Encounters Africa and the Americas, 1450–1550

In 1400, few observers would have predicted that Europeans would become overlords of the Western Hemisphere and dominate trade in Africa. A thousand years after the fall of the Roman empire, Europe remained a mosaic of small and relatively weak kingdoms. Moreover, around 1350, a vicious plague from the subcontinent of India—the Black Death—had killed one-third of Europe's population. Peoples in other regions had stronger economies and governments. China and India together accounted for more than half of world manufacturing output and had the potential to seize control of world commerce. Indian and Arab merchants already controlled most of Europe's trade with southern Asia. And between 1411 and 1422, large Chinese fleets militarily subdued competitors as they traded around the Indian Ocean and along the eastern coast of Africa.

European Agricultural Society

In 1450, there were just a few large cities in Western Europe: Only Paris, London, and Naples had as many as 100,000 residents. Most Europeans were **peasants** who lived in small agricultural communities. Peasant families usually owned or leased a small dwelling in the village center and had the right to farm the surrounding fields. The fields were open, not divided by fences or hedges, so cooperative farming was a necessity. The community decided which crops to grow, and every family followed its dictates. Because output was limited and there were few good roads, most trade was local. Neighboring families exchanged surplus grain and meat and bartered their farm products for the services of local millers, weavers, and blacksmiths. Most peasants yearned to be **yeomen**, to own enough land to support their family in comfort, but relatively few achieved that goal.

For European peasants, as for Native Americans, the rhythm of life followed the seasons. The agricultural year began in late March, when the ground thawed and dried and the villagers began the exhausting work of spring plowing and then planting wheat, rye, and oats. During these busy months, men sheared the thick winter wool of their sheep, which the women washed and spun into yarn. In June, peasants cut the first crop of hay and stored it as winter fodder for their livestock. During the summer, life was more relaxed, and families had the time to repair their houses and barns. Fall brought the strenuous harvest, followed by solemn feasts of thanksgiving and riotous

Artisan Family
Workers made goods by hand in the preindustrial world, and output was slow, so economic survival required the labor of the entire family. Here, a fifteenth-century French woodworker planes a panel of wood while his wife twists flax fibers into linen yarn for the family's clothes and their young son cleans up wood shavings from the workshop floor. Giraudon/Art Resource, New York.

bouts of merrymaking. As winter approached, peasants slaughtered excess livestock and salted or smoked the meat. During the cold months, they threshed grain and wove textiles, visited friends and relatives, and celebrated the winter solstice or the birth of Christ. Just before the farming cycle began again in the spring, they held carnivals, celebrating with drink and dance the end of the long winter night. Even births and deaths followed the seasons: More successful conceptions took place in early summer than at any other time of the year. And many rural people died either in January and February, victims of viral diseases, or in August and September in epidemics of fly-borne dysentery.

For most peasants, survival meant constant labor, breaking the soil with primitive wooden plows and harvesting hay and grain with small hand sickles. In the absence of today's high-quality seeds, chemical fertilizers, and pesticides, output was pitifully small—less than one-tenth of present-day yields. The margin of existence was small, and that corroded family relationships. Malnourished mothers fed their babies sparingly, calling them "greedy and gluttonous," and many newborn girls were "helped to die" so that their older brothers would have enough to eat. Disease killed about half of all peasant children before the age of twenty-one. Assault, murder, and rape were woven into the fabric of daily life, and hunger was a constant companion. "I have seen the latest epoch of misery," a French doctor reported as famine struck. "The inhabitants . . . lie down in a meadow to eat grass, and share the food of wild beasts." Often destitute, usually exploited by landlords and nobles, many peasants drew on strong religious beliefs and an inclination to "count blessings" and accepted their harsh existence.

Others hoped for a better life for themselves and their children. It was the peasants of Spain, Germany, and Britain who would supply the majority of white migrants to the Western Hemisphere.

Hierarchy and Authority

In traditional hierarchical societies—Mesoamerican or European—authority came from above. In Europe, kings and princes owned vast tracts of land, forcibly conscripted men for military service, and lived in splendor off the peasantry's labor. Yet monarchs were far from supreme: Local nobles also owned large estates and controlled hundreds of peasant families. Collectively, these nobles challenged royal authority with both their military power and their legislative institutions, such as the French *parlements* and the English House of Lords.

Just as kings and nobles ruled society, so men governed families. Rich or poor, the man was the head of the house, his power justified by the teachings of the Christian church. As one English clergyman put it: "The woman is a weak creature not embued with like strength and constancy of mind"; consequently, law and custom "subjected her to the power of man." Once she married, an Englishwoman assumed her husband's surname and had to submit to his orders and physical "correction," which was completely legal. Moreover, a wife surrendered to her husband the legal right to all her property. Her sole protection: When he died, she received a **dower**, usually the use during her lifetime of one-third of the family's land and goods.

Men also controlled the lives of their children, who usually worked for their father into their middle or late twenties. Then landowning peasants would give land to their sons and dowries to their daughters and choose marriage partners of appropriate wealth and status. In many regions, fathers bestowed all their land on their eldest son, a practice known as **primogeniture**, forcing many younger children to join the ranks of the roaming poor. In this kind of society, few men—and even fewer women—had much personal freedom or individual identity.

Hierarchy and authority prevailed in traditional European society both because of the power of established institutions—family, church, and village—and because, in a violent and unpredictable world, they offered ordinary people a measure of security. Carried by migrants to America, these security-conscious institutions would shape the character of family and society well into the eighteenth century.

The Power of Religion

For centuries, the Roman Catholic Church was the great unifying institution in Western Europe. The pope in Rome stood at the head of a vast religious hierarchy of cardinals, bishops, and priests. Catholic tracts and theologians preserved Latin, the great language of classical scholarship, and Christian dogma provided a common understanding of God, the world, and human history. Every village had a church, and the holy shrines that dotted the byways of Europe were reminders of the Church's teachings and authority.

Christian doctrine penetrated deeply into the everyday lives of peasants. Originally, most Europeans were **pagans**. Like the Indians of North America, they were animists who believed that elemental forces, such as the sun, rain, and wind, governed the natural world and that these spiritual forces had to be heeded and honored. However, Christian priests taught the peasants that spiritual power came from outside nature, from a supernatural God who had sent his divine son, Jesus Christ, into the world to save humanity from its sins. The Church devised a religious calendar that transformed pagan agricultural festivals into Christian holy days. The winter solstice, which for pagans marked the return of the sun, became the feast of Christmas, to celebrate the birth of Christ. To avert famine and plague, Christianized peasants no longer made ritual offerings to nature; instead, they offered prayers to Christ.

The Church also taught that Satan, a lesser and wicked supernatural being, was constantly challenging God by tempting people to sin. If a devout Christian fell mysteriously ill, the cause might be an evil spell cast by a witch in league with Satan. Prophets who spread **heresies**—doctrines that were inconsistent with the teachings of the Church—were seen as the tools of Satan. Suppressing false doctrines became an obligation of Christian rulers. So did combating Islam, a religion that, like Christianity, proclaimed a single god. Following the death in A.D. 632 of the prophet Muhammad, the founder of Islam, the newly converted Arab peoples of the Mediterranean used force and persuasion to spread the Muslim faith into sub-Saharan Africa, India, Indonesia, and deep into Spain and the Balkan regions of Europe. Between 1096 and 1291, Christian armies undertook a series of Crusades to halt this Muslim advance and win back the holy lands where Christ had lived.

The crusaders had some military successes, but their most profound impact was on European society. Religious warfare intensified Europe's Christian identity and prompted the persecution of Jews and their expulsion from many European countries. The Crusades also broadened the economic horizons of the merchants of Western Europe, who set out to capture the trade routes that stretched from Constantinople to China and from the Mediterranean Sea to the Indian Ocean.

The Renaissance Changes Europe, 1300–1500

The Crusades exposed educated Europeans to Byzantine and Arab learning and reacquainted them with the achievements of classical antiquity. Arabs had access to the silks and spices of the East and had acquired magnetic compasses, water-powered mills, and mechanical clocks, mostly from the Chinese. Moreover, Arab scholars carried on the legacy of Byzantine civilization, which had preserved the great achievements of the Greeks and Romans in medicine, philosophy, mathematics, astronomy, and geography. Stimulated by this knowledge, first Italy and then the countries of northern Europe experienced a rebirth of cultural life and economic energy.

The Renaissance had the most profound impact on the upper classes. Merchants from the Italian city-states of Venice, Genoa, Florence, and Pisa dispatched ships to Alexandria, Beirut, and other eastern Mediterranean ports, where they purchased goods from China, India, Persia, and Arabia to be sold throughout Europe. The enormously profitable commerce created wealthy merchants, bankers, and textile manufacturers who conducted trade, lent vast sums of money, and spurred technological innovation in silk and wool production. These Italian moneyed elites ruled their city-states as **republics**, with no prince or king. They celebrated **civic humanism**, an **ideology** that praised public virtue and service to the state and in time profoundly influenced European and American conceptions of government.

Perhaps no other age in European history has produced such a flowering of artistic genius. Michelangelo, Andrea Palladio, and Filippo Brunelleschi designed and built great architectural masterpieces. Leonardo da Vinci, Jacopo Bellini, and Raphael produced magnificent religious paintings, setting styles and standards that have endured into the modern era.

This creative energy inspired Renaissance rulers. In *The Prince* (1513), Niccolò Machiavelli offered unsentimental advice on how monarchs could increase their political power. The kings of Western Europe followed his advice, creating royal law courts and bureaucracies to reduce the power of the landed nobility and forging alliances with merchants and urban artisans. Monarchs allowed merchants to trade throughout their realms, granted privileges to the artisan organizations called **guilds**, and safeguarded commercial transactions in royal law courts, thereby encouraging domestic manufacturing and foreign trade. In return, kings and princes extracted taxes from towns and loans from merchants to support their armies and officials. This mutually enriching alliance of monarchs and merchants propelled Europe into its first age of overseas expansion.

Under the direction of Prince Henry (1394–1460), Portugal led a surge of maritime expansion. In 1415, as a young soldier of the Crusading Order of Christ, Henry

Astronomers at Istanbul (Constantinople), 1581
Arab and Turkish scholars transmitted ancient texts and learning to Europeans during the Renaissance and provided much of the geographical and astronomical knowledge that European explorers used during the sixteenth century, the great Age of Discovery. Ergun Cagatay, Istanbul.

learned of Arab merchants' rich trade in gold and slaves across the Sahara Desert. Seeking a maritime route to this trade's source in West Africa, Henry drew on the work of Renaissance thinkers and Arab and Italian geographers. In 1420, he founded a center for oceanic navigation and astronomical observation in the south of Portugal. He urged his captains to find a way around Cape Bojador in North Africa, a region of fierce winds and treacherous currents, and to explore the feared "Sea of Darkness" to the south. Eventually, Henry's mariners sailed far into the Atlantic, where they discovered and colonized the Madeira and Azore islands; from there, they sailed to the sub-Saharan African coast. By 1435, Portuguese sea captains had reached Sierra Leone, where they exchanged salt, wine, and fish for African ivory and gold. By the 1440s, the Portuguese were trading in humans as well, the first Europeans to engage in the long-established African trade in slaves. Henry's mission of enhancing Portugal's wealth through trade with West Africa had succeeded.

West African Society and Slavery

Vast and diverse, West Africa stretches along the coast from present-day Senegal to the Democratic Republic of Congo. In the 1400s, tropical rain forest covered much of the coast, but a series of great rivers—the Senegal, Gambia, Volta, Niger, and Congo—provided relatively easy access to the woodlands and savannas of the interior, where most people lived. There were few coastal cities because there was little seaborne trade (Map 1.2).

Most West Africans lived in extended families in small villages and farmed modest plots. Normally, the men cleared the land and the women planted and harvested the crops. On the plains, farmers grew millet and cotton and set their livestock out to graze; the forest peoples planted yams and harvested oil-rich palm nuts. Forest dwellers exchanged palm oil and kola nuts, a highly-valued stimulant, for the textiles and leather goods that savanna dwellers produced. Similarly, merchants collected valuable salt, which was produced along the coast and mined in great deposits in the Sahara, and traded it for iron, gold, and manufactures along the Niger and other rivers.

West Africans lived in diverse ethnic groups and spoke four basic languages, each with many dialects. Among West Atlantic–speakers, the Fulani and Wolof peoples were most numerous. Mande-speakers in the upper Niger region included the Malinke and Bambara peoples; the Yorubas and the Ibos of southern Nigeria spoke varieties of the Kwa language. Finally, the Mossis and other Voltaic-speakers inhabited the area along the upper Volta River. Most of these peoples lived in societies that were similar to those of the Mayans and Aztecs: socially stratified states ruled by kings and princes. Some lived in city-states that produced high-quality metal, leather, textiles, and pottery. Other West African societies were stateless, organized by household and lineage, much like those of the eastern woodland Indians.

Spiritual beliefs varied greatly. West Africans who lived immediately south of the Sahara—the Fulanis in Senegal, Mande-speakers in Mali, and Hausas in northern Nigeria—learned about Islam from Arab merchants and missionaries. Although some West Africans worshipped only the Muslim god, Allah, most recognized other gods as well as spirits that lived in the earth, in animals, and in plants. Many Africans also believed that their kings had divine attributes and could contact the spirit world. They

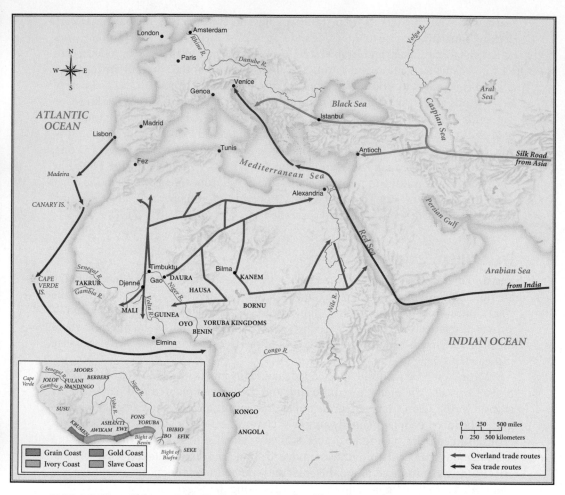

MAP 1.2 West Africa and the Mediterranean in the Fifteenth Century
Trade routes across the Sahara Desert had long connected West Africa with the Mediterranean. Gold, ivory, and slaves moved north and east; fine textiles, spices, and the Muslim faith traveled south and west. Beginning in the 1430s, the Portuguese opened up maritime trade with the coastal regions of West Africa, which were home to many peoples and dozens of large and small states. Within a decade, they would join in the slave trade there.

treated their ancestors with great respect, partly because they believed that the dead resided in a nearby spiritual realm and could intercede in their lives. Most West African peoples had secret societies, such as the Poro for men and the Sande for women, that united people from different lineages and clans. These societies educated their members in sexual practices, conducted adult initiation ceremonies, and used public humiliation to enforce codes of conduct and morality.

Early European traders had a positive impact on West Africa by introducing new plants and animals. Portuguese merchants brought coconuts from East Africa; oranges and lemons from the Mediterranean; pigs from Western Europe; and, after 1492, maize, manioc, and tomatoes from the Americas. They also expanded existing African trade networks. From small, fortified trading posts on the coast, merchants shipped metal products, manufactures, and slaves along the coast and to inland regions and took gold, ivory, and pepper in return. For much of the inland trade, the Portuguese relied on Africans, since Portuguese ships could travel no more than 150 miles up the slow-flowing Gambia and lesser distances on the other rivers. Yellow fever, malaria, and dysentery quickly struck down Europeans who spent time in the interior of West Africa, often killing as many as half of them each year.

Portuguese adventurers continued their quest for an ocean route to Asia. In 1488, Bartholomeu Dias rounded the Cape of Good Hope, the southern tip of Africa; ten years later, Vasco da Gama reached India. Although the Arab, Indian, and Jewish merchants along India's Malabar Coast tried to exclude him from trading there, da Gama acquired a highly profitable cargo of cinnamon and pepper, which were used to flavor and preserve meat. To acquire more spices and Indian textiles, da Gama returned to India in 1502 with twenty-one fighting vessels, which outmaneuvered and outgunned the Arab fleets. That expedition netted 1,700 tons of spices, as much as flowed through Venice in an entire year. Soon the Portuguese government set up fortified trading posts for its merchants at key points around the Indian Ocean, in Indonesia, and along the coast of China. In a transition that began the momentous growth of European wealth and power, the Portuguese replaced the Arabs as the leaders in world commerce.

Portuguese traders joined African states and Arab merchants in the slave trade. Bonded labor—slavery, serfdom, or indentured servitude—was the norm in most premodern societies, and in Africa it took the form of slavery. Some people were held in bondage as security for debts; others were sold into servitude by their kin, often in exchange for food in times of famine; many others were captured in wars. Most slaves worked as agricultural laborers or served in slave armies. And most were treated as property. Sometimes their descendants became low-status members of society, but many others endured hereditary bondage. Sonni Ali, the ruler from 1464 to 1492 of the powerful upper Niger Islamic kingdom of Songhay, personally owned twelve "tribes" of hereditary agricultural slaves, many of them seized in raids against stateless peoples.

A significant number of West Africans became **trade slaves**, sold as agricultural workers from one kingdom to another or carried overland in caravans by Arab traders to the Mediterranean region. When the renowned Tunisian traveler Ibn Battua trekked northward across the Sahara from the Kingdom of Mali around 1350, he traveled with a caravan of 600 female slaves, who were destined for domestic service or concubinage in North Africa, Egypt, and the Ottoman Empire. The first Portuguese in Senegambia found that the Wolof king, who commanded a horse-mounted warrior aristocracy, "supports himself by raids which result in many slaves. . . . He employs these slaves in cultivating the land allotted to him; but he also sells many to the [Arab] merchants in return for horses and other goods."

To exploit this trade in slaves, Portuguese merchants established forts at small port cities—first at Elmina in 1482 and later at Gorée, Mpinda, and Loango—where they bought gold and slaves from African princes and warlords. Initially, they carried a few thousand Africans each year to work on sugar plantations in the Cape Verde

Islands, the Azores, and the Madeira Islands; they also sold slaves in Lisbon, which soon had an African population of 9,000. After 1550, the maritime slave trade—the vast forced diaspora of African peoples—expanded enormously as Europeans set up sugar plantations in the lands of Brazil and the West Indies.

Europeans Explore America

Explorers financed by the Spanish monarchs, King Ferdinand of Aragon and Queen Isabel of Castile, discovered the Western Hemisphere for Europeans. As Renaissance rulers, Ferdinand and Isabel saw national unity and foreign commerce as the keys to power and prosperity. Married in an arranged match to combine their Christian kingdoms, the young rulers (r. 1474–1516) completed the centuries-long *reconquista*. In 1492, their armies captured Granada, the last Islamic state in Western Europe. Using Catholicism to build a sense of "Spanishness," they launched the brutal Inquisition against suspected Christian heretics and expelled or forcibly converted thousands of Jews and Muslims.

Simultaneously, Ferdinand and Isabel sought trade and empire by enlisting the services of Christopher Columbus, a mariner from Genoa. Misinterpreting the findings of Italian geographers, Columbus believed that the Atlantic Ocean, long feared by Arab merchants as a 10,000-mile-wide "green sea of darkness," was a much narrower channel of water separating Europe from Asia. Although dubious about Columbus's theory, Ferdinand and Isabel arranged financial backing from Spanish merchants and dispatched him to find a western route to Asia.

Columbus set sail in three small ships in August 1492. Six weeks later, after a perilous voyage of 3,000 miles, he disembarked on an island in the present-day Bahamas. Believing that he had reached Asia—"the Indies" in fifteenth-century parlance—Columbus called the native inhabitants *Indians* and the islands *the West Indies.* Surprised by the rude living conditions of the native people, Columbus expected them to "easily be made Christians." With ceremony and solemnity, he symbolically claimed the islands for Spain and for Christendom by giving them the names of the Spanish royal family and Catholic holy days. Columbus then explored the neighboring Caribbean islands and demanded tribute from the local Taino [*TIE-no*], Arawak [*air-a-WAK*], and Carib peoples. Buoyed by the natives' stories of rivers of gold lying "to the west," Columbus left forty men on the island of Hispaniola (present-day Haiti and the Dominican Republic) and returned triumphantly to Spain.

Although Columbus brought back no gold, the Spanish monarchs supported three more voyages. During those expeditions, Columbus began the colonization of the West Indies, transporting more than a thousand Spanish settlers—all men—and hundreds of domestic animals. He also began the transatlantic trade in slaves, carrying Indians to bondage in Europe and Africans to work as artisans and farmers in the new Spanish settlements. But Columbus failed to find either golden treasures or great kingdoms, and his death in 1506 went virtually unnoticed.

A German geographer soon labeled the continents "America" in honor of a Genoese explorer, Amerigo Vespucci. Vespucci, who had explored the new-found region around 1500, denied that it was part of Asia. He called it a *nuevo mundo,* a "new world."

For its part, the Spanish crown called the continents *Las Indias* ("the Indies") and wanted to make them a new Spanish world.

The Spanish Conquest

Spanish adventurers ruled the peoples of the Caribbean with an iron hand. After subduing the Arawaks and Tainos on Hispaniola, the Spanish probed the mainland for gold and slaves. In 1513, Juan Ponce de León explored the coast of Florida and gave that peninsula its name. In the same year, Vasco Núñez de Balboa crossed the Isthmus of Darien (Panama) and became the first European to see the Pacific Ocean. Rumors of rich Indian kingdoms in the interior encouraged other Spaniards, including hardened veterans of the *reconquista*, to launch an invasion. They had the support of the Spanish monarchs, who offered successful conquistadors (conquerors) titles, vast estates, and Indian laborers to farm them.

Hernán Cortés (1485–1547) conquered an empire and destroyed a civilization. Cortés came from a family of minor gentry in Spain and, seeking military adventure and material gain, sailed to Santo Domingo in 1506. Ambitious and charismatic, he distinguished himself in battle, putting down a revolt and serving in the conquest of Cuba. These exploits and marriage to a well-connected Spanish woman won Cortés an extensive Cuban estate and a series of administrative appointments.

Eager to increase his fortune, Cortés jumped at a chance in 1519 to lead an expedition to the mainland. He landed with 600 men near the Mayan settlement of Potonchan, which he quickly overpowered. Then Cortés got lucky. The defeated Mayans presented him with slave women to serve as servants and concubines. Among them was Malinali, a young woman of noble birth and, a Spanish soldier noted, "of pleasing appearance and sharp-witted and outward-going." Malinali also spoke Nahuatl, the

Malinche and Cortés
This Aztec pictograph (c. 1540) shows Cortés with Malinche (Mariana in Spanish), his Nahuatl-speaking interpreter, advisor, and mistress. Signifying her dual identity as an Indian and a European, Malinche wears native clothes but holds a rosary. Bibliothèque Nationale de France, Paris.

For more help analyzing this image, see the Online Study Guide at **bedfordstmartins** **.com/henrettaconcise**.

Aztecs' language. Cortés took her as his mistress and interpreter, and soon she became his guide. When the Spanish leader learned from Malinali the extent of the Aztec empire, his goal became power rather than plunder. He would depose its king, Moctezuma [*mok-tah-ZOO-mah*], and take over his realm.

Of Malinali's motives for helping Cortés, there is no record. Like his Spanish followers, she may have been dazzled by his powerful personality. She may have calculated that Cortés was her best hope for escaping slavery and reclaiming her noble status. Whatever her reasons, Malinali's loyalty was complete. As the Spanish marched on the Aztec capital of Tenochtitlán, she risked her life by warning Cortés of a surprise attack in the city of Cholula, and she helped him to negotiate his way into the Aztec capital. "Without her," concluded Bernal Díaz del Castillo, the Spanish chronicler of the conquest, the Spaniards would "have been unable to surmount many difficulties."

Awed by the military prowess of the Spanish invaders, Moctezuma received Cortés with great ceremony, only to become his captive. When the emperor's supporters tried to expel the invaders, they faced superior European military technology. The sight of the Spaniards in full metal armor, with guns that shook the heavens and inflicted devastating wounds, made a deep impression on the Aztecs, who knew how to purify gold but not how to produce iron tools or weapons. Moreover, the Aztecs had no wheeled carts or cavalry, and their warriors, fighting on foot with flint- or obsidian-tipped spears and arrows, were no match for mounted Spanish conquistadors wielding steel swords and aided by vicious attack dogs. Although heavily outnumbered and suffering great losses, Cortés and his men were able to fight their way out of the Aztec capital.

Winning a battle was one thing; conquering an empire was another. Had Moctezuma ruled a united empire, he could have overwhelmed the 600 well-armed Spanish invaders. But many Indian peoples hated the Aztecs, and Cortés deftly exploited their anger. With the help of Malinali, now known by the honorific Nahuatl name Malinche, he formed military alliances with the subject peoples whose wealth had been seized by Aztec nobles and whose people had been sacrificed to the Aztec sun god. The Aztec empire collapsed, the victim not of superior military technology but of a vast internal rebellion instigated by the wily Cortés (see American Voices, p. 25).

The Spanish also had a silent ally: disease. Separated from the Eurasian land mass for thousands of years, the inhabitants of the Americas had no immunities to common European diseases. A massive smallpox epidemic lasting seventy days ravaged Tenochtitlán after the Spanish exodus, "striking everywhere in the city," according to an Aztec source, and killing Moctezuma's brother and thousands more. "They could not move, they could not stir. . . . Covered, mantled with pustules, very many people died of them." Subsequent outbreaks of smallpox, influenza, and measles killed hundreds of thousands of Indians and sapped the survivors' morale. Exploiting this demographic weakness, Cortés quickly extended Spanish rule over the Aztec empire. His lieutenants then moved against the Mayan city-states of the Yucatán Peninsula, eventually conquering them as well.

In 1524, Francisco Pizarro led a Spanish military expedition toward Peru, home of the rich and powerful Inca empire, which stretched 2,000 miles along the Pacific coast of South America. To govern this far-flung empire, the Inca rulers had laid 24,000 miles of roads and built dozens of administrative centers, carefully constructed of

Cortés and Moctezuma Meet BERNAL DÍAZ DEL CASTILLO

Bernal Díaz was an unlikely chronicler of great events. Born poor, he went to America as a common soldier in 1514 and served under conquistadors in Panama and Cuba. In 1519, he joined Cortés's expedition and received an estate in present-day Guatemala, where he lived out his life. In his old age, Díaz wrote *The True History of the Conquest of New Spain,* a compelling memoir written from a soldier's perspective.

When we arrived near to Mexico, . . . the Great Moctezuma got down from his litter, and those great Caciques [aristocrats] supported him with their arms beneath a marvelously rich canopy of green coloured feathers with much gold and silver embroidery . . . which was wonderful to look at. The Great Moctezuma was richly attired according to his usage, and he was shod with sandals, the soles were of gold and the upper part adorned with precious stones. . . .

Many other Lords walked before the Great Moctezuma, sweeping the ground where he would tread and spreading cloths on it, so that he should not tread on the earth. Not one of these chieftains dared even to think of looking him in the face, but kept their eyes lowered with great reverence. . . .

When Cortés was told that the Great Moctezuma was approaching, and he saw him coming, he dismounted from his horse, and when he was near Moctezuma, they simultaneously paid great reverence to one another. Moctezuma bade him welcome and our Cortés replied through Doña Marina [Malinche, Cortés's Indian mistress and interpreter] wishing him very good health. . . . And then Cortés brought out a necklace which he had ready at hand, made of glass stones, . . . which have within them many patterns of diverse colours, these were strung on a cord of gold and with musk so that it should have a sweet scent, and he placed it round the neck of the Great Moctezuma. . . .

Then Cortés through the mouth of Doña Marina told him that now his heart rejoiced having seen such a great Prince, and that he took it as a great honour that he had come in person to meet him. . . .

Thus space was made for us to enter the streets of Mexico, without being so much crowded. But who could now count the multitude of men and women and boys who were in the streets and in canoes on the canals, who had come out to see us. It was indeed wonderful. . . .

They took us to lodge in some large houses, where there were apartments for all of us. . . .

Cortés thanked Moctezuma through our interpreters, and Moctezuma replied, "Malinche, you and your brethren are in your own house, rest awhile," and then he went to his palaces, which were not far away, and we divided our lodgings by companies, and placed the artillery pointing in a convenient direction, and [we were ordered] . . . to be much on the alert, both the cavalry and all of us soldiers. A sumptuous dinner was provided for us according to their use and custom, and we ate it at once. So this was our lucky and daring entry into the great city of Tenochtitlán Mexico on the 8th day of November the year of our Saviour Jesus Christ, 1519.

SOURCE: Bernal Díaz del Castillo, *The True History of the Conquest of New Spain,* trans. A. P. Maudslay (1632; London: Routledge, 1928), 272–275.

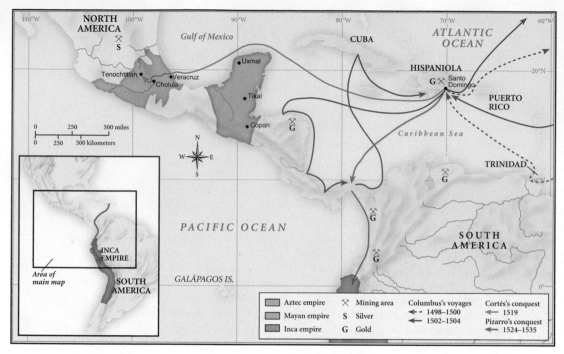

MAP 1.3 The Spanish Conquest of the Great Indian Civilizations

The Spanish first invaded and settled the islands of the Caribbean. Rumors of a golden civilization led to Cortés's invasion of the Aztec empire in central Mexico in 1519. By 1535, other Spanish conquistadors had conquered the Mayan temple cities of the Yucatán Peninsula and the Inca empire in Peru, completing one of the great conquests in world history.

For more help analyzing this map, see the Online Study Guide at **bedfordstmartins.com/henrettaconcise.**

finely crafted stone. An Inca king, claiming divine status, ruled the empire with the help of a bureaucracy staffed by noblemen. By the time Pizarro and his small force of 168 men and 67 horses finally reached Peru in 1532, half of the Inca population had died from European diseases spread by Indian traders. Weakened militarily and fighting over succession to the throne, the Inca nobility was easy prey for Pizarro's army. In only thirteen years, Spain had become the master of the wealthiest and most populous regions of the Western Hemisphere (Map 1.3).

The Spanish invasion changed life forever in the Americas. Disease and warfare wiped out virtually all of the Indians of Hispaniola—at least 300,000 people. In Peru, the population plummeted from nine million in 1530 to fewer than 500,000 a century later. Mesoamerica suffered the greatest losses: In one of the great demographic disasters in world history, its population of thirty million Native Americans in 1500 had dwindled to just three million in 1650.

Once the conquistadors had triumphed, the Spanish monarchs quickly created an elaborate bureaucratic empire. From its headquarters in Madrid, the Council of the Indies issued laws and decrees to viceroys, governors, judges, and other Spanish officials in America. But the conquistadors and their descendants remained powerful because they secured judgeships and other bureaucratic positions for family members and held *encomiendas*, royal grants that gave them legal control of the labor of the native population. They ruthlessly exploited the surviving Native Americans, forcing them to raise crops and cattle both for local consumption and for export to Europe. The Spaniards also permanently altered the natural environment: The livestock (horses, cattle, sheep, and goats), grain crops (wheat, barley, and rice), and human diseases (smallpox, measles, chickenpox, influenza, malaria, and yellow fever) of Africa and Eurasia became part of life in the Americas.

The Spanish conquest had a significant ecological impact on Europe and Africa as well. In a process that historians call the **Columbian Exchange**, the food products of the Western Hemisphere — especially maize, potatoes, manioc, sweet potatoes, and tomatoes — were transferred to other continents, where they significantly increased agricultural yields and population growth. Thus, in the century after these crops reached China (around 1700), the population doubled. A less welcome transfer was the virulent strain of syphilis Columbus's crew members took back to Europe with them. Nor was that all. The gold and silver that had formerly honored Aztec gods now gilded the Catholic churches of Europe and flowed into the countinghouses of Spain. From there, vast amounts of silver flowed to China, home to 125 million people in 1650, where it was in great demand for use as money. In exchange, Spain received valuable silks, spices, and ceramics. As Spain's American wealth flowed around the globe between 1540 and 1640, it made that nation the richest and most powerful in Europe. Indeed, Spain now claimed a "lordship of all the world."

Meanwhile, the once magnificent civilizations of Mexico and Peru lay in ruins. "Of all these wonders" — the great city of Tenochtitlán, the bountiful irrigated fields, the rich orchards, the overflowing markets — "all is overthrown and lost, nothing left standing," recalled Bernal Díaz, who had been a young soldier in Cortés's army. The surviving Indian peoples lost a vital part of their cultural identity when Spanish priests suppressed many traditional religious ceremonies and gave Catholic identities to Indian gods. As early as 1531, an Indian convert reported a vision of a dark-skinned Virgin Mary, later known as the Virgin of Guadalupe, a Christian version of the "corn mother" who traditionally protected the maize crop.

A new society took shape on the lands emptied by disease and exploitation. Between 1500 and 1650, at least 350,000 Spaniards migrated to Mesoamerica and western South America. More than 75 percent were men — at first poor, unmarried, and unskilled refugees from Andalusia and later a broader mix of Castilians — and many of them took Indian women as wives or mistresses. Consequently, a substantial mixed-race population, called **mestizos**, quickly appeared, along with an elaborate race-based **caste system**. Around 1800, near the end of the colonial era, Spanish America stretched from the tip of South America to the northern border of present-day California. It contained about 17 million people: a dominant caste of 3.2 million Spaniards; 5.5 million people of mixed Indian and European genetic

▶ Compare and contrast the main characteristics of traditional European society, West African society, and the Native American societies of the eastern woodlands.

▶ Why and how did Portugal and Spain pursue overseas commerce and conquest?

and cultural heritage; 1.0 million enslaved Africans; and 7.5 million Indians, who lived mostly on marginal lands. The sudden and harsh collision among the peoples of three old worlds—European, African, Native American—transformed them all as it integrated them into a single Atlantic world.

The Protestant Reformation and the Rise of England, 1500–1620

Even as Catholic fervor prompted the forced conversion of Indians in America and Muslims and Jews in Spain, Christianity ceased to be a unifying force in European society. During the 1520s, religious doctrines preached by Martin Luther and other reformers divided Europe between Catholic and Protestant states and plunged the continent into a century-long series of religious wars. During these conflicts, France replaced Spain as the most powerful European state, and Holland and England emerged as Protestant nations determined to colonize the Western Hemisphere.

The Protestant Movement

Over the centuries, the Catholic Church had become a large and wealthy institution. Renaissance popes and cardinals used the Church's wealth to patronize the arts and enrich themselves. Pope Leo X (r. 1513–1521) received half a million ducats (about $20 million in 2008 dollars) a year from the sale of religious offices. Such corruption encouraged ordinary priests and monks to seek economic or sexual favors. One English reformer denounced the clergy as a "gang of scoundrels" who should be "rid of their vices or stripped of their authority," but he was ignored. Other critics of the Church, such as Jan Hus of Bohemia, were executed as heretics.

In 1517, Martin Luther, a German monk and professor at the university in Wittenberg, took up the cause of reform. Luther viewed the world as the site of a primordial combat between God and the devil. His *Ninety-five Theses* condemned the Church for encouraging practices that condoned human depravity, such as the granting of **indulgences**, certificates that allegedly pardoned sinners from punishment in the afterlife. Outraged by Luther's charges, the pope dismissed him from the Church, and the Holy Roman Emperor, King Charles I of Spain (r. 1516–1556), threatened Luther with punishment. However, the princes of northern Germany, who were resisting the emperor's authority for political reasons, protected Luther from arrest, thus allowing the protest movement to survive.

Luther took issue with Roman Catholic doctrine in three major respects. First, he rejected the belief that Christians could secure salvation through good deeds or the purchase of indulgences; instead, Luther argued that people could be saved only by grace, which came as a "free gift" from God. Second, he downplayed the role of the clergy as mediators between God and the people and proclaimed a much more democratic outlook. "Our baptism consecrates us all without exception and makes us all priests." Third, he said that believers must look to the Bible—not to Church officials or doctrine—as the ultimate authority in matters of faith. So that every literate German could read the Bible, for centuries available only in Latin, Luther translated it into German.

Peasants as well as princes heeded Luther's attack on authority and, to his dismay, mounted social protests of their own. In 1524, many German peasants rebelled against their manorial lords. Fearing social revolution, Luther urged obedience to established political institutions and condemned the teachings of the Anabaptists (who rejected the baptism of infants) and other groups of religious dissidents. Assured of Luther's social conservatism, most princes in northern Germany embraced his teachings and broke from Rome, thereby gaining the power to appoint bishops and control the Church's property within their domains. To restore Catholic doctrine and his own political authority, the Holy Roman Emperor dispatched armies to Germany, setting off a generation of warfare. Eventually, the Peace of Augsburg (1555) divided Germany into Lutheran states in the north and Catholic principalities in the south.

John Calvin, a French theologian in Geneva, Switzerland, established the most rigorous Protestant regime. Even more than Luther, Calvin stressed human weakness and God's omnipotence. His *Institutes of the Christian Religion* (1536) depicted God as an awesome and absolute sovereign who governed the "wills of men so as to move precisely to that end directed by him." Calvin preached the doctrine of **predestination**, the idea that God chooses certain people for salvation before they are born and condemns the rest to eternal damnation. In Geneva, he set up a model Christian community, eliminating bishops and placing spiritual power in the hands of ministers chosen by their congregations. Ministers and pious laymen ruled the city, prohibiting frivolity and luxury. "We know," wrote Calvin, "that man is of so perverse and crooked a nature, that everyone would scratch out his neighbor's eyes if there were no bridle to hold them in." Calvin's authoritarian doctrine won converts all over Europe; it became the theology of the Huguenots in France, the Reformed churches in Belgium and Holland, and the Presbyterians and Puritans in Scotland and England.

In England, King Henry VIII (r. 1509–1547) initially opposed Protestantism. However, in 1534, when the pope refused to annul his marriage to the Spanish princess Catherine of Aragon, Henry broke with Rome and placed himself at the head of a national church, the Church of England, which promptly granted the king an annulment. Henry made few changes in Catholic doctrine, organization, and ritual, but he allowed the spread of Protestant teachings. Faced with popular pressure for greater reform, Henry's daughter and successor, Queen Elizabeth I (r. 1558–1603), approved a Protestant confession of faith that incorporated both the Lutheran doctrine of salvation by grace and the Calvinist belief in predestination. To satisfy traditionalists, Elizabeth retained the Catholic ritual of Holy Communion—now conducted in English rather than Latin—as well as the hierarchy of bishops and archbishops.

Elizabeth's compromises angered radical Protestants, who condemned the power of bishops as "proude, pontificall and tyrannous" as well as "anti-Christian and devilish and contrary to the Scriptures." These reformers took inspiration from the presbyterian system pioneered in Calvin's Geneva and developed by John Knox for the Church of Scotland. In Scotland, congregations elected lay elders (presbyters) who helped ministers and participated in the synods (councils) that decided Church doctrine. By 1600, five hundred Church of England clergy demanded the elimination of bishops and a republican-like presbyterian form of church government.

Other radical English Protestants called themselves "unspotted lambs of the Lord" or Puritans. These extraordinarily devout Calvinists wanted to "purify" the church of all Catholic teachings and magical or idolatrous practices. Puritans refused to burn incense or to pray to dead saints; a carefully argued sermon was the focus of their religious service. They placed special emphasis on the "conversion experience," the felt infusion of God's grace, and the "calling," the duty to serve God in one's ordinary life and work. To ensure that all men and women had direct access to God's commands in the Bible, Puritans encouraged literacy and Bible study. Finally, most Puritans wanted authority over spiritual and financial matters to rest primarily with local congregations. Eventually, thousands of Puritans and Presbyterian migrants would establish churches in North America based on these radical Protestant doctrines.

The Dutch and English Challenge Spain

Luther's challenge to Catholicism in 1517 came just two years before Cortés began his conquest of the Aztec empire, and the two events became linked. Gold and silver from Mexico and Peru made Spain the wealthiest nation in Europe and King Philip II (r. 1556–1598) its most powerful ruler. In addition to Spanish America, Philip presided over wealthy states in Italy; the commercial and manufacturing provinces of the Spanish Netherlands (present-day Holland and Belgium); and, after 1580, Portugal and all its possessions in America, Africa, and the East Indies. "If the Romans were able to rule the world simply by ruling the Mediterranean," boasted a Spanish priest, "what of the man who rules the Atlantic and Pacific oceans, since they surround the world?"

An ardent Catholic, Philip tried to root out Islam in North Africa and Protestantism in the Netherlands and England. He failed to do either. A massive Spanish fleet defeated a Turkish armada at Lepanto in the eastern Mediterranean in 1571, freeing 15,000 Christian galley slaves, but Muslims continued to rule all of North Africa. Moreover, the Spanish-controlled Netherlands remained a hotbed of Calvinism. These Dutch- and Flemish-speaking provinces had grown wealthy from trade with the Portuguese empire and from weaving wool and linen. To protect their Calvinist faith and political liberties, they revolted against Spanish rule in 1566. After fifteen years of war, the seven northern provinces declared their independence, becoming the Dutch Republic (or Holland) in 1581.

Elizabeth I of England had aided the Dutch cause by dispatching 6,000 troops to Holland. She also supported military expeditions to extend direct English rule over Gaelic-speaking Catholic regions of Ireland. Calling the Irish "wild savages" who were "more barbarous and more brutish in their customs . . . than in any other part of the world," English troops brutally massacred thousands, prefiguring the treatment of Indians in North America. In 1588, to meet Elizabeth's challenge, Philip sent a Spanish Armada — 130 ships and 30,000 men — against England. Philip intended to restore Catholicism to England and Ireland and then to wipe out Calvinism in Holland. But he failed utterly when English ships and a fierce storm destroyed the Spanish fleet.

Nevertheless, Philip continued to spend his American gold and silver on religious wars. This ill-advised militaristic policy diverted resources from industrial investment in Spain. Oppressed by high taxes on agriculture and fearful of military service, more than 200,000 residents of Castile, the richest region of Spain, migrated to America. By the time of Philip's death in 1598, Spain was in serious economic decline.

Elizabeth I (r. 1558–1603)
Dressed in richly decorated clothes that symbolize her power, Queen Elizabeth I relishes the destruction of the Spanish Armada, which appears in the background. The queen's hand rests on a globe, asserting England's claims in the Western Hemisphere and its imperial ambitions. Woburn Abbey Collection, by permission of the Marquess of Tavistock and the Trustees of the Bedford Estates.

As mighty Spain faltered, tiny Holland prospered—the economic miracle of the seventeenth century. Amsterdam emerged as the financial capital of northern Europe, and the Dutch Republic replaced Portugal as the dominant trader in Indonesia and West Africa. Dutch merchants also looked across the Atlantic: They created the West India Company (1621), which invested in sugar plantations in Brazil and established the fur-trading colony of New Netherland along the Hudson River.

England also emerged as a European power in the sixteenth century, its economy stimulated, as colonial advocate Richard Hakluyt noted, by a "wounderful increase of our people." As England's population soared from three million in 1500 to five million in 1630, its monarchs supported the expansion of commerce and manufacturing. English merchants had long supplied European weavers with high-quality wool; around 1500, they created their own **outwork** textile industry. Merchants bought wool from the owners of great estates and then sent it "out" to landless peasants to spin and weave into cloth in their small cottages. The government aided textile entrepreneurs by setting low rates for wages, and it helped merchants by awarding monopoly privileges in foreign markets. Queen Elizabeth granted monopolies to the Levant Company (to trade tin for silk and spices in Turkey) in 1581, the Guinea Company (to exchange manufactures for slaves in Africa) in 1588, and the East India Company (to import cotton cloth and spices from India) in 1600.

This system of state-assisted manufacturing and trade became known as **mercantilism**. By encouraging textile production, Elizabeth hoped to reduce imports and increase exports, giving England a favorable balance of trade. The queen and her advisors wanted gold and silver to flow into the country in payment for English goods, enriching the merchant community and stimulating further economic expansion. Increased trade also boosted import duties, which swelled the royal treasury and the monarch's power. By 1600, Elizabeth's mercantile policies had laid the foundations for overseas colonization. Now the English, as well as the Dutch, had the merchant fleets and wealth needed to challenge Spain's domination of the Western Hemisphere.

The Social Causes of English Colonization

England sent more than merchant fleets and manufactures to America. The rapid growth of the English population provided a large body of settlers, many of them fleeing economic hardship caused by an upheaval known today as the **Price Revolution**. The massive influx of American gold and silver had doubled the money supply of Europe and sparked a major inflation.

The landed nobility in England was the first casualty of the Price Revolution. Aristocrats customarily rented out their estates on long leases for fixed rents, which provided a secure income and plenty of leisure. As one English nobleman put it, "We eat and drink and rise up to play and this is to live like a gentleman." Then inflation struck. In less than two generations, the price of goods tripled while the nobility's income from rents barely increased. As the purchasing power of the aristocracy fell, that of the **gentry** and the yeomen rose. The gentry, who were nonnoble landholders with substantial estates, kept pace with inflation by renting land on short leases at higher rates. Yeomen, described by a European traveler as "middle people of a condition between gentlemen and peasants," owned small farms that they worked with family labor. As wheat prices tripled, yeomen used the profits to build larger houses and provide their children with land.

Economics influenced politics. As nobles lost wealth, the influence of their branch of Parliament, the House of Lords, weakened. Simultaneously, members of the rising gentry entered the House of Commons, the political voice of the propertied classes, and demanded that the Commons have power over taxation and other policies. Thus the Price Revolution encouraged the rise of representative institutions in which rich commoners and property-owning yeomen had a voice. This development had profound consequences for English — and American — political history.

The Price Revolution likewise transformed the lives of peasants, who made up three-fourths of the English population. The economic stimulus of Spanish gold spurred the expansion of the textile industry. To increase the supply of wool, profit-minded landlords and wool merchants persuaded Parliament to pass **enclosure acts**, laws that allowed owners to kick peasants off their lands, fence in their fields, and put sheep to graze there. The dispossessed peasant families lived on the brink of poverty, spinning and weaving wool or working as agricultural wage laborers. Wealthy men had "taken farms into their hands," an observer noted in 1600, "whereby the peasantry of England is decayed and become servants to gentlemen."

The coming of "The Little Ice Age," a century-long series of remarkably long and cold winters that began about 1600, magnified the impact of these social changes. As crop yields diminished, grain prices soared and social unrest increased. "Thieves and rogues do swarm the highways," warned one justice of the peace, "and bastards be multiplied in parishes." Seeking work, thousands of young men and women migrated to America as **indentured** servants; in exchange for their passage across the Atlantic, they sold their labor (and freedom) for four or five years. Dispossessed peasants and weavers threatened by a recession in the cloth trade were likewise ready to try their luck elsewhere. Thousands of yeomen families were also on the move, looking for affordable land on which to settle their children. By 1640, over 100,000 English and Scots had migrated to Ulster in Ireland, and 50,000 more had moved to North America and the Caribbean Islands. As Puritans looked for religious freedom and peasants for economic security, they formed a powerful migratory movement.

▶ How did Protestant religious doctrine differ from that of Roman Catholicism?

▶ What factors prompted the large-scale migration of English men and women to America?

▶ What was the impact of the Columbian Exchange in food, people, diseases, and gold on the Americas, Europe, and Africa?

SUMMARY

In this chapter, we have seen that the first human inhabitants of the Western Hemisphere were hunter-gatherers from Asia. Their descendants would form many cultures and speak many languages. In Mesoamerica, the Mayan and Aztec peoples developed populous agricultural societies and highly sophisticated religious and political systems; so, too, did the Incas along the western coast of South America. The Hopewell, Pueblo, and Mississippian peoples of North America likewise created complex societies and cultures; but in 1500, most Indians north of the Rio Grande lived in small self-governing communities of foragers, hunters, and farmers.

We have also traced the maritime expansion that brought Europeans to the Americas. The Spanish crown, eager to share in Portugal's mercantile success, financed expeditions to find new trade routes to Asia. When Christopher Columbus revealed a "new world" to Europeans in 1492, Spanish adventurers undertook to conquer it. By 1535, conquistadors had destroyed the civilizations of Mesoamerica and Peru and inadvertently introduced diseases that would kill millions of Native Americans. Through the Columbian Exchange of crops, animals, plants, and diseases, there was a significant alteration in the ecology of much of the world.

Population growth, religious warfare, and American gold and silver transformed European society in the sixteenth century. As the cost of religious warfare sapped Spain's strength, the rise of strong governments in Holland, France, and England, along with a class of increasingly powerful merchants, enhanced the economies of those countries and whetted their appetite for overseas expansion.

Connections: Society

In the essay that opens Part One, we noted that "Europeans, with their steel weapons, attractive trade goods, and diseases, shredded the fabric of most Native American cultures." In this chapter, you have read the first part of that story: the Spanish invasion of Mesoamerica and South America. In Chapter 2, we compare the interaction of Native Americans with various European peoples: the Spanish in New Mexico and Florida, the French in Louisiana, and the Dutch and English in New York and New England. Chapter 2 concludes with an analysis of Native Americans in the English colonies as of 1700. Later chapters explain how Native Americans continued to shape the history of the eastern seaboard, even as their numbers and strength underwent a sharp decline. Part One concludes with the Great War for Empire (1756–1763). That war was known in the British colonies as the French and Indian War and rightly so: It was yet another effort by Native Americans to defend their lands from Anglo-American settlers.

TIMELINE

13,000–3000 B.C. ►	Asian migrants reach North America	**1513** ►	Juan Ponce de León explores Florida
3000 B.C. ►	Farming begins in Mesoamerica	**1517** ►	Martin Luther sparks Protestant Reformation
A.D. 100–400 ►	Flourishing of Hopewell culture	**1519–1521** ►	Hernán Cortés conquers Aztec empire
300 ►	Rise of Mayan civilization	**1520–1650** ►	Price Revolution
500 ►	Zenith of Teotihuacán civilization	**1532–1535** ►	Francisco Pizarro vanquishes Incas
600 ►	Pueblo cultures emerge	**1534** ►	Henry VIII establishes Church of England
632–1100 ►	Arab people adopt Islam and spread its influence	**1536** ►	John Calvin publishes *Institutes of the Christian Religion*
800–1350 ►	Development of Mississippian culture	**1550–1630** ►	English crown supports mercantilism
1096–1291 ►	Crusades link Europe with Arab learning	►	Parliament passes enclosure acts
1300–1450 ►	Italian Renaissance	**1556–1598** ►	Reign of Philip II, king of Spain
1325 ►	Aztecs establish capital at Tenochtitlán	**1558–1603** ►	Reign of Elizabeth I, queen of England
1430 on ►	Portugal trades along West and Central African coasts	**1560–1620** ►	Growth of English Puritan movement
1492 ►	Christopher Columbus makes first voyage to America	**1588** ►	Storms and English ships destroy Spanish Armada
1498 ►	Portugal's Vasco da Gama reaches India		

The coming of those settlers to the Chesapeake region and New England between 1600 and 1675 will be a major theme of Chapter 2.

FOR FURTHER EXPLORATION

Kenneth Pomeranz, *The Great Divergence: Europe, China, and the Making of the Modern World Economy* (2000), examines the impact of the Americas on world history. Brian M. Fagan, *The Great Journey: The People of Ancient America* (1987), and Alvin M. Josephy Jr., ed., *America in 1492: The World of the Indian Peoples Before the Arrival of Columbus* (1991) are reliable and vividly written studies. For the European background of colonization, consult George Huppert's highly readable study, *After the Black Death* (2nd ed., 1998); see also the engaging biography by William D. Phillips, with Carla Rahn Phillips, *The Worlds of Christopher Columbus* (1992). Two Public Broadcasting Service (PBS) videos examine the ancient civilizations of Mesoamerica: *Odyssey: Maya Lords of the Jungle* (1 hour) and *Odyssey: The Incas* (1 hour). Also, log onto "1492: An Ongoing Voyage" (**www.loc.gov/exhibits/1492/intro.html**) for images and analysis of the native cultures of the Western Hemisphere.

Peter Laslett, *The World We Have Lost* (3rd ed., 1984), paints a vivid portrait of seventeenth-century English society; see also Andrew McRae, *God Speed the Plough* (2002), and Ethan Shagan, *Popular Politics and the English Reformation* (2003). "Martin Luther" (**www.luther.de/e/index.html**) offers biographies and striking images of the era of the Protestant Reformation. Giles Milton, *Nathaniel's Nutmeg* (1999), tells the rousing tale of European competition for the spice trade and, subsequently, the New World.

TEST YOUR KNOWLEDGE

To assess your mastery of the material in this chapter and for Web sites, images, and documents related to this chapter, visit **bedfordstmartins.com/henrettaconcise**.

The Invasion and Settlement of North America

1550–1700

Indians are the rock,
European peoples are the
sea, and history seems a
constant storm.

— Richard White,
The Middle Ground (1991)

Establishing colonies in North America was not for the faint of heart. First came a long voyage over stormy, dangerous waters; shipwrecks, spoiled food, and disease claimed many lives along the way. Of three hundred migrants to New France in 1663, for example, seventy died en route. Those who survived had to build shelters and plant crops, and many faced hostile Indian peoples. "We neither fear them nor trust them," declared Puritan settler Francis Higginson, but rely on "our musketeers." Still, despite great risks and uncertain rewards, English, French, and Spanish migrants by the tens of thousands crossed the Atlantic during the seventeenth century. They were either driven by poverty and religious persecution at home or drawn by the promise of land, gold, or — according to one pious migrant — promoting "the Christian religion to such People as yet live in Darkness."

For Native Americans, the European invasion was a catastrophe. Whether they came as settlers, fur traders, or missionaries, the white-skinned people and their African slaves brought new diseases and religions that threatened the Indians' lives and cultures. "Our fathers had plenty of deer and skins, . . . and our coves were full of fish and fowl," Narragansett chief Miantonomi reminded the Montauk people in 1642, "but these English having gotten our land . . . their cows and horses eat the grass, and their hogs spoil our clam banks, and we shall all be starved." Miantonomi called for united resistance: "We [are] all Indians [and must] say brother to one another, . . . otherwise we shall all be gone shortly." The chief's unsuccessful plea foretold the course of North American history: The European invaders would advance, enslaved Africans would endure, and Indian peoples would decline.

The Rival Imperial Models of Spain, France, and Holland

In Mesoamerica, the Spanish seized the Indians' lands, converted many to Catholicism, and made them dig for gold and farm large estates. In the sparsely populated eastern regions of North America, French and Dutch merchants created fur-trading colonies, and the native peoples retained their lands and political autonomy. Whatever the Europeans' goals, Indian peoples diminished in numbers and soon rebelled.

New Spain: Colonization and Conversion

In their ceaseless quest for gold, Spanish explorers penetrated deep into the present-day United States. In the 1540s, Francisco Vásquez de Coronado searched in vain for the fabled seven golden cities of Cíbola; what he discovered instead were the southern reaches of the Grand Canyon, the Pueblo peoples of the Southwest, and the grasslands of Kansas. Meanwhile, Hernán de Soto and a force of 600 Spaniards were cutting a bloody swath across the Southeast, battling the Apalachees in northern Florida and the Coosas in northern Alabama but finding no gold (Map 2.1).

MAP 2.1 New Spain Looks North, 1513–1610
The search for gold drew Spanish explorers first to Florida and then deep into the present-day United States. When the wide-ranging expeditions of Hernán de Soto and Francisco Vásquez de Coronado failed to find gold or flourishing Indian civilizations, authorities in New Spain limited northern settlements to St. Augustine in Florida (to protect the treasure fleet) and Santa Fe in the upper Rio Grande Valley.

For more help analyzing this map, see the Online Study Guide at **bedfordstmartins.com/henrettaconcise.**

By the 1560s, Spanish officials had given up the search for gold and were focusing on the defense of their empire. Roving English "sea dogs" were plundering Spanish treasure ships, and French Protestants were settling in Spanish-claimed Florida. Following King Philip II's order to cast out the Frenchmen "by the best means," Spanish troops massacred 300 members of the "evil Lutheran sect" near the St. John River. To safeguard the route of the treasure fleet, Spain established a fort at St. Augustine in 1565, making it the first permanent European settlement in the future United States. However, raids by the Calusas and Timucuas wiped out a dozen other Spanish military outposts in Florida, and Algonquins destroyed Jesuit religious missions along the Atlantic coast, including one near the Chesapeake Bay.

These military setbacks and the urgings of Franciscan friars prompted Spanish leaders to adopt a new policy: They would conquer the Indian peoples by Christianizing them. The Comprehensive Orders for New Discoveries (1573) placed responsibility for pacification primarily in the hands of missionaries, not conquistadors. Over the next century, scores of Franciscan friars set up missions among the Apalachees in Florida and the Pueblo peoples in the lands the Spanish named Nuevo México. The friars often learned Indian languages, but they also systematically attacked the natives' culture. And their methods were anything but peaceful. Protected by Spanish soldiers, missionaries whipped Indians who continued to practice **polygamy**, smashed the Indians' religious idols, and punished anyone who worshipped traditional gods. On one occasion, forty-seven "sorcerers" in Nuevo México were whipped and sold into slavery.

Conversion in New Mexico
Franciscan friars, aided by nuns of various religious orders, introduced Catholicism to the Indian peoples north of the Rio Grande. This 1631 engraving shows nun María de Jesús de Agreda preaching to nomadic peoples (the Chichimecos) in New Mexico.
Nettie Lee Benson Latin American Collection, University of Texas at Austin.

Religious conversion, cultural assimilation, and forced labor went hand in hand. The Franciscans encouraged the Indians to talk, cook, dress, and walk like Spaniards. They ignored laws that protected the native peoples and allowed privileged Spanish landowners (*encomenderos*) to extract goods and forced labor from the native population. The missions themselves depended on Indian workers to grow crops and carry them to market.

Native Americans initially tolerated the Franciscans because they feared military reprisals and hoped to learn the friars' spiritual secrets. But when Christian prayers failed to protect their communities from European diseases, droughts, and raids by nomadic Apaches and Pawnees, many Pueblo people returned to their ancestral gods. The people of Hawikuh refused to become "wet-heads" (as the Indians called baptized Christians) "because with the water of baptism they would have to die."

In 1598, the tense relations between Indians and Spaniards in New Mexico exploded into open warfare. An expedition of 500 Spanish soldiers and settlers led by Juan de Oñate seized corn and clothing from the Pueblo peoples and murdered or raped those who resisted. When Indians of the Acoma pueblo retaliated by killing 11 soldiers, the Spanish troops destroyed the pueblo and murdered 800 men, women, and children. Faced with bitterly hostile native peoples, most settlers left New Mexico. In 1610, the Spanish returned, founded the town of Santa Fe, and reestablished the system of missions and forced labor. Over the next two generations, European diseases, forced tribute, and raids by nomadic plains Indians reduced the population of Pueblo peoples from 60,000 to just 17,000.

In 1680, in a carefully coordinated rebellion, the Indian shaman Popé and his followers killed more than 400 Spaniards and forced 1,500 colonists (and 500 Pueblo and Apache slaves) to flee 300 miles to El Paso. The Pueblo peoples burned "the seeds which the Spaniards sowed" and planted "only maize and beans, which were the crops of their ancestors." Repudiating Christianity, they desecrated churches and rebuilt the sacred kivas, the round stone structures in which they had long worshiped. Like many later Native American rebels, Popé marched forward while looking backward, hoping to restore the traditional way of life.

It was not to be. A decade later, Spain reasserted control over most of the Pueblo peoples. The oppressed natives rebelled again in 1696 and were again subdued. Exhausted by a generation of warfare, the Pueblos agreed to a compromise that allowed them to practice their own religion and avoid forced labor. In return, they accepted a dependent position in New Mexico and helped the Spanish defend their settlements and farms against nomadic Apaches and Comanches.

Spain had maintained its northern empire, but it failed to assimilate the Indian peoples. Some Pueblo Indians had married Spaniards, and their offspring formed a bicultural mestizo population, but most continued to practice the old ways. As a Franciscan friar admitted, "They are still drawn more by their idolatry and infidelity than by the Christian doctrine."

Spanish officials experienced a similar disappointment in Florida. In the early 1700s, English raids from Carolina destroyed most of the Spanish missions and killed or enslaved most Catholic converts. These setbacks persuaded Spanish officials to halt the settlement of the distant northern province of California. Santa Fe and St. Augustine stood alone as the northern outposts of Spain's American empire.

New France: Furs and Warfare

Far to the northeast, the French were also confronting native peoples. In the 1530s, Jacques Cartier had claimed the lands bordering the Gulf of St. Lawrence for France. The first permanent settlement came in 1608, when Samuel de Champlain founded the fur-trading post of Quebec. But the colony languished until 1662, when King Louis XIV (r. 1643–1714) turned New France into a royal colony and subsidized the migration of indentured servants. Servants served a term of thirty-six months, received a yearly salary, and could eventually lease a farm — terms far more generous than those for indentured servants in the English colonies.

Nonetheless, few people moved to New France, in part because it was a cold and forbidding country "at the end of the world." In addition, state policies and laws discouraged migration. To expand France's boundaries in Europe, Louis XIV drafted tens of thousands of men into military service. The Catholic monarch also barred Huguenots (French Calvinist Protestants) from migrating to New France. Moreover, the legal system gave peasants strong rights to their village lands in France, and migrants to New France found an oppressive, aristocratic- and church-dominated feudal system. In the village of Saint Ours in Quebec's fertile Richelieu Valley, for example, peasants paid 45 percent of their wheat crop to nobles and the Catholic Church. In 1698, the European population of the colony was only 15,200, compared to 100,000 residents in the English settlements.

Lacking settlers, New France became a vast enterprise for acquiring furs, which were in great demand in Europe to make felt hats and fur garments. To secure plush beaver pelts from the Huron Indians, who controlled trade north of the Great Lakes, Champlain provided the Huron with manufactured goods. Selling pelts, an Indian told a French priest, "makes kettles, hatchets, swords, knives, bread." It also made guns, which Champlain sold to the Huron to fight the expansionist-minded Five Iroquois Nations of New York, who wanted to run the fur trade. Searching for more furs, explorer Jacques Marquette reached the Mississippi River in present-day Wisconsin in 1673 and traveled as far south as Arkansas. Then, in 1681, Robert de La Salle traveled down the majestic river to the Gulf of Mexico, trading as he went. As a French priest noted with disgust, La Salle and his associates hoped "to buy all the Furs and Skins of the remotest Savages, who, as they thought, did not know their Value; and so enrich themselves in one single voyage." To honor Louis XIV, La Salle named the region Louisiana, where the port of New Orleans on the Gulf of Mexico was established in 1718.

Despite their small numbers, the French had a disastrous impact. By unwittingly introducing European diseases, they triggered epidemics that killed from 25 to 90 percent of many Indian peoples. Moreover, by bartering guns for furs, the French (and the Dutch) sparked a series of deadly wars. The Five Iroquois Nations were the prime aggressors. From their strategic geographical location in central New York, the Iroquois could obtain guns and goods from Dutch merchants at Albany and quickly attack other Indian peoples. Iroquois warriors moved to the east along the Mohawk River as far as New England and south along the Delaware and Susquehanna rivers as far as the Carolinas. They traveled north via Lake Champlain and the Richelieu River to Quebec. And they journeyed west via the Great Lakes to exploit the rich fur-bearing lands of the upper Mississippi River Valley.

The rise of the Iroquois was breathtakingly rapid. In 1600, the Iroquois numbered about 30,000 and lived in large towns of 500 to 2,000 inhabitants. Over the next two decades, they organized themselves in a confederation of Five Nations: Senecas, Cayugas, Onondagas, Oneidas, and Mohawks. Partly in response to a virulent smallpox epidemic in 1633, which cut their number by one-third, the Iroquois waged a series of devastating wars against the Hurons (1649), Neutrals (1651), Eries (1657), and Susquehannocks (1660)—all Iroquoian-speaking peoples. They razed the villages and killed most of the men, cooking and eating their flesh to gain access to their spiritual powers. They took thousands of women and children as captives and ritually adopted them into Iroquois lineages. The conquered Hurons met a more dire fate: They simply ceased to exist as a distinct people; survivors trekked westward and joined other remnant peoples to form a new tribe, the Wyandots.

Between 1625 and 1763, hundreds of French priests lived among the Iroquois and other peoples of the Great Lakes region. Most were members of the Society of Jesus (or Jesuits), a Catholic religious order founded to combat the Protestant Reformation. These priests—unlike the Spanish Franciscan monks—came to understand and respect the Indians' values. One Jesuit noted the Huron belief that "our souls have desires which are inborn and concealed, yet are made known by means of dreams." For their part, many Indian peoples initially welcomed the French "Black Robes" as powerful spiritual beings with magical secrets, including the ability to forge iron. But when prayers to the Christian god did not protect them from disease, the Indians grew skeptical. A Peoria chief charged that a priest's "fables are good only in his own country; we have our own [religious beliefs], which do not make us die as his do." When a drought struck, Indians lashed out at the missionaries. "If you cannot make rain, they speak of nothing less than making away with you," lamented one Jesuit.

Whatever the limits of their spiritual powers, the French Jesuits did not exploit Indian labor. Moreover, they tried to keep brandy, which wreaked havoc among the natives, from becoming a bargaining chip in the French fur trade. And the Jesuits won converts by adapting Christian beliefs to the Indians' needs. In the 1690s, for example, the Jesuits introduced the cult of the Virgin Mary to the young women of the Illinois people. Its emphasis on chastity reinforced existing beliefs among the Illinois that unmarried women were "masters of their own body."

Despite the Jesuits' efforts, the French fur-trading system brought cultural devastation. Epidemics killed tens of thousands of Indians, and Iroquois warriors murdered thousands more. Nor did the Iroquois escape unscathed. In 1666 and again in the 1690s, French armies invaded their lands, burned villages and cornfields, and killed many warriors. "Everywhere there was peril and everywhere mourning," recalled an oral Iroquois legend.

New Netherland: Commerce and Conquest

By 1600, Holland had emerged as the financial and commercial hub of northern Europe. Exploiting the country's strategic location at the mouth of the great Rhine River and near the Baltic sea, enterprising Dutch merchants controlled the trade of northwestern Europe. Dutch entrepreneurs dominated the European banking, insurance, and textile industries; Dutch merchants owned more tons of shipping and employed more sailors than did the combined fleets of England, France, and Spain. Indeed, the Dutch managed much of the world's commerce. During their struggle for independence from Spain (and its Portuguese dependency), the Dutch seized Portuguese forts in Africa, Brazil, and Indonesia, gaining control of the Atlantic trade in slaves and the Indian Ocean commerce in East Indian spices and Chinese silks and ceramics.

In 1609, Dutch merchants dispatched an Englishman, Henry Hudson, to locate a western route to the riches of the East Indies. After Hudson explored the North American river that bears his name, the merchants built Fort Orange (Albany) in 1614 to trade for furs with the Munsee and Lenape Indians. In 1621, the Dutch government chartered the West India Company and gave it a monopoly over the trade in American furs and West African slaves. Three years later, the company founded the town of New Amsterdam on Manhattan Island and made it the capital of the colony of New Netherland.

The new colony did not thrive. The population of the Dutch Republic was small — just 1.5 million people, compared to 5 million in Britain and 20 million in France — and relatively prosperous. Consequently, few Dutch settlers moved to the fur-trading posts, making them vulnerable to rival European nations. To encourage migration, the West India Company granted huge estates along the Hudson River to wealthy Dutchmen and smaller land grants to English and Dutch settlers. But in 1664, New Netherland had just 5,000 residents, and fewer than half of them were Dutch.

Nonetheless, New Netherland flourished as a fur-trading enterprise. Dutch traders at Fort Orange cultivated good relations with the powerful Iroquois who controlled the fur trade; in 1633, the traders exported 30,000 beaver and otter pelts. Dutch settlers near New Amsterdam were less respectful of their Algonquian-speaking neighbors. They seized prime farming land from the Indians and took over their trading network, in which corn and wampum from Long Island were exchanged for furs from Maine. In response, the Algonquins launched a war that nearly destroyed the colony. "Almost every place is abandoned," the settlers lamented, "whilst the Indians daily threaten to overwhelm us." To defeat the Algonquins, the Dutch waged vicious warfare — maiming, burning, and killing hundreds — and formed an alliance with the Mohawks, who were no less brutal. Thereafter, the Mohawks controlled Indian access to Albany, and their dialect became the language of business in the small fur-trading outpost.

After the crippling Indian war, the West India Company largely ignored New Netherland, focusing instead on the profitable trade in African slaves and Brazilian sugar. In New Amsterdam, Governor Peter Stuyvesant ruled in an authoritarian fashion. He rejected demands of English Puritans on Long Island for a representative system of government and alienated the colony's increasingly diverse population of Dutch, English, and Swedish migrants. Consequently, the residents of New Amsterdam offered little resistance when England invaded the colony in 1664.

The Duke of York, the overlord of the new English colony of New York, initially ruled with a mild hand: He allowed the Dutch residents to retain their property, legal system, and religious institutions. That policy changed after the Dutch briefly recaptured the colony in 1673. The duke's governor, Edmund Andros, shut down the Dutch courts, imposed English law, and demanded an oath of allegiance. Dutch residents responded by avoiding the English courts and resisting cultural assimilation: They spoke Dutch, married among themselves, and worshipped at the Dutch Reformed Church. Once dominant over the Algonquins, the Dutch had themselves become a subject people. As a group of Anglicans noted in 1699, New York "seemed rather like a conquered Foreign Province held by the terror of a Garrison, than an English colony."

▶ What were the colonial goals of the Spanish, French, and Dutch? How successful were they in achieving these goals?

▶ What happened to the Five Nations of the Iroquois between 1600 and 1700? Were the Iroquois better off at the beginning of the period or at the end? Why?

The English Arrive: The Chesapeake Experience

Unlike their European rivals, the English founded settler-colonies in North America. But that was not the plan of the London investors who financed an expedition to Virginia in 1607. They expected to establish a trade factory, like those recently set up in India, Sierra Leone, and Morocco, to buy goods from the native peoples — gold, if possible, or fruits, dyes, olives, and sugar. Not finding such goods, migrants settled in the Chesapeake Bay region and created a tobacco-growing society. Prominent families ruthlessly pursued their dreams of wealth by exploiting the labor of indentured English servants and enslaved Africans.

Settling the Tobacco Colonies

The first English settlements in North America were organized privately, first by minor nobles and later by merchants and religious dissidents. Although the English monarch and ministry approved these ventures, they did not control them. This policy meant that the English settlements, unlike the state-supervised Spanish and French colonies, enjoyed considerable autonomy and developed in astonishingly different ways.

The private ventures organized by the nobles were abject failures. In the 1580s, Sir Humphrey Gilbert's settlement in Newfoundland collapsed for lack of financing, and Sir Ferdinando Gorges's colony along the coast of Maine floundered in the harsh climate. Sir Walter Raleigh's three expeditions to North Carolina likewise ended in disaster when 117 settlers on Roanoke Island vanished without a trace. (Roanoke is still known as the "lost colony.")

Merchants then took charge of English expansion. In 1606, King James I (r. 1603–1625) granted to the Virginia Company of London all the lands stretching from present-day North Carolina to southern New York. To honor the memory of Elizabeth I, the never-married "Virgin Queen," the company's directors named the region Virginia. For the Virginia Company, as for the French and Dutch, trade with the native population was the primary goal. The first expedition, in 1607, was limited to male traders — no women, farmers, or ministers — who were the employees or "servants" of the company. They were to procure their own food and to ship gold, exotic crops, and Indian goods to England. Some employees were young gentlemen with personal ties to the company's shareholders: a bunch of "unruly Sparks, packed off by their Friends to escape worse

The Tobacco Economy

Most farmers in Virginia — poor and rich — raised tobacco. Wealthy planters used indentured servants and slaves, like those pictured here, to grow and process the crop. The workers cured the tobacco stalks by hanging them for several months in a well-ventilated shed; then they stripped the leaves and packed them tightly into large plantation-made barrels, or hogsheads, for shipment to Europe. Library of Congress.

For more help analyzing this image, see the Online Study Guide at **bedfordstmartins.com/henrettaconcise.**

Destinies at home." Others were cynical men looking for a quick profit: All they wanted, one of them said, was to "dig gold, refine gold, load gold."

But there was no gold, and the traders were poorly equipped to deal with the new environment. Arriving in Virginia after an exhausting four-month voyage, they settled on a swampy, unhealthy peninsula, which they named Jamestown to honor the king. Because the adventurers lacked access to fresh water and refused to plant crops, they quickly died off; only 38 of the 120 men were alive nine months later. Death rates remained high. By 1611, the Virginia Company had dispatched 1,200 settlers to Jamestown, but fewer than half had survived. "Our men were destroyed with cruell diseases, as Swellings, Fluxes, Burning Fevers, and by warres," reported one of the settlement's leaders, "but for the most part they died of meere famine."

The local Indians were initially suspicious of the new arrivals. However, Powhatan, the chief of the thirty tribes living between the James and Potomac rivers, treated the English traders as potential allies and a source of valuable goods. A "grave majestical man," according to explorer John Smith, Powhatan allowed his 14,000 Algonquian-speaking followers to exchange their corn for English cloth and iron hatchets. To integrate the English traders into his domain of Tsenacommacah, Powhatan arranged a marriage between his daughter Pocahontas and John Rolfe, an English colonist. This tactic failed because Rolfe had imported tobacco seed from the West Indies and produced a crop of "pleasant, sweet, and strong Tobacco," which fetched a high price in England. Eager to become rich by planting tobacco, thousands of English settlers embarked for Virginia. Now Powhatan accused the English of coming "not to trade but to invade my people and possess my country."

To foster the flow of migrants, the Virginia Company allowed individual settlers to own land, granting 100 acres to every freeman and more to those who imported servants. The company also issued a "great Charter" that created a system of representative government. The House of Burgesses, which first convened in 1619, could make laws and levy taxes, although the governor and the company council in England could veto its acts. By 1622, land ownership, self-government, and a judicial system based on "the lawes of the realme of England" had attracted some 4,500 new recruits. To encourage Virginia's transition to a settler colony, the company recruited dozens of "Maides young and uncorrupt to make wifes to the Inhabitants."

The influx of land-hungry English migrants and conversion-minded ministers sparked an all-out revolt by the Indian peoples. The uprising was led by a mysterious chief named Opechancanough [O-pee-chan-KA-no], who was Powhatan's younger brother and successor. Some evidence suggests that early Spanish explorers had taken Opechancanough to Spain in the 1570s and that when he returned as part of a Jesuit mission, he killed the missionaries. There is no doubt that in 1609, Opechancanough personally confronted the English invaders, captured Captain John Smith, and then spared his life. Subsequently, the Indian chief "stood aloof" from the English settlers and "would not be drawn to any Treaty." In particular, he resisted English proposals to place Indian children in schools where they would be "brought upp in Christianytie." After Opechancanough became the main chief in 1621, he told the chief of the Potomacks: "Before the end of two moons, there should not be an Englishman in all their Countries."

Opechancanough almost succeeded. In 1622, he coordinated a surprise attack by twelve Indian tribes that killed 347 English settlers, nearly one-third of the white population. The English fought back by seizing the fields and food of those they now saw as "naked, tanned, deformed Savages." To secure the safety of their colony, the European invaders declared "a perpetual war without peace or truce" that lasted for a decade. They sold captured warriors into slavery, "destroy[ing] them who sought to destroy us," and took control of "their cultivated places . . . possessing the fruits of others' labour."

Shocked by the Indian uprising, James I revoked the charter of the Virginia Company and, in 1624, made Virginia a royal colony. Now the king and his ministers appointed the governor and a small advisory council. James retained the House of Burgesses but stipulated that his Privy Council, a committee of leading ministers, must ratify all legislation. The king also decreed the legal establishment of the Church of England, which meant that residents had to pay taxes to support its clergy. These institutions—a royal governor, an elected assembly, a formal legal system, and an established Anglican church—became the model for royal colonies throughout English America.

A second tobacco-growing colony, with a very different set of institutions, developed in neighboring Maryland. King Charles I (r. 1625–1649), James's successor, was secretly sympathetic toward Catholicism. In 1632, he granted the lands bordering the vast Chesapeake Bay to Cecilius Calvert, a Catholic aristocrat who carried the title Lord Baltimore. As the territorial lord (or proprietor) of Maryland, Baltimore could sell, lease, or give away the land as he pleased. He also had the authority to appoint public officials and to found churches.

Lord Baltimore wanted Maryland to become a refuge for Catholics, who were subject to persecution in England. In 1634, twenty gentlemen, mostly Catholics, and 200 artisans and laborers, mostly Protestants, established St. Mary's City, which over-looked the mouth of the Potomac River. To minimize religious confrontations, the proprietor instructed the governor (his brother, Leonard Calvert) to allow "no scandall nor offence to be given to any of the Protestants" and to "cause All Acts of Romane Catholicque Religion to be done as privately as may be."

Maryland's population grew quickly because the Calverts imported scores of arti-sans and offered ample lands to wealthy migrants. But political conflict constantly threatened the colony's stability. Disputing Lord Baltimore's lordly powers, settlers demanded that he govern in accordance with the "Advice, Assent, and Approbation" of the freemen. They elected a representative assembly and insisted on the right to initi-ate legislation, which Baltimore grudgingly granted. Anti-Catholic agitation by Prot-estant settlers also threatened the Calverts' religious goals. To protect his coreligionists, who remained a minority, Lord Baltimore persuaded the assembly to enact the Tolera-tion Act (1649), which granted all Christians the right to follow their beliefs and hold church services.

In Maryland, as in Virginia, tobacco quickly became the main crop. Indians had long used tobacco as a medicine and a stimulant, and the English came to crave the nicotine it contained. By the 1620s, they were smoking, chewing, and snorting tobacco with abandon. James I initially condemned tobacco as a "vile Weed" whose "black stinking fumes" were "baleful to the nose, harmful to the brain, and dangerous to the lungs." But the king's attitude changed as taxes on imported tobacco bolstered the royal treasury.

European demand for tobacco set off a forty-year economic boom in the Ches-apeake region. "All our riches for the present do consist in tobacco," a planter remarked in 1630. Exports rose from three million pounds in 1640 to ten million pounds in 1660. Initially, most plantations were small, farmed by families or male partners. But after 1650, migrants from gentry or noble families established large estates along the coastal rivers. Coming primarily from southern England, where tenants and wage laborers farmed large manors, they recreated that hierarchical system by buying indentured servants to work their lands (see Voices from Abroad, p. 47).

For rich and poor alike, life in the Chesapeake colonies was harsh. The scarcity of towns deprived settlers of community (Map 2.2). Families were equally scarce be-cause there were few women, and marriages often ended with the death of a young spouse. Pregnant women were especially vulnerable to malaria, which was spread by the mosquitoes that flourished in the warm climate. Many mothers died after bearing a first or second child, so orphaned children (along with unmarried young men) formed a large segment of the society. Sixty percent of the children born in Middlesex County, Virginia, before 1680 lost one or both of their parents before they were thir-teen. Death was a constant presence. Some 15,000 English migrants arrived in Virginia between 1622 and 1640, but the population rose only from 2,000 to 8,000.

Magisterial Justice in Maryland

Tens of thousands of English indentured servants came to Maryland and Virginia in the seventeenth century, hoping for a better life. Many found only oppressive masters and unforgiving magistrates. When two indentured servants in Lower Norfolk County in Virginia stole some food, the justices of the county court ordered the sheriff to lash them 100 times on their bare backs. English servants who shirked from work and demanded adequate food faced a similar fate at the hands of Maryland magistrates—in this case the governor and council of the colony—who themselves held bound laborers and were determined to enforce strict discipline.

To the honorable the Governor and Council of Maryland:

The humble petition of Richard Preston showeth:

That your petitioner's servants did, upon the 5th day of the last week, called Thursday, peremptorily and positively refuse to go and do their ordinary labor upon the account (as they then alleged) that if they had not flesh [meat], they could not work. Your suppliant's answer then was to them, that if they would not go to work unless they had flesh, I could not help it; for I had not flesh then to give them (. . . And at night returning home, found that his said servants had not been at work upon the account of not having that day some meat, although until that time they have not wanted for the most part, since the crop of tobacco was in, to have meat three times in the week and at least twice . . . And they continuing still in that obstinate rebellious condition, although I have instead of flesh for the present provided sugar, fish, oil, and vinegar for them, am constrained to address myself to this court, that according to equity and their demerits they may receive such censure as shall be judged equal for such perverse servants. . . .

To the honorable the Governor and Council:

The humble Petition of John Smith, Richard Gibbs, Samuel Coplen, Samuel Styles, etc., servants to Mr. Richard Preston, showeth:

That Mr. Preston doth not allow your petitioners sufficient provisions for the enablement to our work, but straitens us so far that we are brought so weak we are not able to perform the employments he puts us upon. We desire but so much as is sufficient, but he will allow us nothing but beans and bread. . . .

Upon these petitions of Mr. Richard Preston and his servants, and upon examination of the said servants present in court: the court, taking the same into serious consideration, ordered that these servants now petitioning . . . be forthwith whipped with 30 lashes each. . . .

And thereupon the said servants, kneeling on their knees, asking and craving forgiveness of their master and the court for their former misdemeanor and promising all compliance and obedience hereafter, their penalty is remitted or suspended at present. But they are to be of good behavior towards their said master ever hereafter.

SOURCE: John Demos, ed., *Remarkable Providences, Readings in Early American History* (Boston: Northeastern University Press, 1972): 135–137.

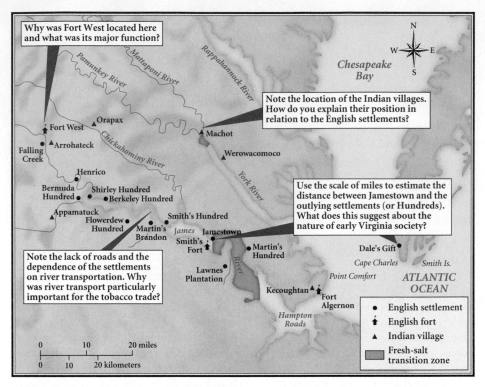

MAP 2.2 River Plantations in Virginia, c. 1640
The first migrants settled in widely dispersed plantations along the James River. The growth of the tobacco economy promoted this pattern: Wealthy planter-merchants would trade with English ship captains from their riverfront plantations. Consequently, few substantial towns or trading centers developed in the Chesapeake region.

Masters, Servants, and Slaves

Still, the prospect of owning land continued to lure settlers. By 1700, more than 100,000 English migrants had come to Virginia and Maryland, mostly as indentured servants. Shipping registers from the English port of Bristol reveal the backgrounds of 5,000 embarking servants. Three-quarters were young men, many of them displaced by the enclosure of their village lands (see Chapter 1). They came to Bristol searching for work; once there, merchants persuaded them to sign contracts to labor in America. The indenture contracts bound the men—and a much smaller number of women—to work for a master for four or five years, after which they would be free to marry and work for themselves.

For merchants, servants were valuable cargo: Their contracts fetched high prices from Chesapeake (and West Indian) planters. For the plantation owners, indentured servants were an incredible bargain. During the tobacco boom, a male servant could produce five times his purchase price in a single year. To maximize their gains, most masters ruthlessly exploited their servants, forcing them to work long hours, beating them without cause, and withholding permission to marry. If servants ran away or became pregnant, masters went to court to increase the term of their service. Female servants were especially vulnerable to abuse. As a Virginia law of 1692 stated, "dissolute masters have gotten their maids with child; and yet claim the benefit of their service." Planters got rid of uncooperative servants by selling their contracts. As one Englishman remarked in disgust, in Virginia, "servants were sold up and down like horses."

Most indentured servants in the Chesapeake colonies did not escape from poverty. Half the men died before completing the term of their contract, and another quarter remained landless. Only one-quarter achieved their quest for property and respectability. Female servants generally fared better. Men had grown "very sensible of the Misfortune of Wanting Wives," so many propertied planters married female servants. By migrating to the Chesapeake, these few—and very fortunate—men and women escaped a life of landless poverty.

Fate was equally mixed for the first African workers. In 1619, John Rolfe noted that "a Dutch man of warre . . . sold us twenty Negars"—slaves shipped from the Portuguese port of Luanda in Angola. For a generation, the number of Africans remained small. About 400 Africans lived in the Chesapeake colonies in 1649, just 2 percent of the population; in 1670, only 5 percent of the population was black. Though some of these early African workers served their English masters for life, they were not legally enslaved. English **common law** did not acknowledge **chattel slavery**, the ownership of a human being as property. Moreover, many of these Africans came from the Kingdom of Kongo, where Portuguese missionaries had converted the king and some of the people to Christianity. Knowing the ways of Europeans, these workers found means to escape their bondage. Some ambitious African freemen even purchased slaves, bought the labor contracts of white servants, or married Englishwomen.

Mobility for Africans ended in the 1660s with the collapse of the tobacco boom. Tobacco had once sold for 24 pence a pound; now it fetched just one-tenth of that. The "low price of Tobacco requires it should bee made as cheap as possible," declared Virginia planter Nicholas Spencer, and "blacks can make it cheaper than whites." As the English-born elite imported fewer English servants and more African slaves, Chesapeake legislators grew more race-conscious and enacted laws that undercut the status of blacks. By 1671, the Virginia House of Burgesses had forbidden Africans to own guns or join the militia. It also barred them—"tho baptized and enjoying their own Freedom"—from owning white servants and from claiming freedom by becoming Christians. Being black was increasingly a mark of inferior legal status, and slavery was becoming a permanent and hereditary condition. As an English clergyman observed, "These two words, Negro and Slave had by custom grown Homogeneous and convertible."

The Seeds of Social Revolt

As the tobacco boom went bust, long-standing social conflicts flared into political turmoil. Falling tobacco prices signaled an imbalance in the market: Exports doubled between 1670 and 1700, outstripping European demand. But it also reflected Parliament's passage of Acts of Trade and Navigation in 1651, 1660, and 1663. The Navigation Acts allowed only English or colonial-owned ships to enter American ports, thereby excluding Dutch merchants, who paid the highest prices for tobacco, sold the best goods, and provided the cheapest shipping services. The legislation also required the colonists to ship tobacco, sugar, and other "enumerated articles" only to England, where monarchs continually raised import duties, stifling market demand. By the 1670s, tobacco planters were getting just a penny a pound for their crop; one Virginian grumbled that the planters had become mere "beneficial Slaves" to England's merchants and monarch.

Despite low prices, Virginians continued to plant tobacco because there was no other cash crop. To preserve soil fertility without costly manuring, yeomen families adopted a long-fallow system (rotating fields over a twenty-year cycle) and pocketed just enough income to scrape by. Worse off were newly freed indentured servants, who could not earn enough to buy tools and seed or to pay the fees required to claim their right to fifty acres of land. Many ex-servants had to sell their labor again, either signing new indentures or becoming wage workers or tenant farmers.

Consequently, after 1670, an elite of planter-merchants dominated the Chesapeake colonies. Like the English gentry, they prospered from the ownership of large estates that they leased to the growing population of former servants. Many well-to-do planters also became commercial middlemen and moneylenders. They set up retail stores and charged commissions for shipping the tobacco produced by smallholding farmers. This elite accumulated nearly half the land in Virginia by securing grants from royal governors. In Maryland, well-connected Catholic planters were equally powerful; by 1720, one of those planters, Charles Carroll, owned 47,000 acres of land, farmed by scores of tenants, indentured servants, and slaves.

Bacon's Rebellion

As these aggressive planter-entrepreneurs confronted a multitude of free, young, and landless laborers, armed political conflict rocked Virginia during the 1670s. This violent struggle left a mixed legacy: a decrease in class conflict among whites and increasing racial divisions because of massive imports of enslaved Africans.

William Berkeley, who first served as governor of Virginia between 1642 and 1652, suppressed a major Indian uprising in 1644. Appointed governor again in 1660, Berkeley bestowed large land grants on members of his council. The councilors promptly exempted their own lands from taxation and appointed their friends as local justices of the peace and county judges. To win the cooperation of the House of Burgesses, Berkeley bought off legislators with land grants and lucrative appointments as sheriffs and tax collectors. But social unrest surfaced when the corrupt Burgesses changed the voting system to exclude landless freemen, who by now constituted half the adult white men. Property-holding yeomen retained the vote, but they were angered by falling tobacco prices, political corruption, and "grievous taxations" that threatened the "utter ruin of us the poor commonalty." Berkeley and his gentry allies were living on borrowed time.

An Indian conflict lit the flame of social rebellion. When the English intruded into Virginia in 1607, there were 30,000 Native Americans living there; by 1675, the number had dwindled to only 3,500. By comparison, the number of Europeans had multiplied to 38,000 and the number of Africans to about 2,500. Most Indians lived on treaty-guaranteed territory along the frontier. Now poor **freeholders** and landless former servants demanded that the natives be expelled or exterminated. Opposition to western expansion came from wealthy river-valley planters, who wanted a ready supply of tenant farmers and wage laborers, and from Berkeley and the planter-merchants, who traded with the Indians for furs.

Fighting broke out late in 1675, when a vigilante band of Virginia militiamen murdered thirty Indians. Defying Berkeley's orders, a larger force of 1,000 militiamen then surrounded a fortified Susquehannock village and killed five chiefs who came out to negotiate. The Susquehannocks, who had recently migrated from the north, retaliated by killing 300 whites on outlying plantations. To avoid an Indian war, Berkeley proposed a defensive military strategy: a series of frontier forts to deter Indian intrusions. The settlers dismissed this scheme as a useless plot by planters and merchants to impose high taxes and take "all our tobacco into their own hands."

Nathaniel Bacon emerged as the leader of the rebels. A young, well-connected migrant from England, Bacon held a position on the governor's council. But residing on a frontier estate, he differed with Berkeley on Indian policy. When the governor refused Bacon a military commission to attack nearby Indians, he used his commanding personal presence to mobilize his neighbors and attack the peaceful Doeg Indians.

Nathaniel Bacon
Condemned as a rebel and a traitor in his own time, Nathaniel Bacon emerged in the late nineteenth century as an American hero, a harbinger of the Patriots of 1776. Famed jeweler and glassmaker Tiffany & Co. of New York probably designed and fabricated this stained-glass window. Installed in a Virginia church, it endowed Bacon with semisacred status.
The Association for the Preservation of Virginia Antiquities.

Condemning the frontiersmen as "rebels and mutineers," Berkeley expelled Bacon from the council and had him arrested. But Bacon's armed men forced the governor to release their leader and to hold legislative elections. The newly elected House of Burgesses enacted far-reaching political reforms that curbed the powers of the governor and the council and restored voting rights to landless freemen.

These much-needed reforms came too late. Bacon remained bitter toward Berkeley, and poor farmers and indentured servants resented years of exploitation by wealthy planters, arrogant justices of the peace, and "wicked & pernicious Counsellors." As one yeoman rebel complained, "A poor man who has only his labour to maintain himself and his family pays as much [in taxes] as a man who has 20,000 acres." Backed by 400 armed men, Bacon issued a "Manifesto and Declaration of the People" that demanded the death or removal of the Indians and an end to the rule of wealthy "parasites." "All the power and sway is got into the hands of the rich," Bacon proclaimed as his army burned Jamestown to the ground and plundered the plantations of Berkeley's allies. When Bacon died suddenly of dysentery in October 1676, the governor took revenge, dispersing the rebel army, seizing the estates of well-to-do rebels, and hanging twenty-three men.

Bacon's Rebellion was a pivotal event in the history of the Chesapeake colonies. Thereafter, landed planters retained their dominance by curbing corruption and appointing ambitious yeomen to public office. They appeased yeomen and tenants by cutting taxes and supporting expansion onto Indian lands. Most important, planters sought to forestall another rebellion by poor whites by cutting the use of indentured servants. Instead, planters imported thousands of African laborers, and in 1705, the Burgesses explicitly legalized chattel slavery. Those fateful decisions committed subsequent generations of Americans to a social system based on racial exploitation.

► What were the various systems of bound labor that took hold in the Chesapeake colonies? What accounts for the appearance of these systems?

► Compare the Indian uprising in Virginia in 1622 with Bacon's Rebellion in 1675. What were the consequences of each for Virginia's development?

Puritan New England

As the scramble for wealth escalated in the Chesapeake, Puritan settlers created colonies in New England that had strong ethical and spiritual goals. Between 1620 and 1640, thousands of Puritans fled to America seeking land and religious freedom. By distributing land broadly, the Puritans built a society of independent farm families. And by establishing a "holy commonwealth," they tried to preserve a "pure" Christian faith. Their "errand into the wilderness" gave a moral dimension to American history that survives today.

The Puritan Migration

New England differed from other European colonies in America. Unruly male adventurers founded New Spain and Jamestown, and male traders dominated life in New France and New Netherland. By contrast, the leaders of the Plymouth and Massachusetts Bay colonies were pious Protestants, and the settlers there included women and children as well as men.

The Pilgrims who settled in Plymouth were religious separatists — Puritans who had left the Church of England. When King James I threatened to drive Puritans "out of the land, or else do worse," some Puritans left England to live among Dutch Calvinists in Holland. Subsequently, thirty-five of these exiles resolved to migrate to America to maintain their English identity. Led by William Bradford and joined by sixty-seven migrants from England, they sailed to America in 1620 aboard the *Mayflower* and settled near Cape Cod in southeastern Massachusetts. Lacking a royal charter, they "combine[d] ourselves together into a civill body politick." The Mayflower Compact, the first American constitution, used the Puritans' self-governing religious congregation as the model for its political structure.

The first winter in Plymouth tested the Pilgrims. Of the 102 migrants who arrived in November, only half survived until spring. But then Plymouth became a healthy and thriving community. The cold climate inhibited the spread of mosquito-borne diseases, and the Pilgrims' religious discipline maintained a strong work ethic. Moreover, a smallpox epidemic in 1618 had killed most of the local Wampanoag people, so the migrants faced few external threats. The Pilgrims built solid houses and planted ample crops, and their number grew rapidly. By 1640, there were 3,000 settlers in Plymouth. To ensure political stability, they issued a written legal code that provided for representative self-government, broad political rights, property ownership, and religious freedom of conscience.

Meanwhile, England plunged deeper into religious turmoil. King Charles I repudiated certain Protestant doctrines, including the role of grace in salvation. English Puritans, now powerful in Parliament, accused the king of "popery" — of holding Catholic beliefs. In 1629, Charles dissolved Parliament, claimed the authority to rule by "divine right," and raised money through royal edicts and the sale of monopolies. When Archbishop William Laud, whom Charles chose to head the Church of England, dismissed hundreds of Puritan ministers, thousands of Puritan families fled to America.

That exodus began in 1630 with the departure of 900 Puritans led by John Winthrop, a well-educated country squire who became the first governor of the Massachusetts Bay Colony. Calling England morally corrupt and "overburdened with people," Winthrop sought land for his children and a place in Christian history for his people. "We must consider that we shall be as a City upon a Hill," Winthrop told the migrants. "The eyes of all people are upon us." Like the Pilgrims, the Puritans envisioned a reformed Christian society with "authority in magistrates, liberty in people, purity in the church," as minister John Cotton put it. By creating a genuinely "New" England, they hoped to inspire religious reform throughout Christendom.

Winthrop and his associates governed the Massachusetts Bay Colony from the town of Boston. They transformed their **joint-stock corporation**, the General Court of shareholders, into a representative political system with a governor, council, and assembly. To ensure rule by the godly, the Puritans limited the right to vote and hold office to men who were church members. Rejecting the Plymouth Colony's policy of religious tolerance, the Massachusetts Bay Colony established Puritanism as the state-supported religion, barred other faiths from conducting services, and used the Bible as a legal guide. "Where there is no Law," they said, magistrates should rule "as near the law of God as they can." Over the next decade, about 10,000 Puritans migrated to the colony, along with 10,000 others fleeing hard times in England.

The New England Puritans emulated the simplicity of the first Christians. They eliminated bishops, censuring them as "traitours unto God," and placed power in the hands of the ordinary members of the congregation—hence the name Congregationalist for their churches. Following the teachings of John Calvin, many Puritans embraced predestination, the doctrine that God had chosen (before their birth) only a few saints for salvation. Many church members lived in great anxiety, uncertain that God had chosen them as members of the "elect." Some hoped for a conversion experience, the intense spiritual sensation of receiving God's grace and being "born again." Other Puritans relied on "preparation," the confidence in salvation that came from spiritual guidance by their ministers. Still others believed that God considered them his chosen people, the new Israelites, who would be saved if they obeyed his laws.

To maintain God's favor, the Massachusetts Bay magistrates purged their society of religious dissidents. One target was Roger Williams, the Puritan minister in Salem, a coastal town north of Boston. Williams opposed the decision to establish Congregationalism as the state religion and praised the Pilgrims' separation of church and state. He advocated toleration, arguing that political magistrates had authority over only the "bodies, goods, and outward estates of men," not their spiritual lives. Moreover, Williams questioned the Puritans' seizure of Indian lands. The magistrates banished him from the colony in 1636.

Williams and his followers settled fifty miles south of Boston, founding the town of Providence on land purchased from the Narragansett Indians. Other religious dissidents settled nearby at Portsmouth and Newport. In 1644, these settlers obtained a corporate charter from Parliament for a new colony—Rhode Island—with full authority to rule themselves. In Rhode Island, as in Plymouth, there was no legally established church, and individuals could worship God as they pleased.

The Massachusetts Bay magistrates sensed a second threat to their authority in Anne Hutchinson. The wife of a merchant and a mother of seven, Hutchinson held weekly prayer meetings for women in her house and accused various Boston clergymen of placing too much emphasis on good behavior. Like Martin Luther, Hutchinson denied that salvation could be earned through good deeds: There was no "covenant of works"; God bestowed salvation only through the "covenant of grace." Moreover, Hutchinson declared that God "revealed" divine truth directly to individual believers, a controversial doctrine that the Puritan magistrates denounced as heretical.

The magistrates also resented Hutchinson because of her sex. Like other Christians, Puritans believed that both men and women could be saved. But gender equality stopped there. Women were inferior to men in earthly affairs, said leading Puritan divines, who instructed married women: "Thy desires shall bee subject to thy husband, and he shall rule over thee." The same was true in church affairs. According to Pilgrim minister John Robinson, women "are debarred by their sex from ordinary prophesying, and from any other dealing in the church wherein they take authority over the man." Puritan women could not be ministers or lay preachers, and they had no vote in the congregation. In 1637, the magistrates put Hutchinson on trial for teaching that inward grace freed an individual from the rules of the church and found her guilty of holding heretical views. Banished, she followed Roger Williams into exile in Rhode Island.

These coercive policies and a desire for better farm land prompted some Puritans to migrate to the Connecticut River Valley. In 1636, pastor Thomas Hooker and his congregation established the town of Hartford, and other Puritans settled along the river at Wethersfield and Windsor. In 1660, they secured a charter from King Charles II (r. 1660–1685) for the self-governing colony of Connecticut. Like Massachusetts Bay, Connecticut had a legally established church and an elected governor and assembly; however, it granted voting rights to most property-owning men, not just church members as in the original Puritan colony.

Meanwhile, England had fallen into a religious war. When Archbishop Laud imposed a Church of England prayer book on Presbyterian Scotland in 1642, a Scottish army invaded England. Thousands of English Puritans (and hundreds of American Puritans) joined the Scots, demanding religious reform and Parliamentary power. After years of civil war, the parliamentary forces led by Oliver Cromwell emerged victorious. In 1649, Parliament executed King Charles I, proclaimed a republican commonwealth, and banished bishops and elaborate rituals from the Church of England.

The Puritan triumph in England was short-lived. Popular support for the Commonwealth ebbed, especially after 1653, when Cromwell took dictatorial control. After his death in 1658, moderate Protestants and a resurgent aristocracy restored the monarchy and the hierarchy of bishops. For many Puritans, Charles II's accession to the throne in 1660 represented the victory of the Antichrist, the false prophet described in the final book of the New Testament.

For the Puritans in America, the restoration of the monarchy began a new phase of their "errand into the wilderness." They had come to New England to preserve the "pure" Christian church, expecting to return to Europe in triumph. When the failure of the English Revolution dashed that sacred mission, ministers exhorted their congregations to create a godly republican society in America. The Puritan colonies now stood as outposts of Calvinism and the Atlantic republican tradition.

Puritanism and Witchcraft

Like Native Americans, Puritans believed that the physical world was full of supernatural forces. Devout Christians saw signs of God's (or Satan's) power in blazing stars, birth defects, and other unusual events. Noting that the houses of many ministers "had been smitten with Lightning," Cotton Mather, a prominent Puritan theologian, wondered "what the meaning of God should be in it."

This belief in "forces" and "spirits" stemmed in part from Christian teachings—the Catholic belief in miracles, for example, and the Protestant faith in grace. It also reflected a pagan influence. When Samuel Sewall, a well-educated Puritan merchant and judge, moved into a new house, he fended off evil spirits by driving a metal pin into the floor. Thousands of ordinary Puritan farmers followed the pagan astrological charts printed in almanacs to determine the best times to plant crops, marry, and make other important decisions.

Zealous ministers attacked these practices as "superstition" and condemned the "cunning" individuals who claimed powers as healers or prophets. Indeed, many Christians believed such conjurers were Satan's "wizards" or "witches." People in the town of Andover "were much addicted to sorcery," claimed one observer, and "there

The PROTESTANT

ALMANACK,

For the Year 1700.

The Creation of the World	5706
The Incarnation of Jesus Christ	1700
England received the Christian Faith	1510
Martin Luther wrote against the Pope	184
Our first Deliverance from Popery by K. Edward VI.	152
Our second deliverance from Popery by Q. Elizabeth	141
The horrid design of the Gun-Powder Plot	95
The Burning of the City of London	34
Our Third Deliverance from Popery, by K.Will. & Q.Mary	12

Being the

BISSEXTILE or LEAP-YEAR.

WHEREIN

The Bloody Aspects, Fatal Oppositions, Diabolical Conjunctions, and Pernicious Revolutions of the Papacy against the Lord and his Anointed, are described.

With the Change of the Moon, some probable Conjectures of the VVeather, the Eclipses, the Moons place in the Zodiack, and an account of some principal Martyrs in each Month.

Calculated according to Art, for the Meridian of Babylon, where the Pope is elevated a hundred and fifty degrees above all Right and Religion; above Kings, Canons, Councils, Conscience, and every thing therein called God. 2 Thess. 2. And may without sensible Errour, indifferently serve the whole Papacy.

By Philoprotess, a well-willer to the Mathematicks.

London, Printed by John Richardson for the Company of STATIONERS. 1700.

The Protestant Almanack, 1700
The conflict between Protestants and Catholics took many forms. To reinforce the religious identity of English Protestants, the Company of Stationers published a yearly almanac that charted not only the passage of the seasons but also the "Pernicious Revolutions of the Papacy against the Lord and his Anointed." By permission of the Syndics of Cambridge University Library.

were forty men in it that could raise the Devil as well as any astrologer." Between 1647 and 1662, civil authorities in New England hanged fourteen people for witchcraft, mostly older women accused of being "double-tongued" or of having "an unruly spirit."

The most dramatic episode of witch-hunting occurred in Salem in 1692. Several young girls experienced strange seizures and then accused various neighbors of bewitching them. When judges at the trials of the accused witches allowed the use of "spectral" evidence — visions seen only by the girls — the accusations spun out of control. Eventually, Massachusetts Bay authorities arrested and tried 175 people for the crime of witchcraft and executed nineteen of them. The causes of this mass hysteria were complex and are still debated. Some historians point to group rivalries: Many of the accusers were the daughters or servants of poor farmers, whereas many of the alleged witches were wealthier church members or their friends. Because eighteen of those put to death were women, other historians claim the trials were part of a broader Puritan effort to subordinate women. Still other scholars focus on political instability in Massachusetts Bay in the early 1690s (see Chapter 3) and on fears raised by recent Indian attacks in nearby Maine, which had killed the parents of some of the young accusers.

Whatever the cause, the Salem episode marked a turning point in the handling of witchcraft accusations. Shaken by the executions, government officials now discouraged legal prosecutions for witchcraft. Equally important was the impact of the European Enlightenment, a major intellectual movement that began around 1675 and promoted a rational, scientific view of the world. Increasingly, educated people explained accidents and sudden deaths by reference to "natural causes," not witchcraft. Thus, unlike Cotton Mather (1663–1728), who believed that lightning was a supernatural sign, Benjamin Franklin (1706–1790) and other well-read men of his generation would conceive of lightning as a natural phenomenon.

A Yeoman Society, 1630–1700

In building their communities, New England Puritans consciously rejected the feudal practices of English society. Many Puritans came from middling families in East Anglia, a region of pasture lands and few manors. They had no desire to live as tenants of wealthy aristocrats or submit to oppressive taxation by a distant government. They had "escaped out of the pollutions of the world," the settlers of Watertown in Massachusetts Bay declared, and vowed "to sit down . . . close togither" in self-governing communities. Accordingly, the General Courts of Massachusetts Bay and Connecticut bestowed the title to each township on a group of settlers, or **proprietors**, who then distributed the land among the male heads of families.

Widespread ownership of land did not mean equality of wealth or status. "God had Ordained different degrees and orders of men," proclaimed Boston merchant John Saffin, "some to be Masters and Commanders, others to be Subjects, and to be commanded." Town proprietors normally awarded the largest plots to men of high social status, who often became selectmen and justices of the peace. However, all families received some land, and most adult men had a vote in the **town meeting**, the main institution of local government (Map 2.3).

In this society of independent households and self-governing communities, ordinary farmers had much more political power than Chesapeake yeomen and European peasants did. Although Nathaniel Fish was one of the poorest men in the town of Barnstable—he owned just a two-room cottage, eight acres of land, an ox, and a cow—he was a voting member of the town meeting. Each year, Fish and other Barnstable farmers levied taxes; enacted ordinances governing fencing, road building, and the use of common fields; and chose the selectmen who managed town affairs. The farmers also selected the town's representatives to the General Court, which gradually displaced the governor as the center of political authority. For Fish and thousands of other ordinary settlers, New England had proved to be a new world of opportunity.

▶ Why did the Puritans of Massachusetts Bay create an established church and persecute dissenters when they had fled England to escape those things?

▶ What were the main characteristics of the social and political structure of the New England colonies? Why did they develop in that fashion?

▶ Why were there were no major witchcraft scares in the Chesapeake colonies and no uprising in New England like Bacon's Rebellion?

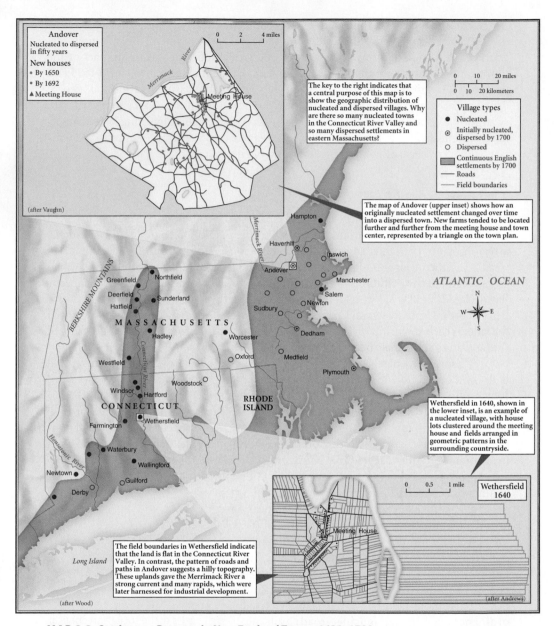

The key to the right indicates that a central purpose of this map is to show the geographic distribution of nucleated and dispersed villages. Why are there so many nucleated towns in the Connecticut River Valley and so many dispersed settlements in eastern Massachusetts?

Andover
Nucleated to dispersed in fifty years
New houses
• By 1650
• By 1692
▲ Meeting House

Meeting House

(after Vaughn)

Village types
• Nucleated
◉ Initially nucleated, dispersed by 1700
○ Dispersed
▨ Continuous English settlements by 1700
— Roads
— Field boundaries

The map of Andover (upper inset) shows how an originally nucleated settlement changed over time into a dispersed town. New farms tended to be located further and further from the meeting house and town center, represented by a triangle on the town plan.

Hampton
Haverhill
Ipswich
Andover
Manchester
Greenfield Northfield
Deerfield Sunderland Salem
Hatfield Newton
Sudbury
MASSACHUSETTS
BERKSHIRE MOUNTAINS
Hadley Worcester Dedham
Oxford Medfield
Westfield
Plymouth
Woodstock
Windsor Hartford
CONNECTICUT **RHODE ISLAND**
Wethersfield
Farmington
Waterbury
Wallingford
Newtown
Guilford
Derby

ATLANTIC OCEAN

N
W   E
S

Wethersfield in 1640, shown in the lower inset, is an example of a nucleated village, with house lots clustered around the meeting house and fields arranged in geometric patterns in the surrounding countryside.

The field boundaries in Wethersfield indicate that the land is flat in the Connecticut River Valley. In contrast, the pattern of roads and paths in Andover suggests a hilly topography. These uplands gave the Merrimack River a strong current and many rapids, which were later harnessed for industrial development.

Long Island

Meeting House

Wethersfield 1640

(after Andrews)

(after Wood)

MAP 2.3 Settlement Patterns in New England Towns, 1630–1700

Initially, most Puritan towns were compact. Regardless of the topography—hills or plains—families lived close to one another in the village center and traveled daily to work in the surrounding fields. This pattern is clear in the 1640 map of Wethersfield, which is situated on the broad plains of the Connecticut River Valley. The first settlers in Andover, Massachusetts, also chose to live in the village center. However, the rugged topography of eastern Massachusetts encouraged the townspeople to disperse; by 1692, many Andover residents were living on their own farms.

The Eastern Indians' New World

Native Americans along the Atlantic coast also lived in a new world, but for them, it was a bleak and dangerous place. Epidemics of smallpox struck with devastating results. In New England, so many Indians were stricken, an observer reported, they were "not able to help one another, no not to make a fire nor fetch a little water to drink, nor any to bury the dead." The European invaders took over the depopulated areas and ejected other Indian peoples from their ancestral lands. A few Indian peoples, most prominently the Iroquois, used European guns and manufactures to resist white intrusion and to dominate other tribes. Still other native peoples retreated into the mountains or moved westward to preserve their traditional cultures.

Puritans and Pequots

As the Puritans embarked for New England, they pondered the morality of intruding on Native American lands. "By what right or warrant can we enter into the land of the Savages?" they asked themselves. Responding to such concerns, John Winthrop detected God's hand in a recent smallpox epidemic: "If God were not pleased with our inheriting these parts," he asked, "why doth he still make roome for us by diminishing them as we increase?" Citing the Book of Genesis, the Massachusetts Bay magistrates declared that the Indians had not "subdued" their land and therefore had no "just right" to it.

Believing they were God's chosen people, the Puritans often treated Native Americans with a brutality equal to that of the Spanish conquistadors and Nathaniel Bacon's frontiersmen. When Pequot warriors attacked English farmers who had intruded onto their Connecticut River Valley lands in 1636, a Puritan militia attacked a Pequot village and massacred some 500 men, women, and children. "God laughed at the Enemies of his People," one soldier boasted, "filling the Place with Dead Bodies."

Like most Europeans, English Puritans saw the Indians as culturally inferior "savages." But the Puritans were not *racists* as the term is understood today. To their minds, Europeans and Native Americans were genetically the same. The Indians were white people with sun-darkened skin and "sin," not race, accounted for their degeneracy. "Probably the devil" delivered these "miserable savages" to America, Cotton Mather suggested, "in hopes that the gospel of the Lord Jesus Christ would never come here." This interpretation of the Indians' history inspired Puritan minister John Eliot to translate the Bible into Algonquian and to convert Indians to Christianity. Because of the rigorous admissions standards, only a few Native Americans became full members of Puritan congregations; nevertheless, Eliot and his colleagues turned fourteen Indian villages, such as Natick (Massachusetts) and Maanexit (Connecticut), into **praying towns**. Like the Franciscan missions in New Mexico, these towns were intended as intensely Christian communities. By 1670, more than 1,000 Indians lived in these settlements, having forsaken much of their independence and traditional culture.

Metacom's Rebellion

By the 1670s, New England whites outnumbered Indians by three to one. The English population had grown to some 55,000, while the number of native peoples had plummeted—from an estimated 120,000 in 1570 to 70,000 in 1620, to barely 16,000.

To Metacom (King Philip), leader of the Wampanoags, the future looked grim. When his people copied English ways by raising hogs and selling pork in Boston, Puritan officials accused them of selling at "an under rate" and placed restrictions on their trade. When Indians killed wandering livestock that damaged their cornfields, authorities denounced them for violating English property rights.

Like Opechancanough in Virginia and Popé in New Mexico, Metacom concluded that the Europeans had to be ousted from Indian lands. In 1675, the Wampanoags' leader forged a military alliance with the Narragansetts and Nipmucks and attacked white settlements throughout New England. They went to war, a group of Indians told Roger Williams, because the English "had forced them to it." Almost every day, settler William Harris fearfully reported, he heard new reports of the Indians' "burneing houses, takeing cattell, killing men & women & Children: & carrying others captive." Bitter fighting continued into 1676 and ended only when the Indian warriors ran short of gunpowder and when the Massachusetts Bay government hired Mohegan and Mohawk warriors, who ambushed and killed Metacom.

The rebellion was a deadly affair. Indians destroyed 20 percent of the English towns in Massachusetts and Rhode Island and killed 1,000 settlers, nearly 5 percent of the adult population. The very future of the Puritan experiment hung in the balance. Had "the Indeans not been divided," remarked one settler, "they might have forced us [to evacuate] to Som Islands: & there to have planted a little Corne, & fished for our liveings." But the natives' own losses—from famine and disease, death in battle, and sale into slavery—were much larger: About 4,500 Indians died, one-quarter of an already-diminished population. Many of the surviving Wampanoag, Narragansett, and Nipmuck peoples migrated farther into the New England backcountry, where they intermarried with Algonquin tribes allied to the French. Over the next century, these displaced Indian peoples would take their revenge, joining with French Catholics to attack their Puritan enemies (see American Voices, p. 61).

The Human and Environmental Impact of the Fur Trade

As English towns filled the river valleys along the Atlantic coast, the Indians who lived in the great forested areas beyond the Appalachian Mountains remained independent. Yet the distant Indian peoples—the Iroquois, Ottawas, Crees, Illinois, and many more—also felt the European presence through the fur trade. As they bargained for woolen blankets, iron cookware, knives, and guns, Indians learned to avoid the French at Montreal, who demanded two beaver skins for a woolen blanket. Instead, they dealt with the Dutch and English merchants at Albany, who asked for only one pelt and who could be played off against one another. "They are marvailous subtle in their bargains to save a penny," an English trader noted with displeasure. "They will beate all markets and try all places . . . to save six pence." Still, because the Indians had no way of knowing the value of their pelts in Europe, they rarely secured the highest possible price.

Nor could they control the European impact on their societies. European diseases, guns, and rum sapped the vitality of many Indian peoples. In South Carolina, a smallpox epidemic killed nearly half of the Catawbas, and "strong spirits" took a toll among the survivors: "Many of our people has Lately Died by the Effects of that Strong Drink."

A Captivity Narrative MARY ROWLANDSON

Mary Rowlandson, a minister's wife in Lancaster, Massachusetts, was one of many settlers taken captive by the Indians during Metacom's war. Mrs. Rowlandson spent twelve weeks in captivity before being ransomed by her family for the considerable sum of £20. Her account of this ordeal, *The Sovereignty and Goodness of God* (1682), was written in part to assert her moral purity (that she had not been sexually exploited), so that she could again live as a respectable Puritan woman. But Mrs. Rowlandson's dramatic and literary skills made it one of the most popular prose works of its time.

On the tenth of February 1675, came the Indians with great numbers upon Lancaster: their first coming was about sunrising; hearing the noise of some guns, we looked out; several houses were burning, and the smoke ascending to heaven. . . . [T]he Indians laid hold of us, pulling me one way, and the children another, and said, "Come go along with us"; I told them they would kill me: they answered, if I were willing to go along with them, they would not hurt me. . . .

The first week of my being among them I hardly ate any thing; the second week I found my stomach grow very faint for want of something; and yet it was very hard to get down their filthy trash; but the third week . . . they were sweet and savory to my taste. I was at this time knitting a pair of white cotton stockings for my [Indian] mistress; and had not yet wrought upon a sabbath day. When the sabbath came they bade me go to work. I told them it was the sabbath-day, and desired them to let me rest, and told them I would do as much more tomorrow; to which they answered me they would break my face. . . .

During my abode in this place, Philip [Metacom] spake to me to make a shirt for his boy, which I did, for which he gave me a shilling. I offered the money to my master, but he bade me keep it; and with it I bought a piece of horse flesh. Afterwards he asked me to make a cap for his boy, for which he invited me to dinner. I went, and he gave me a pancake, about as big as two fingers. It was made of parched wheat, beaten, and fried in bear's grease, but I thought I never tasted pleasanter meat in my life. . . .

My master had three squaws, living sometimes with one, and sometimes with another one. . . . [It] was Weetamoo with whom I had lived and served all this while. A severe and proud dame she was, bestowing every day in dressing herself near as much time as any of the gentry of the land: powdering her hair, and painting her face, going with necklaces, with jewels in her ears, and bracelets upon her hands. When she had dressed herself, her work was to make girdles of wampom and beads. . . .

On Tuesday morning they called their general court (as they call it) to consult and determine, whether I should go home or no. And they all as one man did seemingly consent to it, that I should go home. . . .

SOURCE: C. H. Lincoln, ed., *Original Narratives of Early American History: Narratives of Indian Wars,* 1675–1699 (New York: Barnes and Noble, 1952), 14: 139–41.

Most native societies also lost their economic independence. As they exchanged furs for European-made iron utensils and woolen blankets, Indians neglected their traditional artisan skills, making fewer flint hoes, clay pots, and skin garments. "Every necessity of life we must have from the white people," a Cherokee chief complained. Religious autonomy vanished as well. When French missionaries won converts among the Hurons, Iroquois, and Illinois, they divided Indian communities into hostile religious factions.

Likewise, constant warfare for furs altered the dynamics of tribal politics by shifting power from cautious elders to headstrong young warriors. The sachems (chiefs), a group of young Seneca warriors said scornfully, "were a parcell of Old People who say much but who Mean or Act very little." The position and status of Indian women changed in especially complex ways. Traditionally, eastern woodland women had a voice in political councils because they were the chief providers of food and handcrafted goods. As a French Jesuit noted of the Iroquois, "The women are always the first to deliberate . . . on private or community matters. They hold their councils apart and . . . advise the chiefs . . . , so that the latter may deliberate on them in their turn." The disruption of farming by warfare and the influx of European goods undermined the economic basis of women's power. Yet, paradoxically, among victorious warring tribes such as the Iroquois, the influence of women probably increased in other respects; for example, women were responsible for the cultural assimilation of hundreds of captives.

There is no doubt that the sheer extent of the fur industry—the slaughter of hundreds of thousands of beaver, deer, otter, and other animals—profoundly altered the environment. As early as the 1630s, a French Jesuit worried that the Montagnais people, who lived north of the St. Lawrence, were killing so many beaver that they

An English View of Pocahontas
By depicting the Indian princess Pocahontas as a well-dressed European woman, the artist casts her as a symbol of peaceful assimilation into English culture. In actuality, marriages between white men (often fur traders) and Indian women usually resulted in bilingual families that absorbed elements from both cultures.
National Portrait Gallery, Smithsonian Institution/Art Resource, New York.

would "exterminate the species in this Region, as has happened among the Hurons." As the animal populations died off, streams ran faster (there were fewer beaver dams) and the underbrush grew denser (there were fewer deer to trim the vegetation). The native environment, as well as its animals and peoples, were now part of a new American world of relentless exploitation and little civility.

▶ Compare the causes of the uprisings led by Popé in New Mexico and Metacom in New England. Which was more successful? Why?

▶ What were the major social and environmental developments that made America a new world for both Europeans and Indians?

SUMMARY

We have seen that Spain created a permanent settlement in North America in 1565 and that England, France, and the Dutch Republic did likewise between 1607 and 1614. All of these European incursions spread devastating diseases among the native peoples. All reduced some Indians to subject peoples. And except for the Dutch, all involved efforts to spread Christianity. There were important differences as well. The French and the Dutch established fur-trading colonies, while the Spanish and the English created settler colonies. However, Spanish settlers intermarried with the Indians, but the English did not.

We also saw major differences and similarities between England's Chesapeake colonies, in which bound laborers raised tobacco for export to Europe, and those in New England, where pious Puritan yeoman lived in self-governing farming communities. But both regions boasted representative political institutions. Both experienced Indian wars in the first decades of settlement (in Virginia in 1622 and in New England in 1636) and again in 1675–1676. Indeed, the simultaneous eruption of Bacon's Rebellion and Metacom's War suggests that the histories of the two English regions had begun to converge.

Connections: Religion

In the essay that opens Part One, we stated that

> The American experience profoundly changed religious institutions and values. . . . American Protestant Christianity became increasingly tolerant, democratic, and optimistic.

In Chapter 2, we began our discussion of religion by discussing the migration of Anglicans to Virginia, Catholics to Maryland, and Puritans to New England. We saw how religious diversity and ideological principles thwarted attempts to enforce spiritual conformity in Massachusetts Bay and to create strong established churches in Maryland, Plymouth Colony, and Rhode Island. We will revisit issues of religious uniformity and tolerance in Chapter 3, in a discussion of Quakers in Pennsylvania and West New Jersey in the 1680s, and in Chapter 4, with an analysis of the migration to British North America between 1720 and 1760 of Scots-Irish Presbyterians, German Lutherans, and other European Protestants.

TIMELINE

1539–1543 ▶ Coronado and de Soto lead gold-seeking expeditions	**1630** ▶ Puritans found Massachusetts Bay Colony
1565 ▶ Spain establishes a fort at St. Augustine	**1634** ▶ Maryland settled as Catholic refuge
1598 ▶ Acomas rebel in New Mexico	**1636** ▶ Puritan-Pequot War
1603–1625 ▶ Reign of James I, advocate of "divine right" of kings	**1636** ▶ Roger Williams founds Providence, Rhode Island
1607 ▶ English traders settle Jamestown	**1637** ▶ Anne Hutchinson banished from Massachusetts Bay
1608 ▶ Samuel de Champlain founds Quebec	**1640s** ▶ Iroquois initiate wars over fur trade
1614 ▶ Dutch set up fur-trading post at Fort Orange (Albany)	**1642–1659** ▶ Puritan Revolution in England
1619 ▶ First Africans arrive in the Chesapeake region	**1651** ▶ First Navigation Act
▶ House of Burgesses convenes in Virginia	**1660** ▶ Restoration of English monarchy
1620 ▶ Pilgrims found Plymouth Colony	▶ Tobacco prices fall and remain low
1620–1660 ▶ Chesapeake colonies experience tobacco boom	**1664** ▶ English conquer New Netherland
1621 ▶ Dutch West India Company granted charter	**1675** ▶ Bacon's Rebellion
	1675–1676 ▶ Metacom's uprising
1622 ▶ Opechancanough's uprising	**1680** ▶ Popé's rebellion in New Mexico
1624 ▶ Virginia becomes a royal colony	
1625–1649 ▶ Charles I reigns and is executed	**1692** ▶ Salem witchcraft trials
	1705 ▶ Virginia enacts law defining slavery

The forced migration of hundreds of thousands of Africans, one of the central themes of Chapter 3, will add complexity to our story of colonial religion. Some African slaves were Muslims; many more relied for spiritual substance and moral guidance on African gods and the powers they saw in nature. As we will see in Chapter 4, the Great Awakening, a far-reaching Christian revival during the 1740s and 1750s, brought only a few Africans into Christian churches but significantly increased the diversity of religious institutions and beliefs among Europeans. As the timeline for Part One suggests, key themes of the American experience include religious liberty, pluralism, and tolerance.

FOR FURTHER EXPLORATION

For an insightful narrative of Spain's northern adventures, consult David Weber, *The Spanish Frontier in North America* (1992). Bernard Bailyn, *The Peopling of British North America* (1986), presents a brief, vivid history of English settlement. In *American Slavery, American Freedom* (1975), Edmund Morgan offers a compelling portrait of life in early Virginia. John Demos, *The Unredeemed Captive: A Family Story from Early America* (1994), relates the gripping tale of Eunice Williams, a Puritan girl who was captured by and lived her life among the Mohawks. Two other fine studies of Native American life are James Merrell, *The Indians' New World: Catawbas and Their Neighbors* (1989), and Colin Calloway, *New Worlds for All: Indians, Europeans, and the Remaking of Early America* (1997).

Two fine Web sites are "Caleb Johnson's Mayflower History" (**www.mayflowerhistory .com/**) and "The Plymouth Colony Archive Project" (**etext.lib.virginia.edu/users/deetz/**). For insight into life in colonial New England, see the Web site for *Colonial House* (**www.pbs.org/wnet/colonialhouse/about.html**) and the Web site for the "Salem Witchcraft Trials" (**etext.lib.virginia.edu/salem/witchcraft/**). "Colonial Williamsburg" (**www.colonialwilliamsburg.org/history/**) offers an extensive collection of documents, illustrations, and secondary texts about colonial life. A two-hour-long PBS video, *Surviving Columbus*, traces the history of the Pueblo Indians over 450 years. "First Nations Histories" (**www.tolatsga.org/Compacts.html**) offers information on many North American Indian peoples.

TEST YOUR KNOWLEDGE

To assess your mastery of the material in this chapter and for Web sites, images, and documents related to this chapter, visit **bedfordstmartins.com/henrettaconcise**.

Creating a British Empire in America
1660–1750

These two words, Negro and Slave, [have become] Homogeneous and Convertible; even as Negro and Christian, Englishman and Heathen, are [now] made opposites.

— The Reverend Morgan Godwyn, 1680

When Charles II came to the throne in 1660, England was a second-class commercial power, its merchants picking up the crumbs left by the worldwide maritime empire of the Dutch. "What we want is more of the trade the Dutch now have," declared the Duke of Albemarle, a trusted minister of the king and a proprietor of Carolina. To get it, the English government embarked on a century-long quest for trade and empire. It passed a series of Navigation Acts, designed to exclude Dutch ships from its colonies, and it went to war to destroy Holland's maritime dominance. By the 1720s, Great Britain (the recently unified kingdoms of England and Scotland) had seized control of the transatlantic trade in American sugar and African slaves. The emerging British Empire, boasted the ardent imperialist Malachy Postlethwayt, "was a magnificent superstructure of American commerce and naval power on an African foundation."

That was only the half of it. British commerce increasingly spanned the world. It exported woolen goods to Europe, America, and Africa. Its merchants bought cotton textiles in India to trade for slaves in West Africa and carried silver to China to exchange for tea, ceramics, and silks. To protect the empire's valuable sugar colonies and trade routes, British ministers repeatedly went to war, first against the Dutch and then against the French. The goal—to preserve a mercantile system in British America and win "free entry" into the commerce of other empires—was increasingly successful. Boasted one English pamphleteer: "We are, of any nation, the best situated for trade, . . . capable of giving maritime laws to the world."

That dictum included Britain's North American colonies. When imperial official Edward Randolph reported from New England in the early 1670s that "there is no notice taken of the act of navigation," the home government undertook to impose its political will on the American settlements.

The Politics of Empire, 1660–1713

Before 1660, England governed its New England and Chesapeake colonies haphazardly. Taking advantage of that laxness and the English civil war, local "big men" (oligarchies of Puritan magistrates and tobacco planters) ran their societies as they wished. After the monarchy was restored in 1660, royal bureaucrats tried to impose order on the unruly settlements and, enlisting the aid of Indian allies, warred with rival European powers.

The Great Aristocratic Land Grab

When Charles II (r. 1660–1685) ascended the English throne, he quickly established new settlements: the Restoration Colonies, as historians call them. In 1663, Charles paid off a monetary and political debt to eight loyal noblemen with the gift of Carolina, an area long claimed by Spain and populated by thousands of Indians. He bestowed an equally huge grant on his brother James, the Duke of York, who received New Jersey and the just-conquered Dutch colony of New Netherland (now renamed New York). James quickly conveyed the ownership of New Jersey to two of the Carolina proprietors.

In one of the great land grabs in history, a handful of English nobles had taken title to vast provinces. Like Lord Baltimore's Maryland, their new colonies were proprietorships: The aristocrats owned all the land and could rule as they wished, provided their laws conformed broadly to those of England. Most proprietors envisioned a traditional European society presided over by a landed gentry and the Church of England. The Fundamental Constitutions of Carolina (1669), for example, prescribed a **manorial system**, with a mass of serfs governed by a handful of powerful nobles.

The manorial system proved to be a fantasy. The first settlers in North Carolina were primarily poor families and runaway servants from Virginia and English Quakers, an equality-minded radical Protestant sect (also known as the Society of Friends). Quakers "think there is no difference between a Gentleman and a labourer," complained one Anglican clergyman. Refusing to work on large manors, the settlers raised corn, hogs, and tobacco on modest family farms. In 1677, inspired by Bacon's Rebellion in Virginia, the residents of Albemarle County staged their own uprising. Angered by taxes on tobacco exports to support the Anglican Church, they rebelled again in 1708. The residents were "stubborn and disobedient," a wealthy Anglican landowner charged, and by deposing a series of governors, they forced the proprietors to abandon their dreams of a feudal society.

In South Carolina, the colonists also refused to accept the Fundamental Constitutions. Many of the white settlers there were migrants from the overcrowded sugar-producing island of Barbados, and they wanted to create a hierarchical society based on slavery. They used enslaved workers — both Africans and Native Americans — to raise cattle and food crops for export to the West Indies. Carolina merchants also opened a lucrative trade in deerskins with neighboring Indian peoples. In exchange for rum and guns, the Carolinians' Indian trading partners also provided slaves — captives from other Native American peoples. By 1708,

William Penn's Treaty with the Indians, 1683
In 1771, Benjamin West executed this famous picture of William Penn's meeting with the Lenni-Lanapes, who called themselves "the Common People." As a Quaker, Penn refused to seize Indian lands; instead, he negotiated their purchase. Penn was favorably impressed by the Lenni-Lanapes: "For their persons they are generally tall, straight, well built, and of singular proportion," he wrote in 1683. "They tread strong and clever, and mostly walk with a lofty chin." Pennsylvania Academy of the Fine Arts, Philadelphia.
For more help analyzing this image, see the Online Study Guide at **bedfordstmartins.com/henrettaconcise**.

white Carolinians were working their coastal plantations with 1,400 Indian and 2,900 African slaves, and brutal Indian warfare continued in the backcountry. South Carolina would remain a violent frontier settlement until the 1720s.

In dramatic contrast to the Carolinians, the 15,000 migrants who settled in Pennsylvania in the late seventeenth century pursued a pacifistic policy toward Native Americans and quickly became prosperous. In 1681, Charles II bestowed Pennsylvania (which included present-day Delaware) on William Penn in payment for a large debt owed to Penn's father. The younger Penn was born to wealth, owned substantial estates in Ireland and England, and lived lavishly—with a country mansion, fine clothes, and eight servants. Destined by birth for courtly pursuits, Penn instead joined the Quakers, who condemned extravagance. Penn designed Pennsylvania as a refuge for his fellow Quakers, who were persecuted in England because they refused to serve in the military or pay taxes to support the Church of England. Penn himself spent more than two years in jail for preaching his beliefs.

Like the Puritans, the Quakers wanted to restore Christianity to its early simple spirituality. But they rejected the Puritans' pessimistic Calvinist doctrines, which restricted salvation to a small elect. The Quakers followed the teachings of two English visionaries, George Fox and Margaret Fell, who argued that God had imbued all men — and women — with an "inner light" of grace or understanding. Reflecting this emphasis on gender equality, 350 Quaker women would serve as ministers in the colonies.

Penn's Frame of Government (1681) applied the Quakers' radical beliefs to politics. It ensured religious freedom by prohibiting a legally established church, and it promoted political equality by allowing all property-owning men to vote and hold office. Cheered by these provisions, thousands of Quakers — mostly yeomen families from the north-west Midland region of England — flocked to Pennsylvania. Initially, they settled along the Delaware River near the city of Philadelphia, which Penn himself laid out in a grid with wide main streets and many parks. To attract European Protestants, Penn published pamphlets in Dutch and German promising cheap land and religious toleration. In 1683, migrants from Saxony founded Germantown (just outside Philadelphia), and thousands of other Germans soon followed. Ethnic diversity, pacifism, and freedom of conscience made Pennsylvania the most open and democratic of the Restoration Colonies.

From Mercantilism to Imperial Dominion

As Charles II gave away his American lands, his ministers devised policies to keep colonial trade in English hands. Since the 1560s, the English crown had used government subsidies and charters to stimulate English manufacturing and foreign trade. Now it extended these mercantilist policies to the American settlements through the Navigation Acts.

According to mercantilist theory, the colonies would produce agricultural goods and raw materials, which English merchants would carry to England. Certain goods would be exported immediately to Europe in return for **specie** (gold or silver coin) or goods; other goods would be manufactured into finished products and then exported. The Navigation Act of 1651 kept this trade in English hands. It excluded Dutch merchants from the English colonies and required that goods be carried on ships owned by English or colonial merchants. New parliamentary acts in 1660 and 1663 strengthened the ban on foreign traders, required the colonists to ship sugar and tobacco only to England, and mandated that colonists import European goods only through England. To pay the customs officials who enforced these mercantilist laws, the Revenue Act of 1673 imposed a "plantation duty" on American exports of sugar and tobacco.

The English government backed these policies with military force. In three commercial wars between 1652 and 1674, the English navy drove the Dutch from New Netherland, seized control of commerce in the North Atlantic, and contested Holland's control of the Atlantic slave trade by attacking Dutch forts and ships along the West African coast. Meanwhile, English merchants expanded their fleets, which increased in capacity from 150,000 tons in 1640 to 340,000 tons in 1690.

Many colonists ignored the mercantilist laws and continued to trade with Dutch merchants and to import sugar and molasses from the French West Indies. The Massachusetts Bay assembly boldly declared: "The laws of England are bounded within the seas [surrounding it] and do not reach America." Outraged by this insolence, an English customs official called for troops to "reduce Massachusetts to obedience." Instead, the Lords of Trade—the administrative body charged with colonial affairs—opted for a punitive legal strategy. In 1679, it denied the claim of Massachusetts Bay to New Hampshire and eventually established a completely separate royal colony there. Then, in 1684, the Lords of Trade persuaded an English court to annul the charter of Massachusetts Bay because the Puritan government had violated the Navigation Acts and virtually outlawed the Church of England.

The Puritans' troubles had only begun, thanks to the accession of King James II (r. 1685–1688). The new monarch was an aggressive and inflexible ruler. During the reign of Oliver Cromwell, James had grown up in exile in France, and he admired its authoritarian king, Louis XIV. Believing that monarchs had a "divine right" to rule, James instructed the Lords of Trade to impose strict royal control on the American colonies. In 1686, the Lords revoked the corporate charters of Connecticut and Rhode Island and merged them with the Massachusetts Bay and Plymouth colonies to form a new royal province, the Dominion of New England. As governor of the Dominion, James II appointed Sir Edmund Andros, a hard-edged former military officer. Two years later, James II added New York and New Jersey to the Dominion, creating a vast colony that stretched from Maine to Pennsylvania.

The Target of the Glorious Revolution: James II

In Godfrey Kneller's portrait of James II (r. 1685–1688), the king's stance and facial expression suggest his forceful, arrogant personality. James set out to consolidate England's North American empire, but his arbitrary measures and Catholic sympathies prompted rebellions that cost him the throne. National Portrait Gallery, London.

The Dominion extended to America the authoritarian model of colonial rule the English government had imposed on Catholic Ireland. When England had recaptured New York from the Dutch in 1674, James II refused to allow an elective assembly and ruled by decree. Now he imposed absolutist rule on the entire Dominion by ordering Governor Andros to abolish the existing legislative assemblies. In Massachusetts, Andros immediately banned town meetings, angering villagers who prized local self-rule, and advocated public worship in the Church of England, offending Puritan Congregationalists. Even worse, from the colonists' perspective, the governor challenged all land titles granted under the original Massachusetts Bay charter. Andros offered to provide new deeds, but only if the colonists would agree to pay an annual fee.

The Glorious Revolution in England and America

Fortunately for the colonists, James II angered English political leaders as much as Andros alienated American settlers. The king revoked the charters of English towns, rejected the advice of Parliament, and aroused popular opposition by openly practicing Roman Catholicism. Then, in 1688, James's Spanish Catholic wife gave birth to a son, raising the prospect of a Catholic heir to the throne. To forestall that outcome, Protestant bishops and parliamentary leaders in the Whig Party led a quick and bloodless coup known as the Glorious Revolution. Backed by the populace and the military, they forced James into exile and in 1689 enthroned Mary, his Protestant daughter by his first wife, and her Dutch Protestant husband, William of Orange. The Whigs were not democrats: They wanted political power, especially the power to levy taxes, in the hands of the gentry, merchants, and other substantial property owners. Whig politicians forced King William and Queen Mary to accept a Declaration of Rights, which created a constitutional monarchy that enhanced the powers of the House of Commons at the expense of the crown.

To justify their coup, the members of Parliament relied on political philosopher John Locke. In his *Two Treatises on Government* (1690), Locke rejected the divine right monarchy celebrated by James II; instead, he argued that the legitimacy of government rests on the consent of the governed and that individuals have inalienable natural rights to life, liberty, and property. Locke's celebration of individual rights and representative government had a lasting influence in America, where many political leaders wanted to expand the powers of the colonial assemblies.

The Glorious Revolution sparked rebellions by Protestant colonists in Massachusetts, Maryland, and New York. When news of the coup reached Boston in April 1689, Puritan leaders, supported by 2,000 militiamen, seized Governor Andros, accused him of Catholic sympathies, and shipped him back to England. Heeding American complaints of authoritarian rule, the new monarchs broke up the Dominion of New England. However, they refused to restore the old Puritan-dominated government of Massachusetts Bay; instead, in 1692, they created a new royal colony (which included Plymouth and Maine). The new charter empowered the king to appoint the governor and customs officials; it gave the vote to all male property owners, not just Puritan church members; and it eliminated Puritan restrictions on the Church of England.

The uprising in Maryland had economic as well as religious causes. Since 1660, falling tobacco prices had hurt smallholders, tenant farmers, and former indentured servants. These poorer farmers were overwhelmingly Protestants, and they resented the rising taxes and the high fees imposed by wealthy proprietary officials, who were mostly Catholics. When Parliament ousted James II, a Protestant association mustered 700 men and forcibly removed the Catholic governor. The Lords of Trade supported this Protestant initiative: They suspended Lord Baltimore's proprietorship, imposed royal government, and made the Church of England the legal religion in the colony. This arrangement lasted until 1715, when Benedict Calvert, the fourth Lord Baltimore, converted to the Anglican faith and the king restored the proprietorship to the Calvert family.

In New York, Jacob Leisler led the rebellion against the Dominion of New England. Leisler was a German soldier who had worked for the Dutch West India Company, become a merchant, and married into a prominent Dutch family in New York. He was also a militant Calvinist, rigid and hot tempered. When New England settlers on Long Island, angered by James's prohibition of representative institutions, learned of the king's ouster, they repudiated the Dominion. The rebels quickly won the support of Dutch Protestant artisans in New York City, who welcomed the succession of Queen Mary and her Dutch husband. Led by Leisler, the Dutch militia ousted Lieutenant Governor Nicholson, an Andros appointee and an alleged Catholic sympathizer.

Initially, all classes and ethnic groups rallied behind Leisler, who headed a temporary government. However, Leisler's denunciations of political rivals as "popish dogs" and "Roages, Rascalls, and Devills" soon alienated many English-speaking New Yorkers. When Leisler imprisoned forty of his political opponents, imposed new taxes, and championed the artisans' cause, the prominent Dutch merchants who had traditionally controlled the city's government condemned his rule. In 1691, the merchants found an ally in Colonel Henry Sloughter, the newly appointed governor, who had Leisler indicted for treason. Convicted by an English jury, Leisler was hanged and then decapitated, an act of ethnic vengeance that corrupted New York politics for a generation.

The Glorious Revolution of 1688–1689 began a new, nonauthoritarian political era in both England and America. In England, William and Mary ruled as constitutional monarchs and promoted an empire based on commerce. Because the new Protestant monarchs wanted colonial support for a war against Catholic France, they accepted the overthrow of the Dominion of New England and allowed the restoration of self-government in Massachusetts and New York. Parliament created a Board of Trade in 1696 to supervise the American settlements, but it had limited success. Settlers and proprietors resisted the board's attempt to install royal governments, as did many English political leaders, who feared an increase in monarchical power. The result was another period of lax political administration during which the home government imposed only a few laws and taxes on the mainland settlements. It allowed local elites to rule the American colonies and encouraged English merchants to develop them as sources of trade.

Imperial Wars and Native Peoples

In a world of commercial competition, Britain's success depended on both mercantile skills and military power. Between 1689 and 1815, Britain fought a series of increasingly intense wars with France. To win wars in Western Europe and the Caribbean,

British leaders created a powerful central state that spent three-quarters of its revenue on military and naval expenses. As the wars spread to the North American mainland, they involved colonists and Native Americans, both of whom tried to turn the fighting to their own advantage.

The first significant battles in North America occurred during the War of the Spanish Succession (1702–1713), which pitted Britain against France and Spain. English settlers in the Carolinas armed the Creeks, whose 15,000 members farmed the fertile lands along the present-day border of Georgia and Alabama. A joint English-Creek expedition attacked Spanish Florida, burning the town of St. Augustine but failing to capture the nearby fort. To protect Havana in nearby Cuba, the Spanish reinforced St. Augustine and unsuccessfully attacked Charleston, South Carolina.

The Creeks had their own agenda: To become the dominant tribe in the region, they needed to vanquish their longtime enemies, the pro-French Choctaws to the west and the Spanish-allied Apalachees to the south. Beginning in 1704, a force of Creek and Yamasee warriors destroyed the remaining Franciscan missions in northern Florida, attacked the Spanish settlement at Pensacola, and captured 1,000 Apalachees, whom they sold to South Carolinian slave traders for use in the West Indies. Simultaneously, a Carolina-supplied Creek expedition attacked the Iroquois-speaking Tuscarora people of North Carolina, killing hundreds, executing 160 male captives, and sending 400 women and children into slavery. The surviving Tuscaroras migrated to the north and joined the Iroquois in New York (who now became the Six Iroquois Nations). The Carolinians, having used Indians to kill Spaniards, now died at the hands of their former allies. When English traders demanded the payment of trade debts in 1715, the Creeks and Yamasees revolted. They killed 400 colonists before being overwhelmed by the Carolinians and their new Indian allies, the Cherokees.

Native Americans also joined in the warfare between French Catholics in Canada and English Protestants in New England. With French aid, Catholic Mohawk and Abenaki warriors took revenge on their Puritan enemies. They destroyed English settlements in Maine, and in 1704, they attacked the western Massachusetts town of Deerfield, where they killed 48 residents and carried 112 into captivity. In response, New England militia attacked French settlements and, in 1710, joined with British naval forces to seize Port Royal in French Acadia (Nova Scotia). However, a major British–New England expedition against the French stronghold at Quebec failed miserably.

The New York frontier remained quiet. French and English merchants did not want to disrupt the lucrative fur trade, and the Iroquois, tired of war, had adopted a policy of "aggressive neutrality." In 1701, the Iroquois concluded a peace treaty with France and its Indian allies. Simultaneously, the Iroquois renewed the Covenant Chain, a series of military alliances with the English government in New York and its Indian friends (see Chapter 2). For the next half century, the Iroquois exploited their strategic location between the English and the French colonies by trading with both but refusing to fight for either. The Iroquois's strategy, according to their Delaware ally Teedyuscung, was "to defend our land against both."

Stalemated militarily in America, Britain won major territorial and commercial concessions through its victories in Europe. In the Treaty of Utrecht (1713), Britain obtained Newfoundland, Acadia, and the Hudson Bay region of northern Canada from France, as well as access through Albany to the western Indian trade. From Spain,

▶ What was the role of the colonies in the British mercantilist system?

▶ Explain the causes and the results of the Glorious Revolutions in England and America.

Britain acquired the strategic fortress of Gibraltar at the entrance to the Mediterranean and a thirty-year contract to supply slaves to Spanish America. These gains advanced Britain's quest for commercial supremacy, preserved its Protestant monarchy, and brought peace to eastern North America for a generation.

The Imperial Slave Economy

Britain's focus on America reflected the growth of a new agricultural and commercial order—the South Atlantic System—which produced sugar, tobacco, rice, and other subtropical products for an international market. At its center stood plantation societies ruled by European planter-merchants and worked by hundreds of thousands of enslaved Africans.

The South Atlantic System

The South Atlantic System had its center in Brazil and the West Indies, and sugar was its primary product. Before 1500, the world's people enjoyed few sweeteners—mostly honey and fruit juices. Then European planters developed sugarcane plantations in Brazil and the islands of the Caribbean Sea. The craving for the potent new sweetener was so intense that by 1900, sugar accounted for an astonishing 20 percent of the calories consumed by the world's people.

European merchants, investors, and planters garnered the profits of the South Atlantic System. Following mercantilist principles, they provided the plantations with tools and equipment to grow and process the sugarcane and ships to carry it to Europe. But it was the Atlantic slave trade that made the system run. Between 1520 and 1650, Portuguese traders accounted for 95 percent of the 820,000 Africans carried across the Atlantic—about 4,000 slaves each year before 1600 and 10,000 annually thereafter. Over the next half century, the Dutch dominated the Atlantic slave trade; then, between 1700 and 1800, the British became the prime carriers, transporting about 2.5 million of the total of 6.1 million Africans sent to the Americas. To secure this vast number of workers, European merchants relied on African-run slave-catching systems. These systems extended far into Africa's interior and funneled captives to Elmina, Calabar, Luanda, and other slave ports.

The cultivation of sugar—and, after 1750, coffee—drove the slave trade. In the 1620s, the English colonized a number of small West Indian islands: St. Christopher, Nevis, Montserrat, and especially Barbados, which had an extensive amount of arable land. Until the 1650s, most settlers were English, smallholders and indentured servants, who exported tobacco and livestock hides. In fact, there were more English residents in the West Indies (some 44,000) than in the Chesapeake (12,000) and New England (23,000) colonies combined.

Sugar transformed Barbados and the other islands into slave-based plantation societies. To provide raw sugar for refineries in Amsterdam, Dutch merchants provided English planters with money to buy land, sugar-processing equipment, and

A Sugar Mill in the French West Indies, 1655
Sugar powered the South Atlantic System. Its production demanded hard labor and considerable expertise. As this romanticized view shows, field slaves did the hard work, cutting the sugarcane and carrying or carting it to the oxen- (or wind-) powered mill, where it was pressed to yield the juice. Then skilled slave artisans took over. They carefully heated the juice and, at the proper moment, added ingredients to produce granulated sugar. The remaining liquid was molasses, a bitter-tasting sweetener that could be distilled into rum. The Granger Collection, New York.

slaves. By 1680, an elite group of 175 planters dominated Barbados's economy; they owned more than half the land and half the slaves, who numbered more than 50,000. In 1692, exploited Irish servants and island-born African slaves staged a major uprising, which was brutally suppressed. As social inequality and racial conflict increased, hundreds of English farmers fled to South Carolina and the large island of Jamaica, which England had seized from Spain in 1655. But the days of Caribbean smallholders were numbered. English sugar merchants soon invested heavily in Jamaica; by 1750, it had 700 large sugar plantations worked by more than 105,000 slaves and had become the wealthiest British colony.

Sugar was a rich man's crop because it could be produced most efficiently on large plantations. Scores of slaves planted and cut the sugarcane, which was then processed by expensive equipment—crushing mills, boiling houses, distilling apparatus—into raw sugar, molasses, and rum. The affluent planter-merchants who controlled the sugar industry drew annual profits of more than 10 percent on their investment. As Scottish economist Adam Smith noted in his famous treatise *The Wealth of Nations* (1776), sugar was the most profitable crop in Europe and America.

The South Atlantic System brought wealth to the entire British—and European—economy. Most British West Indian plantations belonged to absentee landlords who lived in England, where they spent their profits and formed a powerful "sugar lobby." Moreover, the Navigation Acts kept the trade in British sugar in the hands of British merchants, who exported it to foreign markets. By 1750, British reshipments of American sugar and tobacco to Europe accounted for half the nation's exports. Enormous profits also flowed into Britain from the slave trade. The value of the guns, iron, rum, cloth, and other European products used to buy slaves was relatively small—only about one-tenth (in the 1680s) to one-third (by the 1780s) of the value of the crops those slaves produced in America. This substantial differential allowed the Royal African Company and other English traders to sell slaves in the West Indies for three to five times what they paid for them in Africa.

These massive profits drove the expansion of the slave trade. At its height in the 1790s, Britain annually exported 300,000 guns to Africa, and a British ship carrying 300 to 350 slaves left an African port every other day. This commerce stimulated the entire British economy. English and Scottish shipyards built hundreds of vessels, and thousands of people worked in trade-related industries: building port facilities and warehouses, refining sugar and tobacco, distilling rum from molasses, and manufacturing textiles and iron products for the growing markets in Africa and America. Over 1,000 British merchant ships plied the Atlantic by 1750, providing a supply of experienced sailors and laying the foundation for the supremacy of the Royal Navy.

Africa, Africans, and the Slave Trade

As the South Atlantic System enhanced European prosperity, it imposed enormous costs on West and Central Africa. Between 1550 and 1870, the Atlantic slave trade uprooted almost eleven million Africans, draining many lands south of the Sahara of people and wealth. Equally important, the slave trade changed African society. By directing commerce away from the savannas and the Islamic world across the Sahara, the Atlantic slave trade diminished the economic and cultural vitality of many interior states and peoples. It also prompted the growth of militaristic centralized states in the coastal areas and the use of European manufactures and Indian textiles throughout the continent (Map 3.1).

Warfare and slaving had been an integral part of African life for centuries, driven by conflicts among numerous states and ethnic groups. But the South Atlantic System dramatically increased the demand for African labor, and slaving wars became a favorite tactic of ambitious kings and plundering warlords. "Whenever the King of Barsally wants Goods or Brandy," an observer noted, "the King goes and ransacks some of his enemies' towns, seizing the people and selling them." Supplying the Atlantic trade became a way of life in

MAP 3.1 Africa and the Atlantic Slave Trade, 1700–1810

The tropical rain forest of West Africa was home to scores of peoples and dozens of kingdoms. Some kingdoms became aggressive slavers. Dahomey's army, for example, seized tens of thousands of captives in wars with neighboring peoples and sold them to European traders. About 15 percent of the captives died during the grueling Middle Passage, the transatlantic voyage between Africa and the Americas. Most of the survivors labored on sugar plantations in Brazil and the British and French West Indies.

the West African state of Dahomey, where the royal house monopolized the sale of slaves and used European guns to create a military despotism. Dahomey's army, which included a contingent of 5,000 women, systematically raided the interior for captives; between 1680 and 1730, Dahomey annually exported 20,000 slaves exported from the ports of Allada and Whydah. The Asante kings along the Gold Coast also used European firearms and slave trading to expand their political dominion during the 1720s. Conquering neighboring states along the coast and Muslim kingdoms in the savanna, they created a prosperous empire of three million to five million people. Yet participation in Atlantic trade remained a choice for Africans, not a necessity. The powerful kingdom of Benin, famous for its cast bronzes and carved ivory, kept its many male slaves for labor at home and, for a time, prohibited the export of all slaves, male and female.

The trade in humans produced untold misery. Hundreds of thousands of young Africans died, and millions more endured a brutal life in the Americas. In Africa itself, class divisions hardened as people of noble birth enslaved and sold those of lesser status. Gender relations shifted as well. Men constituted two-thirds of the slaves sent across the Atlantic because European planters paid more for "men and stout men boys" and because Africans sold women captives in local or Saharan slave markets as agricultural workers, house servants, and concubines. The resulting sexual imbalance prompted men to take several wives, changing the meaning of marriage. Finally, the expansion of the Atlantic trade increased the extent of slavery in Africa. Sultan Mawlay Ismail of Morocco (r. 1672–1727) owned 150,000 black slaves, obtained by trade in Timbuktu and by wars in Senegal. In Africa, as in the Americas, slavery eroded the dignity of human life.

The Africans sold into the South Atlantic System had the bleakest fate. Torn from their villages, they were marched in chains to coastal ports. From there, they made the perilous **Middle Passage** to the New World in hideously overcrowded ships. The captives had little to eat or drink, and some would die from dehydration. The feces, urine, and vomit below deck prompted dangerous outbreaks of dysentery, which took more lives. "I was so overcome by the heat, stench, and foul air that I nearly fainted," reported a European doctor. Some slaves jumped overboard, choosing to drown rather than endure more suffering (see Voices from Abroad, p. 80). Others staged violent revolts. Slave uprisings occurred on 2,000 voyages, roughly one of every ten Atlantic passages. Nearly 100,000 slaves died in these insurrections, and more than a million others—about 15 percent of those transported—died of diseases such as dysentery and smallpox on the month-long journey.

For those who survived the Middle Passage, things only got worse. Life on the sugar plantations of northwestern Brazil and the West Indies was a lesson in relentless exploitation. The slaves worked ten hours a day under the hot semitropical sun; slept in flimsy huts; and lived on a starchy diet of corn, yams, and dried fish. They were subjected to brutal discipline: "The fear of punishment is the principle [we use] . . . to keep them in awe and order," one planter declared. With sugar prices high and the cost of slaves low, many planters simply worked their slaves to death and then bought more. Between 1708 and 1735, British planters on Barbados imported about 85,000 Africans; however, the island's black population increased by only 4,000 (from 42,000 to 46,000). The constant influx of new slaves kept the black population thoroughly "African" in its languages, religions, and culture. "Here," wrote a Jamaican observer, "each different nation of Africa meet and dance after the manner of their own country . . . [and] retain most of their native customs."

Slavery in the Chesapeake and South Carolina

Following Bacon's Rebellion, planters in Virginia and Maryland presided over a "tobacco revolution." They now grew tobacco on large plantations rather than smallholdings and, taking advantage of the British slave trade, staffed them with enslaved Africans rather than white indentured servants. By 1720, Africans made up 20 percent of the Chesapeake population, and slavery had become a core institution, not just one of several forms of unfree

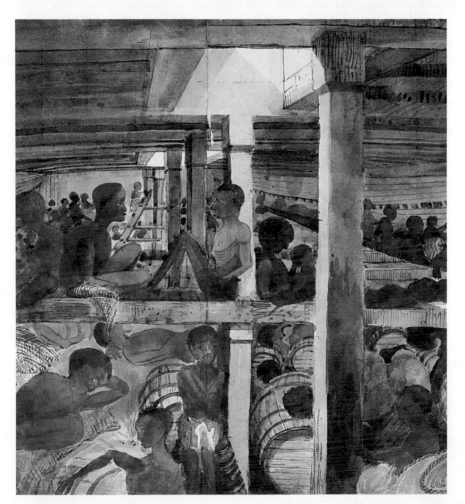

Two Views of the Middle Passage
The 1846 watercolor shows the cargo hold of a slave ship on a voyage to Brazil, which imported large numbers of Africans until the 1860s. Painted by a ship's officer, the picture minimizes the brutality of the Middle Passage — none of the slaves are in chains — and captures the Africans' humanity and dignity. A naval architect's drawing of packed-in slaves in a ship's hold better captures the actual conditions on most slave ships. Peabody and Essex Museum/Bridgeman Art Library.

The Brutal "Middle Passage" OLAUDAH EQUIANO

Olaudah Equiano claimed to have been born in Igboland (in present-day southern Nigeria). But two scholars, one African and one Euro-American, writing independently, have recently argued that Equiano was born into slavery in South Carolina and drew on conversations with African-born slaves to write a fictitious history of an idyllic West African childhood, his enslavement at the age of eleven, and a traumatic passage across the Atlantic. It now appears that Equiano was a plantation slave who was purchased by an English sea captain. He bought his freedom in 1766, settled in London, became an antislavery activist, and, in 1789, published the memoir containing these selections.

My father, besides many slaves, had a numerous family of which seven lived to grow up, including myself and a sister who was the only daughter. . . . One day, when all our people were gone out to their works as usual and only I and my dear sister were left to mind the house, two men and a woman got over our walls, and in a moment seized us both. . . .

At length, after many days' travelling, during which I had often changed masters, I got into the hands of a chieftain in a very pleasant country. This man had two wives and some children, and they all used me extremely well and did all they could to comfort me, particularly the first wife, who was something like my mother. . . . I was again sold and carried through a number of places till . . . at the end of six or seven months after I had been kidnapped I arrived at the sea coast.

The first object which saluted my eyes when I arrived on the coast was the sea, and a slave ship which was then riding at anchor and waiting for its cargo. I now saw myself deprived of all chance of returning to my native country. . . . I was soon put down under the decks, and there I received such a salutation in my nostrils as I had never experienced in my life; so that with the loathsomeness of the stench and crying together, I became so sick and low that I was not able to eat, nor had I the least desire to taste any thing. I now wished for the last friend, death, to relieve me; but soon, to my grief, two of the white men offered me eatables, and on my refusing to eat, one of them held me fast by the hands and laid me across I think the windlass, and tied my feet while the other flogged me severely. . . . One day, when we had a smooth sea and moderate wind, two of my wearied country-men who were chained together (I was near them at the time), preferring death to such a life of misery, somehow made it through the nettings and jumped into the sea.

At last we came in sight of the island of Barbados; the white people got some old slaves from the land to pacify us. They told us we were not to be eaten but to work, and were soon to go on land where we should see many of our country people. This report eased us much; and sure enough soon after we were landed there came to us Africans of all languages.

SOURCE: *The Interesting Narrative of the Life of Olaudah Equiano, or Gustavus Vassa, the African, Written by Himself* (London, 1789), 15, 22–23, 28–29.

labor. Equally important, slavery was now defined in racial terms. Virginia legislators prohibited sexual intercourse between English and Africans in 1692; in 1705, they defined virtually all resident Africans as slaves: "All servants imported or brought into this country by sea or land who were not Christians in their native country shall be accounted and be slaves."

Still, conditions for slaves in Virginia and Maryland were much less severe than those in the West Indies, and slaves in the Chesapeake lived relatively long lives. Unlike sugar and rice, which were "killer crops" that demanded strenuous labor, tobacco cultivation required only steady, careful, physically undemanding labor. Slaves planted the young tobacco seedlings in the spring, hoed and weeded the crop during the summer, and in the fall picked and hung the leaves to cure over the winter. Moreover, diseases did not spread easily among Chesapeake slaves, because plantation quarters were less crowded and more dispersed than those in the West Indies. Finally, because tobacco profits were low, planters avoided the purchase of new slaves and treated their workers less harshly than West Indian planters did.

Some tobacco planters tried to increase their workforce by buying female slaves and encouraging them to have children. In 1720, women made up more than one-third of the Africans in Maryland, and the black population had begun to increase naturally. One absentee owner instructed his plantation agent "to be kind and indulgent to the breeding wenches, and not to force them when with child upon any service or hardship that will be injurious to them." By midcentury, slaves made up one-third of the Chesapeake population, and more than three-quarters of them were American born.

Slaves in South Carolina labored under much more oppressive conditions. The colony grew slowly until 1700, when planters began to plant and export rice to southern Europe, where it was in great demand. To expand production, planters imported thousands of Africans—some of them from rice-growing societies. By 1705, Africans formed a majority of the total population and 80 percent of those in rice-growing areas.

Most rice plantations lay in inland swamps, and the work was dangerous and exhausting. Slaves planted, weeded, and harvested the rice in ankle-deep mud. Pools of putrid water bred mosquitoes, which transmitted diseases that claimed hundreds of African lives. Other slaves, forced to move tons of dirt to build irrigation works, died from exhaustion. "The labour required [for growing rice] is only fit for slaves," a Scottish traveler remarked, "and I think the hardest work I have seen them engaged in." In South Carolina, as in the West Indies and Brazil, there were many slave deaths and few births, and the importation of new slaves constantly "re-Africanized" the black population.

The Emergence of an African American Community

Slaves came from many different states and peoples in West Africa and the Central African regions of Kongo and Angola. White planters welcomed ethnic diversity to deter slave revolts. "The safety of the Plantations," declared a widely read English pamphlet, "depends upon having Negroes from all parts of Guiny, who do not understand each other's languages and Customs and cannot agree to Rebel." By accident or design, most plantations drew laborers of many languages, including Kwa, Mande, and Kikongo. Of the slaves imported after 1730 into the Upper James River region of Virginia, 41 percent came from various ethnic groups in present-day Nigeria, and another 25 percent came from West-Central Africa. The rest hailed from the Windward and Gold coasts, Senegambia, and

Sierra Leone. In South Carolina, many plantation owners preferred laborers from the Gold Coast and Gambia, who had a reputation as hardworking farmers. But as African sources of slaves shifted southward after 1730, more than 30 percent of the colony's workers came from Kongo and Angola.

Initially, the slaves did not think of themselves as Africans or blacks but as members of a specific family, clan, or people—Wolof, Hausa, Ibo, Yoruba, Teke, Ngola—and they associated with others who shared their language and customs. In the Upper James River region, Ibo men and women arrived in equal numbers, married each other, and maintained their Ibo culture.

Over time, the slaves made friendships and married across ethnic lines. In the process, Africans created new languages. One was the Gullah dialect of the South Carolina lowlands, which combined English and African words in an African grammatical structure. "They have a language peculiar to themselves," a missionary reported, "a wild confused medley of Negro and corrupt English." In the Chesapeake region, where there were more American-born slaves, most people of African descent gradually lost their native tongues. In the 1760s, a European visitor to Virginia reported with surprise that "all the blacks spoke very good English."

A common language—Gullah or English or French (in Louisiana and the French West Indies)—was one key to the emergence of an African American community. A nearly equal number of men and women—which encouraged marriage, stable families, and continuity between generations—was another. In South Carolina, the high death rate among slaves undermined ties of family and kinship; but after 1725, Chesapeake-area blacks created strong nuclear families and extended kin relationships. Thus, all but 30 of the 128 slaves on one of Charles Carroll's estates in Maryland were members of two extended families. These African American kin groups passed on family names, traditions, and knowledge to the next generation, and gradually, a distinct culture developed. As one observer suggested, blacks had created a separate world, "a Nation within a Nation."

As the slaves forged a new identity, they carried on certain African practices but let others go. Many Africans arrived in America with ritual scars that white planters called "country markings"; these signs of ethnic identity fell into disuse on culturally diverse plantations. But the slaves' African heritage took tangible forms in hairstyles, the motifs used in wood carvings and pottery, the large wooden mortars and pestles used to hull rice, and the design of houses, in which rooms were arranged from front to back in a distinctive "I" pattern, not side by side as was common in English dwellings.

African values also persisted. Some slaves passed on Muslim beliefs, and many more told their children of the spiritual powers of conjurers, known as obeah or ifa, who knew the ways of the African gods. Thus, enslaved Yorubas consulted Orunmila, the god of fate, and other Africans (a Jamaican planter noted) relied on obeah "to revenge injuries and insults, discover and punish thieves and adulterers; [and] to predict the future."

Resistance and Accommodation

There were drastic limits on creativity among African Americans. Most slaves were denied education, the chance to accumulate material possessions, or the opportunity to create associations. Slaves who challenged these boundaries did so at their peril.

"Virginian Luxuries"
This painting by an unknown artist (c. 1810) depicts the physical and sexual exploitation inherent in a slave society. On the right, an owner chastises a male slave by beating him with a cane; on the left, ignoring the cultural and legal rules prohibiting sexual intercourse between whites and blacks, a white master prepares to bed his black mistress. Abby Aldrich Rockefeller Folk Art Collection, Colonial Williamsburg Foundation.

Planters whipped slaves who refused to work; some turned to greater cruelties. Declaring the chronic runaway Ballazore an "incorrigeble rogue," a Virginia planter ordered all his toes cut off: "Nothing less than dismembering will reclaim him." Thomas Jefferson, who witnessed such punishments on his father's Virginia plantation, noted that each generation of whites was "nursed, educated, and daily exercised in tyranny": The relationship "between master and slave is a perpetual exercise of the most unremitting despotism on the one part, and degrading submission on the other." A fellow Virginian, planter George Mason, agreed: "Every Master is born a petty tyrant."

The extent of white violence depended on the size and density of the slave population. As Virginia planter William Byrd II complained in 1736, "Numbers make them insolent." In the northern colonies, where there were few slaves, white violence was sporadic. But plantation owners and overseers in the sugar- and rice-growing areas, where Africans outnumbered Europeans eight to one, routinely whipped assertive slaves. They prohibited their workers from leaving the plantation without special passes and called on their poor white neighbors to patrol the countryside at night, a duty that (authorities regularly reported) was "almost totally neglected."

Slaves dealt with their plight in several ways. Some newly arrived Africans fled to the frontier, where they established traditional villages or married into Indian tribes. American-born blacks who were fluent in English fled to towns, where they tried to pass as free men and women. The African Americans who remained enslaved bargained continually with their masters over the terms of their bondage. Some blacks bartered extra work for better food and clothes; others seized a small privilege and dared the master to revoke it. In that way, Sundays gradually became a day of rest—asserted as a right, rather than granted as a privilege. When bargaining failed, slaves protested silently by working slowly or stealing. Others, provoked beyond endurance, killed their owners or overseers. In the 1760s, in Amherst County, Virginia, a slave killed four whites; in Elizabeth City County, eight slaves strangled their master in bed. A few blacks even plotted rebellion, despite white superiority in guns and, in many regions, in numbers as well.

Predictably, South Carolina witnessed the largest slave uprising: the Stono Rebellion of 1739. The Catholic governor of the Spanish colony of Florida instigated the revolt by promising freedom to fugitive slaves. By February 1739, at least sixty-nine slaves had escaped to St. Augustine, and rumors circulated "that a Conspiracy was formed by Negroes in Carolina to rise and make their way out of the province." When war between England and Spain broke out in September (see p. 92), seventy-five Africans rose in revolt and killed a number of whites near the Stono River. According to one account, some of the rebels were Portuguese-speaking Catholics from the Kingdom of Kongo attracted by the prospect of life in Catholic Florida. Displaying their skills as soldiers—decades of brutal slave raiding in Kongo had militarized the society there—the rebels marched toward Florida "with Colours displayed and two Drums beating." White militia killed many of the Stono rebels, preventing a general uprising; after this, frightened whites cut slave imports and tightened plantation discipline.

William Byrd and the Rise of the Southern Gentry

As the southern colonies became full-fledged slave societies, life changed for whites as well as for blacks. Consider the career of William Byrd II (1674–1744). Byrd's father, a successful planter-merchant in Virginia, hoped to marry his children into the English gentry. To smooth his son's entry into landed society, Byrd sent him to England for his education. But his status-conscious classmates at the Felsted School shunned young Byrd, calling him a "colonial," a first bitter taste of the gradations of rank in English society.

Other rejections followed. Lacking aristocratic connections, Byrd was denied a post with the Board of Trade, passed over three times for the royal governorship of Virginia, and rejected in his efforts to marry a rich Englishwoman. In 1726, at age fifty-two, Byrd finally gave up and moved back to Virginia, where he sometimes felt he was "being buried alive." Accepting his lesser destiny as a member of the colony's elite, Byrd built an elegant brick mansion on the family's estate at Westover, sat in "the best pew in the church," and won an appointment to the governor's council.

William Byrd II's experience mirrored that of many planter-merchants, trapped in Virginia and South Carolina by the curse of their inferior colonial status. They used their wealth to rule over white yeomen families and tenant farmers and resorted to violence to exploit enslaved blacks, the American equivalent of the oppressed peasants of Europe. The planters used Africans to grow food as well as tobacco; to build houses, wagons, and tobacco casks; and to make shoes and clothes. By making their plantations self-sufficient, the Chesapeake elite survived the depressed tobacco market between 1670 and 1720.

To prevent another uprising like Bacon's Rebellion, the Chesapeake gentry addressed the concerns of middling and poor whites (see Chapter 2). They gradually lowered taxes: In Virginia, the annual head tax (on each adult man) fell from forty-five pounds of tobacco in 1675 to just five pounds in 1750. The gentry encouraged smallholders to improve their economic lot by investing in slaves, and many did so. By 1770, 60 percent of the English families in the Chesapeake colonies owned at least one slave. On the political front, planters now allowed poor yeomen and some tenants to vote. The strategy of the leading families—the Carters, Lees, Randolphs, and Robinsons—was to curry favor with these voters by bribing them with rum, money, and the promise of minor offices in county governments. In return, they expected the yeomen and tenants to elect them to office and defer to their rule. This horse-trading solidified the social position of the planter elite, which used its control of the House of Burgesses to limit the power of the royal governor. Hundreds of yeomen farmers benefited as well, tasting political power and garnering substantial fees and salaries as deputy sheriffs, road surveyors, estate appraisers, and grand jurymen.

Even as wealthy Chesapeake gentlemen formed political ties with smallholders, they consciously set themselves apart culturally. As late as the 1720s, many leading planters were boisterous, aggressive men who enjoyed the amusements of common folk—from hunting, hard drinking, and gambling on horse races to demonstrating their manly prowess by forcing themselves on female servants and slaves. As time passed, the planters began—like William Byrd II—to model themselves on the English aristocracy, remaining sexual predators but learning from advice books how to act like gentlemen in other regards: "I must not sit in others' places; Nor sneeze, nor cough in people's faces. Nor with my fingers pick my nose, Nor wipe my hands upon my clothes." Cultivating **gentility**—a refined but elaborate lifestyle—they replaced their modest wooden houses with mansions of brick and mortar. Robert "King" Carter, who owned hundreds of slaves, built a house that was seventy-five feet long, forty-four feet wide, and forty feet high; he filled it with fine furniture and rugs. Planters sent their sons to London to be educated as lawyers and gentlemen. But unlike Byrd's father, they expected their sons to return to America, marry local heiresses, and assume their fathers' roles: managing plantations, socializing with fellow gentry, and running the political system.

Wealthy Chesapeake and South Carolina women likewise emulated the English elite. They read English newspapers and fashionable magazines, wore the finest English clothes, and dined in the English fashion, with an elaborate afternoon tea. To improve their daughters' marriage prospects, parents hired English tutors to teach them proper etiquette. Once married, planter women deferred to their husbands, reared pious children, and maintained elaborate social networks, in time creating a new ideal: the southern gentlewoman. Using the profits generated by enslaved Africans in the South Atlantic System of commerce, wealthy planters formed an increasingly well educated, refined, and stable ruling class.

The Northern Maritime Economy

The South Atlantic System had a broad geographical reach. As early as the 1640s, New England farmers supplied the sugar islands with bread, lumber, fish, and meat. As a West Indian explained, planters "had rather buy foode at very deare rates than produce it by labour, soe infinite is the profitt of sugar works." By 1700, the economies of the West Indies and New England were closely interwoven. Soon farmers and merchants in New York, New Jersey, and Pennsylvania were also shipping wheat, corn, and bread to the Caribbean. By the 1750s, about two-thirds of New England's exports and half of those from the Middle Colonies went to the British and French sugar islands.

The sugar economy linked Britain's entire Atlantic empire. In return for the sugar they sent to England, West Indian planters received credit — in the form of **bills of exchange** — from London merchants. The planters used these bills to buy slaves from Africa and to pay North American farmers and merchants for their provisions and shipping services. The mainland colonists then exchanged the bills for British manufactures, primarily textiles and iron goods.

The West Indian trade created the first American merchant fortunes and the first urban industries (Map 3.2). Merchants in Boston, Newport, Providence, Philadelphia, and New York invested their profits in new ships; some set up manufacturing enterprises, including twenty-six refineries that processed raw sugar into finished loaves. Mainland distilleries turned West Indian molasses into rum — more than two and a half million gallons in Massachusetts alone by the 1770s. Merchants in Salem, Marblehead, and smaller New England ports built a major fishing industry by selling salted mackerel and cod to the sugar islands and to southern Europe. Baltimore merchants transformed their town into a major port by developing a bustling export business in wheat, while traders in Charleston shipped deerskins, indigo, and rice to European markets.

As transatlantic commerce expanded — from 500 voyages a year in the 1680s to 1,500 annually in the 1730s — American port cities grew in size and complexity. Seeking jobs and excitement, British and German migrants and young people from the countryside (servant girls, male laborers, and apprentice artisans) flocked to urban areas. By 1750, the populations of Newport and Charleston were nearly 10,000; Boston had 15,000 residents; and New York had almost 18,000. The largest port was Philadelphia, whose population by 1776 had reached 30,000, the size of a large European provincial city. Smaller coastal towns emerged as centers of the lumber and shipbuilding industries. Seventy sawmills dotted the Piscataqua River in New Hampshire, providing low-cost wood for homes, warehouses, and especially shipbuilding. Taking advantage of the Navigation Acts, which allowed colonists to build and own trading vessels, hundreds of shipwrights turned out oceangoing vessels, while other artisans made ropes, sails, and metal fittings for the new fleet. By the 1770s, colonial-built ships made up one-third of the British merchant fleet.

The South Atlantic System extended far into the interior. A fleet of small vessels sailed back and forth on the Hudson and Delaware rivers, delivering cargoes of European manufactures and picking up barrels of flour and wheat to carry to New York and Philadelphia for export to the West Indies and Europe. By the 1750s, hundreds of professional teamsters in Maryland were transporting 370,000 bushels of wheat and corn and 16,000 barrels of flour to urban markets each year — more than 10,000 wagon trips.

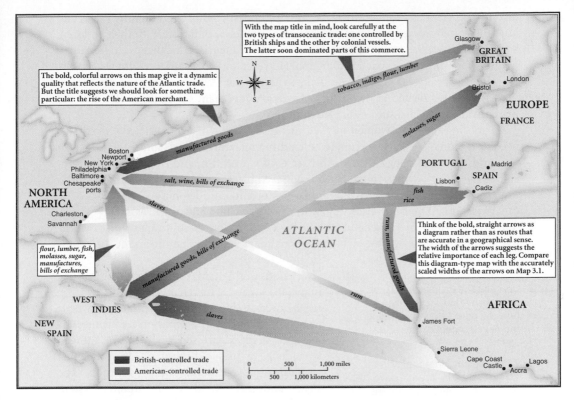

With the map title in mind, look carefully at the two types of transoceanic trade: one controlled by British ships and the other by colonial vessels. The latter soon dominated parts of this commerce.

The bold, colorful arrows on this map give it a dynamic quality that reflects the nature of the Atlantic trade. But the title suggests we should look for something particular: the rise of the American merchant.

Think of the bold, straight arrows as a diagram rather than as routes that are accurate in a geographical sense. The width of the arrows suggests the relative importance of each leg. Compare this diagram-type map with the accurately scaled widths of the arrows on Map 3.1.

British-controlled trade
American-controlled trade

MAP 3.2 The Rise of the American Merchant, 1750
Throughout the colonial era, British merchant houses dominated the transatlantic trade in manufactures, sugar, tobacco, and slaves. However, by 1750, American-born merchants in Boston, New York, and Philadelphia had seized control of the commerce between the mainland and the West Indies. Newport traders played a small role in the slave trade from Africa, and Boston and Charleston merchants grew rich carrying fish and rice to southern Europe.

For more help analyzing this map, see the Online Study Guide at **bedfordstmartins.com/henrettaconcise**.

To service this traffic, entrepreneurs and artisans set up taverns, horse stables, and barrel-making shops in towns along the wagon roads. Lancaster, in a prosperous wheat-growing area of Pennsylvania, boasted more than 200 German and English artisans and a dozen merchants.

Prosperous merchants dominated seaport cities. In 1750, about forty merchants controlled over 50 percent of Philadelphia's trade; they had taxable assets averaging £10,000, a huge sum at the time. Like the Chesapeake gentry, urban merchants modeled themselves after the British upper classes, importing design books from England and building Georgian-style mansions to display their wealth. Their wives created a genteel culture by decorating their houses with fine furniture and entertaining guests at elegant dinners.

Artisan and shopkeeper families, the middle ranks of seaport society, made up nearly half the population. Innkeepers, butchers, seamstresses, shoemakers, weavers, bakers, carpenters, masons, and dozens of other skilled workers toiled to gain a competency—an income sufficient to maintain their families in modest comfort and dignity. Wives and husbands often worked as a team, teaching the "mysteries of the craft" to their children. Some artisans aspired to wealth and status, an entrepreneurial ethic that prompted them to hire apprentices and expand production. However, most artisans were not well-to-do. During his working life, a tailor was lucky to accumulate £30 worth of property, far less than the £2,000 owned at death by an ordinary merchant or the £300 listed in the **probate inventory** of a successful blacksmith.

Laboring men and women formed the lowest ranks of urban society. Merchants needed hundreds of dockworkers to unload manufactured goods and molasses from inbound ships and reload them with barrels of wheat, fish, and rice. Often, the merchants filled these demanding jobs with enslaved blacks and indentured servants, who until the 1750s made up 30 percent of the workforce in Philadelphia and New York City; otherwise, they hired unskilled wageworkers. Poor white and black women—single, married, or widowed—eked out a living by washing clothes, spinning wool, or working as servants or prostitutes. To make ends meet, laboring families sent their children out to work.

▶ Describe the major elements of the South Atlantic System and how it worked. How did it shape the development of the various colonies?

▶ What role did Africans play in the expansion of the Atlantic slave trade? What role did Europeans play?

Periods of stagnant commerce threatened the financial security of merchants and artisans alike. For laborers, seamen, and seamstresses, whose household budgets left no margin for sickness or unemployment, depressed trade meant hunger, dependence on public charity, and—for the most desperate—petty thievery or prostitution. The sugar- and slave-based South Atlantic System brought economic uncertainty as well as opportunity to the people of the northern colonies.

The New Politics of Empire, 1713–1750

The South Atlantic System changed the politics of empire. British ministers, pleased with the wealth produced by the trade in staple crops, ruled the colonies with a gentle hand. The colonists took advantage of that leniency to strengthen their political institutions and eventually challenged the rules of the mercantilist system.

The Rise of Colonial Assemblies

After the Glorious Revolution of 1688–1689, representative assemblies in America followed the example of the English Whigs by limiting the powers of crown officials. In Massachusetts during the 1720s, the assembly repeatedly ignored the king's instructions to provide the royal governor with a permanent salary, and legislatures in North Carolina, New Jersey, and Pennsylvania did the same. Using such tactics, the colonial legislatures gradually took control of taxation and appointments, which angered imperial bureaucrats and absentee proprietors. "The people in power in America," complained William Penn during a struggle with the Pennsylvania assembly, "think nothing taller than themselves but the Trees."

Leading the increasingly powerful assemblies were members of the colonial elite. Although most property-owning white men had the right to vote, only men of wealth and status stood for election. In New Jersey in 1750, 90 percent of assemblymen came from influential political families. In the same decade in Virginia, seven members of the wealthy Lee family sat in the House of Burgesses and, along with other powerful families, dominated its major committees. In New England, affluent descendants of the original Puritans formed a core of political leaders. "Go into every village in New England," John Adams wrote in 1765, "and you will find that the office of justice of the peace, and even the place of representative, have generally descended from generation to generation, in three or four families at most."

However, neither elitist assemblies nor wealthy property owners could impose unpopular edicts on the people. Purposeful crowd actions were a fact of colonial life. An uprising of ordinary citizens overthrew the Dominion of New England in 1689. In New York, mobs closed houses of prostitution; in Salem (Massachusetts), they ran people with infectious diseases out of town; and in New Jersey in the 1730s and 1740s, mobs of farmers battled with proprietors who were forcing tenants off disputed lands. When officials in Boston restricted the sale of farm produce to a single public market, a crowd destroyed the building, and its members defied the authorities to arrest them. "If you touch One you shall touch All," an anonymous letter warned the sheriff, "and we will show you a Hundred Men where you can show one." These expressions of popular discontent, combined with the growing authority of the assemblies, created a political system that was broadly responsive to popular pressure and increasingly resistant to British control.

Salutary Neglect

British colonial policy during the reigns of George I (r. 1714–1727) and George II (r. 1727–1760) allowed the rise of American self-government. Royal bureaucrats, pleased by growing trade and import duties, relaxed their supervision of internal colonial affairs. In 1775, British political philosopher Edmund Burke would praise this strategy as salutary neglect.

Salutary neglect was a by-product of the political system developed by Sir Robert Walpole, the Whig leader in the House of Commons from 1720 to 1742. By providing supporters with appointments and pensions, Walpole won parliamentary approval for his policies. However, his patronage appointments filled the British government, including the Board of Trade and the colonial bureaucracy, with political hacks. When Governor Gabriel Johnson arrived in North Carolina in the 1730s, he vowed to curb the powers of the assembly and "make a mighty change in the face of affairs." Receiving little support from the Board of Trade, Johnson renounced reform and decided "to do nothing which can be reasonably blamed, and leave the rest to time, and a new set of inhabitants."

Walpole's tactics also weakened the empire by undermining the legitimacy of the political system. **Radical Whigs** protested that Walpole had betrayed the Glorious Revolution by using patronage and bribery to create a strong Court (or Kingly) Party. The Country Party—its members were landed gentlemen—likewise warned that Walpole's policies of high taxes and a bloated royal bureaucracy threatened British

Sir Robert Walpole, the King's Minister
All eyes are on Sir Robert Walpole (left) as he offers advice to the Speaker of the House of Commons. A brilliant politician, the treasury secretary held the confidence of George I and George II, the German-speaking monarchs from the duchy of Hanover, and used patronage to command a majority in the Commons. Walpole's personal motto, "Let sleeping dogs lie," helps explain his colonial policy of salutary neglect. © National Trust Photographic Library/John Hammond.

liberties. Heeding these arguments, colonial legislators complained that royal governors abused their patronage powers. To preserve American liberty, the colonists strengthened the powers of the representative assemblies, unintentionally laying the foundation for the American independence movement (see American Voices, p. 91).

Protecting the Mercantile System

Apart from patronage, Walpole's American policy focused on protecting British commercial interests. Initially, Walpole pursued a cautious foreign policy to allow Britain to recover from a generation of war (1689–1713) against Louis XIV of France. But in 1732, he provided a parliamentary subsidy for the new colony of Georgia, situated in a region long claimed by Spain. Georgia's reform-minded trustees envisioned the colony as a refuge for Britain's poor. To create a society of independent family farmers, the trustees limited most land grants to five hundred acres and outlawed slavery.

Walpole had little interest in social reform; he subsidized Georgia to protect the valuable rice-growing colony of South Carolina. It did exactly the opposite. Britain's expansion into Georgia outraged Spanish officials, who were already angry over British intrusions into the trade with New Spain. British merchants had silently taken over the Andalusian firms that held a monopoly on Spanish-American trade, and now—in a massive illegal commerce—provided many of the slaves and manufactures imported by the Spanish colonies. To counter Britain's commercial imperialism, Spanish naval

Confronting the House of Burgesses   ALEXANDER SPOTSWOOD

During the eighteenth century, the American representative assemblies expanded their popular appeal and political power. Many assemblies used their newfound authority to resist imperial governors, who often viewed them with contempt. Alexander Spotswood, who became governor of Virginia in 1710, remarked that the colony's voters had chosen "a set of representatives whom heaven has not generally endowed with the ordinary qualifications requisite to legislators." Spotswood's efforts to reduce the powers of the Burgesses made him few friends; in 1722, his enemies used their influence in London to have him removed from office.

To ye Council of Trade,
October 15, 1712
MY LORDS:
. . . [T]he Mob of this Country, having tried their Strength in the late Election and finding themselves able to carry whom they please, have generally chosen representatives of their own Class, who as their principal Recommendation have declared their resolution to raise no Tax on the people. . . . This is owing to a defect in the Constitution, which allows to every one, tho' but just out of the Condition of a Servant, and that can but purchase half an acre of Land, an equal Vote with the Man of the best Estate in the Country. . . .

December the 17th 1714
. . . The Council declare that they cannot advise the Governor to move for any alteration in the present method of Electing of Burgesses, some being of opinion that this is not a proper time, & others that the present manner of electing of Burgesses & the qualifications of the elected is sufficiently provided for by the Laws now in force. . . .

To Mr. Secretary James Stanhope,
July 15, 1715
I cannot forbear regretting that I must always have to do with ye Representatives of ye Vulgar People, and mostly with such members as are of their Stamp and Understanding, for so long as half an Acre of Land, . . . qualifys a man to be an Elector, the meaner sort of People will ever carry ye Elections, and the humour generally runs to choose such men as are their most familiar Companions, who very eagerly seek to be Burgesses merely for the lucre of the Salary, and who, for fear of not being chosen again, dare in Assembly do nothing that may be disrelished out of the House by ye Common People. Hence it often happens that what appears prudent and feasible to his Majesty's Governors and Council here will not pass with the House of Burgesses. . . .

To the Lords Commissioners of Trade,
May 23, 1716
. . . The behaviour of [Philip Ludwell Jr., the colony's auditor] in constantly opposing whatever I have offered for ye due collecting the Quitt rents . . . [and] his stirring up ye humours of the people before the last election of Burgesses . . . would have made me . . . suspend him from ye Council, but I find by the late Instructions I have received from his Majesty that Power is taken from ye Governor and transferred upon the majority of that Board, and while there are no less than seven of his Relations there, it is impossible to get a Majority to consent to the Suspension of him. . . .

SOURCE: R. A. Brock, ed., *The Official Letters of Alexander Spotswood* (Richmond: Virginia Historical Society, 1885), 2: 1–2, 124, 154–155.

forces had stepped up their seizure of illegal traders, including mutilation of an English sea captain, Robert Jenkins.

Yielding to Parliamentary pressure, Walpole declared war on Spain in 1739. The so-called War of Jenkins's Ear (1739–1741) was a largely unsuccessful attack on Spain's empire in North America. In 1740, British regulars failed to capture St. Augustine because South Carolina whites, still shaken by the Stono Rebellion, refused to commit militia units to the expedition. A year later, a major British and American assault on the prosperous Spanish seaport of Cartagena (in present-day Colombia) also failed. Instead of enriching themselves with Spanish booty, hundreds of troops from the mainland colonies died in the attack, mostly from tropical diseases.

The War of Jenkins's Ear quickly became part of a general European conflict, the War of the Austrian Succession (1740–1748). Massive French armies battled British-subsidized German forces in Europe, and French naval forces roamed the West Indies, vainly trying to conquer a British sugar island. There was little fighting in North America until 1745, when 3,000 New England militiamen, supported by a British naval squadron, captured Louisbourg, a French fortress at the entrance to the St. Lawrence River. To the dismay of New England Puritans, who feared invasion from Catholic Quebec, the Treaty of Aix-la-Chapelle (1748) returned Louisbourg to France. The treaty made it clear to colonial leaders that England would act in its own interests, not theirs.

The American Economic Challenge

The Walpole ministry had its own complaints about American economic activities. The Navigation Acts stipulated that the colonies were to produce staple crops and to consume British manufactured goods. To enforce the British monopoly on manufacturing, Parliament prohibited Americans from selling colonial-made textiles (Woolen Act, 1699), hats (Hat Act, 1732), and iron products such as plows, axes, and skillets (Iron Act, 1750).

However, the Navigation Acts had a major loophole: They allowed Americans to own ships and transport goods. Colonial merchants exploited those provisions to take control of 75 percent of the transatlantic trade in manufactures and 95 percent of the commerce between the mainland and the British West Indies. In fact, by the 1720s, the British sugar islands could not absorb all the flour, fish, and meat produced by mainland settlers. So, ignoring Britain's intense rivalry with France, colonial merchants sold their produce to its sugar islands, the wealth-producing epicenter of its American empire. Soon French planters were producing low-cost sugar that drove British products off the European market. When American rum distillers began to buy cheap molasses from the French islands, the West Indian "sugar lobby" intervened. It persuaded Parliament to enact the Molasses Act of 1733. The act allowed the mainland colonies to export fish and farm products to the French islands but—to give a price advantage to British sugar planters—placed a high tariff on French molasses. American merchants and legislators protested that the Molasses Act would cut off molasses imports, which would cripple the distilling industry, cut farm exports, and, by slashing colonial income, reduce the mainland's purchases of British goods. When Parliament ignored these arguments, American merchants smuggled in French molasses by bribing customs officials. Luckily for the Americans, British sugar prices rose sharply in the late 1730s, so the act was not rigorously enforced.

The lack of currency in the colonies prompted another conflict with British officials. To pay for manufactured goods, American merchants gave British merchants the bills of exchange and the gold and silver coins earned in the West Indian trade. These payments drained the colonial economy of money, which made it difficult for Americans to borrow funds or to buy and sell goods among themselves. To remedy the problem, ten colonial assemblies established public **land banks** that lent paper money to farmers, who pledged their land as collateral for the loans. Farmers used the currency to buy tools or livestock or to pay their creditors, thereby stimulating trade. However, some assemblies, particularly the legislature in Rhode Island, issued huge quantities of paper money (which consequently fell in value) and required merchants to accept it as legal tender. English merchants and other creditors rightly complained that they were being forced to accept devalued money. So in 1751, Parliament passed the Currency Act, which barred the New England colonies from establishing new land banks and prohibited the use of publicly issued paper money to pay private debts.

These conflicts over trade and paper money angered a new generation of English political leaders. In 1749, Charles Townshend of the Board of Trade charged that the American assemblies had assumed many of the "ancient and established prerogatives wisely preserved in the Crown"; he vowed to replace salutary neglect with more rigorous imperial control.

The wheel of empire had come full circle. In the 1650s, England had set out to create a centrally managed Atlantic empire and, over the course of a century, achieved the military and economic aspects of that goal. Mercantilist legislation, maritime warfare, commercial expansion, and the forced labor of a million African slaves brought prosperity to Britain. However, internal unrest (the Glorious Revolution) and a policy of salutary neglect had weakened Britain's political authority over its American colonies. Recognizing the threat self-government posed to the empire, British officials in the late 1740s vowed to reassert their power in America—an initiative that would have disastrous results.

▶ How did the ideas and policies of the English Whigs affect British and colonial politics between 1700 and 1760?

▶ What was the British policy of salutary neglect? Why did the British follow this policy? What consequences did it have for the British colonies in North America?

▶ Describe the connection in the eighteenth century between the South Atlantic System and the politics of empire.

SUMMARY

In this chapter, we examined two processes of change: one in politics and one in society and economy. The political story began in the 1660s with Britain's attempt to centralize control over its American possessions. Parliament passed the Acts of Trade and Navigation to keep colonial products and trade in English hands. Then King James II abolished representative institutions in the northern colonies and created the authoritarian Do-minion of New England. The Glorious Revolution of 1688–1689 reversed these policies, restoring American self-government and ushering in the era of salutary neglect.

The social and economic story centers on the development of the South Atlan-tic System of production and trade. It involved an enormous expansion in African slave raiding; the Atlantic slave trade; and the cultivation of sugar, rice, and tobacco in America. This complex story includes the creation of an exploited African American labor force in the southern mainland and West Indian colonies and of prosperous communities of European American farmers, merchants, and artisans on the North American mainland. How would the two stories turn out? In 1750, slavery and the South Atlantic System seemed firmly in place; however, the days of salutary neglect appeared to be numbered.

Connections: Economy **and** Government

In the essay opening Part One, we noted that

> some European settlements became places of oppressive captivity for Africans. . . .
> [P]lanters in the Chesapeake region imported enslaved African workers to grow tobacco.
> Wealthy British and French planters in the West Indies bought hundreds of thousands
> of slaves . . . and forced them to labor on sugar plantations.

The expansion of the South Atlantic System of slavery and staple-crop produc-tion dramatically changed the British colonies. In 1675, the three major English set-tlements—in the Chesapeake, New England, and Barbados—were small in num-bers and reeling from Indian attacks and social revolts. By 1750, British settlements in North America and the Caribbean had more than 2 million residents; produced vast amounts of sugar, rice, tobacco, wheat, and corn; and were no longer in danger of being destroyed by Indian attacks. The South Atlantic System had brought wealth and opportunity to the white inhabitants not only in the sugar islands but also on the North American mainland.

If expansion solved some problems, it created others. As we have seen in Chapter 3, imperial officials imposed mercantilist laws regulating the increasingly valuable col-onies and repeatedly went to war to safeguard them. This story of expanding imperial authority and warfare continues in Chapter 4, with Britain's "Great War for Empire," a vast military conflict intended to expand British commercial power throughout the world and to establish Britain as the dominant nation in Europe.

FOR FURTHER EXPLORATION

On England's empire, see Michael Kammen, *Empire and Interest: The American Col-onies and the Politics of Mercantilism* (1970), and Linda Colley, *Britons: Forging the Nation, 1707–1837* (1992). For multicultural tensions in early New York, read Joyce Goodfriend, *Before the Melting Pot: Society and Culture in Colonial New York City, 1664–1730* (1992). Richard Bushman, *King and People in Provincial Massachusetts* (1985), explores eighteenth-century imperial politics.

Betty Wood, *Origins of American Slavery* (1998), David Eltis, *The Rise of African Slavery in the Americas* (2000), and Ira Berlin, *Many Thousands Gone: The First Two Centuries of Slavery in North America* (1999), are fine studies. See also Philip D. Morgan,

TIMELINE

1651	▶ First Navigation Act
1660–1685	▶ Reign of King Charles II
1663	▶ Charles II grants Carolina proprietorship
1664	▶ English capture New Netherland, rename it New York
1681	▶ William Penn founds Pennsylvania
1685–1688	▶ Reign of King James II
1686–1689	▶ Dominion of New England
1688–1689	▶ Glorious Revolution in England and America
1689	▶ William and Mary ascend throne in England
	▶ Revolts in Massachusetts, Maryland, and New York
1689–1713	▶ England, France, and Spain at war
1696	▶ Parliament creates Board of Trade
1705	▶ Virginia enacts slavery legislation
1714–1750	▶ British policy of salutary neglect allows American assemblies to gain power
1720–1742	▶ Sir Robert Walpole leads Parliament
1720–1750	▶ African American community forms
	▶ Rice exports from South Carolina soar
	▶ Chesapeake planter aristocracy emerges
	▶ Seaport cities expand
1732	▶ Parliament charters Georgia, challenging Spain
	▶ Hat Act
1733	▶ Molasses Act
1739	▶ Stono Rebellion in South Carolina
1739–1748	▶ War in Europe
	▶ Sporadic warfare against Spain in the Caribbean and France in Canada
1750	▶ Iron Act restricts colonial iron manufactures
1751	▶ Currency Act prohibits land banks in New England and use of paper money as legal tender

Slave Counterpoint: Black Culture in the Eighteenth-Century Chesapeake and Low Country (1998). A good primary source is Olaudah Equiano, *The Interesting Narrative of the Life of Olaudah Equiano* (1789, 1995). On Africa, begin with Paul Bohannan and Philip Curtin, *Africa and the Africans* (3rd ed., 1988).

The PBS video *Africans in America* has a good Web site (**www.pbs.org/wgbh/aia/part1/title.html**). Writings by enslaved and free African Americans are at "Digital History" (**www.digitalhistory.uh.edu/black_voices/black_voices.cfm**). For a "Visual Record" of "The Atlantic Slave Trade and Slave Life in the Americas," go to (**hitchcock.itc.virginia.edu/Slavery/**). Also see the Library of Congress exhibit "African-American Odyssey" at (**lcweb2.loc.gov/ammem/aaohtml/**).

TEST YOUR KNOWLEDGE

To assess your mastery of the material in this chapter and for Web sites, images, and documents related to this chapter, visit **bedfordstmartins.com/henrettaconcise**.

Growth and Crisis in Colonial Society
1720–1765

> To lie low before God, as in the dust, that I might be nothing, and that God might be all.
>
> —Jonathan Edwards

In 1736, Alexander MacAllister left the Highlands of Scotland for the back-country of North Carolina, where his wife and three sisters soon joined him. Over the years, MacAllister prospered as a landowner and mill proprietor and had only praise for his new home. Carolina was "the best poor man's country I have heard in this age," he wrote to his brother Hector, urging him to "advise all poor people . . . to take courage and come." In North Carolina, there were no landlords to keep "the face of the poor . . . to the grinding stone," and so many Highlanders were arriving that "it will soon be a new Scotland." Here, on the far margins of the British empire, people could "breathe the air of liberty, and not want the necessarys of life." Some 300,000 European migrants—primarily Highland Scots, Scots-Irish, and Germans—heeded MacAllister's advice and helped to swell the population of Britain's North American settlements from 400,000 in 1720 to almost two million by 1765.

The rapid increase in white settlers and the arrival of nearly 300,000 enslaved Africans transformed life in every region of British America. Long-settled towns in New England became overcrowded; antagonistic ethnic and religious communities in the Middle Atlantic colonies jostled uneasily with one another; and the influx of the MacAllisters and thousands of other Celtic and German migrants altered the social landscape of the southern backcountry. Everywhere, two European cultural movements—the Enlightenment and Pietism—changed the tone of intellectual and spiritual life. Most important, as the migrants and the landless children of long-settled families moved inland, they sparked wars with the native peoples and with France and Spain, which were also vying for empire in North America. A generation of dynamic growth produced a decade of deadly warfare that would set the stage for a new era in American history.

Freehold Society in New England

In the 1630s, the Puritans left a country in which a small elite of nobles and gentry owned 75 percent of the arable land and farmed it with **leaseholding** tenants and propertyless workers. In New England, the Puritans set out to create a yeoman society of relatively equal landowning farm families. They succeeded all too well. By 1750, the migrants' descendants had parceled out all of the best farmland, threatening the future of the freehold ideal.

Farm Families: Women and the Rural Household Economy

The Puritans' vision of social equality did not extend to women. Puritan ideology placed the husband firmly at the head of the household, with almost complete control over his dependents. The Reverend Benjamin Wadsworth of Boston advised women in *The Well-Ordered Family* (1712) that being richer, more intelligent, or of higher social status than their husbands mattered little: "Since he is thy Husband, God has made him the head and set him above thee." It was a wife's duty "to love and reverence" her husband.

Women learned their subordinate role throughout their lives. Small girls watched their mothers defer to their fathers. As young women, they saw the courts prosecute many women and very few men for the crime of fornication (having sexual intercourse outside of marriage). And they learned that their marriage portions would be inferior in kind and size to those of their brothers. Thus, Ebenezer Chittendon of Guilford (Connecticut) left all his land to his sons, decreeing that "Each Daughter [shall] have half so much as Each Son, one half in money and the other half in Cattle." Because English law had eliminated many customary restrictions on inheritances, fathers could divide their property as they pleased.

In rural New England — and throughout the colonies — women assumed the role of dutiful helpmeets (helpmates) to their husbands. Farmwives tended gardens that provided fresh vegetables and herbs. They spun thread and yarn from flax or wool and then wove it into cloth for shirts and gowns. They knitted sweaters and stockings, made candles and soap, churned milk into butter and pressed curds into cheese, fermented malt for beer, preserved meats, and mastered dozens of other household tasks. "Notable women," the most accomplished practitioners of these domestic arts, won praise and high status in rural communities.

Bearing and rearing children were equally important tasks. Most women in New England married in their early twenties and by their early forties had given birth to six or seven children, usually delivered with the help of a neighbor or a midwife. Such large families sapped the physical and emotional strength of most mothers for twenty or more of their most active years. One Massachusetts woman confessed that she had little time for religious activities because "the care of my Babes takes up so large a portion of my time and attention." Yet most full members of Puritan congregations were women: "In a Church of between *Three* and *Four* Hundred *Communicants*," the eminent minister Cotton Mather noted, "there are but few more than *One* Hundred *Men*; all the Rest are Women." Many women became full members, revivalist Jonathan Edwards suggested, because they feared the dangers of childbirth and because that status meant that "their children may be baptized."

As the size of farms shrank in long-settled communities, many couples chose to have fewer children. After 1750, women in Andover, a typical farm village in Massachusetts, bore an average of only four children and had time and energy to pursue other tasks. Farm women now made yarn, cloth, or cheese to exchange with neighbors or sell to shopkeepers, which raised their families' standard of living. Or, like Susan Huntington of Boston, the wife of a prosperous merchant, they spent more time in "the care & culture of children, and the perusal of necessary books, including the scriptures."

Still, women's lives remained tightly bound by a web of legal and cultural restrictions. Ministers praised women's piety but excluded them from an equal role in the church. When Hannah Heaton, a farmwife in Connecticut, grew dissatisfied with her Congregationalist minister, thinking him unconverted and a "blind guide," she sought out Quaker and evangelist Baptist churches that welcomed questioning women. However, by the 1760s, many evangelical congregations had reinstituted traditional gender roles. "The government of Church and State must be . . . family government" controlled by its "king," declared the Danbury (Connecticut) Baptist Association. Willingly or not, most colonial women abided by the custom that, as essayist Timothy Dwight put it, they should be "employed only in and about the house and in the proper business of the sex."

Farm Property: Inheritance

By contrast, European men who migrated to the colonies escaped many traditional constraints, including the curse of landlessness. "The hope of having land of their own & becoming independent of Landlords is what chiefly induces people into America," an official noted in the 1730s. Owning property gave formerly dependent peasants a new social identity.

Property ownership and family authority were closely related. Most migrating Europeans wanted sizable farms that would provide sustenance for themselves and ample land for their children. Parents who could not provide some of their offspring with land placed them as indentured servants in more prosperous households. When the indentures ended at age eighteen or twenty-one, propertyless sons faced a decades-long climb up the agricultural ladder, from laborer to tenant and finally to freeholder.

Sons and daughters in well-to-do farm families were luckier: They received a marriage portion when they reached the age of twenty-three to twenty-five. That portion—land, livestock, or farm equipment—repaid children for their past labor and allowed parents to choose their children's partners, which they did not hesitate to do. Parents' security during old age depended on a wise choice of son- or daughter-in-law. Although the youths could refuse an unacceptable match, they did not have the luxury of falling in love with and marrying whomever they pleased.

Marriage under eighteenth-century English common law was not a contract between equals. A bride relinquished to her husband the legal ownership of all her property. After his death, she received a dower right—the right to use, but not sell, one-third of the family's property; on the widow's death or remarriage, her portion was divided among the children. The widow's property rights were subordinate to those of the family line, which stretched across the generations.

A father's duty was to provide inheritances for his children, and men who did not do so lost status in the community. Some fathers willed the family farm to a single son, providing their other children with money, an apprenticeship, or uncleared frontier tracts or requiring the inheriting son to do so. Other yeomen moved their families to the frontier, where life was hard but land was cheap and abundant. "The Squire's House stands on the Bank of the Susquehannah," traveler Philip Fithian reported from the Pennsylvania backcountry in the early 1760s. "He tells me that he will be able to settle all his sons and his fair Daughter Betsy on the Fat of the Earth."

These farmers' historic achievement was the creation of whole communities of independent property owners. A French visitor noted the sense of personal dignity in this rural world, which contrasted sharply with that of European peasants. Throughout the northern colonies, he found "men and women whose features are not marked by poverty . . . or by a feeling that they are insignificant subjects and subservient members of society."

The Crisis of Freehold Society

How long would this happy circumstance last? Because of high rates of natural increase, New England's population doubled with each generation. The Puritan colonies had about 100,000 people in 1700, nearly 200,000 in 1725, and almost 400,000 in 1750. In long-settled areas, farms had been divided and then subdivided; now many were so small — fifty acres or less — that parents could provide only one child with an adequate inheritance. In the 1740s, the Reverend Samuel Chandler of Andover was "much distressed for land for his children," seven of whom were young boys. A decade later, in nearby Concord, about 60 percent of the farmers owned less land than their fathers had.

Because parents had less to give their sons and daughters, they had less control over their children's lives. The traditional system of arranged marriages broke down as young people engaged in premarital sex and used the urgency of pregnancy to win permission to marry. Throughout New England, the number of premarital conceptions rose dramatically, from about 10 percent of firstborn children in the 1710s to more than 30 percent in the 1740s. Given another chance, young people "would do the same again," an Anglican minister observed, "because otherwise they could not obtain their parents' consent to marry."

Even as family dynamics changed, New England families maintained the freeholder ideal. Some parents chose to have smaller families and used birth control: abstention, coitus interruptus, or primitive condoms. Other families petitioned the provincial government for frontier land grants and hacked new farms out of the forests of central Massachusetts, western Connecticut, and, eventually, New Hampshire and Vermont. Still others improved their farms' productivity by replacing the traditional English crops of wheat and barley with high-yielding potatoes and maize, known as Indian corn. Corn was an especially wise choice: It yielded a hearty food for people, and its leaves furnished feed for cattle and pigs, which provided farm families with milk and meat. Gradually, New England changed from a grain economy to a livestock economy and became a major exporter of salted meat to the plantations of the West Indies.

Finally, New England farmers adapted their agriculture by developing the full potential of what one historian has called the "household mode of production." In this system of community exchange, families swapped labor and goods with one another. Women and children worked in groups to spin yarn, sew quilts, and shuck corn. Men

▶ In what ways were the lives of women and men in New England similar? In what ways were they different?

▶ What was the threat to the freehold ideal in midcentury New England, and what new strategies did farming families use to preserve it?

loaned one another tools, draft animals, and grazing land. Farmers plowed fields owned by artisans and shopkeepers, who repaid them with shoes, furniture, or store credit. In part because currency was in short supply, no cash changed hands. Instead, farmers, artisans, and shopkeepers recorded their debits and credits and "balanced" the books every few years by transferring small amounts of cash. This system allowed households—and the region's economy—to maximize output and so preserve the freehold ideal.

The Middle Atlantic: Toward a New Society, 1720–1765

The Middle Atlantic colonies—New York, New Jersey, and Pennsylvania—became home to peoples of differing origins, languages, and religions. Scots-Irish Presbyterians, English and Welsh Quakers, German Lutherans and Moravians, and Dutch Reformed Protestants formed ethnic and religious communities that coexisted uneasily with one another.

Economic Growth and Social Inequality

Ample fertile land attracted migrants to the Middle Atlantic colonies, and grain exports to Europe and the West Indies financed their rapid settlement. Between 1720 and 1770, a growing demand for food doubled the price of wheat. By increasing their exports of wheat, corn, flour, and bread, Middle Atlantic farmers brought prosperity to the region. The population of the area surged from 120,000 in 1720 to 450,000 in 1765.

Many migrants refused to settle in New York's fertile Hudson River Valley—and with good reason. There, wealthy Dutch and English families—Van Rensselaers, Philipses, Livingstons, and Clarks—presided over huge manors created by the Dutch West India Company and English governors (Map 4.1). Like Chesapeake planters, the New York landlords aspired to live like European gentry, but few migrants wanted to labor as poor, dependent peasants. To attract tenants, the manorial lords had to grant them long leases and the right to sell their improvements—their houses and barns, for example—to the next tenant. Still, the number of tenant families rose slowly; the vast 100,000-acre Van Rensselaer estate had only 82 tenants in 1714 and 345 in 1752 but jumped to 700 by 1765.

Most tenant families hoped that with hard work, they could sell enough wheat to buy their own farmsteads. But preindustrial technology during the crucial harvest season limited their output. As the wheat ripened, it had to be harvested before it sprouted and became useless. Yet a worker with a hand sickle could reap only half an acre of wheat, rye, or oats a day. The cradle scythe, a tool introduced during the 1750s, doubled or tripled the amount of grain a worker could cut. Even so, a family with two adult workers could reap only about twelve acres of grain—perhaps 150 to 180 bushels of

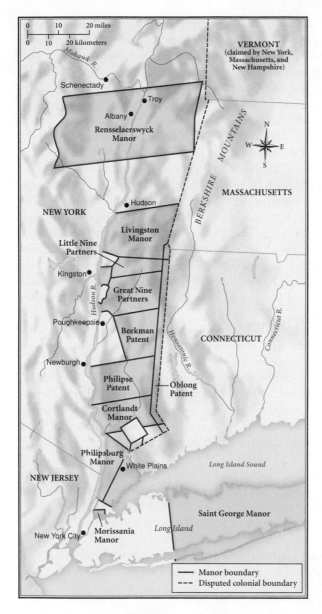

MAP 4.1 The Hudson River Manors

Dutch and English manorial lords owned much of the fertile eastern shore of the Hudson River, where they leased farms on perpetual contracts to German tenants and refused to sell land to freehold-seeking migrants from overcrowded New England. This powerful landholding elite produced Patriot leaders, such as Gouverneur Morris and Robert Livingston, and prominent American families, such as the Roosevelts.

wheat. After reserving enough grain for food and seed, the remainder might be worth £15, enough to buy salt and sugar, tools, and cloth, but little else. The road to land ownership was not an easy one.

In rural Pennsylvania and New Jersey, wealth was initially distributed more evenly. The first Quakers arrived with few resources and lived simply in small houses with one or two rooms, a sleeping loft, a few benches or stools, and some wooden platters and cups. Only the wealthiest families ate off pewter or ceramic plates imported from England or Holland.

However, the expanding trade in wheat and an influx of poor settlers sharpened social divisions. By the 1760s, eastern Pennsylvania landowners with large farms were using the labor of slaves and poor migrants to grow wheat. Other ambitious men were buying up land and dividing it into small tenancies, which they let out on profitable leases. Still others were making money by providing new settlers with farming equipment, sugar and rum from the West Indies, and financial services. These large-scale farmers, rural landlords, speculators, storekeepers, and gristmill operators formed a distinct class of agricultural capitalists. They displayed their wealth by building large stone houses, furnishing them with expensive mahogany tables and four-poster beds, and laying their tables with elegant linen and handsomely decorated Dutch dinnerware.

In sharp contrast, one-half of Middle Atlantic's white men owned no land and little personal property. Some propertyless men were the sons of farmers and would eventually inherit part of the family estate. But many more were Scots-Irish "inmates"—single men or families, explained a tax assessor, "such as live in small cottages and have no taxable property, except a cow." In the predominantly German settlement of Lancaster, Pennsylvania, a merchant noted an "abundance of Poor people" who "maintain their Families with great difficulty by day Labour." Although these Scots-Irish and German settlers hoped eventually to become landowners, sharply rising land prices prevented many from realizing their dreams.

Some hard-pressed migrants turned to crime, which rose sharply after 1720. Previously, merchant Isaac Norris recalled, "we could Safely go to bed with our doors open but now Robberies, housebreaking, Rapes, & other crimes are become Common." In 1732, the Philadelphia Society of Friends publicly identified the perpetrators as "the vicious and scandalous Refuse of other Countries," a charge confirmed by recent scholarship. Pennsylvania's religious peoples—Quakers, Mennonites, Amish, Moravians, and Dunkards—broke relatively few laws; most crimes were committed by people who were propertyless or indentured servants or Scots-Irish (and often all three).

Merchants and artisans took advantage of the ample labor supply to set up an outwork system. They bought wool or flax from farmers and paid propertyless workers and land-poor farm families to spin it into yarn or weave it into cloth. In the 1760s, an English traveler reported that hundreds of Pennsylvanians had turned "to manufacture, and live upon a small farm, as in many parts of England." In both the Middle Atlantic and New England, many communities were now as crowded and socially divided as those in rural England, and many families feared a return to the lowly status of the European peasant.

Cultural Diversity

The middle colonies were not a melting pot. Most European migrants held tightly to their traditions, creating a patchwork of ethnically and religiously diverse communities. In 1748, a traveler counted no fewer than twelve religious denominations in Philadelphia, including Anglicans, Baptists, Quakers, Swedish and German Lutherans, Mennonites, Scots-Irish Presbyterians, and Roman Catholics.

Migrants preserved their cultural identity by marrying within their ethnic groups and maintaining their Old World customs (see Voices from Abroad, p. 103). A major

What, Then, Is the American, This New Man? J. HECTOR ST. JOHN DE CRÈVECOEUR

A Frenchman by birth, Crèvecoeur (1735–1813) came to America during the French and Indian War, married a merchant's daughter, and settled in Orange County, New York, where he lived as a "gentleman farmer." In 1782, he published *Letters from an American Farmer,* a justly famous book of essays that offered a European perspective on the new land and its people.

[The people here] are a mixture of English, Scotch, Irish, French, Dutch, Germans, and Swedes. From this promiscuous breed, that race now called Americans have arisen. The eastern provinces [New England] must indeed be excepted as being the unmixed descendants of Englishmen. I have heard many wish that they had been more intermixed also; I for my part, . . . I respect them for what they have done; for the accuracy and wisdom with which they have settled their territory; for the decency of their manners; for their early love of letters; their ancient college [Harvard], . . . for their industry. . . .

In this great American asylum, the poor of Europe have . . . become men: in Europe they were as so many useless plants, wanting vegetative mould and refreshing showers; they withered, and were mowed down by want, hunger, and war; but now, by the power of transplantation, like all other plants they have taken root and flourished! Formerly they were not numbered in any civil lists of their country, except in those of the poor; here they rank as citizens. . . .

What, then, is the American, this new man? He is either an European or the descendant of an European; hence that strange mixture of blood, which you will find in no other country. I could point out to you a family whose grandfather was an Englishman, whose wife was Dutch, whose son married a French woman, and whose present four sons have now four wives of different nations. *He* is an American, who, leaving behind him all his ancient prejudices and manners, receives new ones from the new mode of life he has embraced, the new government he obeys, and the new rank he holds. . . .

How much wiser, in general, the honest Germans than almost all other Europeans; . . . and [by] the most persevering industry, they commonly succeed. . . . The Scotch and the Irish [are different]. . . . out of twelve families of emigrants of each country, generally seven Scotch will succeed, nine German, and four Irish. The Scotch are frugal and laborious, but their wives cannot work so hard as German women, who on the contrary vie with their husbands, and often share with them the most severe toils of the field. . . . The Irish do not . . . prosper so well; they love to drink and to quarrel; they are litigious and soon take to the gun, which is the ruin of everything; they seem beside to labour under a greater degree of ignorance in husbandry than the others. . . . [In Ireland,] their potatoes, which are easily raised, were perhaps an inducement to laziness . . . and their whisky [there was] too cheap.

SOURCE: J. Hector St. John de Crèvecoeur, *Letters from an American Farmer,* ed. Albert E. Stone (New York: Penguin, 1981) 68–71, 85.

exception were the Huguenots, Calvinists expelled from Catholic France in the 1680s who resettled in Holland, England, and the British colonies. Huguenots in American port cities—Boston, New York, and Charleston—soon lost their French identity by intermarrying with other Protestants. More typical were the Welsh Quakers. Seventy percent of the children of the original Welsh migrants to Chester County, Pennsylvania, married other Welsh Quakers, as did 60 percent of the third generation.

In Pennsylvania and western New Jersey, Quakers shaped the culture, at first because of their numbers and later because of their wealth and social cohesion. Most Quakers came from pastoral farming regions of England and carried with them traditions of local village governance, popular participation in politics, and social equality. Quakers were also pacifists, so Pennsylvania officials negotiated treaties with Native Americans and bought their lands rather than seizing them. However, in 1737, Governor Thomas Penn used sharp tactics to oust the Lenni-Lenape (or Delaware) Indians from a vast area, creating bitterness that would lead to war in the 1750s. By that time, Quakers had extended their religious values of equality and justice to African Americans. Many Quaker meetings (congregations) condemned the institution of slavery, and some expelled members who continued to keep slaves.

The Quaker vision of a "peaceable kingdom" attracted 100,000 German migrants who were fleeing their homelands because of military conscription, religious persecution, and high taxes. First to arrive, in 1683, were the Mennonites, religious dissenters drawn by the promise of religious freedom. In the 1720s, a larger wave of German migrants arrived from southwestern Germany and Switzerland, refugees from religious upheaval and overcrowded villages. "Wages were far better" in Pennsylvania, Heinrich Schneebeli reported to his friends in Zurich, and "one also enjoyed there a free unhindered exercise of religion." A third wave of Germans and Swiss—nearly 40,000 strong—landed in Philadelphia between 1749 and 1756. Some were redemptioners, indentured servants who migrated as individuals or families; but many more were propertied farmers and artisans in search of better opportunities for their children.

Germans soon dominated many districts of eastern Pennsylvania, and thousands more moved down the Shenandoah Valley into the western parts of Maryland, Virginia, and the Carolinas. The migrants carefully guarded their cultural heritage. A minister in North Carolina admonished young people "not to contract any marriages with the English or Irish," emphasizing that "we owe it to our native country to do our part that German blood and the German language be preserved in America." Well beyond 1800, these settlers spoke German, read German-language newspapers, attended church services in German, and preserved German farming practices, which sent women into the fields to plow and reap.

As Germans and Protestants, these settlers readily accepted life as subjects of Britain's German-born and German-speaking Protestant monarchs, George I (1714–1727) and George II (1727–1760). They generally avoided politics except to protect their cultural practices; for example, they insisted that married women should have the right to hold property and write wills, as they did in Germany.

Migrants from Ireland formed the largest group of incoming Europeans, about 115,000 in number. Although some were Irish and Catholic, most were Scots and Presbyterian, the descendants of the Calvinist Protestants sent to Ireland during the seventeenth century to solidify English rule. Once in Ireland, the Scots faced hostility from

German Farm in Western Maryland
Beginning in the 1730s, wheat became a major export crop in Maryland and Virginia. The farm in this engraving is probably owned by Germans because the harvesters are using oxen, not horses, and women are working in the field alongside the men. Using "a new method of reaping," possibly of German origin, the harvesters cut only the grain-bearing tip of the plants, leaving the wheat stalks in the fields to be eaten by livestock. Library of Congress.
For more help analyzing this image, see the Online Study Guide at **bedfordstmartins.com/henrettaconcise**.

both Irish Catholics and English officials and landlords. The Irish Test Act of 1704 restricted voting and office holding to members of the Church of England. English mercantilist regulations placed heavy import duties on the linens made by Scots-Irish weavers, and Scots-Irish farmers paid heavy taxes. "Read this letter, Rev. Baptist Boyd," a migrant to New York wrote back to his minister, "and tell all the poor folk of ye place that God has opened a door for their deliverance . . . all that a man works for is his own; there are no revenue hounds to take it from us here."

Lured by such reports, thousands of Scots-Irish families sailed for the colonies. The first of these migrants landed in Boston in the 1710s and settled primarily in New Hampshire. By 1720, most were sailing to Philadelphia, attracted by the religious tolerance there. Seeking cheap land, they moved to central Pennsylvania and the fertile Shenandoah Valley, which stretched along the backcountry from Maryland to North Carolina. Governor William Gooch of Virginia welcomed the Scots-Irish presence to secure "the Country against the Indians"; but an Anglican planter thought them as dangerous as "the Goths and Vandals of old" had been to the Roman Empire. Like the Germans, the Scots-Irish retained their culture, living in ethnic communities and holding firm to the Presbyterian Church.

Religious Identity and Political Conflict

In Western Europe, the leaders of church and state condemned religious diversity (Map 4.2). "To tolerate all [religions] without controul is the way to have none at all," declared an Anglican clergyman. Both English and German ministers carried such

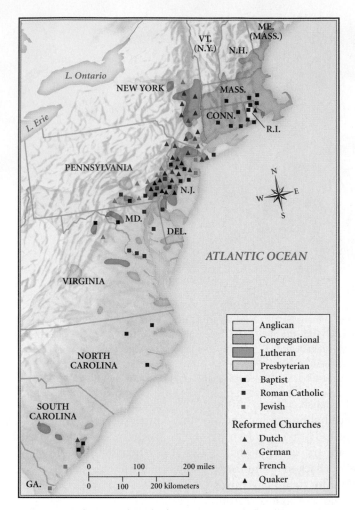

MAP 4.2 Religious Diversity in 1750

By 1750, religious diversity was on the rise, not only in the multiethnic middle colonies but also through-out British North America. Baptists had increased their numbers in New England, long the stronghold of Congregationalists, and would soon become important in Virginia. Already there were good-sized pockets of Presbyterians, Lutherans, and German Reformed in the South, where Anglicanism was the established religion.

For more help analyzing this map, see the Online Study Guide at **bedfordstmartins.com/henrettaconcise.**

sentiments to Pennsylvania. "The preachers do not have the power to punish anyone, or to force anyone to go to church," complained Gottlieb Mittelberger, an influential German minister. As a result, "Sunday is very badly kept. Many people plough, reap, thresh, hew or split wood and the like." He concluded: "Liberty in Pennsylvania does more harm than good to many people, both in soul and body."

Mittelberger was mistaken. Although ministers in Pennsylvania could not invoke government authority to uphold religious values, the result was not social anarchy.

Instead, religious sects enforced moral behavior through communal self-discipline. Quaker families and institutions were tight-knit. Families attended a weekly meeting for worship and a monthly meeting for business. Every three months, a committee from the monthly meeting reminded parents to provide their children with proper religious instruction. Parents took the committee's words to heart. "If thou refuse to be obedient to God's teachings," Walter Faucit of Chester County admonished his son, "thou will be a fool and a vagabond." The committee also supervised adult behavior: A Chester County meeting, for example, disciplined one of its members "to reclaim him from drinking to excess and keeping vain company." Significantly, Quaker meetings allowed couples to marry only if they had land and livestock sufficient to support a family. As a result, the children of well-to-do Friends usually married within the sect, while poor Quakers remained unmarried, wed later in life, or married without permission — in which case they were often ousted from the meeting. These marriage rules helped build a self-contained and prosperous Quaker community.

In the 1740s, Quaker dominance in Pennsylvania came under attack. The flood of German and Scots-Irish migrants reduced Quakers to a mere 30 percent of the residents. Moreover, the Scots-Irish in central Pennsylvania were demanding an aggressive Indian policy, challenging the pacifism of the Quaker-dominated assembly. Quaker politicians sought allies among German settlers, many of whom embraced the Quakers' policies of pacifism and voluntary (not compulsory) militia service. In return, German leaders demanded fair representation in the assembly and legislation that respected their inheritance customs.

By the 1750s, politics throughout the Middle Atlantic had become a steaming cauldron of ethnic-based conflicts. In New York, a Dutchman declared that he "Valued English Law no more than a Turd," while in Pennsylvania, Benjamin Franklin disparaged the "boorish" character and "swarthy complexion" of German migrants. The attempts of Scots-Irish Presbyterians, German Baptists, and German Lutherans to form "a general confederacy" against the Pennsylvania Quakers were likely to fail, a European visitor predicted, because of "a mutual jealousy, for religious zeal is secretly burning." The region's experiment in social diversity prefigured the bitter ethnic conflicts that would characterize much of American society in the centuries to come.

▶ Who were the new migrants to the middle colonies? Why did they leave Europe? What were their goals in British North America?

▶ What were the main issues that divided the ethnic and religious groups of the middle colonies?

The Enlightenment and the Great Awakening, 1720–1765

Two great European cultural movements reached America between the 1720s and the 1760s: the Enlightenment and Pietism. The Enlightenment, which emphasized the power of human reason to understand and shape the world, appealed especially to urban artisans and well-educated men and women from merchant or planter families. Pietism, an evangelical Christian movement that stressed the individual's personal relationship with God, attracted many more adherents, primarily farmers and urban laborers. Together, the two movements transformed American intellectual and cultural life.

The Enlightenment in America

To explain the workings of the natural world, some settlers relied on folk wisdom. Swedish settlers in Pennsylvania, for example, attributed magical powers to the great white mullein, a common wildflower, and treated fevers by tying the plant's leaves around their feet and arms. Others relied on religion. Most Christians believed the earth stood at the center of the universe and that God (and Satan) intervened directly and continuously in human affairs.

The scientific revolution of the sixteenth and seventeenth centuries challenged both folk and traditional Christian worldviews. In the 1530s, the astronomer Copernicus observed that the earth traveled around the sun, not vice versa. Copernicus's discovery suggested that humans occupied a more modest place in the universe than Christian theology assumed. Eventually, Sir Isaac Newton, in his *Principia Mathematica* (1687), used the sciences of mathematics and physics to explain the movement of the planets around the sun. Newton's laws of motion and gravity described how the universe could operate by means of natural forces. This explanation, which did not require the constant intervention of a supernatural being to guide the planets, undermined the traditional Christian understanding of the cosmos.

In the century between the publication of *Principia Mathematica* and the French Revolution of 1789, the philosophers of the European Enlightenment used empirical research and scientific reasoning to study all aspects of life, including social institutions and human behavior. Enlightenment thinkers advanced four fundamental principles: the lawlike order of the natural world, the power of human reason, the "natural rights" of individuals (including the right to self-government), and the progressive improvement of society.

English philosopher John Locke was a major contributor to the Enlightenment. In his *Essay Concerning Human Understanding* (1690), Locke discussed the impact of environment and experience on human behavior and beliefs. He argued that the character of individuals and societies was not fixed but could be changed through education, rational thought, and purposeful action. Locke's *Two Treatises of Government* (1690) advanced the revolutionary theory that political authority was not given by God to monarchs, as James II had insisted (see Chapter 3). Instead, it derived from social compacts that people made to preserve their "natural rights" to life, liberty, and property. In Locke's view, the people should have the power to change government policies — or even their form of government.

Locke's ideas and those of other Enlightenment thinkers came to America by way of books, travelers, and educated migrants. Some clergymen responded to these ideas by devising a rational form of Christianity. Rejecting supernatural interventions and a vengeful Calvinist God, Congregationalist minister Andrew Eliot maintained that "there is nothing in Christianity that is contrary to reason." The Reverend John Wise of Ipswich, Massachusetts, used Locke's political principles to defend the Puritans' practice of vesting power in ordinary church members. Just as the social compact formed the basis of political society, Wise argued, so the religious covenant among the lay members of the congregation made them — not the bishops of the Church of

England or even ministers like himself—the proper interpreters of religious truth. The Enlightenment influenced Puritan minister Cotton Mather as well. When a measles epidemic ravaged Boston in the 1710s, he thought that only God could end it. A decade later, when smallpox struck the town, Mather turned to a scientific remedy by joining with physician Nicholas Boyleston to advocate the new technique of inoculation.

Benjamin Franklin was the exemplar of the American Enlightenment. Born in Boston in 1706 to a devout Calvinist family and apprenticed as a youth to a printer, Franklin was a self-taught man. While working as a printer and journalist in Philadelphia, he formed "a club of mutual improvement" that met weekly to discuss "Morals, Politics, or Natural Philosophy." These discussions and Enlightenment literature, rather than the Bible, shaped Franklin's mind. As Franklin explained in his *Autobiography* (1771), "From the different books I read, I began to doubt of Revelation [God-revealed truth]."

Like many urban artisans, wealthy Virginia planters, and affluent seaport merchants, Franklin became a **deist**. Deism was a way of thinking, not a church. "My own mind is my own church," said deist Thomas Paine. "I am of a sect by myself," added Thomas Jefferson. Influenced by Enlightenment science, deists believed that a Supreme Being (or Grand Architect) had created the world, allowed it to operate through the laws of nature, and did not intervene directly in history or in people's lives. Rejecting the divinity of Christ and the authority of the Bible, deists relied on people's "natural reason," their innate moral sense, to define right and wrong. Thus, Franklin, a onetime slave owner, came to question the morality of racial bondage and repudiated it as he contested the colonists' political bondage to the British.

Franklin popularized the practical outlook of the Enlightenment in *Poor Richard's Almanack* (1732–1757), an annual publication read by thousands, and in the American Philosophical Society (1743–present), an institution devoted to "the promotion of useful knowledge." Taking this message to heart, Franklin invented bifocal lenses for eyeglasses, the Franklin stove, and the lightning rod. His book on electricity, published in England in 1751, won praise as the greatest contribution to science since Newton's discoveries. Inspired by Franklin, ambitious printers in America's seaport cities published newspapers and gentlemen's magazines, the first significant nonreligious publications to appear in the colonies. The European Enlightenment, then, added a secular dimension to colonial cultural life, foreshadowing the great contributions to republican political theory by the American intellectuals of the revolutionary era: John Adams, James Madison, and Thomas Jefferson.

American Pietism and the Great Awakening

As many educated Americans turned to deism, thousands of other colonists embraced Pietism. This Christian movement had its origins in Germany around 1700 and emphasized "pious" behavior (hence the name). In its emphasis on a mystical union with God and in its emotional services, Pietism appealed to the hearts of individuals rather than to their minds. In the 1720s, German migrants carried Pietism to America and sparked a religious **revival**. In Pennsylvania and New Jersey, Dutch minister Theodore Jacob Frelinghuysen moved from church to church, preaching rousing emotional sermons to German settlers and encouraging church members to spread the message of spiritual urgency. A decade later, William Tennent and his son Gilbert copied Frel-inghuysen's approach and led revivals among Scots-Irish Presbyterians throughout the Middle Atlantic region.

Simultaneously, an American-born Pietist movement appeared in Puritan New England. The original Puritans were intensely pious Christians, but over the decades, their spiritual zeal had faded. In the 1730s, Jonathan Edwards restored that zeal to Congregational churches in the Connecticut River Valley. Edwards was born in 1703, the fifth child and only son among the eleven children of Timothy and Esther Stoddard Edwards. Jonathan's father was a poorly paid rural minister, but his mother was the daughter of Solomon Stoddard, a famous preacher who taught that God was compassionate and that sainthood was not limited to a select few.

As a young man, Edwards rejected Stoddard's thinking. Inspired by the harsh the-ology of John Calvin, he preached that men and women were helpless and completely dependent on God. In his most famous sermon, "Sinners in the Hands of an Angry God" (1741), Edwards declared: "There is Hell's wide gaping mouth open; and you have nothing to stand upon, nor any thing to take hold of: there is nothing between you and Hell but the air; 'tis only the power and mere pleasure of God that holds you up." Ac-cording to one observer, the response was electric: "There was a great moaning and crying through the whole house. What shall I do to be saved—oh, I am going to Hell."

Surprisingly, Edwards's writings contributed to Enlightenment thought. The New England minister accepted Locke's argument in the *Essay Concerning Human Under-standing* (1690) that ideas are the product of experience as conveyed by the senses; but Edwards argued that people's ideas also depended on their passions. Edwards used his theory of knowledge to justify his preaching, suggesting that vivid words would "fright persons away from Hell" and promote conversions. News of Edwards's success stimu-lated religious fervor up and down the Connecticut River Valley.

George Whitefield transformed the local revivals of Edwards and the Tennents into a Great Awakening that spanned the British colonies. Whitefield had his awak-ening after reading German Pietists, and he became a follower of John Wesley, the founder of English Methodism. In 1739, Whitefield carried Wesley's fervent mes-sage to America, where he attracted huge crowds of "enthusiasts" from Georgia to Massachusetts. "Religion is become the Subject of most Conversations," the *Pennsylvania Gazette* reported. "No books are in Request but those of Piety and Devotion." Whitefield's preaching so impressed Benjamin Franklin that when the revivalist asked for contributions, Franklin emptied the coins in his pockets "wholly into the collector's dish, gold and all." By the time Whitefield reached Boston, the Reverend Benjamin Colman reported, the people were "ready to receive him as an angel of God" (see American Voices, p. 111).

Whitefield owed his appeal to his compelling presence. "He looked almost angelical; a young, slim, slender youth . . . cloathed with authority from the Great God," wrote a Connecticut farmer. Like most evangelical preachers, Whitefield did not read his sermons but spoke from memory. He gestured eloquently, raised his voice for dramatic effect, and at times assumed a female persona—a woman in labor struggling to deliver the word of God. When the young preacher told his spellbound listeners that they had all sinned and must seek salvation, hundreds of men and women suddenly felt a "new light" within them. As "the power of god come down,"

A Quest for Assurance   SARAH OSBORNE

Born in London in 1714, Sarah Osborne came to the colonies in 1722 with her parents, who settled in Newport, Rhode Island, in 1729. Throughout her youth, Osborne struggled with deep feelings of emotional distress and guilt, which were largely relieved by her conversion experience during the Great Awakening.

I was married to Mr. Samuel Wheaten, being in my eighteenth year, October 21, 1731, and went with my husband, the next winter, to see his friends in the country. . . . After I came home, I met with much affliction in many respects. It seemed to me that the whole world were in arms against me. I thought I was the most despised creature living upon earth. I used to pray to God in secret to relieve me; but did not, as I ought, see his hand in permitting it so to be, as a just punishment for my vile sins: And therefore was not humbled under it as I ought; but let nature rise, and acted very imprudently, in many respects. I was then with child, and often lamented that I was to bring a child into such a world of sorrow. . . .

My child was born on Oct. 27, 1732. The next spring, my husband returned home; but went to sea again, and died abroad in November, 1733.

In Sept. 1740, God in mercy sent his dear servant [George] Whitefield here, which in some measure stirred me up. But when Mr. [Gilbert] Tennent came soon after, it pleased God to bless his preaching so to me, that it roused me. But I was all the winter after exercised with dreadful doubts and fears about my state. I questioned the truth of all I had experienced, and feared I had never yet passed through the pangs of the new birth, or ever had one spark of grace. . . .

I continued thus till March, 1741. and then it pleased God to return Mr. Tennent

to us again. . . . But while he was here, I was more than ever distressed. I had lost the sensible manifestations of Christ's love. . . . And [Mr. Tennent] struck directly at those things, for which I had so foolishly and wickedly pleaded Christian example, such as singing songs, dancing and foolish jesting. . . . He said, he would not say there was no such thing as a dancing Christian, but he had a very mean opinion of such as could bear to spend their time so, when it is so short, and the work for eternity so great. Then, and not till then, was I fully convinced what prodigal wasters of precious time such things were. And, through grace, I have abhorred them all ever since. . . .

About this time I had the offer of a second marriage, with one who appeared to be a real Christian (and I could not think of being unequally yoked with one who was not such). . . . I concluded it was the will of God that I should accept of the offer, and accordingly was married to Mr. Henry Osborn, on the fifth day of May, 1742. . . . Soon after this, we fell into disagreeable and difficult worldly circumstances, with respect to living and paying the debts we owed. . . . [But] God ordered things so that our creditors were paid to their satisfaction.

SOURCE: Samuel Hopkins, ed., *Memoirs of the Life of Mrs. Sarah Osborn* (Worcester, MA: Leonard Worcester, 1799), 39–55.

George Whitefield, Evangelist
No painting could capture Whitefield's magical appeal, although this image conveys his open demeanor, religious intensity, and appeal to listeners. When Whitefield spoke to a crowd near Philadelphia, an observer noted, his words were "sharper than a two-edged sword. . . . Some of the people were pale as death; others were wringing their hands . . . and most lifting their eyes to heaven and crying to God for mercy."
Courtesy, Trustees of the Boston Public Library.

Hannah Heaton recalled, "my knees smote together . . . it seemed to me I was a sinking down into hell . . . but then I resigned my distress and was perfectly easy quiet and calm . . . it seemed as if I had a new soul & body both." Strengthened and self-confident, these "New Lights" were eager to spread Whitefield's message.

Religious Upheaval in the North

Like all cultural explosions, the Great Awakening was controversial. Conservative ministers — "Old Lights" — condemned the "cryings out, faintings and convulsions" in revivalist meetings and the New Lights' claims of "working Miracles or speaking with Tongues." Charles Chauncy, a minister in Boston, also attacked the New Lights for allowing women to speak in public: It was "a plain breach of that commandment of the LORD, where it is said, Let your WOMEN keep silence in the churches." In Connecticut, Old Lights persuaded the legislature to prohibit evangelists from speaking to congregations without their ministers' permission. Although Whitefield insisted, "I am no *Enthusiast*," he found many pulpits closed to him when he returned to Connecticut in 1744. But the New Lights refused to be silenced. Dozens of farmers, women, and artisans roamed the countryside, condemning the Old Lights as "unconverted" sinners and willingly accepting imprisonment: "I shall bring glory to God in my bonds," a dissident preacher wrote from jail.

The Awakening undermined support for legally established churches and their tax-supported ministers. In New England, New Lights left the Congregational Church and founded 125 "separatist" churches that supported their ministers through voluntary contributions. Other religious dissidents joined Baptist congregations, which also condemned government support of churches. "God never allowed any civil state upon earth to impose religious taxes," declared Baptist preacher Isaac Backus. In New York and New Jersey, the Dutch Reformed Church split in two because New Lights refused to accept the doctrines decreed by conservative church authorities in Holland.

Indeed, the Great Awakening challenged the authority of all ministers, whose status had long rested on respect for their education and knowledge of the Bible. In an influential pamphlet, *The Dangers of an Unconverted Ministry* (1740), Gilbert Tennent asserted that ministers' authority should come not from theological training but from the conversion experience. Reaffirming Martin Luther's belief in the priesthood of all Christians, Tennent suggested that anyone who had experienced the redeeming grace of God could speak with ministerial authority. Isaac Backus also celebrated a spiritual democracy, noting with approval that "the common people now claim as good a right to judge and act in matters of religion as civil rulers or the learned clergy." When challenged by her minister, Sarah Harrah Osborne, a New Light "exhorter" in Rhode Island, refused "to shut up my mouth . . . and creep into obscurity."

In many rural villages, revivalism reinforced communal values by challenging the moneygrubbing practices of merchants and land speculators. Jonathan Edwards spoke for many rural farm families when he charged that a miserly spirit was more suitable "for wolves and other beasts of prey, than for human beings."

As religious enthusiasm spread, churches founded new colleges to educate their young men and train ministers. New Light Presbyterians established the College of New Jersey (Princeton) in 1746, and New York Anglicans founded King's College (Columbia) in 1754. Baptists set up the College of Rhode Island (Brown) in 1764; two years later, the Dutch Reformed Church subsidized Queen's College (Rutgers) in New Jersey. However, the main intellectual legacy of the Great Awakening was not education for the privileged few but a new sense of authority among the many. A European visitor to Philadelphia remarked in surprise, "The poorest day-laborer . . . holds it his right to advance his opinion, in religious as well as political matters, with as much freedom as the gentleman."

Social and Religious Conflict in the South

In the southern colonies, where the Church of England was legally established, religious enthusiasm triggered social conflict. Anglican ministers generally ignored the spiritual needs of African Americans (about 40 percent of the population), and landless whites (another 20 percent) attended church irregularly. Middling white freeholders (35 percent of the residents) formed the core of most Church of England congregations. Prominent planters and their families (just 5 percent) held the real power, and they used their control of parish finances to discipline their ministers. One clergyman complained that dismissal awaited any minister who "had the courage to preach against any Vices taken into favor by the leading Men of his Parish."

Consequently, the Great Awakening challenged the dominance of both the Anglican Church and the planter elite. In 1743, bricklayer Samuel Morris, inspired by reading George Whitefield's sermons, led a group of Virginia Anglicans out of the church. Seeking a deeper religious experience, Morris invited New Light Presbyterian ministers to lead their prayer meetings. Soon Presbyterian revivals erupted among the English residents in the Tidewater region, where they threatened the social authority of the Virginia gentry. Traditionally, planters and their well-dressed families arrived at Anglican services in fancy carriages drawn by well-bred horses, and the men flaunted their power by marching in a body to their front-pew seats. Such ritual displays of the gentry's superiority would be meaningless if freeholders attended Presbyterian churches. Moreover, religious pluralism threatened the tax-supported status of the Anglican Church.

To halt the spread of New Light ideas, Virginia's governor William Gooch denounced them as "false teachings," and Anglican justices of the peace closed down Presbyterian meetinghouses. This harassment kept most white yeomen and poor tenants families in the Church of England; so did the fact that many well-educated Presbyterian ministers did not preach in the "enthusiastic" style preferred by illiterate farmers.

New Light Baptist ministers did not hesitate to reach out to ordinary folk. During the 1760s, their vigorous preaching and democratic message converted thousands of white farm families. The Baptists were radical Protestants whose central ritual was adult (rather than infant) baptism. Once men and women had experienced the infusion of grace — had been "born again" — they were baptized in an emotional public ceremony, often involving complete immersion in water.

Even slaves were welcome at Baptist revivals. During the 1740s, George Whitefield had urged Carolina planters to bring their slaves into the Christian fold, but white hostility and the commitment of Africans to their ancestral religions kept the number of converts low. The first significant Christian conversions came in Virginia in the 1760s, as native-born African Americans responded to the Baptists' message that all people were equal in God's eyes. Sensing a threat to the system of racial slavery, the House of Burgesses imposed heavy fines on Baptists who preached to slaves without their owners' permission.

The Baptists' insurgency posed other threats to gentry authority. Their preachers repudiated the social hierarchy, urging followers to call one another "brother" and "sister," and attacked the planters' rakish lifestyle. As planter Landon Carter complained, the Baptists were "destroying pleasure in the Country; for they encourage ardent Prayer; strong & constant faith, & an intire Banishment of *Gaming, Dancing,* & Sabbath-Day Diversions." The gentry responded with violence. Hearing Baptist Dutton Lane condemn "the vileness and danger" of drunkenness and whoring, planter John Giles took the charge personally: "I know who you mean! and by God I'll demolish you." In Caroline County, an Anglican posse attacked Brother John Waller at a prayer meeting. Waller "was violently jerked off the stage; they caught him by the back part of his neck, beat his head against the ground, and a gentleman gave him twenty lashes with his horsewhip."

Despite these attacks, Baptist congregations multiplied. By 1775, about 15 percent of Virginia's whites and hundreds of black slaves had joined Baptist churches. To signify their state of grace, some Baptist men "cut off their hair, like Cromwell's round-headed chaplains." Others forged a new evangelical masculinity—"crying, weeping, lifting up the eyes, groaning" when touched by the Holy Spirit but defending themselves with vigor. "Not able to bear the insults" of a heckler, a group of Baptists "took [him] by the neck and heels and threw him out of doors," setting off a bloody brawl.

The Baptist revival in the Chesapeake challenged traditional authority but did not overturn it. Rejecting the requests of evangelical women, Baptist men kept church authority in the hands of "free born male members"; and Anglican slaveholders retained control of the political system. Still, the Baptist insurgency infused the lives of poor tenant families with spiritual meaning and empowered yeomen to defend their economic interests. Moreover, as Baptist ministers spread Christianity among slaves, the cultural gulf between blacks and whites shrank, undermining one justification for slavery and giving some blacks a new religious identity. Within a generation, African Americans would develop distinctive versions of Protestant Christianity.

▶ In what ways did the Enlightenment and the Great Awakening prompt Americans to challenge traditional sources of authority?

▶ How did the Baptist insurgency in Virginia challenge conventional assumptions about race, gender, and class?

The Midcentury Challenge: War, Trade, and Social Conflict, 1750–1765

Between 1750 and 1765, a series of events transformed colonial life. First, Britain embarked on a war against the French in America, which became a worldwide conflict: the Great War for Empire. Second, a surge in trade boosted colonial consumption and placed Americans deeply in debt to British creditors. Third, westward migration sparked new conflicts with Indian peoples, armed disputes between settlers and speculators, and backcountry rebellions against eastern-controlled governments.

The French and Indian War Becomes a War for Empire

By 1754, France and Britain had laid claim to much of the land west of the Appalachians, but few Europeans had moved into that vast area (Map 4.3). The mountainous terrain discouraged access from the British colonies, and the Indian peoples that inhabited the region firmly opposed white settlement.

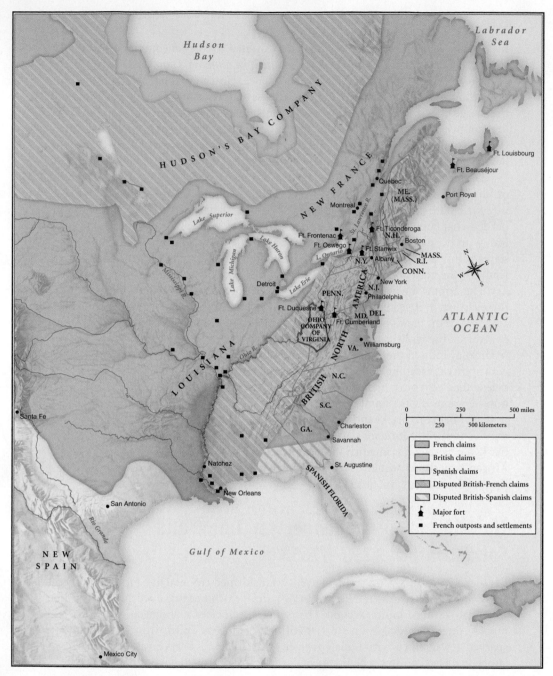

MAP 4.3 European Spheres of Influence in North America, 1754
France and Spain laid claim to vast areas of North America and relied on their Indian allies to combat the numerical superiority of British settlers. For their part, Native Americans played off one European power against another. As a British official observed, "To preserve the Ballance between us and the French is the great ruling Principle of Modern Indian Politics." By expelling the French from North America, the Great War for Empire destroyed this balance and left the Indian peoples on their own to resist encroaching Anglo-American settlers.

For decades, Iroquois and other native peoples had used their control of the fur trade to obtain guns and subsidies from French and British officials. By the 1740s, however, this strategy of playing off the French against the British was breaking down. The Europeans resented the rising cost of "gifts"; equally important, the alliances between the Indians and the British were crumbling as Anglo-American demands for western lands escalated. In the late 1740s, the Mohawks rebuffed attempts by Sir William Johnson, an Indian agent and land speculator, to settle Scottish migrants west of Albany. The Iroquois also responded angrily when Virginia Governor Robert Dinwiddie, along with Virginia land speculators and London merchants, formed the Ohio Company in 1749. The company's royal grant of 200,000 acres lay in the upper Ohio River Valley, an area the Iroquois controlled through alliances with the Delaware and Shawnee peoples. "We don't know what you Christians, English and French intend," the outraged Iroquois complained; "we are so hemmed in by both, that we have hardly a hunting place left."

To repair ties with the Iroquois, the British Board of Trade called a meeting at Albany in June 1754. At the Albany Congress, delegates from Britain's mainland colonies denied any designs on Iroquois lands and asked the Indians for help against New France. Though small in numbers, the French colony had a broad reach. In the 1750s, the 15,000 French farm families who lived along the St. Lawrence River provided food and supplies to the fur-trading settlements of Montreal and Quebec and the hundreds of fur traders, missionaries, and soldiers who lived among the western Indian peoples. To counter French expansion, Benjamin Franklin proposed a Plan of Union. Franklin's plan included a continental assembly that would manage trade, Indian policy, and defense in the West. But neither Franklin's plan nor a proposal by the Board of Trade for a political "union between ye Royal, Proprietary, & Charter Governments" was in the cards. British ministers worried that a union would spark American demands for independence, and provincial leaders feared that a consolidated government would undermine the authority of their assemblies.

Meanwhile, the Ohio Company's land grant alarmed French authorities. To stop British settlers from pouring into the Ohio River Valley, they constructed a series of forts. One, Fort Duquesne, stood at the point where the Monongahela and Allegheny rivers join to form the Ohio River (present-day Pittsburgh). In response, Governor Dinwiddie dispatched a military expedition led by Colonel George Washington, a young Virginia planter and Ohio Company stockholder. In July 1754, French troops seized Washington and his men, prompting Virginian and British expansionists to demand war. Henry Pelham, the British prime minister, urged calm: "There is such a load of debt, and such heavy taxes already laid upon the people, that nothing but an absolute necessity can justifie our engaging in a new War."

Pelham could not control the march of events. In Parliament, William Pitt, a rising British statesman, and Lord Halifax, the new head of the Board of Trade, were strong advocates for expansion. They persuaded Pelham to dispatch military forces to America to attack the French forts. In June 1755, British and New England troops captured Fort Beauséjour in Nova Scotia (Acadia). Soldiers from Puritan Massachusetts then seized nearly 10,000 French Acadians and deported them to France, the West Indies, and Louisiana (where they became known as Cajuns). English and Scottish Protestants took over the farms the French Catholics left behind.

These Anglo-American successes were quickly offset by a stunning defeat. In July 1755, 2,000 British regulars and Virginia militiamen advancing on Fort Duquesne marched into a deadly ambush. A much smaller force of French soldiers and Delaware and Shawnee warriors rained fire on the British force, taking the life of the British commander, General Edward Braddock, and killing or wounding half of his troops. "We have been beaten, most shamefully beaten, by a handfull of Men," Washington complained bitterly as he led the militiamen back to Virginia.

The Great War for Empire

By 1756, the conflict in America had spread to Europe, where it was known as the Seven Years' War. There, it pitted Britain and Prussia against France, Spain, and Austria. When Britain mounted major offensives in India and West Africa as well as in North America, the conflict became a Great War for Empire. Since 1700, Britain had reaped unprecedented profits from its overseas trading empire; now it vowed to crush France, the main obstacle to further expansion.

William Pitt emerged as the architect of the British war effort. Pitt, the grandson of the East Indies merchant "Diamond" Pitt, was a committed expansionist with a touch of arrogance. "I know that I can save this country and that I alone can," he boasted. In fact, Pitt was a master of strategy, both commercial and military, and planned to cripple France by seizing its colonies. In designing the critical campaign against New France, Pitt exploited a demographic advantage: On the North American mainland, King George II's two million subjects outnumbered the French by fourteen to one. To mobilize the colonists, Pitt paid half the cost of their troops and supplied them with arms and equipment, at a cost of £1 million a year. He also committed a fleet of British ships and 30,000 British soldiers to the American conflict.

Beginning in 1758, the powerful Anglo-American forces moved from one triumph to the next. They forced the French to abandon Fort Duquesne (which they renamed Fort Pitt); then they captured Fort Louisbourg, a French stronghold at the mouth of the St. Lawrence. In 1759, a force led by British General James Wolfe sailed down the St. Lawrence and took Quebec, the heart of France's American empire. The Royal Navy prevented French reinforcements from crossing the Atlantic, allowing British forces to complete the conquest of Canada in 1760 by capturing Montreal.

Elsewhere, the British also went from success to success. Fulfilling Pitt's dream, the East India Company ousted French traders from India; and British forces seized French Senegal in West Africa and the sugar islands Martinique and Guadeloupe in the French West Indies. From Spain, the British won Cuba and the Philippine Islands. The Treaty of Paris of 1763 confirmed Britain's triumph. It granted the British sovereignty over half the continent of North America, including French Canada, all French territory east of the Mississippi River, and Spanish Florida. The French empire in North America had shrunk to a handful of sugar islands in the West Indies, and Britain had forged a commercial and colonial empire that was nearly worldwide.

Britain's territorial acquisitions alarmed Indian peoples from New York to Michigan, who rightly feared an influx of British troops and Anglo-American settlers. To encourage the French to return, the Ottawa chief Pontiac declared, "I am French, and I want to die French." Neolin, a Delaware prophet, went further. He taught that the

Pipe of Peace
In 1760, the Ottawa chief Pontiac welcomed British troops to his territory. Here, he is shown offering a pipe of peace to their commander, Major Robert Rogers. Three years later, as British troops built forts in Indian lands and Anglo-American settlers moved west, Pontiac led a coordinated Indian uprising against the new European intruders. Library of Congress.

Indians' decline stemmed from their dependence on European goods, guns, and rum. He called for the expulsion of the white-skinned invaders: "If you suffer the English among you, you are dead men. Sickness, smallpox, and their poison [rum] will destroy you entirely." In 1763, inspired by Neolin's vision, Pontiac led a group of loosely confederated tribes (stretching geographically from the New York Senecas to the Minnesota Chippewas) in a major uprising. In Pontiac's Rebellion, Indian forces seized nearly every British military garrison west of Fort Niagara, besieged the fort at Detroit, and killed or captured more than 2,000 settlers. But the Indian alliance gradually weakened, and British military expeditions defeated the Delawares near Fort Pitt and broke the siege of Detroit. In the peace settlement, Pontiac and his allies accepted the British as their new political "fathers." In return, the British issued the Proclamation of 1763, which prohibited white settlements west of the Appalachians. It was an edict the colonists would ignore.

British Industrial Growth and the Consumer Revolution

Britain owed its military and diplomatic success to its unprecedented economic resources. Since 1700, when it had wrested control of many oceanic trade routes from the Dutch, Britain had become the dominant commercial power in the Atlantic and Indian oceans. By 1750, it had also become the first country to use new manu-facturing technology and work discipline to expand output. This combination of commerce and industry would soon make Britain the most powerful nation in the world.

Mechanical power was key to Britain's Industrial Revolution. British artisans de-signed and built water mills and steam engines that efficiently powered a wide array of machines: lathes for shaping wood, jennies and looms for spinning and weaving tex-tiles, and hammers for forging iron. The new power-driven machinery produced woolen and linen textiles, iron tools, furniture, and chinaware in greater quantities than tradi-tional manufacturing methods—and at lower cost. Moreover, the entrepreneurs who ran the new workshops drove their employees hard, forcing them to work long hours and to keep pace with the machines. To market the abundant factory-produced goods, English and Scottish merchants extended a full year's credit to colonial shopkeepers instead of the traditional six months'. Americans soon were purchasing 30 percent of all British exports.

To pay for British manufactures, the colonists increased their exports of tobacco, rice, indigo, and wheat. In Virginia, farmers moved into the Piedmont, a region of plains and rolling hills inland from the Tidewater counties. Using credit advanced by Scottish merchants, planters bought land, slaves, and equipment and grew tobacco, which they exported to expanding markets in France and central Europe. In South Carolina, rice planters increased their wealth and luxurious lifestyles by using British government subsidies to develop indigo plantations. By the 1760s, they were exporting the deep blue dye to English textile factories and 65 million pounds of rice a year to Holland and southern Europe. Simultaneously, New York, Pennsylvania, Maryland, and Virginia became the breadbasket of the Atlantic world, supplying Europe's ex-ploding population with wheat. In Philadelphia, export prices for wheat jumped al-most 50 percent between 1740 and 1765.

Americans used their profits from agricultural exports to buy English manufac-tures. Although this "consumer revolution" raised living standards, it landed many consumers—and the colonies as a whole—in debt. Even during the booming war-time economy of the 1750s, exports paid for only 80 percent of imported British goods. The remaining 20 percent—the Americans' trade deficit—was financed by Britain through the extension of credit and Pitt's military expenditures. When the military subsidies ended in 1763, the colonies fell into an economic recession. Merchants looked anxiously at their overstocked warehouses and feared bankruptcy. "I think we have a gloomy prospect before us," a Philadelphia trader noted in 1765, "as there are of late some Persons failed, who were in no way suspected." The increase in transatlantic trade had made Americans more dependent on overseas credit and markets.

The Struggle for Land in the East

In good times and bad, the colonial population continued to grow, intensifying the demand for arable land. Consider the experience of Kent, Connecticut. The settlers who founded the town in 1738 were descended from the original Puritan migrants. Like earlier generations, they had moved inland to establish new farms, but Kent stood at the colony's western boundary. To provide for the next generation, many

MAP 4.4 Westward Expansion and Land Conflicts, 1750–1775
Between 1750 and 1775, the mainland population more than doubled — from 1.2 million to 2.5 million — triggering both migration westward and legal battles over land, which had become increasingly valuable. Violence broke out in eastern areas, where tenant farmers and smallholders contested landlords' titles, and in the backcountry, where migrating settlers fought with Indians, rival claimants, and the officials of eastern-dominated governments.

Kent families joined the Susquehanna Company (1749), which speculated in lands in the Wyoming Valley along the upper Susquehanna River in present-day northeastern Pennsylvania. As settlers took up farmsteads there, the company urged the Connecticut legislature to claim the region on the basis of Connecticut's "sea-to-sea" royal charter of 1662. However, King Charles II had also granted the Wyoming Valley region to William Penn, and the Penn family had sold farms there to Pennsylvania residents. By the late 1750s, settlers from Connecticut and Pennsylvania were at war, burning down their rivals' houses and barns.

Simultaneously, three distinct but related land disputes broke out in the Hudson River Valley (Map 4.4). Dutch tenant farmers, Wappinger Indians, and migrants from Massachusetts asserted ownership rights to lands long claimed by the Van Rensselaer, Livingston, and other manorial families. When the manorial lords turned to the legal system to uphold their claims, Dutch and English farmers in Westchester, Dutchess, and Albany counties rioted to close the courts. In response, New York's royal governor ordered British General Thomas Gage and two regiments of troops to assist local sheriffs and manorial bailiffs to put down the mobs. They suppressed the tenant uprisings, intimidated the Wappingers, and evicted the Massachusetts squatters.

Other land disputes erupted in New Jersey and the southern colonies, as landlords and English aristocrats successfully asserted legal claims based on long-dormant seventeenth-century charters. One court decision upheld the right of Lord Granville, an heir of an original Carolina proprietor, to collect an annual tax on land in North Carolina; another decision awarded ownership of the entire northern neck of Virginia (along the Potomac River) to Lord Fairfax.

The revival of proprietary claims by manorial lords and English nobles testified to the rising value of land along the Atlantic coastal plain. It also reflected the maturity of the colonial courts, which now had enough authority to uphold property rights. And it underscored the increasing similarities between rural societies in Europe and America. To avoid being reduced to the status of European peasants, native-born yeomen and tenant families joined the stream of European migrants searching for cheap land near the Appalachian Mountains.

Western Uprisings and Regulator Movements

As would-be landowners moved westward, they sparked conflicts over Indian policy, political representation, and debts. During the war with France, Delaware and Shaw-nee warriors had exacted revenge for Thomas Penn's land swindle of 1737 by de-stroying frontier farms in Pennsylvania and killing hundreds of residents. Scots-Irish settlers demanded the expulsion of all Indians, but Quaker leaders refused. So in 1763, a group of Scots-Irish frontiersmen called the Paxton Boys took matters into their own hands and massacred twenty members of the peaceful Conestoga tribe. When Governor John Penn tried to bring the murderers to justice, 250 armed Scots-Irish advanced on Philadelphia. Benjamin Franklin intercepted the angry mob at Lancaster and arranged a truce, averting a battle with the militia. Prosecution of the Paxton Boys failed for lack of witnesses, and the Scots-Irish dropped their de-mands that the Indians be expelled; but the episode left a legacy of racial hatred and political resentment.

Violence also broke out in the backcountry of South Carolina, where land-hungry Scottish and Anglo-American settlers clashed repeatedly with Cherokees during the war with France. When the war ended in 1763, a group of landowning vigilantes, the Regulators, tried to suppress outlaw bands of whites that were stealing cattle. The Regulators also had political goals: They demanded that the eastern-controlled government provide western districts with more courts, fairer taxation, and greater representation in the assembly. Fearing slave revolts, the lowland rice planters who ran the South Carolina assembly compromised with the Regulators rather than fighting them. In 1767, the assembly created courts in the western coun-ties and reduced the fees for legal documents; but it refused to reapportion the legislature or lower western taxes. Like the Paxton Boys in Pennsylvania, the South Carolina Regulators won attention to western needs but failed to wrest power from the eastern elite.

In 1766, a more radical Regulator movement arose in the backcountry of North Carolina. The economic recession of the early 1760s brought a sharp fall in tobacco prices, and many farmers could not pay their debts. When creditors sued, judges directed sheriffs to seize the debtors' property and sell it to pay debts and court costs.

Governor Tryon and the Regulators Meet at Hillsborough, 1768
Orange County, North Carolina, was home to the Sandy Creek Association, a group of Quakers led
by Herman Husband, a powerful advocate of social justice and a leader of the Regulator movement.
In September 1768, Royal Governor William Tryon and the low-country militia confronted a group of
Regulators near Hillsborough. As this engraving suggests, the potential for violence was high and only
narrowly averted. In 1771, Tryon engaged the Regulators in a battle near the Alamance River, twenty
miles west of Hillsborough. Courtesy, North Carolina State Archives.

Backcountry farmers—including many German and Scots-Irish migrants—
denounced the merchants' lawsuits, both because they generated high fees for lawyers
and court officials and because they violated rural custom, which allowed loans to
remain unpaid in hard times.

To save their farms from grasping creditors and tax-hungry officials, North
Carolina's debtors defied the government's authority. Disciplined mobs of farmers
intimidated judges, closed courts, and freed their comrades from jail. Significantly,
the Regulators proposed a coherent set of reforms. They proposed legislation to
lower legal fees and allow tax payments in the "produce of the country" rather than
in cash. They demanded greater representation in the assembly and a new revenue
system, which would tax each person "in proportion to the profits arising from his
estate." All to no avail. In May 1771, Royal Governor William Tryon decided to suppress the Regulators. Mobilizing British troops and the eastern militia, Tryon defeated
a large Regulator force at the Alamance River. When the fighting ended, thirty men
lay dead, and Tryon summarily executed seven insurgent leaders. Not since Bacon's
Rebellion in Virginia in 1675 (see Chapter 2) had a domestic political conflict
caused so much bloodshed.

▶ What impact did the Industrial Revolution in England have on the American colonies?

▶ What were the causes of unrest in the American backcountry in the mid-eighteenth century?

▶ In what ways were the various regions in British North America—New England, Middle Atlantic, the South (see Chapter 3), the backcountry—becoming increasingly similar between 1720 and 1750? In what ways were they becoming different?

In 1771, as in 1675, colonial conflicts became linked with imperial politics. In Connecticut, the Reverend Ezra Stiles defended the North Carolina Regulators. "What shall an injured & oppressed people do," he asked, when faced with "Oppression and tyranny?" Stiles's remarks reflected growing resistance to recently imposed British policies of taxation and control. In 1771, as in 1686 when James II imposed the Dominion of New England, the American colonies still depended on Britain for their trade and military defense. However, by the 1760s, the mainland settlements had evolved into a complex society with the potential to exist independently. British policies would determine the direction the maturing colonies would take.

SUMMARY

In this chapter, we observed the dramatic transformation of British North America between 1720 and 1765. There was an astonishing surge in population—from 400,000 to almost two million—the combined result of natural increase, European migration, and the trade in African slaves. Three other transatlantic developments brought equally great changes: The European Enlightenment, European Pietism, and substantial imports of consumer goods from England altered the cultural landscape.

We noted that the colonists confronted three major regional challenges. In New England, crowded towns and ever-smaller farms threatened the yeoman ideal of independent farming, prompting families to limit births, move to the frontier, or participate in an "exchange" economy. In the Middle Atlantic colonies, Dutch, English, German, and Scots-Irish residents maintained their religious and cultural identities, which led to bruising ethnic conflicts. Finally, westward migration into the backcountry and the Ohio River Valley set off conflicts with Indian peoples, civil unrest among white settlers, and, ultimately, the Great War for Empire. In the aftermath of the war, Britain stood triumphant in Europe and America.

Connections: Culture

In the essay opening Part One, we provided an outline of cultural changes in America between 1600 and 1765:

> New forms of family and community life arose in the new American society . . . [, which was] increasingly pluralistic, composed of migrants from many European ethnic groups . . . as well as enslaved Africans and Native American peoples. Distinct regional cultures developed in New England, the Middle Atlantic colonies, the Chesapeake, and the Carolinas.

In tracking the trajectory of Britain's North American colonies, we can see a crucial turning point around 1700. Until then, most settlers came from England, bringing with them traditional English social and political structures: Fathers ruled families, and authoritarian leaders dominated politics. Then came a massive wave of migrants: enslaved Africans, Germans, Scots-Irish, and Scots. By 1765, these migrants and their descendants formed a majority of the population. As British North America became more diverse, life became less repressive and more open to innovation.

A second phase of change began around 1740. More farmers sold goods in distant markets; a responsive system of government prompted more men to seek office; declining parental power gave young people greater marriage choices; and an outburst

TIMELINE

1710s–1730s ▶ Enlightenment ideas spread to America

▶ Germans and Scots-Irish settle in Middle Atlantic region

▶ Theodore Jacob Frelinghuysen conducts Pietist revivals

1730s ▶ William and Gilbert Tennent lead Presbyterian revivals

▶ Jonathan Edwards mobilizes piety in New England

1739 ▶ George Whitefield sparks Great Awakening

1740s–1760s ▶ Old Light–New Light conflicts

▶ Small farms in New England threaten freehold ideal

▶ Ethnic and religious conflict in Middle Atlantic region

▶ Religious denominations establish colleges

1743 ▶ Benjamin Franklin founds American Philosophical Society

▶ Samuel Morris starts Presbyterian revivals in Virginia

1749 ▶ Virginia speculators organize Ohio Company; Connecticut farmers form Susquehanna Company

1750s ▶ American consumer imports increase debts to English merchants

1754 ▶ French and Indian War begins

▶ Albany Congress of colonial delegates and Iroquois

1756 ▶ Britain begins Great War for Empire

1759–1760 ▶ Britain completes conquest of Canada

1760s ▶ Land conflicts along New York and New England border

▶ Baptists win converts in Virginia

1763 ▶ Pontiac's Rebellion leads to Proclamation of 1763

▶ Treaty of Paris ends Great War for Empire

▶ Scots-Irish Paxton Boys massacre Indians in Pennsylvania

1771 ▶ Royal governor puts down Regulator revolt in North Carolina of pietistic enthusiasm shook established churches and advanced religious toleration. Together, these developments provided white colonists in British North America (as we stated in the opening essay) with "unprecedented opportunities for economic security, political freedom, and spiritual fulfillment."

FOR FURTHER EXPLORATION

Stories of individuals bring alive the social history of eighteenth-century America. In *Good Wives* (1982) and *A Midwife's Tale* (1990), Laurel Thatcher Ulrich paints a vivid picture of women's experiences. For additional materials on Ballard, see **www .pbs.org/amex/midwife** and **www.DoHistory.org**. Benjamin Franklin's *Autobiography* (1771) shows his Enlightenment sensibility and his pursuit of wealth and fame. See also "Benjamin Franklin . . . in His Own Words" (**www.loc.gov/exhibits/treasures/ franklin-home.html**) and "The Electric Franklin" (**www.ushistory.org/franklin/ index.htm**).

Harry S. Stout's *The Divine Dramatist: George Whitefield and the Rise of Modern Evangelicalism* (1991) evokes the charismatic preacher's flair for theatrics "Jonathan Edwards On-Line" (**www.JonathanEdwards.com/**) presents the writings of the great philosopher and preacher.

"Colonial Currency and Colonial Coin" (**www.coins.nd.edu/ColCurrency/index .html**) suggests the dimensions of daily economic life, and "Bethlehem Digital History Project" (**bdhp.moravian.edu/**) documents the experiences of migrant German religious sectarians. On settler-Indian relations, see Jane T. Merritt, *At the Crossroads: Indians and Empires on a Mid-Atlantic Frontier, 1700–1763* (2003), and Gregory Evans Dowd, *War Under Heaven: Pontiac, the Indian Nations, and the British Empire* (2002). For the French and Indian War, see the PBS series "The War That Made America" and its Web site (**www.thewarthatmadeamerica.com/**).

TEST YOUR KNOWLEDGE

To assess your mastery of the material in this chapter and for Web sites, images, and documents related to this chapter, visit **bedfordstmartins.com/henrettaconcise**.

The New Republic

1763–1820

GOVERNMENT	DIPLOMACY	ECONOMY
Creating republican institutions	**European entanglements**	**Expanding commerce and manufacturing**
1763 ▸ Stamp Act Congress (1765) ▸ Committees of correspondence ▸ First Continental Congress (1774)	▸ Treaty of Paris (1763) gives Britain control of Canada and Florida	▸ Merchants defy Sugar and Stamp Acts ▸ Boycotts spur domestic manufacturing
1775 ▸ Second Continental Congress (1775) ▸ States institute republican constitutions	▸ Independence declared (1776) ▸ Treaty of Alliance with France (1778)	▸ Manufacturing expands during war ▸ Curtailed trade and severe inflation threaten economy
1780 ▸ Articles of Confederation ratified (1781) ▸ Legislatures emerge as supreme in states ▸ Philadelphia convention drafts U.S. Constitution (1787)	▸ Treaty of Paris (1783) ▸ Britain restricts U.S. trade with West Indies ▸ U.S. government signs treaties with Indian peoples	▸ Bank of North America founded (1781) ▸ Commercial recession (1783–1789) ▸ Land speculation continues in West
1790 ▸ Conflict over Alexander Hamilton's economic policies ▸ First national parties: Federalists and Republicans	▸ Wars between France and Britain ▸ Jay's Treaty and Pinckney's Treaty (both 1795) ▸ Undeclared war with France (1798)	▸ First Bank of the United States (1792–1811) ▸ States charter business corporations ▸ Outwork system grows
1800 ▸ Jefferson's "Revolution of 1800" reduces activism of national government ▸ Chief Justice Marshall asserts judicial powers	▸ Napoleonic Wars (1802–1815) ▸ Louisiana Purchase (1803) ▸ Embargo Act (1807)	▸ Cotton output expands ▸ Farm productivity improves ▸ Embargo encourages U.S. manufacturing
1810 ▸ Triumph of Republican Party and end of Federalist Party ▸ State constitutions democratized	▸ War of 1812 (1812–1815) ▸ John Quincy Adams makes border treaties ▸ Monroe Doctrine (1823)	▸ Second Bank of the United States chartered (1816–1836) ▸ Supreme Court guards property ▸ Emergence of a national economy

SOCIETY	CULTURE
Defining liberty and equality	**Pluralism and national identity**
▶ Artisans seek influence ▶ Quebec Act (1774) allows Catholicism	▶ Patriots call for American unity ▶ Concept of "popular sovereignty" takes hold
▶ Judith Sargent Murray writes *On the Equality of the Sexes* (1779) ▶ Emancipation begins in the North	▶ Thomas Paine's *Common Sense* (1776) calls for a republic ▶ Influx of migrants from Europe slows
▶ Virginia enacts religious freedom legislation (1786) ▶ Politicians and ministers praise "republican motherhood"	▶ Noah Webster defines American English ▶ State cessions and land ordinances create national domain in West ▶ German settlers keep own language
▶ Bill of Rights ratified (1791) ▶ Creation of French Republic (1793) sparks ideological debate ▶ Sedition Act limits freedom of press (1798)	▶ Indians form Western Confederacy (1790) ▶ Second Great Awakening (1790–1860) ▶ Divisions emerge between South and North
▶ New Jersey denies suffrage to propertied women (1807) ▶ Atlantic slave trade legally ends (1808)	▶ Tenskwatawa and Tecumseh revive Western Confederacy ▶ Percentage of native-born citizens increases
▶ Suffrage for white men expands ▶ American Colonization Society (1817) ▶ Missouri Compromise (1819–1821)	▶ War of 1812 tests national unity ▶ Religious benevolence produces social reform

"The American war is over," Philadelphia Patriot Benjamin Rush declared in 1787, "but this is far from being the case with the American Revolution. On the contrary, nothing but the first act of the great drama is closed. It remains yet to establish and perfect our new forms of government." As we will suggest in Part Two, the job was even greater than Rush imagined. The republican revolution that began with the Patriot resistance movement of 1765 and took shape with the Declaration of Independence in 1776 reached far beyond politics. It challenged many of the values and institutions of the colonial social order and forced Americans to consider fundamental changes in their economic, religious, and cultural practices. Here, in summary, are the main themes of our discussion of America's new political and social order.

GOVERNMENT

Once Americans had repudiated their allegiance to Britain and its monarch, they faced the task of creating a new system of government. In 1776, no one knew how the states should go about setting up republican institutions. Nor did Patriot leaders know whether there should be a permanent central authority along the lines of the Continental Congress. It would take experimentation stretching over an entire generation to find out. It would take even longer to assimilate a new institution—the political party—into the workings of government. However, by 1820, years of difficult political compromise and constitutional revision had resulted in republican national and state governments that commanded the allegiance of their citizens.

DIPLOMACY

To create and preserve their new republic, Americans of European descent fought two wars against Great Britain, an undeclared war against France, and many battles with Indian peoples. The wars against Britain divided the country into bitter factions—Patriots against Loyalists in the War of Independence and pro-war Republicans versus antiwar Federalists in the War of 1812—and expended much blood and treasure. The extension of American sovereignty and settlements into the trans-Appalachian west was a cultural disaster for Indian peoples, who were brutally displaced from their lands. Despite these wars, by 1820, the United States had emerged as a strong independent state. Freed from a half-century of entanglement in European wars and diplomacy, its people began to exploit the riches of the continent.

ECONOMY

By the 1760s, the expansion of production and commerce had established the foundation for a vigorous national economy. Beginning in the 1780s, northern merchants financed a banking system and organized a rural system of manufacturing. Simultaneously, state governments used charters and other privileges to assist businesses and to improve roads, bridges, and waterways. Meanwhile, southern planters continued to use enslaved African Americans and exported a new staple crop—cotton—to markets in the North and in Europe. Many yeomen farm families migrated westward to grow grain. Those in the East turned out raw materials such as leather and wool for burgeoning manufacturing enterprises and made shoes, textiles, tinware, and other handicrafts for market sale. By 1820, the young American republic was on the verge of achieving economic as well as political independence.

SOCIETY

As Americans confronted the challenges of creating a republican society, they found themselves divided by gender, race, religion, and class. They disagreed over fundamental issues such as legal equality for women, the status of slavery, the meaning of free speech and religious liberty, and the extent of public responsibility for social inequality. As we shall see, political leaders managed to resolve some of these disputes. Legislatures abolished slavery in the North, broadened religious liberty by allowing freedom of conscience, and, except in New England, ended the system of legally established churches. However, Americans continued to argue over social equality, in part because their republican creed placed authority in the family and society in the hands of men of property. This arrangement denied power and status not only to slaves but also to free blacks, women, and poor white men.

CULTURE

The British colonies in North America contained a diversity of peoples and ways of life. This complexity jeopardized the effort to define an American culture and identity. Native Americans still lived in their own clans and nations; and black Americans, one-fifth of the enumerated population, were developing a new, African American culture. White Americans were also enmeshed in vigorous regional cultures — New England, Middle Atlantic, and Southern — and in strong ethnic communities: English, Scottish, Scots-Irish, German, and Dutch. However, over time, the political institutions began to unite Americans of diverse backgrounds, as did their increasing participation in the market economy and in evangelical Protestant churches. By 1820, to be an American meant, for many members of the dominant white population, to be a republican, a Protestant, and an enterprising individual in a capitalist-run market system.

Toward Independence:
Years of Decision
1763–1776

> The said [Stamp] act is contrary to the rights of mankind and subversive of the English Constitution.
>
> — Town meeting of Leicester, Massachusetts, 1765

As the Great War for Empire ended in 1763, Massachusetts soldier Seth Metcalf and other American colonists celebrated the triumph of British arms. Metcalf thanked "the Great Goodness of God" for the "General Peace" that was so "percularly Advantageous to the English Nation." Just two years later, Metcalf was less certain of God's favor. "God is angry with us of this land," the pious Calvinist wrote in his journal, "and is now Smiting [us] with his Rod Especially by the hands of our Rulers."

The rapid disintegration of the bonds uniting Britain and America — an event that Metcalf ascribed to Divine Providence — mystified many Americans. How had it happened, the president of King's College in New York asked in 1775, that such a "happily situated" people were ready to "hazard their Fortunes, their Lives, and their Souls, in a Rebellion"? Unlike other colonial peoples, white Americans lived in a prosperous, self-governing society. They had little to gain and much to lose by rebelling.

Or so it seemed in 1763, before the British government began to reform the imperial system. "This year Came an act from England Called the Stamp Act . . . which is thought will be very oppressive," Metcalf reflected. The British effort to transform a loose empire into more of a transatlantic nation-state prompted violent resistance and a downward spiral of ideological and political conflict that ended in a war for American independence. Could careful statecraft and political compromise have saved the empire? The likely answer is yes. But neither statecraft nor compromise was in evidence. Instead, the inflexibility of British ministers and the passionate determination of Patriot leaders destroyed the British empire in North America.

Imperial Reform, 1763–1765

The Great War for Empire left a mixed legacy. Britain's armies had driven the French out of Canada and the Spanish out of Florida, and Britain now dominated eastern North America (Map 5.1). But the war had been costly, and to reduce the

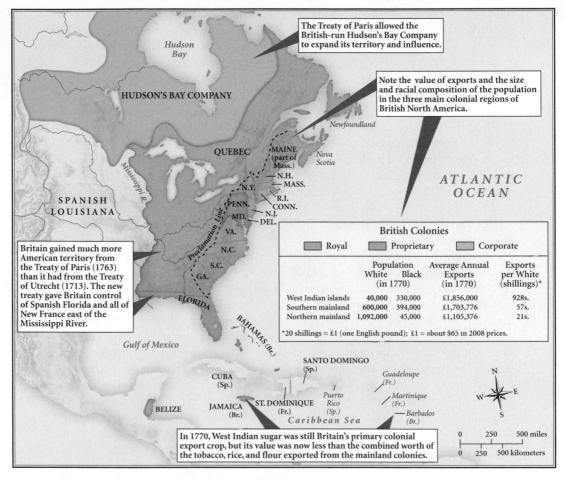

The Treaty of Paris allowed the British-run Hudson's Bay Company to expand its territory and influence.

Note the value of exports and the size and racial composition of the population in the three main colonial regions of British North America.

Hudson Bay

HUDSON'S BAY COMPANY

Newfoundland

QUEBEC

MAINE (part of Mass.)

Nova Scotia

— N.H.

N.Y.

— MASS.

— R.I.

ATLANTIC OCEAN

SPANISH LOUISIANA

Mississippi R.

PENN.

CONN.

MD.

N.J.

— DEL.

VA.

N.C.

S.C.

GA.

Proclamation Line

FLORIDA

Britain gained much more American territory from the Treaty of Paris (1763) than it had from the Treaty of Utrecht (1713). The new treaty gave Britain control of Spanish Florida and all of New France east of the Mississippi River.

BAHAMAS (Br.)

Gulf of Mexico

British Colonies

▢ Royal	▢ Proprietary	▢ Corporate

	Population White (in 1770)	Black	Average Annual Exports (in 1770)	Exports per White (shillings)*
West Indian islands	40,000	330,000	£1,856,000	928s.
Southern mainland	600,000	394,000	£1,703,776	57s.
Northern mainland	1,092,000	45,000	£1,105,376	21s.

*20 shillings = £1 (one English pound); £1 = about $65 in 2008 prices.

SANTO DOMINGO (Sp.)

CUBA (Sp.)

Guadeloupe (Fr.)

Puerto Rico (Sp.)

Martinique (Fr.)

W ✦ E

BELIZE

JAMAICA (Br.)

ST. DOMINIQUE (Fr.)

Barbados (Br.)

Caribbean Sea

In 1770, West Indian sugar was still Britain's primary colonial export crop, but its value was now less than the combined worth of the tobacco, rice, and flour exported from the mainland colonies.

```
0        250      500 miles
0      250   500 kilometers
```

MAP 5.1 Britain's North American and Caribbean Empire in 1763
The Treaty of Paris gave Britain control of the eastern half of North America and strengthened its position in the West Indies. To protect the empire's new territories on the continent, British ministers dispatched troops to Florida and Quebec. They also instructed the troops to uphold the terms of the Proclamation of 1763, which prohibited Anglo-American settlement west of the Appalachian Mountains.

enormous war debt, the British ministry imposed new taxes on the American possessions. More fundamentally, the war spurred Parliament to redefine the empire: Salutary neglect, with its flexible emphasis on trade and colonial self-government, gave way to rigid regulations, imperial administrators, and direct rule by Parliament.

The Legacy of War

The war strained the relationship between Britain and its North American colonies. British generals and American leaders disagreed sharply on military strategy, and the presence of 25,000 British troops revealed sharp cultural differences. The arrogance of British officers and their demands for deference shocked many Americans: British soldiers "are but little better than slaves to their officers," declared a Massachusetts militiaman. The hostility was mutual. British general James Wolfe complained that colonial troops were drawn from the dregs of society and that "there was no depending on them in action."

The war also exposed the weakness of the royal governors. In theory, the governors had extensive political powers, including command of the provincial militia; in reality, they shared power with the colonial assemblies, a situation that outraged British officials. The Board of Trade complained that in Massachusetts "almost every act of executive and legislative power is ordered and directed by votes and resolves of the General Court." To tighten the collection of trade duties, which colonial merchants had evaded for decades by bribing customs officials, Parliament passed the Revenue Act of 1762. The ministry also instructed the Royal Navy to seize American vessels carrying supplies from the mainland to the French West Indies. It was absurd, declared a British politician, that French armies attempting "to Destroy one English province . . . are actually supported by Bread raised in another."

Britain's military victory resulted in a fundamental shift in policy: the peacetime deployment of an army of 10,000 men in North America. King George III (r. 1760–1820) wanted military commands for his friends, and the king's ministers feared a possible rebellion by the 60,000 French residents of Canada, Britain's new northern province. The Native Americans were also a concern. Pontiac's Rebellion had nearly overwhelmed Britain's frontier forts, and it would take a substantial military force to deter land-hungry whites from defying the Proclamation of 1763 by settling west of the Appalachian Mountains (see Chapter 4). Finally, British politicians worried about the colonists' loyalty now that the French no longer controlled Canada. "The main purpose of Stationing a large Body of Troops in America," declared treasury official William Knox, "is to secure the Dependence of the Colonys on Great Britain." By deploying an army in America, the British ministry was prepared to use force against conquered Frenchmen, unruly Indians, or rebellious colonists.

But troops cost money, which was in short supply. Britain's national debt had soared from £75 million in 1756 to £133 million in 1763. Indeed, the interest on the war debt was consuming 60 percent of the national budget. To restore fiscal stability, prime minister Lord Bute decided to raise taxes. The Treasury Department opposed increasing the land tax, which was paid primarily by the gentry and aristocracy, who wielded great influence in Parliament. So Bute taxed the people who had little political power — the poor and middling classes — by imposing higher import duties on tobacco and sugar, thus raising their cost to consumers. Parliament also increased excise levies — essentially sales taxes — on salt, beer, and distilled spirits, once again passing on the cost of the war to the king's ordinary subjects. Left unresolved was the question of taxing the American colonists, who, like Britain's poor, had little influence in Parliament.

To collect the taxes — old and new — the government doubled the size of the tax bureaucracy. Scores of customs agents patrolled the coasts of southern Britain, arresting smugglers and seizing tons of French wines and Flemish textiles. Convicted smugglers faced heavy penalties, including death or forced "transportation" to America. Despite protests by the colonial assemblies, nearly 50,000 English criminals had already been banished to America as indentured servants.

The price of empire abroad had turned out to be higher taxes and government scrutiny at home. These developments confirmed the worst fears of the British opposition parties, the Radical Whigs and Country Party. They complained that the huge war debt placed the treasury at the mercy of the "monied interest," the banks and financiers who reaped millions of pounds in interest from government bonds. They charged that the tax bureaucracy now contained thousands of patronage positions filled with "worthless pensioners and placemen." To reverse the growth of government power — and the consequent threats to personal liberty and property rights — reformers in Britain demanded a more representative Parliament. The Radical Whig John Wilkes called for an end to **rotten boroughs**, tiny electoral districts whose voters were controlled by wealthy aristocrats and merchants. In domestic affairs, as in colonial policy, the war had transformed British political life.

George Grenville: Imperial Reformer

A member of Parliament since 1741, George Grenville was widely conceded to be one of the ablest men in Great Britain. But he faced difficult financial issues. When he became prime minister in 1763, the nation was mired in debt, and British taxpayers were paying nearly five times as much in taxes as free Americans were. Grenville decided that new revenue would have to come from America.

Grenville set out to reform the imperial system. He began by winning passage of the Currency Act of 1764, which banned all the American colonies (not just New

George Grenville, Architect of the Stamp Act
This portrait, painted in 1763, suggests Grenville's energy and ambition. As prime minister, he was determined to reform the imperial system and ensure that the colonists shared the cost of the empire. The Earl of Halifax, Garrowby, Yorkshire.

England) from using paper money as legal tender. Now American shopkeepers, planters, and farmers would have to pay their debts to British merchants in gold or silver coin, which was always in short supply.

Grenville also won parliamentary approval of the Sugar Act of 1764 to replace the widely ignored Molasses Act of 1733 (see Chapter 3). The prime minister and his subordinates understood the pattern of colonial trade: They knew that mainland settlers had to sell at least some of their wheat, fish, and lumber in the French sugar islands to accumulate funds to buy British manufactures. So Grenville resisted demands from British sugar planters, who wanted to cut off all mainland trade with the French islands by levying a duty of 6 pence per gallon on French molasses; instead, he settled on a duty of 3 pence per gallon.

This carefully crafted policy garnered little support in America. New England merchants—among them John Hancock of Boston—had made their fortunes smuggling French molasses. In 1754, Boston merchants paid customs duties on a mere 400 hogsheads of molasses even as they imported the 40,000 hogsheads that were used by sixty-three Massachusetts distilleries. Merchants claimed publicly that the Sugar Act would wipe out trade with the French islands and ruin the distilling industry; privately, they vowed to evade the duty by smuggling or by bribing officials.

More important, the merchants' political allies raised constitutional objections to the Sugar Act. The Speaker of the Massachusetts House of Representatives argued that the new legislation was "contrary to a fundamental Principall of our Constitution: That all Taxes ought to originate with the people." "They who are taxed at pleasure by others cannot possibly have any property, and they who have no property, can have no freedom," warned governor Stephen Hopkins of Rhode Island. The Sugar Act raised other constitutional issues as well. Merchants prosecuted under the act would be tried by a **vice-admiralty court**, a maritime tribunal run by a British-appointed judge. American assemblies had long opposed the vice-admiralty courts and had found ways to have merchants who were accused of violating the Navigation Acts tried by local common-law courts, where they often were acquitted by friendly juries. The Sugar Act closed this legal loophole by extending the jurisdiction of the vice-admiralty courts to all customs offenses.

The new taxes and courts imposed by the Sugar Act revived old American fears of British control. The influential Virginia planter Richard Bland admitted that the colonies were subject to the Navigation Acts, which restricted their manufactures and commerce. But, he protested, the American settlers "were not sent out to be the Slaves but to be the Equals of those that remained behind." John Adams, a young Massachusetts lawyer who was defending John Hancock on a charge of smuggling, claimed that the vice-admiralty courts "degrade every American . . . below the rank of an Englishman."

While the logic of the Americans' arguments appeared compelling, some of their facts were wrong. The Navigation Acts certainly favored British merchants and manufacturers. However, trying accused smugglers in vice-admiralty courts was not discriminatory because similar rules had long been in force in Britain. The real issue was the growing administrative power of the British state. Americans had lived for decades under a policy of salutary neglect and an "unwritten constitution" that encouraged political compromise between the king's officials and his subjects. They understood that the new policies would deprive them "of some of their most essential Rights as British subjects," as a committee of the Massachusetts House of Representatives put it.

For their part, British officials insisted on the supremacy of parliamentary laws and denied that colonists should enjoy the traditional legal rights of Englishmen. When royal governor Francis Bernard of Massachusetts heard that the Massachusetts House had objected to the Sugar Act, claiming that there should be no taxation without representation, he asserted that Americans did not have that constitutional right: "The rule that a British subject shall not be bound by laws or liable to taxes, but what he has consented to by his representatives must be confined to the inhabitants of Great Britain only." To Bernard, Grenville, and other imperial reformers, Americans were second-class subjects of the king, their rights limited by the Navigation Acts, parliamentary laws, and British interests.

An Open Challenge: The Stamp Act

Another new tax, the Stamp Act of 1765, sparked the first great imperial crisis. The new levy would cover part of the cost of keeping British troops in America—some £200,000 a year (about $50 million today). The tax would require stamps on all court documents, land titles, contracts, playing cards, newspapers, and other printed items. A similar stamp tax in England was yielding £290,000 a year; Grenville hoped that the American levy would raise £60,000. The prime minister knew that some Americans opposed the tax on constitutional grounds, so he raised the issue explicitly in the House of Commons: Did any member doubt "the power and sovereignty of Parliament over every part of the British dominions, for the purpose of raising or collecting any tax?" No one rose to object.

Confident of Parliament's support, Grenville threatened to impose a stamp tax unless the colonists paid for their own defense. The London merchants who served as agents for the colonial legislatures immediately protested that Americans lacked a continent-wide body that could raise such funds. Colonial officials had met together officially only once, at the Albany Congress of 1754, and not a single assembly had accepted that body's proposals for a continental union (see Chapter 4). Benjamin Franklin, who was in Britain as the agent of the Pennsylvania assembly, proposed another solution to Grenville's challenge: American representation in Parliament. "If you chuse to tax us," he suggested, "give us Members in your Legislature, and let us be one People."

With the exception of William Pitt, British politicians rejected Franklin's idea as too radical. They maintained that the colonists already had **virtual representation** in Parliament because a number of its members were transatlantic merchants and West Indian sugar planters. Colonial leaders were equally skeptical of Franklin's plan. Americans were "situate at a great Distance from their Mother Country," the Connecticut assembly declared, and therefore "cannot participate in the general Legislature of the Nation."

As Grenville moved forward with the Stamp Act, his goal was not only to raise revenue but also to assert a constitutional principle: "the Right of Parliament to lay an internal Tax upon the Colonies." The House of Commons ignored American petitions and passed the new legislation by an overwhelming vote of 205 to 49. At the request of General Thomas Gage, the British military commander in America, Parliament also passed the Quartering Act, which required colonial governments to provide barracks and food for British troops stationed within their borders. Finally, Parliament approved Grenville's proposal that violations of the Stamp Act be tried in vice-admiralty courts.

The design for reform was complete. Using the doctrine of parliamentary supremacy, Grenville had begun to fashion a centralized imperial system in America much like the one already in place in Ireland: British officials would govern the colonies with little regard for the local assemblies. Consequently, Grenville's plan provoked a constitutional confrontation on both the specific issues of taxation, jury trials, and military quartering and the general question of representative self-government.

► What were the goals of British imperial reformers?

► Why did the colonists object to the new taxes in 1764 and again in 1765? What arguments did they use? How did these conflicts turn into a constitutional crisis?

The Dynamics of Rebellion, 1765–1770

In the name of reform, Grenville had thrown down the gauntlet to the Americans. The colonists had often resisted unpopular laws and arbitrary governors, but they had faced an all-out attack on their institutions only once—in 1686, when James II had unilaterally imposed the Dominion of New England. The danger now was even greater because both the king and Parliament backed the reforms. But the Patriots, as the defenders of American rights came to be called, met the challenge posed by Grenville and his successor, Charles Townshend. They organized protests, both peaceful and violent, and fashioned a compelling ideology of resistance.

Politicians Protest, and the Crowd Rebels

Virginians took the lead. In May 1765, Patrick Henry, a hotheaded young member of the Virginia House of Burgesses, condemned Grenville's legislation and attacked George III for supporting it. In comparing the king to Charles I, whose tyranny had led to his overthrow in the 1640s, Henry seemed to be calling for a new republican revolution. Although the assembly members were shaken by Henry's remarks, which bordered on treason, they condemned the Stamp Act as "a manifest Tendency to Destroy American freedom." In Massachusetts, James Otis, another republican-minded firebrand, persuaded the House of Representatives to call an all-colony congress "to implore Relief" from the act.

Nine colonial assemblies sent delegates to the Stamp Act Congress, which met in New York City in October 1765. The Congress issued a set of resolutions protesting the loss of American "rights and liberties," especially the right to trial by jury. The Stamp Act Resolves also challenged the constitutionality of the Stamp and Sugar Acts by declaring that only the colonists' own elected representatives could tax them. Still, the moderate-minded delegates wanted compromise, not confrontation. They assured Parliament that Americans "glory in being subjects of the best of Kings" and humbly petitioned for repeal of the Stamp Act. But other influential Americans, favoring peaceful resistance, organized a boycott of British goods.

However, popular opposition took a violent form. When the Stamp Act went into effect on November 1, 1765, disciplined mobs demanded the resignation of stamp-tax collectors, most of whom were American-born. In Boston, the **Sons of Liberty** beheaded and burned an effigy of collector Andrew Oliver and then destroyed Oliver's new brick warehouse. Two weeks later, Bostonians attacked the house of Lieutenant Governor

The BOSTONIAN'S Paying the EXCISE-MAN, or TARRING & FEATHERING.

Plate I.   London Printed for Rob.' Sayer & J.Bennett, Map & Printsellers N.053 Fleet Street as the Act directs 31 Oct.r 1774.

A British View of American Mobs

This satiric etching of the Sons of Liberty, published in a British magazine, depicts their brutal treatment of John Malcolm, a commissioner of customs in Boston. The mob threatened to kill Malcolm — notice the noose hanging from the "liberty tree" — but instead tarred and feathered him and forced him to drink huge quantities of tea. In showing this violence and (in the background) the men pouring tea into Boston Harbor, the artist seems to be asking, "Does liberty mean anarchy?" Courtesy, John Carter Brown Library at Brown University.

Thomas Hutchinson, long known as a defender of social privilege and imperial authority; the attackers smashed his furniture, looted his wine cellar, and set fire to his library.

Wealthy merchants such as John Hancock and Patriot lawyers such as John Adams encouraged the mobs, which were usually led by middling artisans and minor merchants. "Spent the evening with the Sons of Liberty," Adams wrote in his diary, "John Smith, the brazier [metalworker], Thomas Crafts, the painter, Edes, the printer, Stephen Cleverly, the brazier; Chase, the distiller; [and] Joseph Field, Master of a vessel." These men knew one another through their work or were drinking buddies at the taverns that became centers of Patriot agitation.

In New York City, nearly 3,000 shopkeepers, artisans, laborers, and seamen marched through the streets breaking streetlamps and windows and crying, "Liberty!" Resistance to the Stamp Act spread far beyond the port cities. In nearly every colony, crowds of angry people — the "rabble," their detractors called them — intimidated royal officials. Near Wethersfield, Connecticut, 500 farmers seized a tax collector, Jared Ingersoll, and forced him to resign his office in "the Cause of the People."

Such crowd actions were common in both Britain and America. Every November 5, Protestant mobs on both sides of the Atlantic burned effigies of the pope to celebrate the failure of a Catholic plot to blow up the Houses of Parliament. Colonial crowds regularly destroyed brothels and rioted against the impressment (forced service) of merchant seamen by the Royal Navy. Governments tolerated the mobs because they usually did little damage and because, short of calling out the militia, there was no means of stopping them.

If rioting was traditional, its political goals were new. In New York City, for example, the leaders of the Sons of Liberty were two minor merchants, Isaac Sears and Alexander McDougall. As Radical Whigs, Sears and McDougall were afraid that imperial reform would undermine political liberty. But many artisans and their journeymen joined the protests because low-priced imports of British shoes and other manufactures (like low-priced Chinese imports today) threatened their livelihood. Some rioters feared new taxes and a parasitic British governing elite. Unlike "the Common people of England," a well-traveled colonist observed, "the people of America . . . never would submitt to be taxed that a few may be loaded with palaces and Pensions . . . while they cannot support themselves and their needy offspring with Bread."

Religion motivated other protesters. Roused by the Great Awakening, evangelical Protestants resented the arrogance of British military officers and the corruption of royal bureaucrats. In New England, where people and memories had long lives, rioters looked back to the antimonarchy sentiments of their great-grandparents. A letter to a Boston newspaper that was signed "Oliver Cromwell," the English republican revolutionary of the 1650s, promised to save "all the Freeborn Sons of America." Finally, the mobs included apprentices, day laborers, and unemployed sailors—young men looking for excitement and, when fortified by drink, eager to resort to violence.

Nearly everywhere, popular resistance nullified the Stamp Act. Fearing a massive assault on Fort George, New York lieutenant governor Cadwallader Colden called on General Gage to use his small military force to protect the stamps. Gage refused. "Fire from the Fort might disperse the Mob, but it would not quell them," he told Colden, and the result would be "an Insurrection, the Commencement of Civil War." Frightened collectors gave up their stamps, and angry Americans forced officials to accept legal documents without them. This popular insurrection gave a democratic cast to the emerging American Patriot movement. "Nothing is wanting but your own Resolution," declared a New York rioter, "for great is the Authority and Power of the People."

Because communication across the Atlantic was slow, the British response to the Stamp Act Congress and the Sons of Liberty would not be known until the spring of 1766. However, royal officials in America already knew that they had lost the popular support that had sustained the empire for three generations. A customs collector in Philadelphia lamented: "What can a Governor do without the assistance of the Governed?"

The Ideological Roots of Resistance

The American resistance movement began in the seaports because British policies directly affected the economic lives of their residents. The Sugar Act raised the cost of molasses to urban distillers; the Stamp Act taxed the newspapers sold by printers and the contracts and other legal documents prepared by lawyers and merchants; and the flood of British manufactures threatened the jobs of seaport artisans. According to one pamphleteer, Americans were being compelled to give the British "our money, as oft and in what quantity they please to demand it."

But some Americans couched their resistance in broader constitutional terms. Many of these men were lawyers drawn into conflict by their economic ties to merchants, who hired them to protect their goods from seizure by customs officials, and by professional motives. As practitioners of English common law, colonial lawyers believed in the importance of trial by jury and generally opposed the extension of judge-run vice-admiralty courts. Composing pamphlets of remarkable political sophistication, Patriot lawyers gave the resistance movement its rationale, its political agenda, and its leaders.

Patriot writers drew on three intellectual traditions. The first was English common law, the centuries-old body of legal rules and procedures that protected the lives and property of the monarch's subjects. In the famous *Writs of Assistance* case of 1761, Boston lawyer James Otis invoked English legal precedents to dispute a general search warrant that allowed customs officials to conduct wide-ranging inspections. And in demanding a jury trial for John Hancock, John Adams appealed to provision in the "29th Chap. of Magna Charta," an ancient document (1215) that "has for many Centuries been esteemed by Englishmen, as one of the . . . firmest Bulwarks of their Liberties." Other lawyers protested that new British measures violated specific "liberties and privileges" embodied in colonial charters as well as Britain's "ancient constitution." They objected as well when the ministry declared that colonial judges served "at the pleasure" of the royal governors, claiming that this would undermine the independence of the judiciary.

A second major intellectual resource was the rationalist thought of the Enlightenment. Virginia planter Thomas Jefferson invoked David Hume and Francis Hutcheson, Enlightenment philosophers who applied reason in their critiques of traditional political practices and in their proposals to correct social ills. Jefferson and other Patriot writers also drew on John Locke, who argued that all individuals possessed certain "natural rights"—among them life, liberty, and property—and that governments must protect those rights (see Chapter 4). And they turned to French philosopher Montesquieu, who argued that a separation of powers among government departments prevented arbitrary rule.

The republican and Whig strands of the English political tradition provided a third ideological source for American Patriots. Puritan New England had long venerated the Commonwealth era, the brief period between 1649 and 1660 when England was a republic (see Chapter 2). After the Glorious Revolution of 1688–1689, many colonists praised the English Whigs for preventing the monarch from imposing taxes and for limiting other monarchical powers. Bostonian Samuel Adams and other Patriot leaders also applauded Britain's Radical Whigs for denouncing political corruption among royal officials and questioning their motives. Joseph Warren, a physician and a Radical Whig Patriot, suggested that the Stamp Act was part of a ministerial plot "to force the colonies into rebellion" and justify the use of "military power to reduce them to servitude" (see American Voices, p. 142).

These arguments—publicized in newspapers and pamphlets—gave intellectual substance to the Patriot movement and turned a series of impromptu riots and tax protests into a formidable political force. The Patriots organized a highly successful boycott of British manufactures to force a repeal of the new imperial measures.

Parliament Compromises, 1766

When news of the Stamp Act riots and the boycott reached Britain, Parliament was already in turmoil. Disputes over domestic policy had led George III to dismiss Grenville as the prime minister, but Grenville's followers demanded that imperial reform

An American View of the Stamp Act SAMUEL ADAMS

Thanks to his education at Harvard College, distiller Samuel Adams had impressive intellectual and literary skills. In this private letter to an English friend, Adams undertakes, in reasoned prose, to refute the arguments used by British ministers to defend the new measures of imperial taxation and control.

To John Smith
December 19, 1765

Your acquaintance with this country . . . makes you an able advocate on her behalf, at a time when her friends have everything to fear for her. . . . The [British] nation, it seems, groaning under the pressure of a very heavy debt, has thought it reasonable & just that the colonies should bear a part; and over & above the tribute which they have been continually pouring into her lap, in the course of their trade, she now demands an internal tax. The colonists complain that this is both burdensome & unconstitutional. They allege, that while the nation has been contracting this debt solely for her own interest, they have [been] subduing & settling an uncultivated wilderness, & thereby increasing her power & wealth at their own expense. . . .

But it is said that this tax is to discharge the colonies' proportion of expense in carrying on the [recent] war in America, which was for their defense. To this it is said, that it does by no means appear that the war in America was carried on solely for the defense of the colonies; . . . there was evidently a view of making conquests, [thereby] . . . advancing her dominion & glory. . . .

There are other things which perhaps were not considered when the nation determined this to be a proportionate tax upon the colonies. . . . The [British] nation constantly regulates their trade, & lays it under what restrictions she pleases. The duties upon the goods imported from her & consumed here . . . amount to a very great sum. . . .

There is another consideration which makes the Stamp Act obnoxious to the people here, & that is, that it totally annihilates, as they apprehend, their essential rights as Englishmen. The first settlers . . . solemnly recognized their allegiance to their sovereign in England, & the Crown graciously acknowledged them, granted them charter privileges, & declared them & their heirs forever entitled to all the liberties & immunities of free & natural born subjects of the realm. . . .

The question then is, what the rights of free subjects of Britain are? . . . It is sufficient for the present purpose to say, that the main pillars of the British Constitution are the right of representation & trial by juries, both of which the Colonists lose by this act. Their property may be tried . . . in a court of Admiralty, where there is no jury. [As for representation], if the colonists are free subjects of Britain, which no one denies, it should seem that the Parliament cannot tax them consistent with the Constitution, because they are not represented. . . .

SOURCE: Harry Alonzo Cushing, ed., *The Writings of Samuel Adams* (New York: G. P. Putnam, 1904).

continue—if necessary, at the point of a gun. The issue for them was the constitutional supremacy of Parliament and its status as one of the few powerful representative bodies in eighteenth-century Europe. "The British legislature," declared Chief Justice Sir James Mansfield, "has authority to bind every part and every subject, whether such subjects have a right to vote or not."

Three other parliamentary factions pushed for repeal of the Stamp Act. The Old Whigs, now led by Lord Rockingham, who had succeeded Grenville as prime minister, had long maintained that America was more important for its "flourishing and increasing trade" than for its tax revenues. A second group, representing British merchants and manufacturers, worried that the American trade boycott was cutting deeply into British exports. A committee of "London Merchants trading to America" had joined with traders in Liverpool, Bristol, and Glasgow to demand repeal. "The Avenues of Trade are all shut up," a Bristol merchant told Parliament. "We have no Remittances and are at our Witts End for want of Money to fulfill our Engagements with our Tradesmen." Finally, former prime minister William Pitt and his allies in Parliament argued that the Stamp Act was a mistake and insisted that it "be repealed absolutely, totally, and immediately." Pitt tried to draw a subtle distinction between taxation and legislation: Parliament lacked the authority to tax the colonies, he said, but its power over America was "sovereign and supreme, in every circumstance of government and legislation whatsoever." As Pitt's ambiguous formula suggested, the Stamp Act raised the difficult constitutional question of Parliament's sovereign powers.

Rockingham was a young and inexperienced minister facing complex issues. He decided on compromise. To mollify the colonists and help British merchants, he repealed the Stamp Act and reduced the duty on molasses imposed by the Sugar Act to a penny a gallon. Then he pacified imperial reformers and hard-liners with the Declaratory Act of 1766, which explicitly reaffirmed Parliament's "full power and authority to make laws and statutes . . . to bind the colonies and people of America . . . in all cases whatsoever." By ending the Stamp Act crisis swiftly, Rockingham hoped that it would be forgotten just as quickly.

Charles Townshend Steps In

Often, the course of history is changed by a small event—an illness, a personal grudge, a chance remark. That was the case in 1767, when Rockingham's government collapsed over domestic issues and George III named William Pitt to head a new government. Pitt was chronically ill with gout, a painful disease of the joints, and often missed parliamentary debates, leaving chancellor of the exchequer Charles Townshend in command. Pitt was sympathetic toward America; Townshend was not. As a member of the Board of Trade, Townshend had demanded restrictions on the colonial assemblies, and he strongly supported the Stamp Act. So in 1767, when Grenville demanded in Parliament that the colonists pay for the British troops in America, Townshend made an unplanned and fateful decision. He promised to find a new source of revenue in America.

The new tax legislation, the Townshend Act of 1767, had both fiscal and political goals. The statute imposed duties on colonial imports of paper, paint, glass, and tea and would raise about £40,000 a year. Townshend allocated some of this revenue for American military expenses but earmarked most of the money to fund a colonial civil list—paying the salaries of royal governors, judges, and other imperial officials. By freeing royal officials from financial dependence on the American assemblies, the ministry would assist them to enforce parliamentary laws and the king's instructions. To strengthen imperial power further, Townshend devised the Revenue Act of 1767. This legislation created a board of customs commissioners in Boston and vice-admiralty courts in Halifax, Boston, Philadelphia, and Charleston. Through taxes imposed by Parliament to finance imperial administration, Townshend intended to undermine the power of American political institutions.

The full implications of Townshend's policies became clear when the New York assembly refused to comply with the Quartering Act of 1765. Fearing an unlimited drain on its treasury, the New York legislature first denied General Gage's requests for barracks and supplies and then offered limited assistance. Townshend demanded full compliance, and to raise the funds, Parliament considered a special duty on New York's imports and exports. The Earl of Shelburne, the new secretary of state, went even further: He proposed the appointment of a military governor with the authority to seize funds from New York's treasury and "to act with Force or Gentleness as circumstances might make necessary." Townshend decided on a less provocative but equally coercive measure: the Restraining Act of 1767, which suspended the New York assembly. Faced with the loss of self-government, New Yorkers reluctantly appropriated funds to quarter the troops.

The Restraining Act raised the stakes for the colonists. Previously, the British Privy Council had invalidated about 5 percent of colonial laws, such as those establishing land banks. Townshend's Restraining Act went much further, declaring that the very existence of American representative assemblies depended on the will of Parliament.

America Debates and Resists Again

The Townshend duties revived the constitutional debate over taxation. During the Stamp Act crisis, some Americans, including Benjamin Franklin, distinguished between external and internal taxes. They suggested that external duties on trade, such as those long mandated by the Navigation Acts, were acceptable to Americans but that direct, or internal, taxes were not. Townshend thought that this distinction was "perfect nonsense," but he indulged the Americans and laid duties only on trade.

Even so, most colonial leaders rejected the legitimacy of Townshend's measures. They agreed with lawyer John Dickinson, author of *Letters from a Farmer in Pennsylvania* (1768), that the real issue was the *intent* of the legislation. Because the Townshend duties were designed to raise revenue (not to regulate trade), they were taxes imposed without consent. In February 1768, the Massachusetts House of Representatives circulated a letter condemning the Townshend Act, and Boston and New York merchants began a new boycott of British goods. Throughout Puritan New England, ministers and public officials discouraged the purchase of "foreign superfluities" and promoted the domestic manufacture of cloth and other necessities.

American women, ordinarily excluded from public affairs, became crucial to the nonimportation movement through their production of **homespun** cloth. During the Stamp Act boycott of 1765, the wives and daughters of Patriot leaders had made more yarn and cloth, but the Townshend boycott mobilized many more patriotic women. Pious farmwives spun yarn at the homes of their ministers. In Berwick, Maine, "true Daughters of Liberty" celebrated American products by "drinking rye coffee and dining on bear venison." Other women's groups supported the boycott by spinning flax and wool to donate to the needy. Just as Patriot men followed tradition by joining crowd actions, so women's protests reflected their customary concern for the well-being of the community.

Newspapers celebrated the exploits of Daughters of Liberty. One Massachusetts town proudly claimed an annual output of 30,000 yards of cloth; East Hartford, Connecticut, reported 17,000 yards. This surge in domestic production hardly replaced British imports, which annually averaged about 10 million yards of cloth, but it brought thousands of women into the public arena.

The boycott mobilized many American men as well. In the seaport cities, the Sons of Liberty published the names of merchants who imported British goods and harassed their employees and customers. By March 1769, the nonimportation movement had spread to Philadelphia; two months later, the members of the Virginia House of Burgesses vowed not to buy dutied articles, luxury goods, or slaves imported by British merchants. Reflecting colonial self-confidence, Benjamin Franklin called for a return to the pre-1763 mercantilist system: "Repeal the laws, renounce the right, recall the troops, refund the money, and return to the old method of requisition."

American resistance only increased British determination. When the Massachusetts House's letter opposing the Townshend duties reached London, Lord Hillsborough,

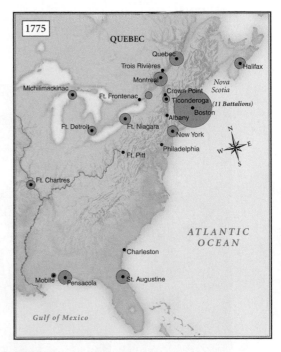

MAP 5.2 British Troop Deployments, 1763 and 1775
As the imperial crisis deepened, British military priorities changed. In 1763, most British battalions were stationed in Canada to deter Indian uprisings and French Canadian revolts. After the Stamp Act riots of 1765, the British established large garrisons in New York and Philadelphia. By 1775, eleven battalions of British regulars occupied Boston, the center of the Patriot movement.

the secretary of state for American affairs, branded it "unjustifiable opposition to the constitutional authority of Parliament." To strengthen the "Hand of Government" in Massachusetts, Hillsborough dispatched General Thomas Gage and 4,000 British troops to Boston. Gage accused Massachusetts leaders of "Treasonable and desperate Resolves" and advised the ministry to "Quash this Spirit at a Blow." Hillsborough proposed isolating Massachusetts from the other colonies and then using the army to bring the rebellious New Englanders to their knees (Map 5.2). In 1765, American resistance had provoked a parliamentary debate; in 1768, it produced a plan for military coercion.

Lord North Compromises, 1770

At this critical moment, the ministry's resolve faltered. A series of harsh winters and dry summers in Great Britain had cut grain output and raised food prices. In Scotland and northern England, thousands of tenants deserted their farms and boarded ships for America; food riots spread across the English countryside. There were also riots in Ireland over the growing military budget there.

Adding to the ministry's difficulties was Radical Whig John Wilkes. Supported by associations of merchants and artisans, Wilkes attacked government corruption and won election to Parliament. Overjoyed, American Patriots drank toasts to Wilkes and

John Wilkes, British Radical
Wilkes won fame on both sides of the Atlantic as the author of *North Briton, Number 45* (depicted on the left), which called for reform of the British political system. At a dinner in Boston, Radical Whigs raised their wineglasses to Wilkes, toasting him forty-five times! But Wilkes had many enemies, including this artist, who depicts him as a cunning demagogue, brandishing the cap of Liberty to curry favor with the mob. Miriam and Ira D. Wallach Division of Art, Prints and Photographs, The New York Public Library. Astor, Lenox and Tilden Foundations.

For more help analyzing this image, see the Online Study Guide at **bedfordstmartins. com/henrettaconcise**.

bought thousands of teapots and mugs emblazoned with his picture. When Wilkes was imprisoned for libel against Parliament, an angry crowd protested his arrest, and troops killed seven protesters in the highly publicized Massacre of Saint George's Field.

The American trade boycott also had a major impact on the British economy. In 1768, the colonies had cut their imports and reduced their trade deficit from £500,000 to £230,000. By 1769, the boycott of British goods and increases in the colonies' exports of goods and shipping services had yielded an American balance-of-payments surplus of £816,000. To end the boycott, British merchants and manufacturers petitioned Parliament for repeal of the Townshend duties. By late 1769, some ministers felt that the Townshend duties were a mistake, and the king no longer supported Hillsborough's plan to use military force against Massachusetts.

Early in 1770, Lord North became prime minister. A witty man and a skillful politician, North set out to save the empire by designing a new compromise. He argued that it was foolish to tax British exports to America (thereby raising their price and decreasing consumption) and persuaded Parliament to repeal most of the Townshend duties. However, North retained the tax on tea as a symbol of Parliament's supremacy. Mollified by the partial repeal, colonial merchants called off the boycott.

Even an outbreak of violence did not destroy North's compromise. During the boycott, New York artisans and workers had taunted British troops, mostly with words but occasionally with stones and fists. In retaliation, the soldiers tore down a Liberty Pole (a Patriot flagpole), setting off a week of street fighting. In Boston, friction over constitutional principles and competition between residents and off-duty British soldiers for jobs triggered a violent conflict. In March 1770, a group of soldiers fired into a crowd of rowdy demonstrators, killing five men. Convinced of a ministerial conspiracy against liberty, Radical Whigs labeled the incident a "massacre" and filled the popular press with accusations that the British had planned the killings.

Although most Americans remained loyal to the empire, five years of conflict over taxes and constitutional principles had taken their toll. In 1765, American leaders had accepted Parliament's authority; the Stamp Act Resolves had opposed only certain "unconstitutional" legislation. By 1770, the most outspoken Patriots — Benjamin Franklin in Pennsylvania, Patrick Henry in Virginia, and Samuel Adams in Massachusetts — had concluded that the British ruling elite was self-interested and indifferent to its colonial responsibilities. So they repudiated parliamentary supremacy and claimed equality for the American assemblies within the empire. Perhaps thinking of various European "composite monarchies," in which kings ruled far-distant provinces acquired by inheritance or conquest, Franklin suggested that the colonies were now "distinct and separate states" with the "the same Head, or Sovereign, the King."

Franklin's suggestion outraged Thomas Hutchinson, the American-born royal governor of Massachusetts. Hutchinson emphatically rejected the idea of "two independent legislatures in one and the same state"; in his mind, the British empire was a whole, its sovereignty indivisible. "I know of no line," he told the Massachusetts assembly, "that can be drawn between the supreme authority of Parliament and the total independence of the colonies."

► If Grenville's and Townshend's initiatives had succeeded, how would the character of the British imperial system have changed?

► Weigh the relative importance of economic and ideological motives in promoting the colonial resistance movement. Which was more important? Why?

There the matter rested. The British had twice imposed revenue acts on the colonies, and American Patriots had twice forced a retreat. If Parliament insisted on a policy of constitutional absolutism by imposing taxes a third time, some Americans were prepared to resist by force. Nor did they flinch when reminded that George III condemned their agitation. As the Massachusetts House told Hutchinson, "There is more reason to dread the consequences of absolute uncontrolled supreme power, whether of a nation or a monarch, than those of total independence." Fearful of civil war, Lord North's government hesitated to force the issue.

The Road to Independence, 1771–1776

Repeal of the Townshend duties in 1770 restored harmony to the British empire, but strong passions and mutual distrust lay just below the surface. In 1773, those emotions erupted, destroying any hope of compromise. Within two years, the Americans and the British clashed in armed conflict, and Patriot legislators created provisional governments and military forces, the two essentials for independence.

A Compromise Ignored

Once aroused, political passions are not easily quieted. In Boston, Samuel Adams and other radical Patriots continued to warn Americans of imperial domination and, late in 1772, persuaded the town meeting to set up a committee of correspondence "to state the Rights of the Colonists of this Province." Soon, eighty Massachusetts towns had similar committees. When the British government threatened to prosecute Americans in British courts following the burning of the *Gaspée*, a customs vessel, the Virginia House of Burgesses set up its own committee of correspondence. By mid-1773, committees had appeared in Connecticut, New Hampshire, and South Carolina.

These committees sprang into action when Lord North and Parliament enacted the Tea Act in May 1773. The act provided financial relief for the East India Company, which was deeply in debt because of military expeditions to extend Britain's influence in India. The Tea Act gave the company a government loan and canceled the English import duty on its tea. The act offended many Americans. Since 1768, when Townshend had placed a duty of 3 pence a pound on tea, most colonists had drunk smuggled Dutch tea. By relieving the East India Company of English duties, the Tea Act made its tea cheaper than that sold by Dutch merchants.

Radical Patriots accused the British government of bribing Americans to give up their principled opposition to the tea tax. As an anonymous woman wrote to the *Massachusetts Spy*, "The use of [British] tea is considered not as a private but as a public evil . . . a handle to introduce a variety of . . . oppressions amongst us." Merchants joined the protest because the East India Company planned to distribute its tea directly to shopkeepers, excluding American vendors from the profits of the trade. "The fear of an Introduction of a Monopoly in this Country," British general Frederick Haldimand reported from New York, "has induced the mercantile part of the Inhabitants to be very industrious in opposing this Step and added Strength to a Spirit of Independence already too prevalent."

The committees of correspondence organized resistance to the Tea Act. They sponsored public bonfires and persuaded their fellow townspeople—sometimes gently, sometimes not—to consign British tea to the flames. When the Sons of Liberty prevented East India Company ships from delivering more tea, Royal Governor Hutchinson hatched a scheme to land the tea and collect the tax. As soon as a shipment of tea arrived in Boston Harbor on the *Dartmouth*, Hutchinson passed the ship through customs. Hutchinson intended to order British troops to unload the tea and supervise its sale by auction. To foil the governor's plan, a group of artisans and laborers disguised as Indians boarded the *Dartmouth* on December 16, 1773; broke open 342 chests of tea (valued at about £10,000, or nearly $900,000 today); and threw them into the harbor. "This destruction of the Tea is so bold and it must have so important Consequences," John Adams wrote in his diary, "that I cannot but consider it as an Epoch in History."

The British Privy Council was furious, as was the king. "Concessions have made matters worse," George III declared. "The time has come for compulsion." Early in 1774, Parliament decisively rejected a proposal to repeal the duty on American tea; instead, it enacted four Coercive Acts to force Massachusetts to pay for the tea and to submit to imperial authority. A Port Bill closed Boston Harbor; a Government Act annulled the Massachusetts charter and prohibited most local town meetings; a new Quartering Act required the colony to build barracks for British troops; and a Justice Act allowed trials for capital crimes to be transferred to other colonies or to Britain.

Patriot leaders branded the measures "Intolerable" and rallied support for Massachusetts. In far-off Georgia, a Patriot warned the "Freemen of the Province" that "every privilege you at present claim as a birthright, may be wrested from you by the same authority that blockades the town of Boston." "The cause of Boston," George Washington declared in Virginia, "now is and ever will be considered as the cause of America." The committees of correspondence had created a firm sense of unity among Patriots.

In 1774, Parliament also passed the Quebec Act, which allowed the practice of Roman Catholicism in Quebec. This concession to Quebec's predominantly Catholic population reignited religious passions in New England, where Protestants associated Catholicism with arbitrary royal government and popish superstition. Because the act extended the boundaries of Quebec into the Ohio River Valley, it likewise angered influential land speculators and politicians in Virginia (Map 5.3). Although the ministry did not intend the Quebec Act as a coercive measure, many colonial leaders saw it as proof of Parliament's intention to control American domestic affairs.

The Continental Congress Responds

In response to the Coercive Acts, Patriot leaders convened a new continent-wide body, the Continental Congress. Twelve mainland colonies sent representatives. Four recently acquired colonies—Florida, Quebec, Nova Scotia, and Newfoundland—refused to participate, as did Georgia, where the royal governor controlled the legislature.

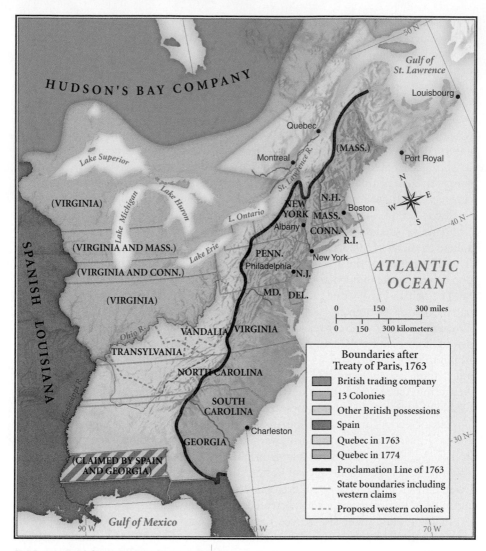

MAP 5.3 British Western Policy, 1763–1774

Despite the Proclamation of 1763, Anglo-American settlers and land speculators proposed two new western colonies: Vandalia and Transylvania. But the Quebec Act of 1774 ruled out the creation of new settlements in the west by reserving most trans-Appalachian lands for Native peoples and by vastly enlarging the boundaries of Quebec, which eliminated the sea-to-sea land claims of many seaboard colonies.

For more help analyzing this map, see the Online Study Guide at **bedfordstmartins.com/henrettaconcise**.

The assemblies of Barbados, Jamaica, and the other British sugar islands, fearful of revolts by their predominately African populations, reaffirmed their allegiance to the crown.

The delegates who met in Philadelphia in September 1774 had distinct agendas. Southern representatives, fearing a British plot "to overturn the constitution and introduce a system of arbitrary government," advocated a new economic boycott.

Independence-minded representatives from New England demanded political union and defensive military preparations. Many delegates from the Middle Atlantic colonies favored a political compromise.

Led by Joseph Galloway of Pennsylvania, these men of "loyal principles" proposed a new political system similar to the plan that Benjamin Franklin had proposed in Albany two decades earlier: Each colony would retain its assembly to legislate on local matters, and a new continent-wide body would handle general American affairs. The king would appoint a president-general to preside over a legislative council selected by the colonial assemblies. Although Galloway's plan gave the council veto power over parliamentary legislation that affected America, the delegates refused to endorse it. With British troops occupying Boston, most thought it was too conciliatory.

Instead, a majority of the delegates passed a Declaration of Rights and Grievances, which demanded the repeal of the Coercive Acts. They repudiated the Declaratory Act of 1766, which had proclaimed Parliament's supremacy over the colonies, and they stipulated that British control be limited to matters of trade. Finally, the Congress approved a program of economic retaliation: Americans would stop importing British goods in December 1774. If Parliament did not repeal the Intolerable Acts by September 1775, the Congress vowed to cut off virtually all colonial exports to Britain, Ireland, and the British West Indies. Ten years of constitutional conflict had culminated in the threat of all-out commercial warfare.

A few British leaders still hoped for compromise. In January 1775, William Pitt, now sitting in the House of Lords as the Earl of Chatham, asked Parliament to renounce its power to tax the colonies and to recognize the Continental Congress as a lawful body. In return for these concessions, he suggested, the Congress should acknowledge parliamentary supremacy and grant a permanent revenue to help defray the British national debt.

The British ministry rejected Chatham's plan. Twice it had backed down in the face of colonial resistance; a third retreat was unthinkable. Branding the Continental Congress an illegal assembly, the ministry rejected Lord Dartmouth's proposal to send commissioners to negotiate a settlement. Instead, Lord North set stringent terms: Americans must pay for their own defense and administration and acknowledge Parliament's authority to tax them. To put teeth in these demands, North imposed a naval blockade on American trade with foreign nations and ordered General Gage to suppress dissent in Massachusetts. "Now the case seemed desperate," the prime minister told Thomas Hutchinson, whom the Patriots had forced into exile in London. "Parliament would not—could not—concede. For aught he could see it must come to violence."

The Countryside Rises Up

Ultimately, the fate of the urban-led Patriot movement would depend on the large rural population. Most farmers had little interest in imperial affairs. Their lives were deeply rooted in the soil, and their prime allegiance was to family and community. But imperial policies had increasingly intruded into the lives of farm families by recruiting their sons for the army and raising their taxes. In 1754, farmers on Long Island, New York, had paid an average of 10 shillings a year in taxes; by 1756, thanks to the Great War for Empire, their taxes had jumped to 30 shillings. Peace brought little relief: The British-imposed Quartering Act kept taxes high, an average of 20 shillings a year, angering farmers in New York and elsewhere.

The urban-led Patriot boycotts of 1765 and 1768 also raised the political consciousness of rural Americans. When the First Continental Congress called for a new boycott of British goods in 1774, it easily established a rural network of committees of safety and inspection to enforce it. In Concord, Massachusetts, 80 percent of the male heads of families and a number of single women signed a "Solemn League and Covenant" supporting nonimportation. In other farm towns, men blacked their faces, disguised themselves in blankets "like Indians," and threatened violence against shopkeepers who traded "in rum, molasses, & Sugar, &c." in violation of the boycott.

Patriots likewise warned that British measures threatened the yeoman tradition of landownership. In Petersham, Massachusetts, the town meeting worried that new British taxes would drain "this People of the Fruits of their Toil." Arable land was now scarce and expensive in older communities, and merchants in new settlements were seizing farmsteads for delinquent debts. By the 1770s, many northern yeomen felt personally threatened by British imperial policies, which, a Patriot pamphlet warned, were "paving the way for reducing the country to lordships."

Despite their higher standard of living, southern slave owners had similar fears. Many Virginia Patriots—including Patrick Henry, George Washington, and Thomas Jefferson—speculated in western lands, and they reacted angrily when first the Proclamation of 1763 and then the Quebec Act of 1774 restricted the land claims of existing colonies. Thanks to their extravagant lifestyle, many Chesapeake planters were deeply in debt to British merchants. Even as planters faced financial disaster, George Washington noted, they lived "genteely and hospitably" and were "ashamed" to adopt frugal ways. Accustomed to being absolute masters on their slave-labor plantations, they resented their financial dependence on British creditors and dreaded the prospect of political subservience to British officials.

That danger now seemed real. If Parliament used the Coercive Acts to subdue Massachusetts, it might turn next to Virginia, dissolving the colony's representative assembly and judicial institutions and assisting British merchants to seize their debt-burdened properties. Consequently, the Virginia gentry supported demands by indebted yeomen farmers to close the law courts so that they could bargain with merchants over debts without the threat of legal action. "The spark of liberty is not yet extinct among our people," declared one planter, "and if properly fanned by the Gentlemen of influence will, I make no doubt, burst out again into a flame."

Loyalist Americans

Other "Gentlemen of influence" worried that resistance to Britain would undermine all political institutions and end in mob rule. Their fears increased when the Sons of Liberty used intimidation and violence to uphold the boycotts. One well-to-do New Yorker complained, "No man can be in a more abject state of bondage than he whose Reputation, Property and Life are exposed to the discretionary violence . . . of the community." As the crisis deepened, such men became Loyalists—so called because they remained loyal to the British crown.

Less affluent Americans also refused to endorse the Patriot cause. In New Jersey and Pennsylvania, thousands of pacifist Quakers and Germans tried to remain neutral. In areas where wealthy landowners became Patriots—the Hudson River Valley of New York, for example—many tenant farmers supported the king because they hated their landlords. Similar social conflicts prompted some Regulators in the North Carolina backcountry and many farmers in eastern Maryland to oppose the Patriots there. Enslaved blacks had little reason to support the cause of their Patriot masters. In November 1774, James Madison reported that some Virginia slaves were planning to escape "when the English troops should arrive."

Prominent Loyalists — royal officials, merchants with military contracts, clergy of the Church of England, and well-established lawyers — tried to mobilize support for the king. Relying on their high status and rhetorical skills, they denounced the Patriot leaders as troublemakers and accused them of working toward independence. But Loyalist leaders found relatively few active followers. A Tory association started by Governor Benning Wentworth of New Hampshire enrolled just fifty-nine members, fourteen of whom were his relatives. At this crucial juncture, Americans who supported resistance to British rule commanded the allegiance — or at least the acquiescence — of the majority of white Americans.

Compromise Fails

When the Continental Congress met in September 1774, Massachusetts was already defying British authority. In August, 150 delegates to an extralegal Middlesex County Congress had advised Patriots to close the existing royal court and to transfer their political allegiance to the popularly elected House of Representatives. After the Middlesex Congress, armed crowds harassed Loyalists and ensured Patriot rule in most of New England.

General Thomas Gage, now the military governor of Massachusetts, tried desperately to maintain imperial power. In September, he ordered British troops in Boston to seize Patriot armories and storehouses in nearby Charlestown and Cambridge. Following that raid, 20,000 colonial militiamen mobilized to safeguard other military supply depots. The Concord town meeting raised a defensive force, the famous **Minutemen**, to "Stand at a minutes warning in Case of alarm." Increasingly, Gage's authority was limited to Boston, where it rested primarily on the bayonets of his 3,500 troops. Meanwhile, the Patriot-controlled Massachusetts House met in defiance of Parliament, collected taxes, bolstered the militia, and assumed the responsibilities of government.

In London, the colonial secretary, Lord Dartmouth, proclaimed Massachusetts to be in "open rebellion" and ordered Gage to march against the "rude rabble." On the night of April 18, 1775, Gage dispatched 700 soldiers to capture colonial leaders and supplies at Concord. Paul Revere and two other Bostonians warned the Patriots; at dawn, local militiamen confronted the British troops first at Lexington and then at Concord. Those skirmishes took a handful of lives. But as the British retreated to Boston, militiamen from neighboring towns repeatedly ambushed them. By the end of the day, 73 British soldiers were dead, 174 had been wounded, and 26 were missing. British fire had killed 49 Massachusetts militiamen and wounded 39 (see Voices from Abroad, p. 154). Too much blood had been spilled to allow another compromise. Twelve years of economic conflict and constitutional debate had culminated in civil violence.

The Second Continental Congress Organizes for War

A month later, in May 1775, Patriot leaders gathered in Philadelphia for the Second Continental Congress. As the Congress opened, 3,000 British troops attacked American fortifications on Breed's Hill and Bunker Hill overlooking Boston. After three assaults

A British View of Lexington and Concord LIEUTENANT COLONEL FRANCIS SMITH

The past vanishes as soon as it occurs and must be reconstructed by historians from documentary evidence. On April 26, 1775, a week after British troops marched on Lexington and Concord, the Patriot-controlled Massachusetts Provincial Congress issued what it called a "true, and authentic account" of the hostilities. The Congress alleged that at Lexington "the regulars rushed on with great violence and first began the hostilities" and that in the retreat of the British troops from Concord, "houses on the road were plundered, . . . women in child-bed were driven by soldiery naked in the streets, [and] old men peaceably in their houses were shot dead." Four days earlier, in his official report to General Gage, British lieutenant colonel Francis Smith offered an account that presented British actions in a much different light. Which version should the historian find more "true, and authentic"?

Sir,—In obedience to your Excellency's commands, I marched on the evening of the 18th inst. with the corps of grenadiers and light infantry for Concord, . . . to destroy all ammunition, artillery, tents &c. . . . Notwithstanding we marched with the utmost expedition and secrecy, we found the country had intelligence or strong suspicion of our coming. . . .

At Lexington . . . [we] found on a green close to the road a body of the country people drawn up in military order, with arms and accoutrements, and, as appeared afterward, loaded. . . . Our troops advanced towards them, without any intention of injuring them . . . ; but they in confusion went off, principally to the left, only one of them fired before he went off, and three or four more jumped over a wall and fired from behind it among the soldiers; on which the troops returned it, and killed several of them. They likewise fired on the soldiers from the Meeting[house] and dwelling-houses. . . .

While at Concord we saw vast numbers assembling in many parts; at one of the bridges they marched down, with a very considerable body, on the light infantry posted there. On their coming pretty near, one of our men fired on them, which they returned; on which an action ensued and some few were killed and wounded. In this affair, it appears that, after the bridge was quitted, they scalped and otherwise ill treated one or two of [our] men who were either killed or severely wounded. . . .

On our leaving Concord to return to Boston they began to fire on us from behind walls, ditches, trees, &c., which, as we marched, increased to a very great degree, and continued . . . for, I believe, upwards of eighteen miles; so that I can't think but it must have been a preconcerted scheme in them, to attack the King's troops the first favorable opportunity that offered; otherwise, I think they could not, in such a short a time from our marching out, have raised such a numerous body. . . .

SOURCE: Massachusetts Historical Society, *Proceedings, 1876* (Boston, 1876), 350ff.

and 1,000 casualties, the British finally dislodged the Patriot militia. Inspired by his countrymen's valor, John Adams exhorted the Congress to rise to the "defense of American liberty" by creating a continental army. He nominated George Washington to lead it. After bitter debate, the Congress approved the proposals, though, Adams lamented, only "by bare majorities."

Despite the bloodshed in Massachusetts, a majority in the Congress still hoped for reconciliation. Led by John Dickinson of Pennsylvania, these moderates won approval of a petition expressing loyalty to George III and asking for repeal of oppressive parliamentary legislation. But Samuel Adams, Patrick Henry, and other zealous Patriots drummed up support for a Declaration of the Causes and Necessities of Taking Up Arms. Americans dreaded the "calamities of civil war," the declaration asserted, but were "resolved to die Freemen rather than to live [as] slaves." George III failed to exploit the divisions among the Patriots; instead, in August 1775, he issued a Proclamation for Suppressing Rebellion and Sedition.

Before the king's proclamation reached America, the radicals in the Congress had won support for an invasion of Canada. They hoped to unleash an uprising among the French inhabitants and add a fourteenth colony to the rebellion. Patriot forces easily defeated the British forces at Montreal; but in December 1775, they failed to capture Quebec City. Meanwhile, American merchants waged the financial warfare promised at the First Continental Congress by cutting off all exports to Britain and its West Indian sugar islands. Parliament retaliated with the Prohibitory Act, which outlawed all trade with the rebellious colonies.

Skirmishes between Patriot and Loyalist forces now broke out. In Virginia, the Patriot-dominated House of Burgesses forced the royal governor, Lord Dunmore, to take refuge on a British warship in Chesapeake Bay. Branding the Patriots "traitors," the governor organized two military forces — one white, the Queen's Own Loyal Virginians, and one black, the Ethiopian Regiment, which enlisted 1,000 slaves who had fled their Patriot owners. In November 1775, Dunmore issued a controversial proclamation promising freedom to black slaves and white indentured servants who joined the Loyalist cause. White planters denounced this "Diabolical scheme," claiming that it "point[ed] a dagger to their Throats." A new rising of the black and white underclasses, as in Bacon's Rebellion in the 1680s, seemed a possibility. In Fincastle County in southwestern Virginia, Loyalist planter John Hiell tried to rouse workers to support the king, telling "a Servant man" that in about a month, "he and all the negroes would get their freedom." Frightened by Dunmore's aggressive tactics, Patriot yeoman and tenant farmers called for a final break with Britain.

In North Carolina, too, military clashes prompted demands for independence. Early in 1776, Josiah Martin, the colony's royal governor, raised a Loyalist force of 1,500 Scottish Highlanders in the backcountry. In response, Patriots mobilized the low-country militia and, in February, defeated Martin's army at the Battle of Moore's Creek Bridge, capturing more than 800 Highlanders. Following this victory, radical Patriots in the North Carolina assembly instructed its delegates in Philadelphia "to concur with the Delegates of other Colonies in declaring Independence, and forming foreign alliances." In May, the Virginia gentry followed suit: Led by James Madison, Edmund Pendleton, and Patrick Henry, the Patriots met in convention and resolved unanimously to support independence.

Thomas Paine's *Common Sense*

As radical Patriots edged toward independence, many colonists retained an affection for the king. Joyous crowds had toasted the health of George III when he ascended the throne in 1760 and again in 1766 when his ministers repealed the Stamp Act. Their loyalty stemmed in part from the character of authority in a patriarchal society. Every father was "a king, and governor in his family," as one group of Baptists put it. Just as people followed the dictates of elders in town meetings and ministers in churches, so they should obey the king, their imperial "father." To deny the king's legitimacy would disrupt the social order.

But by late 1775, many Americans were turning against the monarch. As military conflicts escalated, they accused George III of supporting oppressive legislation and ordering armed retaliation. Surprisingly, agitation became especially intense in Quaker-dominated Philadelphia. Many Philadelphia merchants harbored Loyalist sympathies and refused to join the boycott against the Townshend duties. Consequently, artisans, who made up about half of Philadelphia's workers, became the most powerful force in Philadelphia's Patriot movement. Worried that British imports threatened their small-scale manufacturing enterprises, they organized a Mechanics Association to protect America's "just Rights and Privileges." By February 1776, forty artisans sat with forty-seven merchants on the Philadelphia Committee of Resistance.

Scots-Irish artisans and laborers became Patriots for cultural and religious reasons. They came from Presbyterian families that had fled economic and religious discrimination in British-controlled Ireland, and many of them had embraced the egalitarian message preached by Gilbert Tennent and other New Light ministers (see Chapter 4). As pastor of Philadelphia's Second Presbyterian Church, Tennent had told his congregation that all men and women were equal before God. Applying that idea to politics, New Light Presbyterians shouted in street demonstrations that they had "no king but King Jesus." Republican ideas derived from the European Enlightenment also circulated freely among Pennsylvania artisans. So Patriot leaders Benjamin Franklin and Dr. Benjamin Rush found a receptive audience when they questioned not just the wisdom of George III but the very idea of monarchy.

With popular sentiment in flux, a single pamphlet tipped the balance. In January 1776, Thomas Paine published *Common Sense*, a rousing call for independence and a republican form of government. Paine had served as a minor bureaucrat in the customs service in England and was fired for protesting low wages. In 1774, Paine migrated to Philadelphia, where he met Rush and other Patriots who shared his republican sentiments.

In *Common Sense*, Paine launched an assault on the traditional monarchical order in language that stirred popular emotions. "Monarchy and hereditary succession have laid the world in blood and ashes," Paine proclaimed, leveling a personal attack at George III, "the hard hearted sullen Pharaoh of England." Mixing insults with biblical quotations, Paine blasted the British system of "mixed government" among the three estates of king, lords, and commoners. Paine granted that the system "was noble for the dark and slavish times in which it was created," but now it yielded only "monarchical tyranny in the person of the king" and "aristocratical tyranny in the persons of the peers."

George III and the Royal Family
George III strikes a regal pose, surrounded by his queen and numerous offspring, all brilliantly attired. Patriots repudiated not only monarchy but also the fancy dress and aristocratic manners of the old regime. In its place, they championed a society of republican simplicity. *Family of George III*, by John Zoffany, late eighteenth–early nineteenth century. Royal Collection, St. James's Palace. © H.M. Queen Elizabeth II.

Paine made a compelling case for American independence by turning the traditional metaphor of patriarchal authority on its head: "Is it the interest of a man to be a boy all his life?" he asked. Within six months, *Common Sense* had gone through twenty-five editions and had reached hundreds of thousands of people throughout the colonies. "There is great talk of independence," a worried New York Loyalist noted, "the unthinking multitude are mad for it. . . . A pamphlet called Common Sense has carried off . . . thousands." Paine called on Americans to create independent republican states. "A government of our own is our natural right, 'TIS TIME TO PART."

Independence Declared

Inspired by Paine's arguments and beset by armed Loyalists, Patriot conventions throughout the colonies urged a break from Britain. In June 1776, Richard Henry Lee presented Virginia's resolution to the Continental Congress: "That these United Colonies are, and of right ought to be, free and independent states." Faced with certain defeat, staunch Loyalists and anti-independence moderates withdrew from the Congress, leaving committed Patriots to take the fateful step. On July 4, 1776, the Congress approved the Declaration of Independence (see Documents, p. D-1).

The main author of the Declaration was Thomas Jefferson, a young planter from Virginia. As a Virginia Burgess, Jefferson had mobilized resistance to the Coercive Acts with the pamphlet *A Summary View of the Rights of British America* (1774). Now, to justify independence and republicanism to Americans and the world, Jefferson vilified George III: "He has plundered our seas, ravaged our coasts, burned our towns, and destroyed the lives of our people. . . . A prince, whose character is thus marked by every act which may define a tyrant," Jefferson concluded, conveniently ignoring his own status as a slave owner, "is unfit to be the ruler of a free people."

Employing the ideas of the European Enlightenment, Jefferson proclaimed a series of "self-evident" truths: "that all men are created equal"; that they possess the "unalienable rights" of "Life, Liberty, and the pursuit of Happiness"; that government derives its "just powers from the consent of the governed" and can rightly be overthrown if it "becomes destructive of these ends." By linking these doctrines of individual liberty, **popular sovereignty**, and republican government with American independence, Jefferson established them as the defining political values of the new nation. For Jefferson, as for Paine, the pen proved mightier than the sword. In rural hamlets and seaport cities, crowds celebrated the Declaration by burning effigies of George III and toppling statues of the king. On July 8, 1776, in Easton, Pennsylvania, a "great number of spectators" heard a reading of the Declaration, "gave their hearty assent with three loud huzzahs, and cried out, 'May God long preserve and unite the Free and Independent States of America.'"

▶ Why did the Patriot movement wane in the early 1770s? Why did the Tea Act reignite colonial resistance?

▶ The narrative suggests that the British empire could have been saved. Do you agree? Why or why not? At what point during the imperial crisis did peaceful compromise cease to be possible?

SUMMARY

In this chapter, we have focused on a short span of time — a mere decade and a half — and have laid out the plot of a political drama in three acts. In Act I, the Great War for Empire prompts British political leaders to implement a program of imperial reform and taxation. Act II is full of dramatic action, as colonial mobs riot, Patriot writers articulate ideologies of resistance, and British ministers search for compromise between claims of parliamentary sovereignty and assertions of colonial autonomy. Act III takes the form of tragedy: The once-proud British empire dissolves into civil war, an imminent nightmare of death and destruction.

Why did this happen? More than two centuries later, the answers still are not clear. Certainly, the lack of astute leadership in Britain was a major factor. But British leaders faced circumstances that limited their actions: a huge national debt and a deep commitment to the absolute authority of Parliament. Moreover, in America, decades

TIMELINE

1756–1763	▶ War doubles British national debt
1760	▶ George III becomes king
1762	▶ Revenue Act reforms customs service
1763	▶ Treaty of Paris ends Great War for Empire
	▶ Proclamation Line restricts western settlement
	▶ George Grenville becomes prime minister
1764	▶ Parliament passes Sugar Act and Currency Act
	▶ Colonists oppose vice-admiralty courts
1765	▶ Stamp Act imposes direct tax
	▶ Quartering Act requires aid to British troops
	▶ Sons of Liberty riot
	▶ Stamp Act Congress meets in New York City
	▶ First American boycott of British goods
1766	▶ First compromise: Parliament repeals Stamp Act, passes Declaratory Act
1767	▶ Townshend duties on colonial imports
	▶ Restraining Act suspends New York assembly
1768	▶ Second American boycott of British goods

	▶ Daughters of Liberty make "homespun" cloth
1770	▶ Second compromise: Parliament repeals Townshend Act, retains tax on tea
	▶ Boston Massacre
1773	▶ Tea Act aids East India Company; Boston Tea Party
1774	▶ Coercive Acts and Quebec Act anger Patriots
	▶ First Continental Congress meets in Philadelphia
	▶ Third American boycott of British goods
1775	▶ Skirmishes at Lexington and Concord
	▶ Second Continental Congress creates Continental army
	▶ Lord Dunmore promises freedom to Loyalist slaves
	▶ Patriots invade Canada, skirmish with Loyalists in South
1776	▶ Thomas Paine issues *Common Sense*
	▶ Declaration of Independence

of salutary neglect strengthened Patriots' demands for political autonomy, as did the fears and aspirations of artisans and farmers. The trajectory of their histories placed Britain and its American possessions on course for a disastrous—and fatal—collision.

Connections: Government

It is impossible to understand the Patriot resistance movement without understanding political developments during the colonial era. As we noted in the essay opening Part One after 1689, white settlers in the English mainland colonies devised an increasingly free and competitive political system. Thereafter, local governments and representative assemblies became more powerful and created a tradition of self-rule that would spark demands for political independence from Britain.

As we have seen in Chapter 5 and will see again in Chapters 6 and 7, the traditions of localism and self-rule retained their vitality. During the War of Independence, local communities governed themselves through existing institutions or new Committees of Safety. The states assumed the status of sovereign entities, and their legislatures devised new republican constitutions.

The tradition of local and state rule was so strong that it was only with great difficulty that nationalist-minded politicians secured ratification of the Constitution of 1787, which restored a measure of political centralization to American life. Even then, most citizens looked first to their local and state governments. Having resisted and fought a distant British regime, they were not eager to place their affairs in the hands of a remote national government. When Alexander Hamilton and the Federalist Party increased national authority in the 1790s, voters turned them out of office in favor of Thomas Jefferson and his Republican followers, who wanted political power to reside primarily in local and state governments.

FOR FURTHER EXPLORATION

In *Angel in the Whirlwind: The Triumph of the American Revolution* (1997), Benson Bobrick narrates a grand epic that stretches from the French and Indian War to Washington's inauguration. For more complex accounts, read John Ferling, *A Leap in the Dark: The Struggle to Create the American Republic* (2003) and *Almost a Miracle: The American Victory in the War of Independence* (2007). Gary B. Nash, *The Unknown American Revolution: The Unruly Birth of Democracy* (2005), and Woody Holton, *Forced Founders: Indians, Debtors, Slaves, & the Making of the American Revolution in Virginia* (1999), show how ordinary citizens shaped events.

Edmund Morgan and Helen Morgan tell the story of *The Stamp Act Crisis* (1953), and Philip Lawson offers a sympathetic portrait of *George Grenville* (1984). Benjamin Labaree's *The Boston Tea Party* (1979) suggests how a "small" event can alter the course of history; and David Hackett Fischer explains the rise of the radical Patriots in *Paul Revere's Ride* (1994).

Liberty! The American Revolution, a PBS video, has a fine Web site (**www.pbs .org/ktca/liberty/**). For a British perspective, see "The Sceptered Isle: Empire" (**www .bbc.co.uk/radio4/history/empire/regions/americas.shtml**). For fine collections of pamphlets and images, consult **odur.let.rug.nl/~usa/D/index.htm** and **www.research .umbc.edu/~bouton/Revolution.links.htm**. The Web site of the National Gallery of Art (**www.nga.gov**) shows American paintings of the colonial and Revolutionary periods.

TEST YOUR KNOWLEDGE

To assess your mastery of the material in this chapter and for Web sites, images, and documents related to this chapter, visit **bedfordstmartins.com/henrettaconcise**.

Making War and Republican Governments

1776–1789

> [Societies] and governments are republican only in proportion as they embody the will of their people.
>
> —Thomas Jefferson, 1813

When the Patriots of Frederick County, Maryland, demanded allegiance to the American cause in 1776, Robert Gassaway would have none of it. "It was better for the poor people to lay down their arms and pay the duties and taxes laid upon them by King and Parliament than to be brought into slavery and commanded and ordered about [by you]," he told the local Patriots. The story was much the same in Farmington, Connecticut, where Patriot officials imprisoned Nathaniel Jones and seventeen other men for "remaining neutral." Throughout the colonies, the events of 1776 forced families to choose the Loyalist or the Patriot side.

The Patriots' control of most local governments gave them an edge in that battle. Patriot leaders organized their neighbors into militia units and recruited volunteers for the Continental army, a ragtag force that held its own on the battlefield. "I admire the American troops tremendously!" exclaimed a French officer. "It is incredible that soldiers composed of every age, even children of fifteen, of whites and blacks, almost naked, unpaid, and rather poorly fed, can march so well and withstand fire so steadfastly."

Military mobilization created political commitment—and vice versa. To encourage Americans to support the war—as soldiers, taxpayers, and republican citizens—Patriot leaders encouraged them to take an active role in government. As the common people exerted their influence, the character of politics changed. "From subjects to citizens the difference is immense," remarked South Carolina Patriot David Ramsay. By raising a democratic army and repudiating monarchical rule, the Patriots launched the age of republican revolution that would throw European nations into turmoil and sweep through Spain's American colonies.

The Trials of War, 1776–1778

The Declaration of Independence coincided with a full-scale British military assault. For two years, British forces manhandled the Continental army. A few inspiring American victories kept the rebellion alive, but during the winters of 1776 and 1777, the Patriot cause hung in the balance.

War in the North

Once the British resorted to military force, few European observers gave the rebels a chance. Great Britain had 11 million people compared to the colonies' 2.5 million, 20 percent of whom were enslaved Africans. Britain also possessed the immense wealth generated by the South Atlantic System and the emerging Industrial Revolution. Its financial resources paid for the most powerful navy in the world, a standing army of 48,000 Britons, and thousands of German (Hessian) soldiers. In addition, Britain had an experienced officer corps and the support of thousands of American Loyalists and many Indian tribes: The Cherokees in the Carolinas, were firmly committed to the British, as were four of the six Iroquois Nations of New York.

By contrast, the Americans were economically and militarily weak. They lacked a strong central government and a source of revenue, and their new Continental army, commanded by General George Washington, consisted of about 18,000 poorly trained recruits. The Patriot militia would not march to distant battles, and American officers had never faced a disciplined European army.

To demonstrate its military superiority, Britain's prime minister, Lord North, ordered General William Howe to capture New York City. His goal was to seize control

Joseph Brant
Mohawk chief Thayendanegea, known as Joseph Brant, was a devout Anglican who helped translate the Bible into the Iroquois language. Brant persuaded four of the six Iroquois Nations to support Britain in the war. In 1778 and 1779, he led Iroquois warriors and Tory rangers in devastating attacks on American settlements in the Wyoming Valley of Pennsylvania and Cherry Valley in New York. In this painting from 1797, Charles Willson Peale provided Brant with European features. Independence National Historic Park, Philadelphia.

For more help analyzing this image, see the Online Study Guide at **bedfordstmartins .com/henrettaconcise.**

of the Hudson River, thereby isolating the radical Patriots in New England from the colonies to the south. As the Second Continental Congress declared independence in Philadelphia in July 1776, Howe landed 32,000 troops — British regulars and German mercenaries — outside New York City. In August 1776, Howe defeated the Americans in the Battle of Long Island and forced their retreat to Manhattan Island. There, Howe outflanked Washington's troops and nearly trapped them. Outgunned and outmaneuvered, the Continental army again retreated, eventually crossing the Hudson River to New Jersey. By December, the British army had pushed the rebels across New Jersey and over the Delaware River into Pennsylvania.

From the Patriots' perspective, winter came just in time. Following eighteenth-century military custom, the British halted their campaign for the cold months, allowing the Americans to catch them off guard. On Christmas night 1776, Washington crossed the Delaware River and staged a surprise attack on Trenton, New Jersey, where he forced the surrender of 1,000 German soldiers. In early January 1777, the Continental army won a small victory at nearby Princeton (Map 6.1). Bright stars in a dark sky, these minor triumphs could not mask British military superiority. "These are the times," wrote Tom Paine, that "try men's souls."

Armies and Strategies

Thanks in part to General Howe, the Continental army remained intact, and the rebellion survived. Howe had opposed the Coercive Acts of 1774, and he still hoped for a political compromise. So he did not try to destroy the American army; he wanted simply to show its weakness and thereby persuade the Continental Congress to give up the struggle. Howe's restrained tactics were understandable, but they cost Britain the opportunity to nip the rebellion in the bud. For his part, Washington acted cautiously so as to avoid a major defeat; he told Congress, "On our Side the War should be defensive." His strategy was to draw the British away from the seacoast, extend their lines of supply, and sap their morale.

Congress had promised Washington a regular force of 75,000 men, but the Continental army never reached even a third of that number. Yeomen refused to be "Haras'd with callouts" that took them away from their families and farms; they insisted on serving in local militias. When the Virginia gentry tried to impose a military draft and three years of service on propertyless men — the "Lazy fellows who lurk about and are pests to Society" — they resisted so fiercely that the legislature had to pay them substantial bounties for short terms of service. The Continental soldiers recruited in Maryland by General William Smallwood were either poor American-born youths or older foreign-born men, often British ex-convicts and former indentured servants. Most enlisted for the bonus of $20 in cash (about $2,000 today) and the promise of 100 acres of land. Molding such recruits into a fighting force was difficult. Even brave men panicked in the face of a British artillery bombardment or flank attack; hundreds deserted, unwilling to submit to the discipline of military life.

The soldiers who stayed resented the contempt their officers had for the "camp followers," the women who fed and cared for the troops. These women made do with little because the Continental army was poorly supplied and faintly praised. Radical

MAP 6.1 The War in the North, 1776–1777

In 1776, the British army drove Washington's forces across New Jersey into Pennsylvania. The Americans counterattacked successfully at Trenton and Princeton and then set up winter headquarters in Morristown. In 1777, British forces stayed on the offensive. General Howe attacked the Patriot capital, Philadelphia, from the south and captured it in early October. Meanwhile, General Burgoyne and Colonel St. Leger launched simultaneous invasions from Canada. With the help of thousands of New England militiamen, American troops commanded by General Horatio Gates defeated Burgoyne in August at Bennington, Vermont, and, in October 1777, at Saratoga, New York, the military turning point in the war.

Whig Patriots believed that a standing army was a threat to liberty; even in wartime, they preferred militias to a professional force. General Philip Schuyler of New York complained that his troops were "weak in numbers, dispirited, naked, destitute of provisions, without camp equipage, with little ammunition, and not a single piece of cannon." Given these handicaps, Washington was fortunate to have escaped an overwhelming defeat.

Victory at Saratoga

Howe's failure to achieve an overwhelming victory dismayed Lord North and his colonial secretary, Lord George Germain. So they launched another major military campaign in 1777. Isolating New England remained the primary goal. To achieve it, Germain planned a three-pronged attack converging on Albany, New York. General John Burgoyne would lead a large contingent of British regulars south from Quebec to Albany. Colonel Barry St. Leger and a force of Iroquois warriors would attack from the west, and General Howe would lead a force northward from New York City.

Howe had a different plan, and it led to a disastrous result. He decided to attack Philadelphia, the home of the Continental Congress, hoping to end the rebellion with a single decisive victory. But instead of marching quickly through New Jersey, Howe loaded his troops onto boats, which sailed along the coast and up the Chesapeake Bay to attack Philadelphia from the south. The strategy worked brilliantly. Howe's troops easily outflanked the American positions along Brandywine Creek in Delaware and, in late September, marched triumphantly into Philadelphia. Howe expected that the capture of the rebels' capital would end the uprising, but the Continental Congress, determined to continue the struggle, fled into the interior.

Howe's slow attack against Philadelphia contributed directly to the defeat of Burgoyne's army. Burgoyne's troops had advanced quickly from Quebec, crossing Lake Champlain, overwhelming the American defenses at Fort Ticonderoga in early July, and driving toward the Hudson River. Then they stalled. Burgoyne — "Gentleman Johnny" — fought with style, stopping early each day to pitch comfortable tents and eat elaborate dinners. The American troops led by General Horatio Gates also slowed Burgoyne's progress by felling huge trees and raiding his supply lines to Canada.

At summer's end, Burgoyne's army of 6,000 British and German troops and 600 Loyalists and Indians was stuck near Saratoga, New York. Desperate for food and horses, the British raided nearby Bennington, Vermont, but were beaten back by 2,000 American militiamen. Patriot forces in the Mohawk Valley also forced St. Leger and the Iroquois to retreat. Making matters worse, the British commander in New York City recalled 4,000 troops he had sent toward Albany and sent them to Philadelphia to bolster Howe's force. While Burgoyne waited in vain for help, thousands of Patriot militiamen from Massachusetts, New Hampshire, and New York joined Gates's forces. They "swarmed around the army like birds of prey," reported an English sergeant, and in October 1777, they forced Burgoyne to surrender (see Voices from Abroad, p. 166).

The battle at Saratoga was the turning point of the war. The Patriots captured more than 5,000 British troops, and their victory ensured the success of American diplomats in Paris, who were seeking a military alliance with France.

Social and Financial Perils

The Patriots' triumph at Saratoga was tempered by wartime difficulties. A British naval blockade had cut supplies of European manufactures and disrupted the New England fishing industry; and the British occupation of Boston, New York, and Philadelphia had reduced domestic trade and manufacturing. As unemployed shipwrights, masons,

The Surrender of Burgoyne, 1777   BARONESS VON RIEDESEL

Frederika Charlotte Louise, Baroness Von Riedesel, was the wife of the commander of the Hessian soldiers in Burgoyne's army. An intrepid woman, the baroness was an eyewitness to the Saratoga campaign and a forthright critic of "Gentleman Johnny" Burgoyne. After Saratoga, she, her husband, and their three children (ages six, three, and one) were held as prisoners of war.

We were halted at six o'clock in the morning [of October 9, 1777], to our general amazement. General Burgoyne ordered the artillery to be drawn up in a line, and to have it counted. This gave much dissatisfaction. . . . At length we recommenced our march; but scarcely an hour had elapsed, before the army was again halted, because the enemy was in sight. They were but two hundred in number, who came to reconnoitre, and who might easily have been taken, had not general Burgoyne lost all his presence of mind. . . .

We reached Saratoga about dark, which was but half an hour's march from the place where we had spent the day. I was quite wet, and was obliged to remain in that condition, for want of a place to change my apparel. I seated myself near the fire, and undressed the children, and we then laid ourselves upon some straw.—I asked general Phillips, who came to see how I was, why we did not continue our retreat, my husband having pledged himself to cover the movement, and to bring off the army in safety. "My poor lady," said he, "you astonish me. Though quite wet, you have so much courage as to wish to go farther in this weather. What a pity it is that you are not our commanding general! He complains of fatigue, and has determined upon spending the night here, and giving us a supper."

It is very true, that General Burgoyne liked to make himself easy, and that he spent half his nights in singing and drinking, and diverting himself. . . .

I refreshed myself at 7 o'clock, the next morning, (the 10th of October,) with a cup of tea, and we all expected that we should soon continue our march. About 2 o'clock [the next day] we heard again a report of muskets and cannon, and there was much alarm and bustle among our troops. My husband sent me word, that I should immediately retire into a house which was not far off. Soon after our arrival, a terrible cannonade began, and the fire was principally directed against the house, where we had hoped to find a refuge, probably because the enemy inferred, from the great number of people who went towards it, that this was the headquarters of the generals, while, in reality, none were there except women and crippled soldiers. We were at last obliged to descend into the cellar, where I laid myself in a corner near the door. My children put their heads upon my knees. An abominable smell, the cries of the children, and my own anguish of mind, did not permit me to close my eyes, during the whole night. . . .

On the 17th of October, the capitulation was carried into effect. The generals waited upon the American general Gates, and the troops surrendered themselves prisoners of war and laid down their arms.

SOURCE: Madame de Riedesel, *Letters and Memoirs Relating to the War of American Independence, and the Capture of the German Troops at Saratoga* (New York, 1827), 173–183.

and laborers moved to the countryside, New York City's population declined from 21,000 to 10,000. In the Chesapeake, the British blockade cut tobacco exports, so planters grew grain to sell to the contending armies. All across the land, farmers and artisans adapted to a war economy.

With goods in short supply, governments requisitioned military supplies directly from the people. In 1776, Connecticut officials asked the citizens of Hartford to provide 1,000 coats and 1,600 shirts, and they assessed smaller towns proportionately. After losing all his shirts "except the one on my back" in the Battle of Long Island, Captain Edward Rogers told his wife that "the making of Cloath . . . must go on." In response, Patriot women in Elizabeth, New Jersey, promised "upwards of 100,000 yards of linnen and woolen cloth." Other women assumed the burdens of farm work while their men were away at war and acquired a taste for decision making. "We have sow'd our oats as you desired," Sarah Cobb Paine wrote to her absent husband. "Had I been master I should have planted it to Corn." Their self-esteem boosted by their wartime activities, some women expected greater legal rights in the new republican society.

Still, goods remained scarce and pricey. Hard-pressed consumers assailed shopkeepers as "enemies, extortioners, and monopolizers" and called for government regulation. But when the New England states imposed price ceilings in 1777, many farmers and artisans refused to sell their goods. Ultimately, a government official admitted, consumers had to pay the higher market prices "or submit to starving."

Even more frightening, the fighting exposed tens of thousands of civilians to deprivation and death. "An army, even a friendly one, are a dreadful scourge to any people," a Connecticut soldier wrote from Pennsylvania. "You cannot imagine what devastation and distress mark their steps." British and American armies marched back and forth across New Jersey, forcing Patriot and Loyalist families to flee their homes to escape arrest—or worse. Soldiers and partisans looted farms, and disorderly troops harassed and raped women and girls.

The war divided many communities. Patriots formed committees of safety to collect taxes and seized property from those who refused to pay. In New England, mobs of Patriot farmers beat suspected Tories and destroyed their property. "Every Body submitted to our Sovereign Lord the Mob," a Loyalist preacher lamented. In parts of Maryland, the number of "nonassociators"—those who refused to join either side—was so large that they successfully defied Patriot organizers. "Stand off you dammed rebel sons of bitches," Robert Davis of Anne Arundel County shouted, "I will shoot you if you come any nearer."

Such defiance exposed the financial weakness of Patriot governments. Most states were afraid to raise taxes, so officials borrowed gold or silver currency from wealthy individuals. When those funds ran out, individual states printed so much paper money—some $260 million all told—that it lost worth, and most people refused to accept it at face value. In North Carolina, even tax collectors eventually rejected the state's currency.

The finances of the Continental Congress collapsed too, despite the efforts of Philadelphia merchant Robert Morris, the government's chief treasury official. Because Congress lacked the authority to impose taxes, Morris relied on funds requisitioned from the states, but they paid late or not at all. So Morris secured loans from

Paper Currency
Symbolizing their independent status, the new state governments printed their own currency. Rejecting the English system of pounds and shillings, Virginia based its currency on the Spanish gold dollar, though it showed the equivalent in English pounds. Initially, $1,200 was equal to £360—a ratio of 3.3 to 1. By 1781, Virginia had printed so much paper money to pay its soldiers and wartime expenses that its currency's value had depreciated to a ratio of 40 to 1.
American Numismatic Society, New York City.

France and Holland and sold Continental bonds to wealthy Americans. Then it issued paper money—some $200 million between 1776 and 1779—that quickly fell in value. In 1778, a family needed $7 in Continental bills to buy goods worth $1 in gold or silver. As the rate of exchange deteriorated—to 42 to 1 in 1779, 100 to 1 in 1780, and 146 to 1 in 1781—it sparked social upheaval. In Boston, a mob of women accosted merchant Thomas Boyleston, "seazd him by his Neck," and forced him to sell his wares at traditional prices. In rural Ulster County, New York, women told the committee of safety to lower food prices or "their husbands and sons shall fight no more." As morale crumbled, some Patriot leaders doubted that the rebellion could succeed.

Fears reached their peak during the winter of 1777. While Howe's army lived comfortably in Philadelphia, Washington's army retreated 20 miles to Valley Forge, where 12,000 soldiers and hundreds of camp followers suffered horribly. "The army. . . . now begins to grow sickly," a surgeon confided to his diary. "Poor food—hard lodging—cold weather—fatigue—nasty clothes—nasty cookery. . . . Why are we sent here to starve and freeze?" Nearby farmers refused to help. Some were pacifists, Quakers and German sectarians unwilling to support either side. Others looked out for their own families, selling grain for the gold offered by British quartermasters but refusing depreciated Continental currency. "Such a dearth of public spirit, and want of public virtue," Washington lamented. By spring, 1,000 hungry soldiers had deserted, and another 3,000 had died from malnutrition and disease. One winter at Valley Forge took as many American lives as had two years of fighting.

▶ What accounted for British military superiority in the first years of the war? How did the Americans sustain their military effort between 1776 and 1778?

▶ Who was to blame for Britain's failure to win a quick victory over the American rebels: General Howe, General Burgoyne, or the ministers in London? Explain your answer.

In this dark hour, Baron von Steuben raised the readiness of the American army. A former Prussian military officer, von Steuben was one of a handful of republican-minded foreign aristocrats who helped the American cause. He instituted a strict system of drill and encouraged officers to become more professional. Thanks to von Steuben, the smaller Continental army that emerged from Valley Forge in the spring of 1778 was a much tougher and better-disciplined force.

The Path to Victory, 1778–1783

Wars are often won by astute diplomacy, and so it was with the War of Independence. The Patriots' prospects improved dramatically in 1778, when the Continental Congress concluded a military alliance with France, the most powerful nation in Europe. The alliance gave the Americans desperately needed money, supplies, and, eventually, troops. And it confronted Britain with an international war that challenged its domination of the Atlantic world.

The French Alliance

France and America were unlikely partners. France was Catholic and a monarchy; the United States was Protestant and a federation of republics. From 1689 to 1763, the two peoples had been enemies: New Englanders had brutally uprooted the French population from Acadia (Nova Scotia), and the French and their Indian allies had raided British settlements. But the Comte de Vergennes, the French foreign minister, was determined to avenge the loss of Canada during the Great War for Empire and persuaded King Louis XVI to provide the rebellious colonies with a secret loan and much-needed gunpowder. When news of the rebel victory at Saratoga reached Paris in December 1777, Vergennes sought a formal alliance.

Benjamin Franklin and other American diplomats craftily exploited France's rivalry with Britain to win an explicit commitment to American independence. The Treaty of Alliance of February 1778 specified that once France entered the war, neither partner would sign a separate peace without the "liberty, sovereignty, and independence" of the United States. In return, the Continental Congress agreed to recognize any French conquests in the West Indies.

The alliance gave new life to the Patriots' cause. "There has been a great change in this state since the news from France," a Patriot soldier reported from Pennsylvania. Farmers—"mercenary wretches," he called them—"were as eager for Continental Money now as they were a few weeks ago for British gold." Its confidence bolstered, the Continental Congress addressed the financial demands of the officer corps. Most officers were gentlemen who equipped themselves and often served without pay; in return, they insisted on lifetime military pensions at half pay. John Adams condemned the officers for "scrambling for rank and pay like apes for nuts," but General Washington urged Congress to grant the pensions: "The salvation of the cause depends upon it." Congress reluctantly granted the officers half pay but only for seven years.

Meanwhile, the war had become unpopular in Britain. Radical Whig politicians and republican-minded artisans supported American demands for autonomy and demanded a more representative system of government. The gentry protested increases in the land tax, and merchants condemned new levies on carriages, wine, and imported goods. "It seemed we were to be taxed and stamped ourselves instead of inflicting taxes and stamps on others," a British politician complained.

At first, George III was determined to crush the rebellion. If America won independence, he warned Lord North, "the West Indies must follow them. Ireland would soon follow the same plan and be a separate state, then this island would be reduced to itself, and soon would be a poor island indeed." Stunned by the defeat at Saratoga, the king changed his mind. To thwart an American alliance with France, he authorized North to seek a negotiated settlement. In February 1778, North persuaded Parliament to repeal the Tea and Prohibitory acts and, amazingly, to renounce its power to tax the colonies. But the Patriots, now allied with France and committed to independence, rejected North's overture.

War in the South

The French alliance did not bring a rapid end to the war. When France entered the conflict in June 1778, it tried to capture Barbados or another rich sugar island. Spain, which joined the war against Britain in 1779, wanted to regain Florida and the fortress of Gibraltar at the entrance to the Mediterranean Sea.

For its part, the British government revised its military strategy in America and now focused on the rich tobacco- and rice-growing colonies: Virginia, the Carolinas, and Georgia. The British planned to conquer these colonies and use the Scottish Highlanders in the Carolinas and other Loyalists to hold them. They also hoped to mobilize the Cherokees against the land-hungry Americans and to take advantage of planters' fears of slave uprisings. As a South Carolina delegate explained to the Continental Congress, his state could not contribute recruits to the war "by reason of the great proportion of citizens necessary to remain at home to prevent insurrection among the Negroes."

Implementing Britain's southern strategy became the responsibility of Sir Henry Clinton. Clinton based the main British army in New York City and launched a seaborne attack on Savannah, Georgia; troops commanded by Colonel Archibald Campbell captured the town in December 1778. Mobilizing hundreds of blacks to transport supplies, Campbell moved inland and captured Augusta early in 1779. By year's end, Clinton's forces and local Loyalists controlled coastal Georgia, and 10,000 troops were poised for an assault on South Carolina.

During most of 1780, British forces marched from victory to victory (Map 6.2). In May, Clinton forced the surrender of Charleston, South Carolina, and its American garrison of 5,000 troops. Then Lord Charles Cornwallis assumed control of the British forces and, at Camden, defeated an American force commanded by General Horatio Gates, the hero of Saratoga. Only 1,200 Patriot militiamen joined Gates at Camden—a fifth of the number at Saratoga—and many of them panicked. As Cornwallis took control of South Carolina, hundreds of African Americans fled to freedom behind British lines.

Then the tide of battle turned. Thanks to the Marquis de Lafayette, France finally dispatched troops to the American mainland. A republican-minded aristocrat who had long supported the American cause, Lafayette persuaded Louis XVI to send General Comte de Rochambeau and 5,500 men to Newport, Rhode Island. There, they threatened British forces in New York City.

Meanwhile, Washington dispatched General Nathanael Greene to recapture the Carolinas, where he found "a country that has been ravaged and plundered by both

MAP 6.2 The War in the South, 1778–1781

Britain's southern strategy started well. British forces captured Savannah in December 1778, took control of Georgia during 1779, and vanquished Charleston in May 1780. Over the next eighteen months, brutal warfare between British and Loyalist units and the American army and militia raged in the interior of the Carolinas, ending in a stalemate. Hoping to break the deadlock, British general Charles Cornwallis carried the battle into Virginia in 1781. A Franco-American army led by Washington and Lafayette, with the help of the French fleet under Admiral de Grasse, surrounded Cornwallis's forces on the Yorktown Peninsula and forced their surrender.

For more help analyzing this map, see the Online Study Guide at **bedfordstmartins.com/henrettaconcise**.

friends and enemies." To use local militiamen, who were "without discipline and addicted to plundering," Greene placed them under strong leaders and unleashed them on less-mobile British forces. In October 1780, Patriot militia defeated a regiment of Loyalists at King's Mountain, South Carolina, taking about 1,000 prisoners. American guerrillas commanded by the "Swamp Fox," General Francis Marion, also won a series of small but fierce battles. Then, in January 1781, General Daniel Morgan led an American force to a bloody victory at Cowpens, South Carolina. But Loyalist garrisons, helped by the well-organized Cherokees, remained powerful. "We fight, get beaten, and fight again," General Greene declared doggedly. In March 1781, Greene's soldiers fought Cornwallis's seasoned army to a draw at North Carolina's Guilford Court House. Weakened by this **war of attrition**, the British general decided to concede the Carolinas to Greene and seek a decisive victory in Virginia. There, many Patriot militiamen, claiming that "the Rich wanted the Poor to fight for them," refused to take up arms.

Exploiting these social divisions, Cornwallis moved easily through the Tidewater region of Virginia in the early summer of 1781. British forces from New York commanded by General Benedict Arnold, the infamous Patriot traitor, soon bolstered his ranks. As Arnold and Cornwallis sparred near the York Peninsula with an American force commanded by Lafayette, France sent its West Indian fleet to North America. Emboldened by the French naval forces, Washington devised an audacious plan. Feigning an assault on New York City, he secretly marched General Rochambeau's army from Rhode Island to Virginia. Simultaneously, the French fleet massed off the coast, taking control of Chesapeake Bay. By the time the British discovered Washington's scheme, Cornwallis was surrounded, his 9,500-man army outnumbered 2 to 1 on land and cut off from reinforcement or retreat by sea. In a hopeless position, Cornwallis surrendered at Yorktown in October 1781.

The Franco-American victory broke the resolve of the British government. "Oh God! It is all over!" Lord North exclaimed. Isolated diplomatically in Europe, stymied militarily in America, and lacking public support at home, the British ministry gave up active prosecution of the war.

The Patriot Advantage

Angry members of Parliament demanded an explanation. How could mighty Britain, victorious in the Great War for Empire, lose to a motley rebel army? The ministry blamed the military leadership, pointing to a series of blunders. Why had Howe not ruthlessly pursued Washington's army in 1776? Why had Howe and Burgoyne failed to coordinate their attacks in 1777? Why had Cornwallis marched deep into the Patriot-dominated state of Virginia in 1781?

Historians acknowledge British blunders, but they also attribute the rebels' victory to French aid and the support of the American population. About one-third of the white colonists were zealous Patriots, and another third supported the rebellion by paying taxes and joining the militia. Moreover, George Washington played a crucial role as an inspired military leader and an astute politician. By deferring to the civil authorities, he won the support of the Continental Congress and the state governments. Confident of his military abilities, he maintained the support of his officers and the morale of his men through five long years of war. Finally, Washington had a greater margin for error than the British generals did. Because the Patriots controlled local governments, the American general could mobilize local militias to reinforce the Continental army. Militiamen provided the margin of victory at Saratoga in 1777 and forced Cornwallis from the Carolinas in 1781.

In the end, it was the American people who decided the outcome. Preferring Patriot rule, tens of thousands of farmers and artisans accepted Continental bills in payment for supplies, and thousands of soldiers took them as pay—even as the currency literally depreciated in their pockets. Rampant inflation meant that every paper dollar held for a week lost value, imposing a hidden "currency tax" on those who accepted the paper currency. Each individual tax was small—a few pennies on each dollar. But as millions of dollars changed hands multiple times, these currency taxes paid the huge cost of the American military victory.

Diplomatic Triumph

After Yorktown, diplomats took two years to conclude a peace treaty. Talks began in Paris in April 1782, but the French and Spanish, still hoping for a territorial conquest, stalled for time. Their tactics infuriated the American diplomats: Benjamin Franklin, John Adams, and John Jay. So the Patriot diplomats negotiated secretly with the British, prepared if necessary to ignore the Treaty of Alliance and sign a separate peace. British ministers were eager for a quick settlement because Parliament no longer supported the war, and they feared the loss of a rich sugar island.

Consequently, the American diplomats secured a favorable peace. In the Treaty of Paris, signed in September 1783, Great Britain formally recognized the American independence. Britain retained Canada but relinquished its claims to lands south of the Great Lakes and east of the Mississippi River. The British negotiators did not insist on a separate Indian territory. "In endeavouring to assist you," a Wea Indian complained to a British general, "it seems we have wrought our own ruin."

The treaty also granted Americans fishing rights off Newfoundland and Nova Scotia, prohibited the British from "carrying away any negroes or other property," and guaranteed freedom of navigation on the Mississippi to American citizens "forever." In return, the American government allowed British merchants to pursue legal claims for prewar debts and encouraged the state legislatures to return confiscated property to Loyalists and grant them citizenship.

In the Treaty of Versailles, signed simultaneously, Britain made peace with France and Spain. Neither American ally gained very much. Spain reclaimed Florida from Britain but failed to win back the strategic fortress at Gibraltar. France won control of the Caribbean island of Tobago, small consolation for a war that had sharply raised taxes and quadrupled France's national debt. Just six years later, cries for tax relief and political liberty would spark the French Revolution. Only Americans profited handsomely from the treaties, which gave them independence and access to the trans-Appalachian west.

▶ Why did Britain switch to a southern military strategy? Why did that strategy ultimately fail?

▶ Without the French alliance, would the American rebellion have succeeded? Why or why not?

Creating Republican Institutions, 1776–1787

When the Patriots declared independence, they raised the issue of political power. "Which of us shall be the rulers?" asked a Philadelphia newspaper. The question was multifaceted. Where would power reside: in the national government or the states? Who would control the new republican institutions: traditional elites or average citizens? Would women have greater political and legal rights? What would be the status of the slaves in the new republic?

The State Constitutions: How Much Democracy?

In May 1776, the Second Continental Congress urged Americans to reject royal authority and establish republican governments. Most states quickly complied. "Constitutions employ every pen," an observer noted. Within six months, Virginia, Maryland, North Carolina, New Jersey, Delaware, and Pennsylvania had ratified new constitutions, and Connecticut and Rhode Island had revised their colonial charters by deleting references to the king.

Republicanism meant more than ousting the king. The Declaration of Independence had stated the principle of popular sovereignty: Governments derive "their just powers from the consent of the governed." In the heat of revolution, many Patriots gave this clause a democratic twist. In North Carolina, the backcountry farmers of Mecklenburg County instructed their delegates to the state's constitutional convention to "oppose everything that leans to aristocracy or power in the hands of the rich." In Virginia, voters elected a new assembly that, an eyewitness remarked, "was composed of men not quite so well dressed, nor so politely educated, nor so highly born" as colonial-era legislatures.

This democratic impulse flowered in Pennsylvania, thanks to a coalition of Scots-Irish farmers, Philadelphia artisans, and Enlightenment-influenced intellectuals. In 1776, these insurgents ousted every officeholder of the proprietary government, abolished property ownership as a test of citizenship, and granted all taxpaying men the right to vote and hold office. The Pennsylvania constitution of 1776 also created a unicameral (one-house) legislature with complete power; there was no governor to exercise a veto. Other provisions mandated an extensive system of elementary education and protected citizens from imprisonment for debt.

Pennsylvania's democratic constitution alarmed many leading Patriots. From Boston, John Adams denounced the unicameral legislature as "so democratical that it must produce confusion and every evil work." Along with other conservative Patriots, Adams wanted to restrict office holding to "men of learning, leisure and easy circumstances" and warned of oppression under majority rule: "If you give [ordinary citizens] the command or preponderance in the . . . legislature, they will vote all property out of the hands of you aristocrats."

To counter the appeal of the Pennsylvania Constitution, Adams published *Thoughts on Government* (1776). In that treatise, he adapted the British Whig theory of mixed government (a sharing of power among the monarch, the Houses of Lords, and the Commons) to a republican society. To disperse authority and preserve liberty, he assigned lawmaking, administering, and judging to separate institutions. Legislatures would make laws, the executive would administer them, and the judiciary would enforce them. Adams also called for a bicameral (two-house) legislature with an upper house of substantial property owners to offset the popular majorities in the lower one. As further curbs on democracy, he proposed an elected governor with veto power and an appointed—not elected—judiciary.

Conservative Patriots endorsed Adams's plea for appointed judges, a bicameral legislature, and property qualifications for voting. The property clauses in the New York Constitution of 1777 excluded 20 percent of white men from voting for members of the assembly and 60 percent from casting ballots for the governor and the upper house. In South Carolina, elite planters used property rules to rule out office holding for about 90 percent of white men. The 1778 constitution required candidates for governor to have a debt-free estate of £10,000 (about $700,000 today), senators to be worth £2,000, and assemblymen to own property valued at £1,000.

The political legacy of the Revolution was complex. Only in Pennsylvania and Vermont were radical Patriots able to create truly democratic institutions. Yet everywhere, representative legislatures had acquired more power, and the politics of electioneering and interest-group bargaining had become more responsive to average citizens.

Women Seek a Public Voice

The extraordinary excitement of the Revolutionary era tested the dictum that only men could engage in politics. Men controlled all public institutions—legislatures, juries, government offices—but upper-class women engaged in political debate and, defying men's scorn, filled their letters, diaries, and conversations with opinions on public issues. "The men say we have no business [with politics]," Eliza Wilkinson of South Carolina complained in 1783. "They won't even allow us liberty of thought, and that is all I want."

These American women did not insist on civic equality with men but only on the end of restrictive customs and laws. Abigail Adams, for example, demanded equal legal rights for married women, who under common law could not own property, enter into contracts, or initiate lawsuits. "Men would be tyrants" if they continued to hold such power over women, Adams declared to her husband John, criticizing him and other Patriots for "emancipating all nations" from monarchical despotism while "retaining absolute power over Wives."

Most politicians ignored women's requests, and most husbands remained patriarchs who dominated their households. Even young men who embraced the republican ideal of "companionate marriage" (see Chapter 8) did not support legal equality or a public role for their wives and daughters. Except in New Jersey, which until 1807 allowed unmarried and widowed female property holders to vote, women remained disfranchised.

The republican belief in an educated citizenry created opportunities for some American women. In her 1779 essay "On the Equality of the Sexes," Judith Sargent Murray argued that men and women had an equal capacity for memory and that women had a superior imagination. She conceded that most women were inferior to men in judgment and reasoning, but only because they had not been trained: "We can only reason from what we know," she argued, and most women had been denied "the opportunity of acquiring knowledge." That situation changed in the 1790s, when the attorney general of Massachusetts declared that girls had an equal right to schooling

Judith Sargent (Murray), Age Nineteen
The well-educated daughter of a wealthy Massachusetts merchant, Judith Sargent enjoyed a privileged childhood. As an adult, however, she endured a difficult seventeen-year marriage to John Stevens, who ultimately went bankrupt, fled from his creditors, and died in the West Indies. In 1788, she married John Murray, a minister who became a leading American Universalist. Her portrait, painted around 1771 by John Singleton Copley, captures the young woman's skepticism, which enabled her to question customary gender roles. Terra Museum of American Art, Chicago, Illinois. Daniel J. Terra Collection.

under the state constitution. By 1850, the literacy rates of women and men in the northeastern states were equal, and educated women again challenged their subordinate legal and political status.

The Loyalist Exodus

The success of republican institutions was facilitated by the departure of 100,000 monarchists, many of whom suffered severe financial losses. John Tabor Kempe, the last royal attorney general of New York, sought compensation of £65,000 sterling (about $4.5 million today) from the British government for Patriot land seizures but received a mere £5,000. Refugees often suffered psychologically too. Loyalists who fled to England complained of "their uneasy abode in this country of aliens." The great number of Loyalist evacuees who settled in Canada or the West Indies likewise lamented their loss. An exiled woman in Nova Scotia confessed: "[I had] such a feeling of loneliness . . . I sat down on the damp moss with my baby on my lap and cried bitterly."

Some Patriots demanded revolutionary justice: the seizure of all Loyalist property and its distribution to needy Americans. While every state seized some Loyalists' property, American leaders worried that wholesale confiscation would impair the nation's commercial credit and violate republican principles. In Massachusetts, officials cited the state's constitution of 1780, which protected every citizen "in the enjoyment of his life, liberty, and property, according to the standing laws." When state governments did seize the property of flagrant Loyalists, they often auctioned it to the highest bidders, who were usually wealthy Patriots rather than ambitious yeomen farmers or property-less foot soldiers. In a few cases, confiscation did produce a democratic result: In North Carolina, about half the new owners of Loyalist lands were small-scale farmers; in New York, the state government sold farmsteads on the Philipse manor to longtime tenants. When Frederick Philipse III tried to reclaim his estate, the former tenants told him they had "purchased it with the price of their best blood" and "will never become your vassals again." In general, though, the Revolution did not drastically alter the structure of rural society.

Social turmoil was greater in the cities, where Patriot merchants replaced Tories at the top of the economic ladder. In Massachusetts, the Lowell, Higginson, Jackson, and Cabot families moved their trading enterprises to Boston to fill the vacuum created by the departure of the Loyalist Hutchinson and Apthorp clans. In Philadelphia, small-scale Patriot traders stepped into the void left by the collapse of Anglican and Quaker mercantile firms. The War of Independence replaced a traditional economic elite — who invested profits from trade in real estate — with a group of republican entrepreneurs who promoted new trading ventures and domestic manufacturing. This shift advanced America's economic development in the years to come.

The Articles of Confederation

As Patriots embraced independence in 1776, they envisioned a central government with limited powers. Carter Braxton of Virginia thought the Continental Congress should "regulate the affairs of trade, war, peace, alliances, &c." but "should by no means have authority to interfere with the internal police [governance] or domestic concerns of any Colony."

That thinking — of a limited central government — informed the Articles of Confederation, which were approved by the Continental Congress in November 1777. The Articles provided for a loose confederation in which "each state retains its sovereignty, freedom, and independence." As a union of equals, each state had one vote regardless of its population or wealth. Important laws needed the approval of at least nine of the thirteen states, and changes in the Articles required the consent of all states. In the Confederation government, there was neither an executive nor a judiciary. Still, the Confederation government enjoyed considerable authority: The Confederation Congress could declare war, make treaties with foreign nations, adjudicate disputes between the states, borrow and print money, and requisition funds from the states "for the common defense or general welfare."

Although Congress exercised de facto constitutional authority — raising the Continental army, negotiating foreign treaties, and financing the war — disputes over western lands delayed ratification of the Articles until 1781. Many states, particularly Virginia, Massachusetts, and Connecticut, used their royal charters to claim boundaries stretching to the Pacific Ocean. States without western claims — Maryland and Pennsylvania — refused to accept the Articles until the land-rich states relinquished their claims. Threatened by Cornwallis's army in 1781, Virginia gave up its claims, and Maryland, the last holdout, finally ratified the Articles (Map 6.3).

MAP 6.3 The Confederation and Western Land Claims, 1781–1802
The Confederation Congress faced the conflicting state claims to western lands on the basis of their royal charters. For example, notice the huge—and overlapping—territories claimed by New York and Virginia. Between 1781 and 1802, Congress persuaded all of the states to cede their claims, creating a "national domain" open to all citizens. In the ordinances for the domain north of the Ohio River, Congress divided the area into territories, provided for its survey, prohibited slavery, and set up democratic procedures for territories to join the Union. South of the Ohio River, Congress allowed the existing southern states to play a substantial role in the settling of the ceded lands.

The Confederation had a major weakness: It lacked the authority to tax either the states or the people. By 1780, the central government was nearly bankrupt, and General Washington called urgently for a national tax system, warning Congress that otherwise, "our cause is lost." Led by Robert Morris, who became superintendent of finance in 1781, nationalist-minded Patriots tried to expand the Confederation's authority. They persuaded Congress to charter the Bank of North America, a private institution in Philadelphia, arguing that its notes would stabilize the inflated Continental currency. Morris also created a central bureaucracy that paid army expenses, apportioned war costs among the states, and assumed responsibility for the Confederation's debts. He hoped that the existence of a "national" debt would prompt Congress to enact an import duty to pay it off. However, Rhode Island and New York rejected Morris's proposal for a tax of 5 percent on imports. His state had opposed British duties, New York's representative declared, and it would not accept them from Congress. To raise revenue, Congress looked to the sale of western lands. In 1783, it asserted that the recently signed Treaty of Paris had extinguished the Indians' land rights and made them the property of the United States.

Settlers had already moved to the frontier. In 1784, the residents in what is now eastern Tennessee organized a new state, called it "Franklin," and sought admission to the Confederation. To preserve its authority over the West, Congress refused to recognize Franklin and gave Virginia control over the region. Subsequently, Congress created the Southwest Territory, the future states of Alabama and Mississippi, on lands ceded by North Carolina and Georgia. Because these cessions carried the stipulation that "no regulation . . . shall tend to emancipate slaves," the states that eventually formed in the Southwest Territory (and the entire region south of the Ohio River) allowed slavery.

However, the Confederation Congress banned slavery north of the Ohio River. Between 1784 and 1787, it issued three important ordinances organizing the "Old Northwest." The Ordinance of 1784, written by Thomas Jefferson, divided the region into territories that could become states as their population grew. The Land Ordinance of 1785 promoted settlement by mandating a quick rectangular-grid system of surveying and by encouraging large-scale land purchases. The ordinance specified a minimum price of $1 an acre and required that half of the townships be sold in single blocks of 23,040 acres each, which only large-scale speculators could afford, and the rest in parcels of 640 acres each, which restricted their sale to well-to-do farmers (Map 6.4).

Finally, the Northwest Ordinance of 1787 created the territories that would eventually become the states of Ohio, Indiana, Illinois, Michigan, and Wisconsin. The ordinance prohibited slavery and earmarked funds from land sales for the support of schools. It also specified that Congress would appoint a governor and judges to administer each new territory until the population reached 5,000 free adult men, when the citizens could elect a territorial legislature. When the population reached 60,000, the legislature could devise a republican constitution and apply to join the Confederation.

The land ordinances of the 1780s were a great and enduring achievement of the Confederation Congress. They provided for orderly settlement and the admission of new states on the basis of equality; there would be no dependent "colonies" in the West. But they also perpetuated and extended the geographical division between slave and free areas that would haunt the nation in the coming decades.

Shays's Rebellion

If the future of the West was bright, postwar conditions in the East were grim. The war had crippled the American merchant marine and disrupted the export of tobacco, rice, and wheat. The British Navigation Acts, which had nurtured colonial commerce, now

MAP 6.4 Land Division in the Northwest Territory

Throughout the Northwest Territory, government surveyors imposed a rectangular grid on the landscape, regardless of the local topography, so that farmers bought neatly defined tracts of land. The right-angled property lines in Muskingum County, Ohio (lower left), contrasted sharply with those in Baltimore County, Maryland (lower right), where — as in most of the eastern and southern states — boundaries followed the contours of the land.

barred Americans from legal trade with the British West Indies. Moreover, low-priced British manufactures were flooding American markets, driving urban artisans and wartime textile firms out of business.

The fiscal condition of the state governments was equally fragile, primarily because of political conflicts over war debts. On one side were wealthy merchants and landowners who had invested in state bonds or speculated in debt certificates by buying them from farmers and soldiers for less than their face value. These men demanded that the state governments redeem the bonds quickly and at full value, a policy that would require high taxes. On the other side were the elected state legislators. Because the new state constitutions apportioned seats on the basis of population, many legislators now represented western communities and were men of "middling circumstances." By the mid-1780s, such middling farmers and artisans controlled the lower houses of most northern legislatures and formed a sizable minority in southern assemblies. When their constituents demanded tax relief, these representatives usually reduced levies and refused to redeem war bonds. State legislatures also printed paper currency and enacted laws allowing debtors to pay their private creditors in installments. Although wealthy men deplored these measures, claiming that they destroyed "the just rights of creditors," the measures probably prevented social upheaval.

A case in point was Massachusetts, where lawmakers refused to enact debtor-relief legislation, imposed high taxes to pay off the state's war debt, and cut the supply of paper currency. When cash-strapped farmers could not pay their debts, creditors threatened lawsuits. Debtor Ephraim Wetmore heard that merchant Stephan Salisbury "would have my Body Dead or Alive in case I did not pay." To protect their livelihoods, farmers called extralegal conventions that protested the tax increases and property seizures. Then mobs of angry farmers — including men of high status — closed the courts by force. "[I] had no Intensions to Destroy the Publick Government," declared Captain Adam Wheeler, a former town selectman; his goal was simply to prevent "Valuable and Industrious members of Society [being] dragged from their families to prison" because of their debts. These crowd actions grew into a full-scale revolt led by Captain Daniel Shays, a former officer in the Continental army.

As a struggle against taxes imposed by a distant government, Shays's Rebellion resembled colonial resistance to the British Stamp Act. "The people have turned against their teachers the doctrines which were inculcated to effect the late revolution," complained Fisher Ames, a conservative Massachusetts lawmaker. To link themselves to the Patriot movement, Shays's men placed pine twigs in their hats, just as Continental troops had done. But some of the radical Patriots of 1776 condemned the Shaysites: "Those Men, who . . . would lessen the Weight of Government lawfully exercised must be Enemies to our happy Revolution and Common Liberty," charged Samuel Adams. To put down the rebellion, the Massachusetts legislature passed a Riot Act, and Governor James Bowdoin equipped a formidable fighting force, which dispersed Shays's ragtag army during the winter of 1786–1787.

Shays's Rebellion failed, but it suggested that the costs of war and the fruits of independence were not being evenly shared. Middling Patriot families felt they had exchanged British tyrants for American oppressors. Massachusetts voters turned Governor Bowdoin out of office, and debt-ridden farmers in New York, northern Pennsylvania, Connecticut, and New Hampshire closed courthouses and demanded economic relief. British officials in Canada predicted the imminent demise of the United States, and some Americans

▶ What were the main differences between conservative state constitutions, such as that of Massachusetts, and more democratic constitutions, such as Pennsylvania's?

▶ What were the causes of Shays's Rebellion, and what does it tell us about postwar America?

feared for the future of their republican experiment. Events in Massachusetts, declared nationalist Henry Knox, formed "the strongest arguments possible" for the creation of "a strong general government."

The Constitution of 1787

From its creation, the U.S. Constitution was a controversial document, praised as a solution to the nation's woes and condemned as a perversion of its republican principles. Critics charged that republican institutions worked only in small political units — the states. Advocates answered that the Constitution extended republicanism by adding another level of government elected by the people. In this composite political system, the new national government would exercise limited, delegated powers, and the existing state governments would retain authority over all other matters.

The Rise of a Nationalist Faction

Money questions — debts, taxes, and tariffs — dominated the postwar political agenda. Americans who had served the Confederation as military officers, officials, and diplomats viewed these issues from a national perspective and advocated a stronger central government. George Washington, Robert Morris, Benjamin Franklin, John Jay, and John Adams wanted Congress to control foreign commerce and tariff policy. However, lawmakers in Massachusetts, New York, and Pennsylvania, states with strong commercial traditions, insisted on controlling their own tariffs, either to protect their artisans from low-cost imports or to assist their merchants in expanding trade. Most southern states opposed tariffs because planters wanted to import British textiles and ironware at the lowest possible prices.

Nonetheless, some southern leaders became nationalists because of the economic policies of their state legislatures. During the hard times of the 1780s, lawmakers in Virginia and elsewhere had lowered taxes and delayed the redemption of state war bonds. Such actions, lamented Charles Lee of Virginia, a wealthy bondholder, led taxpayers to believe they would "never be compelled to pay" the public debt. Creditors also complained about state laws that "stayed" (delayed) the payment of mortgages and other private debts. "While men are madly accumulating enormous debts, their legislators are making provisions for their nonpayment," complained a South Carolina merchant. To cut the power of the democratic majorities in the state legislatures, creditors favored a stronger central government.

In 1786, James Madison and other nationalists persuaded the Virginia legislature to call a convention to discuss tariff and taxation policies. Only five state governments sent delegates to the meeting in Annapolis, Maryland. Ignoring their small numbers, the delegates called for another convention in Philadelphia. Spurred on by Shays's Rebellion, nationalists in Congress secured a resolution calling for a revision of the Articles of Confederation. "Nothing but the adoption of some efficient plan from the Convention," a fellow nationalist wrote to James Madison, "can prevent anarchy first & civil convulsions afterwards."

The Philadelphia Convention

In May 1787, fifty-five delegates arrived in Philadelphia. They came from every state except Rhode Island, where the legislature opposed increasing central authority. The delegates were men of property: merchants, slaveholding planters, or "monied men." There were no artisans, backcountry settlers, or tenants, and there was only a single yeoman farmer.

Some delegates, such as Benjamin Franklin, had been early advocates of independence. Others, including George Washington and Robert Morris, had risen to prominence during the war. Some influential Patriots missed the convention. John Adams and Thomas Jefferson were serving as American ministers to Britain and France, respectively. The Massachusetts General Court rejected Sam Adams as a delegate because he opposed a stronger national government, and his fellow firebrand from Virginia, Patrick Henry, refused to attend because he "smelt a rat."

The absence of these experienced leaders allowed capable younger nationalists to set the agenda. Declaring that the convention would "decide for ever the fate of Republican Government," James Madison insisted on increased national authority. Alexander Hamilton of New York likewise demanded a strong central government to protect the republic from "the imprudence of democracy."

The delegates elected Washington as their presiding officer and, to prevent popular interference, met in secret. Rather than revising the Articles of Confederation, they considered a scheme for a powerful national government—the so-called Virginia Plan—devised by James Madison. Just thirty-six years old, Madison had arrived in Philadelphia determined to fashion new political institutions run by men of high character. A graduate of Princeton, he had read classical and modern political theory and served in both the Confederation Congress and the Virginia assembly. Once an optimistic Patriot, Madison had become discouraged by the "narrow ambition" and outlook of many state legislators.

Madison's Virginia Plan differed from the Articles of Confederation in three crucial respects. First, the plan rejected state sovereignty in favor of the "supremacy of national authority," including the power to overturn state laws. Second, the national government would be established by the people (not the states), and national laws would operate directly on citizens of the various states. Third, the plan proposed a three-tier election system. Ordinary voters would elect only the lower house of the national legislature, which would name the members of the upper house; then both houses would choose the executive and judiciary.

From a political perspective, Madison's plan had two fatal flaws. First, the provision allowing the national government to veto state laws was unacceptable to most state politicians and citizens. Second, the plan gave the most power to the populous states, because representation in the lower house depended on population. As a Delaware delegate put it, Madison's scheme would allow the populous states to "crush the small ones whenever they stand in the way of their ambitious or interested views."

So small-state delegates rallied behind a plan devised by William Paterson of New Jersey. The New Jersey Plan gave the Confederation the power to raise revenue, control commerce, and make binding requisitions on the states. But it preserved the states' control of their own laws and guaranteed their equality: Each state would have one vote in a unicameral legislature, as in the Confederation Congress. Delegates from the populous states vigorously opposed this provision. After debating the two plans for a month, a bare majority of the states agreed to use Madison's Virginia Plan as the basis of discussion.

This decision raised the odds that the delegates would create a more powerful national government. Outraged by this prospect, two New York representatives accused the delegates of exceeding their mandate to revise the Articles and left the convention. The remaining delegates met six days a week during the hot summer of 1787, debating high principles and discussing practical details. Experienced politicians, they looked for a plan that would be acceptable to most citizens and existing political interests. Pierce Butler of South Carolina invoked a classical Greek precedent: "We must follow the example of Solon, who gave the Athenians not the best government he could devise but the best they would receive."

Representation of large and small states remained the central problem. The Connecticut delegates suggested that the upper chamber, the Senate, have two members from each state, while seats in the lower chamber, the House of Representatives, be apportioned by population (determined every ten years by a national census). After bitter debate, delegates from the populous states reluctantly accepted this "Great Compromise."

Other state-related issues were quickly settled by restricting (or leaving ambiguous) the extent of central authority. Some delegates opposed a national system of courts, warning that "the states will revolt at such encroachments" on their judicial authority. So the convention defined the judicial power of the United States in broad terms, vesting it "in one supreme Court" and leaving the new national legislature to decide whether to establish lower courts within the states. The convention also refused to set a national property requirement for voting in national elections. "Eight or nine states have extended the right of suffrage beyond the freeholders," George Mason of Virginia pointed out. "What will people there say if they should be disfranchised?" Finally, the convention placed the selection of the president in an electoral college chosen on a state-by-state basis and specified that state legislatures would elect members of the U.S. Senate. By giving state legislatures important roles in the new constitutional system, the delegates hoped their citizens would accept a reduction in state sovereignty.

The shadow of slavery hovered over many debates, and Gouverneur Morris of New York brought it into view. Born into the New York aristocracy, Morris initially opposed independence because he feared the "domination of a riotous mob." Having become a Patriot and a nationalist, he came to the Philadelphia convention convinced that the protection of "property was the sole or primary object of Government & Society." To safeguard property rights, Morris demanded life terms for senators, a property qualification for voting in national elections, and a strong president with veto power. Nonetheless, Morris rejected the legitimacy of two traditional types of property: the feudal dues claimed by aristocratic landowners and the ownership of slaves. An advocate of **free markets** and personal liberty, he condemned slavery as "a nefarious institution."

In response, Southern delegates joined together to defend slavery but split over the Atlantic slave trade. George Mason and other Chesapeake planters, who already owned many slaves, wanted to end the trade. Rice planters from South Carolina and Georgia demanded that slave imports continue; otherwise, their states "shall not be parties to the Union." At their insistence, the delegates denied Congress the power to regulate immigration—and so the slave trade—until 1808 (see American Voices, p. 186).

Gouverneur Morris, Federalist Statesman
When the war with Britain broke out, Morris thought about joining the Loyalist cause: He was a snob who liked privilege and feared the common people. ("The mob begins to think and reason," he once noted with disdain.) Morris later became a Federalist for the same reason. He helped write the Philadelphia constitution and, after 1793, strongly supported the Federalist Party.
National Portrait Gallery, Smithsonian Institution/Art Resource, New York.

To preserve national unity, the delegates devised other compromises on other slavery-related issues. To mollify southern planters, they devised a "fugitive" clause that allowed masters to reclaim enslaved blacks (or white indentured servants) who fled to other states. But acknowledging the antislavery sentiments of Morris and other northerners, the delegates did not use the words "slavery" or "slave" in the Constitution; it spoke of citizens and "all other Persons." Because slaves lacked the vote, antislavery delegates wanted to exclude them in apportioning seats in Congress; southerners demanded that they be counted the same as full citizens. Ultimately, the delegates agreed to count each slave as three-fifths of a free person for purposes of representation and taxation, a compromise that helped southern planters to dominate the national government until 1860.

Having addressed the concerns of small states and slave states, the delegates created a powerful procreditor national government. The Constitution and all national legislation would be the "supreme" law of the land. The national government would have broad powers over taxation, military defense, and external commerce and the authority to make all laws "necessary and proper" to implement those and other provisions. To protect creditors and establish the new government's fiscal integrity, the Constitution required the United States to honor the existing national debt. To prevent state governments from aiding debtors, it prohibited the states from issuing paper money or enacting "any Law impairing the Obligation of Contracts."

The proposed constitution was not a "perfect production," Benjamin Franklin admitted on September 17, 1787, as he urged the delegates to sign it. But the great statesman confessed his astonishment at finding "this system approaching so near to perfection." His colleagues apparently agreed; all but three signed the document.

The Constitution and Slavery   MASSACHUSETTS RATIFYING CONVENTION

In Philadelphia, the Framers of the Constitution agreed on a compromise: They gave Congress the power to tax or prohibit slave imports but withheld that power for twenty years. In the Massachusetts convention, the delegates split on this issue and on many others. They eventually ratified the Constitution by a narrow margin: 187 to 168.

Mr. Neal (from Kittery) [an Antifederalist] went over the ground of objection to . . . the idea that slave trade was allowed to be continued for 20 years. His profession, he said, obliged him to bear witness against any thing that should favor the making merchandize of the bodies of men, and unless his objection was removed, he could not put his hand to the constitution. Other gentlemen said, in addition to this idea, that there was not even a proposition that the negroes ever shall be free: and Gen. Thompson exclaimed—"Mr. President, shall it be said, that after we have established our own independence and freedom, we make slaves of others? Oh! Washington . . . he has immortalized himself! but he holds those in slavery who have a good right to be free as he is. . . ."

On the other side, gentlemen said, that the step taken in this article, towards the abolition of slavery, was one of the beauties of the constitution. They observed, that in the confederation there was no provision whatever for its ever being abolished; but this constitution provides, that Congress may after twenty years, totally annihilate the slave trade. . . .

Mr. Heath (Federalist): . . . I apprehend that it is not in our power to do any thing for or against those who are in slavery in the southern states. No gentleman within these walls detests every idea of slavery more than I do: it is generally detested by the people of this commonwealth, and I ardently hope that the time will soon come, when our brethren in the southern states will view it as we do, and put a stop to it; but to this we have no right to compel them.

Two questions naturally arise: if we ratify the Constitution, shall we do any thing by our act to hold the blacks in slavery or shall we become the partakers of other men's sins? I think neither of them: each state is sovereign and independent to a certain degree, and they have a right, and will regulate their own internal affairs, as to themselves appears proper. . . . We are not in this case partakers of other men's sins, for nothing we do voluntarily encourage the slavery of our fellow men. . . .

The federal convention went as far as they could; the migration or immigration &c. is confined to the states, now existing only, new states cannot claim it. Congress, by their ordnance for erecting new states, some time since, declared that there shall be no slavery in them. But whether those in slavery in the southern states, will be emancipated after the year 1808, I do not pretend to determine: I rather doubt it.

SOURCE: Jonathan Elliot, ed., *The Debates . . . on the Adoption of the Federal Constitution* (Philadelphia: J. B. Lippincott, 1863), 1: 103–105, 107, 112, 117.

The People Debate Ratification

The procedure for ratifying the new constitution was as controversial as its contents. The delegates did not submit the Constitution to the state legislatures for their unanimous consent, as required by the Articles of Confederation, because they knew that Rhode Island (and perhaps other states) would reject it. So they arbitrarily specified that it would take effect when ratified by conventions in nine of the thirteen states. Because of its nationalist sympathies, the Confederation Congress winked at this extralegal procedure; surprisingly, most state legislatures also winked and called ratification conventions.

As the constitutional debate began in early 1788, the nationalists seized the initiative with two bold moves. First, they called themselves **Federalists**, suggesting that they supported a federal union—a loose, decentralized system—and obscuring their commitment to a strong national authority. Second, they launched a coordinated campaign in pamphlets and newspapers to explain and justify the Philadelphia constitution.

The opponents of the Constitution, the Antifederalists, had diverse backgrounds and motives. Some, like Governor George Clinton of New York, feared that state governments would lose power. Rural democrats protested that the proposed constitution, unlike most state constitutions, lacked a declaration of individual rights; they also feared that the central government would be run by wealthy men. "Lawyers and men of learning and monied men expect to be managers of this Constitution," worried a Massachusetts farmer, "they will swallow up all of us little folks . . . just as the whale swallowed up Jonah." Giving political substance to these fears, Melancton Smith of New York argued that the large electoral districts prescribed by the Constitution would restrict office holding to wealthy men, whereas the smaller districts used in state elections usually produced legislatures "composed principally of respectable yeomanry."

Smith spoke for many Americans who held traditional republican values. To keep government "close to the people," they wanted the nation of small sovereign republics tied together only for trade and defense—not the "United States" but the "States United." Citing French political philosopher Montesquieu, Antifederalists argued that republican institutions were best suited to cities or small states, a localist perspective that shaped American political thinking well into the twentieth century. "No extensive empire can be governed on republican principles," declared James Winthrop of Massachusetts. Patrick Henry predicted the Constitution would recreate the worst features of British rule: high taxes, an oppressive bureaucracy, a standing army, and a "great and mighty President . . . supported in extravagant munificence."

In New York, where ratification was hotly contested, James Madison, John Jay, and Alexander Hamilton defended the proposed constitution in a series of eighty-five essays collectively called *The Federalist*. *The Federalist* influenced political leaders throughout the country and was subsequently recognized as an important treatise of practical republicanism. Its authors denied that a centralized government would lead to domestic tyranny. Drawing on Montesquieu's theories and John Adams's *Thoughts on Government*, Madison, Jay, and Hamilton pointed out that authority would be divided among the president, a bicameral legislature, and a judiciary. Each branch of government would "check and balance" the others and so preserve liberty.

In "Federalist No. 10," Madison challenged the traditional belief that republican governments were suited only to small political units; rather, a large state would better protect republican liberty. It was "sown in the nature of man," Madison wrote, for individuals to seek power and form factions. Indeed, "a landed interest, a manufacturing interest, a mercantile interest, a moneyed interest, with many lesser interests, grow up of necessity in civilized nations." A free society should welcome such interests but keep any of them from becoming dominant—an end best achieved in a large republic. "Extend the sphere," Madison concluded, "and you take in a greater variety of parties and interests; you make it less probable that a majority of the whole will have a common motive to invade the rights of other citizens."

The delegates who debated these issues in the state ratification conventions included untutored farmers and middling artisans as well as educated gentlemen. Generally, backcountry delegates were Antifederalists, while those from the coast were Federalists. In Pennsylvania, Philadelphia merchants and artisans joined with commercial farmers to ratify the Constitution. Other early Federalist successes came in four less-populous states—Delaware, New Jersey, Georgia, and Connecticut—where delegates hoped a strong national government would offset the power of large neighboring states (Map 6.5).

The Constitution's first real test came in January 1788 in Massachusetts, a hotbed of Antifederalist sentiment. Influential Patriots, including Samuel Adams and Governor John Hancock, opposed the new constitution, as did many followers of Daniel Shays. But Boston artisans, who wanted tariff protection from British imports, supported ratification. To win over other delegates, Federalist leaders assured the convention that they would enact a national bill of rights. By a close vote of 187 to 168, the Federalists carried the day.

Spring brought Federalist victories in Maryland and South Carolina. When New Hampshire narrowly ratified the Constitution in June, the required nine states had approved it. But it took the powerful arguments advanced in *The Federalist* and more promises of a bill of rights to secure the Constitution's adoption in the essential states of Virginia and New York. The votes were close: 89 to 79 in Virginia and 30 to 27 in New York.

Testifying to their respect for popular sovereignty and majority rule, most Americans accepted the verdict of the ratifying conventions. "A decided majority" of the New Hampshire assembly had opposed the "new system," reported Joshua Atherton, but now they said, "It is adopted, let us try it." In Virginia, Patrick Henry vowed to "submit as a quiet citizen" and fight for amendments "in a constitutional way."

Working against great odds, the Federalists had created a national republic and partly restored an elitist system of political authority. They celebrated their triumph by forming great processions in the seaport cities. By marching in an orderly fashion—in conscious contrast to the riotous Revolutionary mobs—and carrying a copy of the Constitution on an "altar of liberty," Federalist-minded citizens affirmed their allegiance to a self-governing republican community and a **civil religion**.

▶ According to the nationalists, what were the central problems of the Articles of Confederation? How did the delegates to the Philadelphia convention address them?

▶ How did the Philadelphia convention resolve three controversial issues: the representation of large and small states, state power, and slavery?

▶ Who were the Antifederalists and why did they oppose the Constitution?

MAP 6.5 Ratifying the Constitution of 1787

In 1907, geographer Owen Libby mapped the votes of members of the state conventions that ratified the Constitution. His map showed that most delegates from seaboard or commercial farming districts, which sent many delegates to the conventions, supported the Constitution, while those from sparsely represented backcountry areas opposed it. Subsequent research has confirmed Libby's socioeconomic interpretation of the voting patterns in North and South Carolina and in Massachusetts. However, other factors influenced delegates elsewhere. For example, in Georgia, delegates from all regions voted for ratification.

SUMMARY

In this chapter, we examined the unfolding of two related sets of events. The first was the war between Britain and its rebellious colonies that began in 1776 and ended in 1783. Two great battles determined the outcome of that conflict: Saratoga in 1777 and Yorktown in 1781. Surprisingly, given the military might of the British empire, both were American victories. These triumphs testify to the determination of George Washington, the resilience of the Continental army, and support for the Patriot cause from hundreds of local militias and tens of thousands of taxpaying citizens.

This popular support reflected the Patriots' success in building effective institutions of republican government. These institutions had their origins in the colonial period, in the town meetings and assemblies that were responsive to popular pressure and increasingly independent of imperial control. They took on new meaning between 1776 and 1781 in the state constitutions that made British subjects into American citizens and in the first national constitution, the Articles of Confederation. Despite the challenges of the postwar economy, these fledging political institutions laid the foundation for the Constitution of 1787, the national charter that endures today.

Connections: Diplomacy

In the essay that introduces Part Two, we pointed out that

> [t]o create and preserve their new republic, Americans of European descent fought two wars against Great Britain, an undeclared war against France, and many battles with Indian peoples.

As Chapter 6 has revealed, American success in the War of Independence was the result, in substantial measure, of French assistance. The French first provided secret monetary and material aid; then, after 1778 and the formal Treaty of Alliance, French military and naval forces helped the Patriots to secure their great victory at Yorktown. It was astute American diplomacy by Benjamin Franklin and others that obtained this French assistance and negotiated a favorable peace treaty. As we will see in Chapter 7, subsequent American diplomatic efforts produced mixed results: The United States nearly went to war with France in 1798, failed to force the British and French to lift restrictions on American merchant vessels in 1807, and precipitated a second, nearly disastrous, war with Great Britain in 1812. Only the purchase of Louisiana from France in 1803 stands out as an unblemished American diplomatic triumph.

Still, the number of these diplomatic initiatives points out the crucial importance of relationships with foreign nations and Native American peoples in the first decades of the United States. Indian warfare and European entanglements—diplomatic, military, commercial, and ideological—stood at the center of American history and are a major focus of our discussion in Chapter 7.

FOR FURTHER EXPLORATION

For vivid accounts of the war, see John C. Dann, ed., *The Revolution Remembered: Eyewitness Accounts of the War for Independence* (1980). "The Virtual Marching Tour" at **www.ushistory.org/brandywine/index.html** offers a multimedia view of Howe's attack on Philadelphia.

Colin G. Calloway, *The American Revolution in Indian Country* (1995), traces the Revolution's impact on native peoples. "Africans in America: Revolution" (**www.pbs .org/wgbh/aia/part2/title.html**) explores the black wartime experience. For blacks who

TIMELINE

1776
- ▶ Second Continental Congress declares independence
- ▶ Howe forces Washington to retreat from New York and New Jersey
- ▶ Pennsylvania approves a democratic state constitution
- ▶ John Adams publishes *Thoughts on Government*

1777
- ▶ Articles of Confederation devised
- ▶ Patriot women contribute to war economy
- ▶ Howe occupies Philadelphia (September)
- ▶ Gates defeats Burgoyne at Saratoga (October)
- ▶ Severe inflation of paper currency begins

1778
- ▶ Franco-American alliance (February)
- ▶ Lord North seeks political settlement; Congress rejects negotiations
- ▶ British adopt southern strategy, capture Savannah (December)

1779
- ▶ British and American forces battle in Georgia

1780
- ▶ Sir Henry Clinton seizes Charleston (May)
- ▶ Guerrilla warfare in Carolinas
- ▶ French troops land in Rhode Island

1781
- ▶ Lord Cornwallis invades Virginia (April), surrenders at Yorktown (October)
- ▶ States ratify Articles of Confederation
- ▶ Large-scale Loyalist emigration

1783
- ▶ Treaty of Paris (September 3) ends war

1784–1785
- ▶ Congress enacts ordinances for new states

1786
- ▶ Nationalists hold convention in Annapolis, Maryland
- ▶ Shays's Rebellion roils Massachusetts

1787
- ▶ Congress passes Northwest Ordinance
- ▶ Constitutional Convention in Philadelphia

1787–1788
- ▶ Jay, Madison, and Hamilton write *The Federalist*
- ▶ Eleven states ratify U.S. Constitution

emigrated to Canada, see **http://epe.lac-bac.gc.ca/100/205/301/ic/cdc/blackloyalists/index.htm** and **http://museum.gov.ns.ca/blackloyalists/index.htm**.

Two important studies of women are Mary Beth Norton, *Liberty's Daughters: The Revolutionary Experience of American Women, 1750–1800* (1980), and Carol Berkin, *Revolutionary Mothers: Women in the Struggle for America's Independence* (2005). For a woman who went to war, see "Masquerade: Deborah Sampson, Continental Soldier" (**forum.wgbh.org/wgbh/forum.php?lecture_id=1654**).

For a dramatic retelling of the Constitutional Convention, see Catherine Drinker Bowen's *Miracle at Philadelphia* (1966). Jack Rakove's *Original Meanings: Politics and Ideas in the Making of the Constitution* (1996) offers a more complex analysis. Michael Kammen, *A Machine That Would Go by Itself* (1986), surveys the changing reputation of the Constitution. David Waldstreicher, *In the Midst of Perpetual Fetes: The Making of American Nationalism, 1776–1820* (1997), probes the meaning of public celebrations.

TEST YOUR KNOWLEDGE

To assess your mastery of the material in this chapter and for Web sites, images, and documents related to this chapter, visit **bedfordstmartins.com/henrettaconcise**.

Politics and Society in the New Republic
1787–1820

The power of the people,
if uncontroverted, is
licentious and mobbish.

— Fisher Ames, Massachusetts
Federalist, 1794

Like an earthquake, the American Revolution shook the European monarchical order, and its aftershocks reverberated for decades. By "creating a new republic based on the rights of the individual, the North Americans introduced a new force into the world," the eminent German historian Leopold von Ranke warned the king of Bavaria in 1854, a force that might cost the monarch his throne. Before 1776, "a king who ruled by the grace of God had been the center around which everything turned. Now the idea emerged that power should come from below [from the people]."

Other republican-inspired upheavals—England's Puritan Revolution of the 1640s and the French Revolution of 1789—had ended in political chaos and military rule. Similar fates befell many Latin American republics that won independence from Spain in the early nineteenth century. But the American states somehow escaped social anarchy and military dictatorship. When the War of Independence ended in 1783, General George Washington left public life to manage his plantation, astonishing European observers. "'Tis a Conduct so novel," American painter John Trumbull reported from London, that it is "inconceivable to People [here]." Washington's voluntary retirement bolstered the authority of elected Patriot leaders, who were fashioning representative republican governments.

This great task absorbed the energy and intellect of an entire generation. As Americans wrote constitutions and enacted new laws, political leaders worried that the measures were too democratic and self-interested. When a bill came before a state legislature, Connecticut conservative Ezra Stiles grumbled, every elected official "instantly thinks how it will affect his constituents" rather than how it would affect the general welfare. What Stiles criticized as the irresponsible pursuit of personal and group advantage, most Americans welcomed. The concerns of ordinary citizens had taken center stage in the halls of government, and the monarchs of Europe trembled.

The Political Crisis of the 1790s

The final decade of the eighteenth century brought fresh challenges for American politics. The Federalists split into two irreconcilable factions over financial policy and the French Revolution. Their leaders, Alexander Hamilton and Thomas Jefferson, offered contrasting visions of the future. Would the United States remain, as Jefferson hoped, an agricultural nation governed by local and state officials? Or would Hamilton's vision of a strong national government and an economy based on manufacturing become reality?

The Federalists Implement the Constitution

The Constitution expanded the dimensions of political life: Previously, voters had elected local and state officials; now they chose national leaders as well. The Federalists swept the election of 1788, winning forty-four seats in the first House of Representatives; only eight Antifederalists won election. As expected, members of the Electoral College chose George Washington as president. John Adams received the second highest number of electoral votes and became vice president.

Once the military savior of his country, Washington now became its political father. At age fifty-seven, the first president was a man of great personal dignity. Knowing he would be setting precedents, Washington proceeded cautiously. He adopted many of the administrative practices of the Confederation and asked Congress to reestablish the existing executive departments: Foreign Affairs (State), Finance (Treasury), and War. He initiated one important practice: The Constitution required the Senate's approval for the appointment of major officials, but Washington insisted that the president had sole authority to remove them, thus ensuring the executive's control over the bureaucracy. To head the Department of State, Washington chose Thomas Jefferson, a fellow Virginian and an experienced diplomat. For secretary of the treasury, he turned to Alexander Hamilton, a lawyer and Washington's military aide during the war. The president designated Jefferson, Hamilton, and Secretary of War Henry Knox as his cabinet, or advisory body.

The Constitution mandated a supreme court, but the Philadelphia convention left to Congress the task of creating other national courts. The Federalists in Congress wanted strong national institutions, and the Judiciary Act of 1789 reflected their vision. The act established a federal district court in each state and three circuit courts to hear appeals from the districts, with the Supreme Court having the final say. The Judiciary Act also allowed cases involving federal laws and powers that were decided in state courts to be appealed to the Supreme Court. This provision ensured that federal judges would have the final say on the meaning of the Constitution.

The Federalists kept their promise to add a declaration of rights to the Constitution. James Madison, now a member of the House of Representatives, submitted nineteen amendments to the First Congress; by 1791, ten had been approved by Congress and ratified by the states. These ten amendments, known as the Bill of Rights, safeguard fundamental personal rights, including freedom of speech and religion, and mandate trial by jury and other legal procedures that protect individual citizens. By easing Antifederalists' concerns about an oppressive national government, the amendments secured the legitimacy of the Constitution. They also addressed, but did not resolve, the issue of federalism: the proper balance between national and state power. That question was extremely controversial until the Civil War and remains important today.

Hamilton's Financial Program

George Washington's most important decision was his choice of Alexander Hamilton as secretary of the treasury. An ambitious self-made man of great charm and intelligence, Hamilton had married into the Schuyler family, influential Hudson River Valley landowners, and had become a prominent lawyer in New York City. At the Philadelphia convention, he took a strongly conservative stance, condemning the "democratic spirit" and calling for an authoritarian government and a president with near-monarchical powers.

As treasury secretary, Hamilton devised bold policies to enhance national authority and to favor financiers and merchants. He outlined his plans in three path-breaking reports to Congress: on public credit (January 1790), on a national bank (December 1790), and on manufactures (December 1791). These reports outlined a coherent program of national mercantilism—in other words, government-assisted economic development.

The financial and social implications of Hamilton's "Report on the Public Credit" made it instantly controversial. Hamilton asked Congress to redeem at face value the $55 million in securities issued by the Confederation that were held by foreign and domestic investors and speculators. He reasoned that as an underdeveloped nation, the United States was heavily dependent on loans from Dutch and British financiers and needed good credit. However, his redemption plan would give enormous profits to speculators, who had bought up depreciated securities. For example, a Massachusetts merchant firm, Burrell & Burrell, had paid $600 for Confederation notes with a face value of $2,500; it stood to reap a profit of $1,900. Such windfall gains offended a majority of Americans, who worked hard for their living and rejected the speculative practices of capitalist financiers. Equally controversial was Hamilton's proposal to pay the Burrells and other Confederation note holders with new interest-bearing securities, thereby creating a permanent **national debt**.

Hamilton's plan for a national debt owned mostly by wealthy families reawakened the fears of Radical Whigs and "Old Republicans." Speaking for the Virginia House of Burgesses, Patrick Henry condemned this plan "to erect, and concentrate, and perpetuate a large monied interest" and warned that it would prove "fatal to the existence of American liberty." James Madison challenged the morality of Hamilton's redemption proposal. Madison demanded that Congress consider the original owners of Confederation securities: the thousands of shopkeepers, farmers, and soldiers who had bought or accepted the securities during the dark days of the war and later sold them to speculators. However, it would have been difficult to trace the original owners, and nearly half the members of the House of Representatives owned Confederation securities and would profit personally from Hamilton's plan. Melding practicality with self-interest, the House rejected Madison's suggestion.

Hamilton then proposed that the national government enhance the public credit by assuming the war debts of the states, some $22 million, a plan that would also favor wealthy creditors. Knowing Hamilton's intentions in advance, Assistant Secretary of the

Treasury William Duer and his associates secretly bought up the war bonds of southern states at cheap rates. Congressional critics of Hamilton's assumption plan condemned Duer's speculation. They also pointed out that some states had already paid off their war debts; in response, Hamilton promised to reimburse those states. Representatives from Virginia and Maryland worried that assumption would enhance the already excessive financial sway of the national government. To quiet their fears, the treasury chief agreed to locate the permanent national capital along the banks of the Potomac, where suspicious southerners could easily watch its operations. Such astute bargaining gave Hamilton the votes he needed to enact both his redemption and assumption plans.

In December 1790, Hamilton issued a second report asking Congress to charter the Bank of the United States, to be jointly owned by private stockholders and the national government. Hamilton argued that the bank would provide financial stability to the specie-starved American economy by making loans to merchants, handling government funds, and issuing bills of credit. These potential benefits persuaded Congress to grant Hamilton's bank a twenty-year charter and send the legislation to the president for his approval.

At this critical juncture, Secretary of State Thomas Jefferson joined with James Madison to oppose Hamilton's financial initiatives. Jefferson had already condemned Duer and the "corrupt squadron of paper dealers" who speculated in southern war bonds. Now he charged that Hamilton's national bank was unconstitutional. "The incorporation of a Bank," Jefferson told President Washington, was not a power expressly "delegated to the United States by the Constitution." Jefferson's argument rested on a *strict* interpretation of the national charter. Hamilton preferred a *loose* interpretation; he told Washington that Article 1, Section 8, empowered Congress to make "all Laws which shall be necessary and proper" to carry out the provisions of the Constitution. Agreeing with Hamilton, the president signed the legislation.

Hamilton now undertook to raise the revenue to pay the annual interest on the national debt. At his insistence, Congress imposed domestic excise taxes, including a duty on whiskey distilled in the United States. These taxes would yield $1 million a year. To raise another $4 million to $5 million, the treasury secretary proposed higher tariffs on foreign imports. Although Hamilton's "Report on Manufactures" (1791) urged the nation to become self-sufficient in manufacturing, he did not support high **protective tariffs** that would exclude foreign products. Rather, he advocated moderate **revenue tariffs** that would pay the interest on the debt and defray the expenses of the national government.

Hamilton's scheme worked brilliantly. As American trade increased, customs revenue rose steadily and defrayed the annual interest on the national debt. Ample tariff revenues also had the unexpected effect of encouraging rapid settlement of the West. Because import duties covered federal government expenses, Congress sold lands in the national domain at ever-lower prices, a policy outcome opposed by Hamilton and favored by his Jeffersonian opponents. In any event, the treasury secretary had devised a strikingly modern fiscal system that provided the new national government with financial stability.

Jefferson's Agrarian Vision

Hamilton paid a high political price for his success. Even before Washington began his second four-year term in 1793, Hamilton's financial measures had split the Federalists into two irreconcilable factions. Most northern Federalists adhered to Hamilton's faction, while most southern Federalists joined a rival group headed by Madison and Jefferson. By the elections of 1794, the two factions had acquired names. Hamilton's supporters remained Federalists; Madison and Jefferson's allies called themselves Democratic Republicans or simply Republicans.

Thomas Jefferson spoke for southern planters and western farmers. Well-read in architecture, natural history, agricultural science, and political theory, Jefferson embraced the optimism of the Enlightenment. He believed in the "improvability of the human race" and deplored the corruption and social divisions that threatened its progress. Having seen the poverty of laborers in British factories, Jefferson doubted that wageworkers had the economic and political independence needed to sustain a republican polity.

Jefferson therefore set his democratic vision of America in an agricultural society of yeomen farm families. "Those who labor in the earth are the chosen people of God," he wrote in *Notes on the State of Virginia* (1785). The grain and meat from their farms would feed European nations, which "would manufacture and send us in exchange our clothes and other comforts." Jefferson's notion of an international division of labor resembled that proposed by Scottish economist Adam Smith in *The Wealth of Nations* (1776).

Turmoil in Europe brought Jefferson's vision closer to reality. The French Revolution began in 1789; four years later, France's new republican government went to war against a British-led coalition of monarchies. As fighting disrupted European farming, wheat prices leaped from 5 to 8 shillings a bushel and remained high for twenty years, bringing substantial profits to Chesapeake and Middle Atlantic farmers. "Our farmers have never experienced such prosperity," remarked one observer. Simultaneously, a boom in the export of raw cotton, fueled by the invention of the cotton gin and the mechanization of cloth production in Britain (see Chapter 9), boosted the economies of Georgia and South Carolina. As Jefferson had hoped, European markets brought prosperity to American agriculturalists.

The French Revolution Divides Americans

American merchants profited even more handsomely from the European war. In 1793, President Washington issued a Proclamation of Neutrality, allowing U.S. citizens to trade with all belligerents. As neutral carriers, American merchant ships were initially allowed to pass through the British naval blockade of French ports, and Americans quickly took over the lucrative sugar trade between France and its West Indian islands. Commercial earnings rose spectacularly, averaging $20 million annually in the 1790s — twice the value of cotton and tobacco exports. As the American merchant fleet increased from 355,000 tons in 1790 to 1.1 million tons in 1808, northern shipbuilders and merchants provided work for thousands of shipwrights, sailmakers, laborers, and seamen. Carpenters, masons, and cabinetmakers in Boston, New York, and Philadelphia found work building warehouses and fashionable "Federal-style" town houses for newly affluent merchants. In Philadelphia, a European visitor reported, "a great number of private houses have marble steps to the street door, and in other respects are finished in a style of elegance."

Federalist Gentry

A prominent New England Federalist, Oliver Ellsworth served as chief justice of the United States from 1796 to 1800. His wife, Abigail Wolcott Ellsworth, was the daughter of a Connecticut governor. In 1792, portraitist Ralph Earl captured the Ellsworths' aspirations by depicting the couple as landed gentry and prominently displaying their mansion (in the window). Like other Federalists who tried to reconcile their wealth and social authority with republican values, Ellsworth dressed with restraint, and his manners, remarked Timothy Dwight, were "wholly destitute of haughtiness and arrogance." Wadsworth Atheneum, Hartford.

Even as Americans profited from the European struggle, they argued passionately over its ideologies. Most Americans had welcomed the French Revolution of 1789 because it abolished feudalism and established a constitutional monarchy. The creation of the First French Republic in 1792 was more controversial. Some Americans applauded the downfall of the monarchy. Urban artisans embraced the egalitarian ideology of the Jacobins, a radical French group, and followed their example by addressing one another as "citizen" and starting democratic political clubs. However, Americans with strong religious beliefs condemned the new French government for rejecting Christianity, closing churches, and promoting a rational religion based on "natural morality." Fearing social revolution at home, wealthy Americans condemned Robespierre and his radical republican followers for executing King Louis XVI and 3,000 aristocrats (see Voices from Abroad, p. 199).

Their fears were well founded. Ideological conflicts and discontent over Hamilton's economic policies sparked a domestic insurgency. In 1794, western Pennsylvania farmers, already angered by the state's conservative fiscal policies, mounted the so-called

Peter Porcupine Attacks Pro-French Americans   WILLIAM COBBETT

The Democratic Republican followers of Thomas Jefferson declared that "he who is an enemy to the French Revolution, cannot be a firm republican." William Cobbett, a British journalist who settled in Philadelphia and wrote under the pen name "Peter Porcupine," rejected that proposition. A strong supporter of the Federalist Party, Cobbett attacked its opponents in caustic and widely read pamphlets and newspaper articles like this one of 1796.

France is a republic, and the decrees of the Legislators were necessary to maintain it a republic. This word outweighs, in the estimation of some persons (I wish I could say they were few in number), all the horrors that have been and that can be committed in that country. One of these modern republicans will tell you that he does not deny that hundreds of thousands of innocent persons have been murdered in France; . . . that its commerce, its manufactures, its sciences, its arts, and its honour, are no more; but at the end of all this, he will tell you that it must be happy, because it is a republic. I have heard more than one of these republican zealots declare, that he would sooner see the last of the French exterminated, than see them adopt any other form of government. Such a sentiment is characteristic of a mind locked up in a savage ignorance.

Shall we say that these things never can take place among us? . . . We are not what we were before the French revolution. Political projectors from every corner of Europe, troublers of society of every description, from the whining philosophical hypocrite to the daring rebel, and more daring blasphemer, have taken shelter in these States.

We have seen the guillotine toasted to three times three cheers. . . . And what would the reader say, were I to tell him of a Member of Congress, who wished to see one of these murderous machines employed for lopping off the heads of the French, permanent in the State-house yard of the city of Philadelphia?

If these men of blood had succeeded in plunging us into a war; if they had once got the sword into their hands, they would have mowed us down like stubble. The word Aristocrat would have been employed to as good account here, as ever it had been in France. We might, ere this, have seen our places of worship turned into stables; we might have seen the banks of the Delaware, like those of the Loire, covered with human carcasses, and its waters tinged with blood: ere this we might have seen our parents butchered, and even the head of our admired and beloved President rolling on a scaffold.

I know the reader will start back with horror. His heart will tell him that it is impossible. But, once more, let him look at the example before us. The attacks on the character and conduct of the aged Washington, have been as bold, if not bolder, than those which led to the downfall of the unfortunate French Monarch [Louis XVI, executed in 1793]. Can it then be imagined, that, had they possessed the power, they wanted the will to dip their hands in his blood?

SOURCE: William Cobbett, *Peter Porcupine in America*, ed. David A. Wilson (Ithaca: Cornell University Press, 1994), 150–154.

Whiskey Rebellion to protest Hamilton's excise tax on spirits. The tax had cut the demand for the corn whiskey the farmers brewed and bartered for eastern manufactures. Like the Sons of Liberty in 1765 and the Shaysites in 1786, the Whiskey Rebels assailed the tax collectors who sent the farmers' hard-earned money to a distant government. But the protesters also waved banners proclaiming the French revolutionary slogan "Liberty, Equality, and Fraternity!" To deter popular rebellion and uphold national authority, President Washington raised an army of 12,000 troops and dispersed the Whiskey Rebels.

Britain's maritime strategy increased political divisions in America. Beginning in late 1793, the British navy stopped American ships carrying French sugar and other goods, eventually seizing 250 vessels. Hoping to protect merchant property through diplomacy, Washington dispatched John Jay to Britain. But Jay returned with a controversial treaty. It ignored the merchants' argument that "free ships make free goods" and accepted Britain's right to remove French property from neutral ships. The treaty also required the U.S. government to make "full and complete compensation" to British merchants for pre–Revolutionary War debts owed by American citizens. In return, the agreement allowed American merchants to submit claims for illegal seizures and required the British to remove their troops and Indian agents from the Northwest Territory. Republicans attacked Jay's Treaty for being too conciliatory, but in 1795, the Senate ratified it by the bare two-thirds majority required by the Constitution. As long as Hamilton and the Federalists were in power, the United States would have a pro-British foreign policy.

The Rise of Political Parties

The appearance of Federalists and Republicans marked a new stage in American politics — what historians call the First Party System. Although colonial legislatures had often divided into factions based on family, ethnicity, or region, they did not have organized political parties. Nor did the new state and national constitutions make any provision for political societies. In fact, most Americans thought parties were dangerous because they were self-interested. Following classical republican principles, political leaders asserted that voters and legislators should act independently and for the public interest. Thus, Senator Pierce Butler of South Carolina criticized his congressional colleagues as "men scrambling for partial advantage, State interests, and in short, a train of narrow, impolitic measures."

But classical republican principles collapsed in the face of sharp conflicts over Hamilton's fiscal policies. Most merchants, creditors, and urban artisans supported the Federalist party and its policies, as did wheat-exporting slaveholders in the Tidewater districts of the Chesapeake. The emerging Republican coalition was more diverse. It included not only southern tobacco and rice planters and debt-conscious western farmers but also Germans and Scots-Irish in the southern backcountry and subsistence farmers in the Northeast.

Party identity crystallized in 1796. To prepare for the presidential election, Federalist and Republican leaders called caucuses in Congress and conventions in the states. They also mobilized popular support by organizing public festivals and processions: The Federalists held banquets to celebrate Washington's birthday in February, and the

Republicans marched through the streets to honor the Declaration of Independence on July fourth.

In the election, voters favored Federalist candidates, giving them a majority in Congress and electing John Adams to the presidency. Adams continued Hamilton's pro-British foreign policy and reacted sharply to seizures of American merchant ships by the French navy. When the French foreign minister Talleyrand solicited a loan and a bribe from American diplomats to stop the seizures, Adams charged that Talleyrand's agents, whom he dubbed X, Y, and Z, had insulted America's honor. In response to the XYZ Affair, the Federalist-controlled Congress cut off trade with France in 1798 and authorized American privateers to seize French ships. The United States and France were waging an undeclared maritime war.

Constitutional Crisis, 1798–1800

Ominously, the controversial foreign policy of the Federalists prompted domestic protest and governmental repression. Republican-minded immigrants from Ireland vehemently attacked Adams's pro-British foreign policy. A Federalist pamphleteer in Philadelphia responded in kind: "Were I president, I would hang them for otherwise they would murder me." To silence its critics, the Federalist-controlled Congress enacted three coercive laws that limited individual rights and threatened the fledgling party system. The Naturalization Act lengthened the residency requirement for American citizenship from five to fourteen years; the Alien Act authorized the deportation of foreigners; and the Sedition Act prohibited the publication of insults or malicious attacks on the president or members of Congress. "He that is not for us is against us," thundered the Federalist *Gazette of the United States*. Using the Sedition Act, Federalist prosecutors arrested more than twenty Republican newspaper editors and politicians, accused them of sedition, and convicted and jailed a number of them.

What followed was a constitutional crisis. With justification, Republicans charged that the Sedition Act violated the First Amendment's prohibition against "abridging the freedom of speech, or of the press." However, they did not appeal to the Supreme Court because the Court's power to review congressional legislation was uncertain and because most of the justices were Federalists. Instead, Madison and Jefferson looked to the state legislatures. At their urging, the Kentucky and Virginia legislatures issued resolutions in 1798 declaring the Alien and Sedition Acts to be "unauthoritative, void, and of no force." The resolutions set forth a **states' rights** interpretation of the Constitution, asserting that the states had a "right to judge" the legitimacy of national laws.

The conflict over the Sedition Act set the stage for the presidential election of 1800. Jefferson, once opposed on principle to political parties, now saw them as a valuable way "to watch and relate to the people" the activities of an oppressive government. With opposition to the French conflict growing and Jefferson preparing for a presidential bid, John Adams reevaluated his foreign policy. Adams was a complicated man: He was easily offended but had great integrity and a strong will. Rejecting Hamilton's advice to declare war against France (and benefit from an upsurge in patriotism), Adams put country ahead of party and entered into diplomatic negotiations that ended the fighting.

Despite Adams's statesmanship, the campaign of 1800 degenerated into name-calling. The Federalists attacked Jefferson's beliefs, branding him an irresponsible pro-French radical and, because he opposed state support of religion in Virginia, "the arch-apostle of irreligion and free thought." Both parties changed state election laws to favor their candidates. In fact, tensions ran so high that rumors circulated of a Federalist plot to stage a military coup.

The election did not end these worries. Thanks to a low Federalist turnout in Virginia and Pennsylvania and the three-fifths rule (which boosted electoral votes in the southern states), Jefferson won a narrow 73 to 65 victory over Adams in the Electoral College. However, the Republican electors also gave 73 votes to Aaron Burr of New York, who was Jefferson's vice presidential running mate. The Constitution specified that in the case of a tie vote, the House of Representatives would choose between the candidates. For thirty-five rounds of balloting, Federalists in the House blocked Jefferson's election, prompting a rumor that Virginia was raising a military force to put Jefferson into office.

Ironically, arch-Federalist Alexander Hamilton ushered in a more democratic era by supporting Jefferson. Calling Burr an "embryo Caesar" and the "most unfit man in the United States for the office of president," Hamilton persuaded key Federalists to allow Jefferson's election. The Federalists' concern for political stability also played a role. As Senator James Bayard of Delaware explained, "It was admitted on all hands that we must risk the Constitution and a Civil War or take Mr. Jefferson."

▶ What was Hamilton's vision of the future? What policies did he implement to achieve it? How was Jefferson's vision different?

▶ What were the consequences of the French Revolution in America? How did it affect the development of American politics?

Jefferson called the election the "Revolution of 1800," and so it was. The bloodless transfer of power showed that governments elected by the people could be changed in an orderly way, even in times of bitter partisan conflict. In his inaugural address in 1801, Jefferson praised this achievement, declaring, "We are all Republicans, we are all Federalists." Defying the predictions of European conservatives, the American republican experiment of 1776 had survived a quarter century of economic and political turmoil.

The Westward Movement and the Jeffersonian Revolution

The United States "is a country in flux," a visiting French aristocrat observed in 1799, and "that which is true today as regards its population, its establishments, its prices, its commerce will not be true six months from now." Indeed, the American republic was beginning a period of dynamic westward expansion; between 1790 and 1810, farm families settled as much land as they had during the entire colonial period. George Washington, himself a western land speculator, noted approvingly that ordinary men—the Sons of Liberty—were quickly becoming "the lords and proprietors of a vast tract of continent." Unfortunately for Washington's Federalist Party, most western farmers supported Thomas Jefferson's Republicans.

The Expanding Republic and Native American Resistance

In the Treaty of Paris of 1783, Great Britain relinquished its claims to the trans-Appalachian region and, as one British diplomat put it, left the Indian nations "to the care of their [American] neighbours." *Care* was hardly the right term: Many white Americans wanted to destroy native communities and even the native peoples themselves. "Cut up every Indian Cornfield and burn every Indian town," proclaimed William Henry Drayton, a congressman from South Carolina, so that their "nation be extirpated and the lands become the property of the public." Other leaders, including Henry Knox, Washington's first secretary of war, favored assimilating native peoples into Euro-American society. Tribal lands held in common would be divided among individual Indian families, who would become citizens of the various states. This debate among whites over Indian policy would have an important place on the nation's agenda until 1900, and it continues even today.

Not surprisingly, the major struggle between native peoples and whites centered on land. Invoking the Treaty of Paris and regarding Britain's Indian allies as conquered peoples, the U.S. government asserted its ownership of the trans-Appalachian West. Indian nations rejected that claim, insisting that they had not been conquered and had not signed the Paris treaty. Brushing aside those objections, U.S. commissioners threatened military action to force the pro-British Iroquois peoples—Mohawks, Onondagas, Cayugas, and Senecas—to cede huge tracts in New York and Pennsylvania in the Treaty of Fort Stanwix (1784). New York officials and land speculators used liquor and bribes to take title to millions of additional acres, confining the once powerful Iroquois to reservations.

American negotiators used similar tactics to grab western lands. In 1785, they persuaded the Chippewas, Delawares, Ottawas, and Wyandots to sign away most of the future state of Ohio. The tribes quickly repudiated the agreements, justifiably claiming they were made under duress. To defend their lands, they joined with the Shawnee, Miami, and Potawatomi peoples in the Western Confederacy. Led by Miami chief Little Turtle, confederacy warriors crushed American expeditionary forces sent by President Washington in 1790 and 1791.

Fearing an alliance between the Western Confederacy and the British in Canada, Washington doubled the size of the U.S. Army and ordered General "Mad Anthony" Wayne to lead a new expedition. In August 1794, Wayne defeated the Indians in the Battle of Fallen Timbers (near present-day Toledo, Ohio), but the resistance continued. In the Treaty of Greenville (1795), American negotiators acknowledged Indian ownership of the land. But the Western Confederacy ceded most of Ohio and various strategic sites along the Great Lakes; they also agreed to place themselves "under the protection of the United States, and no other Power whatever." Faced with these American advances, Britain reduced its trade with trans-Appalachian Indian peoples and, following Jay's Treaty (1795), slowly removed its military garrisons (Map 7.1).

The Greenville Treaty sparked a wave of white migration. By 1805, Ohio, a state for just two years, had more than 100,000 residents. Thousands more farm families moved into the future states of Indiana and Illinois, sparking new conflicts with native peoples over land and hunting rights. Declared one Delaware Indian: "The Elks are our horses, the buffaloes are our cows, the deer are our sheep, & the whites shan't have them."

Treaty Negotiations at Greenville, 1795

In 1785, a number of Indian tribes formed the Western Confederacy to prevent white settlement north of the Ohio River. The American victory at the Battle of Fallen Timbers (1794) and the subsequent Treaty of Greenville (1795) opened up the region for white farmers. But the treaty acknowledged many Indian rights because of their near equality in military power. The artist suggests this equality: Notice the height and stately bearing of the Indian leaders and their placement slightly in front of the American officers. Unknown, *Treaty of Greenville,* n.d., Chicago Historical Society.

For more help analyzing this image, see the Online Study Guide at **bedfordstmartins.com/henrettaconcise**.

To alleviate such conflicts, the U.S. government encouraged Native Americans to assimilate into white society. The goal, as one Kentucky Protestant minister put it, was to make the Indian "a farmer, a citizen of the United States, and a Christian." But most Indians rejected assimilation. Even those who embraced Christian teachings retained many of their ancestral values. To think of themselves as individuals or members of a nuclear family, as white Americans were demanding, meant repudiating the clan, the very essence of Indian life. To preserve their traditional cultures, many Indian communities expelled white missionaries and forced Christianized Indians to participate in tribal rites. As a Munsee prophet declared, "There are two ways to God, one for the whites and one for the Indians."

A few Indian leaders sought a middle path. Among the Senecas, the prophet Handsome Lake encouraged traditional animistic ceremonies that gave thanks to the sun, the earth, water, plants, and animals. But he included Christian elements in his teachings — the concepts of heaven and hell, for example — to deter his followers from alcohol, gambling, and witchcraft. Handsome Lake's doctrines divided

MAP 7.1 Indian Cessions and State Formation, 1776–1840

By virtue of the Treaty of Paris with Britain (1783), the United States claimed sovereignty over the entire trans-Appalachian West. The Western Confederacy contested this claim, but the U.S. government upheld it with military force. By 1840, armed diplomacy had forced most Native American peoples to move west of the Mississippi River. White settlers occupied their lands, formed territorial governments, and eventually entered the Union as members of separate — and equal — states.

the Senecas into hostile factions. A conservative group, led by Chief Red Jacket, condemned Indians who accepted white ways and demanded a return to ancestral customs.

Most Indians also rejected the efforts of American missionaries to turn warriors into farmers and women into domestic helpmates. Among eastern woodland peoples, women grew corn, beans, and squash — the mainstays of the Indians' diet — and land cultivation rights passed through the female line. Consequently, women exercised considerable political influence, which they were eager to retain. Nor were Indian men interested in becoming farmers. When war raiding and hunting were no longer possible, they turned to grazing cattle and sheep.

Migration and the Changing Farm Economy

Native American resistance slowed the advance of white settlers but did not stop it. In the years between 1790 and 1820, two great streams of migrants moved out of the southern states. One stream, composed primarily of white tenant farmers and struggling yeomen families, flocked through the Cumberland Gap into Kentucky and Tennessee. "Boundless settlements open a door for our citizens to run off and leave us," a worried eastern landlord lamented in the *Maryland Gazette*, "depreciating all our landed property and disabling us from paying taxes." Many migrants were, in fact, fleeing from this planter-controlled society. They wanted more freedom and hoped to prosper by growing cotton and hemp, which were in great demand.

But many settlers in Kentucky and Tennessee lacked ready cash to buy land. Like the North Carolina Regulators in the 1770s, some poor migrants claimed a customary right to occupy "back waste vacant Lands" sufficient "to provide a subsistence for themselves and their posterity." Virginia legislators, who administered the Kentucky Territory, had a more elitist vision. Although they allowed poor settlers to purchase up to 1,400 acres of land at reduced prices, they sold or granted huge estates of 20,000 to 200,000 acres to scores of wealthy men. When Kentucky became a state in 1792, a handful of land speculators owned one-fourth of the state, while half the white men owned no land and lived as squatters or tenant farmers.

Widespread landlessness—and opposition to slavery—prompted a new migration across the Ohio River into the future states of Ohio, Indiana, and Illinois. In a free community, thought Peter Cartwright, a Methodist lay preacher from southwestern Kentucky who moved to Illinois, "I would be entirely clear of the evil of slavery . . . [and] could raise my children to work where work was not thought a degradation."

Meanwhile, a second stream of southern migrants, made up of slave-owning planters and enslaved African Americans from the Carolinas, moved along the coastal plain toward the Gulf of Mexico. The migrants set up new plantations in the interior of Georgia and South Carolina. Then they moved into the Old Southwest, the future states of Alabama, Mississippi, and Louisiana. "The Alabama Feaver rages here with great violence," a North Carolina planter remarked, "and has carried off vast numbers of our Citizens."

Cotton was key to this migratory surge. Beginning around 1750, the demand for raw wool and cotton increased dramatically as water-powered spinning jennies, weaving mules, and other technological innovations boosted textile production in Europe. South Carolina and Georgia planters began growing cotton, and American inventors—including Connecticut-born Eli Whitney—built machines (called gins) that efficiently extracted seeds from strands of cotton. To grow cotton, the planters imported about 115,000 Africans between 1776 and 1808, when Congress cut off the Atlantic slave trade. The cotton boom financed the rapid settlement of Mississippi and Alabama—in a single year, a government land office in Huntsville, Alabama, sold $7 million of uncleared land—and the two states entered the Union in 1817 and 1819, respectively.

As southern whites and blacks moved across the Appalachians and along the Gulf Coast, a third stream of migrants flowed out of the overcrowded communities of New England. Previous generations of Massachusetts and Connecticut farm families had moved north and east, settling New Hampshire, Vermont, and Maine. Now farmers throughout New England were moving west. Seeking land for their children, thousands of parents packed their wagons with tools and household goods and migrated to New York. By 1820, almost 800,000 New England migrants lived in a string of settlements that stretched from Albany to Buffalo, and many others had moved on to Ohio and Indiana. This vast migration was organized by the settlers, who often moved in large family or religious groups. One traveler reported from central New York: "The town of Herkimer is entirely populated by families come from Connecticut. We stayed at Mr. Snow's who came from New London with about ten male and female cousins." Throughout the Northwest Territory, many new communities were fragments of New England communities that had moved inland.

In New York, as in Kentucky, well-connected speculators snapped up much of the best land. In the 1780s, financier Robert Morris acquired 1.3 million acres in the Genesee region of central New York. The Wadsworth family bought thousands of

Hop Picking, 1801
Farm labor was nothing new for rural women and children, who had always worked on the farm. What was different after 1800 was the growing number of outworkers: landless or poor families who labored as wageworkers for shopkeepers and manufacturers. In this romanticized watercolor by Lucy Sheldon, a schoolgirl at the Litchfield Female Academy in Connecticut, a young couple and their children pick hops, which they will deliver to a storekeeper or local brewer to be made into beer. Litchfield Historical Society.

acres, seeking to reproduce the manorial system of the Hudson River Valley. To attract tenants, the Wadsworths leased farms rent-free for the first seven years, after which they charged rents. Many New England families chose to buy farms. They signed contracts with the Holland Land Company, a Dutch-owned syndicate of speculators, which allowed settlers to pay for their farms as they worked them.

The new farm economy in the trans-Appalachian West forced major changes in eastern agriculture. Unable to compete with lower-priced New York grains, farmers in New England switched to potatoes, which were high yielding and nutritious. To compensate for the labor of sons and daughters who had moved inland, Middle Atlantic farmers bought more efficient farm equipment. They replaced metal-tipped wooden plows with cast-iron models that dug deeper and required a single yoke of oxen instead of two. Such changes in crop mix and technology kept production high even with fewer workers.

Easterners also used the progressive farming methods touted by British agricultural reformers. "Improvers" in Pennsylvania doubled their average yield per acre by rotating their crops and planting nitrogen-rich clover to offset nutrient-hungry wheat and corn. Yeomen farmers diversified production by raising sheep and selling the wool to textile manufacturers. Many farmers adopted a year-round planting cycle, sowing corn in the spring for animal fodder and then planting winter wheat in September for market sale. Women and girls milked the family cows and made butter and cheese to sell in the growing towns and cities.

White families now worked harder and longer, but their efforts were rewarded with higher output and a better standard of living. Whether hacking fields out of western forests or carting manure to replenish eastern soils, farmers increased their productivity. Westward migration had boosted the farming economy throughout the country.

The Jeffersonian Presidency

From 1801 to 1825, three Republicans from Virginia—Thomas Jefferson, James Madison, and James Monroe—each served two terms as president. Supported by farmers in the South and West and strong Republican majorities in Congress, this "Virginia Dynasty" completed what Jefferson had called the Revolution of 1800. It reversed many Federalist policies and actively supported westward expansion.

When Jefferson took office in 1801, he became the first chief executive to live in the White House in the District of Columbia, the new national capital. His administration began with an international conflict inherited from the Federalists. Beginning in the 1780s, the Barbary States of North Africa had raided merchant ships in the Mediterranean, and like many European nations, the United States had paid an annual bribe to protect its vessels. Jefferson refused to pay this "tribute" and ordered the U.S. Navy to attack the pirates' home ports. But the president did not want all-out war, which would have increased taxes and the national debt, so he eventually negotiated a settlement that restored the tribute at a lower rate.

At home, Jefferson inherited a national judiciary filled with Federalist appointees, including the formidable John Marshall of Virginia, the new chief justice of the Supreme Court. To add more Federalist judges, the outgoing Federalist Congress had passed the Judiciary Act of 1801. The act created sixteen new judgeships and six additional circuit courts, which President Adams filled at the last moment with "midnight appointees." The Federalists "have retired into the judiciary as a stronghold," Jefferson complained, "and from that battery all the works of Republicanism are to be beaten down and destroyed."

Jefferson's fears were soon realized. When Republican legislatures in Kentucky and Virginia repudiated the Alien and Sedition Acts and claimed the authority to determine the constitutionality of national laws, Federalist John Marshall quickly responded. The Constitution stated that "the judicial Power shall extend to all Cases . . . arising under this Constitution [and] the Laws of the United States," which implied that the Supreme Court held the power of constitutional review. The Court claimed this authority when James Madison, the new secretary of state, refused to deliver the commission of William Marbury, one of Adams's midnight appointees. Marbury petitioned the Supreme Court to compel delivery under the terms of the Judiciary Act of 1789. In *Marbury v. Madison* (1803), Marshall asserted that Marbury had the right to the appointment but that the Court did not have the constitutional power to enforce it. In defining the Court's powers, Marshall voided a section of the Judiciary Act of 1789, in effect asserting the Court's authority to review congressional legislation and interpret the constitution. "It is emphatically the province and duty of the judicial department to say what the law is," the chief justice declared, directly challenging the Republican view that the state legislatures had that power.

Ignoring this setback, Jefferson and the Republicans reversed other Federalist policies. When the Alien and Sedition acts expired in 1801, Congress branded them political and unconstitutional and refused to reenact them. It also amended the Naturalization Act to allow resident aliens to become citizens after five years, the original waiting period. Charging the Federalists with grossly expanding the national government's size and power, Jefferson had the Republican Congress shrink it. He abolished all internal taxes, including the excise tax that had sparked the Whiskey Rebellion of 1794. To quiet "Old Republican" fears of a military coup, Jefferson reduced the size of the permanent army. He also secured repeal of the Judiciary Act of 1801, thereby ousting forty of Adams's midnight appointees. But the Republican president retained competent Federalist officeholders, removing only 69 of 433 properly appointed Federalists during his eight years as president.

Jefferson also governed tactfully in fiscal affairs. He tolerated the economically important Bank of the United States, which he had once condemned as unconstitutional. But he chose as his secretary of the treasury Albert Gallatin, a fiscal conservative who believed that the national debt was "an evil of the first magnitude." By limiting expenditures and using customs revenue to redeem government bonds, Gallatin reduced the debt from $83 million in 1801 to $45 million in 1812. With Jefferson and Gallatin at the helm, the nation was no longer run in the interests of northeastern creditors and merchants.

Jefferson and the West

Jefferson had long championed settlement of the West. He celebrated the yeoman farmer in *Notes on the State of Virginia*, wrote one of the Confederation's western land ordinances, and supported Pinckney's Treaty of 1795 with Spain, which allowed settlers to export crops via the Mississippi River and the Spanish-held port of New Orleans.

As president, Jefferson pursued policies that made it easier for farm families to acquire land. In 1796, a Federalist-dominated Congress had set the price of land in the national domain to $2 per acre; by 1820, Republican Congresses had cut that to $1.25 an acre. Inspired by Jeffersonian policies, subsequent Congresses reduced the price still further and, in the Homestead Act of 1862, gave farmsteads to settlers for free.

But international events challenged Jefferson's vision of westward expansion. In 1799, Napoleon Bonaparte seized power in France and sought to reestablish a French empire in America. In 1801, he coerced Spain into signing a secret treaty that returned Louisiana to France and restricted American access to New Orleans, violating Pinckney's Treaty. Napoleon also launched an invasion to restore French rule in Haiti (then called Saint-Domingue), once the richest sugar colony in the Americas. Beginning in 1791, a massive slave revolt had convulsed the island. After years of civil war and Spanish and British invasions, black Haitians led by Toussaint L'Ouverture seized control of the sugar-rich country in 1798. Now Napoleon wanted it back.

Napoleon's actions in Haiti and Louisiana prompted Jefferson to question his party's pro-French foreign policy. "The day that France takes possession of New Orleans," the president warned, "we must marry ourselves to the British fleet and nation." Jefferson feared that France might close the Mississippi River to western farmers, so he instructed Robert Livingston, the American minister in Paris, to negotiate the purchase of New Orleans. Simultaneously, Jefferson sent James Monroe to Britain to negotiate an alliance in case of war with France.

Toussaint L'Ouverture, Haitian Revolutionary and Statesman
The American Revolution represented a victory for republicanism; the Haitian revolt represented a triumph of liberty and a demand for racial equality. After leading the black army that ousted French sugar planters and expelled British forces from Haiti, Toussaint formed a constitutional government in 1801. A year later, he negotiated a treaty with French invaders, who were seeking to recapture the island; the treaty halted Haitian resistance in exchange for a promise that the French would not reinstate slavery. Subsequently, the French seized Toussaint and sent him to France, where he died in a prison in 1803. Snark/Art Resource, New York.

Jefferson's diplomacy yielded a magnificent prize: the entire territory of Louisiana. By 1802, the French invasion of Haiti was faltering in the face of disease and determined black resistance, a new war threatened in Europe, and Napoleon feared an American takeover of Louisiana. Acting with characteristic decisiveness, the French ruler offered to sell not just New Orleans but the entire territory of Louisiana for $15 million (about $500 million today). "We have lived long," Livingston remarked to Monroe as they concluded the Louisiana Purchase in 1803, "but this is the noblest work of our lives."

The Louisiana Purchase forced Jefferson to reconsider his strict interpretation of the Constitution. He had long believed that the national government possessed only the powers expressly delegated to it in the Constitution, but there was no constitutional provision for adding new territory. So Jefferson became a pragmatist. Accepting a loose interpretation, he used the treaty-making powers in the Constitution to complete the deal with France.

A scientist as well as a statesman, Jefferson wanted detailed information about the physical features of the new territory, its plant and animal life, and its native peoples. In 1804, he sent his personal secretary, Meriwether Lewis, to explore the region with William Clark, an army officer. Aided by Indian guides, Lewis and Clark and their party of American soldiers and frontiersmen traveled up the Missouri River, across the Rocky Mountains, and—venturing beyond the bounds of the Louisiana Purchase—down the Columbia River to the Pacific Ocean. After two years, they returned with the first maps of the immense wilderness and vivid accounts of its natural resources and inhabitants (Map 7.2).

A stunning accomplishment, the Louisiana Purchase created new problems. Some New England Federalists, fearing that western expansion would hurt their region and party, talked openly of leaving the Union. When Alexander Hamilton rejected their scheme for a northern confederacy, the secessionists recruited Aaron Burr, the ambitious vice president. Hamilton accused Burr of planning to destroy the Union, and the two men fought an illegal pistol duel that ended in Hamilton's death.

This tragedy propelled Burr into another secessionist scheme. When his term as vice president ended in 1805, Burr moved west to avoid prosecution for dueling. There, he conspired with General James Wilkinson, the military governor of the Louisiana Territory, either to seize territory in New Spain or to launch a rebellion to establish Louisiana as a separate nation. But Wilkinson betrayed Burr, arresting the former vice president as he led an armed force down the Ohio River. In a highly politicized trial presided over by Chief Justice John Marshall, the jury acquitted Burr of treason.

The Louisiana Purchase had increased party conflict and generated secessionist schemes in both New England and the Southwest. Such regional differences would continue, challenging Madison's argument in "Federalist No. 10" that a large and diverse republic was more stable than a small one.

▶ Was there anything the Western Indian Confederacy could have done to limit white expansion and preserve Indian lands? Explain your position.

▶ Why did Jefferson support expansion to the West? Why did eastern farm families leave their communities to go west? Were their reasons the same as Jefferson's?

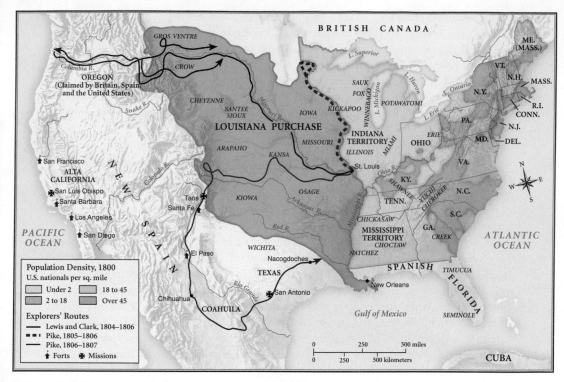

MAP 7.2 U.S. Population Density in 1803 and the Louisiana Purchase

When the United States purchased Louisiana from France in 1803, much of the land between the Appalachian Mountains and the Mississippi River remained in Indian hands: The vast lands west of the Mississippi were virtually unknown, even after the epic explorations of Meriwether Lewis and William Clark and of Zebulon Pike. Still, President Jefferson predicted quite accurately that the vast Mississippi River Valley "from its fertility . . . will ere long yield half of our whole produce, and contain half of our whole population."

The War of 1812 and the Transformation of Politics

Trouble was also brewing in Europe, where war had broken out again in 1802. For the next decade, American politicians tried to safeguard national interests while avoiding war. When this effort finally failed, it sparked dramatic political changes that destroyed the Federalist Party and split the Republicans into National and Jeffersonian factions.

Conflict in the Atlantic and the West

The Napoleonic Wars that ravaged Europe between 1802 and 1815 disrupted American commerce. As Napoleon conquered European countries, he cut off their trade with Britain and seized neutral merchant ships that had stopped there. The British ministry responded with a naval blockade that seized American vessels carrying sugar and molasses from the French West Indies. The British navy also searched American merchant ships for British deserters and used these raids to replenish its crews, a practice known as impressment. Between 1802 and 1811, British naval officers impressed nearly 8,000 sailors, including many American citizens. In 1807, American anger over these seizures turned to outrage when a British warship attacked the U.S. Navy vessel *Chesapeake*, killing three, wounding eighteen, and seizing four alleged deserters. "Never since the battle of Lexington have I seen this country in such a state of exasperation as at present," Jefferson declared.

To protect American interests while avoiding war, Jefferson pursued a policy of peaceful coercion. Working closely with Secretary of State James Madison, he devised the Embargo Act of 1807, which prohibited American ships from leaving their home ports until Britain and France stopped restricting U.S. trade. The embargo was a creative diplomatic measure, probably inspired by the boycotts of the 1760s and 1770s. But it overestimated the reliance of Britain and France on American shipping, and it underestimated the resistance of New England merchants, who feared it would ruin them.

In fact, the embargo weakened the American economy by cutting the gross national product (GNP) by 5 percent. Exports plunged from $108 million in 1806 to $22 million in 1808, hurting farmers as well as merchants. "Would to God," exclaimed one Federalist, "that the Embargo had done as little evil to ourselves as it has done to foreign nations."

Despite popular discontent over the embargo, voters elected Republican James Madison to the presidency in 1808. A powerful advocate for the Constitution, the architect of the Bill of Rights, and a prominent congressman and party leader, Madison had served the nation well. But John Beckley, a loyal Republican, worried that Madison would be "too timid and indecisive as a statesman," and events proved him right. Acknowledging the embargo's failure, Madison replaced it with a series of new economic restrictions, which also failed to persuade Britain or France to respect American interests. "The Devil himself could not tell which government, England or France, is the most wicked," an exasperated congressman declared.

Republican congressmen from the West had no doubt that Britain was the primary offender. They pointed to its continued assistance to the Indians in the Ohio River Valley, a violation of the Treaty of Paris and Jay's Treaty. Bolstered by British guns and supplies, in 1809 the Shawnee war chief Tecumseh [*ta-KUM-sa*] revived the Western Confederacy. His brother, the prophet Tenskwatawa [*tens-QUA-ta-wa*], provided it with a powerful ideology: He urged native peoples to shun Americans, "the children of the Evil Spirit . . . who have taken away your lands"; renounce alcohol; and return to traditional ways. Warriors and wise men from the Kickapoo, Potawatomi, Winnebago, Ottawa, and Chippewa peoples flocked to Tenskwatawa's holy village, Prophetstown, near the juncture of the Tippecanoe and Wabash rivers in the Indiana Territory.

Inspired by the prophet's teachings, Tecumseh mobilized the western Indian peoples for war. William Henry Harrison, the governor of the Indiana territory, decided on a preemptive strike. Taking advantage of Tecumseh's absence in the South (seeking an alliance with the Chickasaws, Choctaws, and Creeks), Harrison mobilized 1,000 troops and militiamen. After trading heavy casualties with the confederacy's warriors at the Battle of Tippecanoe in November 1811, Harrison destroyed Prophetstown.

With Britain assisting Indians in the West and attacking American ships in the Atlantic, Henry Clay of Kentucky, the new Speaker of the House of Representatives, and John C. Calhoun, a rising young congressman from South Carolina, pushed Madison

Tenskwatawa, "The Prophet," 1836
Tenskwatawa added a spiritual dimension to Native American resistance by urging a holy war against the invading whites and by calling for a return to sacred ancestral ways. His dress reflects his teachings: Note the animal skin shirt and the heavily ornamented ears. Tenskwatawa's religious message transcended the cultural differences among Indian peoples and helped his brother, Tecumseh, to create a formidable political and military alliance. Smithsonian American Art Museum, Washington, D.C./Art Resource.

toward war. Like other Republican "war hawks" from the West and South, they wanted to seize territory in British Canada and Spanish Florida. With national elections approaching, Madison issued an ultimatum to Britain. When Britain made no quick response, the president asked Congress for a declaration of war. In June 1812, a sharply divided Senate voted 19 to 13 for war, and the House of Representatives concurred, 79 to 49.

The causes of the War of 1812 have been much debated. Officially, the United States went to war because Britain had violated its neutral rights by seizing merchant ships and sailors. But the Federalists in Congress who represented the merchants voted against the war; and in the election of 1812, New England and the Middle Atlantic states cast their 89 electoral votes for the Federalist presidential candidate, De Witt Clinton of New York. Madison amassed most of his 128 electoral votes in the South and West, where voters and their representatives in Congress strongly supported the war. Many historians therefore argue that the conflict was actually "a western war with eastern labels" (see American Voices, p. 215).

The War of 1812

The War of 1812 was a near disaster for the United States, both militarily and politically. An invasion of British Canada in 1812 quickly ended in a retreat to Detroit. But Americans stayed on the offensive in the West. In 1813, American raiders burned the

Federalists and Republicans Debate "Mr. Madison's War"

The decisions of Lyndon B. Johnson and George W. Bush to pursue wars in Vietnam and Iraq stirred sharp political debates and protests. So too did President James Madison's action in 1812 in leading the nation into war. In 1812, Josiah Quincy and other antiwar Federalist congressmen challenged Madison's justification for the war and the Republicans' proposed military strategy. As the war ended in 1815, Hezekiah Niles, the Republican editor of *Niles's Weekly Register*, came to Madison's defense and blamed New England Federalists for American military reverses.

THE FEDERALIST MANIFESTO: How will war upon the land [an invasion of British Canada] protect commerce upon the ocean? . . .

But it is said that war is demanded by honor. . . . If honor demands a war with England, what opiate lulls that honor to sleep over the wrongs done us by France? On land, robberies, seizures, imprisonments, by French authority; at sea, pillage, sinkings, burnings, under French orders. These are notorious. Are they unfelt because they are French? . . .

There is . . . a headlong rushing into difficulties, with little calculation about the means, and little concern about the consequences. With a navy comparatively [small], we are about to enter into the lists against the greatest marine [power] on the globe. With a commerce unprotected and spread over every ocean, we propose to make a profit by privateering, and for this endanger the wealth of which we are honest proprietors. . . .

What are the United States to gain by this war? . . . Let us not be deceived. A war of invasion [of Canada] may invite a retort of invasion. When we visit the peaceable, and as to us innocent, colonies of Great Britain with the horrors of war, can we be assured that our own coast will not be visited with like horrors?

HEZEKIAH NILES'S REJOINDER: It is universally known that the causes for which

we declared war are no obstruction to peace. The practice of blockade and impressment having ceased by the general pacification of Europe, our government is content to leave the principle as it was. . . .

We have no further business in hostility, than such as is purely defensive; while that of Great Britain is to humble or subdue us. . . .

I did think that in a defensive war — a struggle for all that is valuable — that all parties would have united. But it is not so — every measure calculated to replenish the treasury or raise men is opposed as though it were determined to strike the "star spangled banner" and exalt the bloody cross. Look at the votes and proceedings of congress — and mark the late spirit [to secede from the Union] . . . that existed in Massachusetts, and see with what unity of action every thing has been done [by New England Federalists] to harass and embarrass the government. Our loans have failed; and our soldiers have wanted their pay, because those [New England merchants] who had the greater part of the monied capital covenanted with each other to refuse its aid to the country. . . . History will shock posterity by detailing the length to which they went to bankrupt the republic.

SOURCES: *Annals of Congress*, 12th Cong., 1st sess., vol. 2, cols. 2219–2221; *Niles Weekly Register*, January 28, 1815.

Canadian capital of York (present-day Toronto), Commodore Oliver Hazard Perry defeated a small British flotilla on Lake Erie, and General William Henry Harrison led a new expedition into Canada. There, he defeated a British and Indian force at the Battle of the Thames, taking the life of Tecumseh, now a British general.

Political divisions prevented a major invasion of Canada in the East. New England Federalists opposed the war and prohibited their states' militias from attacking Canada. Boston merchants and banks refused to lend money to the federal government, making the war difficult to finance. In Congress, Daniel Webster, a dynamic young politician from New Hampshire, led Federalist opposition to higher tariffs and to the national conscription of state militiamen.

Gradually, the tide of battle turned in Britain's favor. When the war began, American privateers had quickly captured scores of British merchant vessels, but the Royal Navy soon seized the initiative. By 1813, a flotilla of British warships was harassing American ships and threatening seaports along the Atlantic coast. In 1814, a British fleet sailed up the Chesapeake Bay, and troops stormed ashore and marched north to attack Washington City. In retaliation for the destruction of York, the British burned the U.S. Capitol and government buildings. After two years of fighting, the United States was stalemated along the Canadian frontier and on the defensive in the Atlantic, and its new capital city lay in ruins. The only positive news came from the Southwest. There, a rugged slave-owning planter named Andrew Jackson and a force of Tennessee militiamen defeated the British- and Spanish-supported Creek Indians in the Battle of Horseshoe Bend (1814) and forced the Indians to cede 23 million acres of land (Map 7.3).

American military setbacks strengthened opposition to the war in New England. In 1814, Massachusetts Federalists called for a convention "to lay the foundation for a radical reform in the National Compact." When New England Federalists met in Hartford, Connecticut, some delegates proposed secession, but most wanted to revise the Constitution. To end Virginia's domination of the presidency, the Hartford Convention proposed a constitutional amendment limiting the office to a single four-year term and rotating it among citizens from different states. The convention also suggested amendments restricting commercial embargoes to sixty days and requiring a two-thirds majority in Congress to declare war, prohibit trade, or admit a new state to the Union.

As a minority party in Congress and the nation, the Federalists could prevail only if the war continued to go badly—a very real prospect. Albert Gallatin warned Henry Clay in May 1814 that Britain's triumph over Napoleon in Europe meant that a "well organized and large army is [now] . . . ready together with a super abundant naval force, to act immediately against us." When the British attacked from Canada in the late summer of 1814, only an American naval victory on Lake Champlain averted a British march down the Hudson River Valley. A few months later, thousands of seasoned British troops landed outside New Orleans, threatening American control of the Mississippi River. With the nation politically divided and under military attack from north and south, Gallatin feared that "a continuance of the war might prove vitally fatal to the United States."

Fortunately for the young American republic, by 1815 Britain wanted peace. The twenty-year war with France had sapped its wealth and energy, so it entered into negotiations with the United States in Ghent, Belgium. At first, the American commissioners—John Quincy Adams, Gallatin, and Clay—demanded territory in

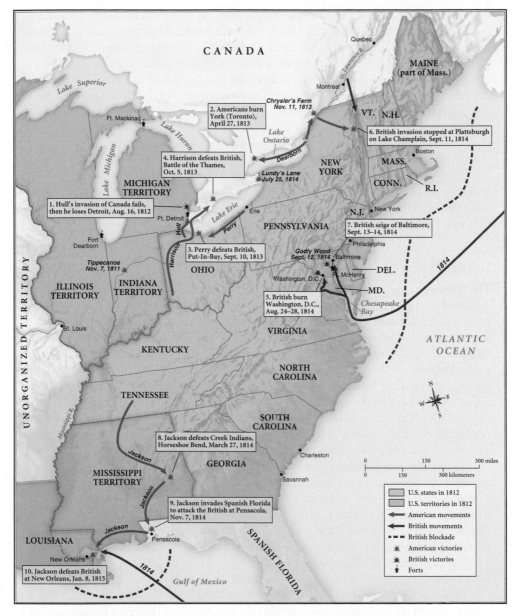

The following text labels appear on the map:

CANADA

Quebec

MAINE
(part of Mass.)

Lake Superior

Montreal

Ft. Mackinac

Lake Huron

Chrysler's Farm
Nov. 11, 1813

VT. N.H.

2. Americans burn York (Toronto), April 27, 1813

Lake Ontario

6. British invasion stopped at Plattsburgh on Lake Champlain, Sept. 11, 1814

Dearborn

Boston

4. Harrison defeats British, Battle of the Thames, Oct. 5, 1813

Lundy's Lane
July 25, 1814

NEW YORK

MASS.

CONN.

R.I.

MICHIGAN TERRITORY

Lake Michigan

Ft. Detroit

Lake Erie

Erie

N.J. New York

1. Hull's invasion of Canada fails, then he loses Detroit, Aug. 16, 1812

Hull

Perry

PENNSYLVANIA

7. British siege of Baltimore, Sept. 13–14, 1814

Fort Dearborn

Tippecanoe
Nov. 7, 1811

Harrison

3. Perry defeats British, Put-In-Bay, Sept. 10, 1813

OHIO

Godly Wood
Sept. 12, 1814 Baltimore

Philadelphia

DEL.

Washington, D.C.

Ft. McHenry

1814

ILLINOIS TERRITORY

INDIANA TERRITORY

5. British burn Washington, D.C., Aug. 24–28, 1814

MD.

Chesapeake Bay

St. Louis

Ohio R.

VIRGINIA

ATLANTIC OCEAN

Mississippi R.

KENTUCKY

NORTH CAROLINA

TENNESSEE

SOUTH CAROLINA

N
W E
S

8. Jackson defeats Creek Indians, Horseshoe Bend, March 27, 1814

Charleston

GEORGIA

| 0 | 150 | 300 miles |
| 0 | 150 | 300 kilometers |

Jackson

MISSISSIPPI TERRITORY

Savannah

Jackson

9. Jackson invades Spanish Florida to attack the British at Pensacola, Nov. 7, 1814

Jackson

LOUISIANA

Pensacola

SPANISH FLORIDA

New Orleans

10. Jackson defeats British at New Orleans, Jan. 8, 1815

1814

Gulf of Mexico

Legend:
- U.S. states in 1812
- U.S. territories in 1812
- ← American movements
- ← British movements
- – – British blockade
- ✳ American victories
- ✴ British victories
- ⚑ Forts

MAP 7.3 The War of 1812

Unlike the War of Independence, the War of 1812 had few large-scale military campaigns. In 1812 and 1813, most of the fighting took place along the Canadian border, as American armies and naval forces attacked British targets with mixed success (#1–4). The British took the offensive in 1814, launching a successful raid on Washington, but their attack on Baltimore failed, and they suffered heavy losses when they invaded the United States along Lake Champlain (#5–7). Near the Gulf of Mexico, American forces moved from one success to another: General Andrew Jackson defeated the pro-British Creek Indians at the Battle of Horseshoe Bend, won a victory in Pensacola, and, in the single major battle of the war, routed an invading British army at New Orleans (#8–10).

Canada and Florida, and British diplomats insisted on an Indian buffer state between the United States and Canada. But both sides quickly realized that these objectives were not worth the cost of prolonged warfare. The Treaty of Ghent, signed on Christmas Eve 1814, retained the prewar borders of the United States.

That result hardly justified three years of warfare, but a final military victory lifted Americans' morale. Before news of the Treaty of Ghent reached the United States, newspaper headlines proclaimed an "ALMOST INCREDIBLE VICTORY!! GLORIOUS NEWS": On January 8, 1815, General Jackson's troops had crushed the British forces attacking New Orleans. Fighting from carefully constructed breastworks, the Americans rained "grapeshot and cannister bombs" on the massed British formations. The British lost 700 men, and 2,000 more were wounded or taken prisoner; just 13 Americans died, and only 58 suffered wounds. The victory made Jackson a national hero, redeemed the nation's battered pride, and undercut the Hartford convention's demands for a significant revision of the Constitution.

The Federalist Legacy

The War of 1812 ushered in a new phase of the Republican political revolution. Before the conflict, Federalists had strongly supported Alexander Hamilton's program of national mercantilism—a funded debt, a central bank, and tariffs—while Jeffersonian Republicans had opposed it. After the war, the Republicans split into two camps. Led by Henry Clay, National Republicans pursued Federalist-like policies. In 1816, Clay pushed legislation through Congress creating a Second Bank of the United States and persuaded President Madison to sign it. The following year, Clay won passage of the Bonus Bill, sponsored by congressman John C. Calhoun of South Carolina, which created a national fund for roads and other internal improvements. Madison vetoed it. Reaffirming traditional Jeffersonian Republican principles, he argued that the national government lacked the constitutional authority to fund internal improvements.

Meanwhile, the Federalist Party was in severe decline. As one Federalist explained, the National Republicans in the eastern states had "destroyed the Federalist party by the adoption of its principles" while the profarmer policies of Jeffersonians maintained the Republican Party's dominance in the South and West. "No Federal character can run with success," Gouverneur Morris of New York lamented, and the election of 1818 proved him right: Republicans outnumbered Federalists 37 to 7 in the Senate and 156 to 27 in the House. Westward expansion and the success of Jefferson's Revolution of 1800 had destroyed the Federalists and shattered the First Party System.

However, the Federalists' nationalist policies lived on because of John Marshall's long tenure on the Supreme Court. Appointed chief justice by President John Adams in January 1801, Marshall had a personality and intellect that allowed him to dominate the Court until 1822 and strongly influence its decisions until his death in 1835. By winning the support of Joseph Story and other National Republican justices, Marshall shaped the evolution of the Constitution.

Three principles informed Marshall's jurisprudence: judicial authority, the supremacy of national laws, and traditional property rights. Marshall claimed the right of judicial review for the Court in *Marbury v. Madison* (1803), but the Supreme Court did not void another law enacted by Congress until the *Dred Scott* decision in 1857 (see Chapter 13). However, the Marshall Court did frequently use the power of review to overturn state laws that, in its judgment, violated the national constitution.

The important case of *McCulloch v. Maryland* (1819) involved one such law. When Congress created the Second Bank of the United States in 1816, it allowed the bank to set up branches in the states, where it competed with state-chartered banks. To enhance the competitiveness of Maryland banks, the state's legislature imposed a tax on notes issued by the Baltimore branch of the Second Bank. The Second Bank claimed that the tax infringed on national powers and was therefore unconstitutional. Lawyers for the state of Maryland replied, using Jefferson's argument, that Congress lacked the constitutional authority to charter a national bank. Even if a national bank was legitimate, the lawyers argued, Maryland could tax its activities within the state.

Marshall and the National Republicans on the Court firmly rejected both arguments. The Second Bank was constitutional, said the chief justice, because it was "necessary and proper," given the national government's control over currency and credit. Like Alexander Hamilton, Marshall was a loose constructionist: If the goal of a law is "within the scope of the Constitution," then "all means which are appropriate" to secure that goal are also constitutional. The chief justice pointed out that "the power to tax involves the power to destroy" and suggested that Maryland's bank tax would render the national government "dependent on the states," an outcome that Marshall claimed was "not intended by the American people" who ratified the Constitution.

The Marshall Court again asserted the dominance of national over state statutes in *Gibbons v. Ogden* (1824). The decision struck down a New York law granting a monopoly to Aaron Ogden for steamboat passenger service across the Hudson River to New Jersey. Asserting that the Constitution gave the federal government authority over interstate commerce, the chief justice sided with Thomas Gibbons, who held a federal license to run steamboats between the two states.

Finally, Marshall used the Constitution to uphold Federalist notions of property rights. During the 1790s, Jefferson Republicans had celebrated "the will of THE PEOPLE," prompting Federalists to worry that popular sovereignty would result in a "tyranny of the majority." Concerned that state legislatures would enact statutes that infringed on the property rights of wealthy citizens, Federalist judges vowed to void such statutes.

Marshall was no exception. Determined to protect individual property rights, he invoked the contract clause of the Constitution to do it. The contract clause (in Article I, Section 10) prohibits the states from passing any law "impairing the obligation of contracts." Economic conservatives at the Philadelphia convention had inserted the clause to prevent states from passing "stay" laws that kept creditors from seizing the lands and goods of debtors. In *Fletcher v. Peck* (1810), Marshall greatly expanded its scope. The Georgia legislature had granted a huge tract of land to the Yazoo Land Company. When a new legislature canceled the grant, alleging fraud and bribery, speculators who had purchased Yazoo lands appealed to the Supreme Court to uphold their titles. Marshall did so by ruling that the legislative grant was a contract that could not be revoked. His decision was controversial and far-reaching. It limited state power, bolstered vested property rights, and, by protecting out-of-state investors, promoted the development of a national capitalist economy.

The Court extended its defense of vested property rights in *Dartmouth College v. Woodward* (1819). Dartmouth College was a private institution established by a royal charter granted by King George III. In 1816, New Hampshire's Republican legislature enacted a statute converting the school into a public university. The Dartmouth trustees opposed the legislation and hired Daniel Webster to plead their case. A renowned constitutional lawyer and a leading Federalist, Webster used the Court's decision in *Fletcher v. Peck* to argue that the royal charter constituted an unalterable contract. The Marshall Court agreed and upheld the claims of the college.

Even as John Marshall incorporated Federalist principles of judicial review, national supremacy, and vested property rights into the American legal system, voting citizens and political leaders embraced the outlook of the Republican Party. The career of John Quincy Adams was a case in point. Although he was the son of Federalist President John Adams, John Quincy Adams joined the Republican Party before the War of 1812. He won national attention negotiating the Treaty of Ghent, which ended the war.

Adams then served brilliantly as secretary of state for two terms under President James Monroe (1817–1825). In 1817, Adams negotiated the Rush-Bagot Treaty, which limited American and British naval forces on the Great Lakes. In 1818, he concluded another agreement with Britain that set the forty-ninth parallel as the border between Canada and the lands of the Louisiana Purchase. Then, in the Adams-Onís Treaty of 1819, Adams persuaded Spain to cede Florida to the United States (Map 7.4). In return, the American government accepted Spain's claim to Texas and agreed on a boundary between New Spain and the state of Louisiana, which had entered the Union in 1812.

Finally, Adams persuaded President Monroe to declare American national policy with respect to the Western Hemisphere. At Adams's behest, Monroe warned Spain and other European powers in 1823 to keep their hands off the newly independent republican nations in Latin America. The American continents were not "subject for further colonization," the president declared—a policy that thirty years later became known as the Monroe Doctrine. In return, Monroe pledged that the United States would not "interfere in the internal concerns" of European nations. Thanks to Adams, the United States had asserted diplomatic leadership of the Western Hemisphere and won international acceptance of its northern and western boundaries.

The appearance of a national consensus after two decades of bitter party politics prompted observers to dub James Monroe's presidency the "Era of Good Feeling." This political harmony was real but transitory. The Republican Party was increasingly split between the National faction, led by Clay and Adams, and the Jeffersonian faction, soon to be led by Martin Van Buren and Andrew Jackson. The two groups differed sharply over federal support for roads and canals and many other issues. As the aging Jefferson complained about the National Republicans, "You see so many of these new republicans maintaining in Congress the rankest doctrines of the old federalists." This division in the ranks of the Republican Party would soon produce a Second Party System, in which national-minded Whigs and

▶ Was the War of 1812 "necessary"? If so, why? If not, why did it occur?

▶ How did the decisions of the Supreme Court between 1801 and 1820 alter the Constitution? How did they change American society?

▶ Explain the rise and fall of the Federalist Party. Why was the Republican triumph so complete?

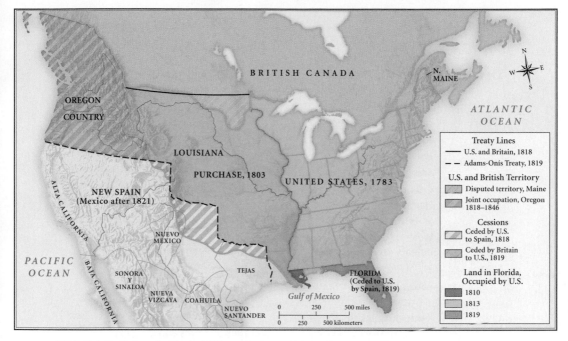

MAP 7.4 Defining the National Boundaries, 1800–1820

After the War of 1812, John Quincy Adams and other American diplomats negotiated treaties with Great Britain and Spain that defined the boundaries between the Louisiana Purchase and British Canada to the north and New Spain (which in 1821 became the independent nation of Mexico) to the south and west. These treaties eliminated the threat of border wars with0 neighboring states, giving the United States a much-needed period of peace and security.

For more help analyzing this map, see the Online Study Guide at **bedfordstmartins.com/henrettaconcise**.

state-focused Democrats would face off against each other (see Chapter 10). By the early 1820s, one cycle of American politics and economic debate had ended, and another was about to begin.

SUMMARY

In this chapter, we have traced three interrelated themes: public policy, westward expansion, and party politics. We began by examining the contrasting public policies advocated by Alexander Hamilton and Thomas Jefferson. A Federalist, Hamilton supported a strong national government and created a fiscal infrastructure (the national debt, tariffs, and a national bank) to spur trade and manufacturing. By contrast, Jefferson wanted to preserve the authority of state governments, and he envisioned an America enriched by farming rather than industry.

The westward movement promoted by Jefferson and his Republican Party sparked new conflicts with the Indian peoples and transformed the agricultural economy by

TIMELINE

1783	▶ Treaty of Paris opens trans-Appalachian West
1784	▶ Iroquois peoples cede lands in New York and Pennsylvania
1787	▶ Northwest Ordinance
1789	▶ Judiciary Act sets up federal courts
	▶ French Revolution begins
1790	▶ Congress approves Hamilton public credit system
1790–1791	▶ Western Confederacy defeats American armies
1791	▶ Bill of Rights ratified
	▶ Bank of the United States chartered
1792	▶ Kentucky joins Union; Tennessee follows (1796)
	▶ French Republic founded
1793	▶ King Louis XVI executed
	▶ Madison and Jefferson create Republican Party
	▶ Washington proclaims neutrality in war between Britain and France
1794	▶ Whiskey Rebellion in western Pennsylvania
	▶ Battle of Fallen Timbers
1795	▶ Jay's Treaty with Great Britain debated
	▶ Pinckney's Treaty with Spain allows U.S. use of Mississippi River
	▶ Treaty of Greenville aids settlement

1798	▶ XYZ Affair sparks conflict with France
	▶ Alien, Sedition, and Naturalization Acts
	▶ Kentucky and Virginia resolutions contest national authority
1800	▶ Jefferson elected president in "Revolution of 1800"
1801	▶ John Marshall becomes chief justice of Supreme Court
1801–1807	▶ Treasury Secretary Gallatin reduces national debt
1802–1807	▶ France and Britain seize American ships
1803	▶ Louisiana Purchase
	▶ Marshall asserts judicial review in *Marbury v. Madison*
1804–1806	▶ Lewis and Clark explore West
1807	▶ Embargo Act cripples American shipping
1809	▶ Tecumseh and Tenskwatawa revive Western Confederacy
1812–1815	▶ War of 1812
1817–1825	▶ Era of Good Feeling
1819	▶ Adams-Onís Treaty annexes Florida and defines Texas boundary
	▶ *McCulloch v. Maryland* increases power of national government
	▶ *Dartmouth College v. Woodward* protects property rights

dramatically increasing the market sale of farm produce. Expansion westward also shaped American diplomatic and military policy, as in the Louisiana Purchase, the War of 1812, and the treaties negotiated by John Quincy Adams.

Finally, there was the unexpected rise of the First Party System. As Hamilton's policies split the political elite, the French Revolution divided Americans into hostile ideological groups. The result was two decades of bitterness over controversial measures: the Federalists' Sedition Act, the Republicans' Embargo Act, and Madison's decision to go to war with Britain. Although the Federalist Party faded away, it left as its enduring legacy Hamilton's financial innovations and John Marshall's constitutional jurisprudence.

Connections: Economy and Society

Before the American Revolution, the northern and southern colonies had distinctly different farming economies: In the North, yeomen families raised grain and livestock; in the South, large scale planters used enslaved laborers to grow tobacco and rice for export. After the Revolution, the northern economy began to diverge in other ways from that of the South. As we noted in the Part Two opening essay:

> Beginning in the 1780s, northern merchants financed a banking system and organized a rural system of manufacturing. . . . Many yeomen farm families . . . turned out raw materials such as leather and wool for burgeoning manufacturing enterprises and made shoes, textiles, tinware, and other handicrafts for market sale.

In Chapter 8, we will explore the creation of a capitalist commonwealth — an increasingly urban, commercial society — in the North. We will show how that society fostered a democratic republican culture that encouraged social mobility for men and new marriage rules and child-rearing practices. In Chapter 8, we also will examine the aristocratic republican culture that remained central to the slave-based society of the South, and we will examine the Missouri crisis of 1819–1821, the first major conflict between these two increasingly distinct societies.

In the part opening, we also noted that many farm families "migrated westward to grow grain." As we will see in Chapter 8, these families were particularly affected by the Second Great Awakening, a religious revival that fundamentally changed American culture.

FOR FURTHER EXPLORATION

James Roger Sharp, *American Politics in the Early Republic* (1993), and Thomas P. Slaughter, *The Whiskey Rebellion* (1986), address the difficulties of the 1790s. Linda Kerber, *No Constitutional Right to Be Ladies: Women and the Obligations of Citizenship* (1999) evaluates the impact of republicanism on women's lives.

Washington's strong leadership is stressed in William Martin's fictionalized biography, *Citizen Washington* (1999). For Washington's correspondence, see **www.virginia .edu/gwpapers/**; for Jefferson's most important writings, go to **http://www.pbs.org/ jefferson/frame5.htm**; and for the impact of the French Revolution, try **chnm.gmu .edu/revolution/**. David McCullough's highly readable biography *John Adams* (2001) draws on the Adams Family Papers (**www.masshist.org/digitaladams/aea/**). For more on Alexander Hamilton, see Ron Chernow's *Alexander Hamilton* (2004) and **www .alexanderhamiltonexhibition.org/**. On the tumultuous election of 1800, read John Ferling, *Adams vs. Jefferson* (2004).

For the explorations of Lewis and Clark, visit **www.pbs.org/lewisandclark** and **www.americanjourneys.org/**. For native peoples' lives in this era, consult Gregory Evans Dowd, *A Spirited Resistance: The North American Indian Struggle for Unity,*

1745–1815 (1992) and Theda Perdue, *Cherokee Women: Gender and Culture Change, 1700–1835* (1998).

Ralph Louis Ketcham's *Presidents Above Party: The First American Presidency, 1789–1829* (1984) probes political ideology, while Donald R. Hickey, *The War of 1812: A Forgotten Conflict* (1989), considers its economic and diplomatic context. Also see "The War of 1812" (**members.tripod.com/~war1812/**).

TEST YOUR KNOWLEDGE

To assess your mastery of the material in this chapter and for Web sites, images, and documents related to this chapter, visit **bedfordstmartins.com/henrettaconcise**.

Creating a Republican Culture

1790–1820

The women, in every free country, have an absolute control of manners: and it is confessed, that in a republic, manners are of equal importance with laws.

— Delaware physician
James Tilton, 1790

B y the 1820s, a sense of optimism pervaded white American society. "The temperate zone of North America already exhibits many signs that it is the promised land of civil liberty, and of institutions designed to liberate and exalt the human race," declared a Kentucky judge in a Fourth of July speech. White Americans had good reason to feel fortunate. They lived under a representative republican government, free from arbitrary taxation and from domination by an established church.

Inspired by their political freedom, these Americans sought to extend republican principles throughout their society. But what *were* those principles? For entrepreneurial-minded merchants, farmers, and political leaders, republicanism meant the advance of **capitalism**: They wanted to use governmental authority to solidify capitalist cultural values and create a dynamic market economy. Using their influence in state legislatures, they secured mercantilist policies that assisted private businesses and, they claimed, enhanced the "common-wealth." Other citizens celebrated republican social values. In the North, they championed democratic republicanism: equality in family and social relationships. In the South, where class and race sharply divided society, politicians and pamphleteers devised an aristocratic republicanism that stressed liberty for whites rather than equality for all. Yet another vision of American republicanism emerged during the massive religious revival that swept the nation between 1790 and 1850. For the many Americans who embraced the Second Great Awakening, the United States was both a great experiment in republican government and an emergent Christian civilization that would redeem the world—a moral mission that, for better or worse, would inform American diplomacy in the centuries to come.

The Capitalist Commonwealth

"If movement and the quick succession of sensations and ideas constitute life," observed a French visitor to the United States, "here one lives a hundred fold more than elsewhere; here, all is circulation, motion, and boiling agitation." Boiling agitation was especially evident in the Northeast, where republican state legislatures actively promoted banking and commerce. "Experiment follows experiment; enterprise follows enterprise," a European traveler noted, and "riches and poverty follow." Of the two, riches were readily apparent. Beginning around 1800, the average per capita income of Americans increased by more than 1 percent a year — more than 30 percent in a single generation.

Banks, Manufacturing, and Markets

America was "a Nation of Merchants," a British visitor reported from Philadelphia in 1798, "keen in the pursuit of wealth in all the various modes of acquiring it." And acquire it they did, making spectacular profits as the wars triggered by the French Revolution (1793–1815) crippled European merchant firms. Fur trader John Jacob Astor and merchant Robert Oliver became the nation's first millionaires. Oliver first worked for an Irish-owned linen firm in Baltimore and then achieved affluence by trading West Indian coffee and sugar. Astor, who migrated from Germany to New York in 1784, became wealthy carrying furs from the Pacific Northwest to markets in China.

To finance such mercantile ventures, Americans needed a banking system. Before the Revolution, farmers relied on government-sponsored land banks for loans, while merchants arranged partnerships or obtained credit from British suppliers. When the War for Independence cut off British credit, Philadelphia merchants persuaded the Confederation Congress to charter the Bank of North America in 1781, and traders in Boston and New York soon founded similar lending institutions. "Our monied capital has so much increased from the Introduction of Banks, & the Circulation of the Funds," Philadelphia merchant William Bingham boasted in 1791, "that the Necessity of Soliciting Credits from England will no longer exist."

That same year, Federalists in Congress chartered the First Bank of the United States to issue notes and make commercial loans. The Bank's profits averaged a handsome 8 percent annually; by 1805, it had branches in eight major cities. However, Jeffersonians claimed the Bank was unconstitutional and oppressive because it created "a consolidated, energetic government supported by public creditors, speculators, and other insidious men lacking in public spirit of any kind." When the bank's twenty-year charter expired in 1811, Jeffersonian Republicans in Congress refused to renew it. To provide credit, merchants, artisans, and farmers persuaded their state legislatures to charter banks. By 1816, when Congress (now run by National Republicans) chartered the Second Bank of the United States, there were 246 state-chartered banks with tens of thousands of stockholders and $68 million in banknotes in circulation. But many of these state banks were shady operations that issued notes without adequate specie reserves and made ill-advised loans to insiders.

Dubious banking policies helped to bring on the financial Panic of 1819. But the most important cause was an abrupt 30 percent drop in world agricultural prices after

The China Trade
After the Revolution, New England merchants took an active role in the long-standing European trade with China. In this painting by George Chinnery (1774–1852), the American flag flies prominently in front of the warehouse district in Canton. There, merchants exchanged bundles of American furs for cargoes of Chinese silks and porcelain plates, cups, and serving dishes. Bridgeman Art Library Ltd.

the Napoleonic Wars. In Charleston, South Carolina, between 1818 and 1819, the sale price for a pound of cotton fell from 34 cents to 15 cents. As their income plummeted, planters and farmers could not pay their debts to storekeepers, wholesale merchants, and banks, sending those businesses into bankruptcy. Many state banks went bust; those that were still solvent in 1821 had just $45 million in circulation. The panic gave Americans their first taste of a **business cycle**, the periodic expansion and contraction of production and employment inherent in an unregulated market economy.

The Panic of 1819 revealed that artisans and yeomen as well as merchants now depended for their prosperity on the market economy. Before 1800, many New England artisans worked part time and sold their handicrafts locally. In central Massachusetts, a French traveler found many houses "inhabited by men who are both cultivators and artisans." In the Middle Atlantic region, artisans bartered products with neighbors. Clockmaker John Hoff of Lancaster, Pennsylvania, exchanged his fine, wooden-cased instruments for a dining table, a bedstead, and labor on his small farm. By 1820, many artisans—shipbuilders in seacoast towns, ironworkers in Pennsylvania and

The Yankee Peddler, c. 1830
Even in 1830, most Americans lived too far from a market town to go there regularly to buy goods.
Instead, they purchased tinware, clocks, textiles, and other manufactured goods from peddlers, often
from New England, who traveled far and wide in small horse-drawn vans like the one pictured in the
doorway. Courtesy, IBM Corporation, Armonk, New York.
For more help analyzing this image, see the Online Study Guide at **bedfordstmartins.com/henrettaconcise**.

Maryland, and shoemakers in Massachusetts—had expanded their output and were
selling their products throughout the nation.

American entrepreneurs encouraged this expansion by developing rural manufacturing networks like those in Europe (see Chapter 1). Enterprising merchants bought raw
materials, hired workers in farm families to process them, and sold the finished manufactures in regional or national markets. "Straw hats and Bonnets are manufactured by many
families," an official in Maine noted in the 1810s. Merchants shipped these products—
shoes, brooms, and palm-leaf hats as well as cups, baking pans, and other tin utensils—to
seaport cities. New England peddlers carried them to the rural South, where the peddlers
earned the dubious reputation of being hard-bargaining "Yankees."

This business expansion stemmed primarily from innovations in organizing production and in marketing; new technology played only a minor role. During the 1780s,
New England and Middle Atlantic merchants had built small mills to power machines
that combed wool—and later cotton—into long strands. But until the 1820s, they used
the household-based outwork system for the next steps in the textile manufacturing
process: Farm women and children spun the strands into thread and yarn on foot-driven
spinning wheels, and men in other households used foot-powered looms to weave the

yarn into cloth. In 1820, more than 12,000 household workers labored full-time weaving woolen cloth, which was then pounded flat and given a smooth finish in water-powered fulling mills. This mixed system of mill and outwork production soon gave way to fully mechanized factories; the number of water-driven cotton spindles soared from 8,000 in 1809 to 333,000 in 1817.

The expansion of manufacturing offered new opportunities—and new risks—to farmers. Ambitious farm families switched from growing crops for subsistence to raising livestock for sale. They sold meat, butter, and cheese to city markets and cattle hides to the booming shoe industry. "Along the whole road from Boston, we saw women engaged in making cheese," a Polish traveler reported from central Massachusetts. Other farm families raised sheep and sold raw wool to textile manufacturers. Processing these raw materials invigorated many farming towns. In 1792, Concord, Massachusetts, had one slaughterhouse and five small tanneries; a decade later, the town boasted eleven slaughterhouses and six large tanneries.

As the rural economy churned out more goods, it significantly altered the environment. Foul odors from stockyards and tanning pits wafted over Concord and many other leather-producing towns. To secure hemlock bark to process stiff hides into pliable leather, tanners cut down thousands of acres of trees each year. Huge herds of livestock—dairy cows, cattle, and especially sheep—brought the destruction of even more trees, felled to create vast pastures and meadows. By 1850, most of the forests in southern New England and eastern New York were gone: "The hills had been stripped of their timber," New York's *Catskill Messenger* reported, "so as to present their huge, rocky projections." Scores of textile milldams dotted New England's rivers, altering their flow and preventing fish from reaching upriver spawning grounds. Even as the income of many farmers rose, the quality of their natural environment deteriorated.

In the new capitalist-run market economy rural parents and their children worked longer and harder. They made yarn, hats, and brooms during the winter and then turned to their regular farming chores during the warmer seasons. More important, these farm families now depended on the income from wage labor and market sales to purchase the textiles, shoes, and hats they had once made for themselves. The new productive system made families and communities more efficient and prosperous—and more dependent on a market they could not control.

Transportation Bottlenecks and Government Initiatives

America's very size threatened to limit its economic growth. Water transport was the quickest and cheapest way to get goods to market, but many new settlements were not near navigable streams. Consequently, improved overland trade became a high priority. Between 1793 and 1812, the Massachusetts legislature granted charters to more than one hundred private turnpike companies. These charters gave the companies special legal status and often included monopoly rights to a transportation route. Pennsylvania issued fifty-five charters, including one to the Lancaster Turnpike Company. The company quickly built a graded gravel road between Lancaster and Philadelphia, a distance of 65 miles. This venture was expensive and yielded only modest profits but gave an enormous boost to the regional economy. Although turnpike investors received about "three percent annually," Henry Clay estimated, society as a whole "actually reap[ed] fifteen or twenty per cent." A farm woman knew what Clay meant: "The turnpike is finished and we can now go to town at all times and in all weather." A boom in turnpike construction soon connected dozens of inland market centers to seaport cities.

Meanwhile, state governments and private entrepreneurs improved water transport. They dredged shallow rivers to make them navigable and constructed canals to bypass waterfalls or rapids. But settlers in the rapidly growing states of Kentucky and Tennessee and in the southern regions of Ohio, Indiana, and Illinois relied on the great Ohio and Mississippi rivers and their tributaries to market their goods. These settlers paid premium prices for farmland near the rivers, and speculators bought up property in the cities along their banks: Cincinnati, Louisville, Chattanooga, and St. Louis. Farmers and merchants built barges to carry cotton, surplus grain, and meat downstream to New Orleans, which by 1815 was handling about $5 million in agricultural products yearly.

Public Policy: The Commonwealth System

Legislative support for road and canal companies reflected the ideology of mercantilism: government-assisted economic development. Just as the British Parliament had used the Navigation Acts to spur prosperity, so American state legislatures passed measures that their members thought would be "of great public utility" and increase the "common wealth." These laws generally took the form of special charters that bestowed valuable legal privileges. For example, most transportation charters included the valuable power of eminent domain, which allowed turnpike, bridge, and canal corporations to force the sale of privately owned land along their routes. State legislatures aided capitalist flour millers and textile manufacturers, who flooded adjacent farmland when they constructed dams to power their water-driven machinery. In Massachusetts, the Mill Dam Act of 1795, deprived farmers of their traditional right under common law to stop the flooding and forced the farmers to accept "fair compensation" for their lost acreage.

Critics condemned these grants to private enterprises as "Scheme[s] of an evident antirepublican tendency," as some "freeholder citizens" in Putney, Vermont, put it. The award of "peculiar privileges" to corporations, they argued, not only violated the "equal rights" of all citizens but also infringed on the sovereignty of the people. As a Pennsylvanian explained, "Whatever power is given to a corporation, is just so much power taken from the State" and its citizens. Nonetheless, judges in state courts, following the lead of John Marshall's Supreme Court (see Chapter 7), consistently upheld corporate charters and grants of eminent domain to private transportation companies. "The opening of good and easy internal communications is one of the highest duties of government," declared a New Jersey judge.

State mercantilism soon encompassed much more than transportation. Following Jefferson's embargo of 1807, which cut off goods and credit from Europe, the New England states awarded charters to two hundred iron-mining, textile-manufacturing, and banking companies, and Pennsylvania granted more than eleven hundred. By 1820, innovative state governments had created a republican political economy: a Commonwealth

► How did promoters of mercantilism (the Commonwealth System) use state and national governments to promote economic growth?

► Why did many Americans believe that the grant of special privileges and charters to private businesses violated republican principles?

System that funneled state aid to private businesses whose projects would improve the general welfare.

Toward a Democratic Republican Culture

After independence, many Americans in the northern states embraced a democratic republicanism that celebrated political equality and social mobility. These citizens, primarily members of the emerging **middle class**, redefined the nature of the family and of education by seeking more egalitarian marriages and more affectionate ways of rearing their children.

Social and Political Equality — for White Men

Between 1780 and 1820, hundreds of well-educated Europeans visitors agreed, almost unanimously, that the American republic embodied a genuinely new social order. In his famous *Letters from an American Farmer* (1782), French-born essayist J. Hector St. Jean de Crèvecoeur wrote that European society was composed "of great lords who possess everything, and of a herd of people who have nothing." The United States, by contrast, had "no aristocratical families, no courts, no kings, no bishops."

The absence of a hereditary aristocracy encouraged Americans to condemn inherited social privilege and to extol legal equality for all free men. "The law is the same for everyone" here, noted one European traveler. Yet Americans willingly accepted social divisions that reflected personal achievement. As individuals used their "talents, integrity, and virtue" to amass wealth, their social standing rose — a phenomenon that astounded many Europeans. "In Europe to say of someone that he rose from nothing is a disgrace and a reproach," remarked an aristocratic Polish visitor. "It is the opposite here. To be the architect of your own fortune is honorable. It is the highest recommendation."

Some Americans from long-distinguished families felt threatened by the nouveau riche and their ideology of wealth-driven social mobility. "Man is estimated by dollars," complained Nathaniel Booth, whose family had once dominated the small Hudson River port town of Kingston, New York, "what he is worth determines his character and his position." However, for most white men, such a merit-based system meant the opportunity to better themselves (Map 8.1).

Old cultural rules — and new laws — denied that opportunity to most women and African American men. When women and free blacks invoked the republican doctrine of equality and asked for voting rights, male legislators wrote explicit race and gender restrictions into the law. In 1802, Ohio disfranchised African Americans, and the New York constitution of 1821 imposed a property-holding requirement on black voters. A striking case of sexual discrimination occurred in New Jersey, where the state constitution of 1776 had granted **suffrage** to all property holders. After 1800, as Federalists and Republicans competed for power, they ignored customary gender rules and encouraged property-owning single women and widows to vote. Sensing a threat to the male-dominated political world, in 1807 the New Jersey legislature limited voting rights to white men only. To justify the exclusion of women, legislators invoked both biology and custom: "Women, generally, are neither by nature, nor habit, nor

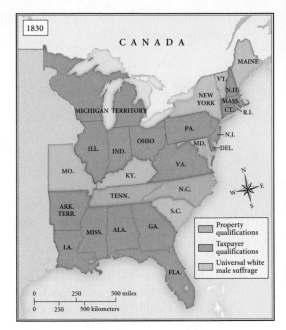

MAP 8.1 The Expansion of Voting Rights for White Men, 1800 and 1830
Between 1800 and 1830, the United States moved steadily toward political equality for white men. Many existing states revised their constitutions and replaced a property qualification for voting with a less-restrictive criterion (the voter must pay taxes or have served in the militia). Some new states in the West extended the suffrage to all adult white men. As parties sought votes from a broader electorate, the tone of politics became more open and competitive, swayed by the interests and values of ordinary people.

education, nor by their necessary condition in society fitted to perform this duty with credit to themselves or advantage to the public."

Toward a Republican System of Marriage

The controversy over women's political rights mirrored a debate over authority within the household. British and American husbands had long claimed patriarchal power and had firm legal control of the family's property. But as John Adams lamented in 1776, the republican doctrine of political equality had "spread where it was not intended," encouraging some white women to speak out on politics and to demand legal and financial rights. These women insisted that their subordinate social position violated the republican principle of equal natural rights. Patriarchy was not a "natural" rule but a social contrivance, argued Patriot author and historian Mercy Otis Warren, and could be justified only "for the sake of order in families."

Economic and cultural changes also eroded customary paternal authority. In colonial America, most property-owning parents had arranged their children's marriages to protect welfare of the entire family. They looked for a son- or daughter-in-law with proper moral values and sufficient financial resources; the physical attraction and emotional compatibility between the young people were secondary considerations.

***The Wedding,* 1805**
Bride and groom stare intently into each other's eyes as they exchange vows, suggesting that their union was a love match, not a marriage based on economic calculation. Given the plain costumes of the guests and the sparse furnishings of the room, the unknown artist may have provided a picture of a rural Quaker wedding. Philadelphia Museum of the Fine Arts.

However, as land holdings shrank in long-settled rural communities, many yeomen fathers lacked farms to leave to their children and lost control over the choice of the children's spouses. Young men and women chose their own partners, influenced by a new cultural attitude: **sentimentalism**.

Sentimentalism originated in Europe as part of the Romantic movement and, after 1800, spread quickly through all classes of American society. Rejecting the Enlightenment's emphasis on rational thought, sentimentalism celebrated the importance of "feeling"—a physical, sensuous appreciation of God, nature, and other human beings. This new sensibility soon permeated the pages of German and English literary works, fell from the lips of actors in popular theatrical melodramas, and infused the emotional rhetoric of revivalist preachers.

As the hot sentimental passions of the heart overwhelmed the cool rational logic of the mind, a new marriage system appeared. Magazines praised marriages "contracted from motives of affection, rather than of interest," and many young people looked for a spouse who was, as Eliza Southgate of Maine put it, "calculated to promote my happiness." As young people "fell in love" and married, many fathers saw their roles change from authoritarian patriarchs to watchful paternalists, from dictating their children's behavior to protecting the children from the consequences of their own actions. To guard against a free-spending son-in-law, a wealthy father often placed his daughter's inheritance in a legal trust, where her husband could not get at it. Wrote one Virginia planter to his lawyer: "I rely on you to see the property settlement properly drawn before the marriage, for I by no means consent that Polly shall be left to the Vicissitudes of Life."

As voluntary agreements between individuals, love marriages conformed more closely to republican principles than did arranged matches. In theory, such **companionate marriages** gave wives "true equality, both of rank and fortune" with their husbands, as one Boston man suggested. In practice, though, husbands continued to dominate most marriages, both because male authority was deeply ingrained in cultural mores and because under American common law, husbands controlled the family's property. Moreover, the new love-based marriage system discouraged parents from protecting the interests of young wives, and governments refused to prevent domestic tyranny. As one lawyer noted, women who would rather "starve than submit" to the orders of their husbands were left to their fate. The marriage contract "is so much more important in its consequences to females than to males," a young man at the Litchfield Law School in Connecticut astutely observed in 1820, "for besides leaving everything else to unite themselves to one man, they subject themselves to his authority. He is their all — their only relative — their only hope" (see American Voices, p. 235).

Young adults who chose partners unwisely were severely disappointed when their spouses failed as providers or faithful companions. Before 1800, little could be done; officials granted divorces only in cases of neglect, abandonment, or adultery — serious offenses against the moral order of society. After 1800, most divorce petitions cited emotional, not moral, grounds. One woman complained that her husband had "ceased to cherish her," while a man grieved that his wife had "almost broke his heart." Responding to changing cultural values, several states expanded the legal grounds for divorce to include drunkenness and personal cruelty.

Republican Motherhood

Traditionally, American women spent most of their active adult years bearing and nurturing children. But by the 1790s, the birthrate in the northern seaboard states was dropping dramatically. In the farming village of Sturbridge in central Massachusetts, women who had married before 1750 usually had eight or nine children; in contrast, women who married around 1810 had an average of six children. In the growing seaport cities, native-born white women bore an average of only four children.

The United States was among the first countries in the world to experience this sharp decline in the birthrate — what historians call the demographic transition. There were several causes. Beginning in the 1790s, thousands of young men migrated to the trans-Appalachian West, which increased the number of never-married women in the East and delayed marriage for many more. Women who married later had fewer children. In addition, thousands of white couples in the urban middle classes deliberately limited the size of their families. Fathers favored smaller families so that they could leave their children an adequate inheritance; mothers, influenced by new ideas of individualism and self-achievement, did not want to spend their entire adulthood rearing children. After having four or five children, these couples used birth control or abstained from sexual intercourse.

Women's lives also changed because of new currents in Christian social thought. Traditionally, many religious writers had suggested that women were morally inferior

Female Submission in Marriage CAROLINE HOWARD GILMAN

The ideal American marriage of the early nineteenth century was republican (a contract between equals) and romantic (a match in which mutual love was foremost). Were these ideals attainable, given the social authority of men and the volatility of human passions? In the following excerpt from *Recollections of a Southern Matron* (1838), novelist Caroline Howard Gilman ponders such issues of domestic life. Caroline Howard was born in Boston in 1794 and moved to Charleston, South Carolina, with her husband, Samuel Gilman, a Unitarian minister.

The planter's bride, who leaves a numerous and cheerful family in her paternal home, little imagines the change which awaits her in her own retired residence. She dreams of an independent sway over her household, devoted love and unbroken intercourse with her husband, and indeed longs to be released from the eyes of others, that she may dwell only beneath the sunbeam of his. And so it was with me. After our bustling wedding and protracted journey, I looked forward to the retirement at Bellevue as a quiet port in which I should rest with Arthur. . . . The romance of our love was still in its glow, as might be inferred by the infallible sign of his springing to pick up my pocket-handkerchief whenever it fell. . . .

There we were together, asking for nothing but each other's presence and love. At length it was necessary for him to tear himself away to superintend his interests. . . . But the period of absence was gradually protracted; then a friend sometimes came home with him, and their talk was of crops and politics, draining the fields and draining the revenue. . . . A growing discomfort began to work upon my mind. I had undefined forebodings; I mused about past days . . . my physical powers enfeebled; a nervous excitement followed: I nursed a moody discontent, and ceased a while to reason clearly.

Woe to me had I yielded to this irritable temperament! . . . [Instead,] I was careful to consult my husband in those points which interested him, without annoying him with mere trifles. If the reign of romance was really waning, I resolved not to chill his noble confidence, but to make a steadier light rise on his affections. . . .

This task of self-government was not easy. To repress a harsh answer, to confess a fault and to stop (right or wrong) in the midst of self-defence, in gentle submission, sometimes requires a struggle like life and death; but these *three* efforts are the golden threads with which domestic happiness is woven. . . .

Men are not often unreasonable; their difficulties lie in not understanding the moral and physical structure of our sex. They often wound through ignorance, and are surprised at having offended. How clear is it, then, that woman loses by petulance and recrimination! Her first study must be self-control, almost to hypocrisy. A good wife must smile amid a thousand perplexities. . . .

Nor in these remarks would I chill the romance of some young dreamer, who is reposing her heart on another. Let her dream on . . . but let her be careful.

SOURCE: Anya Jabour, ed., *Major Problems in the History of American Families and Children* (Boston: Houghton Mifflin, 2005), 109–110.

to men and that many women were sexual temptresses. But by 1800, Protestant ministers were blaming men for sexual and social misconduct and claiming that modesty
and purity were part of women's nature. Soon political leaders echoed that thinking.
In his *Thoughts on Female Education* (1787), Philadelphia physician Benjamin Rush
argued that a young woman should receive intellectual training so that she would be
"an agreeable companion for a sensible man" and ensure her husband's "perseverance
in the paths of rectitude." Rush also called for loyal "republican mothers" who would
instruct "their sons in the principles of liberty and government."

Christian ministers readily embraced the idea of **republican motherhood**. "Preserving virtue and instructing the young are not the fancied, but the real 'Rights of
Women,'" Reverend Thomas Bernard told the Female Charitable Society of Salem,
Massachusetts. He urged his audience to dismiss the public roles for women, such as
voting or serving on juries, that English feminist Mary Wollstonecraft had advocated
in *A Vindication of the Rights of Woman* (1792). Instead, women should care for their
children, a responsibility that gave them "an extensive power over the fortunes of man
in every generation."

Raising and Educating Republican Children

Republican values also changed assumptions about inheritance and child rearing.
Under English common law, when a father died without a will, his property passed to
his eldest son, a practice known as primogeniture (see Chapter 1). After the Revolution, most state legislatures enacted statutes that required that such estates be divided
equally among all the offspring. Most American parents applauded these statutes
because they already treated their children equally and respectfully.

Indeed, many European visitors believed that republican parents gave their children too much respect and freedom. Because of the "general ideas of Liberty and
Equality engraved on their hearts," a Polish aristocrat suggested around 1800, American children had "scant respect" for their parents. Several decades later, a British
traveler stood dumbfounded as an American father excused his son's "resolute disobedience" with a smile and the remark "A sturdy republican, sir." The traveler
guessed that American parents encouraged such independence to help the young
people "go their own way" in the world.

Permissive child rearing was not universal. Foreign visitors interacted primarily
with well-to-do Americans, who were mostly members of Episcopal or Presbyterian
churches. Such parents often followed the teachings of rationalist religious writers
influenced by John Locke and other Enlightenment thinkers. According to these
authors, children were "rational creatures" who should be encouraged to act appropriately by means of advice and praise. The parents' role was to develop their child's
conscience and self-discipline so that the child would act responsibly. This rationalist
method of child rearing was widely adopted by families in the rapidly expanding middle class.

By contrast, many yeomen and tenant farmers, influenced by the Second Great
Awakening, raised their children with authoritarian methods. Evangelical Baptist and
Methodist writers insisted that children were "full of the stains and pollution of sin"
and needed strict rules and harsh discipline. Fear was a "useful and necessary principle

in family government," John Abbott, a minister, advised parents; a child "should sub-mit to your authority, not to your arguments or persuasions." Abbott told parents to instill humility in children and to teach them to subordinate their personal desires to God's will.

The values transmitted within families were crucial because most education still took place within the household. In the 1790s, Bostonian Caleb Bingham, an influential textbook author, called for "an equal distribution of knowledge to make us emphatically a 'republic of letters.'" Both Thomas Jefferson and Benjamin Rush proposed ambitious schemes for a comprehensive system of primary and secondary schooling, followed by college for bright young men. They also envisioned a university in which distinguished scholars would lecture on law, medicine, theology, and political economy.

To ordinary citizens, whose teenage children had to work, talk of secondary and college education smacked of elitism. Farmers, artisans, and laborers wanted elemen-tary schools that would instruct their children in the "three Rs": reading, 'riting, and 'rithmetic. In New England, locally funded public schools offered most boys and some girls such basic instruction in reading and writing. However, in other regions, there were few publicly funded schools, and only 25 percent of the boys and perhaps 10 percent of the girls attended private institutions or had personal tutors. Even in New England, only a small percentage of young men and almost no young women went on to grammar school (high school), and fewer than 1 percent of men attended college. "Let anybody show what advantage the poor man receives from colleges," an anony-mous "Old Soldier" wrote to the *Maryland Gazette*. "Why should they support them, unless it is to serve those who are in affluent circumstances, whose children can be spared from labor, and receive the benefits?"

Although many state constitutions encouraged support for education, few legislatures acted on this issue until the 1820s. Then a new generation of reformers, primarily merchants and manufacturers, successfully campaigned to raise educational standards by certifying qualified teachers and appointing statewide superinten-dents of schools. To encourage self-discipline and individual enterprise in students, the reformers chose textbooks such as *The Life of George Washington* (c. 1800). Its author, Parson Mason Weems, used Washington's life to praise honesty and hard work and to condemn gambling, drinking, and laziness. Believing that patriotic instruction would foster shared cultural ideals, reformers required the study of American history. Thomas Low recalled his days as a New Hampshire schoolboy: "We were taught every day and in every way that ours was the freest, the happiest, and soon to be the greatest and most powerful country of the world."

Like Caleb Bingham, writer Noah Webster believed that education should raise the intellectual skills of his fellow citizens. Asserting that "America must be as inde-pendent in *literature* as she is in politics," he called on his fellow citizens to free themselves "from the dependence on foreign opinions and manners, which is fatal to the efforts of genius in this country." Webster's *Dissertation on the English Lan-guage* (1789) helpfully defined words according to American usage. With less suc-cess, it proposed that words be spelled as they were pronounced, that *labour* (British spelling), for example, be spelled *labur*. Still, Webster's famous "blue-back speller," a compact textbook first published in 1783, sold 60 million copies over the next half-century and served the needs of Americans of all backgrounds. "None of us was 'lowed to see a book," an enslaved African American recalled, "but we gits hold of that Webster's old blue-back speller and we . . . studies [it]."

Despite Webster's efforts, a republican literary culture was slow to develop. Ironically, the most accomplished and successful writer in the new republic was Washington Irving, an elitist-minded Federalist. His essays and histories, including *Salmagundi* (1807) and *Dietrich Knickerbocker's History of New York* (1809), which told the tales of "Rip Van Winkle" and "The Legend of Sleepy Hollow," sold well in America and won praise abroad. Impatient with the slow pace of American literary development, Irving lived for seventeen years in Europe, reveling in its aristocratic culture and intense intellectual life.

Apart from Irving, no American author was well known in Europe or, indeed, in the United States. "Literature is not yet a distinct profession with us," Thomas Jefferson told an English friend. "Now and then a strong mind arises, and at its intervals from business emits a flash of light. But the first object of young societies is bread and covering." Not until the 1830s and 1840s would American authors achieve a professional identity and, in the works of Ralph Waldo Emerson and novelists of the **American Renaissance**, make a significant contribution to Western literature (see Chapter 11).

▶ Did American culture become more democratic — for men, women, and African Americans — in the early nineteenth century? If so, how? If not, why not?

▶ How did republican ideas shape parent-child and marriage relationships and expectations?

Aristocratic Republicanism and Slavery

Republicanism in the South differed significantly from that in the North. Enslaved Africans constituted one-third of the South's population and exposed an enormous contradiction in white Americans' ideology of freedom and equality. "How is it that we hear the loudest yelps for liberty among the drivers of Negroes?" British author Samuel Johnson had chided the American rebels in 1775, a point some Patriots took to heart. "I wish most sincerely there was not a Slave in the province," Abigail Adams confessed to her husband, John. "It always appeared a most iniquitous Scheme to me — to fight ourselves for what we are daily robbing and plundering from those who have as good a right to freedom as we have."

The Revolution and Slavery, 1776–1800

In fact, the whites' struggle for independence raised the prospect of freedom for blacks. As the war began, a black preacher in Georgia told his fellow slaves that King George III "came up with the Book [the Bible], and was about to alter the World, and set the Negroes free." Similar rumors, probably prompted by Governor Dunmore's proclamation of 1775 (see Chapter 5), circulated among slaves in Virginia and the Carolinas, prompting thousands of African Americans to flee behind British lines. Two neighbors of Richard Henry Lee, a Virginia Patriot, lost "every slave they had in the world," as did many other planters. In 1781, when the British army evacuated Charleston, more than 6,000 former slaves went with them; another 4,000 left from Savannah. All told, 30,000

Captain Absalom Boston
Absalom Boston was born in 1785 on the island of Nantucket, Massachusetts, the heart of America's whaling industry. A member of a community of free African American whalers who had been manumitted by their Quaker owners, Boston went to sea at age fifteen. By the age of thirty, he had used his earnings to become the proprietor of a public inn. In 1822, Boston became the first black master with an all-black crew to undertake a whaling voyage from Nantucket. Later, he served as a trustee of the island's African School. Nantucket Historical Association.

blacks may have fled their owners. Hundreds of freed black Loyalists settled permanently in Canada. More than 1,000 others, poorly treated by British officials in Nova Scotia, sought a better life in Sierra Leone, West Africa, a settlement established by English antislavery organizations.

Yet thousands of African Americans supported the Patriot cause. Eager to raise their social status, free blacks in New England volunteered for military service in the First Rhode Island Company and the Massachusetts "Bucks." In Maryland, a significant number of slaves took up arms for the rebels in return for the promise of freedom. Enslaved Virginians struck informal bargains with their Patriot owners, trading loyalty in wartime for the hope of liberty. In 1782, the Virginia assembly passed a **manumission** act, which allowed individual owners to free their slaves; within a decade, planters had released 10,000 slaves.

Quakers took the lead in condemning slavery. Beginning in the 1750s, Quaker evangelist John Woolman urged Friends to free their slaves, and many did so. Rapidly growing evangelical Christian churches, notably the Methodists and the Baptists, initially advocated emancipation and admitted both enslaved and free blacks to their congregations. In 1784, a conference of Virginia Methodists declared that slavery was "contrary to the Golden Law of God on which hang all the Law and Prophets."

Enlightenment philosophy challenged the widespread belief among whites that Africans were inherently inferior to Europeans. John Locke had argued that ideas were not innate but stemmed from a person's experiences in the world. Accordingly, Enlightenment-influenced Americans suggested that the debased condition of blacks reflected their oppressive captivity: "A state of slavery has a mighty tendency to shrink and contract the minds of men." Defying popular opinion, Quaker philanthropist Anthony Benezet declared that African Americans were "as capable of improvement as White People" and funded a Philadelphia school for their education.

These religious and intellectual currents encouraged legal change. In 1784, judicial rulings abolished slavery in Massachusetts; over the next twenty years, every state north of Delaware enacted gradual emancipation legislation. These laws recognized white property rights by requiring slaves to buy their freedom by years—even decades—of additional labor. For example, the New York Emancipation Act of 1799 allowed slavery to continue until 1828 and freed slave children only at the age of twenty-five. As late as 1810, almost 30,000 blacks in the northern states—nearly one-fourth of the African Americans living there—were still enslaved. White opposition to black freedom and equality reflected fears of job competition and racial melding. Even as Massachusetts ended slavery in the state, the legislature reenacted an old law that prohibited whites from marrying blacks, mulattos, or Indians.

The tension in American republican ideology between liberty and property rights was greatest in the South, where enslaved African Americans represented a huge financial investment. Some Chesapeake tobacco planters, moved by religious principles or an oversupply of workers, allowed blacks to buy their freedom through paid work as artisans or laborers. Manumission and self-purchase gradually brought freedom to one-third of the African American residents of Maryland. The Virginia legislature, which had opened the door to manumission in 1782, shut it a decade later. Following the lead of Thomas Jefferson, who owned more than one hundred slaves, the legislators now argued that slavery was a "necessary evil" required to maintain white supremacy and the luxurious planter lifestyle. Resistance to black freedom was even greater in North Carolina, where the legislature condemned Quaker manumissions as "highly criminal and reprehensible." The slave-hungry rice- and cotton-growing states of South Carolina and Georgia totally rejected emancipation. Between 1790 and 1808, merchants and planters in the Lower South imported about 115,000 Africans—nearly half the number introduced into Britain's mainland settlements during the entire colonial period.

The debate over emancipation among Chesapeake whites ended in 1800, when Virginia authorities thwarted an uprising planned by Gabriel Prosser, an enslaved artisan, and hanged him and thirty of his followers. "Liberty and equality have brought the evil upon us," a letter to the *Virginia Herald* proclaimed, denouncing such doctrines as "dangerous and extremely wicked." To preserve their privileged social position, southern whites redefined republicanism: Its principles of individual liberty and legal equality applied only to members of the "master race," creating what historians call a *herrenvolk* (master people) republic.

The North and South Grow Apart

European visitors to the United States agreed that the South formed a distinct society, and many questioned its character. New England was home to religious "fanaticism," according to a British observer, but "the lower orders of citizens" there had "a better education, are more intelligent, and better informed" than those he met in the South. "The state of poverty in which a great number of white people live in Virginia" surprised the Marquis de Chastellux. Other visitors to the South commented on the rude manners, heavy drinking, and weak work ethic of its residents. White tenants and smallholding farmers seemed only to have a "passion for gaming at the billiard table, a cock-fight or cards," and many planters squandered their wealth on extravagant lifestyles while their slaves endured bitter poverty.

Some southerners worried that human bondage corrupted their society by encouraging ignorance and poverty among whites as well as blacks. A South Carolina merchant observed, "Where there are Negroes a White Man despises to work, saying what, will you have me a Slave and work like a Negroe?" Meanwhile, wealthy planters wanted a compliant labor force that was content with the drudgery of agricultural work. Consequently, they trained many of their slaves as field hands, allowing only a few to learn the arts of the blacksmith, carpenter, or bricklayer. Able to hire tutors for their own children, planters did little to provide ordinary whites with elementary schooling. In 1800, the political leaders of Essex County, Virginia, spent about 25 cents per person for local government, including schools, while their counterparts in Acton, Massachusetts, allocated about $1 per person. This difference in support for education mattered: By the 1820s, nearly all native-born men and women in New England could read and write; more than one-third of white southerners lacked these basic skills.

As the northern states ended human bondage, the South's commitment to slavery became a political issue. At the Philadelphia convention in 1787, northern delegates had accepted clauses allowing slave imports for twenty years and guaranteeing the return of fugitive slaves (see Chapter 6). Seeking additional protection for their "peculiar institution," southerners in the new national legislature won approval of James Madison's resolution that "Congress have no authority to interfere in the emancipation of slaves, or in the treatment of them within any of the States."

Nonetheless, slavery remained a contested issue. The black revolt in Haiti brought 6,000 white and mulatto refugees to the United States in 1793, and their stories of atrocities struck fear into the hearts of American slave owners. Simultaneously, northern politicians assailed the British impressment of American sailors as just "as oppressive and tyrannical as the slave trade" and demanded the end of both. When Congress outlawed American participation in the Atlantic slave trade in 1808, some northern representatives called for an end to the interstate trade in slaves. In response, southern leaders mounted a defense of their labor system. "A large majority of people in the Southern states do not consider slavery as even an evil," declared one congressman. The South's political clout—its domination of the presidency and the Senate—ensured that the national government would continue to protect slavery. During the War of 1812, American diplomats vigorously demanded compensation for slaves freed by British troops. Subsequently, Congress enacted legislation upholding the property rights of slave owners in the District of Columbia.

Political conflict increased as the South expanded its slave-based agricultural economy into the lower Mississippi Valley. Antislavery advocates had hoped that slavery would die out naturally as the Atlantic slave trade ended and the tobacco economy declined. Their hopes quickly faded as the cotton boom increased the demand for slaves, and Louisiana (1812), Mississippi (1817), and Alabama (1819) joined the Union with state constitutions that permitted slavery.

These events prompted a group of influential Americans to found the American Colonization Society, which proposed a new solution to the issues of slavery and race. According to Henry Clay—a Society member, Speaker of the House of Representatives, and slave owner—racial bondage had placed his state of Kentucky "in the rear of our neighbors . . . in the state of agriculture, the progress of manufactures, the advance of improvement, and the general prosperity of society." Slaves had to be freed, Clay and other colonizationists argued, and then sent back to Africa. Clay predicted that emancipation without removal would lead to "a civil war that would end in the extermination or subjugation of the one race or the other." To prevent racial chaos, the Colonization Society encouraged planters to emancipate their slaves, who now numbered almost 1.5 million people. But few planters responded to the Society's plea, and in the end, it resettled only about 6,000 African Americans in Liberia, a colony that the Society established on the west coast of Africa.

Most free blacks strongly opposed this and other colonization schemes. As Bishop Richard Allen of the African Methodist Episcopal Church put it, "this land which we have watered with our tears and our blood is now our mother country." Allen spoke from experience. Born into slavery in Philadelphia in 1760 and sold to a farmer in Delaware, Allen had grown up in bondage. In 1777, Freeborn Garretson, an itinerant preacher, converted Allen to Methodism and convinced Allen's owner that on Judgment Day, slaveholders would be "weighted in the balance, and . . . found wanting." Allowed to buy his freedom, Allen paid off his owner and then enlisted in the Methodist cause, becoming a "licensed exhorter" and then a regular minister in Philadelphia. In 1795, Allen formed a separate black congregation, the Bethel Church; in 1816, he became the first bishop of a new denomination: the African Methodist Episcopal Church. Two years later, 3,000 African Americans met in Allen's church to condemn colonization and to claim citizenship. Sounding the principles of democratic republicanism, they vowed to defy racial prejudice and advance in American society using "those opportunities . . . which the Constitution and the laws allow to all."

The Missouri Crisis, 1819–1821

The failure of colonization set the stage for a major battle over slavery. In 1818, Congressman Nathaniel Macon of North Carolina warned slave owners that radical members of the "bible and peace societies" hoped to use the national government to raise "the question of emancipation." And so they did. When Missouri applied for admission to the Union in 1819 with a constitution that allowed slavery, Congressman James Tallmadge of New York proposed an amendment: He would accept Missouri's constitution only if it banned the entry of new slaves and provided for the emancipation of existing slaves. Missouri whites rejected Tallmadge's proposals, and the northern majority in the House of Representatives blocked the territory's admission.

White southerners were horrified. "It is believed by some, & feared by others," Alabama senator John Walker reported from Washington, that Tallmadge's amendment was "merely the entering wedge and that it points already to a total emancipation of the blacks." Mississippi congressman Christopher Rankin warned his northern colleagues, "You conduct us to an awful precipice, and hold us over it." To underline their commitment to slavery, southerners used their power in the Senate—where they held half the seats—to withhold statehood from Maine, which was seeking to separate itself from Massachusetts.

In the ensuing debate over slavery, southerners advanced three constitutional arguments. First, invoking the principle of "equal rights," they argued that Congress could not impose conditions on Missouri that it had not imposed on other territories seeking statehood. Second, they maintained that the Constitution guaranteed a state's sovereignty with respect to its internal affairs and domestic institutions, such as slavery and marriage. Finally, they insisted that Congress had no authority to infringe on the property rights of individual slaveholders. Going beyond these constitutional arguments, southern leaders reaffirmed their commitment to human bondage. Abandoning the argument that slavery was a "necessary evil," they now invoked religion to champion it as a "positive good." "Christ himself gave a sanction to slavery," declared Senator William Smith of South Carolina. "If it be offensive and sinful to own slaves," a prominent Mississippi Methodist added, "I wish someone would just put his finger on the place in Holy Writ."

Controversy raged in Congress and in newspapers for two years before Henry Clay put together a series of political agreements known collectively as the Missouri Compromise. Faced with unwavering southern opposition to Tallmadge's amendment, a group of northern congressmen deserted the antislavery coalition. They accepted a deal that allowed Maine to enter the Union as a free state in 1820 and Missouri to follow as a slave state in 1821. This agreement preserved a balance in the Senate between North and South and set a precedent for future admissions to the Union. For their part, southern senators accepted the prohibition of slavery in the vast northern section of the Louisiana Purchase, the lands north of latitude 36°30′ (the southern boundary of Missouri) (Map 8.2).

As they had in the Constitutional Convention of 1787, white politicians had preserved the Union by compromising over slavery. But the task had become more difficult. The delegates in Philadelphia had resolved their sectional differences in two months; it took Congress two years to work out the Missouri Compromise, and their agreement did not command universal support. "If we

▶ How did the aristocratic republicanism of the South differ from the democratic republicanism of the North?

▶ What compromises over slavery did the members of Congress make to settle the Missouri crisis? Who benefited most from the agreement?

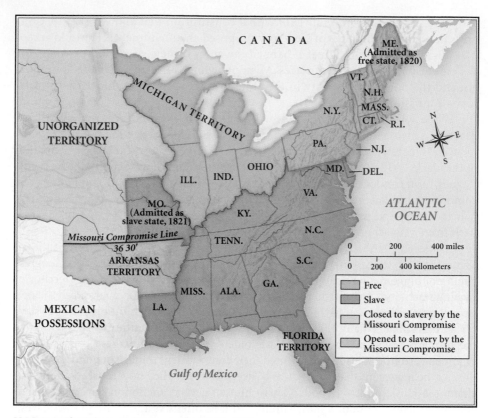

MAP 8.2 The Missouri Compromise, 1820–1821

The Missouri Compromise resolved for a generation the issue of slavery in the lands of the Louisiana Purchase. The agreement prohibited slavery north of the Missouri Compromise line (36°30′ north latitude), with the exception of the state of Missouri. To maintain an equal number of senators from free and slave states in the U.S. Congress, the compromise provided for the nearly simultaneous admission to the Union of Maine and Missouri.

For more help analyzing this map, see the Online Study Guide at **bedfordstmartins.com/henrettaconcise**.

yield now, beware," the *Richmond Enquirer* warned as southern congressmen agreed to exclude slavery from most of the Louisiana Purchase. "What is a *territorial* restriction to-day becomes a *state* restriction tomorrow." The fate of the western lands, enslaved blacks, and the Union itself were now inextricably intertwined, raising the specter of civil war and the end of the American republican experiment. As the aging Thomas Jefferson exclaimed during the Missouri crisis, "This momentous question, like a fire-bell in the night, awakened and filled me with terror."

Protestant Christianity as a Social Force

Throughout the colonial era, religion played a significant role in American life but not an overwhelming one. Then, beginning in 1790, a series of religious revivals planted the values of Protestant Christianity deep in the national character, giving a spiritual definition to American republicanism. These revivals especially changed the lives of blacks and of women. Thousands of African Americans absorbed the faith of white Baptists and Methodists and created a distinctive and powerful institution: the black Christian church. Evangelical Christianity also created new public roles for women, especially in the North, and set in motion a long-lasting movement for social reform.

A Republican Religious Order

The demand for greater liberty unleashed by the republican revolution of 1776 forced American lawmakers to devise new relationships between church and state. Previously, only the Quaker- and Baptist-controlled governments of Pennsylvania and Rhode Island had rejected a legally **established church** and compulsory religious taxes. Then, a convergence of factors—Enlightenment principles, wartime needs, and Baptist ideology—created a new religious regime of toleration and liberty.

Events in Virginia revealed the dynamics of change. In 1776, James Madison and George Mason used Enlightenment ideas of religious toleration to persuade the state's constitutional convention to guarantee all Christians the "free exercise of religion." No longer would the Anglican Church hold a privileged legal status. Virginia's Anglican political elite needed the support of Presbyterians and Baptists in the independence struggle, so it accepted the legitimacy of their churches. Baptists used their growing numbers to oppose the use of taxes to support religion. They convinced lawmakers to reject a bill, supported by George Washington and Patrick Henry, that would have imposed a tax to fund all Christian churches. Instead, in 1786, the Virginia legislature enacted Thomas Jefferson's Bill for Establishing Religious Freedom, which made all churches equal in the eyes of the law and granted direct financial support to none.

Elsewhere, the old order of a single established church crumbled away. In New York and New Jersey, the sheer number of denominations—Episcopalian, Presbyterian, Dutch Reformed, Lutheran, and Quaker, among others—prevented lawmakers from agreeing on an established church or compulsory religious taxes. Congregationalism remained the official state church in New England until the 1830s, but members of other denominations could now pay taxes to their own churches.

The separation of church and state was not complete because many influential Americans believed that religious institutions promoted morality and respect for governmental authority. "Pure religion and civil liberty are inseparable companions," a group of North Carolinians advised their minister. "It is your particular duty to enlighten mankind with the unerring principles of truth and justice, the main props of all civil government." Accepting this premise, most state governments indirectly supported churches by exempting their property and ministers from taxation.

Freedom of conscience also came with sharp cultural limits. In Virginia, Jefferson's Bill for Establishing Religious Freedom prohibited religious requirements for holding public office, but other states discriminated against anyone who dissented from the doctrines of Protestant Christianity. The North Carolina Constitution of 1776 disqualified from public employment any citizen "who shall deny the being of God, or the Truth of the Protestant Religion, or the Divine Authority of the Old or New Testament." No Catholics or Jews need apply. New Hampshire's constitution contained a similar provision until 1868.

Americans influenced by Enlightenment deism and by Evangelical Protestantism condemned these religious restrictions. Jefferson, Franklin, and other American intellectuals maintained that God had given humans the power of reason so that they could determine moral truths for themselves. To protect society from "ecclesiastical tyranny," they demanded complete freedom of conscience. Many evangelical Protestants also demanded religious liberty; their goal was to protect their churches from an oppressive government. Isaac Backus, a New England minister, warned Baptists not to incorporate their churches or accept public funds because that might lead to state control. In Connecticut, a devout Congregationalist welcomed "voluntarism," the uncoerced funding of churches by their members, because it allowed the laity to control the clergy, thereby furthering self-government and "the principles of republicanism."

The Second Great Awakening

Overshadowing such debates, a decades-long series of religious revivals—the Second Great Awakening—made the United States a genuinely Christian society. The churches that prospered during the revivals were primarily those that preached spiritual equality and governed themselves democratically. Because bishops and priests dominated the Roman Catholic Church, it attracted few Protestants, who preferred Luther's doctrine of the priesthood of all believers. Nor did the Catholic Church appeal to the unchurched—the great number of Americans who ignored or repudiated all religious institutions. Likewise, few Americans joined the Protestant Episcopal Church, the successor to the Church of England, because it also had a clerical hierarchy of bishops and was dominated by its wealthiest lay members. The Presbyterian Church attracted more adherents, in part because its churches elected laymen to the synods, the congresses that determined doctrine and practice. Evangelical Methodist and Baptist churches were by far the most popular. The Baptists boasted a republican church organization, with self-governing congregations. Both Baptists and Methodists developed an egalitarian religious culture marked by communal singing and emotional services.

Baptists and Methodists assumed a prominent role in the revivalist movement that began in the 1790s, as they evangelized the cities and the backcountry of New England. A new sect of Universalists, who repudiated the Calvinist doctrine of predestination and preached universal salvation, gained tens of thousands of converts, especially in Massachusetts and northern New England. After 1800, enthusiastic camp meetings swept the frontier regions of South Carolina, Tennessee, Ohio, and Kentucky. The largest gathering, at Cane Ridge in Kentucky in 1801, lasted for nine electrifying days and nights and attracted almost 20,000 people (Map 8.3). With these revivals, Baptist and Methodist preachers reshaped the spiritual landscape throughout the South. Offering a powerful emotional message and the promise of religious fellowship, revivalists attracted both unchurched individuals and pious families searching for social ties in their new frontier communities (see Voices from Abroad, p. 248).

The Second Great Awakening changed the denominational makeup of American religion. The most important churches of the colonial period—the Congregationalists, Episcopalians, and Quakers—grew slowly from the natural increase of their members. But Methodist and Baptist churches expanded spectacularly by winning converts, and soon they were the largest denominations. In the urbanized Northeast,

In the 1820s an intense wave of revivals ignited religious fervor in communities along the Erie Canal, and this region became known as the "burned-over district."

As devout farmers moved west, they established new Protestant churches throughout the Upper South and Midwest.

Student revivals at Yale College and Andover Seminary around 1800 led to the expansion of Protestant missions in the West and also in Africa, India, and Hawaii. Societies supporting the missions combined into the American Home Missionary Society in 1826.

The Second Great Awakening started in the 1790s as Baptists, Methodists, and a new sect called Universalists proselytized in New England. After 1800 the Awakening continued in Kentucky in camp meetings of pioneer farmers, who carried evangelical religion back to their communities.

← Paths of settlement, 1790–1830
▲ Camp meeting, 1801
● Kentucky revival
● New York's "burned-over district"
← Paths of revival

0   125   250 miles
0   125   250 kilometers

MAP 8.3 The Second Great Awakening, 1790–1860

The awakening lasted for decades and invigorated churches in every part of the nation. The revivals in Kentucky and New York State were particularly influential. As thousands of farm families migrated to the West, they carried with them the fervor generated by the Cane Ridge revival in Kentucky in 1801. Between 1825 and 1835, the area along the Erie Canal in New York witnessed so many revivals that it came to be known as the Burned-over District.

pious women aided their ministers by holding prayer meetings and providing material aid to members and potential converts. In the rural South and West, Methodist preachers followed a circuit, "riding a hardy pony or horse" with their "Bible, hymn-book, and Discipline" to visit existing congregations on a regular schedule. These preachers established new churches by searching out devout families, bringing them together for worship, and then appointing lay elders to lead the congregation and enforce moral discipline.

Evangelical ministers copied the "practical preaching" techniques of George Whitefield and other eighteenth-century revivalists (see Chapter 4). To attract converts, preachers spoke from memory in plain language but with a flamboyant style and theatrical gestures. "Preach without papers" and emphasize piety rather than theology, advised one minister, "seem earnest & serious; & you will be listened to with Patience, & Wonder,"

A Camp Meeting in Indiana   FRANCES TROLLOPE

Frances Trollope, the mother of British novelist Anthony Trollope, lived for a time in Cincinnati, where she owned a store that sold imported European goods. Her critical and at times acerbic *Domestic Manners of the Americans* (1832) was a best-seller in Europe and the United States. Here, she provides a vivid description of a revivalist meeting in Indiana around 1830.

We reached the ground about an hour before midnight, and the approach to it was highly picturesque. The spot chosen was the verge of an unbroken forest, where a space of about twenty acres appeared to have been partially cleared for the purpose. . . . Four high frames, constructed in the form of altars, were placed at the four corners of the inclosure; . . . a rude platform was erected to accommodate the preachers, fifteen of whom attended this meeting, and . . . preached in rotation, day and night, from Tuesday to Saturday.

When we arrived, the preachers were silent; but we heard issuing from nearly every tent mingled sounds of praying, preaching, singing, and lamentation. . . . The floor [of one of the tents] was covered with straw, which round the sides was heaped in masses, that might serve as seats, but which at that moment were used to support the heads and arms of the close-packed circle of men and women who kneeled on the floor.

Out of about thirty persons thus placed, perhaps half a dozen were men. One of these [was] a handsome-looking youth of eighteen or twenty. . . . His arm was encircling the neck of a young girl who knelt beside him, with her hair hanging dishevelled upon her shoulders, and her features working with the most violent agitation; soon after they both fell forward on the straw, as if unable to endure in any other attitude the burning eloquence of a tall grim figure in black, who, standing erect in the center, was uttering with incredible vehemence an oration that seemed to hover between praying and preaching. . . .

One tent was occupied exclusively by Negroes. They were all full-dressed, and looked exactly as if they were performing a scene on a stage. . . . One or two [women] had splendid turbans; and all wore a profusion of ornaments. The men were in snow white pantaloons, with gay colored linen jackets. One of these, a youth of coal-black comeliness, was preaching with the most violent gesticulations. . . .

At midnight, a horn sounded through the camp, which, we were told, was to call the people from private to public worship. . . . There were about two thousand persons assembled.

One of the preachers began in a low nasal tone, and, like all other Methodist preachers, assured us of the enormous depravity of man. . . . Above a hundred persons, nearly all females, came forward, uttering howlings and groans so terrible that I shall never cease to shudder when I recall them. They appeared to drag each other forward, and on the word being given, "let us pray," they fell on their knees . . . and they were soon all lying on the ground in an indescribable confusion of heads and legs.

SOURCE: Frances Trollope, *Domestic Manners of the Americans* (London: Whittaker, Treacher, 1832), 139–142.

Women in the Awakening

The Second Great Awakening was a pivotal moment in the history of American women. In this detail from *Religious Camp Meeting*, painted by J. Maze Burbank in 1839, all the preachers are men, but women fill the audience and form the majority of those visibly "awakened." By transforming millions of women into devout Christians, the Awakening provided Protestant churches with dedicated workers, teachers, and morality-minded mothers. When tens of thousands of these women also joined movements for temperance, abolition, and women's rights, they spurred a great wave of social reform. Old Dartmouth Historical Society/New Bedford Whaling Museum, New Bedford, Massachusetts.

In the South, evangelical religion was initially a disruptive force because many ministers spoke of spiritual equality and criticized slavery. Husbands and planters grew angry when their wives became more assertive and when blacks joined their congregations. To retain white men in their churches, Methodist and Baptist preachers gradually adapted their religious message to justify the authority of yeomen patriarchs and slave-owning planters. A Baptist minister declared that a man was naturally at "the head of the woman," and a Methodist conference proclaimed "that a Christian slave must be submissive, faithful, and obedient."

Other evangelists persuaded planters to spread Protestant Christianity among their African Americans slaves. During the eighteenth century, most blacks had maintained the religious practices of their African homelands, giving homage to African gods and spirits or practicing Islam. "At the time I first went to Carolina," remembered Charles Ball, a former slave, "there were a great many African slaves in the country. . . . Many of them believed there were several gods [and] I knew several . . . Mohamedans [Muslims]." Then, in the mid-1780s, Protestant evangelists converted hundreds of African Americans along the James River in Virginia and throughout the Chesapeake region.

Subsequently, black Christians adapted Protestant teachings to their own needs. They generally ignored the doctrines of original sin and Calvinist predestination as well as biblical passages that encouraged unthinking obedience to authority. Some African American converts envisioned the Christian God as a warrior who had liberated the Jews. Their own "cause was similar to the Israelites," preacher Martin Prosser told his fellow slaves as they plotted rebellion in Virginia in 1800. "I have read in my Bible where God says, if we worship him, . . . five of you shall conquer a hundred and a hundred of you a hundred thousand of our enemies." Confident of a special relationship with God, Christian slaves prepared themselves spiritually for emancipation, the first step in their journey to the Promised Land.

Influenced by republican ideology, many whites also rejected the Calvinists' emphasis on human depravity and weakness; instead, they celebrated human reason and free will. In New England, many educated Congregationalists discarded the mysterious concept of the Trinity — Father, Son, and Holy Spirit — and, taking the name Unitarians, worshipped a "united" God. "The ultimate reliance of a human being is, and must be, on his own mind," argued William Ellery Channing, a famous Unitarian minister. A children's catechism conveyed the denomination's optimistic message: "If I am good, God will love me, and make me happy."

Other New England Congregationalists softened traditional Calvinist doctrines. Lyman Beecher, the preeminent Congregationalist clergyman of the early nineteenth century, preached the traditional Christian belief that people had a natural tendency to sin; but, rejecting predestination, he affirmed the capacity of all men and women to choose God. In accepting the doctrine of free will, Beecher testified to the growing belief that people could shape their destiny. "Free Will" Baptists held similar views.

Reflecting this optimism, Reverend Samuel Hopkins linked individual salvation to religious benevolence — the practice of disinterested virtue. As the Presbyterian minister John Rodgers explained, fortunate individuals who had received God's grace had a duty "to dole out charity to their poorer brothers and sisters." Heeding this message, pious merchants in New York City founded the Humane Society and other charitable organizations. By the 1820s, so many devout Protestant men and women had embraced benevolent reform that conservative church leaders warned them not to neglect spiritual matters. Still, improving society emerged as a key element of the new religious sensibility. Said Lydia Maria Child, a devout Christian social reformer: "The only true church organization [is] when heads and hearts unite in working for the welfare of the human-race."

By the 1820s, Protestant Christians were well positioned to undertake that task. Unlike the First Great Awakening, which split churches into warring factions, the Second Great Awakening fostered cooperation among denominations. Religious leaders founded five interdenominational societies: the American Education Society (1815), the Bible Society (1816), the Sunday School Union (1824), the Tract Society (1825), and the Home Missionary Society (1826). Although based in eastern cities—New York, Boston, and Philadelphia—these societies ministered to the nation, dispatching hundreds of missionaries to western regions and distributing tens of thousands of religious pamphlets.

Increasingly, Protestant ministers and laypeople saw themselves as part of a united religious movement that could change the course of history. "I want to see our state evangelized," declared a pious churchgoer near the Erie Canal (where the fires of revivalism were so hot that the region was known as the "Burned-over District"): "Suppose the great State of New York in all its physical, political, moral, commercial, and pecuniary resources should come over to the Lord's side. Why it would turn the scale and could convert the world. I shall have no rest until it is done."

Because the Second Great Awakening aroused such enthusiasm, religion became an important force in political life. On July 4, 1827, the Reverend Ezra Stiles Ely called on the members of the Seventh Presbyterian Church in Philadelphia to begin a "Christian party in politics." Ely's sermon, "The Duty of Christian Freemen to Elect Christian Rulers," proclaimed a religious goal for the American republic—an objective that Thomas Jefferson and John Adams would have found strange and troubling. The two founders had both died precisely a year before, on July 4, 1826, the fiftieth anniversary of the Declaration of Independence, and had gone to their graves believing that America's mission was to spread political republicanism. In contrast, Ely urged the United States to become an evangelical Christian nation dedicated to religious conversion at home and abroad: "All our rulers ought in their official capacity to serve the Lord Jesus Christ." Similar calls for a union of church and state would arise again during the Third (1880–1900) and Fourth (1970–present) Great Awakenings among American Christians.

Women's New Religious Roles

The upsurge in religious enthusiasm prompted women to demonstrate their piety and even to found new sects. Mother Ann Lee organized the Shakers in Britain and then, in 1774, migrated to America, where she attracted numerous recruits; by the 1820s, Shaker communities dotted the American countryside from New Hampshire to Indiana (see Chapter 11). Jemima Wilkinson, a young Quaker woman in Rhode Island, founded a more controversial sect. Stirred by reading George Whitefield's sermons, Wilkinson had a vision that she had died and been reincarnated as Christ. Wilkinson declared herself the "Publick Universal Friend," dressed in masculine attire, and preached a new gospel. Her teachings blended the Calvinist warning of "a lost and guilty, gossiping, dying World" with Quaker-inspired plain dress, pacifism, and abolitionism. Wilkinson's charisma initially won scores of converts, but her radical lifestyle and ambiguous gender aroused hostility, and her sect dwindled away.

These female-led sects were less significant than the activities of thousands of women in mainstream churches. For example, women in New Hampshire managed more than fifty local "cent" societies that raised funds for the Society for Promoting Christian Knowledge, New York City women founded the Society for the Relief of

Poor Widows, and young Quaker women in Philadelphia ran the Society for the Free Instruction of African Females.

Women took charge of religious and charitable enterprises both because they were excluded from other public roles and because of their numbers. After 1800, more than 70 percent of the members of New England Congregational churches were women. This shift in membership prompted Congregational ministers to end traditional gender-segregated prayer meetings, and evangelical Methodist and Baptist preachers encouraged mixed-sex praying. "Our prayer meetings have been one of the greatest means of the conversion of souls," a minister in central New York reported in the 1820s, "especially those in which brothers and sisters have prayed together."

Far from leading to sexual promiscuity, as critics feared, mixing the men and women promoted greater self-discipline. Believing in female virtue, many young women and the men who courted them now postponed sexual intercourse until after marriage—previously a much rarer form of self-restraint. In Hingham, Massachusetts, and many other New England towns, more than 30 percent of the women who married between 1750 and 1800 bore a child within eight months of their wedding day; by the 1820s, the rate had dropped to 15 percent.

As women claimed new spiritual authority, men tried to curb their power. In the North as in the South, evangelical Baptist churches that had once advocated spiritual equality now prevented women from voting on church matters or offering testimonies of faith before the congregation. Those activities, one layman declared, were "directly opposite to the apostolic command in [Corinthians] xiv, 34, 35, 'Let your women learn to keep silence in the churches.'" "Women have a different *calling*," claimed another man. "That they *be chaste, keepers at home* is the Apostle's direction." But such injunctions merely changed the locale of women's activism. Embracing the concepts of republican and Christian motherhood, mothers throughout the United States founded maternal associations to encourage proper child rearing. By the 1820s, *Mother's Magazine* and other newsletters, widely read in hundreds of small towns and villages, were giving women a sense of shared purpose and identity.

Religious activism advanced female education. Churches established academies where girls from the middling classes received intellectual and moral instruction. Emma Willard, the first American advocate of higher education for women, opened the Middlebury Female Seminary in Vermont in 1814 and later founded girls' academies in Waterford and Troy, New York. Beginning in the 1820s, women educated in these seminaries and academies displaced men as public-school teachers, in part because women accepted lower pay than men would. Female schoolteachers earned from $12 to $14 a month with room and board—less than a farm laborer. But as schoolteachers, women had an acknowledged place in public life, a goal that previously had been beyond their reach.

▶ Which American churches were the most republican in their institutions and ideology?

▶ Why did Protestant Christianity and Protestant women emerge as forces for social change?

Just as the ideology of democratic republicanism had expanded voting rights and the political influence of ordinary men in the North, so the values of Christian republicanism had bolstered the public authority of middling women. The Second

Great Awakening made Americans a fervently Protestant people. Along with the values of republicanism and capitalism, this religious impulse formed the core of an emerging national identity.

SUMMARY

Like all important ideologies, republicanism has many facets. We have explored three of them in this chapter. We saw how state legislatures created capitalist commonwealths in which governments actively supported private businesses that contributed to the public welfare. This republican-inspired policy of state mercantilism remained dominant until the 1840s, when it was replaced by classical liberal doctrines (see Chapter 10).

We also saw how republicanism gradually changed social and family values. The principle of legal equality encouraged social mobility among white men and prompted men and women to seek companionate marriages. Republicanism likewise encouraged parents to provide their children with equal inheritances and to allow them to choose their marriage partners. In the South, republican doctrines of liberty and equality coexisted uneasily with slavery and ultimately were restricted to the white population.

Finally, we observed the complex interaction of republicanism and religion. Stirred by republican principles, many citizens joined democratic and egalitarian denominations, particularly Methodist and Baptist churches. Inspired by "benevolent" ideas and the enthusiastic preachers of the Second Great Awakening, many women devoted their energies to religious purposes and social reform organizations. The result of all these initiatives—in economic policy, social relations, and religious institutions—was the creation of a distinctive American republican culture.

Connections: Culture

Between the 1760s and the 1820s, Americans began to create a common culture, a sense of American nationality that would flower in the nineteenth century. As we suggested in the essay that opened Part Two,

> [b]y 1820, to be an American meant, for many members of the dominant white population, to be a republican, a Protestant, and an enterprising individual in a capitalist-run market system.

The creation of a national culture took place in stages. As we saw in Chapter 5, the Patriot movement generated a sense of American identity—in contrast to a Virginian or New York identity—and the republican revolution of 1776 gave it ideological content. In Chapters 6 and 7, we noted how the creation of a national government, first in the Confederation and then under the Constitution of 1787, augmented that political identity even as it generated conflicts between Federalists and Republicans. Simultaneously, the intense focus on financial gain by tens of thousands of entrepreneurial farmers, planters, artisans, and merchants shaped a culture that placed a high value on hard work and economic achievement. Finally, in this chapter, we saw how the Revolution increased religious liberty and set in motion the revivalism and reformism that added Christian and benevolent components to the emergent American identity.

TIMELINE

1782	▶ St. Jean de Crèvecoeur publishes *Letters from an American Farmer* ▶ Virginia allows manumission (reversed in 1792)	**1795**	▶ Massachusetts Mill Dam Act assists textile industry
		1800	▶ Gabriel Prosser plots slave uprising in Virginia
1783	▶ Noah Webster issues his "blue-back" speller	**1800s**	▶ Rise of sentimentalism and of companionate marriages
1784	▶ Massachusetts abolishes slavery; other northern states provide for gradual emancipation		▶ Women's religious activism; founding of female academies ▶ Religious benevolence sparks social reform
1787	▶ Benjamin Rush writes *Thoughts on Female Education*	**1801**	▶ Cane Ridge revival in Kentucky
1790s	▶ States grant charters to corporations	**1807**	▶ New Jersey excludes propertied women from suffrage
	▶ Private companies build toll roads and canals		
	▶ Merchants develop rural outwork system	**1816**	▶ Congress charters Second Bank of the United States
	▶ Chesapeake blacks become Protestants	**1817**	▶ American Colonization Society founded
	▶ Parents limit family size as farms shrink	**1819**	▶ Sharp decline in farm prices sets off panic
	▶ Second Great Awakening expands church membership	**1819–1821**	▶ Missouri Compromise devised
1791	▶ Congress charters First Bank of the United States	**1820s**	▶ States enhance public education
1792	▶ Mary Wollstonecraft's *A Vindication of the Rights of Woman* is published		▶ Women become schoolteachers

FOR FURTHER EXPLORATION

R. Kent Newmyer, *The Supreme Court Under Marshall and Taney* (1968), concisely analyzes constitutional development. Jeffrey L. Pasley, Andrew W. Robertson, and David Waldstreicher, eds., *Beyond the Founders: New Approaches to the Political History of the Early American Republic* (2004), shows how ordinary citizens promoted a democratic polity. Jack Larkin, *The Reshaping of Everyday Life, 1790–1840* (1997), explores the changing texture of daily life, as does the Web site **memorialhall.mass.edu/collection/index.html**.

For changing marriage rules, consult Nancy Cott, *Public Vows: A History of Marriage and the Nation* (2000); for an intimate portrayal of family life in Maine, read Laurel Thatcher Ulrich, *A Midwife's Tale: The Life of Martha Ballard* (1990), and consult the Web sites **www.pbs.org/amex/midwife** and **www.DoHistory.org**.

Jan Lewis's *The Pursuit of Happiness* (1983) explores the lives of the paternalistic slave-owning gentry of the Upper South, while James David Miller, *South by Southwest: Planter Emigration and Identity in the Slave South* (2002), discusses their migration to the Mississippi Valley. For discussions of slavery, see Douglas R. Egerton, *Gabriel's Rebellion: The Virginia Slave Conspiracies of 1800 and 1802* (1995) and the references in Chapter 12.

In *The Democratization of American Christianity* (1987), Nathan Hatch traces the impact of Evangelical Protestantism. Other fine overviews of American religion are Mark A. Noll, *America's God: From Jonathan Edwards to Abraham Lincoln* (2003), and Bernard Weisberger, *They Gathered at the River* (1958).

TEST YOUR KNOWLEDGE

To assess your mastery of the material in this chapter and for Web sites, images, and documents related to this chapter, visit **bedfordstmartins.com/henrettaconcise**.

PART THREE

Economic Revolution and Sectional Strife

1820–1877

ECONOMY	SOCIETY	GOVERNMENT
The economic revolution occurs	A new class structure emerges	Creating a democratic polity
1820 ▸ Waltham textile factory opens (1814) ▸ Erie Canal completed (1825) ▸ Market economy expands nationwide ▸ Cotton belt emerges in South	▸ Business class emerges ▸ Rural women and girls recruited as factory workers ▸ Mechanics form craft unions ▸ Waged work increases	▸ Spread of universal white male suffrage ▸ Rise of Andrew Jackson and Democratic Party ▸ Anti-Masonic Party rises and declines
1830 ▸ Protective tariffs (1828, 1832) trigger nullification crisis ▸ Panic of 1837 ▸ U.S. textiles compete with British	▸ Depression (1837–1843) shatters labor movement ▸ New urban popular culture appears	▸ Whig Party forms (1834) ▸ Second Party System emerges ▸ Jackson expands presidential power
1840 ▸ Irish immigrants join labor force ▸ *Commonwealth v. Hunt* (1842) assists unions; but workers remain "servants"	▸ Working-class districts emerge in cities ▸ Irish and German inflow sparks nativist movement	▸ Log cabin campaign (1840) mobilizes voters ▸ Antislavery parties: Liberty (1840) and Free-Soil (1848)
1850 ▸ Surge of cotton output in South and of railroads in North and Midwest ▸ Manufacturing expands	▸ Expansion of farm society into Midwest and Far West ▸ Free-labor ideology justifies inequality	▸ Whig Party disintegrates ▸ Republican Party founded (1854) ▸ Rise of southern secessionists
1860 ▸ Republicans enact Whigs' policy agenda: Homestead Act (1862), railroad aid, high tariffs, and national banking	▸ Emancipation Proclamation (1863) ▸ Free blacks in the South struggle for control of land	▸ Thirteenth Amendment (1865) ends slavery ▸ Fourteenth Amendment (1868) extends legal and political rights
1870 ▸ Panic of 1873	▸ Rise of sharecropping in the South	▸ Fifteenth Amendment (1870) extends vote to black men

256

CULTURE	SECTIONALISM
Reforming people and institutions	**From compromise to Civil War and Reconstruction**
▶ American Colonization Society (1817) ▶ Benevolent reform movements ▶ Revivalist Charles Finney ▶ Emerson and Transcendentalism	▶ Missouri crisis and compromise (1819–1821) ▶ David Walker's *Appeal . . . to the Colored Citizens of the World* (1829) ▶ Domestic slave trade moves African Americans west
▶ Joseph Smith founds Mormonism ▶ Temperance crusade expands ▶ Female Moral Reform Society (1834)	▶ Ordinance of Nullification (1832) and Force Bill (1833) ▶ W. L. Garrison forms American Anti-Slavery Society (1833)
▶ Fourierist and other communal settlements founded ▶ Seneca Falls women's convention (1848)	▶ Texas annexation (1845), Mexican War (1846–1848), and Wilmot Proviso (1846) increase sectional conflict
▶ Harriet Beecher Stowe's *Uncle Tom's Cabin* (1852) ▶ Anti-immigrant movement grows; Know-Nothing Party	▶ Compromise of 1850 ▶ Kansas-Nebraska Act (1854) and "Bleeding Kansas" ▶ *Dred Scott* decision (1857)
▶ U.S. Sanitary Commission founded (1861) ▶ Freedman's Bureau assists ex-slaves	▶ South Carolina leads secession movement ▶ Confederate States of America (1861–1865)
▶ Freed African Americans create schools and churches	▶ Compromise of 1877 ends Reconstruction

"The procession was nearly a mile long . . . [and] the democrats marched in good order to the glare of torches," a French visitor remarked in amazement during the election of 1832. "These scenes belong to history . . . the wondrous epic of the coming of democracy." As we will see in Part Three, history was being made in many ways between 1820 and 1877. A series of overlapping revolutions were transforming American society. One was political: the creation of a genuinely democratic polity. The second was economic: In 1820, the United States was predominately an agricultural nation; by 1877, the nation boasted one of the world's most powerful industrial economies. Third, there was far-reaching social and cultural change, including the Second Great Awakening, great movements of social reform, and the advent of a complex intellectual culture. These transformations affected every aspect of life in the North and Midwest and brought important changes in the South as well. Here, in brief, is an outline of that story.

ECONOMY

Impressive advances in industrial production, transportation, and trade transformed the nation's economy. Factory owners used high-speed machines and a new system of labor discipline to boost the output of goods dramatically. Manufacturers produced 5 percent of the country's wealth in 1820 but more than 30 percent in 1877. And thanks to enterprising merchants and entrepreneurs, who developed a network of canals and railroads and an integrated system of markets, they now sold their products throughout the nation.

SOCIETY

The new economy created a class-based society in the North and Midwest. A wealthy elite of merchants, manufacturers, bankers, and entrepreneurs rose to the top of the social order. To maintain social stability, they adopted a paternalistic program of benevolent reform. But an expanding urban middle class created a distinct material and religious culture and lent support to movements for radical social reform. A mass of propertyless workers, impoverished immigrants from Germany and Ireland, joined enslaved African Americans at the bottom of the social order. Meanwhile, slavery expanded in numbers and scope as planters created new plantations as far south and west as Texas.

GOVERNMENT

The rapid growth of political parties sparked the creation of a competitive and responsive democratic polity. Farmers, workers, and entrepreneurs persuaded governments to improve transportation, shorten workdays, and award valuable corporate charters. Catholic immigrants from Ireland and Germany entered politics to protect their cultures from restrictive legislation advocated by Protestant nativists and reformers.

With Andrew Jackson at its head, the Democratic Party led a political and constitutional revolution that cut government aid to financiers, merchants, and corporations. To contend with the Democrats, the Whig Party (and, in the 1850s, the Republican Party) devised a competing program that stressed economic development, moral reform, and individual social mobility. This party competition engaged the energies of the electorate and helped to unify a fragmented social order.

Between 1820 and 1860, a series of reform movements, many with religious roots and goals, swept across America. Dedicated men and women preached the gospel of temperance, Sunday observance, prison reform, and many other causes. A few Americans pursued their social dreams in utopian communities, but most reformers worked within the existing society. Abolitionists and women's rights activists demanded radical changes: the overthrow of the patriarchal legal order throughout the nation and the immediate end of slavery in the South. As southerners defended slavery as a "positive good," antislavery advocates demanded free soil in the West and an end to the "slave power."

SECTIONALISM

The economic revolution and social reform sharpened sectional divisions: The North developed into an urban industrial society based on free labor, whereas the South remained a rural agricultural society dependent on slavery. Following the Mexican War (1846–1848), northern and southern politicians struggled bitterly over the introduction of slavery in the vast territories seized from Mexico and the unsettled lands of the Louisiana Purchase. The election of Republican Abraham Lincoln in 1860 prompted the secession of the South from the Union and the Civil War. The conflict became a total war, a struggle between two societies, not just between two armies. Because of new military technology, disease, and huge armies, the two sides endured unprecedented casualties and costs.

The fruits of victory for the North were substantial. The Republican Party ended slavery and imposed its economic policies and constitutional doctrines on the South. But in the face of massive resistance from white southerners during the era of Reconstruction, northerners abandoned the effort to secure full political and civil rights for African Americans. These decades, which began with impressive economic, political, and social achievements, thus ended on the bitter notes of a costly war, an acrimonious peace, and half-won freedoms.

Economic Transformation
1820–1860

The truth was [the American farmer and artisan] believed in Work first of all, so that every human being should stand in his own shoes, indebted only to his own efforts for his living and his place in the world.

— Francis Henry Underwood,
Quabbin, 1893

In 1804, life turned grim for eleven-year-old Chauncey Jerome of Connecticut. His father died suddenly, and Jerome faced indentured servitude on a nearby farm. Knowing that few farmers "would treat a poor boy like a human being," Jerome bought out his indenture by making dials for clocks and became a journeyman clockmaker for Eli Terry. A manufacturing wizard, Terry had designed an enormously popular desk clock with brass parts; his business turned Litchfield, Connecticut, into the clock-making center of the United States. In 1816, Jerome set up his own clock factory. By organizing work more efficiently and using new machines that made interchangeable metal parts, he drove down the price of a simple clock from $20 to $5 and then to less than $2. By the 1840s, he was selling his clocks in England, the hub of the Industrial Revolution; two decades later, his workers were turning out 200,000 clocks a year, clear testimony to American industrial enterprise. By 1860, the United States was not only the world's leading exporter of cotton and wheat but also the third-ranked manufacturing nation behind Britain and France.

"Business is the very soul of an American: the fountain of all human felicity," Francis Grund observed shortly after arriving from Europe. "It is as if all America were but one gigantic workshop, over the entrance of which there is the blazing inscription, 'No admission here, except on business.'" As the editor of *Niles' Weekly Register* in Baltimore put it, there was an "almost universal ambition to get forward." Stimulated by the entrepreneurial culture of early-nineteenth-century America, thousands of artisan-inventors like Eli Terry and Chauncey Jerome and thousands of merchants and traders propelled the country into a new economic era. Two great changes defined that era: the **Industrial Revolution**—the growth and mechanization of industry—and the **Market Revolution**—the expansion and integration of markets.

Not all Americans embraced the new ethic of enterprise, and many did not share in the new prosperity. The spread of industry and commerce created a class-divided society that challenged the founders' vision of an agricultural republic with few distinctions of wealth. As the philosopher Ralph Waldo Emerson warned in 1839: "The invasion of Nature by Trade with its Money, its Credit, its Steam, [and] its Railroad threatens to . . . establish a new, universal Monarchy."

The American Industrial Revolution

Industrialization came to the United States between 1790 and 1820, as merchants and manufacturers reorganized work routines and built factories. Thanks to **mass production**, goods that once had been luxury items became part of everyday life. The rapid construction of turnpikes, canals, and railroads by state governments and private entrepreneurs, working together in the Commonwealth System (see Chapter 8), allowed manufactures to be sold throughout the land.

The Division of Labor and the Factory

Rising rates of production stemmed initially from changes in the organization of work. Consider the shoe industry. Traditionally, New England shoemakers turned leather hides into finished shoes and boots in small wooden shacks called "ten-footers," where they determined the pace of work. During the 1820s and 1830s, the merchants and manufacturers of Lynn, Massachusetts, gradually displaced these independent artisans by introducing an outwork system and a **division of labor**. The employers hired semiskilled journeymen and set them up in large shops cutting leather into soles and uppers. They sent out the upper sections to dozens of rural Massachusetts towns, where women binders sewed in fabric linings. The manufacturers then had other journeymen attach the uppers to the soles and return the shoes to the central shop for inspection, packing, and sale. The new system turned employers into powerful "shoe bosses" and eroded workers' wages and independence. But the division of labor dramatically increased the output of shoes and cut their price.

For products not suited to the outwork system, manufacturers created the modern **factory**, which concentrated production under one roof. For example, in the 1830s, Cincinnati merchants built large slaughterhouses that processed thousands of hogs every month. The technology remained simple: A system of overhead rails moved the hog carcasses past workers; the division of labor made the difference. One worker split the animals, another removed the organs, and others trimmed the carcasses into pieces. Packers then stuffed the cuts of pork into barrels and pickled them to prevent spoilage. The Cincinnati system was so efficient and quick — processing sixty hogs an hour — that by the 1840s, the city was known as "Porkopolis." By 1850, factories were slaughtering hogs at an enormous volume: 334,000 a year. Reported Frederick Law Olmsted:

> We entered an immense low-ceiling room and followed a vista of dead swine, upon their backs, their paws stretching mutely toward heaven. Walking down to the vanishing point, we found there a sort of human chopping-machine where the hogs were converted into commercial pork. . . . Plump falls the hog upon the table, chop, chop; chop, chop; chop,

Pork Packing in Cincinnati
The only modern technology in this Cincinnati pork-packing plant was the overhead pulley that carried hog carcasses past the workers. The plant's efficiency came from its organization, a division of labor in which each worker performed a specific task. Plants like this pioneered the design of the moving assembly line, which would reach a high level of sophistication in the early twentieth century in Henry Ford's automobile factories. Cincinnati Historical Society.

For more help analyzing this image, see the Online Study Guide at **bedfordstmartins.com/henrettaconcise**.

chop, fall the cleavers. . . . We took out our watches and counted thirty-five seconds, from the moment when one hog touched the table until the next occupied its place.

Some factories boasted impressive new technology. In the 1780s, Oliver Evans, a prolific Delaware inventor, built a highly automated flour mill driven by waterpower. His machinery lifted the wheat to the top of the mill, cleaned the grain as it fell into hoppers, ground it into flour, and then cooled the flour as it was poured into barrels. Evans's factory, remarked one observer, "was as full of machinery as the case of a watch." It needed only six men to mill 100,000 bushels of wheat a year — perhaps ten times as much as they could grind in a traditional mill.

By the 1830s, factory owners were using newly improved stationary steam engines to manufacture a wide array of products. Previously, most factories processed agricultural goods: pork, leather, wool, and cotton; by the 1840s, they were fabricating metal goods. Cyrus McCormick of Chicago used power-driven machines to make parts for reaping machines, which workers assembled on a power-driven conveyor belt. In Hartford, Connecticut, Samuel Colt built an assembly line to produce his invention, the six-shooter revolver. These advances in technology and factory organization alarmed British observers: "The contriving and making of machinery has become so common in this country . . . [that] it is to be feared that American manufacturers will become exporters not only to foreign countries, but even to England."

The Textile Industry and British Competition

British textile manufacturers were particularly worried about American competition. They persuaded the British government to prohibit the export of textile machinery and the emigration of **mechanics** who knew how to build it. Lured by high wages, though, thousands of British mechanics disguised themselves as ordinary laborers and sailed to the United States. By 1812, there were at least three hundred British mechanics at work in the Philadelphia area alone.

Samuel Slater was the most important of them. Slater came to America in 1789 after working for Richard Arkwright, who invented the most advanced British machinery for spinning cotton. Slater reproduced Arkwright's innovations in merchant Moses Brown's cotton mill in Providence, Rhode Island; its opening in 1790 symbolized the start of the Industrial Revolution in America.

In competing with British mills, American manufacturers had the advantage of an abundance of natural resources. The nation's farmers produced an abundance of cotton and wool, and the fast-flowing rivers cascading down from the Appalachian foothills to the Atlantic coastal plain provided a cheap source of energy. From Massachusetts to Delaware, these waterways were soon dotted with industrial villages and large textile mills, some as large as 150 feet long, 40 feet wide, and four stories high.

Still, British textile producers easily undersold their American competitors. Thanks to cheap transatlantic shipping and low interest rates in Britain, they could import raw cotton from the United States, manufacture it into cloth, and sell it in America at a bargain price. Moreover, thriving British companies could slash prices to drive fledgling American firms out of business. The most important British advantage was cheap labor: Britain had a larger population—about 12.6 million in 1810 compared to 7.3 million Americans—and thousands of landless laborers who were willing to take low-paying factory jobs. To offset these advantages, American entrepreneurs won help from the federal government. In 1816, 1824, and 1828, Congress passed tariff bills that protected textile manufacturers from imports of cotton and woolen cloth. But in 1833, under pressure from southern planters, western farmers, and urban consumers—who wanted inexpensive imports—Congress began to reduce the tariffs (see Chapter 10), cutting the profits of American firms.

American producers used two other strategies to compete with their British rivals. First, they improved on British technology. In 1811, Francis Cabot Lowell, a wealthy Boston merchant, toured British textile mills, secretly making detailed drawings of their power machinery. Paul Moody, an experienced American mechanic, then copied the machines and improved their design. In 1814, Lowell joined with merchants Nathan Appleton and Patrick Tracy Jackson to form the Boston Manufacturing Company. Having raised the staggering sum of $400,000, they built a textile plant in Waltham, Massachusetts—the first factory in America to perform all the operations of cloth making under one roof. Thanks to Moody's improvements, Waltham's power looms operated at higher speeds than British looms and needed fewer workers.

The second strategy was to tap a new and cheaper source of labor. In the 1820s, the Boston Manufacturing Company recruited thousands of young women from farm families. To appeal to the women, it provided them with rooms in boardinghouses and with evening lectures and other cultural activities. To reassure parents about their daughters' moral welfare, the mill owners enforced strict curfews, prohibited alcoholic beverages, and required regular church attendance. At Lowell (1822), Chicopee (1823), and other sites in Massachusetts and New Hampshire, the company built new cotton factories that used this labor system, known as the Waltham Plan.

Mill Girl, c. 1850
This fine daguerreotype (an early photograph) shows a neatly dressed textile worker about twelve years of age. The harsh working conditions in the mill have taken a toll on her spirit and body: The girl's eyes and mouth show little joy or life, and her hands are rough and swollen. She probably worked either as a knotter, tying broken threads on spinning jennies, or as a warper, straightening out the strands of cotton or wool as they entered the loom. Jack Naylor Collection.

By the early 1830s, more than 40,000 New England women were working in textile mills. As an observer noted, the wages were "more than could be obtained by the hitherto ordinary occupation of housework," the living conditions were better than those in crowded farmhouses, and the women had greater independence. Lucy Larcom became a textile operative at age eleven so that she could support herself and not be "a trouble or burden or expense" to her widowed mother. Other women operatives used their wages to pay off their father's farm mortgages, send their brothers to school, or accumulate a marriage dowry for themselves.

A few operatives just had a good time. Susan Brown, a Lowell weaver, spent half of her earnings on food and lodging and the rest on plays, concerts, lectures, and a two-day excursion to Boston. Like most textile workers, Brown soon tired of the rigor of factory work and the never-ceasing clatter of the machinery, which ran twelve hours a day, six days a week. After eight months, she quit, lived at home for a time, and then moved to another mill. Whatever the hardships, waged work gave young women a sense of freedom and autonomy. "Don't I feel independent!" a woman mill worker wrote to her sister. "The thought that I am living on no one is a happy one indeed to me" (see American Voices, p. 265).

The owners of the Boston Manufacturing Company were even happier. By combining tariff protection with improved technology and cheap female labor, they could undersell their British rivals. Their textiles were also cheaper than those made in New York and Pennsylvania, where farmworkers were better paid than in New England and

Early Days at Lowell LUCY LARCOM

Lucy Larcom (1824–1893) went to work in a textile mill in Lowell, Massachusetts, when she was eleven years old and remained there for a decade. She then migrated to Illinois with her sisters and a great tide of other New Englanders. In later life, Larcom became a teacher and a writer. In her autobiography, she described the contradictory impact of industrial labor— confining and yet liberating—on the lives of young women from farms and rural villages.

I never cared much for machinery. The buzzing and hissing and whizzing of pulleys and rollers and spindles and flyers around me often grew tiresome. I could not see into their complications, or feel interested in them. But in a room below us we were sometimes allowed to peer in through a sort of blind door at the great waterwheel that carried the works of the whole mill. It was so huge we could only watch a few of its spokes at a time, and part of its dripping rim, moving with a slow, measured strength through the darkness that shut it in. It impressed me with something of the awe which comes to us in thinking of the great Power which keeps the mechanism of the universe in motion. . . .

We did not call ourselves ladies. We did not forget that we were working girls, wearing coarse aprons suitable to our work, and that there was some danger of our becoming drudges. I know that sometimes the confinement of the mill became very wearisome to me. In the sweet June weather I would lean far out of the window, and try not to hear the unceasing clash of sound inside. Looking away to the hills, my whole stifled being would cry out

Oh, that I had wings!

Still I was there from choice, and

*The prison unto which we doom
ourselves,
No prison is.*

I regard it as one of the privileges of my youth that I was permitted to grow up among these active, interesting girls, whose lives were not mere echoes of other lives, but had principle and purpose distinctly their own. Their vigor of character was a natural development. The New Hampshire girls who came to Lowell were descendants of the sturdy backwoodsmen who settled that State scarcely a hundred years before. Their grandmothers had suffered the hardships of frontier life. . . . Those young women did justice to their inheritance. They were earnest and capable; ready to undertake anything that was worth doing. My dreamy, indolent nature was shamed into activity among them. They gave me a larger, firmer ideal of womanhood. . . .

Country girls were naturally independent, and the feeling that at this new work the few hours they had of every-day leisure were entirely their own was a satisfaction to them. They preferred it to going out as "hired help." It was like a young man's pleasure in entering upon business for himself. Girls had never tried that experiment before, and they liked it. It brought out in them a dormant strength of character which the world did not previously see.

SOURCE: Lucy Larcom, *A New England Girlhood* (Boston: Houghton Mifflin, 1889), 153–155, 181–183, 196–200.

textile wages consequently were higher. Manufacturers in those states garnered profits by using advanced technology to produce higher-quality cloth. Even Thomas Jefferson, the great champion of yeoman farming, was impressed. "Our manufacturers are now very nearly on a footing with those of England," he boasted in 1825.

American Mechanics and Technological Innovation

By the 1820s, American-born artisans had replaced British immigrants at the cutting edge of technological innovation. Few of these mechanics had a formal education, but they commanded respect as "men professing an ingenious art." In the Philadelphia region, the remarkable Sellars family produced the most important inventors. Samuel Sellars Jr. invented a machine for twisting worsted woolen yarn to give it an especially smooth surface. His son John improved the efficiency of the waterwheels powering the family's sawmills and built a machine to weave wire sieves. John's sons and grandsons ran machine shops that turned out riveted leather fire hoses, papermaking equipment, and eventually locomotives. In 1824, the Sellars family and other mechanics founded the Franklin Institute in Philadelphia. Named after Benjamin Franklin, whom the mechanics admired for his work ethic and scientific accomplishments, the Institute published a journal; provided high-school-level instruction in mechanics, chemistry, mathematics, and mechanical design; and organized exhibits of new products. Crafts-men in Ohio and other states established similar institutes to disseminate technical knowledge and encourage innovation. Around 1820, the U.S. Patent Office issued about two hundred patents for new inventions each year, mostly to gentlemen and merchants. By 1860, the office was awarding four thousand patents annually, mostly to mechanics from modest backgrounds.

American craftsmen pioneered in the development of **machine tools** — machines that made parts for other machines. A key innovator was Eli Whitney (1765–1825), the son of a middling New England farm family. At the age of fourteen, Whitney began manufacturing nails and knife blades; later, he made women's hatpins. Aspiring to wealth and status, Whitney won admission to Yale College and subsequently worked as a tutor on a Georgia cotton plantation. Using his expertise in making hatpins, he built a simple machine that separated cotton seeds from the delicate fibers. Although Whitney patented his cotton "engine" (or "gin," as it became known), other manufac-turers improved on his design and captured the market.

Still seeking his fortune, Whitney decided in 1798 to manufacture military weap-ons. He eventually designed and built machine tools that could rapidly produce inter-changeable musket parts, bringing him the wealth and fame that he had long craved. After Whitney's death, his partner John H. Hall built an array of machine tools to work metal: turret lathes, milling machines, and precision grinders.

Technological innovation now swept through American manufacturing. Mechanics in the textile industry invented lathes, planers, and boring machines that turned out standardized parts for new spinning jennies and weaving looms. Despite being mass-produced, these jennies and looms were precisely made and operated at higher speeds than British equipment. The leading inventor was Richard Garsed: He nearly doubled the speed of the power looms in his father's Delaware factory and patented a cam and harness device that allowed machines to weave damask and other fabrics with elaborate designs. Meanwhile, the mechanics employed by Samuel W. Collins built a machine for pressing and hammering hot metal into dies, or cutting forms. Using this machine, one of Collins's workers could make 300 ax heads a day—compared to twelve using traditional methods. In Richmond, Virginia, Welsh- and American-born mechanics at the Tredegar Iron Works were producing parts for complicated manufacturing equipment at low cost and in great quantities. As a group of British observers noted admiringly, many American products were made "with machinery applied to almost every process . . . all reduced to an almost perfect system of manufacture."

As mass production spread, the American Industrial Revolution came of age. The sheer volume of output elevated some products—such as Remington rifles, Singer sewing machines, and Yale locks—into household names in the United States and abroad. After winning praise at the Crystal Palace Exhibition in London in 1851, the first major international display of industrial goods, Remington, Singer, and other American firms became multinational businesses, building factories in Great Britain and dominating some European markets.

Wageworkers and the Labor Movement

As the Industrial Revolution gathered momentum, it changed the nature of work and of workers' lives. In the early nineteenth century, many American **craft workers** espoused an "artisan-republican" ideology based on the principles of liberty and equality. They saw themselves as a group of small-scale producers, equal to one another and free to work for themselves. The poet Walt Whitman summed up their outlook: "Men must be masters, under themselves."

However, as the outwork and factory systems spread, more and more workers became wage earners. They no longer labored "under themselves" but under the direction of an employer. Unlike young women, who embraced factory work because it freed them from parental control and domestic service, men bridled at their status as coerced wageworkers. To assert their personal independence, male wageworkers repudiated the traditional terms of "master" and "servant"; instead, they used the Dutch word *boss* to refer to their employer. Still, as hired hands, they received meager wages and had little job security. The artisan-republican ideal, a by-product of the American Revolution, was giving way to the harsh reality of waged work—labor as a commodity—in an industrializing capitalist society.

Some wageworkers labored as journeymen carpenters, stonecutters, masons, and cabinetmakers, traditional crafts that required specialized skills and generated a strong sense of identity. This trade-consciousness enabled these workers to form unions and bargain with their master-artisan employers over wages and the increasing length of the workday, which kept them from their families and from educational opportunities. Before 1800, the building trades' workday was twelve hours—6:00 A.M. to 6:00 P.M.—with an hour each for breakfast and lunch. By the 1820s, masters were demanding a longer day during the summer, when it stayed light longer, while paying journeymen the old daily rate. In response, 600 carpenters in Boston went on strike in 1825. The Boston protest failed, but by the mid-1830s, building-trades workers had won a ten-hour day from many employers and from the federal government at the Philadelphia navy yard.

Artisans in other occupations were less successful in preserving their living standards. As aggressive entrepreneurs and machine technology changed the nature of production, shoemakers, hatters, printers, furniture makers, and weavers faced falling income, unemployment, and loss of status. To avoid the regimentation of factory work, some artisans in these trades moved to small towns or set up specialized shops. In New York City, 800 highly skilled cabinetmakers owned small shops that made fashionable or custom-made furniture. In status and income, they outranked a much larger group of 3,200 semitrained workers—disparagingly called "botches"—who labored for wages in factories making cheaper mass-produced tables and chairs. The new industrial system had divided the traditional artisan class into self-employed craftsmen and wage-earning workers.

When wage earners banded together to form unions, they faced a legal hurdle: Under English and American common law, such "combinations" were illegal. As a Philadelphia judge put it, unions were "a government unto themselves" and unlawfully interfered with a "master's" authority over his "servant." Between 1806 and 1847, there were at least twenty-three legal cases accusing unions of "conspiring" to raise wages and thereby injure employers. Despite the legal obstacles, unions bargained over wages and working conditions. In 1830, journeymen shoemakers founded a mutual benefit society in Lynn, Massachusetts, and similar organizations soon appeared in other shoemaking centers. "The division of society into the producing and non-producing classes," the journeymen explained, had made workers like themselves into a mere "commodity" whose labor was bought and sold. As another group of workers put it, "The capitalist has no other interest in us, than to get as much labor out of us as possible. We are hired men, and hired men, like hired horses, have no souls." Indeed, we are "slaves in the strictest sense of the word," declared Lynn shoemakers and Lowell textile workers. But one Lowell worker pointed out, "We are not a quarter as bad off as the slaves of the south. . . . They can't vote nor complain and we can." To exert more pressure on their capitalist employers, in 1834, local unions from Boston to Philadelphia formed the National Trades Union, the first regional union of different trades.

Union leaders criticized the new industrial order by expanding **artisan republicanism** to include waged laborers. Arguing that wage earners were becoming "slaves to a monied aristocracy," they condemned the new outwork and factory systems in which "capital and labor stand opposed." To create a just society in which artisans and waged workers could "live as comfortably as others," they advanced a **labor theory of value**. Under this theory, the price of a good should reflect the labor required to make it, and most of the price should go to those individuals who produced it, not to factory owners, middlemen, or storekeepers. Appealing to the spirit of the American Revolution, which had destroyed the aristocracy of birth, union publicists called for a new revolution to destroy the aristocracy of capital. Armed with this artisan-republican ideology, union men organized nearly fifty strikes for higher wages in 1836.

Women textile operatives were equally active. Competition in the woolen and cotton textile industries was fierce because the mechanization of production caused output to grow faster than demand. As prices fell, manufacturers' revenues declined. To maintain their profits, employers reduced workers' wages and imposed more stringent work rules. In 1828, women mill workers in Dover, New Hampshire, struck against new rules and won some relief; six years later, more than 800 Dover women walked out to protest wage cuts. In Lowell, 2,000 women operatives backed a strike by withdrawing their savings from an employer-owned bank. "One of the leaders mounted a pump," the *Boston Transcript* reported, "and made a flaming . . . speech on the rights of women and the iniquities of the 'monied aristocracy.'" When conditions did not improve, young women in New England refused to enter the mills. Impoverished Irish (and later French Canadian) immigrants took their places.

By the 1850s, workers in many mechanized industries faced unemployment as the supply of manufactures exceeded the demand for them. In 1857, industrial overproduction coincided with a financial panic sparked by the bankruptcies of several railroads. As the economy went into a recession, unemployment rose to 10 percent and reminded Americans of the social costs of the new—and otherwise very successful—system of industrial production.

▶ How did American textile manufacturers compete with British manufacturers? How successful were they?

▶ In what ways did the emerging industrial economy conflict with artisan republicanism? How did wage laborers respond to the new economy?

The Market Revolution

As American factories and farms turned out more goods, businessmen and legislators created faster and cheaper ways to get those products to consumers. Beginning in the late 1810s, they constructed a massive system of canals and roads that linked the states along the Atlantic coast with one another and with the new states in the trans-Appalachian west. This transportation system set in motion both a crucial market revolution and a great migration of people. By 1860, nearly one-third of the nation's citizens lived in the Midwest (the five states carved out of the Northwest Territory—Ohio, Indiana, Illinois, Michigan, and Wisconsin—along with Missouri, Iowa, and Minnesota), where they created a complex society and economy that increasingly resembled those of the Northeast.

The Transportation Revolution Forges Regional Ties

With the Indian peoples in retreat, slave-owning planters from the Lower South settled in Missouri (admitted to the Union in 1821) and pushed on to Arkansas (admitted in 1836). Simultaneously, yeomen farm families from the Upper South joined migrants from New England and New York in farming the fertile lands of the Great Lakes basin. Once Indiana and Illinois were settled, land-hungry farmers poured into Michigan (1837), Iowa (1846), and Wisconsin (1848) (see Voices from Abroad, p. 270). To meet the demand for cheap farmsteads, Congress in 1820 had reduced the price of federal land from $2.00 an acre to $1.25—just enough to cover the cost of the survey and sale. For $100, a farmer could buy 80 acres, the minimum required under federal law. By the 1840s, this generous land distribution policy had enticed about five million people to states and territories west of the Appalachians (Map 9.1).

To link settler-communities to one another, state governments chartered private companies to build toll roads, or turnpikes. In 1806, Congress approved funds for a

German Immigrants in the Midwest ERNST STILLE

Among the thousands of Germans who flooded into the Midwest between 1830 and 1860 were twenty-three members of the interrelated Stille and Krumme families from the Prussian province of Westphalia in northwestern Germany. Most were younger sons and daughters, who could not hope to inherit farms if they stayed in Westphalia. The letters of Ernst Stille reveal the economic opportunities — and the hardships — they found in America.

Cincinäti, May 20th 1847
Dearest friends and relatives,

We went from Bremen to Neu Orleans in 2 months. . . . The trip from Neu Orleans to Cincinäti took 12 days. When I got here . . . I was lucky enough to get a job with Fr. Lutterbeck from Ladbergen [a village near his home in Prussia]. . . . In April all the brickmakers started to work again, many Germans work this trade and earn a good wage and I set to work at this too and earn a dollar a day, of that I have to pay 7 dollars a month for board and washing. . . . We make 8,500 bricks a day and it's hard work but when we start at 4 o'clock in the morning we can be finished by 3 o'clock, if I can stay healthy I will keep working here since if you're healthy and can stand the work, it pays the best.

The only people who are really happy here are those who were used to work in Germany and with toil and great pains could hardly earn their daily bread. . . . But a lot of people come over here who were well off in Germany but were enticed to leave their fatherland by boastful and imprudent letters from their friends or children and thought they could become rich in America, this deceives a lot of people, since what can they do here, if they stay in the city they can only earn their bread at hard and unaccustomed labor? . . .

Cincinäti, July 10th 1848

At the beginning of April, I started working for Ernst Lots in the brickyard. . . . In the winter no one can work at this trade because of the snow and ice, then there's a huge number of idle people. The main work in the winter is with fat livestock, brought in from the country in large herds, on the outer edge of the city there are large buildings where about 1000 a day are slaughtered and cleaned, then they're brought into the city where they are cut up and salted and put in barrels that's how they're sent from here to other countries. This is a pretty hard and dirty job, that's why most people would rather do nothing for $1/4$ year than do this, but if you want to put up with this you can earn 1 to $1^1/2$ dollars a day. . . .

My plan is if I stay in good health for the next couple of years to buy a piece of land and live there, since from my childhood I've been used to farming, I'd rather do that than stay in the city all my life, you can't start very well unless you have 300 dollars.

SOURCE: Walter D. Kamphoefner, Wolfgang Helbid, and Ulrike Sommer, eds., *News from the Land of Freedom: German Immigrants Write Home*, trans. Susan Carter Vogel (Ithaca, NY: Cornell University Press, 1991), 83–87.

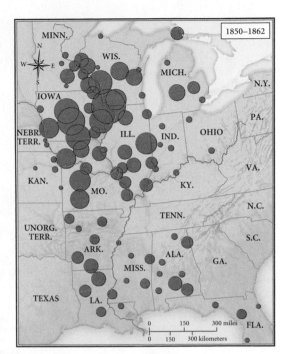

MAP 9.1 Western Land Sales, 1830–1839 and 1850–1862

The federal government set up land offices to sell farmsteads to settlers. During the 1830s, they sold huge amounts of land in the corn and wheat belt of the Old Northwest (Ohio, Indiana, Illinois, and Michigan) and the cotton belt of the Old Southwest (especially Alabama and Mississippi). By the 1850s, most sales of government land were in the upper Mississippi River Valley (particularly Iowa and Wisconsin). Each circle indicates the relative amount of land sold at the land office at its center.

National Road, constructed of compacted gravel, to tie the Midwest to the seaboard states. The project began in Cumberland in western Maryland in 1811; reached Wheeling, Virginia (now West Virginia), on the Ohio River in 1818; and ended in Vandalia, Illinois, in 1839. The National Road and other interregional highways carried migrants and their heavily loaded wagons westward; along the way, they passed herds of livestock destined for eastern markets.

Even on well-built gravel roads, travel over land was slow and expensive. To carry people, crops, and manufactures to and from the Midwest, public money and private businesses developed a water-borne transportation system of unprecedented size, complexity, and cost. The key event was the New York legislature's decision in 1817 to build the Erie Canal, a 364-mile waterway connecting the Hudson River to Lake Erie. At the time, the longest artificial waterway in the United States was just 28 miles long—a reflection of the huge capital cost of canals and the lack of American engineering expertise. But New York's ambitious project had three things in its favor: the vigorous support of New York City's merchants, who wanted access to western markets; the backing of New York's governor, De Witt Clinton, who persuaded the legislature to finance the waterway from tax revenues, tolls, and bond sales to foreign investors; and the relative gentleness of the terrain west of Albany. Even so,

The Erie Canal

This pastoral scene along the Erie Canal near Lockport, New York, only hints at the canal's profound impact on American life. Without the canal, the town in the background would not exist and farmers, such as the man in the foreground, would only have local markets for their cattle and grain. By 1860, the success of the Erie Canal had prompted the construction of a vast system of canals, an infrastructure that was as important to the nation as the railroad network of the late nineteenth century, and the interstate highway and airport transportation systems of the late twentieth century. I. N. Phelps Stokes Collection, Miriam and Ira D. Wallach Division of Art, Prints and Photographs. The New York Public Library. Astor, Lenox and Tilden Foundations.

the task was enormous. Workers — many of them Irish immigrants — had to dig out millions of cubic yards of soil, quarry thousands of tons of rock to build the huge locks that raised and lowered the boats, and construct vast reservoirs to ensure a steady supply of water.

The first great engineering project in American history, the Erie Canal altered the ecology of an entire region. As farming communities and market towns sprang up along the waterway, settlers cut down millions of trees to provide wood for building and heating and land for growing crops and grazing animals. Cows and sheep foraged on pastures that had recently been forests occupied by deer and bears, and spring rains caused massive erosion of the denuded landscape.

Whatever its ecological consequences, the Erie Canal was an instant economic success. The first section, a stretch of 75 miles, opened in 1819 and immediately generated enough revenue to repay its cost. When the canal was completed in 1825, a 40-foot-wide ribbon of water stretched from Buffalo, on the eastern shore of Lake Erie, to Albany, where it joined the Hudson River for a 150-mile trip to New York City. The canal's water "must be the most fertilizing of all fluids," suggested novelist Nathaniel Hawthorne, "for it causes towns with their masses of brick and stone, their churches and theaters, their business and hubbub, their luxury and refinement, their gay dames and polished citizens, to spring up."

The Erie Canal brought prosperity to the farmers of central and western New York and the entire Great Lakes basin. Northeastern manufacturers shipped clothing, boots, and agricultural equipment to farm families; in return, farmers sent grain, cattle, and hogs as well as raw materials (leather, wool, and hemp, for example) to eastern cities and foreign markets. One-hundred-ton freight barges, each pulled by two horses, moved along the canal at a steady 30 miles a day, cutting transportation costs and accelerating the flow of goods. In 1818, the mills in Rochester, New York had processed 26,000 barrels of flour for export to the East; ten years later, their output had soared to 200,000 barrels; and by 1840, it was at 500,000 barrels.

The spectacular benefits of the Erie Canal prompted a national canal boom (Map 9.2). Civic and business leaders in Philadelphia and Baltimore proposed waterways to link their cities to the Midwest. Copying New York's fiscal innovations, they persuaded their state governments to invest in canal companies or to force state-chartered banks to do so. They won state guarantees for canal bonds to encourage British and Dutch investors to buy them. In fact, foreign investors provided almost three-quarters of the $400 million invested in canals by 1840. Soon, a series of waterways connected the farms and towns of the Great Lakes region with the great port cities of New York, Philadelphia, and Baltimore (via the Erie, Pennsylvania, and Chesapeake and Ohio canals) and with New Orleans (via the Ohio and Mississippi Rivers). In 1848, the completion of the Michigan and Illinois Canal, which linked Chicago to the Mississippi River, completed an inland all-water route from New York City to New Orleans.

The steamboat, another product of the industrial age, ensured the economic success of the Midwest's river-borne transportation system. In 1807, engineer-inventor Robert Fulton built the first American steamboat, the *Clermont*, which he piloted up the Hudson River. To navigate shallow western rivers, engineers broadened the steamboats' hulls to reduce their draft and enlarge their cargo capacity. These improved vessels halved the cost of upstream river transport and, along with the canals, dramatically increased the flow of goods, people, and news. In 1830, a traveler or a letter from New York could go by water to Buffalo or Pittsburgh in less than a week and to Detroit or St. Louis in two weeks. Thirty years earlier, the same journeys had taken twice as long.

The states and the national government played key roles in the development of this interregional system of transportation and communication. State legislatures subsidized canals, while the national government created a vast postal system, the first network for the exchange of information. Thanks to the Post Office Act of 1792, the mail system grew rapidly—to more than 8,000 post offices by 1830—and safely carried thousands of letters and millions of dollars of banknotes. The U.S. Supreme Court, headed by John Marshall, likewise encouraged interstate trade by striking down state restrictions on commerce. In *Gibbons v. Ogden* (1824), the Court voided

MAP 9.2 The Transportation Revolution: Roads and Canals, 1820–1850

By 1850, the United States had an effective transportation system with three distinct parts. One system, composed of short canals and navigable rivers running into the Atlantic Ocean, carried cotton, tobacco, and other products from the southern countryside to Northern and European markets. The second system, centered on the Erie, Chesapeake and Ohio, and Pennsylvania Mainline canals, linked the major seaport cities of the Northeast to the vast trans-Appalachian region. Finally, a set of regional canals in the Old Northwest connected much of the Great Lakes region to the Ohio and Mississippi rivers and the port of New Orleans.

For more help analyzing this map, see the Online Study Guide at **bedfordstmartins.com/henrettaconcise**.

a New York law that created a monopoly on steamboat travel into New York City and established federal authority over interstate commerce (see Chapter 7). That decision meant that no local or state monopolies—or tariffs—would impede the flow of goods, services, and news across the nation.

By the 1850s, another product of industrial technology—the railroad—was on its way to replacing canals as the center of the national transportation system (Map 9.3). In 1852, canals carried twice the tonnage transported by railroads. Then capitalists in

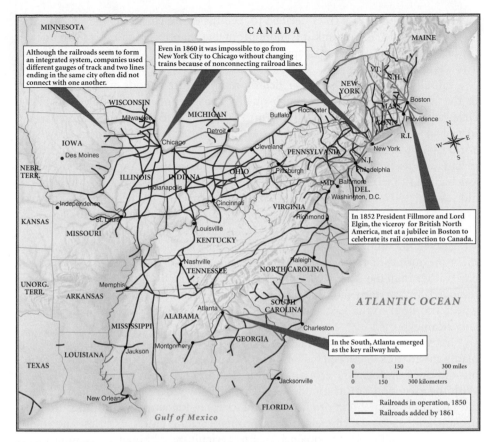

Although the railroads seem to form an integrated system, companies used different gauges of track and two lines ending in the same city often did not connect with one another.

Even in 1860 it was impossible to go from New York City to Chicago without changing trains because of nonconnecting railroad lines.

In 1852 President Fillmore and Lord Elgin, the viceroy for British North America, met at a jubilee in Boston to celebrate its rail connection to Canada.

In the South, Atlanta emerged as the key railway hub.

| | Railroads in operation, 1850 |
| | Railroads added by 1861 |

MAP 9.3 Railroads of the North and South, 1850 and 1861

In the decade before the Civil War, capitalists in the Northeast financed the construction of thousands of miles of new railroad lines in that region and the Midwest, creating an extensive and dense transportation system that stimulated economic development. The South built a more limited system of railroads. In all regions, different railroad companies used different track gauges, which hindered the efficient flow of traffic.

Boston and New York invested heavily in railroad routes; by 1860, railroads were the main carriers of wheat and freight from the Midwest to the Northeast. Serviced by a vast network of locomotive and freight-car repair shops, the Erie Railroad, the Pennsylvania Railroad, the New York Central Railroad, and the Baltimore and Ohio Railroad connected the Atlantic ports — New York, Philadelphia, and Baltimore — with the rapidly expanding Great Lakes cities of Cleveland and Chicago.

The railroad boom of the 1850s expanded commerce in a vast territory around Chicago. Trains carried huge quantities of lumber from Michigan to the treeless prairies of Indiana, Illinois, Iowa, and Missouri, where settlers built 250,000 new farms (covering 19 million acres) and hundreds of small towns. The rail lines moved millions of bushels of wheat to Chicago for transport by boat or rail to eastern markets. Increasingly, they also carried hogs and cattle to Chicago's growing stockyards. In

Jacksonville, Illinois, a farmer decided to feed his entire corn crop of 1,500 bushels "to hogs & cattle, as we think it is more profitable than to sell the corn." "In ancient times," boasted a Chicago newspaper, "all roads led to Rome; in modern times all roads lead to Chicago."

Initially, midwestern settlers relied on manufactured goods made in Britain or in the Northeast. They bought high-quality shovels and spades fabricated at the Delaware Iron Works and the Oliver Ames Company in Easton, Massachusetts; axes forged in Connecticut factories; and steel horseshoes manufactured in Troy, New York. By the 1840s, midwestern entrepreneurs were producing such manufactures: machine tools, hardware, furniture, and especially agricultural implements. Working as a blacksmith in Grand Detour, Illinois, John Deere made his first steel plow out of old saws in 1837; ten years later, he opened a factory in Moline, Illinois, that mass produced the plows. Stronger than the existing cast-iron models built in New York, Deere's steel plows allowed midwestern farmers to cut through the thick sod of the prairies. Other midwestern companies—McCormick and Hussey, for example— mass-produced self-raking reapers that enabled farmers to harvest 12 acres of grain a day (rather than the 2 acres that could be cut by hand). With the harvest bottleneck removed, midwestern farmers planted more acres and shipped vast quantities of wheat and flour to the East and Europe. Flour soon accounted for 10 percent of all American exports.

Extraregional trade also linked southern cotton planters to northeastern textile plants and foreign markets. This commerce in cotton bolstered the wealth of the South but did not transform the economic and social order there as it did in the Midwest. With the exception of Richmond, Virginia, and a few other places, southern planters did not invest their cotton profits in manufacturing. Rather, they continued to invest in land and slaves, which yielded high profits. Lacking cities, factories, and highly trained workers, the South remained tied to agriculture. Although its economy produced more than two-thirds of the world's cotton and accounted for almost two-thirds of American exports (see Chapter 12), the South provided a high standard of living only to the 25 percent of the white population that owned plantations and slaves. In 1860, the annual per capita income in the South was $103, while that of the Northeast was $141. By facilitating the transport of the staple crops of wheat, corn, cotton, and tobacco, the national system of commerce deepened the South's commitment to agriculture and slavery, even as it promoted diversified economies in the Northeast and Midwest.

The Growth of Cities and Towns

The expansion of industry and trade dramatically increased America's urban population. In 1820, there were only 58 towns with more than 2,500 inhabitants in the United States; by 1840, there were 126 urban centers, located mostly in the Northeast and Midwest. During those two decades, the total number of city dwellers grew more than fourfold, from 443,000 to 1,844,000.

The fastest growth occurred in the new industrial towns that sprouted along the "fall line," where rivers began their rapid descent from the Appalachian Mountains to the coastal plain. In 1822, the Boston Manufacturing Company expanded north from its base in Waltham and built a complex of mills in a sleepy Merrimack River village, which was quickly transformed into the bustling textile factory town of Lowell, Massachusetts. The towns of Hartford, Connecticut; Trenton, New Jersey; and Wilmington, Delaware, also became urban centers as mill owners exploited the waterpower of their rivers and recruited workers from the countryside.

Western commercial cities such as Pittsburgh, Cincinnati, and New Orleans grew almost as rapidly. These cities expanded because of their location at points where goods were transferred from one mode of transport to another — from farmers' rafts and wagons, for example, to steamboats or sailing vessels. As the midwestern population grew during the 1830s and 1840s, St. Louis, Detroit, and especially Buffalo and Chicago emerged as dynamic centers of commerce. "There can be no two places in the world," journalist Margaret Fuller wrote from Chicago in 1843, "more completely thoroughfares than this place and Buffalo. . . . the life-blood [of commerce] rushes from east to west, and back again from west to east." To a German visitor, Chicago seemed "for the most part to consist of shops . . . [as if] people came here merely to trade, to make money, and not to live." Chicago's merchants and bankers developed the marketing, provisioning, and financial services that were essential to farmers and small-town merchants in the surrounding countryside. "There can be no better [market] any where in the Union," declared a farmer in Paw Paw, Illinois.

These midwestern commercial hubs quickly became manufacturing centers as well. Capitalizing on the cities' locations as key junctions for railroad lines and steamboats, entrepreneurs built docks, warehouses, flour mills, and packing plants, creating work for hundreds of artisans and factory laborers. In 1846, Cyrus McCormick moved his reaper factory from western Virginia to Chicago to be closer to his midwestern customers. By 1860, St. Louis and Chicago had become the nation's third and fourth largest cities, respectively, after New York and Philadelphia.

The old Atlantic seaports — Boston, Philadelphia, Baltimore, Charleston, and especially New York City — remained important for their foreign commerce and, increasingly, as centers of finance and manufacturing. New York City and nearby Brooklyn grew at a phenomenal rate: Between 1820 and 1860, their combined populations increased nearly tenfold to one million people as tens of thousands of German and Irish immigrants poured into the two cities. Drawing on this abundant supply of labor, New York became a center of small-scale manufacturing and the ready-made clothing industry, which relied on thousands of low-paid seamstresses. "The wholesale clothing establishments are . . . absorbing the business of the country," a "Country Tailor" complained to the *New York Tribune*, "casting many an honest and hardworking man out of employment [and allowing] . . . the large cities to swallow up the small towns."

New York's growth stemmed primarily from its dominant position in foreign and domestic trade. It had the best harbor in the United States and, thanks to the Erie Canal, was the best gateway to the Midwest for immigrants and manufactures and the best outlet for shipments of western grain. Exploiting the city's prime location, in 1818 four Quaker merchants founded the Black Ball Line, a shipping company whose fleet carried cargo, people, and mail between New York and the European ports of Liverpool, London, and Le Havre. It was the first transatlantic service to run on a regular

▶ What roles did state and national government play in the development of America's transportation networks?

▶ Describe the different types of cities that emerged in the United States in the first half of the nineteenth century. How do you explain the differences in their development?

schedule. New York merchants likewise dominated trade with the newly independent South American nations of Brazil, Peru, and Venezuela. New York–based traders took over the cotton trade by offering finance, insurance, and shipping to export merchants in southern ports. By 1840, the port of New York handled almost two-thirds of foreign imports into the United States, almost half of all foreign trade, and much of the immigrant traffic.

Changes in the Social Structure

The Industrial Revolution and the Market Revolution improved the material lives of many Americans by enabling them to live in larger houses, cook on iron stoves, and wear better-made clothes. But especially in the cities, the new economic order spawned distinct social classes: a small but wealthy industrial and commercial elite, a substantial middle class, and a mass of propertyless wage earners. By creating a class-divided society, industrialization posed a momentous challenge to America's republican ideals.

The Business Elite

Before industrialization, white Americans thought of their society in terms of rank: "Notable" families had higher status than families of the "lower orders." Yet in many rural areas, people of different ranks shared a common culture. Gentlemen farmers talked easily with yeomen about crop yields, while their wives conversed about the art of quilting. In the South, humble tenants and aristocratic slave owners enjoyed the same amusements: gambling, cockfighting, and horse racing. Rich and poor attended the same Quaker meetinghouse or Presbyterian church. "Almost everyone eats, drinks, and dresses in the same way," a European visitor to Hartford, Connecticut, reported in 1798, "and one can see the most obvious inequality only in the dwellings."

The Industrial Revolution shattered this agrarian social order, creating a fragmented society composed of distinct classes and cultures. The new economic system pulled many Americans into large cities, thereby accentuating the differences between rural and urban life. Moreover, it made a few city residents—the merchants, manufacturers, bankers, and landlords who made up the business elite—very rich. In 1800, the top 10 percent of the nation's families owned about 40 percent of the wealth; by 1860, the richest 10 percent held nearly 70 percent of the wealth. In large cities such as New York, Chicago, Baltimore, and New Orleans, the superrich—the top 1 percent—owned more than 40 percent of all tangible property (land and buildings, for example) and an even higher share of intangible property (stocks and bonds).

Government tax policies facilitated the accumulation of wealth. In an era before federal taxes on individual and corporate income, the U.S. Treasury raised most of its revenue from tariffs—regressive taxes on textiles and other imported goods that were purchased mostly by ordinary citizens. State and local governments also favored the wealthier classes. They taxed real estate (farms, city lots, and buildings) and tangible personal property (furniture, tools, and machinery) but almost never taxed the stocks and bonds owned by the rich or the inheritances that they passed on to their children.

Consequently, cities that were once socially homogeneous took on an increasingly fragmented character. The wealthiest families consciously set themselves apart. They dressed in well-tailored clothes, rode in fancy carriages, and lived in expensively furnished houses tended by butlers, cooks, and other servants. The women no longer socialized with those of lesser wealth, and the men no longer labored side by side with their journeymen. Instead, they became managers and directors and relied on trusted subordinates to issue orders to hundreds of factory operatives. Increasingly, merchants, manufacturers, and bankers placed a premium on privacy and lived in separate neighborhoods, often at the edge of the city. The geographic isolation of privileged families and the massive flow of immigrants into other districts divided cities spatially along lines of class, race, and ethnicity.

The Middle Class

Standing between wealthy owners and propertyless wage earners was a growing middle class—the social product of the economic revolution. The bulk of the "middling class," a Boston printer explained, was made up of "the farmers, the mechanics, the manufacturers, the traders, who carry on professionally the ordinary operations of buying, selling, and exchanging merchandize." Other members of the middle class came from various professional groups—building contractors, lawyers, and surveyors—who suddenly found their services in great demand and financially profitable. Middle-class business owners, white-collar employees, and professionals were most numerous in the Northeast, where in the 1840s they numbered about 30 percent of the population. But they also could be found in the agrarian South. In 1854, Oglethorpe, Georgia (population: 2,500), a cotton boomtown, had eighty "business houses" and eight hotels.

The growing size, wealth, and cultural influence of the middle class reflected a dramatic rise in urban prosperity. Between 1830 and 1857, the per capita income of Americans increased by about 2.5 percent a year, a remarkable rate never since matched. This surge in income, along with the availability of inexpensive mass-produced goods, fostered a distinct middle-class urban culture. Middle-class husbands earned enough to save about 15 percent of their income, which they used to buy a well-built house in a "respectable part of town." They purchased handsome clothes and drove to work and play in smart carriages. Relieved of much household labor, middle-class wives became purveyors of genteel culture, buying books, pianos, lithographs, and commodious furniture for their front parlors. Affluent middle-class families hired Irish or African American domestic servants, while less prosperous ones relied on the new industrial technology. The middle class outfitted their residences with furnaces that heated water for bathing and for radiators that warmed entire rooms; they bought cooking stoves with ovens and treadle-operated sewing machines. Prosperous urban families now kept their perishable food in iceboxes, which ice-company wagons filled periodically, and bought many varieties of packaged goods. As early as 1825, the Underwood Company of Boston was marketing well-preserved Atlantic salmon in jars.

If material comfort was one distinguishing mark of the middle class, moral and mental discipline was another. Middle-class writers denounced carnivals and festivals as a "chaos of sin and folly, of misery and fun" and, by the 1830s, had managed to suppress them. Ambitious parents were equally concerned with their children's moral and intellectual development. To help their offspring succeed in life, middle-class parents often provided them with a high school education (in an era when most white children received only five years of schooling), and stressed the importance of discipline and hard work. American Protestants had long believed that diligent work in an earthly "calling" was a duty owed to God. Now the business elite and the middle class gave this idea a secular twist by celebrating work as the key to individual social mobility and national prosperity.

Benjamin Franklin gave classical expression to the secular work ethic in his *Autobiography*, which was published in full in 1818 (thirty years after his death) and immediately found a huge audience. Heeding Franklin's suggestion that an industrious man would become a rich one, tens of thousands of young American men saved their money, adopted temperate habits, and aimed to rise in the world. Warner Myers, a Philadelphia housepainter, raised funds from family, friends, and loans and became a builder, constructing sixty houses and garnering ample profits. Countless magazines, children's books, self-help manuals, and novels recounted the stories of similar individuals. The **self-made man** became a central theme of American popular culture and inspired many men (and a few women) to seek wealth. Just as the rural-producer ethic had united the social ranks in pre-1800 America, personal achievement linked the upper and middle classes of the new industrializing society.

Urban Workers and the Poor

As thoughtful business leaders surveyed their industrializing society, they concluded that the yeoman farmer and artisan-republican ideal — a society composed of independent producers — was no longer possible. "Entire independence ought not to be wished for," Ithamar A. Beard, the paymaster of the Hamilton Manufacturing Company, told a mechanics' association in 1827. "In large manufacturing towns, many more must fill subordinate stations and must be under the immediate direction and control of a master or superintendent, than in the farming towns."

Beard had a point. In 1840, all of the nation's slaves and about half of its white workers were laboring for others. The bottom 10 percent of wage earners consisted of casual workers, who were hired on a short-term basis for the most arduous jobs. Poor women washed clothes; their husbands and sons carried lumber and bricks for construction projects, loaded ships, and dug out dirt and stones to build canals. When they could find jobs, these men earned "their dollar per diem," a longtime resident told readers of the *Baltimore American*, but he cautioned that such workers could never save enough "to pay rent, buy fire wood and eatables" when the harbor froze up and they had no work. During business depressions, casual laborers bore the brunt of unemployment; even in good times, their jobs were temporary and dangerous.

Other laborers had greater security of employment, but few were prospering. In Massachusetts in 1825, an unskilled worker earned about two-thirds as much as a mechanic did; two decades later, it was less than half as much. A journeyman carpenter in

Philadelphia reported that he was about "even with the World" after several years of work but that many of his coworkers were in debt. The 18,000 women who made men's clothing in New York City in the 1850s earned just a few pennies a day, less than $80 a year. Such meager wages barely paid for food and rent, so few wage earners could take advantage of the rapidly falling prices of manufactured goods. Only the most fortunate working-class families could afford to educate their children, buy apprenticeships for their sons, or accumulate small dowries for their daughters. Most families sent their ten-year-old children out to work, and the death of a parent often threw the survivors into dire poverty. As a charity worker noted, "What can a bereaved widow do, with 5 or 6 little children, destitute of every means of support but what her own hands can furnish (which in a general way does not amount to more than 25 cents a day)."

Impoverished urban workers gradually congregated in dilapidated housing in bad neighborhoods. Single men and women lived in crowded boardinghouses, while families jammed themselves into tiny apartments in the basements and attics of small houses. As immigrants poured into the nation after 1840, urban populations soared, and developers squeezed more and more dwellings and foul-smelling outhouses onto a single lot. Venturing into the slums of New York City in the 1850s, shocked state legislators found gaunt, shivering people with "wild ghastly faces" living amid "hideous squalor and deadly effluvia, the dim, undrained courts oozing with pollution, the dark, narrow stairways, decayed with age, reeking with filth, overrun with vermin."

Many wage earners sought solace in alcohol. Beer and rum had long been standard fare in many American rituals: patriotic ceremonies, work breaks, barn raisings, and games. But during the 1820s and 1830s, the consumption of intoxicating beverages reached new heights, and alcoholism killed Daniel Tomkins, vice president under James Monroe, and undermined Henry Clay's bid for the presidency. Heavy drinking had an especially devastating impact on urban wage earners, who could ill afford its cost. Although Methodist artisans and ambitious craft workers swore off liquor to protect their work skills, health, and finances, other workers drank heavily on the job—and not just during the traditional 11 A.M. and 4 P.M. "refreshers." A baker recalled how "one man was stationed at the window to watch, while the rest drank." Long before the arrival of spirit-drinking Irish and beer-drinking German immigrants, grogshops dotted almost every block in working-class districts and were focal points of disorder. Unrestrained drinking by young men led to fistfights, brawls, and robberies. The urban police, mostly low-paid watchmen and untrained constables, were unable to contain the lawlessness.

The Benevolent Empire

The disorder among urban wage earners alarmed members of the rising middle class, who wanted safe cities and a disciplined workforce. To improve the world around them, many upwardly mobile men and women embraced religious benevolence. Led by Congregational and Presbyterian ministers, they created organizations of conservative social reform that historians call the **Benevolent Empire**. The ultimate purpose of the reforms was to restore "the moral government of God," explained Presbyterian minister Lyman Beecher, by reducing intemperance and poverty. Reform-minded individuals first regulated their own behavior and then tried to impose discipline into the lives of working people. They would regulate popular behavior—by persuasion if possible, by law if necessary.

The Benevolent Empire targeted age-old evils such as drunkenness, adultery, prostitution, and crime, but its methods were new. Instead of relying on church sermons and the suasion of community leaders, the reformers set out to institutionalize charity and systematically combat evil. They established large-scale organizations: the Prison Discipline Society and the American Society for the Promotion of Temperance, among many others. Each organization had a managing staff, a network of hundreds of chapters, thousands of volunteer members, and a newspaper.

Often acting in concert, these benevolent groups worked to improve society. First, they encouraged people to lead well-disciplined lives by drinking less alcohol and acquiring "regular habits." They persuaded local governments to ban carnivals of drink and dancing, such as Negro Election Day (festivities in which African Americans symbolically took over the government), which had been enjoyed by whites as well as blacks. Second, they devised new institutions to help the needy and to control the unruly. Reformers provided homes of refuge for abandoned children and asylums for the insane, who previously had been confined by their families in attics and cellars. They campaigned to end corporal punishment and to rehabilitate criminals in new, specially designed penitentiaries.

Women formed a crucial part of the Benevolent Empire. Since the 1790s, upper-class women had sponsored charitable organizations such as the Society for the Relief of Poor Widows with Small Children, which was founded in 1797 in New York by Isabella Graham, a devout Presbyterian widow. Her daughter Joanna Bethune set up other charitable institutions, including the Orphan Asylum Society and the Society for the Promotion of Industry, which found jobs for hundreds of poor women as spinners and seamstresses.

Some reformers argued that the decline of the traditional Sabbath was the greatest threat to the "moral government of God." As the market revolution spread, merchants and storekeepers conducted business on Sundays, and urban saloons provided drink and entertainment. To halt these activities, Lyman Beecher and other ministers founded a General Union for Promoting the Observance of the Christian Sabbath in 1828. General Union chapters, replete with women's auxiliaries, sprang up from Maine to Cincinnati and beyond. To rally Christians, the General Union demanded repeal of a law Congress had enacted in 1810 allowing mail to be transported—though not delivered—on Sundays. The Union's members boycotted shipping companies that did business on the Sabbath and campaigned for municipal laws forbidding games and festivals on the Lord's day.

The Benevolent Empire's efforts to impose its Sabbatarian beliefs aroused opposition from workers and freethinkers. Men who labored twelve or fourteen hours a day for six days a week wanted the freedom to spend their one day of leisure as they wished. Shipping company managers wanted to keep goods moving and demanded that the Erie Canal provide lockkeepers on Sundays. They argued that using laws to enforce a particular set of moral beliefs was "contrary to the free spirit of our institutions." When some evangelical reformers proposed teaching Christianity to slaves, they aroused hostility among white southerners. This popular resistance by workers and planters limited the success of the Benevolent Empire.

Charles Grandison Finney: Revivalism and Reform

Presbyterian minister Charles Grandison Finney found a new way to propagate religious values. Finney was not part of the traditional religious elite. Born into a poor farming family in Connecticut, he had planned to become a lawyer and rise into the middle class. But in 1823, Finney underwent an intense conversion experience and chose the ministry as his career. Beginning in towns along the Erie Canal, the young minister conducted emotional revival meetings that stressed conversion rather than doctrine and discipline. Repudiating traditional Calvinist beliefs, he maintained that God would welcome any sinner who submitted to the Holy Spirit. Finney's ministry drew on — and greatly accelerated — the Second Great Awakening, the wave of Protestant revivalism that had begun after the Revolution (see Chapter 8).

Finney's central message was that "God has made man a moral free agent" who could choose salvation. This doctrine of free will was particularly attractive to members of the new middle class, who had already chosen to improve their material lives. But Finney also had great success in converting people at the ends of the social spectrum: the haughty rich, who had placed themselves above God, and the abject poor, who seemed lost to drink and sloth. Finney celebrated their common fellowship in Christ and identified them spiritually with pious middle-class respectability.

Charles Grandison Finney, Evangelist (1792–1875)
When an unknown artist painted this flattering portrait in 1834, Finney was forty-two years old and at the height of his career as an evangelist. Handsome and charismatic, Finney had just led a series of enormously successful revivals in Rochester, New York, and other cities along the Erie Canal. In 1835, he established a theology department at newly founded Oberlin College in Ohio, where he trained a generation of ministers and served as president from 1851 to 1866. Oberlin College Archives.

Finney's most spectacular triumph came in 1830, when he moved his revivals from small towns to Rochester, New York, now a major milling and commercial city on the Erie Canal. Preaching every day for six months and promoting group prayer meetings in family homes, Finney won over the influential merchants and manufacturers of Rochester, who pledged to reform their lives and those of their workers. They promised to attend church, give up intoxicating beverages, and work hard. To encourage their employees to do the same, wealthy businessmen founded a Free Presbyterian church—"free" because members did not have to pay for pew space. Other Evangelical Protestants founded churches to serve transient canal laborers, and pious businessmen set up a savings bank to encourage thrift among the working classes. Meanwhile, Finney's wife Lydia and other pious middle-class women carried the Christian message to the wives of the unconverted, set up Sunday schools for poor children, and formed the Female Charitable Society to assist the unemployed.

Finney's efforts to create a harmonious community of morally disciplined Christians were not completely successful. Skilled workers who belonged to strong craft organizations—boot makers, carpenters, stonemasons, and boatbuilders—protested that they needed higher wages and better schools more urgently than sermons and prayers. Poor people ignored Finney's revival, as did the Irish Catholic immigrants who had recently begun arriving in Rochester and other northeastern cities, bringing with them a hatred of Protestants as religious heretics and political oppressors.

Ignoring this resistance, revivalists from New England to the Midwest copied Finney's evangelical message and techniques. In New York City, wealthy silk merchants Arthur and Lewis Tappan founded a magazine, *The Christian Evangelist*, which promoted Finney's ideas. The revivals swept through Pennsylvania, North Carolina, Tennessee, and Indiana, where, a convert reported, "you could not go upon the street and hear any conversation, except upon religion." The success of the revivals "has been so general and thorough," concluded a Presbyterian general assembly, "that the whole customs of society have changed."

The **temperance movement** proved to be the most successful evangelical social reform. Evangelicals took over the American Temperance Society in 1832; soon the society boasted 2,000 chapters and more than 200,000 members. The society employed the methods of the revivals—group confession and prayer, a focus on the family and the spiritual role of women, and sudden emotional conversion—and took them to northern towns and southern villages. On one day in New York City in 1841, more than 4,000 people took the temperance "pledge." Throughout America, the annual consumption of spirits fell dramatically, from an average of five gallons per person in 1830 to two gallons in 1845.

Evangelical reformers celebrated religion as the key to temperate behavior and moral improvement. Laziness and drinking could not be cured by self-discipline, as Benjamin Franklin had argued; rather, people had to experience a profound change of heart through religious conversion. This evangelical message of individual enterprise and moral discipline appealed to both middle-class Americans and wage-earning citizens. Religion and the ideology of social mobility served as a powerful cement, bonding people to one another in face of economic divisions created by industrialization, market expansion, and increasing cultural diversity.

Immigration and Cultural Conflict

Cultural diversity was the result of vast wave of immigrants. Between 1840 and 1860, about 2 million Irish, 1.5 million Germans, and 750,000 Britons poured into the United States. The British migrants were primarily Protestant and relatively prosperous; their ranks included trained professionals, propertied farmers, and skilled workers. Many German immigrants also came from property-owning farming and artisan families and had sufficient resources to move to the midwestern states of Wisconsin, Iowa, and Missouri. Other Germans and most of the Irish settled in the Northeast, where by 1860, they accounted for nearly one-third of white adults. Most immigrants avoided the South because they opposed slavery or feared competition from enslaved workers.

The poorest migrants were Irish peasants and laborers, who were fleeing a famine caused by severe overpopulation and a devastating blight that destroyed the potato crop. Arriving in dire poverty, the Irish settled mostly in the cities of New England and New York. The men took low-paying jobs as factory hands, construction workers, and canal diggers, while the women became washerwomen and domestic servants. Irish families crowded into cheap tenement buildings with primitive sanitation systems and were the first to die when disease struck. In the summer of 1849, a cholera epidemic took the lives of thousands of poor immigrants in St. Louis and New York City.

In times of hardship and sorrow, immigrants turned to their churches. Many Germans and virtually all the Irish were Catholics, and they fueled the growth of the American Catholic Church. In 1840, there were sixteen Catholic dioceses and 700 churches; by 1860, there were forty-five dioceses and 2,500 churches. Under the guidance of their priests and bishops, Catholics built an impressive network of institutions — charitable societies, orphanages, militia companies, parochial schools, and political organizations — that helped them to maintain both their religion and their German or Irish identity.

The Protestant fervor stirred up by the Second Great Awakening meant that a barrage of anti-Catholic publications greeted the immigrants. One of the most militant critics of Catholicism was artist and inventor Samuel F. B. Morse. In 1834, Morse published *Foreign Conspiracy Against the Liberties of the United States*, which warned of a Catholic threat to American republican institutions. Morse believed that Catholic immigrants would obey the dictates of Pope Gregory XVI, who in an official papal declaration (encyclical) in 1832 had condemned liberty of conscience, freedom of publication, and the separation of church and state. Gregory instructed Catholics to repudiate republicanism and acknowledge the "submission due to princes." Republican-minded Protestants of many denominations shared Morse's fears, and *Foreign Conspiracy* became their handbook.

The social tensions stemming from industrialization intensified anti-Catholic sentiment. During business recessions, unemployed Protestant mechanics and factory workers joined mobs that attacked Catholics, accusing them of taking jobs and driving down wages. These cultural conflicts inhibited the creation of unions, because many Protestant wage earners felt that they had more in common with their Protestant employers than with their Catholic coworkers. Other Protestants formed clubs limited to

RIOT IN PHILADELPHIA
JULY 7ᵗʰ 1844.

Anti-Catholic Riots

When riots against Irish Catholics broke out in Philadelphia in July 1844, the governor of Pennsylvania called out the militia to protect Catholic churches and residential neighborhoods. In the foreground, Protestant rioters, depicted by the artist as well-dressed gentlemen, do battle with the militia. The riots resulted in fifteen deaths and dozens of serious injuries. Historical Society of Pennsylvania.

native-born citizens and called for a halt to immigration. Benevolent-minded Protestants supported the anti-Catholic movement for reasons of public policy. As crusaders for public education, they opposed the diversion of tax resources to Catholic schools; as advocates of a civilized society, they condemned the rowdyism of drunken Irish men.

In many northeastern cities, religious and cultural tensions led to violence. In 1834, in Charlestown, Massachusetts, a quarrel between Catholic laborers repairing a convent owned by the Ursuline order of nuns and Protestant workers in a neighboring brickyard turned into a full-scale riot and led to the destruction of the convent. In 1844, in Philadelphia, riots erupted when the Catholic bishop persuaded public-school officials to use both Catholic and Protestant versions of the Bible. Anti-Irish violence incited by

▶ What were the social classes created by the economic revolution? Describe their defining characteristics.

▶ What were the main goals of the Benevolent Empire? To what extent were they achieved?

▶ Weigh the relative importance of the Industrial and Market Revolutions in changing the American economy.

the city's nativist clubs lasted for two months and escalated into open warfare between Protestants and the Pennsylvania militia. Even as the economic revolution brought prosperity to many Americans and attracted millions of immigrants, it divided society along lines of class, ethnicity, and religion.

SUMMARY

In this chapter, we examined the causes of the economic transformation of the first half of the nineteenth century. That transformation had two facets: the increase in production known as the Industrial Revolution and the expansion of commerce known as the Market Revolution. Water and steam were crucial ingredients in both revolutions — driving factory machinery, carrying goods to market on canals and rivers, and propelling steamboats and railroad engines.

We also explored the consequences of that transformation: the rise of an urban society, the increasing similarity between the Northeast and Midwest and their growing difference from the South, and the creation of a class-divided society. Seeking to shape the emerging society, benevolent reformers and evangelical revivalists worked to instill moral discipline and Christian values. But artisan republicans, unionized workers, Irish and German immigrants had their own economic or cultural goals. The result was a fragmented society. Differences of class and culture now split the North just as race and class had long divided the South. As the next chapter suggests, Americans looked to the political system, which was becoming increasingly democratic, to address these divisions. In fact, the tensions among economic inequality, cultural diversity, and political democracy became a troubling — and enduring — part of American life.

Connections: Economy and Society

In 1820, most Americans lived in a rural, agricultural society much like the world of their grandparents. Then, as we noted in the opening essay for Part Three, came dramatic changes that "affected every aspect of life in the North and Midwest and brought important changes in the South as well." In this chapter, we have described the role of industry and commerce in creating a new economy and a new society in the Northeast and the Midwest. Our in-depth analysis of changes in the South appears in Chapter 12, where we describe the enormous expansion in plantation agriculture and cotton production between 1820 and 1860 and the devastating impact of the domestic slave trade on millions of African Americans.

In the opening essay, we also noted that

> The new economy created a class-based society in the North and Midwest. A wealthy elite of merchants, manufacturers, bankers, and entrepreneurs rose to the top of the social order. To maintain social stability, they adopted a paternalistic program of benevolent reform.

The discussion of social reform begun in this chapter continues in Chapter 11, which describes how advocates of temperance, religious utopianism, abolitionism, and women's rights took the reform movement in new directions. The radical outlooks and activities of these new reformers were the result, in part, of the overthrow of the traditional political system and the rise of Jacksonian democracy, the subjects of Chapter 10.

TIMELINE

1782	▶ Oliver Evans builds automated flour mill	**1820s**	▶ New England women head to textile factories
1790	▶ Samuel Slater opens spinning mill in Rhode Island		▶ Benevolent Empire leads conservative social reform
1792	▶ Congress passes Post Office Act	**1824**	▶ *Gibbons v. Ogden* promotes interstate trade
1793	▶ Eli Whitney manufactures cotton gins	**1830s**	▶ Emergence of western commercial cities
1800–1830	▶ Entrepreneurs in shoe industry impose division of labor		▶ Labor movement gains strength
			▶ Cities segregate by class
1807	▶ Robert Fulton's *Clermont*, the first American steamboat		▶ Middle-class culture emerges
1814	▶ Boston Manufacturing Company opens cotton mill in Waltham, Massachusetts		▶ Growth of temperance movement
			▶ Charles Grandison Finney's revivalist crusade
1816–1828	▶ Congress places protective tariffs on textiles and other imports	**1840s**	▶ Irish and German immigration sparks ethnic riots
1817	▶ Erie Canal begun (completed in 1825)		▶ Rise of machine-tool industry
1820	▶ Minimum federal land price reduced to $1.25 per acre	**1850s**	▶ Expansion of railroads in Northeast and Midwest
1820–1840	▶ Fourfold increase in city residents in Northeast and Midwest	**1857**	▶ Overproduction and speculation trigger a financial panic

FOR FURTHER EXPLORATION

Charles G. Sellers, *The Market Revolution: Jacksonian America, 1815–1846* (1991), focuses on the social impact of economic change. Scott A. Sandage, *Born Losers: A History of Failure in America* (2005), explores the fate of the unsuccessful. David Freeman Hawke, *Nuts and Bolts of the Past: A History of American Technology, 1776–1860* (1988), offers an entertaining account, as does "The Eli Whitney Museum & Workshop" (**www .eliwhitney.org/**).

Stephen Aron, *How the West Was Lost: The Transformation of Kentucky from Daniel Boone to Henry Clay* (1996), and Peter Way, *Common Labor: Workers and the Digging of North American Canals, 1780–1860* (1993), assess the underside of westward expansion. For first-person accounts, see "Pioneering the Upper Midwest" (**memory.loc.gov/ammem/umhtml/umhome.html**).

Stuart M. Blumin's *The Emergence of the Middle Class* (1989), discusses urban class formation. Stephen P. Rice, *Minding the Machine: Languages of Class in Early Industrial America* (2004), and David Grimsted, *American Mobbing* (1998), examine the culture wars of the nineteenth century. In *Home and Work* (1990), Jeanne Boydston critically examines changes in women's lives. For the story of a woman in the mills, log onto **www.fordham.edu/halsall/mod/robinson-lowell.html**.

For Evangelical Protestantism, consult Mark A. Noll, *America's God: From Jonathan Edwards to Abraham Lincoln* (2003), Bernard Weisberger's classic study *They Gathered at the River* (1958), and William R. Hutchison, *Religious Pluralism in America: The Contentious History of a Founding Ideal* (2003).

TEST YOUR KNOWLEDGE

To assess your mastery of the material in this chapter and for Web sites, images, and documents related to this chapter, visit **bedfordstmartins.com/henrettaconcise**.

A Democratic Revolution

1820–1844

No free country can exist
without political parties.

— Martin Van Buren (1856)

Europoean visitors to the United States
in the 1830s generally praised its republican society but not its political
parties and politicians. "The gentlemen spit, talk of elections and the price of produce,
and spit again," Frances Trollope reported in *Domestic Manners of the Americans*
(1832). In her view, American politics was the sport of self-serving party politicians
who reeked of "whiskey and onions." Other Europeans lamented the low intellectual
level of American political debate. The "clap-trap of praise and pathos" voiced by a
Massachusetts politician "deeply disgusted" Harriet Martineau. Basil Hall was aston-
ished by the shallow arguments and the "conclusions in which nothing was concluded"
advanced by the inept "farmers, shopkeepers, and country lawyers" who sat in the New
York assembly.

The verdict was unanimous and negative. "The most able men in the United States
are very rarely placed at the head of affairs," French aristocrat Alexis de Tocqueville
observed in *Democracy in America* (1835). The reason, Tocqueville suggested, lay in
the character of democracy itself. Most citizens simply ignored important political issues, refused out of jealousy to elect their intellectual superiors, and listened in awe to
"the clamor of a mountebank [a charismatic fraud] who knows the secret of stimulating their tastes."

The European visitors were witnessing the unfolding of the American Democratic
Revolution. Before 1815, men of great ability had sat in the seats of government, and
the prevailing ideology had been republicanism, rule by "men of TALENTS and VIRTUE,"
as a newspaper put it. By the 1820s and 1830s, the watchword was *democracy*, which in
practice meant rule by popularly elected party politicians. "That the majority should
govern was a fundamental maxim in all free governments," declared Martin Van Buren,
the most talented of the middle-class professional politicians. The new party politicians often pursued selfish goals, but by encouraging ordinary Americans to burn with
"election fever" and support party principles, they provided a sense of identity and
purpose amid a fragmented social order.

The Rise of Popular Politics, 1820–1829

Expansion of the **franchise** dramatically symbolized the Democratic Revolution. By the 1830s, most states had opened the franchise to most white men. Nowhere else in the world did ordinary farmers and wage earners exercise such political influence. In England, for example, the Reform Bill of 1832 extended the vote to only 600,000 out of 6 million English men — a mere 10 percent.

The Decline of the Notables and the Rise of Parties

The American Revolution weakened the deferential society of the colonial era but did not overthrow it. Only two state constitutions — those of Pennsylvania and Vermont — allowed all male taxpayers to vote; even in those states, families of low rank continued to accept the leadership of their social "betters." Consequently, wealthy notables — northern landlords, slave-owning planters, and seaport merchants — dominated the political system in the new republic. And rightly so, thought John Jay, the first chief justice of the Supreme Court. As Jay put it in 1810: "Those who own the country are the most fit persons to participate in the government of it." Jay and other notables managed local elections by building up an "interest": lending money to small farmers, giving business to storekeepers, and treating their tenants to rum at election time. An outlay of $20 for refreshments, remarked one poll watcher, "may produce about 100 votes." This gentry-dominated system kept men who lacked wealth and powerful family connections from running for office.

The struggle to expand the suffrage began in the 1810s. Reformers in Maryland invoked the egalitarian language of republicanism: Property qualifications were a "tyranny" because they endowed "one class of men with privileges which are denied to another." To defuse this criticism and deter migration to the West, legislators in Maryland and other seaboard states grudgingly accepted a broader franchise. But the new voters quickly changed the tone of politics, rejecting politicians who flaunted their high social status by wearing "top boots, breeches, and shoe buckles," their hair in "powder and queues." Instead, they elected men who dressed simply and endorsed democracy, even if those politicians favored policies that benefited the wealthy.

Smallholding farmers and ambitious laborers in the Midwest and Southwest likewise challenged the old hierarchical order. In Ohio, a traveler reported, "no white man or woman will bear being called a servant." The constitutions of the new states of Indiana (1816), Illinois (1818), and Alabama (1819) prescribed a broad male franchise, and voters usually elected middling men to local and state offices. A well-to-do migrant in Illinois was surprised to learn that the man who plowed his fields "was a colonel of militia, and a member of the legislature." Once in public office, men from modest backgrounds enacted laws that restricted imprisonment for debt, kept taxes low, and allowed farmers to claim squatters' rights to unoccupied land.

By the mid-1820s, many states had instituted universal white male suffrage or had given the vote to all white men who paid taxes or served in the militia. Only a few — North Carolina, Virginia, and Rhode Island — still required the ownership of freehold property for voting. Moreover, between 1818 and 1821, Connecticut, Massachusetts, and New York wrote more democratic constitutions that reapportioned legislative districts on the basis of population and mandated the popular election (rather than the appointment) of judges and justices of the peace.

Democratic politics was contentious and, because it was run by men on the make, often corrupt. Powerful entrepreneurs and speculators—both notables and self-made men—demanded government assistance for their business enterprises and paid bribes to get it. Speculators won land grants by paying off the members of key committees, and bankers distributed shares of stock to key legislators. When the Seventh Ward Bank of New York City received a charter in 1833, the supervising commissioners set aside one-third of the bank's 3,700 shares of stock for themselves and their friends and almost two-thirds for state legislators and officials, leaving just 40 shares for public sale.

More contention broke out when religious reformers turned to political action to advance the cultural agenda of the Benevolent Empire. In Utica, New York, evangelical Presbyterians called for a town ordinance restricting Sunday entertainment. In response, a local Universalist—a member of a freethinking Protestant denomination—denounced the measure as coercive and called for "Religious Liberty."

The appearance of political parties encouraged such debates over government policy. Revolutionary-era Americans had condemned political "factions" as anti-republican and did not even mention political parties in the national and state constitutions. But as the power of notables waned, political parties came to the fore. By the 1820s, a number of states had disciplined parties managed by professional politicians, often middle-class lawyers and journalists. One observer compared the new organizations to a well-designed textile loom, calling them "machines" that wove the interests of diverse social and economic groups into a coherent legislative program.

Martin Van Buren of New York was the chief architect of the emerging system of party government, at both the state and national levels. The son of a Jeffersonian tavern keeper, Van Buren grew up in the landlord-dominated society of the Hudson River Valley. To get his training as a lawyer, he relied on the powerful Van Ness clan; then, determined not to become a dependent "tool" of a notable family, he repudiated their tutelage. His goal was to create a political order based on party, not family. To justify party government, Van Buren rejected the traditional republican belief that political parties were dangerous; instead, he claimed that the opposite was true: "All men of sense know that political parties are inseparable from free government," because they check a government's inherent "disposition to abuse power."

Between 1817 and 1821, Van Buren turned his "Bucktail" supporters (so called because they wore a deer's tail on their hats) into the first statewide **political machine**. He purchased a newspaper, the *Albany Argus*, and used its pages to promote his policies and get out the vote. **Patronage** was an even more important tool. When Van Buren's Bucktails won control of the New York legislature in 1821, they acquired a political "interest" much greater than that of the notables: the power to appoint some six thousand of their followers to positions in New York's legal bureaucracy of judges, justices of the peace, sheriffs, deed commissioners, and coroners. This **spoils system** was fair, Van Buren suggested, because it "would operate sometimes in favour of one party, and sometimes of another." And party government was thoroughly republican, he added, based as it was on majority rule. To enact important legislation, Van Buren insisted on disciplined voting as determined by a **party caucus**. On one crucial occasion, the "Little Magician"—a nickname referring to Van Buren's height and political dexterity—held an elaborate banquet to praise seventeen New York legislators for sacrificing "individual preferences for the general good."

The Election of 1824

The advance of political democracy and party government in the states undermined the old notable-dominated system of national politics. After the War of 1812, the aristocratic Federalist Party virtually disappeared, and the Republican Party splintered into competing factions (see Chapter 7). As the election of 1824 approached, no fewer than five Republican candidates campaigned for the presidency. Three were veterans of President James Monroe's cabinet: Secretary of State John Quincy Adams, the son of former president John Adams; Secretary of War John C. Calhoun; and Secretary of the Treasury William H. Crawford. The fourth candidate was Henry Clay of Kentucky, the dynamic Speaker of the House of Representatives; the fifth was General Andrew Jackson, now a senator from Tennessee.

When a caucus of Republicans in Congress selected Crawford as the party's official nominee, the other candidates refused to withdraw and sought popular support. Because of democratic reforms, eighteen of the twenty-four states required popular elections (rather than a vote of the state legislature) to choose their representatives to the Electoral College. Each candidate had strengths. Thanks to his diplomatic successes as Secretary of State (see Chapter 7), John Quincy Adams enjoyed national recognition; and his Massachusetts origins gave him the electoral votes of New England. Henry Clay based his candidacy on his **American System**, an integrated program of national economic development similar to the Commonwealth policies pursued by state governments. Clay wanted to enhance the powers of the Second Bank of the United States and to use tariff revenues to build roads and canals. His nationalistic program won praise in the West, which needed transportation improvements, but elicited sharp criticism in the South, which relied on rivers to market its cotton and had few manufacturing industries to protect. William Crawford of Georgia, an ideological heir of Thomas Jefferson, denounced Clay's American System as a scheme that would "consolidate" political power in Washington. Recognizing Crawford's appeal in the South, John C. Calhoun of South Carolina withdrew from the presidential race and endorsed Andrew Jackson.

As the hero of the Battle of New Orleans, Jackson benefited from the wave of patriotism that flowed from the War of 1812. Born in the Carolina backcountry, Jackson had settled in Nashville, Tennessee, where he formed ties to influential families through marriage and his career as an attorney and slave-owning cotton planter. His rise from common origins symbolized the new democratic age, and his reputation as a "plain solid republican" attracted voters in all regions.

Still, Jackson's strong showing in the election surprised most political leaders. The Tennessee senator received 99 of the 261 votes cast by members of the Electoral College; Adams garnered 84 votes; Crawford, who had suffered a stroke during the campaign, won 41; and Clay finished with 37 (Map 10.1). Because no candidate received an absolute majority, the Twelfth Amendment to the Constitution (ratified in 1804) specified that the House of Representatives would choose the president from among the three highest vote-getters. This procedure worked against Jackson because many congressmen

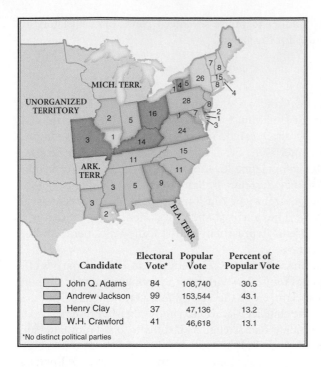

MAP 10.1 The Presidential Election of 1824

Regional voting dominated the presidential election of 1824. John Quincy Adams captured every electoral vote in New England and most of those in New York. Henry Clay carried Ohio and Kentucky, the most populous trans-Appalachian states; and William Crawford took the southern states of Virginia and Georgia. Only Andrew Jackson claimed a national constituency, winning Pennsylvania and New Jersey in the East, Indiana and most of Illinois in the Midwest, and much of the South. Only 356,000 Americans voted, about 27 percent of the eligible electorate.

Candidate	Electoral Vote*	Popular Vote	Percent of Popular Vote
John Q. Adams	84	108,740	30.5
Andrew Jackson	99	153,544	43.1
Henry Clay	37	47,136	13.2
W.H. Crawford	41	46,618	13.1

*No distinct political parties

feared that the rough-hewn "military chieftain" might become a tyrant. Out of the race himself, Henry Clay used his influence as Speaker to thwart Jackson's election. Clay assembled a coalition of congressmen from New England and the Ohio River Valley that voted Adams into the presidency. Adams showed his gratitude by appointing Clay his secretary of state, which was the traditional steppingstone to the presidency.

Clay's appointment was a politically fatal mistake for both men. Jackson supporters accused Clay and Adams of making a secret deal. Condemning what Calhoun labeled a "corrupt bargain" that thwarted the popular will, they vowed that Clay would never become president.

The Last Notable President: John Quincy Adams

As president, Adams called for bold national leadership. "The moral purpose of the Creator," he told Congress, was to use the president and all public officials to "improve the conditions of himself and his fellow men." Adams called for the establishment of a national university in Washington, extensive scientific explorations in the Far West, and a uniform standard of weights and measures. Most important, he endorsed Henry Clay's American System of national economic development and its three key elements: protective tariffs to stimulate manufacturing, federally subsidized roads and canals to facilitate commerce, and a national bank to control credit and provide a uniform currency.

Manufacturers, entrepreneurs, and farmers in the Northeast and Midwest welcomed Adams's proposals. But those policies won little support in the South, where planters opposed protective tariffs, which raised the price of manufactures, and smallholders feared powerful banks that could force them into bankruptcy. From his deathbed,

John Quincy Adams
This famous daguerreotype of the former president, taken about 1843 by Philip Haas, conveys his rigid personality and high moral standards. Although these personal attributes contributed to Adams's success as an antislavery congressman from Massachusetts in the 1830s and 1840s, they hindered his effectiveness as the nation's chief executive. Metropolitan Museum of Art, New York. Gift of I. N. Phelps Stokes, Edward S. Hawes, Alice Mary Hawes, Marion Augusta Hawes.

Thomas Jefferson condemned Adams for promoting "a single and splendid government of aristocracy [of money] . . . riding and ruling over the plundered ploughman and beggared yeomanry."

Other politicians objected to the American System on constitutional grounds. In 1817, President Madison had vetoed the Bonus Bill, which would have used the national government's income from the Second Bank of the United States to fund improvement projects in the states. Such projects, Madison had argued, were the sole responsibility of the states, a sentiment widely shared among Old Republicans. After a trip to Monticello to meet Thomas Jefferson, Martin Van Buren declared his allegiance to the constitutional "doctrines of the Jefferson School." Now a member of the U.S. Senate, Van Buren joined the Old Republicans in defeating most of Adams's proposals for national subsidies for roads and canals.

The farthest-reaching battle of the Adams administration came over tariffs. The Tariff of 1816 placed relatively high duties on imports of cheap English cotton cloth, allowing New England textile producers to dominate that market. In 1824, Adams and Clay secured a new tariff that protected manufacturers in New England and Pennsylvania against imports of iron goods and more expensive English woolen and cotton textiles. Without these tariffs, the U.S. producers might have faced the fate of the once world-dominant textile industry in India, which was destroyed in the early nineteenth century by the free trade policies imposed by the British imperial regime.

Recognizing the appeal of tariffs, Van Buren and his Jacksonian allies hopped on the bandwagon. By placing higher tariffs on wool, hemp, and other imported raw materials, they hoped to win the support of the wool- and hemp-producing farmers in New York, Ohio, and Kentucky for Jackson's presidential candidacy in 1828. The tariff had become a prisoner of politics. "I fear this tariff thing," remarked Thomas Cooper, the president of the College of South Carolina and an advocate of free trade, which has become "by some strange mechanical contrivance . . . a machine for manufacturing Presidents, instead of broadcloths, and bed blankets." Disregarding southern protests, northern Jacksonians joined with supporters of Adams and Clay to enact the Tariff of 1828, which significantly raised duties on raw materials, textiles, and iron goods.

The new tariff enraged the South. As the world's cheapest producer of raw cotton, the South did not need a tariff to protect its main industry. Moreover, by raising the price of manufactures, the tariff cost southern planters about $100 million a year. Planters had to buy either higher-cost American textiles and iron goods, thus enriching northeastern businesses and workers, or highly dutied British imports, thus paying the expenses of the national government. The new tariff was "little less than legalized pillage," an Alabama legislator declared, calling it a "Tariff of Abominations."

Ignoring the Jacksonians' support for the Tariff of 1828, most southerners blamed President Adams for the new act. They also criticized Adams's Indian policy. A deeply moral man, the president supported the land rights of Native Americans against expansionist whites. In 1825, U.S. commissioners had secured a treaty from one Creek faction to cede Creek lands in Georgia to the United States for eventual sale to the citizens of Georgia. When the Creek National Council repudiated the treaty, claiming that it was fraudulent, Adams called for new negotiations. Eager to acquire the Creeks' land, Georgia governor George M. Troup attacked the president as a "public enemy . . . the unblushing ally of the savages." Joining with Georgia's representatives in Congress, Troup persuaded Congress to extinguish the Creeks' land titles, forcing most Creeks to leave the state.

Elsewhere in the nation, Adams's primary weakness was his out-of-date political style. The last notable to serve in the White House, he acted the part: aloof, moralistic, and paternalistic. When Congress rejected his activist economic policies, Adams questioned the wisdom of the people and advised elected officials not to be "palsied [enfeebled] by the will of our constituents." Ignoring his waning popularity, the president did not use patronage to reward his supporters and allowed hostile federal officials to remain in office. Rather than "run" for reelection in 1828, Adams "stood" for it, telling supporters, "If my country wants my services, she must ask for them."

"The Democracy" and the Election of 1828

Martin Van Buren and the professional politicians handling Andrew Jackson's campaign had no reservations about running for office. The Little Magician's goal was to recreate the national political coalition that Thomas Jefferson had formed; he therefore championed policies that appealed both to northern farmers and artisans (the "plain Republicans of the North") and to southern slave owners and smallholding planters. John C. Calhoun, Jackson's vice-presidential running mate, brought his South

Carolina allies into Van Buren's party, and Jackson's close friends in Tennessee rallied voters there and throughout the Old Southwest. By forming a national political party, Jackson's friends hoped to reconcile the diverse economic and social "interests" that, as James Madison had predicted in "Federalist No. 10," would inevitability exist in a large republic.

At Van Buren's direction, the Jacksonians orchestrated a massive publicity campaign. In New York, fifty newspapers declared their support for Jackson on the same day. Elsewhere, Jacksonians organized mass meetings, torchlight parades, and barbecues to celebrate their candidate's frontier origin and rise to fame. With the cry of "Jackson for ever!," they praised "Old Hickory" as a "natural" aristocrat, a self-made man.

The Jacksonians called themselves Democrats or "the Democracy," names that conveyed their egalitarian message. As Thomas Morris told the Ohio legislature, he and other Democrats believed that the republic had been corrupted by legislative charters that gave "a few individuals rights and privileges not enjoyed by the citizens at large." The Democracy would destroy such "artificial distinction in society," Morris promised. Jackson himself declared that "equality among the people in the rights conferred by government" was the "great radical principle of freedom."

Jackson's message of equal rights and popular rule appealed to many social groups. His hostility to business corporations and to Clay's American System won support from northeastern artisans and workers who felt threatened by industrialization. Jackson also captured the votes of Pennsylvania ironworkers and New York farmers who had been enriched by the controversial Tariff of Abominations. Yet by astutely declaring his preference for a "judicious" tariff that would balance regional interests, Jackson remained popular in the South as well. In the Southeast and the Midwest, Old Hickory garnered votes because his well-known hostility toward Native Americans reassured white farmers who favored Indian removal.

The Democrats' celebration of popular rule carried Jackson into office. In 1824, about one-quarter of the eligible electorate had voted; in 1828, more than one-half went to the polls, and 56 percent of voters cast their ballots for the senator from Tennessee (Figure 10.1). Jackson received 178 of 261 electoral votes and became the first president from a trans-Appalachian state. As the president-elect traveled to Washington, he cut a dignified figure. According to an English observer, he "wore his hair carelessly but not ungracefully arranged, and in spite of his harsh, gaunt features looked like a gentleman and a soldier." Still, Jackson's popularity frightened men of wealth. Senator Daniel Webster of Massachusetts, a former Federalist and now a corporate lawyer, warned his clients that the new president would "bring a breeze with him. Which way it will blow, I cannot tell [but] . . . my fear is stronger than my hope." Supreme Court Justice Joseph Story shared Webster's apprehensions. Watching an unruly Inauguration Day crowd climb over the elegant furniture in the White House to congratulate Jackson, Story lamented: "the reign of King 'Mob' seemed triumphant."

▶ Was there a necessary connection between the growth of democracy and the emergence of disciplined political parties, or was it just a coincidence? Explain your answer.

▶ How do you explain John Quincy Adams's great success as secretary of state (see Chapter 7) and his relative lack of success as president?

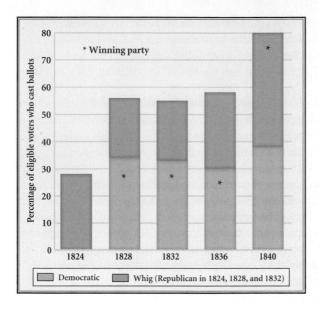

FIGURE 10.1 Changes in Voting Patterns, 1824–1840 Voter participation soared in 1828 and again in 1840 as competition heated up between Democrats and Whigs, who advocated different policies and philosophies of government.

The Jacksonian Presidency, 1829–1837

American-style political democracy—a broad franchise, a disciplined political party, and policies favoring specific groups of voters—ushered Andrew Jackson into office. Jackson used his popular mandate to transform the presidency and the policies of the national government. During his two terms in the White House, he enhanced presidential authority, destroyed the nationalistic American System, and implemented a new ideology of government. An Ohio supporter summarized Jackson's vision: "the Sovereignty of the People, the Rights of the States, and a Light and Simple Government."

Jackson's Agenda: Rotation and Decentralization

Although Jackson had a formal cabinet, for policymaking he relied primarily on an informal group of advisors: his "Kitchen Cabinet." Its most influential members were Kentuckians Francis Preston Blair, who edited the *Washington Globe*, and Amos Kendall, who wrote Jackson's speeches; Roger B. Taney of Maryland, who became attorney general, treasury secretary, and then chief justice of the Supreme Court; and, most important, Secretary of State Martin Van Buren.

Following Van Buren's practice in New York, Jackson used patronage to create a disciplined national party. He insisted on replacing "property in office" (a view that officials held office just as individuals held land) with rotation of officeholders: When an administration was voted out, its bureaucratic appointees would have to leave government service. Rotation would not lessen expertise, Jackson insisted, because public duties were "so plain and simple that men of intelligence may readily qualify themselves for their performance." William L. Marcy, a New York Jacksonian, put it more bluntly: Government jobs were like the spoils of war, and "to the victor belong the

President Andrew Jackson, 1830
The new president came to Washington with a well-deserved reputation as an aggressive Indian fighter and dangerous military leader. But in this official portrait, he looks "presidential": His dress and posture, and the artist's composition, created the image of a calm, deliberate statesman. Subsequent events would show that Jackson had not lost his hard-edged authoritarian personality. Library of Congress.

spoils of the enemy." Using the spoils system, Jackson dispensed government jobs to reward friends and win backing for his policies.

Jackson's priority was to destroy the American System and all national plans for economic development. As Henry Clay noted apprehensively, the new president wanted "to cry down old constructions of the Constitution . . . to make all Jefferson's opinions the articles of faith of the new Church." Declaring that the "voice of the people" called for "economy in the expenditures of the Government," Jackson rejected national subsidies for transportation projects, which he also opposed on constitutional grounds. In 1830, he vetoed four internal improvement bills, including an extension of the National Road, arguing that they infringed "the reserved powers of states." These vetoes also represented an indirect attack on the protective tariffs, another controversial part of the American System, because Clay proposed to use them to fund canals and roads. As Senator William Smith of South Carolina noted, "destroy internal improvements and you leave no motive for the tariff."

The Tariff and Nullification

The Tariff of 1828 had helped Jackson to win the presidency, but it saddled him with a major political crisis. There was fierce opposition to high tariffs throughout the South, especially in South Carolina. South Carolina was the only state with an African American majority—56 percent of the population in 1830—and its slave owners, like the white sugar planters in the West Indies, feared a black rebellion. They also worried about the legal abolition of slavery. The British Parliament was on track to end slavery in the West Indies in 1833; South Carolina planters, remembering attempts to limit slavery in Missouri (see Chapter 8), worried that the U.S. Congress might do the same. So they attacked the tariff, both to lower rates and to discourage other uses of federal power.

The crisis began in 1832, when high-tariff congressmen ignored southern warnings that they were "endangering the Union" and reenacted the Tariff of Abominations. In response, leading South Carolinians called a state convention in November, which boldly adopted an Ordinance of Nullification. The ordinance declared the tariffs of 1828 and 1832 to be null and void; prohibited the collection of those duties in South Carolina after February 1, 1833; and threatened secession if federal officials tried to collect them.

South Carolina's act of **nullification** rested on the constitutional arguments developed in *The South Carolina Exposition and Protest* (1828). Written anonymously by Vice President John C. Calhoun, the *Exposition* gave a localist interpretation to the federal union. Because each geographic region had distinct interests, localists argued, protective tariffs and other national legislation that operated unequally on the various states lacked fairness and legitimacy—in fact, they were unconstitutional. An obsessive defender of the interests of the white South, Calhoun exaggerated the frequency of such legislation, declaring, "Constitutional government and the government of a majority are utterly incompatible."

Advancing an alternative interpretation of the Constitution, Calhoun used the arguments first advanced by Jefferson and Madison in the Kentucky and Virginia resolutions of 1798. Because the U.S. Constitution had been ratified by conventions in the various states, the resolutions suggested, sovereignty lay in the states, not in the people. Beginning from this premise, Calhoun developed a states' rights interpretation of the Constitution, arguing that a state convention could declare a congressional law to be unconstitutional and therefore void within the state's borders. Replying to this argument, which had no support in the text of the Constitution, Senator Daniel Webster of Massachusetts presented a nationalist interpretation that celebrated popular sovereignty and congressional legislation securing the "general welfare."

Jackson hoped to find a middle path between Webster's strident nationalism and Calhoun's radical doctrine of localist federalism. The Constitution clearly gave the federal government the authority to establish tariffs, and, Jackson would enforce that power, whatever the cost. The president declared that South Carolina's Ordinance of Nullification not only violated the letter of the Constitution but also was "unauthorized by its spirit . . . and destructive of the great object for which it was formed." "Disunion by armed force is treason," he warned. At Jackson's request, Congress passed a Force Bill early in 1833; it authorized the president to use military means to compel South Carolina's obedience to national laws. Simultaneously, Jackson addressed the South's objections to high import duties by winning passage of an act that, by 1842, reduced tariff rates to the modest levels of 1816. They remained low because western wheat farmers joined southern planters in advocating cheap imports and abundant exports. "Illinois wants a market for her agricultural products," declared Senator Sidney Breese in 1846, "she wants the market of the world."

Having won the *political* battle by securing a reduction in duties, the South Carolina convention gave up its *constitutional* quest and rescinded its nullification of the tariff. Jackson was satisfied. He had addressed the economic demands of the South while upholding the constitutional principle that no state could nullify a law of the United States—a principle that Abraham Lincoln would embrace to defend the Union during the secession crisis of 1861.

The Bank War

In the middle of the tariff crisis, Jackson faced a major challenge from the political supporters of the Second Bank of the United States. Founded in Philadelphia in 1816 (see Chapter 7), the bank was a privately managed institution that operated under a twenty-year charter from the federal government, which owned 20 percent of its stock. The Second Bank's most important role was to stabilize the nation's money supply, which consisted primarily of notes and bills of credit—in effect, paper money—issued by state-chartered banks. Those banks promised to redeem the notes on demand with "hard" money—that is, gold or silver coins (also known as specie). By collecting those notes and regularly demanding specie, the Second Bank kept the state banks from issuing too much paper money and depreciating its value.

This cautious monetary policy pleased creditors—the bankers and entrepreneurs in Boston, New York, and Philadelphia, whose capital investments were underwriting economic development. However, ordinary Americans were afraid that the Second Bank would force the closure of state banks, leaving people holding worthless paper notes. Some politicians opposed the Second Bank because of the arrogance of its president, Nicholas Biddle. "As to mere power," Biddle boasted, "I have been for years in the daily exercise of more personal authority than any President habitually enjoys." Fearing Biddle's influence, bankers in New York and other states wanted the specie owned by the federal government deposited in their own institutions rather than in the Second Bank. Other expansion-minded bankers, including friends of Jackson's in Nashville, wanted to escape supervision by any central bank.

Although the Bank had many enemies, a political miscalculation by its friends brought its downfall. In 1832, Henry Clay and Daniel Webster persuaded Biddle to seek an early extension of the bank's charter (which still had four years to run). They had the votes in Congress to enact the required legislation and hoped to lure Jackson into a veto that would split the Democrats just before the 1832 elections.

Jackson turned the tables on Clay and Webster. He vetoed the rechartering bill and issued a masterful veto message that blended constitutional arguments with class rhetoric and patriotic fervor. Adopting Thomas Jefferson's position, Jackson declared that Congress had no constitutional authority to charter a national bank, which was "subversive of the rights of the States." He also attacked the Second Bank as "dangerous to the liberties of the people." Employing the populist republican rhetoric of the American Revolution, Jackson condemned the Bank as a nest of special privilege and monopoly power that promoted "the advancement of the few at the expense of . . . farmers, mechanics, and laborers." Finally, the president evoked patriotic sentiment by pointing out that British aristocrats owned much of the bank's stock. Such a powerful institution should be "purely American," Jackson declared.

Jackson's attack on the bank carried him and Martin Van Buren, his long-time ally and new running mate, to victory in 1832. Old Hickory and "Little Van" overwhelmed Henry Clay, who headed the National Republican ticket, by 219 to 49 electoral votes. Jackson's most fervent supporters were eastern workers and western farmers, who blamed the Second Bank for urban price increases and stagnant farm prices. "All the flourishing cities of the West are mortgaged to this money power," charged Senator Thomas Hart Benton, a Jacksonian from Missouri. "They may be devoured by it at any moment." But many of Jackson's supporters had prospered during a decade of strong economic growth. Along with thousands of middle-class Americans — lawyers, clerks, shopkeepers, and artisans — they wanted an equal opportunity to rise in the world and cheered Jackson's attack on privileged corporations.

Early in 1833, Jackson called on Roger B. Taney to weaken the Second Bank, which still had four years left on its charter. A strong opponent of corporate privilege, Taney assumed control of the Treasury Department and promptly withdrew the government's gold and silver from the Second Bank. He deposited the specie in various state banks, which critics called Jackson's "pet banks." To justify this abrupt (and probably illegal) transfer, Jackson declared that his reelection represented "the decision of the people against the bank" and gave him a mandate to destroy it. This sweeping claim of presidential power was new and radical. Never before had a president claimed that victory at the polls allowed him to pursue a controversial policy or to act independently of Congress.

The "bank war" escalated into an all-out political battle. In March 1834, Jackson's opponents in the Senate passed a resolution written by Henry Clay that censured the president and warned of executive tyranny: "We are in the midst of a revolution, hitherto bloodless, but rapidly descending towards a total change of the pure republican character of the Government, and the concentration of all power in the hands of one man." Jackson was not deterred by Clay's charges or Congress's censure. "The Bank is trying to kill me but I will kill it," he vowed to Van Buren. And so he did. When the Second Bank's national charter expired in 1836, Jackson prevented its renewal.

Jackson had destroyed both national banking — the creation of Alexander Hamilton — and the American System of protective tariffs and internal improvements that Henry Clay and John Quincy Adams had instituted. The result was a profound reduction in economic activism and creative policymaking by the national government. "All is gone," observed a Washington newspaper correspondent. "All is gone, which the General Government was instituted to create and preserve."

Indian Removal

The status of Native American peoples posed an equally complex political problem. By the late 1820s, white voices throughout the South and Midwest were calling for the Indian peoples to be resettled west of the Mississippi River. Many easterners who were sympathetic to Native Americans also favored resettlement. Removal to the West seemed the only way to protect Indian peoples from alcoholic devastation and financial exploitation and to preserve the Indians' culture.

However, most Indians did not want to leave their ancestral lands. The Old Southwest was home to the Cherokees and Creeks in Georgia, Tennessee, and Alabama; the

Chickasaws and Choctaws in Mississippi and Alabama; and the Seminoles in Florida. During the War of 1812, Andrew Jackson had forced the Creeks to relinquish millions of acres of land, but Indian peoples still controlled vast tracts. Moreover, the mixed-blood offspring of white traders and Indian women had assumed the leadership of many peoples. Growing up in a bicultural world, mixed-bloods knew the political ways of whites. Most of them strongly resisted removal, and some favored assimilation into white society.

A number of mixed-blood Indians had already adopted the institutions and the lifestyle of southern planters. James Vann, a Georgia Cherokee, owned more than twenty black slaves, two trading posts, and a gristmill. Forty other mixed-blood Cherokee families each owned twenty or more African American slaves. To protect their property and the lands of their people, the mixed-bloods promoted a strong Indian identity. Sequoyah perfected a system of writing for the Cherokee language in 1821; six years later, he and other mixed-bloods devised a new charter of Cherokee government modeled directly on the U.S. Constitution. Full-blood Cherokees, who made up 90 percent of the population, resisted many of these cultural and political innovations but were equally determined to retain their ancestral lands. "We would not receive money for land in which our fathers and friends are buried," one full-blood chief declared. "We love our land; it is our mother."

What the Cherokees wanted carried no weight with the Georgia legislature. In 1802, Georgia had given up its western land claims in return for a federal promise to extinguish Indian landholdings in the state. Now it demanded fulfillment of that pledge. Having spent his military career fighting Indians and seizing their lands, Andrew Jackson gave full support to Georgia. On assuming the presidency, he withdrew the federal troops that had protected Indian enclaves there and in Alabama and Mississippi. The states, he declared, were sovereign within their borders.

Jackson then pushed the Indian Removal Act of 1830 through Congress. The act granted money and land in present-day Oklahoma and Kansas to Native American peoples who would give up their ancestral holdings (see American Voices, p. 304). To persuade Indians to move, government officials promised that they could live on the new lands, "they and all their children, as long as grass grows and water runs." When Chief Black Hawk and his Sauk and Fox followers refused to move from rich farmland in western Illinois in 1832, Jackson sent troops to expel them. Rejecting Black Hawk's offer to surrender, the American army pursued him into the Wisconsin Territory and, in the brutal eight-hour Bad Axe Massacre, killed 850 of Black Hawk's 1,000 warriors. Over the next five years, American diplomatic pressure and military power forced seventy Indian peoples to sign treaties and move west of the Mississippi (Map 10.2).

In the meantime, the Cherokees had carried their case to the Supreme Court, where they claimed the status of a "foreign nation." In *Cherokee Nation v. Georgia* (1831), Chief Justice John Marshall denied the Cherokees' claim of independence and declared that Indian peoples were "domestic dependent nations." However, in *Worcester v. Georgia* (1832), Marshall and the court sided with the Cherokees against Georgia. Voiding Georgia's extension of state law over the Cherokees, the court held that Indian nations were "distinct political communities, having territorial boundaries, within which their authority is exclusive [and this is] guaranteed by the United States."

A Sacred Reverence for Our Lands   BLACK HAWK

Black Hawk (1767–1838), or Makataimeshekiakiak in the language of his people, was a chief of the Sauk and Fox. In 1833, he dictated his life story to a government interpreter, and a young newspaper editor published it. Here, Black Hawk describes the coming of white settlers to his village, near present-day Rock Island, Illinois, and his decision to resist removal to lands west of the Mississippi River.

We had about eight hundred acres in cultivation. The land around our village . . . was covered with bluegrass, which made excellent pasture for our horses. . . . The rapids of Rock river furnished us with an abundance of excellent fish, and the land, being good, never failed to produce good crops of corn, beans, pumpkins, and squashes. We always had plenty—our children never cried with hunger, nor our people were never in want. Here our village had stood for more than a hundred years.

[In 1828] Nothing was now talked of but leaving our village. Ke-o-kuck [the principal chief] had been persuaded to consent to . . . remove to the west side of the Mississippi. . . . [I] raised the standard of opposition to Ke-o-kuck, with full determination not to leave my village. . . . I was of the opinion that the white people had plenty of land and would never take our village from us. . . .

During the [following] winter, I received information that three families of whites had arrived at our village and destroyed some of our lodges, and were making fences and dividing our corn-fields for their own use. . . . I requested them [to leave, but some weeks later] we came up to our village, and found that the whites had not left it—but that others had come, and that the greater part of our corn-fields had

been enclosed. . . . Some of the whites permitted us to plant small patches in the fields they had fenced, keeping all the best ground for themselves. . . . The white people brought whiskey into our village, made people drunk, and cheated them out of their homes, guns, and [beaver] traps!

That fall [1829] I paid a visit to the agent, before we started to our hunting grounds. . . . He said that the land on which our village stood was now ordered to be sold to individuals; and that, when sold, our right to remain, by treaty, would be at an end, and that if we returned next spring, we would be forced to remove! I refused . . . to quit my village. It was here, that I was born—and here lie the bones of many friends and relatives. For this spot I felt a sacred reverence, and never could consent to leave it, without being forced therefrom.

[In the spring of 1831] I directed my village crier to proclaim, that my orders were, in the event of the [Indian] war chief coming to our village to remove us [to honor the treaty], that not a gun should be fired, nor any resistance offered. That if he determined to fight, for them to remain quietly in their lodges, and let them kill them if he chose.

SOURCE: David Jackson, ed., *Black Hawk: An Autobiography* (Urbana: University of Illinois Press, 1964), 88–90, 95–97, 111–113.

MAP 10.2 The Removal of Native Americans, 1820–1846

Beginning in the 1820s, the U.S. government forced scores of Native American peoples to sign treaties that exchanged Indian land in the East for money and designated reservation land west of the Mississippi River. In the 1830s, the government used military force to expel the Cherokees, Chickasaws, Choctaws, Creeks, and many Seminoles from their ancestral homes in the Old Southeast and to resettle them in the Indian Territory, in the present-day states of Oklahoma and Kansas.

For more help analyzing this map, see the Online Study Guide at **bedfordstmartins.com/henrettaconcise**.

Instead of guaranteeing the Cherokees' territory, the U.S. government took it from them. In 1835, American officials negotiated the Treaty of New Echota with a minority Cherokee faction and insisted that all Cherokees abide by it and move to the new Indian Territory. When only 2,000 of 17,000 Cherokees had moved by the deadline of May 1838, President Martin Van Buren ordered General Winfield Scott to enforce the treaty. Scott's army rounded up some 14,000 Cherokees and forcibly marched them 1,200 miles to the Indian Territory, an arduous journey that they described as the Trail of Tears. Along the way, 3,000 Indians died of starvation and exposure.

After the Creeks, Chickasaws, and Choctaws moved west of the Mississippi, the Seminoles were the only numerically significant Indian people remaining in the Old Southwest. With the aid of runaway slaves who had married into the tribe, the Seminoles fought a successful guerrilla war against the U.S. Army during the 1840s

Raising Public Opinion Against the Seminoles
During the eighteenth century, hundreds of enslaved blacks fled South Carolina and Georgia and found refuge in Spanish Florida, where they lived among and intermarried with the Seminole people. This color engraving from the 1830s, showing red and black Seminoles butchering respectable white families, was intended to bolster political support for the forced removal of the Seminoles to the Indian Territory. By the mid-1840s, after a decade of warfare, the U.S. Army had forced 2,500 Seminoles to migrate to Oklahoma. However, another 2,500 Seminoles continued their armed resistance and eventually won a new treaty allowing them to live in Florida. Granger Collection.
For more help analyzing this image, see the Online Study Guide at **bedfordstmartins.com/henrettaconcise**.

and retained their lands in Florida, which was still a sparsely settled frontier region. The Seminoles were an exception. The Jacksonians had forced the removal of most eastern Indian peoples.

The Jacksonian Impact

Jackson's legacy, like that of every great president, is complex and rich. On the institutional level, he permanently expanded the authority of the nation's chief executive by identifying it with the voice of the people. As Jackson put it, "The President is the direct representative of the American people." Assuming that role during the nullification crisis, he upheld national authority by threatening the use of military force, laying the foundation for Lincoln's defense of the Union a generation later. At the same time (and somewhat contradictorily), Jackson curbed the reach of the national government. By undermining Henry Clay's American System of national banking, protective tariffs, and internal improvements, Jackson reinvigorated the Jeffersonian tradition of a limited and frugal central government.

Jackson also undermined the constitutional jurisprudence of John Marshall by appointing Roger B. Taney as Marshall's successor. During his long tenure as chief justice from 1835 to 1864, Taney partially reversed the nationalist and vested-property-rights decisions of the Marshall Court and gave constitutional legitimacy to Jackson's policies of states' rights and free enterprise. In the landmark case *Charles River Bridge Co. v. Warren Bridge Co.* (1837), Taney declared that a legislative charter—in this case, to build and operate a toll bridge—did not necessarily bestow a monopoly and that a legislature could charter a competing bridge to promote the general welfare: "While the rights of private property are sacredly guarded, we must not forget that the community also has rights." This decision directly challenged Marshall's interpretation of the contract clause of the Constitution in *Dartmouth College v. Woodward* (1819), which had stressed the binding nature of public charters (see Chapter 7). By limiting the property and monopoly claims of existing canal and turnpike companies, the decision allowed legislatures to charter competing railroads that would provide cheaper and more efficient transportation.

Other decisions by the Taney Court limited Marshall's nationalistic interpretation of the commerce clause by enhancing the regulatory role of state governments. For example, in *Mayor of New York v. Miln* (1837), the Taney Court ruled that New York State could use its "police power" to inspect the health of arriving immigrants. The Court also restored to the states some of the economic powers they had exercised before 1787. In *Briscoe v. Bank of Kentucky* (1837), for example, the justices allowed a bank owned by the state of Kentucky to issue currency, despite the wording of the U.S. Constitution (Article I, Section 10) that prohibits states from issuing "bills of credit."

Inspired by Jackson and Taney's example, Democrats in the various states mounted their own constitutional revolutions. Between 1830 and 1860, twenty states called conventions to write new constitutions to extend democracy. Most of these constitutions gave the vote to all white men and reapportioned state legislatures on the basis of population. They also brought government "near to the people" by mandating the election, rather than the appointment, of most public officials, including sheriffs, justices of the peace, and judges.

The new constitutions also embodied the principles of **classical liberalism**, or **laissez-faire**, by limiting the government's role in the economy. (Twentieth-century social-welfare liberalism endorses the opposite principle: that government should intervene in economic and social life. See Chapter 24.) As president, Jackson had destroyed the American System; his disciples in the states now attacked the Commonwealth philosophy: the use of chartered corporations and state funds to promote economic development. Most Jackson-era constitutions prohibited states from granting special charters to corporations or extending loans and credit guarantees to private businesses. "If there is any danger to be feared in . . . government," declared a New Jersey Democrat, "it is the danger of associated wealth, with special privileges." The revised constitutions also protected taxpayers by setting strict limits on state debt and encouraging judges to enforce them. Said one New York reformer, "We will not trust the legislature with the power of creating indefinite mortgages on the people's property."

"The world is governed too much," the Jacksonians proclaimed as they embraced a small-government, laissez-faire outlook. The first American populists, they celebrated the power of ordinary people to make decisions in the marketplace and the voting booth.

▶ What were Andrew Jackson's policies on banking and tariffs? Did they help or hurt the American economy? Why?

▶ Why did Jackson support Indian removal? Did removal help to preserve or to destroy Native American cultures? Explain your answer.

▶ How did the constitutional interpretations of the Taney Court and the new Jacksonian state constitutions alter the American legal and constitutional system?

Class, Culture, and the Second Party System

The rise of the Democracy and Jackson's tumultuous presidency sparked the creation in the mid-1830s of a second national party: the **Whigs**. For the next two decades, Whigs and Democrats competed fiercely for votes and won support from different cultural groups. Many Evangelical Protestants became Whigs, while most Catholic immigrants and traditional Protestants joined the Democrats. By debating issues of economic policy, class power, and moral reform, party politicians offered Americans a choice between competing programs and political leaders. "Of the two great parties," remarked philosopher and essayist Ralph Waldo Emerson, the Democracy "has the best cause . . . for free trade, for wide suffrage." The Whig party, he said, "has the best men."

The Whig Worldview

The Whig Party arose in 1834, when a group of congressmen banded together to oppose Andrew Jackson's policies and his high-handed, "kinglike" conduct. They took the name *Whigs* to identify themselves with the pre-Revolutionary American and British parties — also called Whigs — that had opposed the arbitrary actions of British monarchs. The Whigs accused "King Andrew I" of violating the Constitution by creating a spoils system and increasing presidential authority. Jackson's "executive usurpation," they charged, undermined government by elected legislators, who were the true representatives of the sovereign people.

Initially, the Whigs were a diverse group drawn from various political factions. However, under the leadership of Senators Webster of Massachusetts, Clay of Kentucky, and Calhoun of South Carolina, the Whigs gradually articulated a distinct vision. Their goal, like that of the Federalists of the 1790s, was a political world dominated by men of ability and wealth; unlike the Federalists, though, the Whig elite would be chosen by talent, not birth.

The Whigs celebrated the entrepreneur and the enterprising individual: "This is a country of self-made men," they boasted, pointing to the relative absence of permanent distinctions of class and status among white citizens. Embracing the Industrial Revolution, northern Whigs welcomed the investments of "moneyed capitalists," which provided workers with jobs and so "bread, clothing and homes." Whig Congressman Edward Everett told a Fourth of July crowd in Lowell, Massachusetts, that there should be a "holy alliance" among laborers, owners, and governments. Many workers agreed, especially those who labored in the New England textile factories and Pennsylvania iron mills that benefited from protective tariffs. To ensure prosperity, Everett and other northern Whigs called for a return to the American System.

Support for the Whigs in the South rested on the appeal of specific policies and politicians, not the Whigs' social vision. Some southern Whigs were wealthy planters who invested in railroads and banks or sold their cotton to New York merchants. The majority were yeomen whites who resented the grip over state politics held by low-country planters, most of whom were Democrats. In addition, some Virginia and South Carolina Democrats became Whigs because, like John C. Calhoun, they favored states' rights and condemned Andrew Jackson's crusade against nullification.

Like Calhoun, most southern Whigs rejected the Whig Party's enthusiasm for high tariffs and social mobility. Calhoun was extremely conscious of class divisions in society. He believed that the northern Whig ideal of equal opportunity was contradicted not only by slavery, which he considered a fundamental American institution, but also by the wage-labor system of industrial capitalism. "There is and always has been in an advanced state of wealth and civilization a conflict between labor and capital," Calhoun declared in 1837. He urged slave owners and factory owners to unite against their common foe: a working class composed of enslaved blacks and propertyless whites.

Most northern Whigs rejected Calhoun's class-conscious social ideology. "A clear and well-defined line between capital and labor" might fit the slave South or class-ridden European societies, Daniel Webster conceded, but in the North, "this distinction grows less and less definite as commerce advances." Ignoring the ever-increasing mass of propertyless immigrants, Webster focused on the growing size of the northern middle class, whose members generally supported Whig candidates. In the election of 1834, the Whigs won a majority in the House of Representatives by appealing to Evangelical Protestants and upwardly mobile families — prosperous farmers, small-town merchants, and skilled industrial workers in New England, New York, and the new communities along the Great Lakes.

Many of these Whig voters had previously supported the Anti-Masonic Party, a powerful but short-lived political party that formed in the late 1820s. As their name implies, Anti-Masons opposed the Order of Freemasonry, a republican organization that arose in eighteenth-century Europe. The order was a secret society of men whose rituals were closely guarded. Freemasonry spread rapidly in America and attracted political leaders — including George Washington, Henry Clay, and Andrew Jackson — and ambitious businessmen. By the mid-1820s, there were 20,000 Masons in New York State, organized into 450 local lodges. Following the kidnapping and murder in 1826 of William Morgan, a New York Mason who had threatened to reveal the order's secrets, the Freemasons fell into disrepute. Thurlow Weed, a Rochester newspaper editor, spearheaded the Anti-Masonic Party, which condemned the order as a secret aristocratic fraternity and ousted its members from local and state offices.

The Whigs recruited Anti-Masons to their party by endorsing the Anti-Masons' support for temperance, equality of opportunity, and evangelical morality. Throughout the Northeast and Midwest, Whig politicians advocated legal curbs on the sale of alcohol and local ordinances that preserved Sunday as a day of worship. The Whigs also won congressional seats in the Ohio and Mississippi valleys, where farmers, bankers, and shopkeepers favored Henry Clay's American System. For these citizens of the growing Midwest, the Whigs' program of government subsidies for roads, canals, and bridges was as important as their moral agenda.

In the election of 1836, the Whig Party faced Martin Van Buren, the architect of the Democratic Party and Jackson's handpicked successor. Van Buren denounced the American System and warned that its revival would create an oppressive system of "consolidated government." Positioning himself as a defender of individual rights, Van Buren opposed the efforts of Whigs and moral reformers to use state laws to impose temperance and national laws to abolish slavery. "The government is best which governs least" became his motto in economic, cultural, and racial matters.

Celebrating a Political Triumph, 1836

To commemorate Martin Van Buren's election in 1836 and to reward his supporters, the Democrat Party distributed thousands of snuffboxes inscribed with the new president's portrait. By using gifts and other innovative measures to enlist the loyalty of voters, Van Buren and his allies transformed American politics from an upper-class avocation to a democratic contest for votes and power. Collection of Janice L. and David J. Frent.

To oppose Van Buren, the Whigs ran four candidates, each with a strong regional reputation. Their plan was to garner enough electoral votes to throw the contest into the House of Representatives. However, the Whig tally — 73 electoral votes collected by William Henry Harrison of Ohio, 26 by Hugh L. White of Tennessee, 14 by Daniel Webster of Massachusetts, and 11 by W. P. Magnum of Georgia — fell far short of Van Buren's 170 votes. Still, the four Whig candidates won 49 percent of the popular vote, showing that the party's message of economic and moral improvement had a broad appeal (see Voices from Abroad, p. 311).

Labor Politics and the Depression of 1837–1843

As the Democrats struggled with Whigs on the national level, they faced a challenge from urban artisans and workers. In 1827, artisans and workers in Philadelphia organized the Mechanics' Union of Trade Associations, a group of fifty unions with 10,000 members. The following year, they founded a Working Men's Party to secure "a just balance of power . . . between all the various classes." The new party campaigned for the abolition of banks, fair taxation, and universal public education and blazed the trail for similar organizations: By 1833, laborers had established Working Men's Parties in fifteen states.

The new parties had a clear agenda. The Industrial Revolution and the Market Revolution had brought prosperity to bankers and entrepreneurs, but rising prices and stagnant wages had cut the living standards of many urban artisans and wage earners. Seeing "the glaring inequality of society," workers organized for political action. "Past experience teaches us that we have nothing to hope from the aristocratic orders of society," declared the New York Working Men's Party. It vowed "to send men of our own description, if we can, to the Legislature at Albany" to secure laws that would abolish private banks, chartered monopolies, and debtors' prisons. In Philadelphia, the Working Men's Party demanded higher taxes on the wealthy and, in 1834, persuaded the Pennsylvania legislature to authorize tax-supported schools so that workers' children could rise in the world.

The goal of the workingmen's parties was a society without dependent wage earners. In this republic of artisans, said labor intellectual Orestes Brownson, "All men will be

Parties in the United States ALEXIS DE TOCQUEVILLE

In *Democracy in America* (1835), Alexis de Tocqueville presented both a philosophical analysis of American society and an astute description of its political institutions. Here, the republican-minded French aristocrat explains the role of lawyers in American politics, why there are no "great political parties," and how regional and class interests threaten the political system.

We perceive that the authority they have entrusted to the members of the legal profession, and the influence that these individuals exercise in the government, are the most powerful existing security against the excesses of democracy. . . . Men who have made a special study of the laws derive from [that] occupation certain habits of order, a taste for formalities, . . . which naturally render them very hostile to the revolutionary spirit and the unreflecting passions of the multitude. . . . Lawyers belong to the people by birth and interest, and to the aristocracy by habit and taste; they may be looked upon as the connecting link between the two great classes of society. . . .

The political parties that I style great are those which cling to principles rather than to their consequences. . . . Great political parties . . . are not to be met with in the United States at the present time. Parties, indeed, may be found which threaten the future of the Union; but there is none which seems to contest the present form of government or the present course of society. The parties by which the Union is menaced do not rest upon principles, but upon material interests. These interests constitute, in the different provinces of so vast an empire, rival nations rather than parties. Thus, upon a recent occasion [the Tariff of 1832 and the nullification crisis]

the North contended for the system of commercial prohibition, and the South took up arms in favor of free trade, simply because the North is a manufacturing and the South an agricultural community; and the restrictive system that was profitable to the one was prejudicial to the other. . . .

The deeper we penetrate into the inmost thought of these parties, the more we perceive that the object of the one [the Whigs] is to limit and that of the other [the Democrats] to extend the authority of the people. . . .

To quote a recent example, when President Jackson attacked the Bank of the United States, the country was excited, and parties were formed; the well-informed classes rallied round the bank, the common people round the President. But it must not be imagined that the people had formed a rational opinion upon a question which offers so many difficulties to the most experienced statesmen. By no means. The bank is a great establishment, which has an independent existence; and the people . . . are startled to meet with this obstacle to their authority [and are] led to attack it, in order to see whether it can be shaken, like everything else.

SOURCE: Alexis de Tocqueville, *Democracy in America* (1835; New York: Random House, 1981), 1: 94–99.

independent proprietors, working on their own capitals, on their own farms, or in their own shops." Like Jacksonian Democrats, artisan republicans demanded equal rights and attacked chartered corporations. "The only safeguard against oppression," argued William Leggett, a leading member of the New York Loco-Foco (Equal Rights) Party, "is a system of legislation which leaves to all the free exercise of their talents and industry." Working Men's candidates won office in many cities, but divisions over policy and the parties' weakness in statewide contests soon took a toll. By the mid-1830s, most politically active workers had joined the Democratic Party and were urging it to eliminate protective tariffs and tax the stocks and bonds of wealthy capitalists.

When equality-conscious workers formed unions to bargain for higher wages for themselves, employers attacked the union movement. In 1836, clothing manufacturers in New York City agreed to dismiss workers who belonged to the Society of Journeymen Tailors and circulated a list—a so-called **blacklist**—of the society's members. The employers also brought lawsuits to overturn **closed-shop agreements** that required them to hire only union members. They argued that these contracts violated both the common law and legislative statutes that prohibited "conspiracies" in restraint of trade.

Judges usually sided with the employers. In 1835, the New York Supreme Court found that a shoemakers' union in Geneva had illegally caused "an industrious man" to be "driven out of employment" because he would not join the union. "It is important to the best interests of society that the price of labor be left to regulate itself," the court declared. When a court in New York City upheld a conspiracy verdict against a tailors' union, a crowd of 27,000 people denounced the decision in a mass meeting, and tailors circulated handbills warning that the "Freemen of the North are now on a level with the slaves of the South." Workers found allies among jurors. In 1836, local juries hearing conspiracy cases acquitted shoemakers in Hudson, New York; carpet makers in Thompsonville, Connecticut; and plasterers in Philadelphia.

At this juncture, the Panic of 1837 threw the American economy—and the union movement—into disarray. The panic began when the Bank of England, hoping to boost the faltering British economy, sharply curtailed the flow of money and credit to the United States. Since 1822, British manufacturers had extended credit to southern planters to expand cotton production, and British investors had purchased millions of dollars of the canal bonds issued by northern states. Suddenly deprived of British funds, American planters, merchants, and canal corporations had to withdraw specie from domestic banks to pay their commercial debts and interest on their foreign loans. When British textile mills drastically reduced their purchases of raw cotton from the South, cotton prices plummeted from 20 cents a pound to 10 cents or less.

The drain of specie to Britain and falling cotton prices set off a financial panic. On May 8, the Dry Dock Bank of New York City closed its doors, and worried depositors began to withdraw gold and silver coins from other banks. Within two weeks, every bank in the United States stopped trading specie and curtailed credit, turning a financial panic into an economic crisis. "This sudden overthrow of the commercial credit" had a "stunning effect," observed Henry Fox, the British minister in Washington. "The conquest of the land by a foreign power could hardly have produced a more general sense of humiliation and grief."

A second, longer-lasting downturn began in 1839. To revive the economy after the Panic of 1837, state governments had increased their investments in canals and railroads. As they issued more and more bonds to finance these ventures, bond prices fell sharply in Europe, sparking a four-year-long financial crisis. The international crisis engulfed state governments in America, which were unable to meet the substantial interest payments on their bonds. Nine states defaulted on their obligations, prompting foreign creditors to cut the flow of new capital to the United States. Bumper crops drove down cotton prices even further, bringing more bankruptcies.

The American economy fell into a deep depression. By 1843, canal construction had dropped by 90 percent, and prices had fallen by nearly 50 percent. Unemployment reached almost 20 percent of the workforce in seaports and industrial centers. Minister Henry Ward Beecher described a land "filled with lamentation . . . its inhabitants wandering like bereaved citizens among the ruins of an earthquake, mourning for children, for houses crushed, and property buried forever."

By creating a surplus of unemployed workers, the depression devastated the labor movement. In 1837, 6,000 masons, carpenters, and other building-trades workers lost their jobs in New York City, depleting unions' rosters and destroying their bargaining power. By 1843, most local unions and all the national labor organizations had disappeared, along with their newspapers.

The subsequent decades brought few gains for workers or their unions. In *Commonwealth v. Hunt* (1842), Chief Justice Lemuel Shaw of the Massachusetts Supreme Judicial Court upheld the rights of workers to form unions. Shaw's decision overturned common-law precedents by ruling that a union was not an inherently illegal organization and could strike to enforce a closed-shop agreement. But courts found other ways to deter unions, such as issuing **injunctions** that prohibited workers from picketing or striking. Moreover, judges continued to apply the traditional common-law principles to the workplace; this meant, as one legal treatise put it, that "all who are in the employ of another" were "servants" and hence subject to their master-employer. Still, workers won some political victories. Continuing Jackson's effort to recruit laboring men and women to the Democratic Party, President Van Buren signed an executive order in 1840 setting a ten-hour day for federal employees. Increasingly, workers' struggles — like conflicts over tariffs, banks, and internal improvements — were fought out in the political arena.

"Tippecanoe and Tyler Too!"

Many Americans blamed the Democrats for the depression of 1837–1843. In particular, they criticized Jackson for destroying the Second Bank and for issuing the Specie Circular of 1836, which required western settlers to use gold and silver coins to pay for farms in the national domain.

The public turned its anger on Van Buren, who took office just as the panic struck. Ignoring the pleas of influential bankers, the new president refused to revoke the Specie Circular or take other actions that might have reversed the downturn. Holding to his philosophy of limited government, Van Buren advised Congress that "the less government interferes with private pursuits the better for the general prosperity."

As the depression deepened in 1839, this laissez-faire policy commanded less and less political support. Worse, Van Buren's major piece of economic legislation, the Independent Treasury Act of 1840, actually delayed recovery. The act pulled federal specie out of Jackson's pet banks (which had used it to back loans) and placed it in government vaults, where it did no economic good at all.

Determined to exploit Van Buren's weakness, the Whigs organized their first national convention in 1840 and nominated William Henry Harrison of Ohio for president and John Tyler of Virginia for vice president. A military hero of the Battle of Tippecanoe and the War of 1812, Harrison was well advanced in age (sixty-eight) and had little political experience. But the Whig leaders in Congress, Clay and Webster, wanted a president who would rubber-stamp their program for protective tariffs and a national bank. An unpretentious, amiable man, Harrison told voters that Whig policies were "the only means, under Heaven, by which a poor industrious man may become a rich man without bowing to colossal wealth."

Panic and depression stacked the political cards against Van Buren, but the election turned as much on style as on substance. It became the great "log cabin campaign"—the first time two well-organized parties competed for the loyalties of a mass electorate through a new style of campaigning. Whig songfests, parades, and well-orchestrated mass meetings drew new voters into politics. Whig speakers assailed "Martin Van Ruin" as a manipulative politician with aristocratic tastes—a devotee of fancy wines and elegant clothes, as indeed he was. Less truthfully, they portrayed Harrison as a self-made man who was happy living in a log cabin and quaffing hard cider, a drink of the common people. In fact, Harrison's father was a wealthy Virginia planter who had signed the Declaration of Independence, and Harrison himself lived in a series of elegant mansions.

The Whigs boosted their electoral hopes by welcoming women to campaign festivities. Previously, women had been excluded not only from voting but also from marching in political parades. Jacksonian Democrats were particularly committed to politics as a "manly" affair and insinuated that politically minded females were akin to "public" women, the prostitutes who plied their trade in theaters and other public places. But the Whigs recognized that Christian women from Yankee families, a key Whig constituency, had already entered American public life through the temperance movement and other benevolent activities. In October 1840, Daniel Webster addressed a meeting of 1,200 Whig women, praised their efforts for moral reform, and urged them to back Whig candidates. "This way of making politicians of their women is something new under the sun," noted one Democrat, worried that it would bring more Whig men to the polls. And it did: More than 80 percent of the eligible male voters cast ballots in 1840, up from fewer than 60 percent in 1832 and 1836. Heeding the Whig campaign slogan "Tippecanoe and Tyler Too," they voted Harrison into the White House with 53 percent of the popular vote and gave the Whigs a majority in Congress.

Led by Clay and Webster, the Whigs in Congress were poised to reverse the Jacksonian revolution. But their hopes were short-lived; barely a month after his inauguration, Harrison died of pneumonia, and the nation got "Tyler Too." But in what capacity: as acting president or as president? The Constitution was vague on the issue.

The Log Cabin Campaign, 1840

During the Second Party System, politics became more responsive to the popular will as ordinary people voted for candidates who shared their values and lifestyles. The barrels of hard cider framing this homemade campaign banner evoke the drink of the common man, while the central image falsely portrays William Henry Harrison as a poor and simple frontier farmer. New-York Historical Society, New York City.

Ignoring his Whig associates in Congress, who feared a strong president like Jackson, Tyler took the presidential oath of office and declared his intention to govern as he pleased. As it turned out, that would not be like a Whig.

Tyler had served in the House and the Senate as a Jeffersonian Democrat, firmly committed to slavery and states' rights. He had joined the Whigs only to protest Jackson's stance against nullification. On economic issues, Tyler shared Jackson's hostility to the Second Bank and the American System. So the new president vetoed Whig bills that would have raised tariffs and created a new national bank. Disgusted, most of Tyler's cabinet resigned in 1842, and the Whigs expelled Tyler from their party. "His Accidency," as he was called by his critics, was now a president without a party.

The split between Tyler and the Whigs allowed the Democrats to regroup. The party vigorously recruited supporters among subsistence farmers in the North, smallholding planters in the South, and former members of the Working Men's parties in the cities. It also won support among Irish and German Catholic immigrants—whose numbers had increased during the 1830s—by backing their demands for religious and cultural freedom. This pattern of **ethnocultural politics**, as historians refer to the practice of voting along ethnic and religious lines, now became a prominent feature of American life. Thanks to these urban and rural recruits, the Democrats remained the majority party in most parts of the nation. Their program of equal rights, states' rights, and cultural liberty was more attractive than the Whig platform of economic nationalism, moral reform, and individual mobility.

▶ How did the ideology of the Whigs differ from that of the Jacksonian Democrats?

▶ Chapter 10 argues that a democratic revolution swept America in the decades after 1820. What evidence does the text present to support this argument? How persuasive is it?

SUMMARY

In this chapter, we have examined the causes and the consequences of the democratic political revolution that accompanied the economic transformation of the early nineteenth century. We saw that the expansion of the franchise weakened the political system run by notables of high status. In its place emerged a system managed by professional politicians, men like Martin Van Buren, who were mostly of middle-class origin.

We also witnessed a revolution in government policy, as Andrew Jackson and his Democratic party dismantled the political foundation of the mercantilist system. On the national level, Jackson destroyed Henry Clay's American System; on the state level, Democrats wrote new constitutions that ended the Commonwealth System of government charters and subsidies to private businesses.

Finally, we watched the emergence of the Second Party System. Following the splits in the Republican Party during the election of 1824, two new parties—the Democrats and the Whigs—developed on the national level and eventually absorbed the members of the Anti-Masonic and Working Men's parties. The new party system established universal suffrage for white men and a mode of representative government that was responsive to ordinary citizens. In their scope and significance, these political innovations matched the economic advances of the Industrial and Market Revolutions.

Connections: Government

In this chapter, we witnessed the process that transformed the elite-dominated republican polity described in Chapters 7 and 8 into a democratic political culture and the Second Party System of Whigs and Democrats. As we observed in the essay that opened Part Three:

> The rapid growth of political parties sparked the creation of a competitive and responsive democratic polity. . . . This party competition engaged the energies of the electorate and helped to unify a fragmented social order.

TIMELINE

1810s	▶ State constitutions expand voting rights for white men	**1833**	▶ Congress passes Force Bill and compromise tariff
	▶ Martin Van Buren creates a disciplined party in New York	**1834**	▶ Whig Party formed by Henry Clay, John C. Calhoun, and Daniel Webster
1825	▶ John Quincy Adams elected president, adopts Henry Clay's American System		
1828	▶ Artisans in Philadelphia organize Working Men's Party	**1835**	▶ Roger Taney named Supreme Court chief justice
	▶ Tariff imposes high duties on imported goods	**1836**	▶ Martin Van Buren elected president
	▶ Andrew Jackson elected president	**1837**	▶ *Charles River Bridge Co. v. Warren Bridge Co.* weakens chartered monopolies
	▶ John C. Calhoun's *The South Carolina Exposition and Protest*		
1830	▶ President Jackson vetoes extension of National Road		▶ Panic of 1837 derails labor movement
	▶ Congress enacts Jackson's Indian Removal Act	**1838**	▶ Thousands of Cherokees die on Trail of Tears
1831	▶ *Cherokee Nation v. Georgia* denies Indians' claim of national sovereignty	**1839–1843**	▶ International financial crisis; American economic depression
1832	▶ President Jackson vetoes renewal of Second Bank's charter	**1840**	▶ Whigs triumph in log cabin campaign
	▶ South Carolina adopts Ordinance of Nullification	**1841**	▶ John Tyler succeeds William Henry Harrison as president
	▶ *Worcester v. Georgia* upholds political autonomy of Indian peoples	**1842**	▶ *Commonwealth v. Hunt* legitimizes trade unions

We will continue the story of America's political development in Chapter 13, which covers the years between 1844 and 1860. There, we will watch the disintegration of the Second Party System over the issue of slavery. Such slavery-related political crises were not new; as the discussion in Chapter 8 showed, the North and the South quarreled bitterly between 1819 and 1821 over the extension of slavery into Missouri. At that time, notable politicians raised in the old republican culture resolved the issue through compromise. Would democratic politicians be equally adept at fashioning a compromise over slavery in the territories seized from Mexico in 1848? Even more important, would their constituents accept that compromise? By 1848, the United States had become a more complex and contentious society, a change that reflected the appearance of new cultural movements and radical reform organizations, which are the subject of Chapter 11.

FOR FURTHER EXPLORATION

George Dangerfield, *The Era of Good Feelings* (1952), remains the classic study, but see Sean Wilentz, *The Rise of American Democracy: Jefferson to Lincoln* (2005). For a concise survey, read Harry L. Watson, *Liberty and Power: The Politics of Jacksonian America* (1990). The Internet Public Library (**www.ipl.org/div/potus/jqadams.html**) covers the election of 1824 and the Adams administration. For the Whigs, consult Merrill D. Peterson, *The Great Triumvirate: Webster, Clay, and Calhoun* (1987).

Robert V. Remini, *The Life of Andrew Jackson* (1988), highlights Jackson's triumphs and shortcomings. Robert J. Conley, *Mountain Windsong: A Novel of the Trail of Tears* (1992), evokes the impact of Jackson's Indian policy, as does Sean Michael O'Brien, *In Bitterness and in Tears: Andrew Jackson's Destruction of the Creeks and Seminoles* (2003). For material on the Cherokees, see **cherokeehistory.com/**.

Alexis de Tocqueville's classic, *Democracy in America* (1835), incisively views American society and political institutions and is available online at **xroads.virginia .edu/~hyper/detoc/home.html**. For political cartoons, go to "American Political Prints, 1766–1876" at **loc.harpweek.com/**.

TEST YOUR KNOWLEDGE

To assess your mastery of the material in this chapter and for Web sites, images, and documents related to this chapter, visit **bedfordstmartins.com/henrettaconcise**.

Religion and Reform
1820–1860

Slavery must fall because it stands in direct hostility to all the grand movements, principles, and reforms of our age, because it stands in the way of an advancing world.

— Unitarian minister William Ellery Channing (1848)

"The spirit of reform is in every place," the children of legal reformer David Dudley Field wrote in their handwritten monthly *Gazette* in 1842:

The labourer with a family says "reform the common schools"; the merchant and the planter say, "reform the tariff," the lawyer "reform the laws," the politician "reform the government," the abolitionist "reform the slave laws," the moralist "reform intemperance," . . . the ladies wish their legal privileges extended, and in short, the whole country is wanting reform.

Like many Americans, the young Field children sensed that the political whirlwind of the 1830s had transformed the way people thought about themselves and about society. Suddenly, thousands of men and women, inspired by the economic progress and democratic spirit of the age and by the religious optimism of the Second Great Awakening, believed that they could improve both their personal lives and society as a whole. Some dedicated themselves to the cause of reform. William Lloyd Garrison began as an antislavery advocate and then went on to embrace women's rights, pacifism, and the abolition of prisons. Such obsessive individuals, warned Unitarian minister Henry W. Bellows, were pursuing "an object, which in its very nature is unattainable—the perpetual improvement of the outward condition."

Reform was complex and contradictory. Some reformers wanted to improve society by promoting morality and preventing certain types of behavior. The first wave of American reformers, the benevolent religious improvers of the 1820s, championed regular church attendance, temperance, and a strict moral code. Their righteousness prompted one critic to protest, "A peaceable man can hardly venture to eat or drink, . . . to correct his child or kiss his wife, without obtaining the permission . . . of some moral or other reform society."

A second wave of reformers, which emerged during the 1830s and 1840s, was more intent on liberating people from archaic customs and encouraging new lifestyles. These reformers were mostly middle-class northerners and midwesterners who promoted a bewildering assortment of radical ideals: extreme individualism, common ownership of property, the immediate emancipation of slaves, and sexual equality. Although their numbers were small, these reformers challenged the legitimacy of well-established cultural practices and belief, winning the attention—and often the horrified opposition—of the majority of Americans. As one fearful southerner saw it, radical reformers favored a chaotic world in which there would be "No-Marriage, No-Religion, No-Private Property, No-Law and No-Government."

Individualism: The Ethic of the Middle Class

Those fears were not exaggerated. Rapid economic development and geographical expansion had weakened many traditional institutions and social rules, forcing individuals to fend for themselves. In 1835, Alexis de Tocqueville coined a new word, *individualism,* to describe the social relations in the United States. Native-born white Americans were "no longer attached to each other by any tie of caste, class, association, or family," the French aristocrat lamented, and so lived in social isolation. Unlike Tocqueville who mourned the breakdown of social ties, the New England transcendentalist Ralph Waldo Emerson (1803–1882) celebrated the liberation of the individual from traditional constraints. Emerson's vision influenced thousands of ordinary Americans and a generation of important artists.

Ralph Waldo Emerson and Transcendentalism

Emerson was the leading voice of **transcendentalism**, an intellectual movement rooted in the religious soil of New England. Its first advocates were Unitarian ministers from well-to-do New England families, who questioned the constraints of their Puritan heritage (see Chapter 8). For inspiration, they turned to European romanticism, a new conception of self and society. Romantic thinkers, such as German philosopher Immanuel Kant and English poet Samuel Taylor Coleridge, rejected the ordered, rational world of the eighteenth-century Enlightenment. They searched for the passionate aspects of the human spirit and sought deeper insight into the mysteries of existence. By tapping their intuitive powers, the young Unitarians believed, people could come to know the infinite and the eternal.

As a Unitarian, Emerson already stood outside the mainstream of American Protestantism. Unlike most Christians, Unitarians believed that God was a single being, not a trinity of Father, Son, and Holy Spirit. In 1832, Emerson took a more radical step by resigning his Boston pulpit and rejecting all organized religion. He moved to Concord, Massachusetts, and gradually worked out his transcendentalist beliefs. In influential essays, Emerson explored what he called "the infinitude of the private man," the idea of the radically free individual.

The Founder of Transcendentalism
As this painting of Ralph Waldo Emerson by an unknown artist indicates, the young philosopher was an attractive man, his face brimming with confidence and optimism. With his radiant personality and incisive intellect, Emerson deeply influenced dozens of influential writers, artists, and scholars and enjoyed great success as a lecturer to the emerging middle class. The Metropolitan Museum of Art, bequest of Chester Dale, 1962 [64.97.4].

The young philosopher argued that people were trapped by inherited customs and institutions. They wore the ideas of earlier times—the tenets of New England Calvinism, for example—as a kind of "faded masquerade," and they needed to shed those values. "What is a man born for but to be a Reformer, a Remaker of what man has made?" Emerson asked. In his view, an individual could be remade only by discovering his or her "original relation with Nature" and entering into a mystical union with the "currents of Universal Being." The ideal setting for this transcendent discovery was under an open sky, in solitary communion with nature.

Emerson's genius lay in his ability to translate such abstract ideas into examples that made sense to middle-class Americans. His essays suggested that nature was saturated with the presence of God, a pantheistic outlook that departed from traditional Christian doctrine. Emerson also warned that the new market society was diverting the nation's emotional energy—that the focus on work, profits, and consumption was debasing Americans' spiritual lives. "Things are in the saddle," he wrote, "and ride mankind."

The transcendentalist message of self-realization reached hundreds of thousands of people, primarily through Emerson's writings and lectures. Public lectures had become a spectacularly successful way of spreading information and fostering discussion among the middle classes. Beginning in 1826, the Lyceum movement promoted "the general diffusion of knowledge" through lecture tours by hundreds of poets, preachers, scientists, and reformers. The movement took its name and inspiration from the public hall where the ancient Greek philosopher Aristotle taught. The Lyceum became an important cultural institution in the North and Midwest—but not in the South, where the middle class was smaller and popular education was a lower priority. In 1839, nearly 150 lyceums in Massachusetts invited lecturers to address more than 33,000 subscribers. Emerson was the most popular speaker, delivering 1,500 lectures in more than 300 towns in twenty states.

Emerson celebrated individuals who rejected tradition and exhibited both self-discipline and civic responsibility. His words spoke directly to the personal experience of many middle-class Americans, who had left family farms to make their way in the urban world. The great revivalist Charles Grandison Finney described his own religious conversion in Emersonian terms: as taking place in the woods, alone, the mystical union of an individual with God. Like Emerson, Finney told his listeners to transcend old doctrines and constraints. "God has made man a moral free agent," Finney declared, endowing individuals with the ability—and the responsibility—to determine their spiritual fate.

Emerson's Literary Influence

Emerson took as one of his tasks the remaking of American literature. In an address entitled "The American Scholar" (1837), the philosopher issued a literary declaration of independence. He urged American writers to free themselves from the "courtly muse" of Old Europe; instead, they should celebrate democracy and individual freedom and should find inspiration in the experiences of ordinary Americans: "the ballad in the street; the news of the boat; the glance of the eye; the form and gait of the body."

One young New England intellectual, Henry David Thoreau (1817–1862), heeded Emerson's call and sought inspiration from the natural world. In 1845, depressed by his beloved brother's death, Thoreau built a cabin near Walden Pond in Concord, Massachusetts, and lived alone there for two years. In 1854, he published *Walden, or Life in the Woods,* an account of his search for meaning beyond the artificiality of "civilized" society:

> I went to the woods because I wished to live deliberately, to front only the essential facts of life, and see if I could not learn what it had to teach, and not, when I came to die, discover that I had not lived.

Thoreau's book had little impact during his lifetime but has become an essential text of American literature. *Walden*'s most famous metaphor provides an enduring justification for independent thinking: "If a man does not keep pace with his companions, perhaps it is because he hears a different drummer." Beginning from this premise, Thoreau advocated social nonconformity and civil disobedience against unjust laws.

As Thoreau was seeking independence and self-realization for men, Margaret Fuller (1810–1850) was exploring the possibilities of freedom for women. Born into a wealthy Boston family, Fuller mastered six languages, read broadly in classic works of literature, and educated her four siblings. Becoming interested in Emerson's ideas, she started a transcendental "conversation," or discussion group, for educated Boston women in 1839. Soon Fuller was editing the leading transcendentalist journal, *The Dial*. In 1844, she published *Woman in the Nineteenth Century*, which proclaimed that a "new era" was changing the relationships between men and women.

Fuller's philosophy began with the transcendental belief that women, like men, could develop a mystical relationship with God that gave them identity and dignity. Every woman therefore deserved psychological and social independence — the ability "to grow, as an intellect to discern, as a soul to live freely and unimpeded." "We would have every arbitrary barrier thrown down," she wrote, and "every path laid open to Woman as freely as to Man." Embracing that vision, Fuller became the literary critic of the *New York Tribune* and traveled to Italy to report on the Revolution of 1848. Her adventurous life led to an early death; in 1850, she drowned in a shipwreck while returning to the United States. But Fuller's life and writings inspired a rising generation of women writers and reformers.

Another writer who responded to Emerson's call was the poet Walt Whitman (1819–1892). When Whitman first met Emerson, he said, he had been "simmering, simmering"; then Emerson "brought me to a boil." Whitman worked as a printer, a teacher, a journalist, an editor of the *Brooklyn Eagle*, and an influential publicist for the Democratic Party. But poetry was the "direction of his dreams." In *Leaves of Grass*, a collection of wild, exuberant poems first published in 1855 and constantly revised and expanded, Whitman recorded in verse his efforts to transcend various "invisible boundaries": between solitude and community, between prose and poetry, even between the living and the dead. At the center of *Leaves of Grass* is the individual — the figure of the poet — "I, Walt." He begins alone: "I celebrate myself, and sing myself." But because he has an Emersonian "original relation" with nature, Whitman claims perfect communion with others: "For every atom belonging to me as good belongs to you." Whitman celebrates democracy as well as himself by seeking an intimate, mystical relationship with a mass audience. For Emerson, Thoreau, and Fuller, the individual had a divine spark; for Whitman, the individual had expanded to become divine, and democracy assumed a sacred character.

The transcendentalists were optimistic but not naive. Whitman wrote about human suffering with passion, and Emerson laced his accounts of transcendence with twinges of anxiety. "I am glad," he once said, "to the brink of fear." Thoreau was gloomy about everyday life: "The mass of men lead lives of quiet desperation." Still, dark murmurings remain muted in their work, overshadowed by assertions that nothing was impossible for the individual who could break free from tradition.

Emerson's writings also influenced two great novelists, Nathaniel Hawthorne and Herman Melville, who had more pessimistic worldviews. Both sounded powerful warnings that unfettered egoism could destroy individuals and those around them. Hawthorne brilliantly explored the theme of excessive individualism in his novel *The Scarlet Letter* (1850). The two main characters, Hester Prynne and Arthur Dimmesdale, challenge their seventeenth-century New England community in the most blatant way: by committing adultery and producing a child. Their decision to ignore social restraints results not in liberation but in degradation: a profound sense of guilt and the condemnation of the community.

Herman Melville explored the limits of individualism in even more extreme and tragic terms and emerged as a scathing critic of transcendentalism. His most powerful statement was *Moby Dick* (1851), the story of Captain Ahab's obsessive hunt for a mysterious white whale that ends in death for Ahab and all but one member of his crew. Here, the quest for spiritual meaning in nature brings death, not transcendence, because Ahab, the liberated individual, lacks inner discipline and self-restraint.

Moby Dick was a commercial failure. The middle-class audience that read American fiction refused to follow Melville into the dark, dangerous realm of individualism gone mad. Readers also lacked enthusiasm for Thoreau's advocacy of civil disobedience during the U.S. war with Mexico (see Chapter 13) and for Whitman's boundless claims of a mystical union between the man of genius and the democratic masses. What middle-class readers emphatically preferred were the more modest examples of individualism offered by Emerson and Finney: personal improvement through spiritual awareness and self-discipline.

Brook Farm

To escape the constraints of America's emerging market society, transcendentalists and other reformers created ideal communities, or utopias. They hoped these planned societies, which organized life in new ways, would allow people to realize their spiritual potential. The most important transcendentalist communal experiment was Brook Farm, founded just outside Boston in 1841. Intellectual life at Brook Farm was electric. Hawthorne lived there for a time and later used the setting for his novel *The Blithedale Romance* (1852); Emerson, Thoreau, and Fuller were residents or frequent visitors. A former member recalled that they "inspired the young with a passion for study, and the middle-aged with deference and admiration, while we all breathed the intellectual grace that pervaded the atmosphere."

Whatever its spiritual rewards, Brook Farm was an economic failure. The residents hoped to escape the ups and downs of the market economy by becoming self-sufficient in food and exchanging their surplus milk, vegetables, and hay for manufactures. However, most members were ministers, teachers, writers, and students who had few farming skills; only the cash of affluent residents kept the enterprise afloat. After a devastating fire in 1846, the organizers disbanded the community and sold the farm.

► What were the main beliefs of transcendentalism, and how did American writers incorporate them into their work?

► What is the relationship between transcendentalism and individualism? Between transcendentalism and social reform? Between transcendentalism and the middle class?

With the failure of Brook Farm, the Emersonians abandoned their quest for a new social system. They accepted the brute reality of the emergent industrial order and tried to reform it, especially through the education of workers and the movement to abolish slavery.

Rural Communalism and Urban Popular Culture

Even as Brook Farm collapsed, thousands of Americans were joining communal settlements in rural areas of the Northeast and Midwest (Map 11.1). Many communalists were farmers and artisans seeking refuge during the economic depression that began

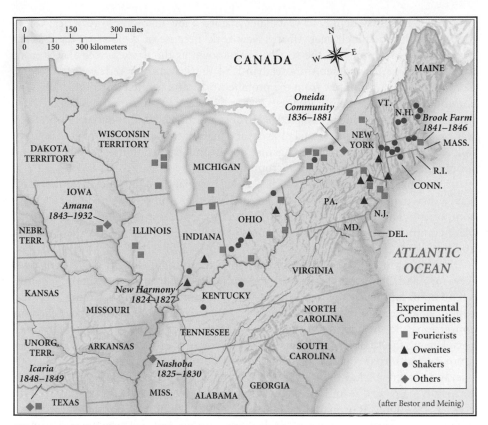

MAP 11.1 Major Communal Experiments Before 1860
Some experimental communities settled along the frontier, but the vast majority chose relatively secluded areas in well-settled regions of the North and Midwest. Because of their opposition to slavery, communalists usually avoided the South. Most secular experiments failed within a few decades, as the founders lost their reformist enthusiasm or died off; religious communities, such as those of the Shakers and the Mormons, were longer-lived.

with the Panic of 1837 and lasted seven years. However, these rural utopias were also symbols of social protest and experimentation. By advocating the common ownership of property and unconventional forms of marriage and family life, the communalists challenged capitalist values and traditional gender roles.

Simultaneously, tens of thousands of rural Americans and European immigrants poured into the larger cities of the United States. There, they created a popular culture that repudiated customary sexual norms, reinforced traditional racist feelings, and encouraged new styles of dress and behavior.

Mother Ann Lee and the Shakers

The Shakers were the first successful American communal movement. In 1770, Ann Lee Stanley (Mother Ann), a young cook in Manchester, England, had a vision that she was an incarnation of Christ and that sexual lust had caused Adam and Eve to be banished from the Garden of Eden. Four years later, she led a few followers to America, where they established a church near Albany, New York. Because of the ecstatic dances that were part of their worship, the sect became known as the Shakers (see Voices from Abroad, p. 327). After Mother Ann's death in 1784, the Shakers honored her as the Second Coming of Christ, withdrew from the profane world, and formed disciplined religious communities. Members embraced the common ownership of property; accepted strict oversight by church leaders; and pledged to abstain from alcohol, tobacco, politics, and war. Shakers also repudiated sexual pleasure and marriage. Their commitment to celibacy followed Mother Ann's testimony against "the lustful gratifications of the flesh as the source and foundation of human corruption."

The Shakers' theology was as radical as their social thought. They held that God was "a dual person, male and female" and that Mother Ann represented God's female component. This doctrine prompted Shakers to repudiate male leadership and to place community governance in the hands of both women and men — the Eldresses and the Elders.

Beginning in 1787, Shakers founded twenty communities, mostly in New England, New York, and Ohio. Their agriculture and crafts, especially furniture making, acquired a reputation for quality that made most Shaker communities self-sustaining and even comfortable. Because the Shakers did not engage in sexual intercourse, they relied on conversions and the adoption of thousands of young orphans to increase their numbers. During the 1830s, 3,000 adults joined the Shakers, attracted by their communal intimacy and sexual equality. Women converts outnumbered men more than two to one, and converts included blacks as well as whites. To Rebecca Cox Jackson, an African American seamstress from Philadelphia, the Shakers seemed to be "loving to live forever." As the supply of orphans dried up during the 1840s and 1850s (with the increase in public and private orphanages), Shaker communities stopped growing and eventually began to decline. By 1900, the Shakers had virtually disappeared, leaving as their material legacy a distinctive plain but elegant style of wood furniture.

Arthur Brisbane and Fourierism

As the Shakers' growth slowed during the 1840s, the American Fourierist movement mushroomed. Charles Fourier (1777–1837) was a French reformer who devised an eight-stage theory of social evolution that predicted the imminent decline of individualism and capitalism. According to Arthur Brisbane, Fourier's leading disciple in America, Fourierism would free workers from the "menial and slavish system of Hired Labor or Labor for Wages," just as republicanism had freed Americans from the slavish monarchical system of government. In a Fourierist society, men and women would not work for themselves or employers but for the community, in cooperative groups called phalanxes. The members of a phalanx would be its shareholders; they would own its property in common, including stores and a bank, a school, and a library.

Fourier and Brisbane saw the phalanx as a humane **socialistic** system that would liberate women as well as men. "In society as it is now constituted," Brisbane wrote, individual freedom was possible only for men, while "woman is subjected to unremitting and slavish domestic duties." In the "new Social Order . . . based upon Associated households," men would share women's domestic labor and thereby increase sexual equality.

The Mystical World of the Shakers

Foreigners were both attracted to and distressed by the strange religious practices that they observed in the United States. In a passage written in the early 1840s, an anonymous British visitor describes a Shaker dance and the sect's intimate contact with spiritual worlds inaccessible to those without faith.

At half past seven P.M. on the dancing days, all the members . . . assemble in the large hall. . . . The chief Elder stepped into the center of the space, and gave an exhortation for about five minutes, concluding with an invitation to them all to "go forth, old men, young men and maidens, and worship God with all [your] might in the dance." . . .

First they formed a procession and marched around the room in double-quick time, while four brothers and sisters stood in the center singing for them. . . . They commenced dancing, and continued it until they were pretty well tired. During the dance the sisters kept on one side, and the brothers on the other, and not a word was spoken by any one of them. . . . [Then] each one took his or her place in an oblong circle formed around the room, and all waited to see if anyone had received a "gift," that is, an inspiration to do something odd. Then two of the sisters would commence whirling round like a top, with their eyes shut; and continued this motion for about fifteen minutes. . . .

On some occasions when a sister had stopped whirling, she would say, "I have a communication to make." . . . The first message I heard was as follows[:] "Mother Ann has sent two angels to inform us that a tribe of Indians has been round here two days, and want the brothers and sisters to take them in. They are outside the building there, looking in at the windows." I shall never forget how I looked round at the windows, expecting to see the yellow faces, when this announcement was made; but I believe some of the old folks who eyed me, bit their lips and smiled. . . .

The next dancing night we again assembled in the same manner as before. . . . The elder then urged upon the members the duty of "taking them in." Whereupon eight or nine sisters became possessed of the spirits of Indian squaws, and about six of the brethren became Indians. Then ensued a regular pow-wow, with whooping and yelling and strange antics, such as would require a Dickens to describe. . . . These performances continued till about ten o'clock: then the chief Elder requested the Indians to go away, telling them they would find someone waiting to conduct them to the Shakers in the heavenly world. . . .

At one of the meetings . . . two or three sisters commenced whirling . . . and revealed to us that Mother Ann was present at the meeting, and that she had brought a dozen baskets of spiritual fruit for her children; upon which the Elder invited all to go forth to the baskets in the center of the floor, and help themselves. Accordingly they all stepped forth and went through the various motions of taking fruit and eating it. You will wonder if I helped myself to the fruit, like the rest. No; I had not faith enough to see the baskets or the fruit.

SOURCE: Noel Rae, ed., *Witnessing America* (New York: Penguin Press, 1966), 372–373.

Brisbane skillfully promoted Fourier's ideas in his influential book *The Social Destiny of Man* (1840), a regular column in Horace Greeley's *New York Tribune*, and hundreds of lectures, many of them in towns along the Erie Canal. Fourierist ideas found a receptive audience among educated farmers and craftsmen, who yearned for economic stability and communal solidarity in the wake of the Panic of 1837. During the 1840s, Fourierists started nearly one hundred cooperative communities, mostly in western New York and the Midwest. However, most of these communities collapsed within a decade because of disputes over work responsibilities and social policies. The decline of Fourierism revealed the difficulty of establishing a utopian community in the absence of a charismatic leader or a compelling religious vision.

John Humphrey Noyes and the Oneida Community

John Humphrey Noyes (1811–1886) was both charismatic and deeply religious. He ascribed the Fourierists' failure to their secular outlook and took as his model the pious Shakers, the true "pioneers of modern Socialism." The Shakers' marriageless society also appealed to Noyes and inspired him to create a community that defined sexuality and gender roles in radically new ways.

Noyes was a well-to-do graduate of Dartmouth College who became a minister after hearing a sermon by Charles Grandison Finney. Dismissed as the pastor of a Congregational church for holding unorthodox beliefs, Noyes turned to perfectionism. Perfectionism was an Evangelical Protestant movement of the 1830s that attracted thousands of New Englanders who had moved to New York and Ohio. Perfectionists believed that Christ had already returned to earth (the Second Coming); consequently, as the Bible suggested, people could aspire to sinless perfection in their earthly lives. Unlike most perfectionists, who lived conventional personal lives, Noyes rejected marriage, seeing it as the major barrier to perfection. "Exclusiveness, jealousy, quarreling have no place at the marriage supper of the Lamb," Noyes wrote. Like the Shakers, Noyes wanted to liberate individuals from sin by reforming sexual relationships. But instead of the Shakers' celibacy, Noyes and his followers embraced "complex marriage," in which all the members of the community were married to one another.

Noyes's marriage system highlighted the growing debate over the legal and cultural constraints on women. One reason for his rejection of monogamy was to free women from their status as the property of their husbands, as they were by custom and by common law. To give women the time and energy to participate fully in the community, Noyes urged them to avoid multiple pregnancies. He asked men to assist in this effort by avoiding orgasm during intercourse. To raise the children of the community, Noyes set up nurseries run by both men and women. Symbolizing their quest for equality, Noyes's women followers cut their hair short and wore pantaloons under calf-length skirts.

In 1839, Noyes established a perfectionist community near his hometown of Putney, Vermont. When he introduced the practice of complex marriage in the mid-1840s, local outrage forced Noyes to relocate the community to an isolated area near Oneida, New York. By the mid-1850s, the Oneida settlement had 200 residents; it became financially self-sustaining when the inventor of a highly successful steel animal trap joined the community. With the profits from trap making, the Oneidians diversified into the production of silverware. When Noyes fled to Canada in 1879 to avoid prosecution for adultery, the community abandoned complex marriage but retained its cooperative spirit. Its members founded Oneida Community, Ltd., a jointly owned silverware-manufacturing company that maintained some of its communal features until the middle of the twentieth century.

The historical significance of the Oneidians, Shakers, and Fourierists does not lie in their numbers, which were small, or in their fine crafts. Rather, their importance stems from their radical repudiation of traditional sexual norms and of the capitalist principles and class divisions of the emerging market society. Their utopian communities stood as countercultural blueprints for a more egalitarian social and economic order.

Joseph Smith and the Mormon Experience

The Shakers and the Oneidians were radical utopians because they rejected traditional definitions of marriage and family. But because their communities remained small, they aroused relatively little hostility. The Mormons, members of the Church of Jesus Christ of Latter-day Saints, were utopians with a conservative social agenda: to perpetuate the traditional patriarchal family. But because of their cohesive organization and substantial numbers, the Mormons provoked more animosity than the radical utopians did.

Like many social movements of the era, Mormonism emerged from the religious ferment among families of Puritan descent who lived along the Erie Canal. The founder of the Mormon Church was Joseph Smith Jr. (1805–1844). Smith was born in Vermont to a poor farming and shop-keeping family, who migrated to Palmyra in central New York. In a series of religious experiences that began in 1820, Smith came to believe that God had singled him out to receive a special revelation of divine truth. In 1830, he published *The Book of Mormon*, which he claimed to have translated from ancient hieroglyphics on gold plates that an angel named Moroni had shown to him. *The Book of Mormon* told the story of ancient civilizations from the Middle East that had migrated to the Western Hemisphere and of the visit of Jesus Christ, soon after the Resurrection, to one of them. Smith's account explained the presence of native peoples in the Americas and integrated them into the Judeo-Christian tradition.

Smith proceeded to organize the Church of Jesus Christ of Latter-day Saints. Seeing himself as a prophet in a sinful, excessively individualistic society, Smith revived traditional social doctrines, among them patriarchal authority within the family. Like many Protestant ministers, he encouraged practices that were central to individual success in the age of capitalist markets and factories: frugality, hard work, and enterprise. But Smith also placed great emphasis on communal discipline that would safeguard the Mormon "New Jerusalem" from individualism and rival religious doctrines. His goal was a church-directed society that would ensure moral perfection.

Smith struggled for years to establish a secure home for his new religion. Constantly harassed by hostile anti-Mormons, Smith and his growing congregation trekked west and eventually settled in Nauvoo, Illinois, a town they founded on the Mississippi River (Map 11.2). By the early 1840s, Nauvoo had become the largest utopian community in the United States, with 30,000 inhabitants. The rigid discipline and secret rituals of the Mormons—along with their prosperity, hostility toward other sects, and bloc

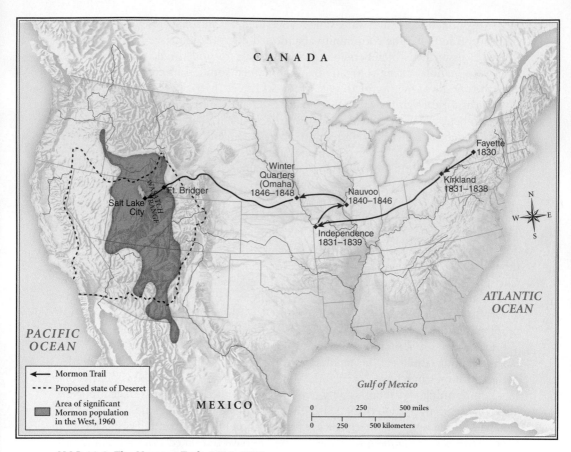

MAP 11.2 The Mormon Trek, 1830–1848

Because of their unorthodox religious views and communal solidarity, Mormons faced hostility first in New York and then in Missouri and Illinois. After founder Joseph Smith Jr. was murdered, Brigham Young led the polygamist faction of Mormons into lands thinly populated by Native American peoples. From Omaha, the migrants followed the path of the Oregon Trail to Fort Bridger and then struck off to the southwest. In 1847, they settled along the Wasatch Mountains in the basin of the Great Salt Lake, on Indian lands that were then part of Mexico and are now in Utah.

voting in Illinois elections—fueled resentment among their neighbors. Resentment turned to overt hostility when Smith refused to abide by any Illinois law of which he disapproved, asked Congress to turn Nauvoo into a separate federal territory, and declared himself a candidate for president of the United States.

Moreover, Smith claimed to have received a new revelation that justified polygamy, the practice of a man having multiple wives. When leading Mormon men took several wives, they sparked a contentious debate within the Mormon community and enraged Christians in neighboring towns. In 1844, Illinois officials arrested Smith and charged him with treason for allegedly conspiring to create a Mormon colony in Mexican territory. An anti-Mormon mob stormed the jail in Carthage, Illinois, where Smith and his brother were being held and murdered them.

A Mormon Man and His Wives
The practice of polygamy split the Mormon community and, because it deviated from traditional religious principles, enraged other Christian denominations. This Mormon household, pictured in the late 1840s, was unusually prosperous, partly because of the labor of the husband's multiple wives. Although the cabin provides cramped quarters for such a large family, it boasts a brick chimney and — a luxury for any pioneer home — a glass window. Library of Congress.

Led by Brigham Young, Smith's leading disciple and an energetic missionary, about 10,000 Mormons fled the United States. Beginning in 1847, they crossed the Great Plains into Mexican territory and settled in the Great Salt Lake Valley in present-day Utah. Using cooperative labor and an elaborate irrigation system based on communal water rights, the Mormon pioneers quickly spread planned agricultural communities along the base of the Wasatch mountain range. Many Mormons who rejected polygamy remained in the United States. Under the leadership of Smith's son, Joseph Smith III, they formed the Reorganized Church of Jesus Christ of Latter-day Saints and settled throughout the Midwest.

When the United States acquired title to Mexico's northern territories in 1848 (see Chapter 13), the Salt Lake Mormons petitioned Congress to create a vast new state, Deseret, which would stretch from present-day Utah to the Pacific coast. Instead, Congress set up the much smaller Utah Territory in 1850 and named Brigham Young its governor. In 1858, President James Buchanan responded to pressure from Protestants to eliminate polygamy by removing Young from the governorship and sending a small army to Salt Lake City. However, the "Mormon War" proved bloodless. Fearing that the forced abolition of polygamy would serve as a precedent for ending slavery, the pro-South Buchanan withdrew the troops. (To enable Utah to win admission to the Union in 1896, its citizens ratified a constitution that "forever" banned the practice of polygamy. But the state government has never strictly enforced that ban.)

Mormons had succeeded even as other social experiments had failed. By endorsing private property and individual enterprise, Mormons became prosperous contributors to the new market society. However, their leaders resolutely used strict religious controls to create patriarchal families and disciplined communities, reaffirming traditional values. This blend of economic innovation, social conservatism, and hierarchical leadership, in combination with a strong missionary impulse, created a wealthy and expansive church that now claims a worldwide membership of about twelve million people.

Urban Popular Culture

As utopian reformers organized communities in the countryside, rural migrants and foreign immigrants created a new urban culture. In 1800, American cities were overgrown towns with rising death rates: New York had only 60,000 residents, and Philadelphia had 41,000; and life expectancy at birth was a mere twenty-five years. Then urban growth accelerated as a huge in-migration outweighed the high death rates. By 1840, New York's population had ballooned to 312,000; Philadelphia and its suburbs had 150,000 residents; and three other cities — New Orleans, Boston, and Baltimore — each had about 100,000. By 1860, New York had become a metropolis with more than a million residents: 813,000 in Manhattan and another 266,000 in the adjacent community of Brooklyn.

These new cities, particularly New York, generated a new urban culture. Thousands of young men and women from rural areas had flocked to the city searching for adventure and fortune, but many found only a hard life. Young men labored for meager wages in the construction crews that erected thousands of new buildings each year. Others worked as low-paid clerks or operatives in hundreds of mercantile and manufacturing firms. The young women had an even harder time. Thousands toiled as live-in domestic servants, ordered about by the mistress of the household and often sexually exploited by their masters. Thousands more scraped out a bare living as needlewomen in New York's booming clothes manufacturing industry. Unwilling to accept the humiliations of domestic service or the subsistence wages of the needlewoman, many of these and other young girls turned to prostitution. In the 1850s, Dr. William Sanger's careful survey found 6,000 women engaged in commercial sex. Three-fifths of them were native-born whites, and the rest were foreign immigrants; most were between fifteen and twenty years old. Half were or had been domestic servants, half had children, and half were infected with syphilis.

Commercialized sex — and sex in general — formed one facet of the new urban culture. "Sporting men" engaged freely in sexual conquests; otherwise respectable married men kept mistresses in handy apartments; and working men frequented bawdy houses. New York City had some two hundred brothels in the 1820s and five hundred by the 1850s. Prostitutes openly advertised their wares on Broadway, the city's most fashionable thoroughfare, and welcomed clients on the infamous "Third Tier" of the theaters. Many men considered access to illicit sex to be a right. "Man is endowed by nature with passions that must be gratified," declared the *Sporting Whip*, a working-class magazine. Reverend William Berrian, pastor of the ultra-respectable Trinity Episcopal Church, did not disagree; he remarked from the pulpit that he had resorted to "a house of ill-fame" a mere ten times.

Promiscuity formed only the tip of the urban sexual iceberg. Freed from family oversight, young working men and women in the city pursued romantic adventure. Many moved from partner to partner until they chanced on an ideal mate. To enhance their attractiveness, they strolled along Broadway in the latest fashions: elaborate bonnets and silk dresses for young women; flowing capes, leather boots, and silver-plated walking sticks for young men. Rivaling the elegance on Broadway was the colorful dress on the Bowery, the broad avenue that ran up the east side of lower Manhattan. By day, the "Bowery Boy" worked as an apprentice or journeyman; by night, he prowled the streets as a "consummate dandy," his hair cropped at the back of his head "as close as scissors could cut," with long front locks "matted by a lavish application of *bear's grease*, the ends tucked under so as to form a roll and brushed until they shone like glass bottles." The "B'hoy," as he was called, cut a dashing figure as he walked along with a "Bowery Gal" in a striking dress and shawl: "a light pink contrasting with a deep blue" or "a bright yellow with a brighter red."

Popular entertainment was a third facet of the new urban culture in New York. Workingmen could partake of traditional rural blood sports—rat and terrier fights—at Sportsmen Hall, or they could crowd into the pit of the Bowery Theatre to see the "Mad Tragedian," Junius Brutus Booth, deliver a stirring performance of Shakespeare's *Richard III*. Middle-class couples looked forward to an evening at the huge Broadway Tabernacle, where they could hear an abolitionist lecture and see the renowned Hutchinson Family Singers of New Hampshire lead the audience in a roof-raising rendition of their antislavery anthem, "Get Off the Track." Or they could visit the museum of oddities (and hoaxes) created by P. T. Barnum, the great cultural entrepreneur and founder of the Barnum & Bailey Circus.

The most popular theatrical entertainments were the minstrel shows. Performed by white actors in blackface, minstrel shows were a complex blend of racist caricature and social criticism. Minstrelsy began around 1830, when a few individual actors put on blackface and performed comic song-and-dance routines. The most famous was John Dartmouth Rice, whose "Jim Crow" blended a weird shuffle-dance-and-jump with unintelligible lyrics delivered in "Negro dialect." By the 1840s, there were hundreds of minstrel troupes, whose members sang rambling improvised songs. The actor-singers poked racist fun at the African Americans they caricatured, portraying them as lazy, sensual, and irresponsible while simultaneously using them to criticize white society. The minstrels ridiculed the drinking habits of Irish immigrants, parodied the speech of recent German arrivals, denounced women's demands for political rights, and mocked the arrogance of upper-class men.

Still, by performing in blackface, the minstrels declared the importance of being white. In particular, their racism encouraged Irish and German immigrants to identify with the dominant culture of native-born whites and eased their entry into New York society. Foreign-born migrants piled into New York beginning in the 1830s; by 1855, 200,000 Irish men and women lived there, along with 110,000 Germans. German-language shop signs dominated entire sections, and German foods (sausages, hamburgers, sauerkraut) and food customs (such as drinking beer in family *biergärten*) became part of the city's culture. The mass of impoverished Irish migrants found allies in the American Catholic Church, which soon became an Irish-dominated institution, and the Democratic Party, which gave them a foothold in the political process.

Rampant Racism
Minstrel shows and music were immensely popular among whites and hugely damaging to the status and self-respect of blacks. Still, minstrelsy had so much appeal that a group of black entertainers, Gavitt's Original Ethiopian Serenaders, joined the circuit. Black abolitionist Frederick Douglass was not impressed. "It is something gained when the colored man in any form can appear before a white audience," he remarked after watching the group perform, "but they must represent the colored man rather as he is, than as Ethiopian Minstrels usually represent him to be. They will *then* command the respect of both races; whereas *now* they only shock the taste of the one, and provoke the disgust of the other." Courtesy, The Library Company of Philadelphia.

For more help analyzing this image, see the Online Study Guide at bedfordstmartins.com/henrettaconcise.

Many native-born New Yorkers took alarm as hordes of ethnically diverse migrants altered the city's traditional culture. They organized a nativist movement—a final aspect of the new urban world. Beginning in the mid-1830s, nativists called for a halt to immigration and mounted a cultural and political assault on foreign-born residents (see Chapter 9). Gangs of B'hoys assaulted Irish youths in the streets, employers restricted Irish workers to the most menial jobs, and temperance reformers denounced the German fondness for beer. In 1844, the American Republican Party, with the endorsement of the Whigs, swept the city elections by highlighting the emotional issues of temperance, anti-Catholicism, and nativism.

► What accounts for the proliferation of rural utopian communities in nineteenth-century America?

► In what respects were the new cultures of the mid-nineteenth century—those of utopian communalists and of urban residents—different from the mainstream culture described in Chapters 8 and 9? How were they alike?

In the city, as in the countryside, new values were challenging old beliefs. The sexual freedom that Noyes advocated at Oneida had its counterpart in the commercialized sex and male promiscuity in New York City. Similarly, the disciplined rejection of tobacco and alcohol by the Shakers and the Mormons found a parallel in the Washington Temperance Society and other urban reform organizations. American society was in ferment, and the outcome was far from clear.

Abolitionism

Like other reform movements, abolitionism drew on the religious enthusiasm of the Second Great Awakening. Around 1800, reformers had argued that human bondage was contrary to republicanism and liberty. By the 1830s, abolitionists were condemning slavery as a sin that it was their moral duty to end. Their demands for an immediate end to slavery led to fierce political debates, urban riots, and sectional conflicts.

Black Social Thought: Uplift, Race Equality, and Rebellion

Beginning in the 1790s, leading African Americans in the North advocated a strategy of social uplift. They encouraged free blacks to "elevate" themselves through education, temperance, and hard work. By securing "respectability," they argued, blacks could assume a position of equality with whites. To promote that goal, black leaders—men such as James Forten, a Philadelphia sailmaker; Prince Hall, a Boston barber; and ministers Hosea Easton and Richard Allen (see Chapter 8)—founded an array of churches, schools, and self-help associations. Capping this effort in 1827, John Russwurm and Samuel D. Cornish of New York published the first African American newspaper, *Freedom's Journal*.

The black quest for respectability elicited a violent response from whites in Boston, Pittsburgh, and other northern cities, who refused to accept African Americans as their social equals. "I am Mr. _____'s *help*," a white maid informed a British visitor, "I am no *sarvant*; none but *negers* are *sarvants*." Such racial contempt prompted white mobs to terrorize black communities. The attacks in Cincinnati were so violent and destructive that several hundred African Americans fled to Canada for safety.

Responding to the attacks, David Walker published a stirring pamphlet: *An Appeal . . . to the Colored Citizens of the World* (1829). Walker was a free black from North Carolina who had moved to Boston, where he sold secondhand clothes and *Freedom's Journal*. A self-educated man, Walker used history and morality to attack racial slavery. His *Appeal* ridiculed the religious pretensions of slaveholders, justified slave rebellion, and in Christian Biblical language warned of a slave revolt if justice were delayed. "We must and shall be free," he told white Americans. "And woe, woe, will be it to you if we have to obtain our freedom by fighting. . . . Your DESTRUCTION is at hand, and will be speedily consummated unless you REPENT." Walker's pamphlet quickly went through three printings and, carried by black merchant seamen, reached free African Americans in the South.

In 1830, Walker and other African American activists called a national convention in Philadelphia. The delegates refused to endorse Walker's radical call for a slave revolt, but they were not any happier with the program of uplift among free blacks. Instead, this new generation of activists demanded freedom and "race-equality" for all those of African descent. They urged free blacks to use every legal means, including petitions and other forms of political protest, to break "the shackles of slavery."

As Walker threatened violence in Boston, Nat Turner, a slave in Southampton County, Virginia, staged a bloody revolt—a chronological coincidence that had far-reaching consequences. As a child, Turner had taught himself to read and had hoped for emancipation, but a new master forced him into the fields, and another new owner separated him from his wife. Becoming deeply spiritual, Turner had a religious vision in which "the Spirit" explained that "Christ had laid down the yoke he had borne for the sins of men, and that I should take it on and fight against the Serpent, for the time was fast approaching when the first should be last and the last should be first." Taking an eclipse of the sun in August 1831 as an omen, Turner and a handful of relatives and friends rose in rebellion and killed at least fifty-five white men, women, and children. Turner hoped that hundreds of slaves would rally to his cause, but he mustered only sixty men. The white militia quickly dispersed his poorly armed force and took their revenge. One company of cavalry killed forty blacks in two days and put the heads of fifteen of them on poles to warn "all those who should undertake a similar plot." Turner died by hanging, still identifying his mission with that of his Savior. "Was not Christ crucified?" he asked.

Deeply shaken by Turner's Rebellion, the Virginia assembly debated a law providing for gradual emancipation and colonization abroad. When the assembly rejected the bill by a vote of 73 to 58, the possibility that southern planters would voluntarily end slavery was gone forever. Instead, the southern states toughened their slave codes, limited black movement, and prohibited anyone from teaching slaves to read. They would meet Walker's radical *Appeal* with radical measures of their own.

Evangelical Abolitionism

Concurrently with Walker's and Turner's religiously suffused attacks on slavery, a cadre of northern Evangelical Christians launched a moral crusade to abolish the institution immediately. If planters did not allow slaves their God-given status as free moral agents, these radical Christians warned, they faced revolution in this world and damnation in the next.

The most determined abolitionist was William Lloyd Garrison (1805–1879). A Massachusetts-born printer, Garrison had worked in Baltimore during the 1820s helping to publish the *Genius of Universal Emancipation*, an antislavery newspaper. In 1830, Garrison went to jail, convicted of libeling a New England merchant engaged in the domestic slave trade. The following year, Garrison moved to Boston, where he started his own weekly, *The Liberator*, and founded the New England Anti-Slavery Society.

From the outset, *The Liberator* demanded the immediate abolition of slavery without compensation to slaveholders. His goal was absolute, Garrison declared: "I will not retreat a single inch—AND I WILL BE HEARD." Garrison accused the American Colonization Society (see Chapter 8) of perpetuating slavery because of its voluntary approach, and assailed the U.S. Constitution as "a covenant with death and an agreement with Hell" because it implicitly accepted racial bondage.

In 1833, Garrison met with Theodore Weld and sixty other abolitionists, black and white, and established the American Anti-Slavery Society. The society received financial support from Arthur and Lewis Tappan, wealthy silk merchants in New York City. Women abolitionists established separate organizations, including the Philadelphia Female Anti-Slavery Society, founded by Lucretia Mott in 1833, and the Anti-Slavery Conventions of American Women, formed by a network of local societies in the late 1830s. The women raised money for *The Liberator* and carried the movement to the farm villages of the Midwest, where they distributed abolitionist literature and collected thousands of signatures on antislavery petitions.

Abolitionist leaders developed a three-pronged plan of attack. They began by appealing to religious Americans. In 1837, Weld published *The Bible Against Slavery*, which used passages from Christianity's holiest book to discredit slavery. Two years later, Weld teamed up with the Grimké sisters—Angelina, whom he married, and Sarah. The Grimkés had left their father's plantation in South Carolina, converted to Quakerism, and taken up the abolitionist cause in Philadelphia. In *American Slavery as It Is: Testimony of a Thousand Witnesses* (1839), Weld and the Grimkés addressed a simple question: "What is the actual condition of the slaves in the United States?" Using reports from southern newspapers and firsthand testimony, they presented a mass of incriminating evidence. Angelina Grimké told of a treadmill that South Carolina slave owners used for punishment:

> One poor girl, [who was] sent there to be flogged, and who was accordingly stripped naked and whipped, showed me the deep gashes on her back— I might have laid my whole finger in them—large pieces of flesh had actually been cut out by the torturing lash.

The book sold more than 100,000 copies in a single year.

To distribute their message, the abolitionists used the latest techniques of mass communication. With the help of new steam-powered printing presses, the American Anti-Slavery Society distributed thousands of pieces of literature in 1834. In 1835, the society launched a "great postal campaign" to flood the nation, including the South, with a million pamphlets.

The abolitionists' second tactic was to aid African Americans who had fled from slavery. They provided lodging and jobs for escaped blacks in free states and created the Underground Railroad, an informal network of whites and free blacks in Richmond, Charleston, and other southern towns that assisted fugitives from the Lower South. In Baltimore, a free African American sailor loaned his identification papers to future abolitionist Frederick Douglass, who used them to escape to New York. Harriet Tubman and other runaway slaves risked reenslavement or death by returning repeatedly to the South to help others escape. "I should fight for . . . liberty as long as my strength lasted," Tubman explained, "and when the time came for me to go, the Lord would let them take me." Thanks to the Railroad, about 1,000 African Americans reached freedom in the North each year.

There, they faced an uncertain future, because most whites did not favor civic equality for African Americans. Voters in six northern and midwestern states adopted constitutional amendments that denied or limited the franchise for free blacks. "We want no masters," declared a New York artisan, "and least of all no negro masters."

Moreover, the Fugitive Slave Law (1793) allowed owners and their hired slave catchers to seize suspected runaways and carry them back to bondage. To thwart these efforts, white abolitionists and free blacks in northern cities formed mobs that attacked slave catchers and released their captives.

A political campaign was the final element of the abolitionists' program. In 1835, the American Anti-Slavery Society bombarded Congress with petitions demanding the abolition of slavery in the District of Columbia, an end to the interstate slave trade, and a ban on admission of new slave states. By 1838, petitions with close to 500,000 signatures had arrived in Washington.

Such activities drew support from thousands of deeply religious farmers and small-town proprietors. The number of local abolitionist societies grew from 200 in 1835 to 2,000 by 1840, with nearly 200,000 members, including many leading transcendentalists. Emerson condemned Americans for supporting slavery, and Thoreau, claiming that the Mexican War was an attempt to extend slavery, refused to pay taxes and submitted to arrest. In 1848, he published "Resistance to Civil Government," an essay urging individuals to follow a higher moral law.

Opposition and Internal Conflict

Still, abolitionists remained a small minority. Perhaps 10 percent of northerners and midwesterners strongly supported the movement, and another 20 percent were sympathetic to its goals. The opponents of abolition were more numerous and equally aggressive. The abolitionists' agitation, they warned, risked "embroiling neighborhoods and families — setting friend against friend, overthrowing churches and institutions of learning, embittering one portion of the land against the other." Wealthy men feared that the attack on slaves as property might become a general assault on all property rights; conservative clergymen condemned the public roles that abolitionist women assumed; and northern merchants and textile manufacturers supported the southern planters who supplied them with cotton. Northern wage earners feared that freed blacks would work for lower wages and take their jobs. Finally, whites almost universally opposed "amalgamation," the racial mixing and intermarriage that Garrison seemed to support by holding meetings of black and white abolitionists of both sexes.

Racial fears and hatreds led to violent mob actions. White workers in northern towns laid waste to places where blacks and whites mixed, such as taverns and brothels; and they attacked "respectable" African American institutions such as churches, temperance halls, and orphanages. In 1833, a mob of 1,500 New Yorkers stormed a church in search of Garrison and Arthur Tappan. Another white mob swept through Philadelphia's African American neighborhoods, clubbing and stoning residents and destroying homes and churches. Fearing change, "gentlemen of property and standing" — lawyers, merchants, and bankers — broke up an abolitionist convention in Utica, New York, in 1835. Two years later, a mob in Alton, Illinois, shot and killed Elijah P. Lovejoy, editor of the abolitionist *Alton Observer*. By pressing for emancipation and equality, the abolitionists revealed the extent of racial prejudice and the impossibility of integrating "respectable" blacks into the white middle class. In fact, the abolitionist crusade had heightened race consciousness, which prompted whites — and blacks — to identify across class lines with members of their own race.

Racial solidarity was especially strong in the South, where whites banned abolitionists and demanded that northern states do the same. The Georgia legislature offered a $5,000 reward to anyone who would kidnap Garrison and bring him south to be tried for inciting rebellion. In Nashville, vigilantes whipped a northern college student for distributing abolitionist pamphlets; in Charleston, a mob attacked the post office and destroyed sacks of abolitionist mail. After 1835, southern postmasters simply refused to deliver mail suspected to be of abolitionist origin.

Politicians joined the fray. President Andrew Jackson, a longtime slave owner, asked Congress in 1835 to restrict the use of the mails by abolitionist groups. Congress refused, but in 1836, the House of Representatives adopted the so-called gag rule. Under this informal rule, which remained in force until 1844, antislavery petitions to the House were automatically tabled and not discussed, keeping the explosive issue of slavery off the congressional stage.

Assailed by racists from the outside, abolitionists fought among themselves over policy and gender issues. Many antislavery clergymen opposed an activist role for women and condemned the Grimké sisters for lecturing to mixed-sex audiences. But Garrison had broadened his reform agenda to include pacifism, the abolition of prisons, and women's rights: "Our object is universal emancipation, to redeem women as well as men from a servile to an equal condition." In 1840, Garrison's demand that the American Anti-Slavery Society support women's rights helped to split the abolitionist movement. Abby Kelley, Lucretia Mott, Elizabeth Cady Stanton, and other women's rights advocates remained with Garrison in the American Anti-Slavery Society and assailed both the institutions that bound blacks and the customs that constrained free women.

Garrison's opponents founded a new organization, the American and Foreign Anti-Slavery Society, which focused its energies on ending slavery through political means. Its members mobilized their churches to oppose racial bondage and established the Liberty Party, the first antislavery political party. In 1840, the new party nominated James G. Birney, a former Alabama slave owner, for president. Birney and the Liberty Party argued that the Constitution did not recognize slavery and, consequently, that slaves automatically became free when they entered areas of federal authority, including the District of Columbia and the national territories. However, Birney won few votes, and the future of political abolitionism appeared dim.

Popular violence in the North, government suppression in the South, and internal schisms stunned the abolitionist movement. By melding the energies and ideas of Evangelical Protestants, moral reformers, and transcendentalists, it had raised the banner of antislavery to new heights, only to face a hostile and widespread backlash. "When we first unfurled the banner of *The Liberator*," Garrison admitted, "it did not occur to us that nearly every religious sect, and every political party would side with the oppressor."

▶ How did black social thought change over the first half of the nineteenth century? What role did black activists play in the abolitionist movement?

▶ How did the abolitionists' proposals and methods differ from those of earlier antislavery movements (see Chapter 8)? Why did those proposals and methods arouse such hostility in the South and in the North?

The Women's Rights Movement

The prominence of women among the abolitionists reflected a broad shift in American culture. By joining religious revivals and reform movements such as the temperance crusade and the abolitionist movement, women entered public life. Their activism caused issues of gender—sexual behavior, marriage, family authority—to become subjects of debate. The debate entered a new phase in 1848, when some reformers focused on women's rights and demanded complete equality with men.

Origins of the Women's Movement

"Don't be afraid, not afraid, fight Satan; stand up for Christ; don't be afraid." So spoke Mary Walker Ostram on her deathbed in 1859. Her religious convictions were as firm at the age of fifty-eight as they had been in 1816, when she helped to found the first Sunday school in Utica, New York. Married to a lawyer-politician but childless, Ostram had devoted her life to Evangelical Presbyterianism and its program of benevolent social reform. In his eulogy after her death, her minister, Philemon Fowler, celebrated Ostram as a "living fountain" of faith, an exemplar of "Women's Sphere of Influence" in the world.

Even as the Reverend Fowler heaped praise on Ostram, he rejected a public presence for women. Like men of the Revolutionary era, Fowler believed that women should limit their political role to that of "republican mother," instructing "their sons in the principles of liberty and government." Women inhabited a "separate sphere" and had no place in "the markets of trade, the scenes of politics and popular agitation, the courts of justice and the halls of legislation." "Home is her peculiar sphere and members of her family her peculiar care," Fowler concluded.

But Ostram and many other middle-class women had already transcended these roles by participating in the Second Great Awakening. Their spiritual activism bolstered their authority within the household and allowed them to influence many areas of family life, including the timing of pregnancies. Publications like *Godey's Lady's Book*, a popular monthly periodical, and Catherine Beecher's *Treatise on Domestic Economy* (1841) taught women how to make their homes examples of middle-class efficiency and domesticity. Women in propertied farm families were equally vigilant. To protect their homes and husbands from alcoholic excess, they joined the Independent Order of Good Templars, a family-oriented temperance organization that granted them full membership.

Some women used their religious activities to enhance other women's lives. In 1834, a group of middle-class women in New York City founded the Female Moral Reform Society and elected Lydia Finney, the wife of revivalist Charles Grandison Finney, as its president. The society sought to curb prostitution in New York City and to protect single women from moral corruption. Rejecting the sexual double standard, its members demanded chastity for men as well as for women. By 1840, the Female Moral Reform Society had grown into a national association, with 555 chapters and 40,000 members throughout the North and Midwest. Employing only women as agents, the society provided moral guidance for young women who were living away from their families and working as factory operatives, seamstresses, or servants. Society members visited brothels, where they sang hymns, offered prayers, searched for runaway girls, and noted the names of clients. They also founded homes of refuge for prostitutes and won the passage of laws in Massachusetts and New York that made seduction a crime.

Other women set out to improve public institutions, and Dorothea Dix (1801–1887) was their model. Dix's paternal grandparents were prominent Bostonians, but her father, a Methodist minister, ended up an impoverished alcoholic. Poor and emotionally abused as a child, Dix grew into a compassionate young woman with a strong sense of moral purpose. She used her grandparents' resources to set up charity schools to "rescue some of America's miserable children from vice" and became a successful author. By 1832, she had published seven books, including *Conversations on Common Things* (1824), an enormously successful treatise on natural science and moral improvement.

In 1841, Dix took up a new cause. Discovering that insane women were jailed alongside male criminals, she persuaded Massachusetts lawmakers to enlarge the state hospital to accommodate indigent mental patients. Exhilarated by that success, Dix began a national movement to establish separate state hospitals for those with mental illness. By 1854, she had traveled more than 30,000 miles and had visited eighteen state penitentiaries, 300 county jails, and more than 500 almshouses in addition to innumerable hospitals. Issuing dozens of reports, Dix prompted many states to expand their public hospitals and improve their prisons.

Both as reformers and as teachers, other northern women transformed public education. From Maine to Wisconsin, women vigorously supported the movement led by Horace Mann to increase the number of elementary schools and improve the quality of instruction. As secretary of the Massachusetts Board of Education from 1837 to 1848, Mann lengthened the school year; established teaching standards in reading, writing, and arithmetic; and improved instruction by recruiting well-educated women as teachers. The intellectual leader of the new women educators was Catherine Beecher, who founded academies for young women in Hartford and Cincinnati. In widely read publications, Beecher argued that "energetic and benevolent women" were better qualified than men were to impart moral and intellectual instruction to the young. By the 1850s, most teachers were women, both because local school boards heeded Beecher's arguments and because the boards could hire women at a lower salary than men. As teachers as well as reformers, women were now part of public life.

Abolitionist Women

Women were central to the antislavery movement. One of the first abolitionists recruited by William Lloyd Garrison was Maria W. Stewart, an African American, who spoke to mixed audiences of men and women in Boston in the early 1830s. As abolitionism blossomed, scores of white women delivered lectures condemning slavery, and thousands more made home "visitations" to win converts to their cause (Map 11.3).

Women abolitionists were particularly aware of the special horrors of slavery for their sex. In her autobiography, *Incidents in the Life of a Slave Girl*, black abolitionist Harriet Jacobs described being forced to have sexual relations with her white owner: "I cannot tell how much I suffered in the presence of these wrongs." According to Jacobs and the other female slaves, such sexual assaults were compounded by the cruel treatment they suffered at the hands of their owners' wives, who were enraged by their husbands' promiscuity. In her best-selling novel, *Uncle Tom's Cabin* (1852), Harriet

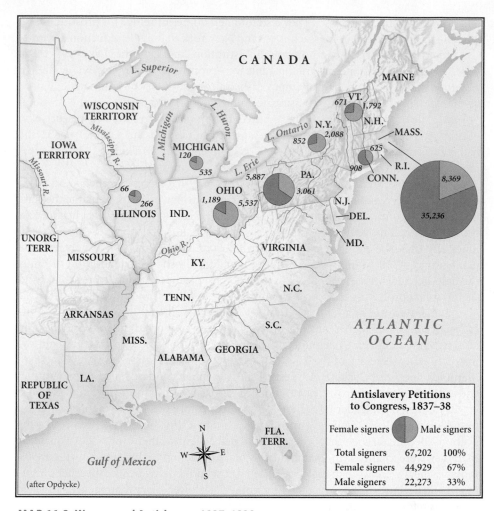

MAP 11.3 Women and Antislavery, 1837–1838

Beginning in the 1830s, antislavery advocates dispatched dozens of petitions to Congress demanding an end to human bondage. Women accounted for two-thirds of the 67,000 signatures on the petitions submitted in 1837–1838, suggesting the importance of women in the antislavery movement and the extent of female organizations and social networks. Lawmakers, eager to avoid sectional conflict, had devised the so-called gag rule, an informal agreement to table the petitions without discussion.

For more help analyzing this map, see the Online Study Guide at **bedfordstmartins.com/henrettaconcise**.

Beecher Stowe charged that one of the greatest moral failings of slavery was the degradation of slave women.

When men challenged their public activism, white abolitionist women grew increasingly conscious of their own degraded social and legal status. In 1836, Congregationalist clergymen in New England assailed Angelina and Sarah Grimké for addressing mixed male and female audiences. For justification, Sarah Grimké turned to the Bible: "The Lord Jesus defines the duties of his followers in his Sermon on the Mount . . .

Sojourner Truth
Few women had as interesting a life as Sojourner Truth. Born "Isabella" in Dutch-speaking rural New York about 1797, she labored as a slave until 1827. Following a religious vision, Isabella moved to New York City, learned English, and worked for deeply religious — and ultimately fanatical — Christian merchants. In 1843, in search of further spiritual enlightenment, she took the name "Sojourner Truth" and left New York. After briefly joining the Millerites (who believed the world would end in 1844), Truth became famous as a forceful speaker on behalf of abolitionism and women's rights. This illustration, showing Truth addressing an antislavery meeting, suggests her powerful personal presence. Miriam and Ira D. Wallach Division of Art, Prints and Photographs. The New York Public Library.

without any reference to sex or condition," she wrote. "Men and women are CREATED EQUAL! They are both moral and accountable beings and whatever is right for man to do is right for woman." In a pamphlet debate with Catherine Beecher (who believed that women should exercise power primarily as wives, mothers, and schoolteachers), Angelina Grimké pushed the argument beyond religion, invoking Enlightenment principles to claim equal civic rights for women:

> It is a woman's right to have a voice in all the laws and regulations by which she is governed, whether in Church or State. . . . The present arrangements of society on these points are a violation of human rights, a rank usurpation of power, a violent seizure and confiscation of what is sacredly and inalienably hers.

By 1840, female abolitionists were asserting that traditional gender roles amounted to the "domestic slavery" of women. "How can we endure our present marriage relations," asked Elizabeth Cady Stanton, since they gave a woman "no charter of rights, no individuality of her own?" Said another female reformer: "The radical difficulty . . . is that women are considered as *belonging* to men" (see American Voices, p. 344). Having acquired a public voice and political skills in the crusade for African American freedom, thousands of northern women now advocated greater rights for themselves.

The Program of Seneca Falls and Beyond

During the 1840s, women's rights activists devised a pragmatic program of reform. They did not challenge the institution of marriage or the conventional division of labor within the family. Instead, they tried to strengthen the legal rights of married women, especially

A Farm Woman Defends the Grimké Sisters KEZIAH KENDALL

The Grimké sisters' abolitionist lecture tour of New England sparked an enormous outcry from ministers and social conservatives, who questioned the propriety of women assuming public roles and demanding civic equality. In a Lyceum lecture in 1839, titled "The Legal Rights of Women," Simon Greenleaf, Royall Professor of Law at Harvard College, defended legal and customary restrictions on women's lives. Replying to Greenleaf, Keziah Kendall—possibly a fictional person created by a women's rights advocate—sent him the following letter, which two historians recently found among his papers.

My name is Keziah Kendall. I live not many miles from Cambridge, on a farm with two sisters, one older, one younger than myself. I am thirty two. Our parents and only brother are dead—we have a good estate—comfortable house—nice barn, garden, orchard &c and money in the bank besides. . . . Under these circumstances the whole responsibility of our property, not less than twenty five thousand dollars rest upon me. . . .

Well—our milkman brought word when he came from market that you were a going to lecture on the legal rights of women, and so I thought I would go and learn. Now I hope you wont think me bold when I say, I did not like that lecture much . . . [because] there was nothing in it but what every body knows. . . .

What I wanted to know, was good reasons for some of those laws that I cant account for. . . . One Lyceum lecture that I heard in C[ambridge] stated that the Americans went to war with the British, because they were taxed without being represented in Parliament. Now we [women] are taxed every year to the full amount of every dollar we possess—town, county, state taxes—taxes for land, for movable [property], for money and all. Now I don't want to [become a legislative] representative [or] . . . a "constable or a

sheriff," but I have no voice about public improvements, and I don't see the justice of being taxed any more than the "revolutionary heroes" did.

Nor do I think we are treated as Christian women ought to be, according to the Bible rule of doing to others as you would others should do unto you. I am told (not by you) that if a woman dies a week after she's married that her husband takes all her personal property and the use of [all] her real estate as long as he lives—if a man dies his wife can have her thirds [use of only one-third of the estate]—*this* does not come up to the Gospel rule. . . .

Another thing . . . women have joined the Antislavery societies, and why? Women are kept for slaves as well as [black] men—it is a common cause, deny the justice of it, who can! To be sure I do not wish to go about lecturing like the Misses Grimkie, but I have not the knowledge they have, and I verily believe that if I had been brought up among slaves as they were . . . and felt a call from humanity to speak, I should run the venture of your displeasure, and that of a good many others like you.

SOURCE: Dianne Avery and Alfred S. Konefsky, "The Daughters of Job: Property Rights and Women's Lives in Mid-Nineteenth-Century Massachusetts," *Law and History Review* 10 (Fall 1992): 323–356.

Crusading Women Reformers
Elizabeth Cady Stanton (1815–1902) and Susan B. Anthony (1820–1906) were a dynamic duo of social reformers. Cady was the well-educated daughter of a New York judge and an early abolitionist. In 1840, she married abolitionist lawyer Henry Stanton, by whom she had seven children. Anthony was raised as a Quaker, taught school for ten years, and then became a temperance activist. Stanton and Anthony became intimate friends and led a successful struggle to expand New York's Married Women's Property Law of 1848. During the Civil War, they set up the Women's Loyal National League, which supported the Union war effort and helped to win passage of the Thirteenth Amendment. In 1866, they were among the founders of the American Equal Rights Association, which demanded the vote for women as well as African American men.
©Bettmann/ Corbis.

with respect to property. This initiative won crucial support from affluent men, who wanted to protect their family's assets in case their businesses went bankrupt in the volatile market economy. By ensuring that their married daughters had property rights, fathers also hoped to protect them (and their inheritances) from financially irresponsible sons-in-law. These considerations prompted legislatures in three states—Mississippi, Maine, and Massachusetts—to enact married women's property acts between 1839 and 1845. Three years later, women activists in New York won a more comprehensive statute that became the model for laws in fourteen other states. This statute of 1848 gave women full legal control over the property they brought to a marriage.

That same year, Elizabeth Cady Stanton and Lucretia Mott organized a gathering of women's right activists in the small New York town of Seneca Falls. Seventy women and thirty men attended the meeting, which issued a rousing manifesto for women's equality. Taking the Declaration of Independence as a model, the attendees extended its republican ideology to women. "All men and women are created equal," the Declaration of Sentiments declared, yet "the history of mankind is a history of repeated injuries and usurpations on the part of man toward woman" and "the establishment of an absolute tyranny over her." To persuade Americans to right this long-standing wrong, the activists resolved to "employ agents, circulate tracts, petition the State and National legislatures, and endeavor to enlist the pulpit and the press on our behalf." By staking out claims for equality for women in public life, the Seneca Falls reformers repudiated both the natural inferiority of women and the ideology of **separate spheres**.

Most men dismissed the Seneca Falls declaration as nonsense, and many women also repudiated the activists and their message. Writing in her diary, one small-town mother and housewife lashed out at the female reformer who "aping mannish manners . . . wears absurd and barbarous attire, who talks of her wrongs in harsh tone, who struts and strides, and thinks that she proves herself superior to the rest of her sex."

Still, the women's rights movement grew in strength and purpose. In 1850, delegates to the first national women's rights convention in Worcester, Massachusetts, hammered out a program of action. The women called on churches to revise notions of female inferiority in their theology. Addressing state legislatures, they proposed laws to guarantee the custody rights of mothers in the event of divorce or a husband's death and to allow married women to institute lawsuits and testify in court. Finally, they began a concerted campaign to win the vote for women. The national women's rights convention of 1851 declared that suffrage was "the corner-stone of this enterprise, since we do not seek to protect woman, but rather to place her in a position to protect herself."

The activists' legislative campaign required talented organizers and lobbyists. The most prominent political operative was Susan B. Anthony (1820–1906). Anthony came from a Quaker family and, as a young woman, participated in the temperance and anti-slavery movements. That experience, Anthony explained, had given her political skills and taught her "the great evil of woman's utter dependence on man." Joining the women's right movement, she worked closely with Elizabeth Cady Stanton. Anthony created a network of political "captains," all women, who relentlessly lobbied state legislatures. In 1860, her efforts secured a New York law granting women the right to control their own wages (which fathers or husbands had previously managed), to own property acquired by "trade, business, labors, or services," and, if widowed, to assume sole guardianship of their children. Genuine individualism for women, the dream of transcendentalist Margaret Fuller, had moved a tiny step closer to reality. Both in such small and much larger ways, the midcentury reform movements had altered the character of American culture.

▶ Why did religious women such as Mary Walker Ostram and the Grimké sisters become social reformers?

▶ How do you explain the appearance of the women's rights movement? What were its goals, and why did they arouse intense opposition?

▶ Did the era of reform increase or decrease the American commitment to, and practice of, liberty? In what ways?

SUMMARY

In this chapter, we examined four major cultural movements of the mid-nineteenth century and analyzed the new popular culture in New York City. Our discussion of the transcendentalists highlighted the influence of Ralph Waldo Emerson on the great literary figures of the era; we also linked transcendentalism to the rise of individualism and the character of middle-class culture.

Our analysis of communal movements probed the efforts of communalists to devise new rules for sexual behavior, gender relationships, and property ownership.

We saw that successful communal experiments—Mormonism, for example—began with a charismatic leader and a religious foundation and endured if they developed strong, authoritarian institutions.

We also traced the personal and ideological factors that linked the abolitionist and women's rights movements. Lucretia Mott, Elizabeth Cady Stanton, and the Grimké sisters began as antislavery advocates; but, denied access to lecture platforms by male abolitionists, they gradually became staunch defenders of women's rights. This transition was a logical one: Both enslaved blacks and married women were "owned" by men, either as property or as their legal dependents. Consequently, the efforts of women's rights advocates to abolish the legal prerogatives of husbands were as controversial as the abolitionists' efforts to end the legal property rights of slave owners. As reformers took aim at these deeply rooted institutions and customs, many Americans feared that such activism would not perfect society but destroy it.

Connections: Culture

Before 1800, the United States contained three distinct regional cultures: those of New England, the Middle Atlantic, and the South. The presence (or absence) of three eighteenth-century migrant cultures—African, German, and Scots-Irish—in a region partially explained its distinct character. As we saw in Chapter 8, between 1790 and 1820, the migrant societies slowly acquired an American identity, and all of the regions integrated republican ideology and Protestant Christianity into their cultural outlook. Then, as we noted in the essay opening Part Three,

> a series of reform movements, many with religious roots and goals, swept across America. Dedicated men and women preached the gospel of temperance, Sunday observance, prison reform, and many other causes.

These reform movements sparked a series of culture wars, as temperance advocates won laws regulating drink, Sabbatarians curtailed Sunday amusements, white mobs rioted against abolitionists, and community hostility forced Mormons westward. The arrival of millions of Catholic migrants from Germany and Ireland sparked more cultural conflicts. Meanwhile, in the South, a vast movement of peoples—white and black—into the lower Mississippi Valley created a new "cotton states" culture, which we discuss in the next chapter.

FOR FURTHER EXPLORATION

Ronald Walters, *American Reformers, 1815–1860* (1978), and Robert H. Abzug, *Cosmos Crumbling* (1994), cover the reform movements and their religious roots. Peter S. Field, *Ralph Waldo Emerson* (2003), Charles Capper, *Margaret Fuller* (1992), and David S. Reynolds, *Walt Whitman's America* (1995), are fine biographies. Good Web sites include **www.vcu.edu/engweb/transcendentalism/** and **religiousmovements.lib.virginia.edu/**. For religious utopianism gone mad, read Paul E. Johnson and Sean Wilentz, *The Kingdom of Matthias* (1995).

On abolitionism, read James B. Stewart, *Holy Warriors: The Abolitionists and American Slavery* (1976); Mark Perry, *Lift Up Thy Voice: The Grimké Family's Journey* (2001); and Catherine Clinton, *Harriet Tubman: The Road to Freedom* (2004). Nat

TIMELINE

1826 ► Lyceum movement begins	► Commercial sex flourishes in New York City
1829 ► David Walker's *Appeal . . . to the Colored Citizens of the World*	**1841** ► Transcendentalists found Brook Farm
1830 ► Joseph Smith issues *The Book of Mormon*	► Dorothea Dix reforms prisons and hospitals
1830s ► Ralph Waldo Emerson defines transcendentalism	**1844** ► Margaret Fuller publishes *Woman in the Nineteenth Century*
► Emergence of minstrelsy shows	**1845** ► Henry David Thoreau withdraws to Walden Pond
► Nativists denounce immigration	
1831 ► William Lloyd Garrison founds *The Liberator* and American Anti-Slavery Society (1833)	**1846** ► Mormon followers of Brigham Young reach Salt Lake
► Nat Turner's uprising in Virginia	**1848** ► John Humphrey Noyes founds Oneida Community
1834 ► New York women create Female Moral Reform Society	► Seneca Falls convention advocates women's equality
1835 ► Abolitionists launch mail campaign; antiabolitionists riot against them	**1850** ► Nathaniel Hawthorne publishes *The Scarlet Letter*
1836 ► House of Representatives adopts gag rule on antislavery petitions	**1851** ► Herman Melville issues *Moby Dick*
► Grimké sisters defend public roles for women	**1852** ► Harriet Beecher Stowe writes *Uncle Tom's Cabin*
1840 ► Liberty Party candidate James G. Birney runs for president	**1855** ► Walt Whitman publishes *Leaves of Grass*
1840s ► Fourierist communities arise in Midwest	**1858** ► "Mormon War" over polygamy

Turner's uprising is the focus of Stephen B. Oates, *The Fires of Jubilee* (1975). For antiabolitionism and minstrelsy, read David Roediger, *The Wages of Whiteness* (1995).

On the women's rights movement, begin with Mary C. Kelley, *Learning to Stand and Speak: Women, Education, and Public Life in America's Republic* (2006); Ellen DuBois, *Feminism and Suffrage* (1978); and Kathleen Barry, *Susan B. Anthony* (1988). See also the Web site for Seneca Falls (**www.nps.gov/wori/home.htm**).

TEST YOUR KNOWLEDGE

To assess your mastery of the material in this chapter and for Web sites, images, and documents related to this chapter, visit **bedfordstmartins.com/henrettaconcise**.

The South Expands: Slavery and Society
1820–1860

A prime able-bodied slave is worth three times as much to the cotton or sugar planter as to the Maryland agriculturalist.

— *Frederick [Maryland] Examiner*, 1858

Life in South Carolina had been good to James Lide. A slave-owning planter who lived near the Pee Dee River, Lide and his wife had raised twelve children and lived in relative comfort. Content with his lot, Lide had long resisted the "Alabama Fever" that had prompted thousands of Carolina families to move west. Finally, at age sixty-five, probably seeking land for his many offspring, he moved his slaves and family—including six children and six grandchildren—to a plantation near Montgomery, Alabama. There, the family took up residence in a squalid double log cabin with airholes but no windows. Even as their living conditions improved, the Lides' family life remained unsettled. "Pa is quite in the notion of moving somewhere," his daughter Maria reported a few years later; "his having such a good crop seems to make him more anxious to move." Although James Lide lived out his years in Alabama, many of his children did not. In 1854, at the age of fifty-eight, Eli Lide moved to Texas, telling his father, "Something within me whispers onward and onward."

The story of the Lide family was the story of American society. Between 1800 and 1860, white planters from the South as well as yeomen farmers from the North were moving west. The South's "master class was one of the most mobile in history," notes historian James Oakes. The planters' goal was to make the West into a "slave society" similar to those their fathers and grandfathers had built in Virginia and South Carolina. Using their own muscles and those of thousands of enslaved African Americans, the planters brought millions of acres of land into cultivation. By 1840, the South was at the cutting edge of the American Market Revolution. The region annually produced and exported 1.5 million bales of raw cotton—over two-thirds of the world's supply—and its economy was larger and richer than those of most nations. "Cotton is King," boasted the *Southern Cultivator*, the leading Georgia farm journal, "and wields an astonishing influence over the world's commerce."

No matter how rich they were, few cotton planters in the southwestern states of Alabama, Mississippi, and Texas lived in elegant houses or led cultured lives. The slave owners of the Cotton South largely abandoned the aristocratic gentility of the Chesapeake region and the Carolinas. These agricultural capitalists wanted to make money. "To sell cotton in order to buy negroes—to make more cotton to buy more negroes, 'ad infinitum,' is the aim . . . of the thorough-going cotton planter," a New England traveler reported from Mississippi in 1835. "His whole soul is wrapped up in the pursuit." A generation later, Frederick Law Olmsted found that little had changed: In Mississippi, "the plantations are all large" but their owners do not live well, he observed; "the greater number have but small and mean residences." Plantation women were especially aware of the loss of genteel surroundings and polite society. Raised in North Carolina, where she was "blest with every comfort, & even luxury," a "discontented" Mary Drake found Mississippi and Alabama "a dreary waste."

Tens of thousands of enslaved African Americans in the Lower Mississippi River Valley knew what "dreary waste" really meant: unremitting toil, unrelieved poverty, and profound sadness. Sold south from Maryland, where his family had lived for generations, Charles Ball's father became "gloomy and morose" and, when threatened again with sale, ran off and disappeared. He had good reason: On new cotton plantations, slaves labored from "sunup to sundown" and from one end of the year to the other. As one field hand put it, there was "no time off [between] de change of de seasons. . . . Dey was allus clearin' mo' lan' or sump'." Day by day, the forced labor of unwilling black migrants produced the great wealth of the Cotton South. Always wanting more, southern planters and politicians plotted to extend their plantation economy across the continent.

Creating the Cotton South

American slavery took root on the tobacco plantations of the Chesapeake and in the rice fields of the Carolina Low Country. It grew to maturity on the sugar fields of Louisiana, the hemp farms of Kentucky and Tennessee, and especially on the cotton plantations of the states bordering the Gulf of Mexico: Alabama, Mississippi, and Texas (Figure 12.1). The transplantation of slavery to these new lands brought vast changes to the lives of enslaved blacks, slave-owning planters, and white farmers. And it led

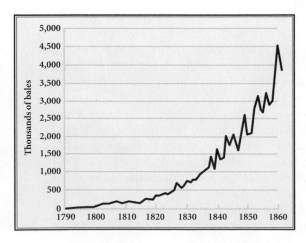

FIGURE 12.1 The Surge in Cotton Production, 1835–1860

Between 1835 and the mid-1840s, southern planters doubled their output of 500-pound bales of cotton from one million per year to two million. Production doubled again in the 1850s, reaching four million bales per year by the end of the decade. Because the price of raw cotton rose slightly (from about 11 cents a pound in the 1830s to 13 cents in the 1850s), planters reaped substantial profits, reinforcing their commitment to the slave system.

SOURCE: Robert William Fogel and Stanley L. Engerman, *Time on the Cross* (Boston: Little, Brown, 1974), fig. 25.

planters to believe that American slavery could keep expanding. "We want land, and have a right to it," declared a Georgia planter on the eve of the Civil War.

The Domestic Slave Trade

In 1817, when the American Colonization Society announced its plan to return freed blacks to Africa (see Chapter 8), the southern plantation system was expanding rapidly, as was the demand for slave labor. In 1790, the western boundary of the plantation system ran through the middle of Georgia; by 1830, it stretched through western Louisiana; by 1860, the slave frontier extended far into Texas (Map 12.1). That advance of 900 miles more than doubled the geographical area cultivated by slave labor and nearly increased the number of slave states from eight in 1800 to fifteen by 1850. The federal government promoted this expansion by buying Louisiana from the French in 1803, removing Native Americans from the southeastern states in the 1830s, and annexing Texas and Mexican lands in the 1840s.

To cultivate this vast area, white planters looked for enslaved laborers first in Africa and then in the Chesapeake region. Between 1776 and 1809, when Congress outlawed the Atlantic slave trade, planters imported about 115,000 Africans. "The Negro business is a great object with us," one slave trader declared, "the Planter will . . . sacrifice every thing to attain Negroes." Despite the influx, the demand for labor far exceeded the supply. Consequently, cotton planters imported new African workers illegally, through the Spanish colony of Florida until 1819 and then through the Mexican province of Texas. Yet these Africans—about 50,000 between 1810 and 1869—did not satisfy the demand for labor.

So planters looked to the Chesapeake region, home in 1800 to nearly half of the nation's black population. Throughout this region, the African American population was growing rapidly from natural increase—an average of 27 percent a decade—and creating a surplus of enslaved laborers. Before the War of 1812, so-called Georgia traders had exploited this surplus; after 1815, the internal trade expanded vastly in scope and size. Between 1818 and 1829, planters in just one Maryland county—Frederick—sold at least 952 slaves to traders or cotton planters. Each decade, about 10 percent of the African Americans in the main exporting states of the Upper South—Maryland and Virginia before 1820, plus the Carolinas by 1830, plus Kentucky by 1840—suffered a similar fate.

The "mania for buying negroes" resulted in a massive forced migration. Seventy-five thousand slaves left Virginia during the 1810s and another 75,000 during the 1820s. The number of unwilling Virginia migrants jumped to nearly 120,000 during the 1830s and then averaged 85,000 during the 1840s and 1850s. In Virginia alone, then, 440,000 African Americans were ripped from communities where their families had lived for three or four generations. By 1860, more than one million slaves had been forced to leave the Upper South.

This movement of African Americans took two forms: transfer and sale. Looking for new opportunities, thousands of Chesapeake and Carolina planters—men like James Lide—sold their plantations and moved to the Southwest with their slaves. Many other planters in the Old South gave slaves to sons and daughters who were moving west. This transfer of entire or partial plantations accounted for about 40 percent of the African American migrants. The rest—about 60 percent of the one million

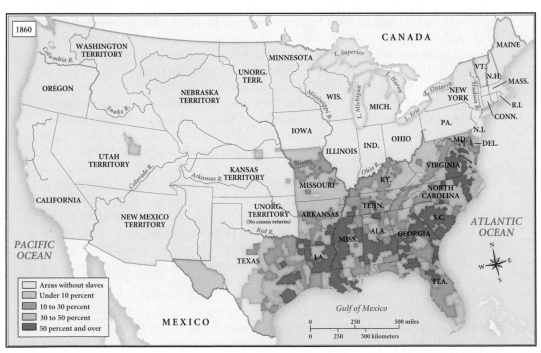

Areas without slaves
Under 10 percent
10 to 30 percent
30 to 50 percent
50 percent and over

migrants—were "sold south." By 1860, a majority of African Americans lived and worked in the Deep South, the lands that stretched from Georgia to Texas.

Just as the Atlantic slave trade was a major eighteenth-century business, so the domestic slave trade emerged as a crucial commercial enterprise between 1800 and 1860. The trade took two forms: a coastal system through the Atlantic seaports and inland commerce using rivers and roads. The coastal system sent thousands of slaves to the sugar plantations in Louisiana, the former French territory that entered the Union in 1812. Slave traders scoured the countryside near the port cities of the Chesapeake and the Carolinas—Baltimore, Alexandria, Richmond, and Charleston—searching, as one of them put it, for "likely young men such as I think would suit the New Orleans market." Each year, hundreds of muscular young slaves passed through the auction houses of the port cities bound for the massive trade mart in New Orleans. Because this traffic in laborers was highly visible, it elicited widespread condemnation by northern abolitionists.

Sugar was a "killer" crop, and Louisiana (like the West Indies) soon had a well-deserved reputation among African Americans "as a place of slaughter," where hundreds died each year from disease, overwork, and brutal treatment. A Maryland farmer refused to consent to his daughter's marriage to a Louisiana sugar planter, remarking, "Mit has never been used to seeing negroes flayed alive and it would kill her."

The inland system that sent slaves to the Cotton South was less apparent than the coastal trade but much more extensive. It also relied on professional slave traders, who went from one rural village to another buying "young and likely Negroes." The traders then marched their purchases in coffles—columns of slaves bound to one another—to Alabama, Mississippi, and Missouri in the 1830s and to Arkansas and Texas in the 1850s. One slave described the arduous journey: "Dem Speculators would put the chilluns in a wagon usually pulled by oxens and de older folks was chained or tied together sos dey could not run off." Once a coffle reached its destination, the trader would sell slaves "at every village in the county."

Chesapeake and Carolina planters provided the trade with its human cargo. Some planters sold slaves when poor management or their own extravagances threw them into debt. "Trouble gathers thicker and thicker around me," Thomas B. Chaplin of South Carolina lamented in his diary, "I will be compelled to send about ten prime Negroes to Town on next Monday, to be sold." Many more planters doubled as slave traders, earning substantial profits by traveling south to sell some of their slaves and those of their neighbors. Prices marched in step with those for cotton; during the boom years of the 1850s, said one planter, a slave that "wouldn't bring over $300, seven years ago, will fetch $1000, cash, quick, this year." Exploiting this demand, Thomas Weatherly of South Carolina drove his surplus slaves to Hayneville, Alabama, where he

◀ **MAP 12.1 Distribution of the Slave Population in 1790, 1830, and 1860**

The cotton boom shifted many African Americans to the Old Southwest. In 1790, most slaves lived and worked on the tobacco plantations of the Chesapeake and on the rice and indigo plantations of South Carolina and Georgia. By 1830, hundreds of thousands of enslaved blacks labored on the cotton and sugar lands of the Lower Mississippi Valley. Three decades later, the centers of slavery lay along the Mississippi River and in an arc of fertile cotton land — the "black belt" — sweeping from Mississippi through Georgia.

For more help analyzing this map see the Online Study Guide at **bedfordstmartins.com/henrettaconcise** lived "in his tents" and "sold ten negroes last week." Colonel E. S. Irvine, a member of the South Carolina legislature and "a highly respected gentleman" in white circles, likewise traveled frequently "to the west to sell a drove of Negroes."

The domestic slave trade was crucial to the prosperity of the southern economy. It provided thousands of workers to fell the forests and plant cotton in the Gulf states, and it bolstered the economy of the Upper South. By selling their surplus workers, tobacco, rice, and grain planters in the Chesapeake and Carolinas added about 20 percent to their income. The domestic slave trade, remarked a Maryland newspaper, served as "an almost universal resource to raise money."

For African American families, the domestic slave trade was a personal disaster that accentuated their status—and vulnerability—as property. On this issue, blacks and whites agreed. W. C. Pennington, a former slave, reflected, "The being of slavery, its soul and its body, lives and moves in the chattel principle, the property principle, the bill of sale principle." A South Carolina master put it more crudely: The slave's earnings "belong to *me* because I bought him." There was an "immense amount of capital which is invested in slave property," Henry Clay observed. "It is owned by widows and orphans, by the aged and infirm, as well as the sound and vigorous. It is the subject of mortgages, deeds of trust, and family settlements." The Whig politician concluded, "I know that there is a visionary dogma, which holds that negro slaves cannot be the subject of property. I shall not dwell long on this speculative abstraction. That is property which the law declares to be property."

As a slave owner himself, Clay knew that property rights were a key to slave discipline. As one master put it, "I govern them . . . without the whip by stating . . . that I should sell them if they do not conduct themselves as I wish." The threat was effective. "The Negroes here dread nothing on earth so much as this," an observer in Maryland noted. "They regard the south with perfect horror, and to be sent there is considered as the worst punishment that could be inflicted on them."

But such sales were inflicted on thousands of families and destroyed about one in every four slave marriages. "I am Sold to a man by the name of Peterson a trader," lamented a Georgia slave. "My Dear wife for you and my Children my pen cannot Express the griffe I feel to be parted from you all." The trade encompassed children and young people as well as adults; in northern Maryland, boys and girls were sold away at an average age of seventeen years. "Dey sole my sister Kate," Anna Harris remembered decades later, "and I ain't seed or heard of her since." The trade also separated almost one-third of all slave children under the age of fourteen from one or both of their parents. Sarah Grant remembered, "Mamma used to cry when she had to go back to work because she was always scared some of us kids would be sold while she was away." Well might she worry, for slave traders worked quietly and quickly. "One night I lay down on de straw mattress wid my mammy," Vinny Baker recalled, "an' de nex' mo'nin I woke up an' she wuz gone." When their owner sold seven-year-old Laura Clark and ten other children from their plantation in North Carolina, Clark sensed that she would see her mother "no mo' in dis life."

Despite these sales, 75 percent of slave marriages remained unbroken, and the majority of children lived with one or both parents until puberty. Consequently, the sense of family among African Americans remained strong. Sold from Virginia to

BY HEWLETT & RASPILLER,

On Saturday, 14th April, inst.

At 1-2 12 o'clock, at Hewlett's Exchange,
WILL BE SOLD,

24 HEAD OF SLAVES,

Lately belonging to the Estate of Jno. Erwin, of the parish of Iberville. These Slaves have been for more than 10 years in the country, and are all well acclimated, and accustomed to all kinds of work on a Sugar Plantation. There are among them a first rate cooper, a first rate brick maker, and an excellent hostler and coachman. They will be sold chiefly in families.

TERMS-----One year's credit, payable in notes endorsed to the satisfaction of the vendor, and bearing mortgage until final payment. Sales to be passed before Carlisle Pollock, Esq. at the expense of the purchasers.

Fielding,	aged 27 years,	field hand,	
Sally,	aged 24	do. field hand and cook,	150
Levi, aged 26 years,		cooper and field hand,	
Aggy, do. 24 do.		house servant and field hand.	2100
James, do. 6 do.			
Emeline, 8 do.			
Stephen, 3 do.			
Priscilly, 1 do.			
Bill, aged 24 years,	field hand,		1600
Leah, do. 22 do.	field hand,		
Rosette, do. 3 do.			
Infant child.			
Alfred, aged 22 years,	brick maker, servant and field hand,		1800
Charlotte, do. 20 years,	house servant and field hand,		
Infant.			
Forrester, aged 41 years,	hostler, house servant and field hand,		1300
Mary, aged 22 years,	field hand and cook.		
Infant.			
Harry, aged 24 years,	field hand,		1400
Charity, aged 24 years,	field hand,		
Polly, aged 22 years,	house servant and seamstress,		800
Sam, aged 2 years,			
Bedford, aged 14 years,	field hand,		700
Mahaly, aged 12 years,	field hand,		500
			11200

The Business of Slavery

In the 1850s, Virginia slaves were still being "sold South." The painting, *Slave Auction in Richmond, Virginia* (1852), captures the apprehension of the enslaved women and the discontent of the man, none of whom can control their fate. Whites — plantation overseer, slave trader, top-hatted aristocratic planter — lurk in the background, where they are completing the commercial transaction. The illustration to the left, a public notice for a slave auction to be held in Iberville, Louisiana, advertises "24 Head of Slaves" as if they were cattle — a striking statement on the business of slavery. The Granger Collection, New York / Library of Congress.

For more help analyzing this image, see the Online Study Guide at **bedfordstmartins .com/henrettaconcise**.

Texas in 1843, Hawkins Wilson carried with him a detailed mental picture of his family. Twenty-five years later, a freedman, Wilson set out to find his "dearest relatives" in Virginia. "My sister belonged to Peter Coleman in Caroline County and her name was Jane. . . . She had three children, Robert[,] Charles and Julia, when I left— Sister Martha belonged to Dr. Jefferson. . . . Sister Matilda belonged to Mrs. Botts."

During the quarter century between sale and freedom, Hawkins Wilson and thousands of other African American migrants constructed new lives for themselves in the Mississippi River Valley. Undoubtedly, many of them did so with a sense of foreboding. From personal experience, they knew that their lives could be shaken to the core at any moment. Like Charles Ball, some "longed to die, and escape from the bonds of my tormentors." Even moments of joy were shadowed by the darkness of slavery. Knowing that sales often ended slave marriages, a white minister blessed one couple "for so long as God keeps them together."

Many white planters "saw" only the African American marriages that endured and ignored those they had broken. Consequently, many slave owners considered themselves benevolent masters, committed to the welfare of "my family, black and white." Some masters gave substance to this paternalist ideal by treating with kindness various "loyal and worthy" slaves: the drivers who commanded their workers, the mammy who raised their children, and the house servants who catered to their needs. By safeguarding the families of these slaves from sale, planters convinced themselves that they "sold south" only "coarse" troublemakers and uncivilized slaves who had "little sense of family." Other owners were more honest about the human cost of their pursuit of wealth. "Tomorrow the negroes are to get off" to Kentucky, a slave-owning woman in Virginia wrote to a friend, "and I expect there will be great crying and morning, with children Leaving there mothers, mothers there children, and women there husbands."

Whether or not they acknowledged the slaves' pain, few southern whites questioned the morality of the domestic slave trade. As a committee of the Charleston City Council responded to abolitionist criticism, slavery was completely consistent "with moral principle and with the highest order of civilization," as was "the removal of slaves from place to place, and their transfer from master to master, by gift, purchase, or otherwise."

The Dual Cultures of the Planter Elite

Westward movement profoundly affected the small elite of extraordinarily wealthy planter families who stood at the top of southern society. These families—about 3,000 in number—each owned more than 100 slaves and huge tracts of the most fertile lands. Their ranks included many of the richest families in the United States. On the eve of the Civil War, southern planters accounted for nearly two-thirds of all American men with wealth of $100,000 or more.

The plantation elite consisted of two distinct groups. The first group consisted of the traditional aristocrats of the Old South. As tobacco and rice production soared after 1700, a wealthy elite dominated the social and political life of the Tidewater region of the Chesapeake and the low country of South Carolina and Georgia. During the eighteenth century, these planters built impressive mansions and adopted the manners and values of the English landed gentry (see Chapter 3). Their aristocratic culture survived the revolution of 1776 and soon took on a republican character. Classical republican theorists had long

A Louisiana Plantation, 1861
This view of a Louisiana plantation by Marie Adrien Persac, a French-born artist, presents an exquisitely detailed but romanticized vision of the planter lifestyle. Well-dressed slaves stand amid neatly spaced rows of cotton as the women of the household prance by on well-groomed horses. Off to the right, smoke rises from the chimneys of a small mill, probably used to process the sugarcane grown elsewhere on the plantation. Louisiana State University Museum of Art.

identified political tyranny as a major threat to liberty, and southern aristocrats, who feared government interference with their property in slaves, embraced this ideological outlook. To prevent despotic rule by democratic demagogues or radical legislatures, planters demanded that authority rest in the hands of incorruptible men of "virtue."

Affluent planters cast themselves as the embodiment of this ideal—a republican aristocracy (see Chapter 8). "The planters here are essentially what the nobility are in other countries," declared James Henry Hammond of South Carolina. "They stand at the head of society & politics . . . [and form] an aristocracy of talents, of virtue, of generosity and courage." These wealthy planters criticized the increasingly democratic polity and middle-class society that was developing in the Northeast and Midwest. "Inequality is the fundamental law of the universe," declared one aristocratic-minded planter. Others condemned professional politicians as "a set of demagogues" and questioned the legitimacy of universal suffrage. "Times are sadly different now to what they were when I was a boy," lamented South Carolinian David Gavin. Then, the "Sovereign people, alias mob" had little influence; now they vied for power with the elite. How can "I rejoice for a freedom," Gavin demanded to know, "which allows every bankrupt, swindler, thief, and scoundrel, traitor and seller of his vote to be placed on an equality with myself?"

To maintain their privileged identity, aristocratic planters married their sons and daughters to one another and taught them to follow in the parents' footsteps: the men working as planters, merchants, lawyers, newspaper editors, and ministers and the women hosting plantation balls and church bazaars. To confirm their social preeminence, planters lived extravagantly and entertained graciously. James Henry Hammond built a Greek Revival mansion with a center hall spanning 53 feet by 20 feet, its floor embellished with stylish Belgian tiles and expensive Brussels carpets. "Once a year, like a great feudal landlord," a guest recounted, Hammond "gave a fete or grand dinner to all the country people."

Rice planters remained at the apex of the plantation aristocracy. In 1860, the fifteen proprietors of the vast plantations in All Saints Parish in the Georgetown District of South Carolina owned 4,383 slaves, who annually grew and processed fourteen million pounds of rice. As inexpensive Asian rice entered the world market and cut the profit margins of Carolina planters, they sold some slaves and worked the others harder, two strategies that allowed them to sustain their luxurious lifestyle. The "hospitality and elegance" of Charleston and Savannah impressed savvy English traveler John Silk Buckingham. Buckingham likewise found "polished" families among long-established French Catholic planters in New Orleans and along the Mississippi River. There, "the sugar and cotton planters live in splendid edifices, and enjoy all the luxury that wealth can impart" (see Voices from Abroad, p. 359).

In tobacco-growing regions, the lives of the planter aristocracy followed a different trajectory, in part because slave ownership was widely diffused. In the 1770s, about 60 percent of white families in the Chesapeake region owned at least one African American slave. As many wealthy tobacco planters moved their plantations and slaves to the Cotton South, middling planters (who owned between five and twenty slaves) came to dominate the economy. The descendants of the old planter aristocracy remained influential in the Chesapeake, but increasingly as slave-owning grain farmers, lawyers, merchants, industrialists, and politicians. The slaves they didn't need for their businesses, they hired out, sold, or allowed to purchase their freedom.

Although this genteel planter aristocracy flourished primarily around the periphery of the South — in Virginia, South Carolina, and Louisiana — its members took the lead in defending slavery. Ignoring the old Jeffersonian defense of slavery as a "necessary evil" (see Chapter 8), southern apologists now maintained that slavery was a positive good that allowed a civilized lifestyle for whites and provided tutelage for genetically inferior Africans. "As a race, the African is inferior to the white man," declared Alexander Stephens, the future vice president of the Confederacy. "Subordination to the white man, is his normal condition." Stephens and other apologists depicted planters and their wives as aristocratic models of "disinterested benevolence," who provided food and housing for their workers and cared for them in old age. One wealthy Georgian declared that "Plantation government should be eminently patriarchal"; the planter, as

The Racial Complexities of Southern Society BERNHARD, DUKE OF SAXE-WEIMAR-EISENACH

In 1828, Bernhard, Duke of the German principality of Saxe-Weimar-Eisenach, published an account of his *Travels . . . Through North America*. Subsequently, Bernhard compiled a distinguished military record in the Royal Dutch Army and then ruled his principality from 1853 until his death in 1862. In this selection, Bernhard describes the racial intricacies of New Orleans society.

In New Orleans we were invited to a subscription ball. These affairs are held twice a week, on Tuesdays and Fridays, in the same hall, the French theater. Only good society is invited to these balls. The first to which we came was not very well attended; but most of the ladies were very nice looking and well turned out in the French manner. Their clothing was elegant after the latest Paris fashions. They danced very well and did credit to their French dancing masters. . . .

The native men are far from matching the women in elegance. And they stayed only a short time, preferring to escape to a so-called "Quarterons Ball" which they find more amusing and where they do not have to stand on ceremony.

A "quarteron" (octoroon) is the offspring of a mestizo mother and a white father, just as the mestizo is the child of a mulatto and a white man. The "quarterons" are almost completely white. There would be no way of recognizing them by their complexion, for they are often fairer than the Creoles. Black hair and eyes are generally the signs of their status, although some are quite blond. The ball is attended by the free "quarterons." Yet the deepest prejudice reigns against them on account of their colored origin; the white women particularly feel or affect to feel a strong repugnance to them.

Marriage between colored and white people is forbidden by the laws of the state.

Yet the "quarterons," for their part, look upon the Negroes and mulattoes as inferiors and are unwilling to mix with them. The girls therefore have no other recourse than to become the mistresses of white men. The "quarterons" regard such attachment as the equivalent of marriage. They would not think of entering upon it other than with a formal contract in which the man engages to pay a stipulated sum to the mother or father of the girl. The latter even assumes the name of her lover and regards the affair with more faithfulness than many a woman whose marriage was sealed in a church.

Some of these women have inherited from their fathers and lovers, and possess considerable fortunes. Their status is nevertheless always very depressed. They must not ride in the street in coaches, and their lovers can bring them to the balls in their own conveyances only after nightfall. They must never sit opposite a white lady, nor may they enter a room without express permission. . . . But many of these girls are much more carefully educated than the whites, behave with more polish and more politeness, and make their lovers happier than white wives their husbands.

SOURCE: C. J. Jeronimus, ed., *Travels by His Highness Duke Bernhard of Saxe-Weimar-Eisenach Through North America in the Years 1825 and 1826*, trans. William Jeronimus (Lanham, MD: University Press of America, 2001), 343, 346–347.

"the *pater-familias*, or head of the family, should, in one sense, be the father of the whole concern, negroes and all."

Taking this ideology to heart, many planters tried to influence their slaves' behavior. Some built cabins for their workers and insisted that the buildings be whitewashed regularly. Many others supervised their slaves' religious lives. They built churches on their plantations, welcomed evangelical preachers, and often required their slaves to attend services. A few planters encouraged African Americans who had spiritual "gifts" to serve as exhorters and deacons. The motives of the slaveowners were mixed. Some acted from sincere Christian belief; others wanted to counter abolitionist criticism or to use religious teachings to control their workers.

Indeed, religion served increasingly as a justification for human bondage. Protestant ministers in the South pointed out that the Hebrews, God's chosen people, had owned slaves and that Jesus Christ had never condemned slavery. As Hammond told a British abolitionist in 1845, "What God ordains and Christ sanctifies should surely command the respect and toleration of man." But many aristocratic apologists were absentee owners or delegated authority to overseers and rarely glimpsed the day-to-day brutality of the slave regime. "I was at the plantation last Saturday and the crop was in fine order," an absentee's son wrote to his father, "but the negroes are most brutally scarred & several have run off."

The Inherent Brutality of Slavery
Like all systems of forced labor, American racial slavery relied on physical coercion. Slave owners and overseers routinely whipped slaves who worked slowly or defied the orders of whites. On occasion, the whip was applied with such ferocity that the slave died or was permanently injured. This photograph of a slave named Gordon stands as graphic testimony to the inherent brutality of the system. National Archives.

There was much less hypocrisy and far less elegance among the second group of elite planters: the market-driven entrepreneurs of the Cotton South. "The glare of expensive luxury vanishes" in the black soil regions of Alabama and Mississippi, John Silk Buckingham noted as he traveled through the Cotton South, and aristocratic paternalism vanished as well. A Mississippi planter put it plainly: "Everything has to give way to large crops of cotton, land has to be cultivated wet or dry, negroes [must] work, hot or cold." Angry at being sold south and pressed to hard labor, many slaves grew "mean" and stubborn. Those who would not labor were subject to the lash. "Whiped all the hoe hands," Alabama planter James Torbert wrote matter-of-factly in his journal. Overseers pushed their workers hard because their salaries often depended on the quantity of cotton they were able "to make for the market." "When I wuz so tired I cu'dnt hardly stan'," a Mississippi slave recalled, "I had to spin my cut of cotton befor' I cu'd go to sleep. We had to card, spin, an' reel at nite."

Cotton was a demanding crop because of its long growing season. Slaves plowed the land in March, dropped seeds into the ground in early April, and, once the plants began to grow, continually chopped away the surrounding grasses. In between these tasks, they planted the corn and peas that would provide food for them and the plantation's hogs and chickens. When the cotton bolls ripened in late August, the long four-month picking season began. Slaves in the Cotton South, concluded traveler Frederick Law Olmsted, worked "much harder and more unremittingly" than those in the tobacco regions. Moreover, fewer slaves acquired craft skills. No coopers were needed to make casks for tobacco or sugar; no engineers were required to build the irrigation systems for the rice fields.

To increase output, profit-conscious cotton planters began during the 1820s to use a rigorous **gang-labor system**. Previously, many planters had either supervised their workers sporadically or assigned them jobs and let them work at their own pace. Now masters with twenty or more slaves organized disciplined teams, or "gangs," supervised by black drivers and white overseers. They instructed the supervisors to work the gangs at a steady pace, clearing and plowing land or hoeing and picking cotton. A traveler in Mississippi described two gangs returning from work:

> First came, led by an old driver carrying a whip, forty of the largest and strongest women I ever saw together; they were all in a simple uniform dress of a bluish check stuff, the skirts reaching little below the knee; . . . they carried themselves loftily, each having a hoe over the shoulder, and walking with a free, powerful swing.

Next marched the plow hands with their mules, "the cavalry, thirty strong, mostly men, but a few of them women." Finally, "a lean and vigilant white overseer, on a brisk pony, brought up the rear."

The cotton planters' quest for profits was enormously successful. Cotton monoculture and the failure to rotate crops on a regular basis depleted the nutrients in the soil and gradually reduced the output per acre. Still, because slaves working in gangs finished as much work in thirty-five minutes as white yeomen planters did in an hour, the gang-labor system produced impressive profits and became ever more prevalent. In one Georgia county, the percentage of slaves working in gangs doubled between 1830 and 1850 and increased further during the 1850s. As the price of raw cotton surged after 1846, the wealth of the planter class exploded in size. It was no wonder: Nearly two million enslaved African Americans now labored on the plantations of the Cotton South and annually produced four million bales of the valuable fiber.

Planters, Smallholding Yeomen, and Tenants

Although the South was a "slave society"—that is, the institution of slavery affected all aspects of life there—most white southerners did not own slaves. The absolute number of slave owners increased constantly between 1800 and 1860, but the white population of the South rose even faster. Consequently, the percentage of white families who held blacks in bondage continually decreased: from 36 percent in 1830, to 31 percent in 1850, to about 25 percent a decade later. However, slave ownership varied by region. In some cotton-rich counties, 40 percent or more of the white families owned slaves; in the hill country near the Appalachian Mountains, the proportion dropped to 10 percent.

Among the privileged minority of 395,000 families who owned slaves in 1860, there was a strict hierarchy. The top one-fifth of these families—a planter elite numbering just 5 percent of the South's white population—owned twenty or more slaves. This elite dominated the economy, owning over 50 percent of the entire slave population of four million and growing 50 percent of the South's cotton crop. The average wealth of these planters was $56,000; by contrast, the average southern yeoman or northern farmer owned property worth a mere $3,200.

Substantial proprietors, another fifth of the slave-owning population, held title to six to twenty slaves. These "middle-class" planters played a significant role in the slave society: They owned almost 40 percent of the African American population and produced more than 30 percent of the cotton. Many owners pursued dual careers as skilled artisans or professional men. For example, many of the fifteen slaves owned by Samuel L. Moore worked in his brick factory; the others labored on his Georgia farm. In Macon County, Alabama, James Tolbert owned a plantation that yielded 50 bales of cotton a year, but Tolbert also ran a sawmill, "which pays as well as making Cotton." Dr. Thomas Gale used the income from his medical practice to buy a Mississippi plantation that annually produced 150 bales of cotton. In Alabama, lawyer Benjamin Fitzpatrick used the profits from his legal practice to buy ten slaves.

Many other lawyers joined Fitzpatrick as slave-owning planters, and some became influential politicians. Throughout the Cotton South, lawyers became wealthy by handling the affairs of elite planters, representing merchants and storekeepers in suits for debt, and settling disputes over property. They became well known by helping smallholders and tenants register their deeds and contracts. Standing at the legal crossroads of their small towns and personally known by many residents, lawyers regularly won election to public office. Fewer than 1 percent of the male population, lawyers made up 16 percent of the Alabama legislature in 1828 and an astounding 26 percent in 1849.

The smallholders who made up the majority of slave owners were much less visible than the wealthy grandees and the lawyer-planters. Because they worked the land themselves, they were similar in some respects to yeomen farmers in the North. These slave owners held from one to five black laborers in bondage and claimed title to a few hundred acres of land. Some smallholders were well-connected young men, who would rise to wealth when their father's death blessed them with more land and slaves. Others were poor but ambitious men trying to pull themselves up by their bootstraps, encouraged to do so by elite planters and proslavery advocates. "Ours is a pro-slavery form of Government, and the pro-slavery element should be increased," declared a Georgia newspaper. "We would like to see every white man at the South the owner of a family of negroes."

Taking this advice to heart, aspiring planters saved or borrowed enough to acquire more land and more laborers. Many achieved modest prosperity. One German settler in Alabama reported in 1855 that "nearly all his countrymen" who emigrated with him were now slaveholders. "They were poor on their arrival in the country; but no sooner did they realize a little money than they invested it in slaves," whose labor made them well-to-do.

Influenced by the patriarchal ideology of the planter class, yeomen farmers ruled their smallholdings with a firm hand. According to a South Carolina judge, the male head of the household had authority over all the dependents—wives, children, and slaves—and the legal right on his property "to be as churlish as he pleases." The wives of southern yeomen had very little power; like women in the North, they lost their legal identity when they married. Looking for ways to express their concerns and interests, southern women turned to religion and usually outnumbered male church members by a ratio of two to one. Women welcomed the message of spiritual equality preached in Evangelical Baptist and Methodist churches, and they hoped that the church community would hold their husbands to the same standards of Christian behavior to which they were held. But most churches supported patriarchal rule and told female members to remain in "wifely obedience," whatever the actions of their husbands.

Lords of their own households, most southern yeomen nevertheless lived and died hardscrabble farmers. They worked alongside their slaves in the fields, struggled to make ends meet as their families grew, and moved regularly in search of opportunity. In 1847, James Buckner Barry left North Carolina with his new wife and two slaves to settle in Bosque County, Texas. There, he worked part-time as an Indian fighter while his slaves toiled on a drought-ridden farm that barely kept the family in food. In South Carolina, W. J. Simpson struggled for years as a smallholding cotton planter and then gave up. He hired out one of his two slaves and went to work as an overseer on his father's farm.

Other smallholders fell from the privileged ranks of the slave-owning classes. Having sold their land and slaves to pay off debts, they joined the large group of propertyless tenants who farmed the estates of wealthy landlords. In 1860, in Hancock County, Georgia, there were 56 slave-owning planters and 300 propertyless white farm laborers and factory workers; in nearby Hart County, 25 percent of the white farmers were tenants. Across the South, about 40 percent of the white population worked as tenants or farm laborers; as the *Southern Cultivator* observed, they had "no legal right nor interest in the soil [and] no homes of their own."

Propertyless whites enjoyed few of the benefits of slavery and suffered many of the same ill consequences. Because hard labor was deemed fit only for enslaved blacks, white workers received little respect. Nor could they hope for a better life for their children, because planters refused to pay taxes to fund public schools. Moreover, wealthy planters bid up the price of slaves, depriving white laborers and tenants of easy access to the slave labor required to accumulate wealth. Finally, planter-dominated legislatures forced all white men—whether they owned slaves or not—to serve in the patrols and militias that deterred black uprisings. For their sacrifices, poor whites gained only the psychological satisfaction that they ranked above blacks. As Alfred Iverson, a U.S. senator from Georgia, explained: A white man "walks erect in the dignity of his color and race, and feels that he is a superior being, with the more exalted powers and privileges than others." To reinforce this sense of racial and social superiority, planter James Henry Hammond told his poor white neighbors, "In a slave country every freeman is an aristocrat."

Rejecting that half-truth, many southern whites fled planter-dominated counties and sought farms in the Appalachian hill country and beyond—in western Virginia, Kentucky, Tennessee, Missouri, and the southern regions of Illinois and Indiana. Living as yeomen farmers, they used family labor to grow foodstuffs for sustenance. To obtain cash or store credit to buy agricultural implements, cloth, shoes, salt, and other necessities, yeomen families sold their surplus crops, raised hogs for market sale, and—when the price of cotton rose sharply in the 1850s—grew a few bales. Their goals were modest: On the family level, they wanted to preserve their holdings and buy enough land to set up their children as small-scale farmers. As citizens, smallholders wanted to control their local government and elect men of their own kind to public office. But thoughtful yeomen realized that the cotton revolution had undercut the democratic potential of the Revolutionary era and sentenced family farmers to a subordinate place in the southern social order. They could hope for a life of independence and dignity only by moving north or farther west, where labor was "free" and hard work was respectable.

The Politics of Democracy

Despite their economic and social prominence, the slave-owning elite could not easily control the political life of the Cotton South. Unlike the planter-aristocrats of the eighteenth century, they lived in a republican society with representative institutions. The Alabama Constitution of 1819 granted suffrage to all white men. It also provided for a **secret ballot**; apportionment based on population; and the election of county supervisors, sheriffs, and clerks of court. Given these democratic provisions, political factions in Alabama had to compete with one another for popular favor. When a Whig newspaper sarcastically asked whether the state's policies should "be governed and controlled by the whim and caprice of the majority of the people," Democrats stood forth as champions of the common folk whose hands were callused from hard work. They called on "Farmers, Mechanics, laboring men" to repudiate Whig "aristocrats . . . the soft handed and soft headed gentry."

To curry favor among voters, Alabama Democrats chose candidates and policies that would command popular support, such as low taxes. Their Whig opponents favored higher taxes in order to provide government subsidies for banks, canals, roads, and other internal improvements; but they also turned to candidates who appealed to the common people. Most candidates from both parties were men of substance. In the early 1840s, nearly 90 percent of Alabama's legislators owned slaves, testimony to the power of the slave-owning minority. But relatively few lawmakers—only about 10 percent—were rich planters, a group voters by and large distrusted. "A rich man cannot sympathize with the poor," declared one candidate. Consequently, the majority of elected state officials and most county officials in the Cotton South came from the ranks of middle-class planters and planter-lawyers.

Whatever their social rank, Alabama's legislators usually enacted policies that reflected the interests of the slave-owning population. However, they took care not to anger the mass of yeomen farmers and propertyless whites by favoring too many expensive measures, such as the public works projects that the Whigs favored. "Voting against appropriations is the safe and popular side," one senator declared, and his colleagues agreed; until the 1850s, they rejected most of the bills that would have granted subsidies to railroads, canals, and banks. They also refrained from laying "oppressive" taxes on the people, particularly the poor white majority who owned no slaves. Between 1830 and 1860, the Alabama legislature obtained about 70 percent of the state's revenue from taxes on slaves and land. Another 10 to 15 percent came from levies on carriages, gold watches, and other luxury goods and on the capital invested in banks, transportation companies, and manufacturing enterprises.

If taxes in Alabama had a democratic thrust, those elsewhere in the South did not. In some states, wealthy planters used their political influence to exempt slave property from taxation. And they shifted the burden of land taxes to backcountry yeomen by taxing farms on the basis of acreage rather than value. Planter-legislators also spared themselves the cost of building fences around their crops by enacting laws that required yeomen to fence in their livestock. Moreover, during the 1850s, wealthy legislators throughout the South used public funds to subsidize the canals and railroads in which they had invested.

Seen from one perspective, these government subsidies were desperately needed. Even as the top 10 percent of the white population grew rich from the cotton, rice, tobacco, and sugar produced by their slaves, the economic well-being of ordinary southerners—white and black—did not improve significantly. In fact, the South's standard of living fell behind that of the North. Both in 1840 and in 1860, the per capita wealth of the South was only 80 percent of the national average, while that in the industrializing Northeast was 139 percent of the average.

This comparison between the South and the Northeast tells only part of the story. If the South had been a separate nation in 1860, its economy would have been the fourth most prosperous in the world, with a per capita income higher than that of France and Germany. As a contributor to a Georgia newspaper argued in the 1850s, it was beside the point to complain about "tariffs, and merchants, and manufacturers" because "the most highly prosperous people now on earth, are to be found in these very [slave] States."

The paradox is that this judgment was both right and wrong. Many white southerners did enjoy higher living standards than other peoples of the world, but most African Americans—30 percent of the population—lived in dire and permanent poverty. Perceptive southerners recognized that their plantation-based economy and slave system failed to provide rising incomes for the majority of the population. Pointing to South Carolina's fixation on an "exclusive and exhausting" system of agriculture, textile entrepreneur William Gregg asked, "Who can look forward to the future destiny of our State . . . without dark forebodings?" Other leaders acknowledged the South's predicament but blamed it on outsiders: "Purely agricultural people," intoned planter-politician James Henry Hammond, "have been in all ages the victims of rapacious tyrants grinding them down."

Such thinking discouraged purposeful private or government action that might have created a more diversified economy. Wealthy southerners continued to invest in land and slaves, a strategy that brought substantial short-run profits from the booming cotton market but diverted capital resources and entrepreneurial energies from more productive forms of economic activity. In particular, southerners failed to take advantage of the technological innovations of the nineteenth century—water- and steam-powered factories, machine tools, steel plows, and crushed-gravel roads, for example—that would have raised the region's productivity. Urban growth, the key to prosperity in Europe and the North, occurred mostly in the commercial cities around the periphery of the South: New Orleans, St. Louis, and Baltimore. Factories, often staffed by slave labor, likewise appeared primarily in the Chesapeake region, which had already diversified its economy and had a surplus of bound workers. Within the Cotton South, a few wealthy planters invested in railroads but only to open up new lands for commercial farming; when the Western & Atlantic Railroad reached the Georgia upcountry, the cotton crop quickly doubled. Cotton—and agriculture—remained "King."

Slavery worked in yet another way to deter industrialization. Fearing competition from slave labor, European immigrants refused to settle in the South. Their absence deprived the region of hardworking families and of laborers who could have drained swamps, dug canals, smelted iron, and worked on railroads. When entrepreneurs tried to hire slaves for such tasks, planters said that "a negro's life is too valuable to be risked" at the dangerous work. Other slave owners feared that being hired out would make their slaves too independent. As a planter explained to Frederick Law Olmsted, such workers "had too much liberty . . . and got a habit of roaming about and taking care of themselves."

Despite the enormous expansion in the territory and exports of the South between 1800 and 1860, it remained an economic colony: Great Britain and the North bought its staple crops and provided its manufactures, financial services, and shipping facilities. In 1860, most southerners—some 84 percent—still worked in agriculture, more than double the percentage in the northern states; and southern factories turned out only 10 percent of the nation's manufactured goods. Textile entrepreneur William Gregg lamented that the combination of cotton and slavery had been to the South

► How would you explain the large and expanding domestic trade in slaves between 1800 and 1860? What combination of factors produced this result?

► By 1860, what different groups made up the South's increasingly complex society? How did these groups interact in the political arena?

> what the [gold and silver] mines of Mexico were to Spain. It has produced us such an abundant supply of all the luxuries and elegances of life, with so little exertion on our part, that we have become enervated, unfitted for other and more laborious pursuits.

The African American World

By the 1820s, the cultural life of most slaves consisted of a complex blend of African and American influences. It reflected both the values and customs of their West African ancestors and the language, laws, and religious beliefs of the dominant white society. This mix of cultural values persisted for decades, both because whites discouraged blacks from assimilating into their society and because slaves prized many aspects of their African heritage.

Evangelical Black Protestantism

The appearance of Black Christianity exemplified the synthesis in the United States of African and European cultures. Evangelical Protestantism came to the white South with the Second Great Awakening between 1790 and 1840. Baptist and Methodist preachers converted thousands of white families and hundreds of enslaved blacks (see Chapter 8). Until that time, African-born blacks, often identifiable by their ritual scars, had maintained the religious practices of their homelands: Some practiced Islam, but the majority called on African gods and spirits. As late as 1842, Charles C. Jones, a Presbyterian minister, noted that the blacks on his family's plantation in Georgia believed "in second-sight, in apparitions, charms, witchcraft . . . [and other] superstitions brought from Africa." Fearing "the consequences" for their own souls if they withheld "the means of salvation from them," Jones and other zealous white Protestant preachers and planters set out to save African American souls for Christ.

Other Protestant crusaders came from the ranks of pious black men and women. Converted to Christianity in the Chesapeake and then swept off to the Cotton South by the domestic slave trade, they carried the evangelical message of emotional conversion, ritual baptism, and communal spirituality with them. Equally important, they adapted Protestant doctrines to black needs. Enslaved Christians pointed out that masters and slaves were all "children of God" and should be dealt with according to the Golden Rule: Treat others as you would be treated by them. Moreover, black preachers generally ignored the doctrines of original sin and predestination as well as biblical passages that encouraged unthinking obedience to authority. A white minister in Liberty County, Georgia, reported that when he urged slaves to obey their masters, "one half of my audience deliberately rose up and walked off."

Indeed, many African American converts envisioned the deity as the Old Testament warrior who had liberated the Jews and saw themselves as Chosen People: "de people dat is born of God." Charles Davenport, a Mississippi slave, recalled black preachers' "exhort[ing] us dat us was the chillum o' Israel in de wilderness an' de Lawd done sont us to take dis lan' o' milk an' honey." It was a vision of Christ that impelled Nat Turner to lead a bloody rebellion against slavery in Virginia (see Chapter 11).

As successive generations of slaves worshiped a European Christian god, they continued to express their religiosity in distinctively African ways. The thousands of African Americans who joined the Methodist Church respected its ban on profane dancing but praised the Lord in the African-derived "ring shout." Minister Henry George Spaulding explained the "religious dance of the Negroes" this way:

> Three or four, standing still, clapping their hands and beating time with their feet, commence singing in unison one of the peculiar shout melodies, while the others walk around in a ring, in single file, joining also in the song.

The songs themselves were usually collective creations, devised spontaneously from bits of old hymns and tunes. Recalled an ex-slave:

> We'd all be at the "prayer house" de Lord's day, and de white preacher he'd splain de word and read whar Esekial done say — *Dry bones gwine ter lib ergin.* And, honey, de Lord would come a-shinin' thoo dem pages and revive dis ole nigger's heart, and I'd jump up dar and den and holler and shout and sing and pat, and dey would all cotch de words and I'd sing it to some ole shout song I'd heard 'em sing from Africa, and dey'd all take it up and keep at it, and keep a-addin' to it, and den it would be a spiritual.

By such African-influenced means, black congregations devised a distinctive and joyous brand of Protestant worship to sustain them on the long journey to emancipation and the Promised Land. "O my Lord delivered Daniel," the slaves sang, "O why not deliver me too?"

Forging Families and Creating Culture

Black Protestantism was one facet of an increasingly homogeneous African American culture in the rural South. Even in South Carolina, a major point of entry for imported slaves, only 20 percent of the black residents in 1820 had been born in Africa. The transfer of slaves into the Lower Mississippi Valley encouraged the decline of regional practices and the emergence of a core black culture. A prime example was the fate of the Gullah dialect (see Chapter 3). Long spoken by residents of the Carolina low country, Gullah did not take root on the cotton plantations of Alabama and Mississippi, because there were many more speakers of the black English spoken in the Chesapeake. Black English, like Gullah, used double-negatives and other African grammatical forms but consisted primarily of English words rendered with a West African pronunciation (for example, with "th" spoken as "d," as in "de preacher").

As the black population was becoming more culturally homogeneous, African influences remained important. At least one-third of the slaves who entered the United States between 1776 and 1809 came from the Congo region of West-Central Africa, and they brought their culture with them. As traveler Isaac Holmes reported in 1821, "In Louisiana, and the state of Mississippi, the slaves . . . dance for several hours during Sunday afternoon. The general movement is in what they call the Congo dance." Similar descriptions of blacks who "danced the Congo and sang a purely African song to the accompaniment of . . . . a drum" appeared as late as 1890.

African Americans also continued to respect African incest taboos by shunning marriages between cousins. On the Good Hope Plantation on the Santee River in South Carolina, nearly half of the slave children born between 1800 and 1857 were related by blood to one another; yet when they married, only one union (out of forty-one) took place between cousins. This taboo was not learned from their white owners: Among the 440 South Carolina men and women who owned at least one hundred slaves in 1860, cousin marriages were frequent, in part because they kept wealth and political power within an extended family.

Unlike white marriages, slave unions were not recognized by law. Southern legislatures and courts prohibited legal marriages among slaves so that their sale would not break a legal bond. Still, many African Americans had their marriages performed by Christian ministers. Others publicly marked their married state by following the African custom of jumping over a broomstick together. Once married, young couples in the Cotton South who had been seized from their parents in the Chesapeake region often adopted older slaves in their new communities as their "aunts" and "uncles." The slave trade had destroyed their family but not their family values.

The creation of such fictive kinship ties was part of a complex community-building process. Naming children was another. Recently imported slaves frequently

Antebellum Slave Quarters
During the colonial period, owners often housed their slaves in communal barracks by gender. In the nineteenth century, slaves usually lived in family units in separate cabins. The slave huts on this South Carolina plantation were sturdily built but had few windows. Inside, they were sparsely furnished. William Gladstone.

gave their children African names. Males who were born on Friday, for example, were often called Cuffee—the name of that day in several West African languages. Many American-born parents chose names of British origin, but they usually named sons after fathers, uncles, or grandfathers and daughters after grandmothers. Those who were transported to the Cotton South often named their children for relatives they had left behind. Like incest rules and marriage rituals, this intergenerational sharing of names evoked memories of a lost world and solidified kin ties in the present one.

Negotiating Rights

By forming stable families and strong communities, African Americans gradually created a sense of order in the harsh and arbitrary world of slavery. In a few regions, slaves won substantial control over their lives. Blacks in the rice-growing lowlands of South Carolina successfully asserted the right to labor by the "task" rather than to work under constant supervision. Each day, task workers had to complete a precisely defined job—for example, turn over a quarter-acre of land, hoe half an acre, or pound seven mortars of rice. By working hard, many finished their tasks "by one or two o'clock in the afternoon," a Methodist preacher reported, and had "the rest of the day for themselves, which they spend in working their own private fields . . . planting rice, corn, potatoes, tobacco &c. for their own use and profit." Slaves on sugar and cotton plantations were less fortunate. The gang-labor system imposed a regimented work schedule, and many owners prohibited slaves from growing crops on their own. "It gives an excuse for trading," explained one slave owner, and that encouraged roaming and independence.

Planters worried constantly that enslaved African Americans—a majority of the population in most counties of the Cotton South—would rise in rebellion. They knew that, legally speaking, masters had virtually unlimited power over their slaves. Justice Thomas Ruffin of the North Carolina Supreme Court wrote in a decision in 1829: "The power of the master must be absolute to render the submission of the slave perfect." But absolute power required unremitting and brutal coercion, and only the most hardened or most sadistic masters had the stomach for that. Some southern whites wanted no part of such violence. "These poor negroes, receiving none of the fruits of their labor, do not love work," explained one farm woman, "if we had slaves, we should have to . . . beat them to make use of them."

Moreover, passive resistance by African Americans seriously limited the power of their owners. Slaves slowed the pace of work by feigning illness and "losing" or breaking tools. Some blacks insisted that people be sold "in families." One Maryland slave, faced with transport to Mississippi and separation from his wife, "neither yields consent to accompany my people, or to be exchanged or sold," his owner reported. Because of the bonds of community among African Americans in the Chesapeake and Carolinas and the increasing black majorities in the Gulf states, masters ignored slaves' feelings at their peril. A slave (or his relatives) might retaliate by setting fire to the master's house and barns, poisoning the white family's food, or destroying crops or equipment. Fear of resistance, as well as the increasingly critical scrutiny of abolitionists, prompted many masters to reduce their reliance on the lash. Instead, they tried to devise "a wholesome and well regulated system" of work discipline by using positive incentives such as food and special privileges to manage their laborers. As Frederick Law Olmsted noted, "Men of sense have discovered that it was better to offer them rewards than to whip them." Nonetheless, owners always had the option of resorting to violence, and many masters continued to satisfy themselves sexually by raping their female slaves.

Slavery remained an exploitative system grounded in fear and coercion. Over the decades, hundreds of individual slaves responded to this violence by attacking their masters and overseers. Blacks such as Gabriel and Martin Prosser in Virginia (1800) plotted mass uprisings, but only a few—among them, Nat Turner (1831)—mounted revolts that took revenge on their white captors. Most slaves recognized that uprisings would be futile; they lacked the strong institutions—such as the communes of free peasants or serfs in Europe, for example—needed to organize a successful rebellion. Moreover, whites were numerous, well armed, and determined to maintain their position of racial superiority (see American Voices, p. 372).

Escape was equally problematic. Blacks in the Upper South could flee to the North, but that meant leaving their family and kin. Slaves in the Lower South could seek freedom in Spanish Florida until 1819, when the United States annexed that territory. Even then, hundreds of blacks continued to flee to Florida, where they intermarried with the Seminole Indians. Elsewhere in the South, small groups of escaped slaves eked out a meager existence in deserted marshy areas or mountain valleys.

Given these limited options, most slaves chose to build the best possible lives for themselves on the plantations where they lived. To do so, they gradually evolved a positive mode of resistance by demanding—and, in many cases, winning—a greater share of the product of their labor, much as unionized workers in the North were trying to do. Thus, slaves insisted on getting paid for "overwork" and on their right to cultivate a garden and sell its produce. "De menfolks tend to de gardens round dey own house," recalled a Louisiana slave. "Dey raise some cotton and sell it to massa and git li'l money dat way." That money was theirs to do with as they wished. An Alabama slave remembered buying "Sunday clothes with dat money, sech as hats and pants and shoes and dresses." By the 1850s, thousands of African Americans were reaping the rewards of this underground economy. But even as their material circumstances improved, few slaves accepted the legitimacy of their fate. Although he was well fed and never whipped, a former slave explained to an English traveler, he knew he had been oppressed: "I was cruelly treated because I was kept in slavery."

The Free Black Population

Some African Americans managed to escape slavery through flight or manumission. The proportion of free blacks rose from 8 percent of the African American population in 1790 to about 13 percent between 1820 and 1840 and then fell to 11 percent by 1860. Of all free blacks in 1840 (some 386,000) and again in 1860 (488,000), nearly half lived in the North. Many of these African Americans were refugees from the South—either runaway slaves or, more often, free blacks who feared reenslavement.

Few free blacks in the North enjoyed unfettered freedom. Most whites regarded African Americans as their social inferiors and did all they could to confine blacks to low-paying jobs. In rural areas, free blacks worked as farm laborers or tenant farmers; in towns and cities, they toiled as domestic servants, laundresses, or day laborers. Only a small number of free African Americans owned land. "You do not see one out of a

Memories of Slavery   MOLLIE DAWSON

Mollie Dawson was born into slavery in 1852 in Texas, to which her owner had migrated from Tennessee. When Dawson told her story to the Writers' Project of the Work Projects Administration in the 1930s, she was eighty-five years old.

Mah maw was de slave of Nath Newman and dat made me his slave. Mah maw's name was Sarah Benjamin. Mah father's name was Carrol Benjamin, and he belonged ter different white folks. . . .

Mah mother and father was slavery time married darkies. Dat didn't mean nuthin' dem days, but jest raisin' mo' darkies, and every slave darkie woman had ter do dat whether she wanted to or not. Dey would let her pick out a man, or a man pick him out a woman, and dey was married, and if de woman wouldn't have de man dat picks her, dey would take her ter a big stout high husky nigger somewhere and leave her a few days, jest lak dey do stock now'days, and she bettah begin raisin' chilluns, too. . . .

Mah mother and father never did love each other lak dey ought to, so dey separated as soon as dey was free. Mah father married another woman by law. Mah mother married George Baldwin, and dey lives together fer about twelve years. Dey separated den, and she married Alfred Alliridge and dey lives together till she dies. . . .

I was too young ter do much work durin' slavery time, but I picks lots of cotton, and all de pay we got fer it was a place ter stay, water ter drink, wood ter burn, food ter eat, and clothes ter wear, and we made de food and clothes ourselves. We eats corn pones three times a day, 'ceptin' Sunday and Christmas mornings; Maser Newman lets us have flour fer biscuits, den.

In de summah we wore cotton clothes. All of dem was made on de plantation. Some of de women would spin and some would weave and some would make clothes. . . .

Maser Newman was a tall, slender man nearly six foot tall and was blue-eyed. He sho' was good ter all us slaves, but we all knew he means fer us ter work. He never whipped any of us slaves, but he hit one of de men wid a leather line 'bout two times once, 'cause dis slave kinda talked back ter him. . . .

Maser Newman was a slow easy-goin' sort of a man who took everything as it comes, takin' bad and good luck jest alak. . . . Maser Newman was lots older dan his wife. She was a real young woman, and they 'peared ter think quite a bit of each other. . . . Maser and Missus Newman jest had two chilluns and both of dem was little girls. . . . Dey sho' was pretty little gals and dey was smart, too. Dey played wid de little slave chilluns all de time, and course dey was de boss, same as deir mother and father.

Maser Newman was a poor man, compared wid some of de other slave owners. He only had about seven slaves big enough ter work all de year round in de fields. . . . He didn't have no drivah; he would jest start dem all out ter work, and dey kept at it all day. But he generally worked around pretty close ter dem.

SOURCE: James Mellon, ed., *Bullwhip Days* (New York: Weidenfeld & Nicolson, 1988), 421–428.

A Master Bridge Builder
Horace King (1807–1885) was
a self-made man of color, a rare
achievement in the nineteenth-
century South. Born a slave of
mixed European, African, and Native
American (Catawba) ancestry, King
built major bridges in Georgia,
Alabama, and Mississippi during
the early 1840s. After winning his
freedom in 1846, he built and ran a
toll bridge across the Chattahoochee
River in Alabama. During the Civil
War, King worked as a contractor
for the Confederacy; during
Reconstruction, he served two terms
as a Republican in the Alabama
House of Representatives. Collection of
the Columbus Museum, Columbus, Georgia;
Museum Purchase.

hundred . . . that can make a comfortable living, own a cow, or a horse," a traveler in New Jersey noted. In addition, northern blacks were usually forbidden to vote, attend public schools, or sit next to whites in churches. Only a few states extended the vote to free blacks, and blacks could testify against whites in court only in Massachusetts. The federal government did not allow free African Americans to work for the postal service, claim public lands, or hold a U.S. passport. As black activist Martin Delaney remarked in 1852, "We are slaves in the midst of freedom."

Of the few African Americans who were able to make full use of their talents, several achieved great distinction. Mathematician and surveyor Benjamin Banneker (1731–1806) published an almanac and helped to lay out the new capital in the District of Columbia; Joshua Johnston (1765–1832) won praise for his portraiture; and merchant Paul Cuffee (1759–1817) acquired a small fortune from his business enterprises. More impressive and enduring were the community institutions that the early generations of free African Americans created. Throughout the North, these largely unknown men and women founded schools, mutual-benefit organizations, and fellowship groups, often called Free African Societies. Discriminated against by white Protestants, they formed their own congregations and a new religious denomination: the African Methodist Episcopal Church, headed by Bishop Richard Allen (see Chapter 8).

These institutions gave free African Americans a sense of cultural autonomy. They also institutionalized sharp social divisions within the black community. "Respectable" blacks tried, through their dress, conduct, and attitude, to win the "esteem and patronage" of prominent whites—first Federalists and then Whigs and abolitionists—who were sympathetic to their cause. Such efforts separated these blacks from their impoverished fellows, who distrusted both whites and blacks who "acted white."

In the slave states the free black population numbered approximately 94,000 in 1810 and 245,000 in 1860. Most of these men and women lived in coastal cities — Mobile, Memphis, New Orleans — and in the Upper South. In Maryland on the eve of the Civil War, half of the black population was free, and many more were "term" slaves, guaranteed their freedom in exchange for a few more years of work. But free blacks faced many dangers. Those accused of crimes were often denied a jury trial, and those charged with vagrancy were sometimes forced back into slavery. To prove their free status, African Americans had to carry manumission documents, which did not protect them from being kidnapped and sold. However, because skilled Europeans generally would not migrate to the South, free blacks formed the backbone of the region's urban artisan workforce. African American carpenters, blacksmiths, barbers, butchers, and shopkeepers played prominent roles in the economies of Baltimore, Richmond, Charleston, and New Orleans.

As a privileged group among African Americans, free blacks had divided loyalties. To advance the welfare of their families, they were tempted to distance themselves from plantation slaves and absorb white culture and values. Some privileged blacks adopted the perspective of the planter class. David Barland, one of twelve children born to a white Mississippi planter and his black slave Elizabeth, owned no fewer than eighteen slaves. In neighboring Louisiana, some free blacks supported secession because they "own slaves and are dearly attached to their native land."

These men were exceptions. Most free African Americans acknowledged their ties to the great mass of slaves, some of whom were their relatives. "We's different [from whites] in color, in talk and in 'ligion and beliefs," said one. White planters reinforced unity among blacks by justifying slavery as a "positive good" and, in the 1840s and 1850s, by calling for the reenslavement of free African Americans. Knowing that their own liberty was not secure as long as slavery existed, free blacks sought liberty for everyone of African ancestry. As a delegate to the National Convention of Colored People in 1848 noted, "Our souls are yet dark under the pall of slavery." In the rigid caste system of American race relations, free blacks stood as symbols of hope to enslaved African Americans and as symbols of danger to most whites.

▶ Why do certain African practices (the ring shout and incest taboos, for example) persist in the United States, and why have others (such as ritual scarring) disappeared?

▶ What were the successes of African Americans in building families, creating a culture, and winning rights? In what endeavors did they not succeed?

▶ Why in 1860 did white southerners remain committed to the institution of slavery and its expansion?

SUMMARY

In this chapter, we have focused on the theme of an expanding South. Beginning about 1800, the plantation system expanded from its traditional home in the Upper South to the Mississippi Valley and beyond. Powered by cotton, this movement westward divided the planter elite into aristocratic paternalists and entrepreneurial capitalists and involved the forced migration of more than one million enslaved African Americans.

We also examined the character of white and black societies in the Cotton South. After 1820, fewer than one-third of white families owned slaves, and another third were yeomen farmers; propertyless tenant farmers and laborers made up the rest. Many whites joined Evangelical Protestant churches, as did blacks, who infused their churches with African modes of expression. Indeed, church and family became core institutions of African American society, providing strength and solace amid the tribulations of slavery.

Connections: Society and Culture

Following the Tobacco and Rice Revolutions around 1700 and the importation of thousands of enslaved Africans, the South became a dual society. People of English and African ancestry shared geographical space but little else. As we discovered in Chapter 3, they spoke different languages, worshipped different gods, and had a different legal status. Coercion — forced work and forced sex — characterized most interactions between the two peoples.

This dual society began to break down during the Revolutionary era (see Chapter 8). By 1780, most slaves had been born in America, and most spoke English; some had become Christians; and thousands would soon become free, the result of gradual emancipation in the North and individual manumissions in the Chesapeake region. Coercion remained a potent force, but as masters and slaves negotiated work rules, the use of physical force became a measure of last resort. Thus, as we noted in the essay that opened Part Three, it was not surprising that "southern planters increasingly defended slavery as a 'positive good'" and considered slaves to be a part of their extended family.

Of course, as we saw in this chapter, the behavior of most planters contradicted their words. They callously sold hundreds of thousands of African Americans and treated black members of their "families" far differently than they did their white kin. Still, the social and cultural differences between the two peoples continued to diminish. By the 1840s, slaves spoke black English, practiced black Protestantism, and were on their way to becoming a black peasantry — a dependent agricultural people similar to the oppressed peasant peoples of Ireland and Central Europe. Indeed, as we shall see in Chapter 15, the abolition of slavery and the events of Reconstruction (1865–1877) would leave most African Americans as poor sharecroppers, a peasantry in fact if not in name.

FOR FURTHER EXPLORATION

Studies of slave owners include Charlene M. Boyer Lewis, *Ladies and Gentlemen on Display: Planter Society at the Virginia Springs, 1790–1860* (2001); William Kauffman Scarborough, *Masters of the Big House* (2003); Jeffrey Robert Young, *Domesticating Slavery: The Master Class in Georgia and South Carolina, 1670–1837* (1999); and James David Miller, *South by Southwest: Planter Emigration and Identity* (2002). On plantation discipline and resistance, see Sally E. Hadden, *Slave Patrols: Law and Violence in Virginia and the Carolinas* (2001), and John Hope Franklin and Loren Sweninger, *Runaway Slaves, Rebels on the Plantation* (1999). Edward Ball discusses his slaveholding ancestors in *Slaves in the Family* (1998). Stephanie McCurry's *Masters of Small Worlds* (1995) offers fine analysis of southern yeomen families.

TIMELINE

1810s ► Africans from Congo region influence black culture

► Natural increase produces surplus of slaves in Old South

► Domestic slave trade expands, disrupting black family life

1812 ► Louisiana becomes a state; its sugar production increases

1817 ► Mississippi admitted to the Union; Alabama follows (1819)

1820s ► Substantial growth in free black population in North and South

► Slave-owning aristocrats in Old South adopt paternalistic ideology

► Entrepreneurial planters in Cotton South turn to gang labor

► Southern Methodists and Baptists become socially conservative

► More African Americans adopt Christian beliefs

1830s ► Defenders of slavery argue it is a "positive good"

► Boom in cotton production

► Percentage of slave-owning families falls

► Slaves in Deep South develop strong families and core culture

► Yeomen farm families in South retreat to hill country

► Lawyers become influential in southern politics

1840s ► Southern Whigs advocate economic diversification

► Gradual emancipation completed in North

1850s ► Price of slaves and cotton rises; production expands

► Underground black economy grows

► Southern states subsidize railroads, but industrialization remains limited

Ira Berlin's *Generations of Captivity* (2003) details the changing character of slavery and African American society. See also "Slavery and the Making of America" at **www.pbs.org/wnet/slavery/about/index.html** and "The Church in the Southern Black Community" at **docsouth.unc.edu/church/index.html**. Marcus Wood, *Blind Memory: Visual Representations of Slavery in England and America, 1780–1865* (2000), and Walter Johnson, *Soul by Soul: Life Inside the Antebellum Slave Market* (1999), are important studies. Two document-rich Web sites are "The African-American Mosaic" at **www.loc.gov/exhibits/african/intro.html** and "Slaves and the Courts, 1740–1860" at **lcweb2.loc.gov/ammem/aaohtml/**.

TEST YOUR KNOWLEDGE

To assess your mastery of the material in this chapter and for Web sites, images, and documents related to this chapter, visit **bedfordstmartins.com/henrettaconcise**.

CHAPTER

13

The Crisis of the Union
1844–1860

This government was made by our fathers, by white men for the benefit of white men and their posterity forever.

— Illinois Senator Stephen Douglas, 1858

Throughout the nation during the 1850s, crusaders for temperance and abolition battled defenders of personal liberties and property rights. The struggle in South Carolina was especially intense. When temperance activists demanded a "Maine law" to prohibit the sale of intoxicants, Randolph Turner, a candidate for the South Carolina assembly, was outraged: "Legislation upon Liquor would cast a shade on my character which as a Caucassian [sic] and a white man, I am not willing to bear." Indeed, Turner vowed to shoulder his musket and, with "hundreds of men in this district, . . . fight for individual rights, as well as State Rights."

In Washington, South Carolina Congressman Preston Brooks battled for "Southern Rights." In an inflammatory speech in 1856, Senator Charles Sumner of Massachusetts denounced the South and, mixing invective with metaphor, declared that Senator Andrew P. Butler of South Carolina had taken "the harlot slavery" as his mistress. Outraged by Sumner's verbal attack on his uncle, Brooks accosted the Massachusetts legislator in the Senate chamber and beat him unconscious with a walking cane. As the impact of Brooks's attack reverberated throughout Washington and the nation, Axalla Hoole of South Carolina and other proslavery migrants in the Kansas Territory leveled their guns at an armed force of abolitionist settlers. Passion and violence had replaced political compromise as the hallmark of American public life.

The upsurge in political violence in the 1850s had complex roots. The immediate catalyst was the admission of Texas to the Union in 1845 and the acquisition of vast territories from Mexico in 1848. But the fuel for the fire was the increasing friction between the northern and southern states and the South's alarm about the potential consequences of this animosity. As John C. Calhoun told the Senate in 1850, white southerners feared the North's increasing wealth, political power, and moral righteousness, especially its "long-continued agitation of the slavery question."

A population surge in the West added another dimension to this sectional conflict. Inspired by the nation's growing population and wealth, many Americans supported the idea of **Manifest Destiny**, believing that it was their duty to extend republican institutions to the Pacific Ocean. But whose republican institutions: the aristocratic traditions of the slaveholding South or the more democratic customs of the reform-minded North and Midwest? Beginning in 1844, leading politicians in the North, South, and West addressed this question. The task of answering it was much more difficult than they expected or had the political sagacity to resolve. Ultimately, their failures would rip the nation apart.

Manifest Destiny: South and North

The crisis over slavery in Missouri in 1819 (see Chapter 8) threw a fright into the nation's politicians. For the next two decades, the professional politicians who managed the Second Party System avoided policies that would lead to another such regional confrontation. This strategy worked as long as the geographical boundaries of the United States remained unchanged. But during the 1840s, as the ideology of Manifest Destiny led Americans toward the Pacific Ocean, the threat of a new clash loomed large.

The Independence of Texas

By the 1830s, settlers from the Ohio River Valley and the South had carried both yeoman farming and plantation slavery into Arkansas and Missouri. Between those states and the Rocky Mountains stretched the semiarid lands of the Great Plains. An army explorer, Major Stephen H. Long, thought the area "almost wholly unfit for cultivation" and called it the Great American Desert. Settlers looking for land therefore turned south, to the Mexican province of Texas.

Texas was occupied primarily by Indian peoples, but it had long been a zone of European conflict. In the eighteenth century, Spanish authorities in Mexico had installed a military garrison in Texas to deter the French in Louisiana from moving into the region. After the Louisiana Purchase (1803), the Spanish worried that Americans would migrate into Texas. However, the Adams-Onís Treaty of 1819 guaranteed Spanish sovereignty over the region.

After winning independence from Spain in 1821, the Mexican government encouraged the settlement of Texas by offering land grants both to its own citizens and to Americans. One early grantee was Moses Austin, an American land speculator who settled white tenants and smallholding farmers on his vast estate. His son, Stephen F. Austin, acquired even more land from the Mexican government—some 180,000 acres—which he sold to incoming settlers. These American residents resisted assimilation into Mexican society. In 1829, Austin and other grantees requested—and won—an exemption from a law that ended slavery in Mexico. By 1835, about 27,000 white Americans and 3,000 African American slaves were raising cotton and cattle in eastern and central Texas. They far outnumbered the

3,000 Mexican residents, who lived primarily near the western towns of Goliad and San Antonio.

When the Mexican government asserted greater political control over Texas in the 1830s, the Americans split into two groups. Members of the "peace party," led by Stephen Austin and other longtime settlers, accepted Mexican rule but campaigned for greater political autonomy. The "war party," headed mostly by recent migrants from Georgia, demanded independence. Austin won significant concessions from Mexican authorities, but in 1835, Mexico's president, General Antonio López de Santa Anna, nullified them. Santa Anna's goal was to strengthen the authority of the national government throughout Mexico. Fearing that outcome, the war party provoked a rebellion that most of the American settlers ultimately supported. On March 2, 1836, the American rebels proclaimed the independence of Texas and adopted a constitution that legalized slavery.

President Santa Anna vowed to put down the rebellion. On March 6, he led an army that wiped out the rebel garrison defending the Alamo in San Antonio and then

Assault on the Alamo

After a thirteen-day siege, on March 6, 1836, a Mexican army of 4,000 stormed the wall of the small fort — originally a Spanish mission — in San Antonio. "The first to climb were thrown down by bayonets . . . or by pistol fire," reported a Mexican officer. After a half-hour of continuous and costly assaults, the attackers won control of the wall. This contemporary woodcut shows the fierceness of the battle, which took the lives of all 250 Texan defenders; 1,500 Mexicans were killed or wounded in the fighting. Archives Division, Texas State Library.

For more help analyzing this image, see the Online Study Guide at **bedfordstmartins.com/henrettaconcise**.

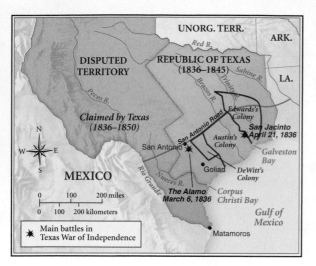

MAP 13.1 American Settlements and the Texas War of Independence

During the 1820s, Mexican officials granted huge tracts of land in Texas to Stephen F. Austin and other land speculators, who encouraged Americans to migrate to Texas and grow cotton. By 1835, the nearly 30,000 American settlers in Texas far outnumbered Mexican residents. To put down the American revolt, General Santa Anna led an army of 6,000 men into Texas in early 1836. Overwhelming the Texans at the Alamo in March, the Mexicans set out in pursuit of the Texas Provisional Government, which had fled to Galveston. But in April, Santa Anna was captured, and his army was defeated at the Battle of San Jacinto by a Texan force commanded by Sam Houston.

took control of Goliad (Map 13.1). Santa Anna thought that he had crushed the rebellion, but New Orleans and New York newspapers romanticized the heroism of the Texans and the deaths at the Alamo of folk heroes Davy Crockett and Jim Bowie. Drawing on anti-Catholic sentiment aroused by Irish immigration, journalists described the Mexicans as tyrannical butchers in the service of the pope. Hundreds of American adventurers, lured by offers of land grants, flocked to Texas to join the rebel army. Led by General Sam Houston, the Texas rebels routed the Mexican army in the Battle of San Jacinto in April 1836, establishing de facto independence. The Mexican government refused to recognize the Texas Republic but abandoned efforts to reconquer it.

The Texans voted by plebiscite (a vote of the people) for annexation by the United States, but President Martin Van Buren refused to bring the issue before Congress. As a Texas diplomat reported, Van Buren and other American politicians feared that annexation would spark a war with Mexico and, beyond that, a "desperate death-struggle . . . between the North and the South; a struggle involving the probability of a dissolution of the Union."

The Push to the Pacific

The annexation of Texas became a pressing issue in the 1840s, as expansionists developed continental ambitions. The term *Manifest Destiny*, coined in 1845 by John L. O'Sullivan, the editor of the *Democratic Review*, captured those dreams. As O'Sullivan put it, "Our manifest destiny is to overspread the continent allotted by Providence for the free development of our yearly multiplying millions." Underlying the rhetoric of Manifest Destiny was a sense of American cultural and racial superiority: The "inferior" peoples who lived in the Far West—Native Americans and Mexicans—were to be brought under American dominion, taught republicanism, and converted to Protestantism.

MAP 13.2 Territorial Boundaries in Oregon, 1819–1846

As nearly 10,000 American settlers arrived in the Oregon Country in the early 1840s, British officials tried to keep them south of the Columbia River. However, the migrants — and fervent midwestern expansionists — asserted that Americans could settle anywhere in the territory, raising the prospect of armed conflict. In 1846, British and American diplomats resolved the dispute by dividing the region at the forty-ninth parallel.

Residents of the Ohio River Valley had already cast their eyes westward to the fertile lands of the Oregon Country. This region, which stretched along the Pacific Coast between Russian-occupied lands in Alaska and the Mexican province of California, was claimed by both Britain and the United States. Since 1818, a British-American agreement had allowed fur traders and settlers from both nations to live there. The British-run Hudson's Bay Company developed a lucrative fur trade north of the Columbia River, while several hundred Americans settled to the south, in the fertile Willamette Valley (see Chapter 16). On the basis of this settlement, the United States claimed sovereignty of the area between California and the Columbia River (Map 13.2).

In 1842, American interest in Oregon increased dramatically. The U.S. Navy published a glowing report of fine harbors in the Puget Sound, which were already being used by New England merchants plying the China trade. In the same year, a party of one hundred farmers journeyed along the Oregon Trail, which fur traders and explorers had blazed through the Great Plains and the Rocky Mountains (Map 13.3). Their letters from Oregon told of a mild climate and fertile soil.

"Oregon fever" suddenly raged. In May 1843, 1,000 men, women, and children — in more than one hundred wagons and with 5,000 oxen and cattle — gathered in Independence, Missouri, for the six-month trek to Oregon. The migrants were mostly yeomen farming families from the southern border states (Missouri, Kentucky, and Tennessee) looking for free land and a new life. These pioneers overcame flooding streams, dust storms, dying livestock, and a few armed encounters with Indians before reaching the Willamette Valley, a journey of 2,000 miles. Over the next two years, another 5,000 settlers reached Oregon, and the numbers continued to grow.

MAP 13.3 Routes to the West, 1835–1860

By the 1840s, a variety of trails spanned the arid zone between the ninety-fifth meridian and the Pacific Coast. From the south, El Camino Real linked Mexico City to the California coast and to Santa Fe. From the east, the Mormon, Oregon, and Santa Fe trails carried more than 250,000 Americans from departure points on the Mississippi and Missouri rivers to Utah communities, the California gold fields, and Oregon farms. By the 1860s, the Pony Express and Butterfield Overland Company were providing reliable communication between the eastern states and California.

By 1860, about 250,000 Americans had braved the Oregon Trail, 65,000 heading for Oregon and the rest to California in the Gold Rush. More than 34,000 of them died in the effort, mostly from disease and exposure; fewer than 500 deaths resulted from Indian attacks. The walking migrants wore three-foot-deep paths, and their wagons carved five-foot-deep ruts across sandstone formations in southern Wyoming—tracks that are visible today. Women found the trail especially difficult because it boosted the authority of their husbands, who directed the enterprise, and added the labor of driving wagons and animals to their usual chores. About 2,500 women endured pregnancy or gave birth during the long journey, and some did not survive. "There was a woman died in this train yesterday," Jane Gould Tortillott noted in her diary. "She left six children, one of them only two day's old."

About 3,000 of the pioneers of the 1840s ended up in the Mexican province of California. They left the Oregon Trail along the Snake River, trudged down the California Trail, and settled in the interior along the Sacramento River. The region had few Native peoples and even fewer Mexicans. California was a remote outpost of Spain's American empire and was settled only in the 1770s, when Spanish authorities built a chain of religious missions and forts (presidios) along the coast. New England merchants struck up trade with the Spanish settlers, buying sea otter pelts and carrying them to China.

Settlement and commerce increased after Mexican independence. To promote California's development, the Mexican government took over the Franciscan-run missions and liberated the 20,000 Indians who had been persuaded to work on them. Some mission Indians rejoined their Native American tribes, but many intermarried with mestizos (Mexicans of mixed Spanish and Indian ancestry) and worked on the large cattle ranches that Mexican entrepreneurs set up in California.

These ranches linked California to the American economy. New England merchants dispatched dozens of agents westward to buy leather and tallow for use in the booming Massachusetts boot and shoe industry. Many of those agents married into the families of the elite Mexican landowners and ranchers—the *Californios*—and adopted their dress, manners, outlook, and Catholic religion (see Chapter 16). A crucial exception was Thomas Oliver Larkin, the most successful merchant in the coastal town of Monterey. Larkin worked closely with Mexican ranchers, but he remained an American in outlook and hoped that California would be peacefully annexed to the United States.

Like Larkin, the American migrants in the Sacramento River Valley did not want to assimilate into Mexican society. Many were squatters or held land grants of dubious legality. Others hoped to emulate the Americans in Texas by colonizing the country and then seeking annexation to the United States. However, in the early 1840s, these settlers numbered only about 700; by contrast, 7,000 Mexicans and 300 American traders lived along the coast.

The Fateful Election of 1844

The election of 1844 determined the American government's policy toward California, Oregon, and Texas. Since 1836, when Texas requested annexation, many southern leaders had advocated territorial expansion to extend slavery. Cautious party politicians and northern abolitionists resisted their efforts. Now there were rumors that Britain wanted the Mexican government to cede California in payment for large debts owed to British investors. Southern leaders also believed that Britain was encouraging Texas to remain independent and had designs on Spanish Cuba, which some southerners wanted to annex. To thwart possible British schemes, southern expansionists demanded the immediate annexation of Texas.

At this crucial juncture, Oregon fever and Manifest Destiny altered the political and diplomatic landscape in the North. In 1843, Americans in the Ohio River Valley and the Great Lakes states organized "Oregon conventions." In July, Democratic and Whig politicians attended a national meeting that demanded that the United States seize Oregon all the way to 54°40' north latitude, the southern border of Russian Alaska. With northern Democrats demanding expansion in Oregon, southern Democrats seized the opportunity to champion the annexation of Texas. The southerners had the strong support of President John Tyler, a proslavery zealot. Disowned by the Whigs because of his opposition to Henry Clay's nationalist economic program, Tyler hoped to win reelection in 1844 as a Democrat. To curry favor among northern expansionists, Tyler proposed to seize all of Oregon.

In April 1844, Tyler and John C. Calhoun, a southern expansionist and the new secretary of state, sent the Senate a treaty to bring Texas into the Union. Two rival presidential candidates, Democrat Martin Van Buren and Whig Henry Clay, quickly declared their opposition. Knowing that annexation would raise the controversial issue of the expansion of slavery, these cautious party politicians persuaded the Senate to reject the treaty.

Expansion into Texas and Oregon became the central issue in the election of 1844. The Democrats passed over Tyler, whom they did not trust, and Van Buren, whom southerners despised for his opposition to annexation. They selected as their candidate Governor James K. Polk of Tennessee, a slave owner who favored the acquisition of Texas. Widely known as "Young Hickory," Polk was a protégé of Andrew Jackson and, like his mentor, a man of iron will and boundless ambition for the nation. Accepting the claim in the Democratic Party platform that both areas already belonged to the United States, Polk campaigned for the "Re-occupation of Oregon and the Re-annexation of Texas." He insisted that the United States claim "the whole of the territory of Oregon" to the Alaskan border. "Fifty-four forty or fight!" became his jingoistic cry.

The Whigs nominated Henry Clay, who again championed his American System of high tariffs, internal improvements, and national banking. Clay initially dodged the issue of Texas but ultimately supported annexation. His position disappointed thousands of antislavery northern Whigs, who cast their ballots for James G. Birney of the Liberty Party (see Chapter 11). Birney garnered less than 3 percent of the national vote but took enough Whig votes in New York to cost Clay that state. By narrowly winning New York's thirty-six electoral votes, Polk captured the presidency; without New York, he would have lost by seven electoral votes.

► What ideas did the term *Manifest Destiny* reflect? Did it cause historical events, or was it merely a description of events? What were those events?

► Why, after two decades of hesitation, did some politicians support territorial expansion in the 1840s? What was the fate of those who supported and those who opposed expansion?

Following Polk's victory, Democrats in Congress called for the immediate annexation of Texas. However, they lacked the two-thirds majority in the Senate needed to ratify a treaty of annexation with the Republic of Texas. So the Democrats admitted Texas to the Union with a joint resolution of Congress, which required just a majority vote in each house. Following a convention in Austin, which drafted a constitution, Texas citizens again voted for annexation, and Texas became the twenty-eighth state in December 1845. Polk's strategy of linking Texas and Oregon had put him in the White House and Texas in the Union. Shortly, it would make the expansion of the South—and its system of slavery—the central topic of American politics.

War, Expansion, and Slavery, 1846–1850

The acquisition of Texas whetted Polk's appetite. The president now saw the possibility of acquiring all the Mexican lands between Texas and the Pacific Ocean. If necessary, he was ready to go to war to get them. What he and the majority of the Democratic Party consciously ignored was the crisis over slavery that this expansion would unleash. Like other American presidents, Polk learned that war is a dangerous military and political option.

The War with Mexico, 1846–1848

Since gaining independence in 1821, Mexico had not prospered. Its stagnant economy yielded few surpluses and only modest tax revenues, which were quickly devoured by a bloated bureaucracy and interest payments on foreign debts. The distant northern provinces of California and New Mexico contributed little to the national economy and remained sparsely settled, with a Spanish-speaking population of only 75,000 in 1840. Still, Mexican officials vowed to preserve their nation's historic boundaries; so when the Texas constitutional convention voted on July 4, 1845, to enter the American Union, Mexico broke off diplomatic relations with the United States.

Taking advantage of this diplomatic rupture, President Polk set in motion his plans to acquire Mexico's northern provinces. To intimidate the Mexican government, he ordered General Zachary Taylor and an American army of 2,000 soldiers to occupy disputed lands between the Nueces River (the historic southern boundary of Spanish Texas) and the Rio Grande, which the Republic of Texas had claimed as its border with Mexico. Simultaneously, Polk launched a secret diplomatic initiative. He sent John Slidell, a Louisiana congressman, to Mexico in December 1845 and told him to secure the Rio Grande boundary and to buy the Mexican provinces of California and New Mexico for $30 million. But Mexican officials, arguing that the annexation of Texas was illegal, refused to see Slidell. Purchasing New Mexico and California was not an option.

Anticipating Slidell's failure, Polk had already embarked on an alternative plan. He hoped to foment a revolution in California that, like the rebellion in Texas, would lead to a request for annexation. In October 1845, Secretary of State James Buchanan told merchant Thomas Oliver Larkin, now the U.S. consul in the port of Monterey, to encourage influential Mexican residents to seek independence and union with the United States. To add military muscle to this scheme, Polk ordered American naval commanders to seize San Francisco Bay and California's coastal towns in case of war with Mexico. The president also had the War Department dispatch Captain John C. Frémont and an "exploring" party of heavily armed soldiers into Mexican territory. By December 1845, Frémont had reached California's Sacramento River Valley.

Events now moved quickly toward war. Polk ordered General Taylor toward the Rio Grande to incite an armed response by Mexico. "We were sent to provoke a fight," recalled Ulysses S. Grant, then a young officer serving with Taylor, "but it was essential that Mexico should commence it." When the armies clashed near the Rio Grande in May 1846, Polk delivered the war message he had drafted long before. Taking liberties with the truth, the president declared that Mexico "has passed the boundary of the United States, has invaded our territory, and shed American blood upon the American soil." Ignoring Whig pleas for a negotiated settlement, the Democratic majority in Congress voted for war, a decision that was greeted with great popular acclaim. To avoid a simultaneous conflict with Britain, Polk retreated from his demand for "fifty-four forty or fight" and accepted a British proposal to divide the Oregon Country at the forty-ninth parallel.

American forces in Texas quickly established their military superiority. Zachary Taylor's army crossed the Rio Grande, occupied Matamoros, and, after a fierce six-day battle in September 1846, took the interior Mexican town of Monterrey. Two months later, a U.S. naval squadron in the Gulf of Mexico seized Tampico, Mexico's second most important port. By the end of 1846, the United States controlled much of northeastern Mexico (Map 13.4).

Fighting had also broken out in California. In June 1846, naval commander John Sloat landed 250 marines in Monterey and declared that California "henceforward will be a portion of the United States." Almost simultaneously, American settlers in the Sacramento River Valley staged a revolt and, supported by Frémont's forces, captured the town of Sonoma, where they proclaimed an independent "Bear Flag Republic." To cement these victories, Polk ordered army units to capture Santa Fe in New Mexico and then march to California. Despite stiff Mexican resistance, American forces secured control of California early in 1847.

Polk expected these American victories to end the war, but he had underestimated the Mexicans' national pride and the determination of President Santa Anna. Santa Anna attacked Taylor's army in northeastern Mexico and, in the battle of Buena Vista in February 1847, nearly defeated it.

To bring Santa Anna to terms, Polk accepted General Winfield Scott's plan to capture the Mexican capital. In March 1847, Scott captured the port of Veracruz and began a 260-mile march to Mexico City. Leading Scott's 14,000 troops was a cadre of talented West Point officers who would become famous in the Civil War: Robert E. Lee, George Meade, and P. G. T. Beauregard. Scott's troops crushed Santa Anna's forces at Cerro Gordo and at Churubusco, just outside Mexico City, and seized the Mexican capital in September 1847. Those defeats cost Santa Anna his presidency, and a new Mexican government made peace with the United States.

A Divisive Victory

Initially, the war with Mexico ignited an explosion of patriotic support. Politicians and newspaper editors hailed the conflict as a noble struggle to extend American republican institutions. However, the war soon divided the nation. A few Whigs—among them Charles Francis Adams of Massachusetts (the son of President John Quincy Adams) and Joshua Giddings of Ohio—opposed the war from the beginning on moral grounds. Known as **conscience Whigs**, they warned of a southern conspiracy to add

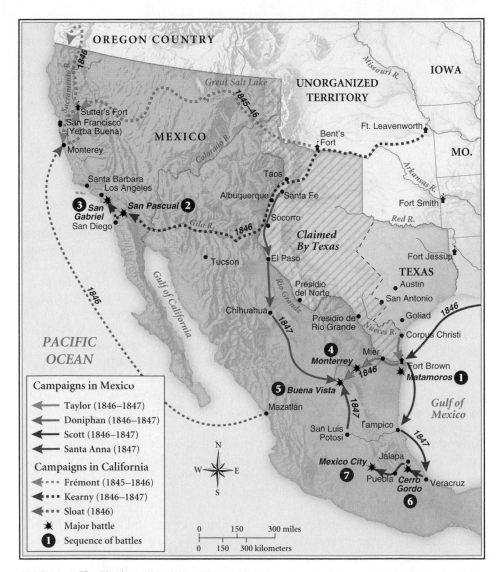

MAP 13.4 The Mexican War, 1846–1848

Departing from Fort Leavenworth in present-day Kansas, American forces commanded by Captain John C. Frémont and General Stephen Kearny defeated Mexican armies in California in 1846 and early 1847. Simultaneously, U.S. troops under General Zachary Taylor and Colonel Alfred A. Doniphan won victories over General Santa Anna's forces far to the south of the Rio Grande. In mid-1847, General Winfield Scott mounted a successful attack on Mexico City, ending the war.

new slave states and ensure permanent control of the federal government by slave-holding Democrats. Antislavery Whigs grew bolder when voters repudiated Polk's war policy in the elections of 1846 and gave their party control of Congress.

Polk's expansionist policies split the Democrats into sectional factions. As early as 1839, Democratic Senator Thomas Morris of Ohio had warned that "the power of slavery is aiming to govern the country, its Constitutions and laws." In 1846, David Wilmot, a Democratic congressman from Pennsylvania, took up that refrain. To check the power of southern slave owners, Wilmot proposed the prohibition of slavery in any territories that might be acquired from Mexico. His plan rallied antislavery northerners. In the House of Representatives, northern Democrats joined forces with antislavery Whigs to pass the Wilmot Proviso. "The madmen of the North . . . ," grumbled the *Richmond Enquirer*, "have, we fear, cast the die and numbered the days of this glorious Union." Fearing just such an outcome, southerners and proslavery Democrats in the Senate killed the proviso.

Fervent Democratic expansionists now became even more aggressive. Polk, Secretary of State Buchanan, and Senators Stephen A. Douglas of Illinois and Jefferson Davis of Mississippi called for the United States to take Mexican territory south of the Rio Grande. However, John C. Calhoun and other southern leaders wanted to avoid a longer war and the need to assimilate a huge number of Mexicans. So they called for the annexation only of New Mexico and California, Mexico's most sparsely populated provinces. "Ours is a government of the white man," Calhoun proclaimed, and should never incorporate "into the Union any but the Caucasian race."

To unify the Democratic Party before the next election, Polk and Buchanan abandoned their hyperexpansionist dreams and accepted Calhoun's policy. In February 1848, Polk signed the Treaty of Guadalupe Hidalgo, in which the United States agreed to pay Mexico $15 million in return for more than one-third of its territory: Texas, New Mexico, and California. The Senate ratified the treaty in March 1848.

The passions that the war had aroused dominated the election of 1848. The Senate's rejection of the Wilmot Proviso prompted antislavery advocates to revive Thomas Morris's charge of a massive "Slave Power" conspiracy. To thwart any such plan, thousands of ordinary northerners, including farmer Abijah Beckwith of Herkimer County, New York, joined the **free-soil movement**. To Beckwith, slavery was an institution of "aristocratic men" and a danger to "the great mass of the people [because it] . . . threatens the general and equal distribution of our lands into convenient family farms."

The free-soilers quickly organized as a political party. They abandoned the Liberty Party's emphasis on the sinfulness of slavery and the natural rights of African Americans. Instead, like Beckwith, they depicted slavery as a threat to republican liberties and the Jeffersonian ideal of a freeholder society. The Wilmot Proviso and the call for free soil were the first antislavery proposals to attract broad popular support. Hundreds of women in the Great Lakes states joined the female free-soil organizations formed by the American and Foreign Anti-Slavery Society. Still, the free-soilers' shift in emphasis—from freeing slaves toward preserving the West for white freehold farming—led abolitionist William Lloyd Garrison to denounce free-soil doctrine as racist "whitemanism."

Nonetheless, Frederick Douglass, the foremost black abolitionist, endorsed the free-soil movement. Born to an enslaved woman on a Maryland plantation in 1818, Douglass grew up as Frederick Bailey. He never knew the identity of his father, though it was undoubtedly his owner, Thomas Auld. Auld had Frederick raised by his brother in Baltimore, where he learned to read and mingled with free blacks. Later, when Frederick faced deportation to the Deep South for attempting to escape from plantation labor, Auld again intervened. In 1835, he returned Frederick to Baltimore, allowed him to hire himself out as a caulker, and promised him freedom in eight years, at the age of twenty-five.

Frederick plunged enthusiastically into the life of Baltimore's free African American community. He courted a free black woman, Anna Murray; joined the East Baltimore Mental Improvement Society; and hatched a plan of escape. In 1838, he borrowed the identification papers of a free African American sailor and sailed to New York City. He took the last name Douglass, married Murray, and settled in New Bedford, Massachusetts. Inspired by Garrison, Douglass lectured for the American Anti-Slavery Society and quickly became a celebrity. His partly African ancestry drew crowds to his lectures, as did his commanding presence, dramatic rhetoric, and forceful intellect.

Gradually, Douglass's views diverged from those of Garrison. To rid America of the sin of slavery, Garrison wanted to expel the southern states from the Union. To Douglass, that policy was madness because it would perpetuate slavery. Rejecting Garrison's moral radicalism, he founded an antislavery newspaper, the *North Star*, and became a political abolitionist, dedicated to using political agitation and government power to overthrow slavery. In 1848, Douglass attended the Buffalo convention that established the Free-Soil Party and endorsed its political strategy of confronting the South.

The conflict over slavery took a toll on Polk and the Democratic Party. Scorned by Whigs and Free-Soilers and exhausted by his rigorous dawn-to-midnight work regime, Polk refused to run for a second term; he would die just three months after leaving office. In his place, the Democrats nominated Senator Lewis Cass of Michigan, an avid expansionist who had advocated buying Cuba, annexing Mexico's Yucatán Peninsula, and taking all of Oregon. To maintain party unity, Cass deliberately took a vague position on the question of slavery in the West. He promoted a new idea—squatter sovereignty—that would allow settlers in each territory to determine its status as free or slave.

Cass's political ingenuity failed to unify the Democracy. Demanding unambiguous opposition to the expansion of slavery, some northern Democrats joined the newly formed Free-Soil Party, which nominated Martin Van Buren for president. Van Buren genuinely supported free soil, but he also wanted to punish southern Democrats for denying him the presidential nomination in 1844. To attract Whig votes, the Free-Soilers chose conscience-Whig Charles Francis Adams as their candidate for vice president.

To keep their party intact, the Whigs nominated General Zachary Taylor for president. Taylor was a Louisiana slave owner, but he had not taken a position on the charged issue of slavery in the territories. Moreover, the general's military exploits had made him a popular hero. Known as "Old Rough and Ready," Taylor had a common touch that won him the affection of his troops. In 1848, as in 1840, running a military hero worked for the Whigs. Taylor took 47 percent of the popular vote to Cass's 42 percent. However, Taylor won a majority in the Electoral College (163 to 127) only because Van Buren and the Free-Soil ticket took the votes of enough Democrats to cause Cass to lose New York's electoral votes. The bitter debate over the Wilmot Proviso had fractured the Democratic Party in the North and changed the dynamics of national politics.

1850: Crisis and Compromise

Even before Taylor took office, events in California triggered a new political crisis over slavery. In January 1848, workmen building a mill for John A. Sutter in the Sierra Nevada foothills in northern California discovered flakes of gold. Sutter was a Swiss

A ROAD SCENE IN CALIFORNIA.

The Gold Rush Creates a Mix of Peoples
This well-composed drawing by German-born artist and California prospector Charles Nahl captures the racial complexity of the gold rush. Displaced from their home by a horde of newcomers, a Native American family trudges away from the gold fields (left). Meanwhile, a contingent of Chinese miners marches toward the diggings (center), and a group of American men struggle to right their overturned wagon. University of California at Berkeley, Bancroft Library.

immigrant who had arrived in California in 1839, became a Mexican citizen, and established an estate in the Sacramento River Valley. He tried to keep the discovery a secret; but by May 1848, Americans from Monterey and San Francisco were pouring into the foothills. When President Polk confirmed the discovery in December, the gold rush was on. By January 1849, 61 crowded ships had left northeastern ports to sail around Cape Horn to San Francisco; by May, 12,000 wagons had crossed the Missouri River bound for the gold fields. By the end of 1849, more than 80,000 people (the "forty-niners") had arrived in California (see Chapter 16).

The rapid settlement of California revived the national debate over free soil. The forty-niners, who lived in crowded, chaotic towns and mining camps, demanded the formation of a territorial government to protect their lives and property. Hoping to prevent a debate over slavery, President Taylor advised the Californians to apply for statehood immediately; in November 1849, they ratified a state constitution that prohibited slavery. Taylor had never believed that the defense of slavery in the South required its expansion into the territories. Now, urged on by William H. Seward, the former Whig governor of New York, Taylor tried to strengthen the Whig Party in the North by appealing to Free-Soilers and northern Democrats.

As part of this political strategy, he urged Congress to admit California as a free state.

The resulting political impasse produced passionate debates in Congress and four distinct positions with respect to slavery in the territories. On the verge of death, John C. Calhoun took his usual extreme stance. Like Senator Albert Gallatin Brown of Mississippi, Calhoun had long resented the "social and sectional degradation" of the South by northern critics. To uphold southern honor, he proposed a constitutional amendment that would permanently balance the political power of the North and the South by creating a dual presidency. Calhoun also advanced the radical position that Congress had no constitutional authority to regulate slavery in the territories. That argument ran counter to a half century of practice. In 1787, Congress had prohibited slavery in the Northwest Territory; and in the Missouri Compromise of 1820, it had extended that ban to most of the Louisiana Purchase.

Calhoun's assertion that the territories were open to slavery won support in the Deep South, but many southerners favored a more moderate proposal to extend the Missouri Compromise line to the Pacific Ocean. This plan won the backing of Pennsylvanian James Buchanan, the former secretary of state, and other influential northern Democrats. Because such an extension would guarantee slave owners access to some western territory, including a separate state in southern California, they saw it as a an easy way to resolve the crisis.

A third alternative was squatter sovereignty — allowing territorial residents to decide the issue. Lewis Cass had advanced this idea in 1848, and Democratic Senator Stephen Douglas of Illinois was now its champion. Douglas called his plan *popular sovereignty* to emphasize its roots in republican ideology, and it had considerable appeal. Politicians liked the fact that it would remove the explosive issue of slavery from national politics; local settlers welcomed the power it would put in their hands. However, popular sovereignty was a vague and slippery concept. Could residents accept or ban slavery when a territory was first organized? Or must they delay that decision until a territory had enough people to frame a constitution and apply for statehood?

For their part, antislavery advocates were unwilling to accept any plan for California that might allow the expansion of slavery there or elsewhere. Senator Salmon P. Chase of Ohio, elected by a Democratic–Free-Soil coalition, and Senator William H. Seward, a New York Whig, urged a fourth position: that federal authorities restrict slavery within its existing boundaries and then extinguish it completely. Condemning slavery as "morally unjust, politically unwise, and socially pernicious" and invoking "a higher law than the Constitution," Seward demanded bold action to protect freedom, "the common heritage of mankind."

Standing on the brink of disaster, senior Whig and Democratic politicians worked desperately to preserve the Union. With the help of Millard Fillmore, who became president in 1850 after Zachary Taylor's sudden death, Whig leaders Henry Clay and Daniel Webster and Democrat Stephen A. Douglas secured the passage of five separate laws known collectively as the Compromise of 1850. To mollify the South, the Compromise included a new Fugitive Slave Act that enlisted federal magistrates in the task of returning runaway slaves. To satisfy the North, the legislation admitted California as a free state, resolved a boundary dispute between

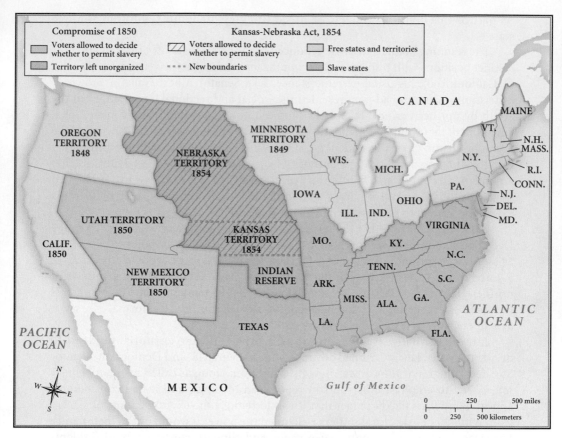

MAP 13.5 The Compromise of 1850 and the Kansas-Nebraska Act of 1854

Vast territories were at stake in the contest over the expansion of slavery. The Compromise of 1850 resolved the status of lands in the Far West: California would be a free state, and the settlers of the Utah and New Mexico territories would vote for or against slavery (the concept of popular sovereignty). The decision in 1854 to void the Missouri Compromise of 1820 and use popular sovereignty to decide the fate of slavery in the Kansas and Nebraska territories sparked a bitter local war and revealed a fatal flaw in the concept.

For more help analyzing this map, see the Online Study Guide at **bedfordstmartins.com/henrettaconcise**.

New Mexico and Texas in favor of New Mexico, and abolished the slave trade (but not slavery) in the District of Columbia. Finally, the Compromise organized the rest of the lands acquired from Mexico into the territories of New Mexico and Utah and left the decision over slavery in those vast areas to popular sovereignty (Map 13.5).

The Compromise averted a secession crisis in 1850, but only barely. During the debate, the governor of South Carolina warned that there was not "the slightest doubt" that his state would leave the Union. He and other militant secessionists (known as "fire-eaters") in Georgia, Mississippi, and Alabama organized special conventions to safeguard "Southern Rights" through secession. In Georgia, U.S. Congressman Alexander H. Stephens called on the delegates to make "the necessary preparations of men and money, arms and munitions, etc. to meet the emergency." However, most convention delegates remained committed to the Union — though now only conditionally. Accepting the principle of secession, they agreed to leave the Union if Congress abolished slavery anywhere or refused to grant statehood to a territory with a proslavery constitution. Political wizardry had solved the immediate crisis, but the underlying issue of slavery remained unresolved.

▶ Why did President Polk go to war with Mexico? Why did the war become so divisive in Congress and the country?

▶ What issues were resolved by the Compromise of 1850? Who benefited more from its terms: the North or the South? Why?

The End of the Second Party System, 1850–1858

The architects of the Compromise of 1850 expected it to last for a generation, as the Missouri Compromise had. Their hopes were quickly dashed. Demanding freedom for fugitive slaves and free soil in the West, antislavery northerners refused to accept the Compromise. For their part, proslavery southerners plotted to extend slavery into the West, the Caribbean, and Central America. The resulting disputes destroyed the Second Party System and deepened the crisis of the Union.

Resistance to the Fugitive Slave Act

The Fugitive Slave Act proved the most controversial element of the Compromise. Under its terms, federal magistrates in the northern states determined the status of alleged runaway slaves. The law denied a jury trial to the accused blacks and even the right to testify. Using its provisions, southern owners reenslaved about 200 fugitives (as well as some free northern blacks).

The plight of the runaways and the appearance of slave catchers in the North and Midwest aroused popular hostility. Ignoring the threat of substantial fines and prison sentences, free blacks and white abolitionists aided fugitive slaves and interfered with their capture. In October 1850, Boston abolitionists helped two slaves to escape and drove a Georgia slave catcher out of town. Rioters in Syracuse, New York, broke into a courthouse to free a fugitive slave. Abandoning his commitment to nonviolence, Frederick Douglass declared, "The only way to make a Fugitive Slave Law a dead letter is to make half a dozen or more dead kidnappers." As if in response, a deadly confrontation took place in the Quaker village of Christiana, Pennsylvania, in September 1851. About twenty African Americans exchanged gunfire with Maryland slave catchers, killing two of them. Federal authorities indicted thirty-six blacks and four whites for treason and other crimes. But a Pennsylvania jury acquitted one defendant, and public opinion in the North forced the government to drop the charges against the rest.

Upping the ante was Harriet Beecher Stowe's abolitionist novel, *Uncle Tom's Cabin* (1852), which boosted northern opposition to the Fugitive Slave Act. By imbedding the moral principles of abolitionism into heartrending personal situations, Stowe's melodramatic book evoked empathy and outrage throughout the North. Legislators in northern states added their opposition to the fugitive act, claiming that it violated state sovereignty by interfering in their legal affairs. In response, they enacted a new set of

personal-liberty laws that increased the legal rights of their residents, including accused fugitives. In 1857, the Wisconsin Supreme Court went even further. In *Ableman v. Booth*, it ruled that the Fugitive Slave Act was void in Wisconsin because it violated state law and the constitutional rights of Wisconsin's citizens. Taking a states' rights stance—a position usually associated with the South—the Wisconsin court denied the authority of federal courts to review its decision. When the case reached the U.S. Supreme Court in 1859, Chief Justice Roger B. Taney led a unanimous Court in affirming the supremacy of federal courts over state courts—a position that has stood the test of time—and upheld the constitutionality of the Fugitive Slave Act. But by then, as Frederick Douglass had hoped, popular opposition had made the act a "dead letter."

The Political System in Decline

The conflict over slavery split both major political parties along sectional lines. The Whigs, weakened by the death of Henry Clay, chose General Winfield Scott, another hero of the war with Mexico, as their presidential candidate in 1852. But many southern Whigs refused to support Scott because northern Whigs opposed slavery. The Democrats were equally divided: Southerners wanted a candidate who accepted Calhoun's constitutional argument that all territories were open to slavery; but northern and midwestern Democrats advocated popular sovereignty, as did the three leading candidates—Lewis Cass of Michigan, Stephen Douglas of Illinois, and James Buchanan of Pennsylvania. Ultimately, the party settled on a compromise nominee, Franklin Pierce of New Hampshire, a congenial man who was sympathetic to the South. Thanks to the Democrats' cautious strategy, they swept the election. Many Free-Soilers voted for Pierce, reuniting the Democratic Party; still split over slavery, the Whig Party fragmented into sectional wings and would never again wage a national campaign.

As president, Pierce pursued an expansionist foreign policy. To assist northern merchants, he sent a mission to Japan to negotiate a commercial treaty. To mollify southern expansionists, he tried to buy Mexican lands south of the Rio Grande. When Mexico rejected his offer, Pierce settled for the purchase of a narrow slice of land that enabled his negotiator, James Gadsden, to build a transcontinental rail line from New Orleans to California.

Pierce's most controversial foreign policy initiatives came in the Caribbean and Central America. American slave traders, financed from New York City, carried about 25,000 slaves to Spanish-owned Cuba annually during the 1850s; southern expansionists were equally active there, funding clandestine military expeditions and encouraging Cuban slave owners to declare independence and join the United States. Beginning in 1853, Pierce covertly supported new military expeditions to Nicaragua and Cuba and threatened war with Spain over the seizure of an American ship. Northern Democrats in Congress denounced this aggressive diplomacy, and Pierce and Secretary of State William L. Marcy backed down. When Marcy's attempt to buy the island from Spain for $130 million also failed, he arranged in 1854 for American diplomats in Europe to issue the so-called Ostend Manifesto, which urged Pierce to seize Cuba. Leaked to newspapers, the Ostend Manifesto revived northern fears of a "Slave Power" conspiracy. Determined resistance by northern politicians scuttled the planters' dreams of an American slave empire in the Caribbean.

The Kansas-Nebraska Act and the Rise of New Parties

The Caribbean was a sideshow. The main stage was the West, where a major controversy in 1854 destroyed the Second Party System and sent the Union spinning toward disaster. The Missouri Compromise prohibited new slave states in the Louisiana Purchase north of 36°30′; consequently, southern senators had long delayed its division into territories. Now residents of the Ohio River Valley and the Upper South demanded its settlement. Senator Stephen A. Douglas of Illinois led the charge, partly because he wanted a transcontinental railroad to run through the area and link Chicago to California. In 1854, Douglas introduced a bill to extinguish Native American rights on the central Great Plains and organize the large free territory of Nebraska.

Douglas's bill conflicted with the plans of southern politicians. They wanted to open up the Louisiana Purchase to slavery and to have a southern city — New Orleans, Memphis, or St. Louis — as the eastern terminus of a transcontinental railroad. To win southern support, Douglas made two major concessions. First, he amended his bill so that it explicitly repealed the Missouri Compromise and organized the region on the basis of popular sovereignty. Second, Douglas agreed to the formation of two territories, Nebraska and Kansas, giving southerners the hope that Kansas would become a slave state. Douglas knew that his bill would "raise a hell of a storm" in the North. To win over northern congressmen, he argued that Kansas was not suited to plantation agriculture and would become a free state. After weeks of bitter debate, the Senate enacted the Kansas-Nebraska Act. To get the act through the House of Representatives, where sixty-six northern Democrats defied party policy and initially opposed it, President Pierce used pressure and patronage to persuade twenty-two members to change their votes, allowing the measure to squeak through.

The Kansas-Nebraska Act was a disaster for the American political system. It finished off the Whig Party and nearly destroyed the Democrats (as 70 percent of the northern Democrats who voted for the act lost their seats in the election of 1854). Denouncing the act as "part of a great scheme for extending and perpetuating supremacy of the slave power," northern Whigs and "anti-Nebraska" Democrats abandoned their old parties. They joined with Free-Soilers and abolitionists in a new Republican Party.

The new party was a coalition of "strange, discordant and even hostile elements," one Republican observed, but its leaders shared an economic philosophy that reflected their bitter opposition to slavery. Republicans condemned slavery because it degraded the dignity of manual labor and drove down the wages and working conditions of free white workers. Like Thomas Jefferson, they praised the morality of a society based on "the middling classes who own the soil and work it with their own hands." Abraham Lincoln, an Illinois Whig who became a Republican, conveyed the party's vision of social justice. "There is no permanent class of hired laborers among us," he declared; consequently, every free man had a chance to become a property owner. Ignoring the increasing class divisions in the industrializing North and Midwest, Lincoln and his fellow Republicans celebrated the values of republican liberty and individual enterprise.

The Republicans faced strong competition from the American, or Know-Nothing, Party. The party had its origins in the anti-immigrant and anti-Catholic movements of the 1840s (see Chapter 9). In 1850, these secret nativist societies banded together as the Order of the Star-Spangled Banner; the following year, they entered politics, forming the American Party. Its secrecy-conscious members often replied, "I know nothing" to outsiders' questions, thus giving the party its nickname. The party's program was far from secret: It wanted to unite all native-born Protestants against the "alien menace" of Irish and German Catholics, prohibit further immigration, and institute literacy tests for voting. In 1854, voters elected dozens of Know-Nothing candidates to the House of Representatives and gave the American Party control of the state governments of Massachusetts and Pennsylvania. The emergence of a major nativist party suddenly became a real possibility.

Meanwhile, thousands of settlers rushed into the Kansas Territory, putting Douglas's theory of popular sovereignty to the test. On the side of slavery, Missouri Senator David R. Atchison encouraged residents of his state to cross temporarily into Kansas to vote in crucial elections there. Opposing Atchison was the abolitionist New England Emigrant Aid Society, which dispatched hundreds of free-soilers to Kansas. In March 1855, the Pierce administration stepped into the fray by accepting the legitimacy of the proslavery territorial legislature meeting in Lecompton, Kansas, which had been elected primarily by border-crossing Missourians. However, the majority of Kansas residents favored free soil and refused allegiance to the Lecompton government.

In May 1856, both sides turned to violence, prompting Horace Greeley of the *New York Tribune* to label the territory as "Bleeding Kansas." A proslavery gang, seven hundred strong, sacked the free-soil town of Lawrence, wrecking two newspaper offices, looting stores, and burning buildings. The attack enraged John Brown, a fifty-six-year-old abolitionist from New York and Ohio, who commanded a volunteer free-state

Armed Abolitionists in Kansas, 1859
The confrontation between North and South in Kansas took many forms. In the spring of 1859, Dr. John Doy (seated) slipped across the border into Missouri and tried to lead thirteen slaves to freedom in Kansas, only to be captured and jailed in St. Joseph, Missouri. The serious-looking men standing behind Doy, well armed with guns and Bowie knives, attacked the jail and carried Doy back to Kansas. The photograph memorialized their successful exploit. Kansas State Historical Society.

militia that had arrived too late to save the town. Brown was a complex man with a long record of failed businesses, but he had an intellectual and moral intensity that won the trust of influential people. Taking vengeance for the sack of Lawrence, Brown and a few followers murdered five proslavery settlers at Pottawatomie. Abolitionists must "fight fire with fire" and "strike terror in the hearts of the proslavery people," Brown declared. The southerners' attack on Lawrence and the Pottawatomie killings started a guerrilla war in Kansas that took nearly two hundred lives (see American Voices, p. 398).

Buchanan's Failed Presidency

The violence in Kansas dominated the presidential election of 1856. The two-year-old Republican Party counted on anger over Bleeding Kansas to boost the party's fortunes. Its platform denounced the Kansas-Nebraska Act and, alleging a Slave Power conspiracy, demanded that the federal government prohibit slavery in all the territories. Republicans called for federal subsidies for transcontinental railroads, reviving an element of the Whig's economic program that was popular among midwestern Democrats. For president, the Republicans nominated Colonel John C. Frémont, a free-soiler who had won fame in the conquest of Mexican California.

The American Party entered the election with equally high hopes, but like the Whigs and Democrats, it split along sectional lines over slavery. The southern faction of the American party nominated former Whig president Millard Fillmore, while the northern contingent endorsed Frémont — thanks to clever maneuvering by Republican political operatives. During the campaign, Frémont and the Republicans won the votes of many Know-Nothing workingmen in the North by demanding a ban on foreign immigrants and high tariffs on foreign manufactures. As a Pennsylvania Republican put it, "Let our motto be, protection to everything American, against everything foreign." In New York, Republicans likewise shaped their policies "to cement into a harmonious mass . . . all of the Anti-Slavery, Anti-Popery and Anti-Whiskey" voters.

The Democrats reaffirmed their support for popular sovereignty and the Kansas-Nebraska Act, and nominated James Buchanan of Pennsylvania. A tall, dignified man, Buchanan was an experienced but unimaginative politician with a prosouthern outlook. Thanks to southern support and the Democrats' organizational strength in the North, Buchanan won the three-way race with 1.8 million votes (45 percent) and 174 electoral votes. Frémont polled 1.3 million votes (33 percent) and 114 electoral votes; but a small shift to Frémont in the popular vote in Illinois and Pennsylvania would have given him those states and the presidency.

The dramatic restructuring of parties was now apparent. With the splintering of the American Party over slavery, the Republicans had replaced the Whigs as the second major party. However, the Republican Party had no support in the South, so it was a sectional rather than a national party; consequently, a Republican triumph in the next presidential election might destroy the Union. A North Carolina newspaper threatened as much during the election of 1856: "If the Republicans should succeed, the result will be a separation of the states. No human power can prevent it." The fate of the republic hinged on President Buchanan's ability to quiet the passions of the past decade.

Events — and his own values and weaknesses — conspired against Buchanan. In 1856, the Supreme Court had heard the case of *Dred Scott v. Sandford*, which raised the controversial issue of Congress's constitutional authority over slavery in the territories.

"Bleeding Kansas": A Southern View AXALLA JOHN HOOLE

Early in 1856, Axalla John Hoole and his bride left South Carolina to build a new life in the Kansas Territory (K.T.). These letters from Hoole to his family show that things did not go well from the start and gradually got worse; after eighteen months, the Hooles returned to South Carolina. A Confederate militia captain during the Civil War, Axalla Hoole died in the Battle of Chickamauga in September 1863.

Kansas City, Missouri, Apl. 3d., 1856. The Missourians . . . are very sanguine about Kansas being a slave state & I have heard some of them say it shall be . . . but generally speaking, I have not met with the reception which I expected. Everyone seems bent on the Almighty Dollar, and as a general thing that seems to be their only thought. . . . [T]he supper bell has rung and I must close. Give my love to [the family] and all the Negroes. . . .

Lecompton, K.T., Sept. 12, 1856. I have been unwell ever since the 9th of July. . . . I thought of going to work in a few days, when the Abolitionists broke out and I have had to stand guard of nights when I ought to have been in bed, took cold which . . . caused diarrhea. . . . Betsie is well. . . . I am now in Lecompton, almost all of the Proslavery party between this place and Lawrence are here. We brought our families here, as we thought that we would be better able to defend our-selves. . . .

Lane [and a force of abolitionists] came against us last Friday (a week ago to-day). As it happened we had about 400 men with two cannon — we marched out to meet him, though we were under the impression at the time that we had 1,000 men. We came in gunshot of each other, but the regular [U.S. Army] soldiers came and

interfered, but not before our party had shot some dozen guns, by which it is reported that five of the Abolitionists had been killed or wounded. We had strict orders . . . not to fire until they made the attack, but some of our boys would not be restrained. I was a rifleman and one of the skirmishers, but did all that I could to restrain our men though I itched all over to shoot myself. . . .

July the 5th., 1857. I fear, Sister, that [our] coming here will do no good at last, as I begin to think that this will be made a Free State at last. 'Tis true we have elected Proslavery men to draft a state constitu-tion, but I feel pretty certain, if it is put to a vote of the people, it will be rejected, as I feel pretty confident that they have a majority here at this time. The South has ceased all efforts, while the North is redoubling her exertions. We nominated a candidate for Congress last Friday — Ex-Gov. Ransom of Michigan. I must confess I have not much faith in him, tho he professes to hate the abolitionists bitterly. . . . If we had nominated a Southern man, he would have been sure to have been beaten. . . .

SOURCE: William Stanley Hoole, ed., "A Southerner's Viewpoint of the Kansas Situation, 1856–1857," *Kansas Historical Quarterly* 3 (1934): 43–65, 149–171, passim.

Dred Scott was an enslaved African American who had lived for a time with his owner, an army surgeon, in the free state of Illinois and in the Wisconsin Territory, where the Northwest Ordinance (1787) prohibited slavery. Seeking freedom for himself and his family, Scott claimed that residence in a free state and a free territory had made him free. Buchanan hoped that the Court would reject Scott's appeal and pressured the two justices from his home state of Pennsylvania to side with their southern colleagues. Then, learning of the justices' vote in advance, the President urged Americans to accept the court's decision as permanently settling the issue of slavery in the territories. In the event, seven of the nine justices issued opinions declaring that Scott was still a slave. But they could not agree on the legal issues, so the case did not result in a binding principle of constitutional law.

Chief Justice Roger B. Taney of Maryland, a slave owner himself, wrote the most influential opinion. He declared that Negroes, whether enslaved or free, could not be citizens of the United States and that Scott therefore had no right to sue in federal court. That argument was controversial enough, given that free blacks were citizens in many states, which presumably gave them access to the federal courts. But then Taney proceeded to make two even more controversial claims. First, he endorsed John C. Calhoun's argument: Relying on the Fifth Amendment, which prohibited "takings" of property without due process of law, Taney ruled that Congress could not prevent southern citizens from taking their slave property into the territories and owning it there. Consequently, the chief justice concluded, the provisions of the Northwest Ordinance and the Missouri Compromise that prohibited slavery had never been constitutional. Second, Taney declared that Congress could not give to territorial governments any powers that it did not possess. Because Congress had no authority to prohibit slavery in a territory, neither did a territorial government. Taney thereby endorsed Calhoun's interpretation of popular sovereignty: Only when settlers wrote a constitution and requested statehood could they prohibit slavery.

In a single stroke, Taney had declared the Republicans' antislavery platform to be unconstitutional. The Republicans could never accept the legitimacy of Taney's broader arguments. Led by Senator Seward of New York, they accused the Chief Justice and President Buchanan of participating in the Slave Power conspiracy.

Buchanan then added fuel to the raging constitutional fire. Ignoring reports that antislavery residents held a clear majority in Kansas, he refused to allow a referendum on the constitution written by the proslavery Lecompton legislature. Instead, early in 1858, the president recommended the admission of Kansas as a slave state. Angered by Buchanan's machinations, Stephen Douglas, the most influential Democratic senator, broke with the president and persuaded Congress to deny statehood to Kansas. (Kansas would enter the Union as a free state in 1861.) Still determined to aid the South, Buchanan informed Congress in December 1858 that he was resuming negotiations to buy Cuba. By pursuing a proslavery agenda — first in *Dred Scott* and then in Kansas and Cuba — Buchanan widened the split in his party and the nation.

▶ Did the Compromise of 1850 fail? Or would it have succeeded if the Kansas-Nebraska Act of 1854 had either not been enacted or contained different provisions?

▶ What were the main constitutional arguments advanced during the debate over slavery in the territories? Which of those arguments influenced Chief Justice Taney's opinion in *Dred Scott*?

Abraham Lincoln and the Republican Triumph, 1858–1860

As the Democratic Party split along sectional lines, the Republicans gained support in the North and Midwest. Abraham Lincoln of Illinois emerged as the pivotal figure in American politics—the only Republican leader whose policies and temperament might have saved the Union. But few southerners trusted Lincoln, and his presidential candidacy revived secessionist agitation in the Deep South.

Lincoln's Political Career

The middle-class world of storekeepers, lawyers, and entrepreneurs in the small towns of the Ohio River Valley shaped Lincoln's early career. He came from a hardscrabble yeoman farm family that was continually on the move—from Kentucky, where Lincoln was born in 1809, to Indiana and then to Illinois. In 1831, Lincoln rejected his father's life as a subsistence farmer and became a store clerk in New Salem, Illinois. Socially ambitious, Lincoln sought entry into the middle class by mastering its literary and professional culture; he joined the New Salem Debating Society, read Shakespeare, and studied law.

Admitted to the bar in 1837, Lincoln moved to Springfield, the new state capital. There, he met Mary Todd, the cultured daughter of a Kentucky banker; they married in 1842. The couple was a picture in contrasts: Her tastes were aristocratic; his were humble. She was volatile; he was easygoing but suffered bouts of depression that tried her patience and tested his character.

Abraham Lincoln, 1859
Lincoln was not a handsome man, and he photographed poorly. In fact, his campaign photographs were often retouched to hide his prominent cheekbones and nose. More important, no photograph ever captured Lincoln's complex personality, verbal wit, and intensity of spirit and intellect. To grasp Lincoln, it is necessary to read his words. Chicago Historical Society.

Lincoln's ambition was "a little engine that knew no rest," his closest associate re-marked, and it prompted him to seek fame and fortune in politics. An admirer of Henry Clay, Lincoln joined the Whig Party and won election to four terms in the Illinois legislature, where he promoted education, banks, canals, and railroads. He became a dexterous party politician, adept in the distribution of patronage and the passage of legislation.

In 1846, the rising lawyer-politician won election to a Congress that was bitterly divided over the Wilmot Proviso. Lincoln had long felt that human bondage was unjust but did not believe that the federal government had the constitutional authority to tamper with slavery in the South. With respect to the war with Mexico, he took a middle ground. He supported bills for military appropriations but voted for Wilmot's proposal to prohibit slavery in any acquired territories. And he personally proposed that Congress enact legislation for the gradual (and thus compensated) emancipation of slaves in the District of Columbia. Lincoln argued that a series of measures — firm opposition to the expansion of slavery, gradual emancipation, and the colonization of freed blacks in Africa — was the only practical solution to the problems of slavery and racial diversity. Both abolitionists and proslavery activists heaped scorn on Lincoln's pragmatic policies, and he lost his bid for reelection. Dismayed by the rancor of ideological politics, he withdrew from politics and prospered as a lawyer representing railroads and manufacturers.

Lincoln returned to the political fray after passage of Stephen Douglas's Kansas-Nebraska Act. Shocked by the act's repeal of the Missouri Compromise, Lincoln warned that the American "republican robe is soiled and trailed in the dust" and called on the citizens of Illinois to "repurify it and wash it white in the spirit, if not the blood of the Revolution." Rejecting Stephen Douglas's advocacy of popular sovereignty, Lincoln reaffirmed his position that slavery be allowed to continue in the South but that the national government should exclude it from the territories. Beyond that, Lincoln likened slavery to a cancer that had to be cut out if the nation's republican ideals and moral principles were to endure.

Abandoning the Whig Party in favor of the Republicans, Lincoln quickly emerged as their leader in Illinois. Campaigning for the U.S. Senate against Douglas in 1858, Lincoln alerted his audiences to the threat posed by the Slave Power. He warned that the proslavery Supreme Court might soon declare that the Constitution "does not permit a state to exclude slavery from its limits," just as it had decided in *Dred Scott* that "neither Congress nor the territorial legislature" could ban slavery in the territories. In that event, "we shall awake to the reality . . . that the Supreme Court has made Illinois a slave state." This prospect of slavery spreading into the North informed Lincoln's famous "House Divided" speech. Quoting from the Bible, "A house divided against itself cannot stand," he predicted that American society "cannot endure permanently half slave and half free. . . . It will become all one thing, or all the other."

The Senate race in Illinois attracted national interest because of Douglas's prominence in the Democratic Party and Lincoln's reputation as a formidable speaker. During a series of seven debates, Douglas declared his support for white supremacy: "This government was made by our fathers, by white men for the benefit of white men," he asserted, attacking Lincoln for supporting "negro equality." Put on the defensive by Douglas's racial rhetoric, Lincoln advocated economic opportunity for free blacks but not equal political rights. He asked how Douglas could accept the *Dred Scott* decision (which protected slave owners' property in the territories) yet advocate popular sovereignty (which asserted settlers' power to exclude slavery). Douglas responded with the so-called Freeport Doctrine: that a territory's residents could exclude slavery simply by not adopting laws to protect it. That position pleased neither proslavery advocates nor antislavery activists, but the Democrats won a narrow victory in Illinois, and the state legislature reelected Douglas to the U.S. Senate.

The Union Under Siege

His debates with Douglas gave Lincoln a national reputation, and the election of 1858 established the Republican Party as a formidable political force, as it won control of the House of Representatives and various state legislatures. Shaken by the Republican advance, southern Democrats divided into moderates and fire-eaters. The moderates, who included Senator Jefferson Davis of Mississippi, strongly defended "Southern Rights;" they wanted ironclad political or constitutional protections for slavery. The fire-eaters—men such as Robert Barnwell Rhett of South Carolina and William Lowndes Yancey of Alabama—repudiated the Union and actively promoted the secession of the southern states. Radical antislavery northerners played into their hands. Senator Seward of New York declared that freedom and slavery were locked in "an irrepressible conflict," and militant abolitionist John Brown showed what that might mean. In October 1859, Brown led eighteen heavily armed black and white men in a raid on the federal arsenal at Harpers Ferry, Virginia. Brown hoped to arm local slaves with the arsenal's weapons and lead a black rebellion that would end slavery and establish a new constitutional regime of racial equality.

Republican leaders condemned Brown's unsuccessful raid, but Democrats called his plot "a natural, logical, inevitable result of the doctrines and teachings of the Republican party." The state of Virginia charged Brown with treason, tried him in court, and sentenced him to be hanged. But transcendentalist reformers Henry David Thoreau and Ralph Waldo Emerson called Brown "an angel of light" and a "saint awaiting his martyrdom," and antislavery northerners leaped to Brown's defense. The slaveholding states looked to the future with fear. "The aim of the present black republican organization is the destruction of the social system of the Southern States, without regard to consequences," warned one newspaper. Once Republicans came to power, another southern paper warned, they "would create insurrection and servile war in the South—they would put the torch to our dwellings and the knife to our throats." Brown predicted as much. As he faced the gallows, Brown apocalyptically warned "that the crimes of this guilty land will never be purged away but with blood."

Nor could the South count on the Democratic Party to protect its interests. At the party's convention in April 1860, northern Democrats rejected Jefferson Davis's proposal to protect slavery in the territories, prompting the delegates from eight southern states to quit the meeting. At a second Democratic convention in Baltimore, northern and midwestern delegates nominated Stephen Douglas for president; meeting separately, southern Democrats nominated the sitting vice president, John C. Breckinridge of Kentucky.

A French Banker Analyzes the Election of 1860 and the Threat of Secession SALOMON DE ROTHSCHILD

Salomon de Rothschild, the son of Baron James de Rothschild of Paris, traveled around the United States from 1859 to 1861. In a series of detailed letters to his cousin Nathaniel in London, Rothschild offered an astute and often cynical analysis of the sectional crisis. Although his comments are generally evenhanded, Rothschild feared social revolution and so favored the South.

You know that the . . . United States was made up of two great parties, the Democrats and the Republicans. These two parties were subdivided into groups, only a few, but extremely violent ones. The abolitionists were the extremist Republicans; the "fire-eaters" or secessionists, the extremist Democrats. Fanaticism and the extremist parties always win out, and, exactly as I expressed my forebodings to you a very long time ago, abolitionism on one side and secession on the other dragged along the moderate neutrals despite themselves.

The point of departure was, as you know, the slavery question. Naturally, this institution, on which the wealth of the South was based, was defended to the limit by those who profited from it. Two reasons pushed the people of the North to seek to destroy slavery by any means. The first . . . was a simple humanitarian reason. In a free country like America, there must be no slaves, and complete equality must reign in all ranks of society. . . . But the real sentiment that guided them . . . was the spirit of leveling; everyone must be equal in abjection. They cannot tolerate someone in the South having 200 arms for his use while they have only their own two. This sentiment was the first seed of the social revolution which is at this very moment taking giant strides behind the political revolution.

You doubtless have read in the newspapers about the first effects of Lincoln's election; . . . several Southern states — Florida, Georgia, Alabama, and Mississippi, with South Carolina as their guide — have for all practical purposes seceded from the United States and are going to form a new confederation. . . .

[A compromise to restore the Union is unlikely, Rothschild writes in another letter, because] the South is simply a producer and consumer; the West and the North, and especially the East, are almost entirely manufacturers, but they need strong [tariff] protection. The South could supply itself with all necessary items in Europe, at prices from twenty-five to forty percent lower. . . . Therefore it wants to escape from this tax. . . . [But] a strong reduction in these duties would completely ruin the eastern states of New Jersey and Pennsylvania, which could not compete with the cheap prices attained by England and even by France. Thousands of men would find themselves unemployed and would therefore threaten the well-being and the very existence not only of their employers, but even of the merchants and the producers in those areas, leading to an imminent danger of social revolution, which the North must avoid at all costs. . . .

The future is as black as it can be. . . .

SOURCE: Sigmund Diamond, ed., *A Casual View of America, 1859–1861: The Home Letters of Salomon de Rothschild* (Stanford, CA: Stanford University Press, 1961), 82–83, 118–119.

With the Democrats divided, the Republicans sensed victory in 1860. They courted white voters with a free-soil platform that opposed both slavery and racial equality: "Missouri for white men and white men for Missouri," declared that state's Republican platform. The national Republican convention chose Lincoln as its presidential candidate because his position on slavery was more moderate than that of the best-known Republicans, Senators William Seward of New York and Salmon Chase of Ohio, who demanded abolition. Lincoln also conveyed a compelling egalitarian image that appealed to small-holding farmers and wage earners. And Lincoln's home territory—the rapidly growing Midwest—was crucial in the competition between Democrats and Republicans.

The Republican strategy worked. Although Lincoln received only 40 percent of the popular vote, he won an absolute majority in the Electoral College by carrying every northern and western state except New Jersey. Douglas took 30 percent of the popular ballot but won electoral votes only in Missouri and New Jersey. Breckinridge captured every state in the Deep South as well as Delaware, Maryland, and North Carolina. Finally, John Bell, a former Tennessee Whig nominated by the compromise-seeking Constitutional Union Party, carried the Upper South states of Kentucky, Tennessee, and Virginia (see Voices from Abroad, p. 403).

The Republicans had united voters in the Northeast, the Midwest, and the Pacific Coast behind free soil and had gained national power. A revolution was in the making. Slavery had permeated the American federal republic for so long and so thoroughly that southerners had come to see it as part of the constitutional order—an order that was now under siege. "I am old enough to remember the horrors of St. Domingo [Haiti]," Chief Justice Taney noted, fearful of a massive black uprising. At the very least, warned John Townsend of South Carolina, a Republican administration in Washington might well suppress "the inter-State slave trade" and thereby "*cripple this vital Southern institution* of slavery." To many southerners, it seemed time to think carefully about Lincoln's statement in 1858 that the Union must "become all one thing, or all the other."

▶ What was Lincoln's position on slavery during the 1850s? Did it differ from that of Stephen Douglas? Explain your answer.

▶ What was the relationship between the collapse of the Second Party System of Whigs and Democrats and the Republican victory in the election of 1860?

▶ Some historians claim that the mistakes of a "Blundering Generation" of political leaders led, by 1860, to the imminent breakup of the Union. Do you agree? Why or why not?

SUMMARY

In this chapter, we examined three related themes: the movement of Americans into Texas and Oregon in the 1830s and 1840s, the causes and consequences of the Mexican war of the late 1840s, and the disintegration of the Second Party System during the 1850s. We saw that the political agendas of Presidents John Tyler and James Polk—their determination to add territory and slave states to the Union—pushed the United States into the Mexican war. The consequences of the war were immense because the acquisition of new territory raised the explosive question of the expansion of slavery.

To resolve the resulting crisis, Henry Clay, Daniel Webster, and Stephen Douglas devised the Compromise of 1850. Their efforts were in vain. Antislavery northerners defied the Fugitive Slave Act, and expansionist-minded southerners sought new slave states in the Caribbean. Ideology (the pursuit of absolutes) replaced politics (the art of compromise) as the ruling principle of American politics.

The Second Party System rapidly disintegrated. The Whig Party vanished, and two issue-oriented parties, the nativist American Party and the antislavery Republican Party, competed for its members. As the Republicans gained strength, the Democratic Party splintered into sectional factions over Bleeding Kansas and other slavery-related issues. The stage was set for Lincoln's victory in the climactic election of 1860.

Connections: Sectionalism

Sectionalism has been an enduring factor in American history. In the seventeenth century, English migrants created distinct societies in the Chesapeake and in New England; after 1700, those regions and that of Middle Atlantic developed along different lines. Then, as we pointed out in the essay that began Part Three, in the early nineteenth century,

> economic revolution and social reform sharpened sectional divisions: The North developed into an urbanizing society based on free labor, whereas the South remained a rural agricultural society dependent on slavery.

As we saw in Chapter 8, the first major conflict between North and South came in 1819–1821 over the admission of Missouri to the Union as a slave state. Then, as we learned in Chapter 10, the conflict over the Tariff of Abominations and Nullification from 1829 to 1832 revived the sectional struggle. Both crises ended with a compromise. As we have just seen, political leaders crafted the Compromise of 1850 to resolve yet another sectional conflict. However, as Chapter 14 will reveal, the crisis sparked by the election of Republican Abraham Lincoln could not be peacefully resolved. Nor did the Union's triumph in the Civil War end sectional strife. As Chapter 15 will demonstrate, Reconstruction created new sectional antagonisms and ended only with the Compromise of 1877—yet another political bargain struck to paper over divisive social differences and conflicts.

FOR FURTHER EXPLORATION

Patricia Nelson Limerick, *The Legacy of Conquest* (1989), offers a provocative analysis of the West; see also **www.pbs.org/thewest**. For California pioneer stories, log onto **lcweb2.loc.gov/ammem/cbhtml/cbhome.html**. On early Texas history, see **www.tsl .state.tx.us/treasures/**. For a dual American and Mexican perspective on the war with Mexico, consult **www.pbs.org/usmexicanwar**.

David Potter, *The Impending Crisis, 1848–1861* (1976), covers political history. For slavery's impact on the crisis, see **www.pbs.org/wgbh/aia/home.html**. Two recent works—John Patrick Daly, *When Slavery Was Called Freedom* (2002), and Leonard L. Richards, *The Slave Power: The Free North and Southern Domination, 1780–1860* (2000)—offer broad cultural analyses. See also William A. Link, *Roots of Secession: Slavery and Politics in Antebellum Virginia* (2003) and Manisha Sinha, *The Counterrevolution of Slavery* (2000).

TIMELINE

1844	▶ James Polk is elected president	**1851**	▶ American (Know-Nothing) Party forms
1845	▶ John Slidell's diplomatic mission fails	**1852**	▶ Harriet Beecher Stowe publishes *Uncle Tom's Cabin*
	▶ Texas is admitted into the Union	**1854**	▶ Ostend Manifesto argues for seizure of Cuba
1846	▶ United States declares war on Mexico		▶ Kansas-Nebraska Act tests popular sovereignty
	▶ Treaty with Britain divides Oregon Country		▶ Republican Party forms
	▶ Wilmot Proviso is approved by House but not by Senate	**1856**	▶ Turmoil in Kansas undermines popular sovereignty
1847	▶ American troops capture Mexico City		▶ James Buchanan is elected president
1848	▶ Gold is discovered in California	**1857**	▶ *Dred Scott v. Sandford* allows slavery in U.S. territories
	▶ In Treaty of Guadalupe Hidalgo, Mexico cedes its provinces of California, New Mexico, and Texas to United States	**1858**	▶ President Buchanan backs Lecompton constitution
	▶ Free-Soil Party forms		▶ Abraham Lincoln and Stephen Douglas debate in U.S. Senate race
1850	▶ Compromise of 1850 seeks to preserve the Union	**1859**	▶ John Brown leads armed raid on federal arsenal at Harpers Ferry
	▶ Northern abolitionists reject Fugitive Slave Act		
	▶ South seeks to acquire Spanish Cuba	**1860**	▶ Abraham Lincoln is elected president in four-way contest

Eric Foner, *Free Soil, Free Labor, Free Men* (1970), probes the ideology of the Republican Party. For an evocative treatment of Lincoln, read Stephen Oates, *With Malice Toward None: A Life of Abraham Lincoln* (1977). The justices' opinions in the *Dred Scott* case are at **odur.let.rug.nl/~usa/D/1851-1875/dredscott/dredxx.htm**; for Lincoln's response, see **www.usconstitution.com/AbrahamLincolnonDredScottDecision.htm**. "*Uncle Tom's Cabin* and American Culture: A Multi-Media Archive" (**jefferson.village .virginia.edu/utc/**) neatly places the novel in its literary and cultural context.

TEST YOUR KNOWLEDGE

To assess your mastery of the material in this chapter and for Web sites, images, and documents related to this chapter, visit **bedfordstmartins.com/henrettaconcise**.

Two Societies at War
1861–1865

No, you dare not make
war on cotton. No power
on earth dares to make
war upon it. Cotton is
king.

— South Carolina Senator James
H. Hammond (1858)

"What a scene it was," Union soldier Elisha Hunt Rhodes wrote in his diary at Gettysburg in July 1863. "Oh the dead and the dying on this bloody field." Thousands of men had already died, and the slaughter would continue for two more years. "What is this all about?" asked Confederate lieutenant R. M. Collins as another gruesome battle ended. "Why is it that 200,000 men of one blood and tongue . . . [are] seeking one another's lives? We could settle our differences by compromising and all be at home in ten days." But there was no compromise, an outcome that President Lincoln found beyond human comprehension. "God wills this contest, and wills that it shall not yet end," he reflected in 1862; even on the eve of victory in 1865, Lincoln confessed his uncertainty: "The Almighty has His own purposes."

To explain why Southerners seceded and then fought to the bitter end is not simple, but racial slavery is an important part of the answer. For southern politicians, the Republican victory in 1860 presented an immediate danger to the slave-owning republic that had existed since 1776. Lincoln won not a single electoral vote in the South, and his Republican Party had vowed to prevent the extension of slavery.

Moreover, Southerners did not believe Lincoln when he promised not "directly or indirectly, to interfere with the institution of slavery in the States where it exists." To the contrary, a southern newspaper declared: "The mission of the Republican party was to meddle with everything — to meddle with the domestic institutions of other States, and to meddle with family arrangements in their own states — to overthrow Democracy, Catholicism and Slavery." Soon, a southern senator warned, "cohorts of Federal office-holders, Abolitionists, may be sent into [our] midst" to mobilize enslaved blacks. The result would be bloody slave revolts and racial intermixture — by which Southerners meant sexual relations between black men and white women, given that white owners had already fathered untold thousands of children by their black women slaves.

"Better, far better! endure all horrors of civil war," insisted a Confederate recruit from Virginia, "than to see the dusky sons of Ham leading the fair daughters of the South to the altar." To preserve black slavery and the supremacy of white men, radical Southerners chose the dangerous enterprise of secession.

Lincoln and the North would not let them go in peace. Living in a world still ruled by kings and princes, northern leaders believed that the collapse of the American Union might destroy for all time the possibility of a democratic republican government. "We cannot escape history," the new president eloquently declared. "We shall nobly save, or meanly lose, the last best hope of earth." A young Union army recruit from Ohio put the issue simply: "If our institutions prove a failure . . . of what value will be house, family, or friends?"

And so came the Civil War. Called the "War Between the States" by Southerners and the "War of the Rebellion" by Northerners, the struggle continued until the great issues of the Union and slavery had finally been resolved. The cost was incredibly high: more lives lost than the combined total in all the nation's other wars and a century-long legacy of bitterness between the triumphant North and the vanquished South.

Fields of Death
Fought with mass armies and new weapons, the Civil War took a huge toll in human lives, as is evidenced by this grisly photograph of a small section of the battlefield at Antietam, Maryland. At Shiloh, Tennessee, General Ulysses Grant surveyed a field "so covered with dead that it would have been possible to walk . . . in any direction, stepping on dead bodies, without a foot touching the ground." Library of Congress.

For more help analyzing this image, see the Online Study Guide at **bedfordstmartins.com/henrettaconcise**.

Secession and Military Stalemate, 1861–1862

After Lincoln was elected in November 1860, secessionist fervor swept through the Deep South. But the veteran party leaders in Washington, who had run the country for a generation, still hoped to save the Union. In the four months between Lincoln's election and his inauguration on March 4, 1861, they struggled to forge a new compromise.

The Secession Crisis

Secession occurred first in South Carolina, the home of John C. Calhoun, Nullification, and Southern Rights. Robert Barnwell Rhett and other fire-eaters had called for secession since the crisis of 1850, and their goal was now within reach. "Our enemies are about to take possession of the Government," warned a South Carolinian, and will act like a "conqueror over a subjugated and craven people." Frightened by that prospect, a special state convention voted unanimously on December 20 to dissolve "the union now subsisting between South Carolina and other States."

Fire-eaters elsewhere in the Deep South quickly called similar conventions and mobilized vigilantes to suppress local Unionists. In early January, white Mississippians joyously enacted a secession ordinance. Within a month, Florida, Alabama, Georgia, Louisiana, and Texas had also left the Union (Map 14.1). In February, the jubilant secessionists met in Montgomery, Alabama, to proclaim a new nation: the Confederate States of America. Adopting a provisional constitution, the delegates named Jefferson Davis of Mississippi, a former U.S. senator and secretary of war, as the Confederacy's president and Alexander Stephens, a congressman from Georgia, as vice president.

Secessionist fervor was less intense in the four states of the Middle South (Virginia, North Carolina, Tennessee, and Arkansas), where there were fewer slaves. White opinion was also sharply divided in the four border slave states (Maryland, Delaware, Kentucky, and Missouri), where yeomen farmers had greater political power. During the 1850s, journalist Hinton Helper of North Carolina had warned yeomen that "the slaveholders . . . have hoodwinked you." Influenced partly by such sentiments, the legislatures of Virginia and Tennessee refused to join the secessionist movement and urged a compromise.

Meanwhile, the Union government floundered. Addressing Congress in December 1860, President Buchanan declared secession illegal. But the president, timid and indecisive, claimed that the federal government lacked authority to restore the Union by force. Buchanan's weakness prompted South Carolina to demand the surrender of Fort Sumter, a federal garrison in Charleston Harbor. When the South Carolinians would not allow a merchant ship to resupply the fort, Buchanan refused to order the navy to escort it into the harbor.

Instead, the outgoing president urged Congress to find a compromise. The plan proposed by Senator John J. Crittenden of Kentucky received the most support. Crittenden's plan had two parts. The first, which Congress approved, called for a constitutional amendment to protect slavery from federal interference in any state where it already existed. Crittenden's second provision called for the westward extension of the Missouri Compromise line (36°30′ north latitude) to the California border. Slavery would be barred north of the line and protected to the south, including any territories

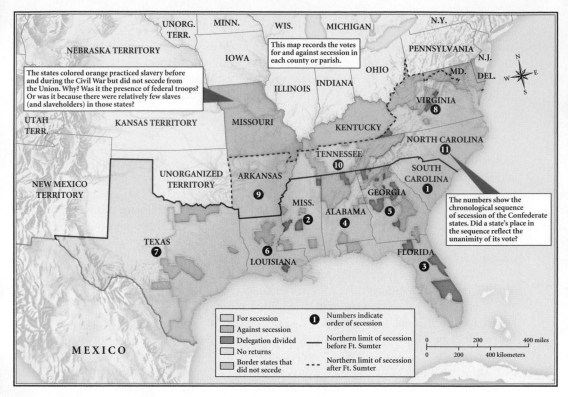

MAP 14.1 The Process of Secession, 1860–1861
The states of the Deep South had the highest concentration of slaves, and they led the secessionist movement. After the attack on Fort Sumter in April 1861, the states of the Middle South joined the Confederacy. Yeomen farmers in Tennessee and the backcountry of Alabama, Georgia, and Virginia opposed secession but, except in the region that became West Virginia, rallied to the Confederate cause. Consequently, the South entered the Civil War with its white population relatively united.

"hereafter acquired," thus raising the prospect of expansion into Cuba or Central America. On strict instructions from President-elect Lincoln, congressional Republicans rejected this part of Crittenden's plan. Lincoln was firmly committed to free soil and — with good reason — feared that this provision would allow new imperialist adventures. Senator Albert G. Brown of Mississippi had candidly stated in 1858: "I want Cuba . . . I want Tamaulipas, Potosi, and one or two other Mexican States; and I want them all . . . for the planting or spreading of slavery." In 1787, 1821, and 1850, the North and South had managed to resolve their differences over slavery. In 1861, there would be no compromise.

In his inaugural address in March 1861, Lincoln carefully outlined his views on slavery and the Union. He promised to safeguard slavery where it existed but vowed to prevent its expansion. Beyond that, Lincoln declared that the Union was "perpetual"; consequently, the secession of the Confederate states was illegal. The Republican president declared his intention to "hold, occupy, and possess" federal property in the seceded states and "to collect duties and imposts" there. If military force was necessary to preserve the Union, Lincoln—like Andrew Jackson during the nullification crisis—would use it. The choice was the South's: Return to the Union or face war.

The Upper South Chooses Sides

The South's decision came quickly. The garrison at Fort Sumter urgently needed food and medicine. Upholding his promise to defend federal property, Lincoln dispatched an unarmed ship to supply the fort. However, Jefferson Davis and his Confederate associates wanted a military confrontation, so Davis demanded the surrender of the fort. Major Robert Anderson refused, and the Confederate forces opened fire on April 12. An ardent fire-eater named Edmund Ruffin supposedly shot off the first cannon. Two days later, the Union defenders capitulated. On April 15, Lincoln called 75,000 state militiamen into federal service for ninety days to put down an insurrection "too powerful to be suppressed by the ordinary course of judicial proceedings."

Northerners responded to Lincoln's call to arms with wild enthusiasm. Asked to provide thirteen regiments of volunteers, Republican governor William Dennison of Ohio sent twenty regiments. Many northern Democrats supported the Union. "Every man must be for the United States or against it," Democratic leader Stephen Douglas declared. "There can be no neutrals in this war, only patriots—or traitors." How then might the Democratic Party function as a "loyal opposition," supporting the Union while challenging many of Lincoln's policies? It would not be an easy task.

Whites in the Middle and Border South now had to choose between the Union and the Confederacy, and their decision was crucial. Those eight states accounted for two-thirds of the South's white population, more than three-fourths of its industrial production, and well over half of its food. They were home to many of the nation's best military leaders, including Colonel Robert E. Lee of Virginia, a career officer whom veteran General Winfield Scott recommended to Lincoln to lead the new Union army. These states were also geographically strategic. Kentucky, with its 500-mile border on the Ohio River, was essential to the movement of troops and supplies. Maryland was vital to the Union's security because it bordered the nation's capital on three sides.

The weight of history decided the outcome in Virginia, the original home of American slavery. Three days after the fall of Fort Sumter, a Virginia convention approved secession by a vote of 88 to 55, the dissenters being drawn mainly from the yeomen-dominated northwestern counties. Elsewhere, Virginia whites rallied to the Confederate cause. "The North was the aggressor," declared Richmond lawyer William Poague as he enlisted. "The South resisted her invaders." Refusing Scott's offer of the Union command, Robert E. Lee resigned from the U.S. Army. "Save in defense of my native state," Lee told Scott, "I never desire again to draw my sword." Arkansas, Tennessee, and North Carolina quickly joined Virginia in the Confederacy.

Lincoln moved aggressively to hold the states of the Border South, where relatively few families owned slaves. To secure the railway line connecting Washington to the Ohio River Valley, the president ordered General George B. McClellan to take control of northwestern Virginia. In October 1861, yeomen voters there overwhelmingly approved the creation of a separate breakaway territory, West Virginia, which was admitted to the Union in 1863. Unionists easily carried the day in Delaware but not in Maryland, where slavery was still entrenched. A pro-Confederate mob attacked

Massachusetts troops traveling through Baltimore, causing the war's first combat deaths: four soldiers and twelve civilians. When Maryland secessionists destroyed railroad bridges and telegraph lines, Lincoln ordered Union troops to occupy the state and arrest Confederate sympathizers, including legislators. He released them only in November 1861, after Unionists had secured control of Maryland's government.

Lincoln was equally energetic and resourceful in the Southwest. To win Missouri (and control of the Missouri and upper Mississippi rivers), Lincoln mobilized the German American militia, which strongly opposed slavery; in July, it defeated a force of Confederate sympathizers commanded by the state's governor. Despite continuing raids by Confederate guerrilla bands, the Union retained control of Missouri (see Voices from Abroad, p. 413). In Kentucky, secessionist and Unionist sentiment was evenly balanced, so Lincoln moved cautiously. He allowed Kentucky's thriving trade with the Confederacy to continue until August, when Unionists took over the state government. When the Confederacy responded to the cutoff of trade by invading Kentucky in September, Illinois volunteers commanded by Ulysses S. Grant drove them out. Mixing military force with political persuasion, Lincoln had kept four border states (Delaware, Maryland, Missouri, and Kentucky) and the northwestern portion of Virginia in the Union.

Setting War Objectives and Devising Strategies

In his first speeches as President of the Confederacy, Jefferson Davis identified the Confederates' cause with that of the Americans of 1776: Like their grandfathers, white Southerners were fighting for the "sacred right of self-government." The Confederacy sought "no conquest, no aggrandizement . . . ; all we ask is to be let alone." Davis's implicit renunciation of western expansion was ironic, because it was the slave owners' quest to extend slavery that had sparked Lincoln's election and southern secession. Still, this decision simplified the Confederacy's military strategy; it needed only to defend its boundaries to achieve independence as a slave-owning republic. Ignoring the strong antislavery sentiment among potential European allies, the Confederate constitution explicitly ruled out gradual emancipation or any other law "denying or impairing the right of property in negro slaves." Confederate Vice President Alexander Stephens insisted that his nation's "cornerstone rests upon the great truth that the Negro is not equal to the white man, that slavery—subordination to the superior race—is his natural or normal condition."

Lincoln responded to Davis in a speech to Congress on July 4, 1861. Portraying secession as an attack on popular government, America's great contribution to world history, Lincoln saw the struggle as a test of "whether a constitutional republic . . . [can] maintain its territorial integrity against a domestic foe." Determined to crush the rebellion, Lincoln rejected General Winfield Scott's strategy of peaceful persuasion through economic sanctions and a naval blockade. Instead, the president insisted on an aggressive military campaign and a policy of unconditional surrender.

Lincoln hoped that a quick strike against the Confederate capital of Richmond, Virginia, would end the rebellion. Many Northerners were equally optimistic. "What a picnic," thought one New York volunteer, "to go down South for three months and clean up the whole business." So in July 1861, Lincoln ordered General Irvin McDowell and an army of 30,000 men to attack General P. G. T. Beauregard's force of 20,000 troops at Manassas, a rail junction in Virginia 30 miles southwest of Washington.

German Immigrants and the Civil War Within Missouri ERNEST DUVERGIER DE HAURANNE

Thousands of German immigrants settled in Missouri in the two decades before the Civil War; and as this letter written by Ernest Duvergier de Hauranne indicates, most of them supported the Union cause. Duvergier de Hauranne (1843–1877), a Frenchman, traveled widely, and his letters home offer intelligent commentary on American politics and society.

St. Louis, September 12, 1864

Missouri is to all intents and purposes a rebel state, an occupied territory where the Federal forces are really nothing but a garrison under siege; even today it is not certain what would happen if the troops were withdrawn. Party quarrels here are poisoned by class hatreds. . . . The old Anglo-French families, attached to Southern institutions, harbor a primitive, superstitious prejudice in favor of slavery. Conquered now, but full of repressed rage, they exhibit the implacable anger peculiar to the defenders of lost causes.

The more recent German population is strongly abolitionist. They have brought to the New World the instincts of European democracy, together with its radical attitudes and all-or-nothing doctrines. Ancient precedents and worn-out laws matter little to them. They have not studied history and have no respect for hallowed injustices; but they do have, to the highest degree, that sense of moral principle which is more or less lacking in American democracy. They aren't afraid of revolution: to destroy a barbarous institution they would, if necessary, take an axe to the foundations of society.

Furthermore, their interests coincide with their principles. . . . The immigrant arrives poor and lives by his work. A newcomer, having nothing to lose and caring little for the interests of established property owners, sees that the subjection of free labor to the ruinous competition of slave labor must be ended. At the same time, his pride rebels against the prejudice attached to work in a land of slavery; he wants to reestablish its value. . . .

There is no mistaking the hatred the two parties, not to say the two peoples, have for each other. . . . As passions were coming to a boil, the Federal government sent General [John C.] Frémont here as army commander and dictator. . . . An abolitionist and a self-made man, he put himself firmly at the head of the German party, determined to crush the friends of slavery. . . . He left the abolitionist party in the West organized, disciplined, stronger and more resolute, but he also left the pro-Southern party more exasperated than ever, and society divided, without intermediaries, into two hostile camps . . . .

Bands of guerrillas hold the countryside, where they raid as much as they please; politics serves as a fine pretext for looting. Their leaders are officers from the army of the South who receive their orders from the Confederate government. . . . These "bushwackers," who ordinarily rob indiscriminately, maintain their standing as political raiders by occasionally killing some poor, inoffensive person. . . . You can see what emotions are still boiling in this region that is supposed to be pacified.

SOURCE: Ernest Duvergier de Hauranne, *A Frenchman in Lincoln's America* (Chicago: Lakeside Press, 1974), 1: 305–309.

McDowell launched a strong assault near Manassas Creek (also called Bull Run), but panic swept his troops when the Confederate soldiers counterattacked, shouting the hair-raising rebel yell. "The peculiar corkscrew sensation that it sends down your backbone under these circumstances can never be told," one Union veteran wrote. "You have to feel it." McDowell's troops — along with the many civilians who had come to observe the battle — retreated in disarray to Washington.

The rout at Bull Run made it clear that the rebellion would not be easily crushed. Lincoln replaced McDowell with General McClellan and enlisted an additional million men, who would serve for three years in the newly created Army of the Potomac. A cautious military engineer, McClellan spent the winter of 1861 training the recruits; then, early in 1862, he launched a major offensive. With great logistical skill, the Union general transported 100,000 troops by boat down the Potomac River to the Chesapeake Bay and landed them on the peninsula between the York and James rivers (Map 14.2). Ignoring Lincoln's advice to "strike a blow" quickly, McClellan advanced slowly toward the South's capital, allowing the Confederates to mount a counterstroke. To relieve the pressure on Richmond, a Confederate army under Thomas J. "Stonewall" Jackson marched rapidly northward through the Shenandoah Valley in western Virginia and threatened Washington. Lincoln recalled 30,000 troops from McClellan's army to protect the Union's capital, and Jackson returned quickly to Richmond to bolster the main Confederate army commanded by General Robert E. Lee. Lee launched a ferocious attack that lasted for days (from June 25 to July 1), in which the Confederates suffered 20,000 casualties to the Union's 10,000. When McClellan failed to exploit the Confederates' losses, Lincoln ordered a withdrawal, and Richmond remained secure.

Hoping for victories that would humiliate Lincoln's government, Lee went on the offensive. Joining with Jackson in northern Virginia, he routed Union troops in the Second Battle of Bull Run (August 1862) and then struck north through western Maryland. There, he nearly met with disaster. When Lee divided his force, sending Jackson to capture Harpers Ferry in West Virginia, a copy of Lee's orders fell into McClellan's hands. But the Union general again failed to exploit his advantage. He delayed his attack, allowing Lee's depleted army to occupy a strong defensive position behind Antietam Creek, near Sharpsburg, Maryland. Outnumbered 87,000 to 50,000, Lee desperately fought off McClellan's attacks until Jackson's troops arrived and saved the Confederates from a major defeat. Appalled by the number of Union casualties, McClellan allowed Lee to retreat to Virginia.

The fighting at Antietam was savage. A Wisconsin officer described his men "loading and firing with demoniacal fury and shouting and laughing hysterically." A sunken road — nicknamed Bloody Lane — was filled with Confederate bodies two and three deep, and the advancing Union troops knelt on "this ghastly flooring" to shoot at the retreating Confederates. The battle at Antietam on September 17, 1862, remains the bloodiest single day in U.S. military history. Together, the Confederate and Union dead numbered 4,800 and the wounded 18,500, of whom 3,000 soon died. (By comparison, there were 6,000 American casualties on D-Day, which began the invasion of Nazi-occupied France in World War II.)

In public, Lincoln claimed Antietam as a Union victory; privately, he criticized McClellan for not fighting Lee to the bitter end. A masterful organizer of men and supplies, McClellan lacked the stomach for all-out warfare. Lincoln dismissed McClellan as his chief commander and began what turned out to be a long search for an effective

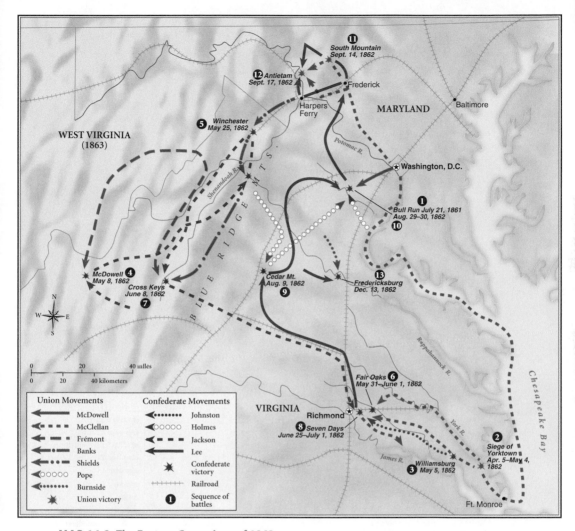

MAP 14.2 The Eastern Campaigns of 1862
Many of the great battles of the Civil War took place in the 125 miles separating the Union capital, Washington, D.C., and the Confederate capital, Richmond, Virginia. During 1862, Confederate generals Thomas J. "Stonewall" Jackson and Robert E. Lee won defensive victories that protected the Confederate capital (3, 6, 8, and 13) and launched offensive strikes against Union forces guarding Washington (1, 4, 5, 7, 9, and 10). They also suffered a defeat — at Antietam (12), in Maryland — that was almost fatal. The victors in these battles were usually either too bloodied or too timid to exploit their advantage.

replacement. His first choice was Ambrose E. Burnside, who proved to be more daring but less competent than McClellan. In December, after heavy losses in futile attacks against well-entrenched Confederate forces at Fredericksburg, Virginia, Burnside resigned his command, and Lincoln replaced him with Joseph "Fighting Joe" Hooker. As 1862 ended, the Confederates were optimistic: They had won a stalemate in the East.

In the West, Union commanders were more successful (Map 14.3). Their goal was to control the Ohio, Mississippi, and Missouri rivers, dividing the Confederacy and reducing

MAP 14.3 The Western Campaigns, 1861–1862

As the Civil War intensified in 1862, Union and Confederate military and naval forces fought to control the great valleys of the Ohio, Tennessee, and Mississippi rivers. From February through April 1862, Union armies moved south through western Tennessee (1–3 and 5). By the end of June, Union naval forces controlled the Mississippi River north of Memphis (4, 10, and 11) and from the Gulf of Mexico to Vicksburg (6, 7, 9, and 12). These military and naval victories gave the Union control of crucial transportation routes, kept Missouri in the Union, and carried the war to the borders of the states of the Deep South.

the mobility of its armies. Because Kentucky did not join the rebellion, the Union already dominated the Ohio River Valley. In 1862, the Union army launched innovative land and water operations to take charge of the Tennessee and Mississippi rivers as well. General Ulysses S. Grant used riverboats clad with iron plates to capture Fort Henry on the Tennessee River and Fort Donelson on the Cumberland River. When Grant moved south to seize critical railroad lines, a Confederate army led by Albert Sidney Johnston and P. G. T. Beauregard caught him by surprise near a small log church named Shiloh. But Grant relentlessly committed troops until he forced a Confederate withdrawal. As the fighting at Shiloh ended on April 7, Grant surveyed a large field "so covered with dead that it would have been possible to walk over the clearing in any direction, stepping on dead bodies, without a foot touching the ground." The cost in lives was high, but Lincoln was pleased: "What I want . . . is generals who will fight battles and win victories."

Three weeks later, Union naval forces commanded by David G. Farragut struck the Confederacy from the Gulf of Mexico. They captured New Orleans and took control of 1,500 plantations and 50,000 slaves in the surrounding region. The Union now held the South's financial center and largest city and had struck a strong blow against slavery. Workers on many plantations looted their owners' mansions and refused to labor unless they were paid wages. Slavery there "is forever destroyed and worthless," declared one Northern reporter. Union victories in the West had significantly undermined Confederate strength in the Mississippi River Valley.

> ▶ Why was there no new compromise over slavery in 1861? How important was the conflict at Fort Sumter? Would the Confederacy — and the Union — have decided to go to war in any event?
>
> ▶ In the first years of the war, what were the political and military strategies of each side? Which side was the more successful? Why?

Toward Total War

The military carnage in 1862 revealed that the war would be long and costly. After Shiloh, Grant later remarked, he "gave up all idea of saving the Union except by complete conquest." The Civil War increasingly resembled the **total wars** that would come in the twentieth century, conflicts that drew on the entire resources of the society and made civilian lives and property legitimate objects of attack. Aided by the Republican Party and a talented cabinet, Lincoln skillfully organized an effective central government and promoted ruthless generals prepared to wage all-out war. Jefferson Davis had less success at harnessing the resources of the South, because the eleven states of the Confederacy remained suspicious of centralized rule and southern yeomen grew increasingly skeptical of the war effort.

Mobilizing Armies and Civilians

Initially, patriotic fervor filled both armies with eager young volunteers. All he heard "was War! War! War!" recalled one Union recruit. Even those of sober minds joined up. "I don't think a young man ever went over all the considerations more carefully than I did," reflected William Saxton of Cincinnatus, New York. "It might mean sickness, wounds, loss of limb, and even life itself. . . . But my country was in danger." The call for volunteers was equally successful in the South, which boasted a strong military tradition, a supply of trained officers, and a culture that stressed duty and honor. "Would you, My Darling, . . . be willing to leave your Children under such a [despotic Union] government?" James B. Griffin of Edgefield, South Carolina, asked his wife. "No—I know you would sacrifice every comfort on earth, rather than submit to it." However, enlistments declined as potential recruits learned the realities of mass warfare: heavy losses to epidemic diseases in the camps and wholesale death on the battlefields. Both governments soon faced the need for conscription.

The Confederacy was the first to act. In April 1862, following the bloodshed at Shiloh, the Confederate Congress imposed the first legally binding draft in American history. Laws extended existing enlistments for the duration of the war and required three years of military service from all men between the ages of eighteen and thirty-five. In September 1862, after the heavy casualties at Antietam, the Confederacy raised the age limit to forty-five. The South's draft had two loopholes, both controversial. First, it exempted one white man—the planter, a son, or an overseer—for each twenty slaves, allowing some whites on large plantations to avoid military service. This provision, Mississippi Senator James Phelan warned Jefferson Davis, "has aroused a sprit of rebellion in some places." Second, draftees could hire substitutes. By the time this loophole was closed in 1864, the price of a substitute had risen to $300 in gold, three times the annual wage of a skilled worker. Laborers and yeomen farmers angrily complained that it was "a rich man's war and a poor man's fight."

Consequently, some Southerners refused to serve. Because the Confederate constitution vested sovereignty in the individual states, the government in Richmond could not compel military service. Strong governors such as Joseph Brown of Georgia and Zebulon Vance of North Carolina simply ignored President Davis's first draft call in early 1862. Elsewhere, state judges issued writs of **habeas corpus**—a legal instrument used to protect people from arbitrary arrest—and ordered the Confederate army to release reluctant draftees. However, the Confederate Congress overrode the judges' authority to free conscripted men, so the government was able to keep substantial armies in the field well into 1864.

The Union government acted more ruthlessly toward reluctant recruits and potential foes. To deter resistance by Confederate sympathizers, Lincoln suspended habeas corpus and, over the course of the war, imprisoned about 15,000 people without trial. The president also placed civilians who discouraged enlistments or resisted the draft under the jurisdiction of military courts, preventing acquittals by sympathetic local juries. But Union governments primarily used incentives to fill the ranks. When the Militia Act of 1862 set local recruitment quotas, many states, counties, and towns avoided conscription by using cash bounties of as much as $600 (about $11,000 today) and signed up nearly one million men. The Union also allowed men to avoid military service by providing a substitute or paying a $300 fee.

When the Enrollment Act of 1863 finally initiated conscription in the North, recent German and Irish immigrants often refused to serve. It was not their war, they said. Northern Democrats used the furor over conscription to bolster support for their party, which took an increasingly critical stance toward Lincoln's policies. Using racist invective, they accused Lincoln of drafting poor whites to free blacks, who would flood the cities and take their jobs. "Slavery is dead," declared a Democratic newspaper in Cincinnati, "the negro is not, there is the misfortune." In July 1863, the immigrants' hostility brought violence to New York City. For five days, Irish and German workers ran rampant, burning draft offices, sacking the homes of influential Republicans, and attacking the police. The rioters lynched and mutilated a dozen African Americans, drove hundreds of black families from their homes, and burned down the Colored Orphan Asylum. Lincoln rushed in Union troops who had just fought at Gettysburg; they killed more than one hundred rioters and suppressed the immigrant mobs.

The Union government won greater support among native-born middle-class citizens. In 1861, prominent New Yorkers established the U.S. Sanitary Commission to provide medical services and prevent the spread of epidemic diseases among the troops. Through its network of 7,000 local auxiliaries, the commission collected clothing and food. "I almost weep," reported a local agent, "when these plain rural people come to send their simple offerings to absent sons and brothers." The Commission also recruited battlefield nurses and doctors for the Union Army Medical Bureau. Despite these efforts, dysentery, typhoid, and malaria spread through the camps, as did mumps and measles, viruses that were dangerous to nonimmune rural recruits. Diseases and infections killed about 250,000 Union soldiers, roughly twice the number who died in combat. Still, thanks to the Sanitary Commission, Union troops had a much lower mortality rate than did the soldiers in nineteenth-century European wars. Confederate armies were less fortunate. Thousands of women volunteered as nurses, but the Confederate health system was poorly organized. Scurvy was a special problem for southern soldiers, who lacked vitamin C in their diets, and they died from camp diseases at a high rate.

War relief had a significant impact on women's lives. More than 200,000 northern women worked as volunteers in the Sanitary Commission and the Freedman's Aid Society, which collected supplies for liberated slaves, and some women took leading roles in wartime agencies. Dorothea Dix (see Chapter 11) served as superintendent of

Hospital Nursing
Working as nurses in battlefront hospitals, thousands of Union and Confederate women gained firsthand experience of the horrors of war. A sense of calm prevails in this behind-the-lines Union hospital in Nashville, Tennessee, as nurse Anne Belle tends to the needs of soldiers recovering from their wounds. Most Civil War nurses were volunteers; they spent time cooking and cleaning for their patients as well as tending their injuries. U.S. Army Military History Institute.

female nurses and, by successfully combating the prejudice against women's providing medical treatment to men, opened a new occupation to women. Thousands of educated Union women became clerks in the expanding government bureaucracy, while southern women staffed the efficient Confederate postal service. In both societies, millions of women assumed new economic responsibilities. They took over many farm tasks; filled jobs in schools and offices; and served as operatives in textile, shoe, and food-processing factories. A few women even took on military duties as spies, scouts, and (disguising themselves as men) soldiers. As nurse Clara Barton, who later founded the American Red Cross, recalled, "At the war's end, woman was at least fifty years in advance of the normal position which continued peace would have assigned her."

Mobilizing Resources

Wars are usually won by the side that has greater resources and better economic organization. In this regard, the Union had a distinct advantage. With nearly two-thirds of the nation's population, two-thirds of the railroad mileage, and almost 90 percent of the industrial output, the North's economy was far superior to the South's. The North had a great advantage in the manufacture of cannon and rifles because many of its arms factories were equipped for mass production.

But the Confederate position was far from weak. Virginia, North Carolina, and Tennessee had substantial industrial capacity. Richmond, with its Tredegar Iron Works, was already an important manufacturing center, and in 1861, the city received the gun-making machinery from the U.S. armory at Harpers Ferry. The production at the Richmond armory, the purchase of Enfield rifles from Britain, and the capture of 100,000 Union guns enabled the Confederacy to provide every infantryman with a modern rifle-musket by 1863.

Moreover, with nine million people, the Confederacy could mobilize enormous armies. The one-third of Southerners who were slaves contributed to the war effort by producing food for the army and cotton for export. Confederate leaders counted on **"King Cotton"** to provide the revenue to purchase clothes, boots, blankets, and weapons from abroad. They also intended to use cotton as a diplomatic weapon to persuade Britain and France, whose textile factories needed raw cotton, to grant the Confederacy diplomatic recognition. However, British manufacturers had stockpiled cotton, and they found new sources in Egypt and India. Still, the South's hope was partially fulfilled. Although Britain never recognized the Confederacy as an independent nation, it granted the rebel government the status of a belligerent power—with the right under international law to borrow money and purchase weapons. The odds, then, did not necessarily favor the Union, despite its superior resources.

To mobilize northern resources, the Republican-dominated Congress enacted a program of government-assisted economic development that far surpassed Henry Clay's American System. The Republicans imposed huge tariffs (averaging nearly 40 percent) on various foreign goods, thereby winning the political support of northeastern manufacturers and workers. They also provided northern and midwestern farmers with "free land." The Homestead Act of 1862 gave settlers the title to 160 acres of public land after five years of residence. Secretary of the Treasury Salmon P. Chase created an integrated national banking system (far more powerful than the First and

Second Banks of the United States) by forcing thousands of local banks to accept federal charters and regulations. Finally, the Republican Congress implemented Clay's program for a nationally financed system of internal improvements. In 1862, it chartered the Union Pacific and Central Pacific companies to build a transcontinental railroad line and granted them lavish subsidies. This comprehensive economic program won the Republican Party the allegiance of farmers, workers, and entrepreneurs and bolstered the Union's ability to fight a long war.

New industries sprang up to meet the army's need for guns, clothes, and food. More than 1.5 million men served in the Union army, and they consumed more than half a billion pounds of pork and other packed meats. To meet this demand, Chicago railroads built new lines to carry thousands of hogs and cattle to the city's ever-larger stockyards and slaughtering houses. By 1862, Chicago had passed Cincinnati as the meatpacking capital of the nation, bringing prosperity to thousands of midwestern farmers and great wealth to Philip D. Armour and other meatpacking entrepreneurs.

A similar concentration of capital occurred in many industries. The war, an observer noted, gave a few men "the command of millions of money"; such massed financial power threatened not only the prewar society of small producers but also the future of democracy. Americans "are never again to see the republic in which we were born," lamented abolitionist and social reformer Wendell Phillips.

The Confederate government took longer to develop a coherent economic policy. True to its states' rights philosophy, the Confederacy initially left most economic matters to the state governments. However, as the realities of total war became clear, the Davis administration took some extraordinary measures: It built and operated shipyards, armories, foundries, and textile mills; commandeered food and scarce raw materials such as coal, iron, copper, and lead; requisitioned slaves to work on fortifications; and exercised direct control over foreign trade. Ordinary southern citizens increasingly resented and resisted these measures by the central government in Richmond, forcing Confederate leaders to rely increasingly on white solidarity: President Davis warned that a Union victory would destroy slavery "and reduce the whites to the degraded position of the African race."

For both sides, the cost of fighting a total war was enormous. The annual spending of the Union government shot up from $63 million in 1860 to more than $865 million in 1864. To raise that enormous sum, the Republicans established a powerful modern state that secured funds in three ways. First, the government increased tariffs; placed high excise duties on alcohol and tobacco; and imposed direct taxes on business corporations, large inheritances, and incomes. These levies paid for about 20 percent of the cost. Treasury bonds financed another 65 percent. The National Banking Acts of 1863 and 1864 forced most banks to buy and hold those bonds; and Jay Cooke, a Philadelphia banker working for the Treasury Department, used newspaper ads and 2,500 subagents to persuade nearly one million northern families to buy them.

The Union paid the remaining cost of the war by printing paper money. The Legal Tender Act of 1862 authorized $150 million in paper currency—which soon became known as **greenbacks**—and required the public to accept them as legal tender. Like the Continental currency issued during the Revolution, the greenbacks were not backed by specie; but they were issued in relatively limited amounts and so did not depreciate disastrously in value. By imposing broad-based taxes, borrowing from the middle classes, and creating a national monetary system, the Union government had created a modern fiscal state.

The financial demands on the South were equally great, but it lacked a powerful central government that could tax and borrow. The Confederate Congress fiercely opposed taxes on cotton exports and slaves, the most valuable property held by wealthy planters; and the urban middle class and yeomen farm families refused to bear the entire tax burden. Consequently, the Confederacy covered less than 5 percent of its expenditures through taxation. The government paid for another 35 percent by borrowing, although wealthy planters and foreign bankers grew increasingly wary of investing in Confederate bonds that might never be redeemed.

So the Confederacy had to pay about 60 percent of its expenses by printing paper money. The flood of currency created a spectacular inflation: By 1865, prices had risen to ninety-two times their 1861 level. As the vast supply of money (and a shortage of goods) caused food prices to soar, riots broke out in more than a dozen southern cities and towns. In Richmond, several hundred women broke into bakeries, crying, "Our children are starving while the rich roll in wealth." In Randolph County, Alabama, women confiscated grain from a government warehouse "to prevent starvation of themselves and their families." As inflation increased, Southerners refused to accept Confederate money, sometimes with serious consequences. When South Carolina storekeeper Jim Harris rejected the currency presented by a group of soldiers, they raided his storehouse and "robbed it of about five thousand dollars worth of goods." Army supply officers likewise seized goods from merchants and offered payment in worthless IOUs. Facing a public that feared strong government and high taxation, the Confederacy could sustain the war effort only by seizing its citizens' property.

▶ Which government — the Union or the Confederacy — imposed greater military and economic burdens on its citizens? How successful were their respective strategies?

▶ What were the main economic policies enacted by the Republican-controlled Congress?

The Turning Point: 1863

By 1863, the Lincoln administration had finally created an efficient war machine, an integrated financial system, and a set of strategic priorities. Henry Adams, the grandson of John Quincy Adams and a future novelist and important historian, noted the change from his diplomatic post in London: "Little by little, one began to feel that, behind the chaos in Washington power was taking shape; that it was massed and guided as it had not been before." Slowly but surely, the tide of the struggle shifted toward the Union.

Emancipation

When the war began, antislavery Republicans demanded that their party make abolition — as well as restoration of the Union — a goal of the war. The fighting should continue, declared a Massachusetts abolitionist, "until the Slave power is completely subjugated, and *emancipation made certain*." Because slave-grown crops sustained the Confederacy, activists justified black emancipation on military grounds. As Frederick Douglass put it, "Arrest that hoe in the hands of the Negro, and you smite the rebellion in the very seat of its life."

As abolitionists pressed their case, enslaved African Americans exploited the disorder of wartime to seize freedom for themselves. When three slaves reached the camp of General Benjamin Butler in Virginia in May 1861, he labeled them "contraband of war" (a term for goods that can be legitimately seized, according to international law) and refused to return them. Butler's term stuck, and within a few months, thousands of "contrabands" were camping with Union armies. Near Fredericksburg, Virginia, an average of 200 blacks appeared every day, "with their packs on their backs and handkerchiefs tied over their heads—men, women, little children, and babies." To provide these fugitives with legal status, Congress passed the Confiscation Act in August 1861, authorizing the seizure of all property, including slaves, used to support the rebellion.

Radical Republicans—Treasury Secretary Salmon Chase, Senator Charles Sumner of Massachusetts, and Representative Thaddeus Stevens of Pennsylvania—now saw a way to use wartime legislation to destroy slavery. A longtime member of Congress, Stevens was a masterful politician, skilled at fashioning legislation that could win majority support. In April 1862, Stevens and the Radicals persuaded Congress to end slavery in the District of Columbia by providing compensation for owners. In June, Congress outlawed slavery in the federal territories (finally enacting the Wilmot Proviso of 1846); and in July, it passed a second Confiscation Act. This act overrode the property rights of Confederate planters by declaring "forever free" all fugitive slaves and all slaves captured by the Union army. Emancipation had become an instrument of war.

Initially, Lincoln had rejected emancipation as a war aim, but faced with thousands of contrabands and Radical Republican pressure, he moved cautiously toward that goal. In July 1862, Lincoln drafted a general proclamation of emancipation, and in August, he wrote a public letter to Horace Greeley of the *New York Tribune* linking black freedom to the war effort. "If I could save the Union without freeing any slave, I would do it," the president stated, "and if I could save it by freeing all the slaves, I would do it." By implicitly raising the issues of military necessity and his constitutional authority, Lincoln was laying the foundation for the destruction of slavery.

Now he waited for a Union victory. Considering the Battle of Antietam "an indication of the Divine Will," Lincoln issued the proclamation of emancipation five days later, on September 22, 1862. The president based its legal authority on his responsibility as commander in chief to suppress the rebellion. The proclamation stated that slavery would be legally abolished in all states that remained out of the Union on January 1, 1863. The rebel states could preserve slavery by renouncing secession. None chose to do so.

The proclamation was politically astute. Lincoln wanted to avoid opposition from slave owners in the Union-controlled border states, such as Maryland and Missouri, so the proclamation left slavery intact in those states. It also permitted slavery to continue in areas occupied by Union armies: western and central Tennessee, western Virginia, and southern Louisiana. Consequently, the Emancipation Proclamation did not immediately free a single slave. Yet, as abolitionist Wendell Phillips understood, Lincoln's proclamation had moved slavery to "the edge of Niagara," and it would soon be swept over the brink. Advancing Union troops became the agents of slavery's destruction. "I became free in 1863, in the summer, when the yankees come by and said I could go work for myself," recalled Jackson Daniel of Maysville, Alabama. As Lincoln now saw it, "the old South is to be destroyed and replaced by new propositions and ideas."

Emancipation was extraordinarily controversial. In the Confederacy, Jefferson Davis labeled it the "most execrable measure recorded in the history of guilty man"; in the North, it produced a racist backlash among white voters. During the congressional election of 1862, the Democrats denounced emancipation as unconstitutional, warned of slave uprisings, and claimed that freed blacks would take white jobs. If slaves became free, a nativist New Yorker suggested, "every one" of them should "shoulder an Irishman and leave the Continent." Such sentiments propelled Democrat Horatio Seymour into the governor's office in New York; if abolition was a war goal, Seymour argued, the South should not be conquered. Other Democrats swept to victory in Pennsylvania, Ohio, and Illinois, and the party gained thirty-four seats in Congress. But the Republicans still held a twenty-five-seat majority in the House and had gained five seats in the Senate. Lincoln refused to retreat. On New Year's Day 1863, he signed the Emancipation Proclamation. To reassure Northerners, Lincoln urged slaves to "abstain from all violence" and justified emancipation as an "act of justice." "If my name ever goes into history," he said, "it was for this act."

Vicksburg and Gettysburg

The fate of the proclamation would depend on Republican political success and Union military victories. The outlook was not encouraging on either front. Democrats had gained significantly in the election of 1862, and popular support was growing for a negotiated peace. Two brilliant victories in Virginia by Lee, whose army defeated Hooker's forces at Fredericksburg (December 1862) and Chancellorsville (May 1863), further eroded northern support for the war.

At this critical juncture, General Grant mounted a major offensive in the West to split the Confederacy in two. Grant drove south along the west bank of the Mississippi and then crossed the river near Vicksburg, Mississippi. There, he defeated two Confederate armies and laid siege to the city. After repelling Union assaults for six weeks, the exhausted and starving Vicksburg garrison surrendered on July 4, 1863. Five days later, Union forces took Port Hudson, Louisiana (near Baton Rouge), and seized control of the Mississippi River. Grant had taken 31,000 prisoners; cut off Louisiana, Arkansas, and Texas from the rest of the Confederacy; and prompted thousands of slaves to desert their plantations or demand wages.

As Grant had advanced toward Mississippi in May, Confederate leaders had argued over the best strategic response. President Davis and other politicians wanted to reinforce Vicksburg and send an army to Tennessee to relieve pressure on Mississippi. But General Robert E. Lee, buoyed by his victories over Hooker, favored a new invasion of the North. That strategy, Lee suggested, would either draw Grant's forces to the east or give the Confederacy a major victory that would destroy the North's will to fight.

MAP 14.4 Lee Invades the North, 1863
After Lee's victories at Chancellorsville (1) in May and Brandy Station (2) in June, the Confederate forces moved northward, constantly shadowed by the Union army. On July 1, the two armies met accidentally near Gettysburg. In the ensuing battle (3), the Union army, commanded by General George Meade, emerged victorious, primarily because it was much larger than the Confederate force and held well-fortified positions along Cemetery Ridge, which gave its units a major tactical advantage.

Lee won out. In June 1863, he maneuvered his army north through Maryland into Pennsylvania. The Army of the Potomac moved along with him, positioning itself between Lee and Washington, D.C. On July 1, the two great armies met by accident at Gettysburg, Pennsylvania, in what became a decisive confrontation (Map 14.4). On the first day of battle, Lee drove the Union's advance guard to the south of town. General George G. Meade, who had just replaced Hooker as the Union commander, placed his troops in well-defended hilltop positions and called up reinforcements. By the morning of July 2, Meade had 90,000 troops to Lee's 75,000. Aware that he was outnumbered but intent on victory, Lee ordered assaults on Meade's flanks but failed to turn them. General Richard B. Ewell refused to risk his men in an all-out assault on the Union's right flank, and General Longstreet, on the Union's left, failed to dislodge Meade's forces from the hill known as Little Round Top.

On July 3, Lee decided on a dangerous frontal assault against the center of the Union line. After the heaviest artillery barrage of the war, Lee ordered General George E. Pickett and his 14,000 men to take Cemetery Ridge. Anticipating this attack, Meade had reinforced his line with artillery and his best troops. When Pickett's men charged across a mile of open terrain, they were met by deadly fire from artillery and rifle-muskets; thousands were killed, wounded, or captured. As the three-day battle ended, the Confederates had suffered 28,000 casualties, one-third of the Army of Northern Virginia, while 23,000 of Meade's soldiers lay killed or wounded. Shocked by the bloodletting, Meade allowed the Confederate units to escape. Lincoln was furious. "As it is," the president brooded, "the war will be prolonged indefinitely."

Still, Gettysburg was a great Union victory and, together with the simultaneous triumph at Vicksburg, was the major turning point in the war. Southern armies would never again invade the North, and Southern citizens began to criticize the military effort. The Confederate elections of 1863 went sharply against the politicians who supported Jefferson Davis.

Vicksburg and Gettysburg also transformed the political situation in the North and in Europe. In the fall of 1863, Republicans swept state and local elections in Pennsylvania, Ohio, and New York. Equally important, American diplomats finally cut the flow of advanced weapons to the Confederacy. In 1862, British shipbuilders had supplied the Confederacy with an ironclad cruiser, the *Alabama*, which had sunk or captured more than one hundred Union merchant ships; and the delivery of two more ironclad cruisers was imminent. News of the Union victories changed everything. Charles Francis Adams, the American minister, persuaded the British government to impound the ships; the ministry did not want to risk Canada or its merchant ships by provoking the United States. Moreover, Britain had become increasingly dependent on imports of wheat and flour from the American Midwest, and British workers and reformers were strongly opposed to slavery. "King Cotton" diplomacy had failed; "King Wheat" stood triumphant. "Rest not your hopes in foreign nations," President Jefferson Davis now advised his nation, "This war is ours; we must fight it ourselves."

▶ What prompted Lincoln to issue the Emancipation Proclamation: the pressure exerted by antislavery Republican politicians or the pressure exerted by the thousands of "contrabands" who had freed themselves? Explain your answer.

▶ Why were the battles at Gettysburg and Vicksburg significant? How did they change the tide of war strategically? How did they change it diplomatically? How did they change it psychologically?

The Union Victorious, 1864–1865

The Union victories of 1863 meant that the South could not win its independence through a decisive military triumph. However, the Confederacy could still hope for a battlefield stalemate and a negotiated peace. Lincoln faced the daunting task of winning an overwhelming victory, or he would lose the support of northern voters.

Soldiers and Strategy

Two developments allowed the Union to prosecute the war with continued vigor: the enlistment of African American soldiers and the emergence of capable and determined generals. As early as 1861, free African Americans and fugitive slaves had volunteered for the Union army, hoping to end slavery and, as Frederick Douglass put it, win "the right to citizenship in the United States." The prospect of military service for blacks offended many northern whites. "I am as much opposed to slavery as any of them," a New York officer wrote to his local newspaper, "but I am not willing to be put on a level with the negro and fight with them." Moreover, most Union generals doubted that former slaves would make good soldiers. So the Lincoln administration initially refused to enlist African Americans; nonetheless, free and contraband blacks, eager to fight, formed regiments in New England, South Carolina, Louisiana, and Kansas.

The Emancipation Proclamation changed popular thinking and military policy. The proclamation invited former slaves to serve in the Union army, and northern whites, their ranks depleted by thousands of casualties, now accepted that blacks should share in the fighting and dying. The valor exhibited by the first African American regiments to go into combat also influenced northern opinion. In January 1863, Thomas Wentworth Higginson, the white abolitionist commander of the First South Carolina Volunteers, wrote a glowing newspaper account of the black regiment's military prowess. In July, a heroic and costly attack on Fort Wagner, South Carolina, by the Fifty-fourth Massachusetts Infantry convinced many Union officers of the value of black soldiers. The War Department authorized black enlistment, and as white resistance to conscription mounted, the Lincoln administration recruited as many African Americans as it could. Without black soldiers, the president suggested late in 1864, "we would be compelled to abandon the war in three weeks." By the spring of 1865, nearly 200,000 African Americans were serving the Union.

Military service did not end racial discrimination. Initially, black soldiers were paid less than white soldiers ($10 a month versus $13); they won equal pay only by threatening

Black Soldiers in the Union Army
Determined to end racial slavery, 200,000 African Americans volunteered for service in the Union army in 1864 and 1865, boosting the northern war effort at a critical moment. These proud soldiers were members of the 107th Colored Infantry, stationed at Fort Corcoran near Washington, D.C. In January 1865, their regiment participated in the daring capture of Fort Fisher, which protected Wilmington, North Carolina, the last Confederate port open to blockade runners. Library of Congress.

to lay down their arms. Moreover, blacks served under white officers in segregated regiments and were used primarily to build fortifications, garrison forts, and guard supply lines. Despite this treatment, African Americans volunteered for military service in disproportionate numbers because they were fighting for freedom and a new social order. "Hello, Massa," said one black soldier to his former master, who had been taken prisoner. "Bottom rail on top dis time." The worst fears of the secessionists had come true: Through the agency of the Union army, blacks had risen in a great rebellion against slavery.

As African Americans bolstered the army's ranks, Lincoln finally found an efficient and ruthless commanding general. In March 1864, Lincoln placed General Ulysses S. Grant in charge of all Union armies and created a unified structure of command. From then on, the president determined the general strategy, and Grant implemented it. Lincoln favored a simultaneous advance against all the major Confederate armies, a strategy that Grant had long favored, to achieve a decisive victory before the election of 1864.

As the successful western campaign of 1863 showed, Grant knew how to fight a war that relied on industrial technology and targeted an entire society. At Vicksburg, he had besieged the whole city and forced its surrender. Then, in November 1863, he had used railroads to charge to the rescue of an endangered Union army near Chattanooga, Tennessee. Moreover, Grant argued that the efforts of earlier Union commanders "to conserve life" through cautious tactics had merely prolonged the war. He was willing to accept heavy casualties, an aggressive stand that earned him a reputation as a butcher of both enemy armies and his own men.

In May 1864, Grant ordered two major offensives. Personally taking charge of the 115,000-man Army of the Potomac, he set out to destroy Lee's force of 75,000 troops in Virginia. Simultaneously, Grant instructed General William Tecumseh Sherman, who shared his ruthless outlook, to invade Georgia and take Atlanta. "All that has gone before is mere skirmish," Sherman wrote as he prepared for battle. "The war now begins."

Grant advanced toward Richmond, hoping to force Lee to fight in open fields, where the Union's superior manpower and artillery would prevail. Remembering his tactical errors at Gettysburg, Lee remained in strong defensive positions and attacked only when he held an advantage. The Confederate general seized that opportunity twice, winning narrow victories in early May 1864 at the extraordinarily bloody battles of the Wilderness and Spotsylvania Court House. At Spotsylvania, the soldiers fought at point-blank range, often using their bayoneted rifles as spears. Despite heavy losses in these battles and then at Cold Harbor, Grant drove on (Map 14.5). Although his attacks severely eroded Lee's forces, which suffered 31,000 casualties, Union losses were even higher: 55,000 men.

The fighting took a heavy psychological toll. "Many a man has gone crazy since this campaign began from the terrible pressure on mind and body," observed a Union captain. As the morale of the soldiers weakened, many deserted. In June 1864, Grant laid siege to Petersburg, an important railroad center near Richmond. Protracted trench warfare—like that in France in World War I—took a terrible toll. Union and Confederate soldiers built complex networks of trenches, tunnels, and artillery emplacements stretching for forty miles along the eastern edge of Richmond and Petersburg. Invoking the intense imagery of the Bible, an officer described the continuous artillery barrages and sniping as "living night and day within the 'valley of the shadow of death.'" The stress was especially great for the outnumbered Confederate troops, who spent months in the muddy, hellish trenches without rotation to the rear.

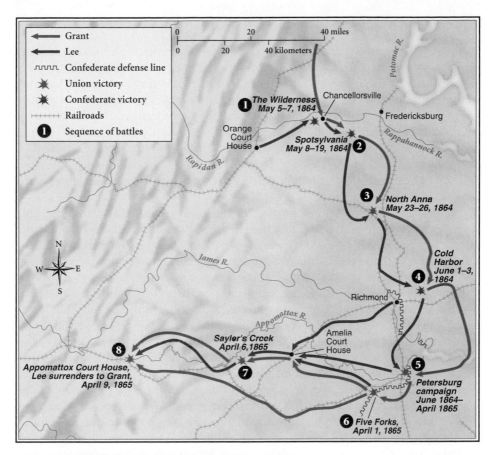

MAP 14.5 The Closing Virginia Campaign, 1864–1865

Beginning in May 1864, General Ulysses S. Grant launched an all-out campaign against Richmond. By threatening General Robert E. Lee's lines of supply from Richmond, Grant tried to lure him into open battle. Lee avoided a major test of strength. Instead, he retreated to defensive positions and inflicted heavy casualties on Union attackers at the Wilderness, Spotsylvania Court House, North Anna, and Cold Harbor (1–4). From June 1864 to April 1865, the two armies faced each other across defensive fortifications outside Richmond and Petersburg (5), a protracted siege that was finally broken by Grant's flanking maneuver at Five Forks (6). Lee's surrender followed shortly.

As time passed, Lincoln and Grant felt pressures of their own. The enormous casualties and continued military stalemate threatened Lincoln with defeat in the November election. The Republican outlook worsened in July, when a raid near Washington by Jubal Early's cavalry forced Grant to divert his best troops from the Petersburg campaign. To punish farmers in the Shenandoah Valley, who had provided aid to Early and Lee, Grant ordered General Philip H. Sheridan to turn the region into "a barren waste." Sheridan's troops conducted a scorched-earth campaign, destroying grain, barns, and gristmills. These terrorist tactics violated the military norms of the day, which treated civilians as noncombatants. Grant's practice of carrying the war to Confederate citizens was changing the definition of conventional warfare.

The Election of 1864 and Sherman's March

As the siege at Petersburg dragged on, Lincoln's hopes for reelection depended on General Sherman in Georgia. Sherman had gradually penetrated to within about thirty miles of Atlanta, a great railway hub at the heart of the Confederacy. Although his army outnumbered that of General Joseph E. Johnston—90,000 men to 60,000 men—Sherman avoided a direct attack and slowly pried the Confederates out of one defensive position after another. Finally, on June 27, at Kennesaw Mountain, Sherman engaged Johnston in a set battle, only to suffer 3,000 casualties—five times the Confederates' losses. By late July 1864, the Union general had advanced to the northern outskirts of Atlanta, but the next month brought little gain. Like Grant, Sherman seemed bogged down in a hopeless campaign.

Meanwhile, the presidential campaign of 1864 was well under way. In June, some delegates to the Republican convention tried to prevent Lincoln's renomination. But the convention endorsed the president's war strategy, demanded the Confederacy's unconditional surrender, and called for a constitutional amendment to abolish slavery. It likewise accepted Lincoln's political strategy. To attract border-state and Democratic voters, the Republicans took a new name, the National Union Party, and chose Andrew Johnson, a Tennessee slave owner and Unionist Democrat, as Lincoln's running mate. The Democratic convention met in late August and nominated General George B. McClellan for president. Lincoln had twice removed McClellan from military commands: first for an excess of caution and then for his opposition to emancipation. Like McClellan, the Democratic delegates rejected freedom for blacks and condemned Lincoln's repression of domestic dissent. However, they split into two camps over the issue of continuing the war until the Union was restored. A substantial contingent of Peace Democrats called for a "cessation of hostilities" and a constitutional convention to restore peace. Although personally a War Democrat, McClellan promised if elected to recommend to Congress an immediate armistice and a peace convention. Hearing this news, Confederate vice president Alexander Stephens celebrated "the first ray of real light I have seen since the war began." He predicted that if Atlanta and Richmond held out, Lincoln could be defeated and McClellan could be persuaded to accept an independent Confederacy.

Stephens's hopes collapsed on September 2, 1864, as Atlanta fell to Sherman's army. In a stunning move, the Union general pulled his troops from the trenches, swept around the city, and destroyed its rail links to the south. Fearing that Sherman would encircle his army, Confederate general John B. Hood abandoned the city. "Atlanta is ours, and fairly won," Sherman telegraphed Lincoln, sparking hundred-gun salutes and wild Republican celebrations in northern cities. "We are *gaining* strength," Lincoln warned Confederate leaders, "and may, if need be, maintain the contest indefinitely."

A deep pessimism settled over the Confederacy. Mary Chesnut, a plantation mistress and general's wife, "felt as if all were dead within me, forever" and foresaw the end of the Confederacy: "We are going to be wiped off the earth," she wrote in her diary. Recognizing the dramatic change in the military situation, McClellan repudiated the Democratic peace platform, and dissident Republicans abandoned efforts to dump Lincoln. The National Union Party went on the offensive, attacking McClellan's inconsistency and attacking Peace Democrats as "copperheads" (poisonous snakes) who were hatching treasonous plots.

Lincoln won a clear-cut victory in November. The president received 55 percent of the popular vote and won 212 of 233 electoral votes. Republicans and National

Unionists captured 145 of the 185 seats in the House of Representatives and increased their Senate majority to 42 of 52 seats. Many Republicans owed their victory to the votes of Union troops, who wanted to crush the rebellion and end slavery.

Legal emancipation was already under way at the edges of the South. In 1864, Maryland and Missouri amended their constitutions to free their slaves, and the three occupied states—Tennessee, Arkansas, and Louisiana—followed suit. Still, abolitionists worried that the Emancipation Proclamation, which was based on the president's wartime powers, would lose its force at the end of the war. Urged on by Lincoln and National Equal Rights League, the Republican Congress approved the Thirteenth Amendment, ending slavery, in January 1865 and sent it to the states for ratification. Slavery was nearly dead.

Thanks to William Tecumseh Sherman, the Confederacy was nearly dead as well. As a young military officer stationed in the South, Sherman had been sympathetic to the outlook of the planter class, and felt that slavery upheld social stability. But Sherman was also a firm supporter of the Union. Secession meant "anarchy," he told his southern friends in early 1861. "If war comes . . . I must fight your people whom I best love." Serving under Ulysses S. Grant, Sherman distinguished himself at Shiloh and Vicksburg. Taking command of a Union army in Tennessee, he developed the philosophy and tactics of "hard war." "When one nation is at war with another, all the people of one are enemies of the other," Sherman declared, turning his troops loose against civilians suspected of helping Confederate guerrillas. After guerrillas fired on a boat with Unionist passengers near Randolph, Tennessee, Sherman sent a regiment to destroy the town, asserting, "We are justified in treating all inhabitants as combatants."

After capturing Atlanta, Sherman decided on a bold hard-war strategy. Instead of pursuing the retreating Confederate army northward into Tennessee, he proposed to move south, live off the land, and "cut a swath through to the sea." To persuade Lincoln and Grant to approve his unconventional plan, Sherman argued that his march would devastate Georgia and be "a demonstration to the world, foreign and domestic, that we have a power [Jefferson] Davis cannot resist." The Union general lived up to his pledge. "We are not only fighting hostile armies," Sherman wrote, "but a hostile people, and must make old and young, rich and poor, feel the hard hand of war." He left Atlanta in flames and, during his 300-mile march to the sea (Map 14.6), his army consumed or demolished everything in its path. A Union veteran wrote, "[We] destroyed all we could not eat, stole their niggers, burned their cotton & gins, spilled their sorghum, burned & twisted their R.Roads and raised Hell generally." The havoc so demoralized Confederate soldiers that many deserted their units and fled home to protect their farms and families (see American Voices, p. 433). When Sherman reached Savannah in mid-December, the city's 10,000 defenders left without a fight.

Georgia's African Americans treated Sherman as a savior. "They flock to me, old and young, they pray and shout and mix up my name with Moses . . . as well as 'Abram Linkom', the Great Messiah of 'Dis Jubilee.'" To provide for the hundreds of blacks now following his army, Sherman issued Special Field Order No. 15, which set aside 400,000 acres of prime rice-growing land for the exclusive use of freedmen. By June 1865, some 40,000 blacks were cultivating "Sherman lands." Many freedmen believed that the lands were to be theirs forever, belated payment for generations of unpaid labor: "All the land belongs to the Yankees now and they gwine divide it out among de coloured people."

In February 1865, Sherman invaded South Carolina, both to link up with Grant at Petersburg and to punish the instigators of nullification and secession. His troops

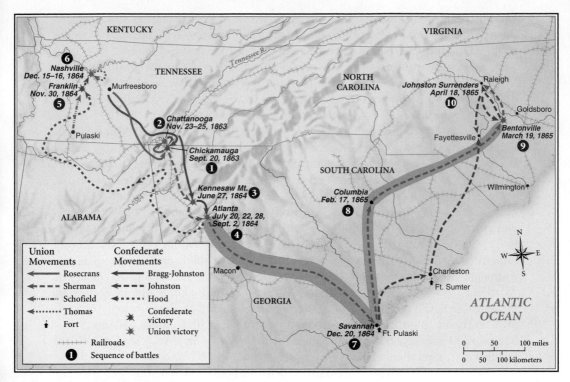

MAP 14.6 Sherman's March Through the Confederacy, 1864–1865

The Union victory in November 1863 at Chattanooga, Tennessee (2), was almost as critical as the victories in July at Gettysburg and Vicksburg because it opened up a route of attack into the heart of the Confederacy. In mid-1864, General Sherman advanced on the railway hub of Atlanta (3 and 4). After finally taking the city in September 1864, Sherman relied on other Union armies to stem General Hood's invasion of Tennessee (5 and 6) while he began a devastating "March to the Sea." By December, Sherman had reached Savannah (7); from there, he cut a swath through the Carolinas (8–10).

For more help analyzing this map, see the Online Study Guide at **bedfordstmartins.com/henrettaconcise**.

ravaged the countryside as they cut a comparatively narrow swath across the state. After capturing South Carolina's capital, Columbia, they burned the business district, most churches, and the wealthiest residential neighborhoods. "This disappointment to me is extremely bitter," lamented Jefferson Davis. By March, Sherman had reached North Carolina and was on the verge of linking up with Grant and crushing Lee's army.

Grant's war of attrition in Virginia had already exposed a weakness in the Confederacy: rising class resentment among poor whites. Angered by slave owners' exemptions from military service and fearing that the Confederacy was doomed, ordinary southern farmers now repudiated the draft. "All they want is to git you . . . to fight for their infurnal negroes," grumbled an Alabama hill farmer. More and more soldiers fled their units. "I am now going to work instead of to the war," vowed David Harris, another backcountry yeoman. By 1865, at least 100,000 men had deserted from Confederate armies, prompting a reluctant Confederate Congress to allow the enlistment of black soldiers and President Davis to issue an executive order granting freedom to blacks who served. But the fighting finished too soon to reveal whether any slaves would have fought for the Confederacy.

Sherman's March Through Georgia DOLLY SUMNER LUNT

"We must make old and young, rich and poor, feel the hand of war," General William Tecumseh Sherman wrote to General Grant late in 1864, indicating his intention to carry the war to the South's civilian population. Dolly Sumner Lunt of Covington, Georgia, soon found out what Sherman meant. Born in Maine in 1817, Dolly Sumner went south to teach school, married a slave owner, and, after his death, ran the family's plantation, apparently in a benevolent fashion. Her wartime journal describes the plantation's fate at Sherman's hands.

November 19, 1864

Slept in my clothes last night, as I heard that the Yankees went to neighbor Montgomery's on Thursday night at one o'clock, searched his house, drank his wine, and took his money and valuables. As we were not disturbed, I walked after breakfast . . . up to Mr. Joe Perry's, my nearest neighbor, where the Yankees were yesterday. Saw Mrs. Laura [Perry] in the road surrounded by her children . . . looking for her husband. . . . Before we were done talking, up came Joe and Jim Perry from their hiding-place. Jim was very much excited. Happening to turn and look behind, as we stood there, I saw some blue-coats coming down the hill. Jim immediately raised his gun, swearing he should kill them anyhow.

"No, don't" said I, and ran home as fast as I could.

I could hear them cry "Halt! Halt!" and their guns went off in quick succession. Oh God, the time of trial has come. . . .

I hastened back to my frightened servants [slaves] and told them they had better hide, and then went back to the gate to claim protection and a guard. But like demons they [Sherman's troops] rushed in! . . . The thousand pounds of meat in my smokehouse is gone in a twinkling, my flour, my meat, my lard, butter, eggs . . . all gone. My eighteen fat turkeys, hens, chickens . . . are shot down in my yard and hunted as if they were rebels themselves. Utterly powerless I ran out and appealed to the guard.

"I cannot help you, Madam; it is orders."

As I stood there, from my lot I saw driven, first, old Dutch, my dear old buggy horse . . . ; then came old May, my brood mare, . . . with her three-year-old colt. . . . There they go! There go my mules, my sheep, and worse than all, my boys [younger slaves]. . . . Their parents are with me, and how sadly they lament the loss of their boys. Their cabins are rifled of every valuable. . . . Poor Frank's chest was broken open, his money and tobacco taken. He has always been a money-making and saving boy, not infrequently has his crop brought him five hundred dollars and more. . . .

Sherman himself and a greater portion of his army passed my house that day . . . ; they tore down my garden palings, made a road through my back-yard and lot field . . . desolating my home—wantonly doing it when there was no necessity for it. . . .

As night drew its sable curtains around us, the heavens from every point were lit up with flames from burning buildings.

SOURCE: *Eyewitnesses and Others: Readings in American History* (New York: Holt, Rinehart and Winston, 1991), 1: pp. 413–417.

The symbolic end of the war took place in Virginia. In April 1865, Grant finally gained control of the crucial railroad junction at Petersburg and cut off Lee's supplies. Lee abandoned Richmond and retreated toward North Carolina to join up with Confederate forces there. While Lincoln visited the ruins of the Confederate capital and was mobbed by joyful ex-slaves, Grant cut off Lee's escape route. On April 9, almost four years to the day after the attack on Fort Sumter, Lee surrendered at Appomattox Court House, Virginia. By late May, all the Confederate generals had stopped fighting, and the Confederate army and government simply melted away.

The hard and bitter conflict was finally over. Union armies had destroyed slavery and the Confederate armies and governments; the South's factories, warehouses, and railroads were in ruins, as were many of its farms and some of its most important cities. Almost 260,000 Confederate soldiers had paid for secession with their lives. On the other side, more than 360,000 Northerners had died for the Union, and thousands more had been maimed. Was it all worth the price? Delivering his second inaugural address as the fighting entered its final phase, Abraham Lincoln could not justify the hideous carnage and fell back on his religious faith: "so still it must be said 'the judgments of the Lord are true and righteous altogether.'"

But what of the war's results? A New York census taker suggested that the conflict had undermined "autocracy" and had an "equalizing effect" on society. Slavery was gone from the South, he reflected, and in the North, "military men from the so called 'lower classes' now lead society, having been elevated by real merit and valor." However perceptive these remarks, they ignored the wartime emergence of a new financial aristocracy that would soon preside over a "Gilded Age" of wealth and excess. Nor was the sectional struggle yet concluded. As the North began to reconstruct the South and the Union, it found those tasks to be almost as hard and bitter as the war itself.

▶ How did the emancipation edict affect the politics and military affairs of the North?

▶ What were the strengths and weaknesses of Grant's and Sherman's military strategy and tactics? How were their ways of warfare different from traditional military practice?

▶ Why did the North win the Civil War?

SUMMARY

In this chapter, we surveyed the dramatic events of the Civil War. Looking at the South, we watched the fire-eaters declare secession, form a new Confederacy, and attack Fort Sumter. Subsequently, we saw its generals repulse Union attacks against Richmond and go on the offensive. However, as the war continued, the inherent weaknesses of the Confederacy came to the fore. Enslaved workers fled or refused to work, and yeomen farmers refused to fight for an institution that primarily benefited wealthy planters.

Examining the North, we witnessed its initial military failure. Its generals—McClellan and Meade—moved slowly to attack and refused to pursue their weakened foes. But over time, the Union's significant advantages in industrial output, financial resources, and military manpower became manifest. Congress created efficient systems of banking and war finance; Lincoln found efficient and ruthless generals; and the emancipation and recruitment of African Americans provided an abundant sup-ply of soldiers determined to preserve their freedom.

We explored the impact of the war on civilians in both regions: the imposition of conscription and high taxes; the increased workload of farm women; and the constant food shortages and soaring prices. Above all else, there was the omnipresent fact of death—a tragedy that touched nearly every family, North and South.

Connections: Government

Since the beginning of the American republic, political leaders have argued over the scope and powers of the national government. As we learned in Chapter 7, Alexander Hamilton interpreted the Constitution expansively and devised a policy of national mercantilism. In response, Thomas Jefferson and James Madison created the Repub-lican Party, which subsequently reduced the scope of the national government and relied on state governments to promote economic development. In the 1820s, as we discussed in Chapter 10, Henry Clay and John Quincy Adams revived Hamilton's nationalistic program. Their American System proposed a national bank to over-see the financial system, national tariff protection for American manufacturers, and national subsidies for roads, canals, and other internal improvements. As we noted in the essay that opened Part Three, in the Jacksonian revolution of the 1830s and 1840s,

> the Democratic Party led a political and constitutional revolution that cut government
> aid to financiers, merchants, and corporations.

We saw in this chapter that the Republican administration of Abraham Lincoln re-versed those Jacksonian policies by extending aid to farmers, railroads, and corpora-tions. Indeed, as we will see in Chapter 17, these Hamilton-Clay-Lincoln initiatives continued in the late nineteenth century. By enacting and upholding legislation favor-able to banks and corporations, Congress and the federal judiciary actively promoted the development of a powerful industrial economy. The Jeffersonian-Jacksonian ide-ology of small government remained strong in the South but, after the Civil War, it receded as a significant force in national life.

FOR FURTHER EXPLORATION

James M. McPherson, *The Battle Cry of Freedom* (1988), and Charles P. Roland, *An American Iliad* (1991), narrate wartime events. For the outbreak of the war, read Richard Current, *Lincoln and the First Shot* (1963). John Hope Franklin, *The Emanci-pation Proclamation* (1963), explains that important edict.

Nancy Scott Anderson and Dwight Anderson, *The Generals: Ulysses S. Grant and Robert E. Lee* (1988), provide a vivid popular account. Good scholarly analyses include Mark Grimsley, *The Hard Hand of War* (1995), and Gary W. Gallagher, *The Confederate War* (1997). William W. Freehling, *The South vs. the South* (2001), explores anti-Confederate sentiment.

For firsthand accounts, see James M. McPherson, *For Cause and Comrades* (1997); Ira Berlin et al., eds., *Freedom's Soldiers: The Black Military Experience* (1998); and Earl J. Hess, *The Union Soldier in Battle* (1997). Michael Shaara's *Killer Angels* (1974) is a masterful novel about the Battle of Gettysburg.

TIMELINE

1860 ► Abraham Lincoln elected president (November 6)

► South Carolina votes to secede (December 20)

1861 ► President Lincoln inaugurated (March 4)

► Confederates fire on Fort Sumter (April 12)

► Virginia leads Upper South into Confederacy (April 17)

► General Butler labels fugitive slaves "contraband of war" (May)

► Confederates rout Union at Bull Run (July 21)

► First Confiscation Act allows seizure of Confederate property (August)

1862 ► Legal Tender Act authorizes greenbacks (February)

► Battle of Shiloh: Union advances in West (April 6–7)

► Confederacy introduces first draft (April)

► Congress passes Homestead (free land) Act (May)

► Congress provides subsidies to transcontinental railroads (July)

► Second Confiscation Act frees contraband slaves (July)

► Union halts Confederate offensive at Antietam (September 17)

► Lincoln issues preliminary Emancipation Proclamation (September 22)

1863 ► Lincoln signs Emancipation Proclamation (January 1)

► Union wins battles at Gettysburg (July 1–3) and Vicksburg (July 4)

► Enrollment Act prompts immigrant riots in New York City (July)

1864 ► Lincoln gives Ulysses S. Grant command of all Union armies (March)

► Grant begins advance on Richmond (May)

► William Tecumseh Sherman takes Atlanta (September 2)

► President Lincoln is reelected (November 8)

► Sherman marches through Georgia (November and December)

1865 ► Congress passes Thirteenth Amendment, ending slavery (January)

► Robert E. Lee surrenders at Appomattox Court House (April 9)

► Lincoln assassinated by John Wilkes Booth (April 14)

► Thirteenth Amendment ratified by states (December 6)

For women's lives, look at *Mary Chesnut's Civil War*, edited by C. Vann Woodward (1981); Jane E. Schultz, *Women at the Front* (2004); and Laura F. Edwards, *Scarlett Doesn't Live Here Anymore* (2000).

For Civil War photographs, log onto **memory.loc.gov/ammem/ndlpcoop/nhihtml/cwnyhshome.html** and **memory.loc.gov/ammem/cwphtml/cwphome.html**. Edward L. Ayers, *In the Presence of Mine Enemies* (2003), explores wartime life in two communities and has a fine Web site at **jefferson.village.virginia.edu/vshadow2/**. For the black experience, go to **www.history.umd.edu/Freedmen/home.html**.

TEST YOUR KNOWLEDGE

To assess your mastery of the material in this chapter and for Web sites, images, and documents related to this chapter, visit **bedfordstmartins.com/henrettaconcise**.

15 Reconstruction
1865–1877

I felt like a bird out of a cage. Amen. Amen. Amen. I could hardly ask to feel better than I did on that day.

— Houston H. Holloway, a former slave recalling his emancipation in 1865

In his second inaugural address, President Lincoln spoke of the need to "bind up the nation's wounds." No one knew better than Lincoln how daunting a task that would be. Slavery was finished. That much was certain. But what system of labor should replace plantation slavery? What rights should the freedmen be accorded beyond emancipation? How far should the federal government go to settle these questions? And, most immediately pressing, on what terms should the rebellious states be restored to the Union?

The last speech that Lincoln delivered, on April 11, 1865, demonstrated his command of these issues. Reconstruction, he said, had to be regarded as a practical problem, not a theoretical one. It could be solved only if Republicans remained united, even if that meant compromising on principled differences that divided them, and only if the defeated South gave its consent, even if that came at the price of forgiving the South's transgressions. The speech revealed the middle ground, both magnanimous and open-minded, on which Lincoln hoped to reunite a wounded nation.

What course Reconstruction might have taken had Lincoln lived is one of the unanswerable questions of American history. On April 14, 1865—five days after Lee's surrender at Appomattox—Lincoln was shot in the head at Ford's Theatre in Washington by John Wilkes Booth, a prominent Shakespearian actor and Confederate sympathizer who had been plotting to abduct Lincoln and rescue the South. After Lee's surrender, Booth became bent on revenge. Without regaining consciousness, Lincoln died on April 15, 1865.

With one stroke, John Wilkes Booth sent Lincoln to martyrdom, hardened many Northerners against the South, and handed the presidency to a man utterly lacking in Lincoln's moral sense and political judgment: Vice President Andrew Johnson.

Presidential Reconstruction

The problem of Reconstruction—how to restore rebellious states to the Union—had not been addressed by the Founding Fathers. The Constitution does not contemplate the possibility of secession. Had the Confederate states, upon seceding, legally left the Union? If so, their reentry surely required legislative action by Congress. If not, if even in defeat they retained their constitutional status, then the terms for restoring them to the Union might be considered an administrative matter best left to the president. In a constitutional system based on the **separation of powers**, the absence of clarity on so fundamental a matter made for explosive politics. The ensuing battle between the White House and Capitol Hill over who was in charge became one of the fault lines in Reconstruction's stormy history.

Lincoln's Way

As wartime president, Lincoln had the elbow room to take the lead, offering in December 1863 a general amnesty to all but high-ranking Confederates. When 10 percent of a rebellious state's voters had taken an oath of loyalty, the state would be restored to the Union, provided that it approved the Thirteenth Amendment abolishing slavery (see Chapter 14). The Confederate states rejected Lincoln's Ten Percent Plan, however, and congressional Republicans proposed a harsher substitute. The Wade-Davis Bill, passed on July 2, 1864, laid down, as conditions, an oath of allegiance to the Union by a majority of each state's adult white men; new governments formed only by those who had never borne arms against the North; and permanent disfranchisement of Confederate leaders. The Wade-Davis Bill served notice that the congressional Republicans were not about to hand over Reconstruction policy to the president.

Lincoln **pocket vetoed** the Wade-Davis Bill by leaving it unsigned when Congress adjourned. At the same time, he initiated informal talks with congressional leaders aimed at a compromise. It was this effort that Lincoln was addressing when he appealed for Republican flexibility in his last speech. Lincoln's successor, however, had no such inclination. Andrew Johnson took the view that Reconstruction was the president's prerogative. By an accident of timing, he was free to act on his convictions. Although the 38th Congress had adjourned in March 1865, under leisurely rules that went back to the early republic the 39th Congress was not scheduled to convene until December 1865.

Johnson Seizes the Initiative

Johnson was a self-made man from the hills of eastern Tennessee. Born in 1808, he was apprenticed as a boy to a tailor. With no formal schooling—his wife was his teacher—Johnson prospered. His tailor shop became a political meeting place, and natural leader that he was, he soon entered local politics with the backing of Greeneville's small farmers and laborers. In 1857, he became a U.S. senator.

Loyal to the Union, Johnson refused to leave the Senate when his state seceded. In this, he was utterly alone; no southern colleague joined him. When federal forces captured Nashville in 1862, Lincoln appointed Johnson Tennessee's military governor.

Andrew Johnson
The president was not an easy man.
This photograph of Andrew Johnson
(1808–1875) conveys some of the
prickly qualities that contributed so
centrally to his failure to reach an
agreement with Republicans on a
moderate Reconstruction program.
Library of Congress.

Tennessee was bitterly divided—Unionist in the east and Rebel in the west. Johnson's assignment was to hold the state together, and he did so, with an iron hand. He was rewarded by being named Lincoln's running mate in 1864. Choosing this war Democrat seemed a smart move, designed to promote wartime unity and court southern Unionists.

In May 1865, just a month after Lincoln's death, Johnson advanced his version of Reconstruction. He offered amnesty to all Southerners who took an oath of allegiance to the Constitution except for high-ranking Confederate officials. Johnson appointed provisional governors for the southern states, requiring as conditions for their restoration only that they revoke their ordinances of secession, repudiate their Confederate debts, and ratify the Thirteenth Amendment. Within months, all the former Confederate states had met Johnson's terms and had functioning elected governments.

At first, Republicans responded favorably. The moderates were sympathetic to Johnson's argument that it was up to the states, not the federal government, to define the rights of the freedmen. Even the Radicals—Republicans who demanded a hard line toward the South—held their fire. The stern treatment of Confederate leaders pleased them, and they awaited signs of good faith such as generous treatment of the freed slaves.

Nothing of the sort happened. The South lay in ruins (see Voices from Abroad, p. 440), but Southerners held fast to the old order. The newly seated legislatures moved to restore slavery in all but name. They enacted laws—known as **Black Codes**—designed to drive the former slaves back to the plantations by imposing severe penalties on vagrancy, placing heavy restrictions on black workers, and legalizing forms of apprenticeship that came close to slavery. The new governments had been formed mostly by southern Unionists, but when it came to racial attitudes, little distinguished these loyalists from the Confederates. Despite his hard words, moreover, Johnson

The Devastated South   DAVID MACRAE

In this excerpt from *The Americans at Home* (1870), an account of his tour of the United States, Scottish clergyman David Macrae describes the war-stricken South as he found it in 1867–1868, at a time when the crisis over Reconstruction was boiling over.

I was struck with a remark made by a Southern gentleman in answer to the assertion that Jefferson Davis [the president of the Confederacy] had culpably continued the war for six months after all hope had been abandoned.

"Sir," he said, "Mr. Davis knew the temper of the South as well as any man in it. He knew if there was to be anything worth calling peace, the South must win; or, if she couldn't win, she wanted to be whipped—well whipped—thoroughly whipped."

The further south I went, the oftener these remarks came back upon me. Evidence was everywhere that the South had maintained the desperate conflict until she was utterly exhausted. . . . Almost every man I met at the South, especially in North Carolina, Georgia, and Virginia, seemed to have been in the army; and it was painful to find many who had returned were mutilated, maimed, or broken in health by exposure. When I remarked this to a young Confederate officer in North Carolina, and said I was glad to see that he had escaped unhurt, he . . . pulled up one leg of his trousers, and showed me that he had an iron rod there to strengthen his limb, and enable him to walk without limping, half of his foot being off. He showed me on the other leg a deep scar made by a fragment of a shell; and these were two of but seven wounds which had left their marks upon his body. When he heard me speak of relics, he said, "Try to find a North Carolina gentleman without a Yankee mark on him."

Nearly three years had passed when I traveled through the country, and yet we have seen what traces the war had left in such cities as Richmond, Petersburg, and Columbia. The same spectacle met me at Charleston. Churches and houses had been battered down by heavy shot and shell hurled into the city from Federal batteries at a distance of five miles. . . . Over the country districts the prostration was equally marked. Along the track of Sherman's army especially, the devastation was fearful—farms laid waste, fences burned, bridges destroyed, houses left in ruins, plantations in many cases turned into wilderness again.

The people had shared in the general wreck, and looked poverty-stricken, careworn, and dejected. Ladies who before the war had lived in affluence, with black servants round them to attend to their every wish, were . . . so utterly destitute that they did not know when they finished one meal where they were to find the next. . . . Men who had held commanding positions . . . were filling humble situations—struggling, many of them, to earn a bare subsistence. . . . I remember dining with three cultured Southern gentlemen . . . all living together in a plain little wooden house, such as they would formerly have provided for their servants. Two of them were engaged in a railway office, the third was seeking a situation, frequently, in his vain search, passing the large blinded house where he had lived in luxurious ease before the war.

SOURCE: Allan Nevins, ed., *America Through British Eyes* (Gloucester, MA: Peter Smith, 1968), 345–347.

forgave ex-Confederate leaders easily, as long as he got the satisfaction of humbling them when they appealed for pardons. Soon the ex-Confederates, emboldened by Johnson's indulgence, were filtering back into the halls of power. Old comrades packed the delegations to the new Congress, including even Alexander Stephens, the former vice president of the Confederacy. This was the last straw for the Republicans.

Under the Constitution, Congress is "the judge of the Elections, Returns and Qualifications of its own Members" (Article 1, Section 5). With this power, the Republican majorities in both houses refused to admit the southern delegations when Congress convened in early December 1865, effectively blocking Johnson's Reconstruction program. The southern states then backed away from the Black Codes, replacing them with regulatory ordinances that were silent on race yet, in practice, applied only to blacks. On top of that, racial violence erupted across the South. In Tennessee, a Nashville newspaper reported that white gangs "are riding about whipping, maiming and killing all negroes who do not obey the orders of their former masters, just as if slavery existed." Congressional Republicans concluded that the South was intent on circumventing the Thirteenth Amendment and that the federal government had to intervene.

Back in March 1865, before adjourning, the 38th Congress had established the Freedmen's Bureau to aid ex-slaves during the transition from war to peace. Now, in early 1866, Congress voted to extend the Freedmen's Bureau's life, gave it direct funding for the first time, and authorized its agents to investigate mistreatment of blacks.

More extraordinary was a civil rights bill, which declared the ex-slaves to be citizens; granted them, along with every other citizen, equal rights of contract, access to the courts, and protection of person and property; and authorized U.S. attorneys to bring enforcement suits in the federal courts. Provoked by an unrepentant South, Republicans demanded that the federal government, not the individual states, assume responsibility for the civil rights of the freedmen.

Acting on Freedom

While Congress debated, emancipated slaves acted on their own ideas about freedom (see American Voices, p. 442). Freedom meant many things — the end of punishment by the lash; the ability to move around; the reuniting of families; and the opportunity to found schools, to form churches and social clubs, and, not least, to engage in politics. Across the South, blacks held mass meetings, paraded, and formed organizations. Topmost among their demands was the right to vote — "an essential and inseparable element of self-government." No less than their former masters, ex-slaves intended to be actors in the savage drama of Reconstruction.

Ownership of land, the ex-slaves believed, was the basis for true freedom. In the chaotic final months of the war, freedmen seized control of plantations where they could. In Georgia and South Carolina, General William T. Sherman had reserved large coastal tracts for liberated slaves and settled them on forty-acre plots. Sherman just did not want to be bothered with the refugees as his army drove across the Lower South, but the freedmen assumed that Sherman's order meant that the land would be theirs. When the war ended, resettlement became the responsibility of the Freedmen's Bureau. Many black families stayed on their old plantations, awaiting redistribution of

Relishing Freedom JOURDON ANDERSON

Folklorists have recorded the sly ways that slaves found, even in bondage, for "puttin' down" their masters. But only in freedom—and beyond reach in a northern state—could Jourdon Anderson's sarcasm be expressed so openly, with the jest that his family might consider returning if they first received the wages due them, calculated to the dollar, for all those years in slavery. Anderson's letter, although probably written or edited by a white friend in Dayton, surely is faithful to what the ex-slave wanted to say.

Dayton, Ohio
August 7, 1865.
To My Old Master, Colonel P. H. Anderson,
Big Spring, Tennessee.
Sir:

I got your letter, and was glad to find that you had not forgotten Jourdon. . . . I thought the Yankees would have hung you long before this, for harboring Rebs they found at your house. I suppose they never heard about your going to Colonel Martin's house to kill the union soldier that was left by his company in their stable. Although you shot at me twice before I left you, I did not want to hear of your being hurt, and am glad you are still living. It would do me good to go back to the dear old home again, and see Miss Mary and Miss Martha and Allen, Esther, Green, and Lee. Give my love to them all, and tell them I hope we will meet in the better world, if not in this. . . .

I want to know particularly what the good chance is you propose to give me. I am doing tolerably well here. I get twenty-five dollars a month, with victuals and clothing; have a comfortable home for Mandy,—the folks call her Mrs. Anderson,—and the children—Milly, Jane, and Grundy—go to school and are learning well. . . . We are kindly treated. Sometimes we overhear others saying, "Them colored people were slaves" down in Tennessee. The children feel hurt when they hear such remarks; but I tell them it was no disgrace in Tennessee to belong to Colonel Anderson. Many darkeys would have been proud, as I used to be, to call you master. . . .

Mandy says she would be afraid to go back without some proof that you were disposed to treat us justly and kindly; and we have concluded to test your sincerity by asking you to send us our wages for the time we served you. . . . I served you faithfully for thirty-two years, and Mandy twenty years. At twenty-five dollars a month for me and two dollars a week for Mandy, our earnings would amount to eleven thousand six hundred and eighty dollars. Add to this the interest for the time our wages have been kept back, and deduct what you paid for our clothing, and three doctor's visits to me, and pulling a tooth for Mandy, and the balance will show what we are in justice entitled to. . . .

In answering this letter, please state if there would be any safety for my Milly and Jane, who are now grown up, and both good-looking girls. . . . I would rather stay here and starve—and die, if it come to that—than have my girls brought to shame by the violence and wickedness of their young masters. . . .

Say howdy to George Carter, and thank him for taking the pistol from you when you were shooting at me.

From your old servant,
Jourdon Anderson

SOURCE: Stanley I. Kutler, ed., *Looking for America: The People's History*, 2nd ed., 2 vols. (New York: W. W. Norton, 1979), 2: 4–6, 24–27.

the land. When the South Carolina planter Thomas Pinckney returned home, his freed slaves told him: "We ain't going nowhere. We are going to work right here on the land where we were born and what belongs to us."

Johnson's amnesty plan, entitling pardoned Confederates to recover property seized during the war, blasted these hopes. In October 1865, Johnson ordered General Oliver O. Howard, head of the Freedmen's Bureau, to restore the plantations on the Sea Islands off the South Carolina coast to their white owners. The dispossessed blacks protested: "Why do you take away our lands? You take them from us who have always been true, always true to the Government! You give them to our all-time enemies! That is not right!" On the Sea Islands and elsewhere, former slaves resisted efforts to evict them. Led by black army veterans, they fought pitched battles with plantation owners and bands of ex-Confederate soldiers. Landowners struck back hard. Often aided by federal troops, the local whites generally prevailed in this land war.

In early 1866, as planters prepared for a new growing season, a battle took shape over the labor system that would replace slavery. Convinced that blacks needed supervision, planters wanted to retain the **gang-labor system** of the past, but with wages replacing the food, clothing, and shelter that the slaves had once received. The Freedmen's Bureau, although watchful against exploitative labor contracts, sided with the planters.

Wage Labor of Former Slaves
This photograph, taken in South Carolina shortly after the Civil War, shows former slaves leaving the cotton fields. Ex-slaves were organized into work crews that were probably not very different from earlier slave gangs, although they now labored for wages and their plug-hatted boss bore little resemblance to the slave drivers of the past. New-York Historical Society.

The main thing, its reform-minded founders had always believed, was that dependency not be encouraged "in the guise of guardianship." Rely on your "own efforts and exertions," an agent told a large crowd of freedmen in North Carolina; "make contracts with the planters" and "respect the rights of property."

This was advice given with little regard for the world in which those North Carolina freedmen lived. It was not only their unequal bargaining power they worried about or even that their ex-masters' real desire was to reenslave them under the guise of "free" contracts. In their eyes, the condition of wage labor was, by definition, debasing. The rural South was not like the North, where working for wages had become the norm and qualified a man as independent. In the South, selling one's labor to another—in particular, selling one's labor to work another's land—implied not freedom, but dependency. "I mean to own my own manhood," responded one South Carolina freedman to an offer of wage work. "I'm going to own my own land."

The wage issue cut to the core of the former slaves' struggle for freedom. Nothing had been more horrifying than the condition of slavery, in which their persons had been the property of others. When a master cast his eye on a slave woman, her husband had no recourse, nor, for that matter, was rape of a slave a crime. In a famous oration celebrating the anniversary of emancipation, the Reverend Henry M. Turner spoke bitterly of the time when "our wives were sold and husbands bought, children were begotten and enslaved by their fathers." That was why formalizing marriage was so urgent a matter and why, when planters demanded that freedwomen go back into the fields, blacks resisted so resolutely. "I seen on some plantations," one freedman recounted, "where the white men would . . . tell colored men that their wives and children could not live on their places unless they work in the fields. The colored men [answered that] whenever they wanted their wives to work they would tell them themselves; and if he could not rule his own domestic affairs on that place he would leave it and go someplace else."

The reader will see the irony in this definition of freedom: It assumed the wife's subordinate role and designated her labor the husband's property. But if that was the price of freedom, freedwomen were prepared to pay it. Far better to take a chance with their own men than with their ex-masters.

Many former slaves voted with their feet, abandoning their old plantations and seeking better lives in the towns and cities of the South. Those who remained in the countryside refused to work the cotton fields under the hated gang-labor system. Whatever system of labor finally might emerge, it was clear that the freedmen would never settle for anything resembling the old plantation system.

The efforts of former slaves to control their own lives challenged deeply entrenched white attitudes. "The destiny of the black race," asserted one Texan, could be summarized "in one sentence—subordination to the white race." And when freedmen resisted, white retribution was swift and often terrible. In Pine Bluff, Arkansas, "after some kind of dispute with some freedmen," whites set fire to their cabins and hanged twenty-four of the inhabitants—men, women, and children. The toll of murdered and beaten blacks mounted into untold thousands.

The governments established under Johnson's plan put the stamp of legality on these efforts to enforce white supremacy. Blacks "would be *just as well* off with no law at all or no Government," concluded a Freedmen's Bureau agent, as with the justice they got under the restored white rule.

In this unequal struggle, blacks turned to Washington. "We stood by the government when it wanted help," a black Mississippian wrote President Johnson. "Now . . . will it stand by us?"

Congress Versus President

Andrew Johnson was not the man to ask. In February 1866, he vetoed the Freedmen's Bureau bill. The bureau, Johnson charged, was an "immense patronage," showering benefits on blacks that were never granted to "our own people." Republicans could not muster enough votes to override his veto. A month later, again rebuffing his critics, Johnson vetoed the civil rights bill, arguing that federal protection of black rights constituted "a stride toward centralization." His racism, hitherto muted, now blazed forth: "This is a country for white men, and by God, as long as I am president, it shall be government for white men."

Galvanized by Johnson's attack, the Republicans went into action. In early April, they got the necessary two-thirds majorities in both houses and enacted the Civil Rights Act. Republican resolve was reinforced by news of mounting violence in the South, culminating in three days of rioting in Memphis. Forty-six blacks were left dead, and hundreds of homes, churches, and schools were burned. In July, an angry Congress renewed the Freedmen's Bureau over a second Johnson veto.

Anxious to consolidate their gains, Republicans moved to enshrine black civil rights in an amendment to the Constitution. The heart of the Fourteenth Amendment was Section 1, which declared that "all persons born or naturalized in the United States" were citizens. No state could abridge "the privileges or immunities of citizens of the United States"; deprive "any person of life, liberty, or property, without due process of law"; or deny anyone "the equal protection of the laws." These phrases were intentionally vague, but they established the constitutionality of the Civil Rights Act and, more important, the basis on which the courts and Congress could erect an enforceable standard of equality before the law in the states.

For the moment, however, the Fourteenth Amendment was most important as a factor in partisan politics. With the 1866 congressional elections approaching, Johnson somehow figured he could turn the Fourteenth Amendment to his advantage. He urged the states not to ratify it. Months earlier, Johnson had begun maneuvering against the Republicans. He failed in his attempt at building a coalition of white Southerners, northern Democrats, and conservative Republicans under the banner of a new National Union Party, however, and his campaign against the Fourteenth Amendment became, effectively, a campaign for the Democratic Party.

Republicans responded furiously, unveiling a practice that would become known as "waving the bloody shirt." The Democratic Party was traitorous, charged Indiana governor Oliver Morton, "a common sewer and loathsome receptacle, into which is emptied every element of treason North and South." In late August, Johnson embarked on a disastrous "swing around the circle"—a railroad tour from Washington to Chicago and St. Louis and back—that violated the custom that presidents not campaign personally. Johnson made matters worse by engaging in shouting matches with hecklers and insulting the hostile crowds.

The 1866 elections inflicted a humiliating defeat on Johnson and gave the Republicans a three-to-one majority in Congress. They considered themselves "masters of the situation" and free to proceed "entirely regardless of [Johnson's] opinions or wishes." The Republican Party emerged with a new sense of unity—a unity that coalesced not at the center but at the extreme, around the unbending program of the Radical minority. The Radicals represented the abolitionist strain within the Republican Party. Most of them hailed from New England or from the upper Midwest, an area settled by New Englanders. They were led in the Senate by Charles Sumner of Massachusetts and in the House by Thaddeus Stevens of Pennsylvania. For them, Reconstruction was never primarily about restoring the Union. It was about remaking southern society.

Only a handful of Radicals went as far as Stevens in demanding that the plantations be treated as "forfeited estates of the enemy" and broken up into small farms for the former slaves. About securing the freedmen's civil and political rights, however, there was agreement. In this endeavor, Radicals had no qualms about expanding the powers of the national government. "The power of the great landed aristocracy in those regions, if unrestrained by power from without, would inevitably reassert itself," warned Congressman George W. Julian of Indiana. Radicals regarded the Republican Party as God's instrument for regenerating the South.

▶ Why can the enactment of southern Black Codes in 1865 be considered a turning point in the course of Reconstruction?

▶ Why did ex-slaves, struggling for freedom after emancipation, resist working for wages?

▶ To what extent was President Johnson responsible for the radicalization of the Republican Party in 1866?

At first, in the months after Appomattox, few but the Radicals themselves imagined that so extreme a program had any chance of enactment. Yet as fury mounted against the unrepentant South, Republicans became ever more radicalized until, in the wake of the smashing congressional victory of 1866, they embraced the Radicals' vision of a reconstructed South.

Radical Reconstruction

Afterward, thoughtful Southerners admitted that the South had brought radical Reconstruction on itself. "We had, in 1865, a white man's government in Alabama," remarked Johnson's provisional governor, "but we lost it." The "great blunder" was not to "have at once taken the negro right under the protection of the laws." Remarkably, the South remained defiant even after the 1866 elections. Every state legislature but Tennessee's rejected the Fourteenth Amendment. It was as if they could not imagine that fully functioning governments sanctioned by the president might be swept away. But that, in fact, is just what the Republicans intended to do.

Congress Takes Command

The Reconstruction Act of 1867, enacted in March, treated the South as a conquered land, dividing it into five military districts, each under the command of a Union general (Map 15.1). The price for reentering the Union was granting the vote to the freedmen and disfranchising any of the South's leaders who had participated in the rebellion. Each military commander was ordered to register all eligible adult males, black as well as white; supervise the election of state conventions; and make certain that the new constitutions

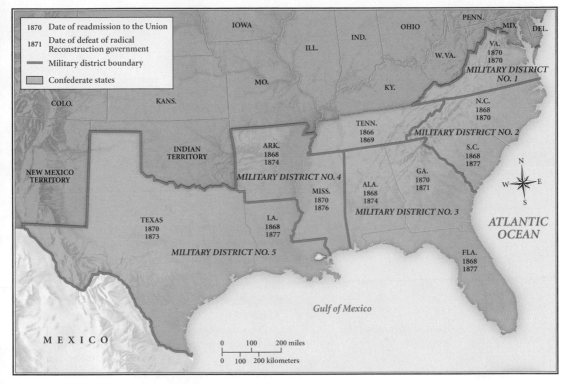

MAP 15.1 Reconstruction

The federal government organized the Confederate states into five military districts during radical Reconstruction. For each state, the first date indicates when that state was readmitted to the Union; the second date shows when Radical Republicans lost control of the state government. All the ex-Confederate states rejoined the Union from 1868 to 1870, but the periods of radical rule varied widely. Republicans lasted only a few months in Virginia; they held on until the end of Reconstruction in Louisiana, Florida, and South Carolina.

For more help analyzing this map, see the Online Study Guide at **bedfordstmartins.com/henrettaconcise**.

contained guarantees of black **suffrage**. Congress would readmit a state to the Union once these conditions were met and the new state legislature approved the Fourteenth Amendment (thus ensuring the needed ratification by three-fourths of the states). A companion bill, the Tenure of Office Act, restricted the president's authority to dismiss senior officials without senatorial consent (Table 15.1).

Seemingly defeated, Johnson was just biding his time. In August 1867, after Congress adjourned, he "suspended" Secretary of War Edwin M. Stanton, a supporter of radical Reconstruction, and replaced him with the commander of the army, Ulysses S. Grant. Next, Johnson replaced four of the commanding generals. Johnson, however, had misjudged Grant, who publicly objected to the president's machinations. When the Senate reconvened in the fall, it overruled Stanton's suspension. Grant, now an open enemy of Johnson's, resigned so that Stanton could resume his office.

On February 21, 1868, Johnson formally dismissed Stanton. The feisty secretary of war responded by barricading the door of his office. Three days later, for the first

TABLE 15.1	Primary Reconstruction Laws and Constitutional Amendments
Law (Date of Congressional Passage)	**Key Provisions**
Thirteenth Amendment (January 1865*)	Prohibited slavery
Civil Rights Act of 1866 (April 1866)	Defined citizenship rights of freedmen
	Authorized federal authorities to bring suit against those who violated those rights
Fourteenth Amendment (June 1866†)	Established national citizenship for persons born or naturalized in the United States
	Prohibited the states from depriving citizens of their civil rights or equal protection under the law
	Reduced state representation in House of Representatives by the percentage of adult male citizens denied the vote
Reconstruction Act of 1867 (March 1867‡)	Divided the South into five military districts, each under the command of a Union general
	Established requirements for readmission of ex-Confederate states to the Union
Tenure of Office Act (March 1867)	Required Senate consent for removal of any federal official whose appointment had required Senate confirmation
Fifteenth Amendment (February 1869)	Forbade states to deny citizens the right to vote on the grounds of race, color, or "previous condition of servitude"
Ku Klux Klan Act (April 1871)	Authorized the president to use federal prosecutions and military force to suppress conspiracies to deprive citizens of the right to vote and enjoy the equal protection of the law

*Ratified by three-fourths of all states in December 1868.
†Ratified by three-fourths of all states in July 1868.
‡Ratified by three-fourths of all states in March 1870.

time in U.S. history, House Republicans introduced articles of **impeachment** against a sitting president, employing the power granted the House of Representatives by the Constitution to charge high federal officials with "Treason, Bribery, or other high Crimes and Misdemeanors." The House serves, in effect, as the prosecutor in such cases, and the Senate serves as the court. Eleven counts of presidential misconduct were brought against Johnson, nine of them violations of the Tenure of Office Act.

The case went to the Senate, with Chief Justice Salmon P. Chase presiding. After an eleven-week trial, thirty-five senators on May 15 voted for conviction—one vote short of the two-thirds majority required. Seven moderate Republicans voted for acquittal along with twelve Democrats. The dissenting Republicans felt that removing a president for defying Congress was too damaging to the constitutional system of checks and balances, even for the sake of punishing Johnson. And they were wary of the alternative: the Radical Republican Benjamin F. Wade, the president pro tem of the Senate, who, since there was no vice president, stood next in line for the presidency. Despite his acquittal, however, Johnson had been defanged. For the remainder of his term, he was powerless to alter the course of Reconstruction.

The impeachment controversy made Grant, already the North's war hero, a Republican hero as well, and he easily won the party's presidential nomination in 1868. Although he supported radical Reconstruction, Grant also urged reconciliation between the sections. His Democratic opponent, Horatio Seymour, a former governor of New York, almost declined the nomination because he doubted that the Democrats could overcome the stain of disloyalty.

As Seymour feared, the Republicans "waved the bloody shirt," stirring up old wartime emotions against the Democrats to great effect. Grant did about as well in the North (55 percent) as Lincoln had in 1864. Overall, Grant won by a margin of 52.7 percent and received 214 of 294 electoral votes. The Republicans also retained two-thirds majorities in both houses of Congress.

In the wake of their smashing victory, the Republicans produced the last major piece of Reconstruction legislation: the Fifteenth Amendment, which forbade either the federal government or the states to deny citizens the right to vote on the basis of race, color, or "previous condition of servitude." The amendment left room for **poll taxes** and property requirements, a necessary concession to northern and western states that already relied on such provisions to keep immigrants and the "unworthy" poor from the polls. A California senator warned that in his state, with its rabidly anti-Chinese sentiment (see Chapter 16), any restriction on that power would "kill our party as dead as a stone."

Despite grumbling by Radical Republicans, the amendment passed without modification in February 1869. Congress required the states still under federal control—Virginia, Mississippi, Texas, and Georgia—to ratify it as a condition for being readmitted to the Union. A year later, the Fifteenth Amendment became part of the Constitution.

Woman Suffrage Denied

If the Fifteenth Amendment troubled some proponents of black suffrage, this was nothing compared to the outrage felt by women's rights advocates. They had fought the good fight for the abolition of slavery for so many years, only to be abandoned when the chance finally came to get the vote for women. All it would have taken was one more word in the Fifteenth Amendment so that the protected categories for voting would have read "race, color, *sex*, or previous condition."

In a decisive debate in May 1869 at the Equal Rights Association, the black abolitionist Frederick Douglass pleaded for understanding. "When women, because they are women, are hunted down . . . dragged from their homes and hung upon lamp posts . . . when their children are not allowed to enter schools; then they will have an urgency to obtain the ballot equal to our own." Not even all his black sisters agreed. "If colored men get their rights, and not colored women theirs," protested Sojourner Truth, "you see the colored men will be masters over the women, and it will be just as bad as it was before." As for white women in the audience, remarked Frances Harper in support of Douglass, they "all go for sex, letting race occupy a minor position," or worse. In her despair, Elizabeth Cady Stanton lashed out in ugly racist terms against "Patrick and Sambo and Hans and Ung Tung," aliens who were ignorant of the Declaration of Independence and yet entitled to vote while the most accomplished of American women remained voteless. Douglass's resolution in support of the Fifteenth Amendment failed, and the Equal Rights convention broke up in acrimony.

At this searing moment, a rift opened in the women's movement. The majority, led by Lucy Stone and Julia Ward Howe, reconciled themselves to disappointment. Organized into the American Woman Suffrage Association, these moderates remained loyal to the Republican Party in hopes that once Reconstruction had been settled, it would be time for the woman's vote. The group led by Elizabeth Cady Stanton and Susan B. Anthony, however, struck out in a new direction. The embittered Stanton declared that woman "must not put her trust in man." The new organization that she headed, the New York–based National Woman Suffrage Association, accepted only women, focused exclusively on women's rights, and resolutely took up the battle for a federal woman suffrage amendment.

The fracturing of the women's movement obscured the common ground the two sides shared. Both appealed to constituencies beyond the narrow confines of evangelical reform. Both elevated suffrage as the preeminent women's issue. And both were energized for the battles that lay ahead. "If I were to give vent to all my pent-up wrath concerning the subordination of woman," Lydia Maria Child wrote to Republican Senator Charles Sumner in 1872, "I might frighten *you*. . . . Suffice it, therefore, to say, either the theory of our government is *false*, or women have a right to vote." If radical Reconstruction seemed a barren time for women's rights, in fact it had planted the seeds of the modern feminist movement.

Republican Rule in the South

Between 1868 and 1871, all the southern states met the congressional stipulations and rejoined the Union. Protected by federal troops, state Republican organizations set up Reconstruction administrations that remained in power for periods ranging from a few months in Virginia to nine years in South Carolina, Louisiana, and Florida. Their core support came from African Americans, who constituted a majority of registered voters in Alabama, Florida, South Carolina, and Mississippi.

Ex-Confederates called Southern whites who supported Reconstruction **scalawags**—an ancient Scots-Irish term for runty, worthless animals. Northern whites they denounced as **carpetbaggers**—self-seeking interlopers who carried all their property in cheap suitcases called carpetbags. Such labels glossed over the actual diversity of these white Republicans.

Some carpetbaggers, while motivated by personal profit, also brought capital and skills. Others were Union army veterans who found the climate, people, and economic opportunities of the South appealing. And interspersed with the self-seekers were many idealists anxious to advance the cause of emancipation.

The scalawags were even more diverse. Some were former slave owners, ex-Whigs and even ex-Democrats drawn to Republicanism as the best way to attract northern capital to southern railroads, mines, and factories. But most hailed from the backcountry districts and wanted to rid the South of its slaveholding aristocracy. They had generally fought against, or at least refused to support, the Confederacy, believing that slavery had victimized whites as well as blacks. "Now is the time," a Georgia scalawag wrote, "for every man to come out . . . and vote for liberty as we have been in bondage long enough."

Hiram R. Revels

In 1870, Hiram R. Revels (1822–1901) was elected to the U.S. Senate from Mississippi to fill Jefferson Davis's former seat. Revels was a free black man from North Carolina who had migrated to the North and attended Knox College in Illinois. He recruited blacks for the Union army and, as an ordained Methodist minister, served as chaplain of a black regiment in Mississippi, where he settled after the war. Library of Congress.

The Democrats' scorn for black leaders, whom they regarded as ignorant field hands, was just as misguided as stereotypes about white Republicans. The first African American leaders in the South came from an elite of free blacks. They were joined by northern blacks who moved south to join the battle for radical Reconstruction. Like their white allies, many were Union army veterans. Some were employed by the Freedmen's Bureau or northern missionary societies. Others had escaped from slavery and were returning home. One of these ex-slaves was Blanche K. Bruce, who had been tutored on the Virginia plantation of his white father. During the war, Bruce escaped and established a school for ex-slaves in Missouri. In 1869, he moved to Mississippi and became active in politics; in 1874, he became Mississippi's second black U.S. senator.

As the reconstructed Republican governments of 1867 began to function, African American speakers, some financed by the Republican Party, fanned out into the old plantation districts and recruited ex-slaves. Still, few of the new leaders were field hands; most had been preachers or artisans. The literacy of one ex-slave, Thomas Allen, who was a Baptist minister and shoemaker, helped him to win election to the Georgia legislature. "In my county," he recalled, "the colored people came to me for instructions, and I gave them the best instructions I could. I took the *New York Tribune* and other papers, and in that way I found out a great deal, and I told them whatever I thought was right."

Although never proportionate to their numbers in the population, blacks became officeholders across the South. In South Carolina, African Americans constituted a majority in the lower house of the legislature in 1868. Three were elected to Congress; another joined the state supreme court. Over the entire course of Reconstruction, 20 African Americans served in state administrations as governor, lieutenant governor, secretary of state, treasurer, or superintendent of education; more than 600 served as state legislators; and 16 were congressmen.

The Republicans had ambitious plans. They wanted to end the South's dependence on cotton agriculture, build an entrepreneurial economy like the North's, and make a better life for all southerners. Although they fell short, they accomplished more than their critics gave them credit for. The new constitutions expanded the rights of married women, enabling them to hold property and earnings independent of their husbands'—"a wonderful reform," a Georgia woman wrote, for "the cause of Women's Rights." Property qualifications for the vote were eliminated, as were the ordinances restricting the lives of the freedmen. Republican social programs called for the establishment of hospitals, more humane penitentiaries, and asylums for orphans and the insane. Money poured into road-building projects and the region's shattered railroad network.

Freedmen's School, c. 1870

This rare photograph shows the interior of one of the 3,000 freedmen's schools established across the South after the Civil War. Although many of these schools were staffed by white missionaries, a main objective of northern educators was to prepare blacks to take over the classrooms. The teacher shown here is surely one of the first. Library of Congress.

For more help analyzing this image, see the Online Study Guide at **bedfordstmartins.com/henrettaconcise**.

The Reconstruction governments overreached, however. State debts mounted rapidly, and as crushing interest on bonds fell due, public credit collapsed. On top of that, much spending was wasted or ended up in the pockets of public officials. Corruption was ingrained in American politics and rampant everywhere in this era, not least in the Grant administration itself. Still, in the free-spending atmosphere of the southern Republican regimes, corruption was especially luxuriant and damaging to the cause of radical Reconstruction.

Nothing, however, could dim the achievement in public education, where the South had lagged woefully. Republican state governments vowed to make up for lost time, viewing education as the foundation for a democratic order. African Americans of all ages rushed to the newly established schools, even when they had to pay tuition. An elderly man in Mississippi explained his hunger for education: "Ole missus used to read the good book [the Bible] to us . . . on Sunday evenin's, but she mostly read dem places where it says, 'Servants obey your masters.' . . . Now we is free, there's heaps of tings in that old book we is just suffering to learn."

The building of schools was joined by a larger effort to fortify the institutions that had sustained the African Americans in the slave days, most especially Christianity. Now, in freedom, they left the white-dominated congregations, where they had sat in segregated balconies, and built churches of their own. These churches joined together to form African American versions of the Southern Methodist and Baptist denominations, including, most prominently, the National Baptist Convention and the African Methodist Episcopal Church. Everywhere, the black churches served not only as places of worship but also as schools, social centers, and political meeting halls.

Black clerics were community leaders and often political leaders as well. As Charles H. Pearce, a Methodist minister in Florida, declared, "A man in this State cannot do his whole duty as a minister except he looks out for the political interests of his people." Calling forth the special destiny of the ex-slaves as the new "Children of Israel," black ministers provided a powerful religious underpinning for the Republican politics of their congregations.

The Quest for Land

In the meantime, the freedmen were locked in a great economic struggle with their former owners. In 1869, the Republican government of South Carolina had established a land commission empowered to buy property and resell it on easy terms to the landless. In this way, about 14,000 black families acquired farms. South Carolina's land distribution plan showed what was possible, but it was the exception and not the rule. Despite a lot of rhetoric, Republican regimes elsewhere did little to help the freedmen fulfill their dreams. Federal efforts proved equally feeble. The Southern Homestead Act of 1866 offered eighty-acre grants to settlers, limited for the first year to freedmen and southern Unionists. The advantage was mostly symbolic, however, since only marginal land was made available, off the beaten track in swampy, infertile parts of the Lower South.

There was no reversing President Johnson's order restoring confiscated lands to ex-Confederates. Property rights, it seemed, trumped everything else, even for most Radical Republicans. The Freedmen's Bureau, which had earlier championed the land claims of the ex-slaves, now devoted itself to teaching them how to be good agricultural laborers.

While yearning for farms of their own, most freedmen started out with no option but to work for their former owners. But not, they vowed, under the conditions of slavery; there would be no gang work, no overseers, no fines or punishments, no regulation of their private lives. In certain parts of the South, wage work became the norm—for example, on the great sugar plantations of Louisiana financed by northern capital. But cotton planters lacked the money to pay wages, at least until the crop came in, and sometimes, in lieu of a straight wage, they offered a share of the crop. As a wage, this was a bad deal for the freedmen, but if they could be paid in shares for their work, why could they not pay in shares to rent the land they worked?

Planters resisted, believing, as one wrote, that "wages are the only successful system of controlling hands." But in a battle of wills that broke out all across the cotton South, the planters yielded to "the inveterate prejudices of the freedmen, who desire to be masters of their own time."

Thus sprang up the distinctive laboring system of cotton agriculture known as **sharecropping**, in which the freedmen worked as renters, exchanging their labor for the use of land, house, implements, and sometimes secd and fertilizer and typically turning over half of their crops to the landlord (Map 15.2). The sharecropping system joined laborers and land owners in a common sharing of risks and returns. But it was

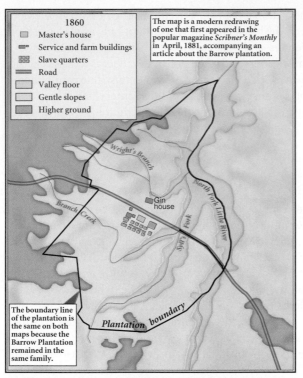

1860

- ☐ Master's house
- ◼▫ Service and farm buildings
- ▦ Slave quarters
- ═ Road
- ☐ Valley floor
- ☐ Gentle slopes
- ▨ Higher ground

The map is a modern redrawing of one that first appeared in the popular magazine *Scribner's Monthly* in April, 1881, accompanying an article about the Barrow plantation.

The boundary line of the plantation is the same on both maps because the Barrow Plantation remained in the same family.

1881

- ☐ Landlord's house
- ◼ Service and farm buildings
- ▦ Houses of former slaves
- ═ Road
- ☐ Valley floor
- ☐ Gentle slopes
- ▨ Higher ground

1. Syrup 4%
2. Wheat 5%
3. Fodder 6%
4. Corn 28%
5. Cotton 57%

Crop share of income for Handy Barrow (ex-slave, 1881)

The boundary also indicates that the land was surveyed according to the old "metes-and-bounds" system, not the rectangular pattern created by the Land Ordinance of 1785 for the division of federal lands.

MAP 15.2 The Barrow Plantation, 1860 and 1881

Comparing the 1860 map of this central Georgia plantation with the 1881 map reveals the impact of sharecropping on patterns of black residence. In 1860, the slave quarters were clustered near the planter's house. In contrast, the sharecroppers scattered across the plantation's 2,000 acres, building cabins on the ridges of land between the low-lying streams. The name Barrow was common among the sharecropping families, which almost certainly means that they had been slaves on the Barrow plantation who, years after emancipation, had not moved away. For all the sharecroppers, freedom surely meant not only their individual lots and cabins but also the school and church shown on the map.

a very unequal relationship, given the force of southern law and custom on the white landowner's side and the sharecroppers' dire economic circumstances. Starting out penniless, they had no way of making it through the first growing season without borrowing for food and supplies.

Country storekeepers stepped in. Bankrolled by their northern suppliers, they furnished the sharecropper with provisions and took as collateral a **lien** on the crop, effectively assuming ownership of the cropper's share and leaving him only the proceeds that remained after his debts had been paid. Once indebted at one store, share-croppers were no longer free to shop around. They became easy targets for exorbitant prices, unfair interest rates, and crooked bookkeeping. As cotton prices declined during the 1870s, more and more sharecroppers failed to settle accounts and fell into permanent debt.

And if the merchant was also the landowner or conspired with the landowner, the debt became a pretext for forced labor, or **peonage**, although evidence now suggests that sharecroppers generally managed to pull up stakes and move on once things became hopeless. Sharecroppers always thought twice about moving, however, because part of their "capital" was being known and well regarded in their home communities. Freedmen who lacked that local standing generally found sharecropping hard going and ended up in the ranks of agricultural laborers.

In the face of so much adversity, black families struggled to better themselves. The saving advantage of sharecropping was that it mobilized husbands and wives in a common enterprise while shielding both from personal subordination to whites. Wives were doubly blessed. Neither field hands for their ex-masters nor dependent house-wives, they became partners laboring side by side with their husbands. The trouble with sharecropping, one planter grumbled, was that "it makes the laborer too independent; he becomes a partner, and has to be consulted."

The battle between planters and freedmen was by no means unique to the American South. Whenever slavery ended—in Haiti after the slave revolt of 1791, in the British Caribbean by abolition in 1833, in Cuba and Brazil by gradual emancipation during the 1880s—planters bent on restoring a gang-labor system battled ex-slaves bent on gaining economic autonomy. The outcome depended on the ex-slaves' access to land. Where vacant land existed, as in British Guiana, or where plantations could be seized, as in Haiti, the ex-slaves became subsistence farmers. Where land was beyond reach, as in British Barbados or Antigua, the ex-slaves returned to plantation labor as wage-workers, although often in some combination with customary rights to housing and garden plots. The cotton South fit neither pattern. The freedmen did not get the land, but neither did the planters get field hands. What both got was sharecropping.

There are two ways of explaining this outcome. One is political. In other countries, emancipated slaves rarely got political rights. Even in the British islands, where substantial self-government existed, high property qualifications effectively disfranchised the ex-slaves. In the United States, however, hard on the heels of emancipation came, for a brief era, a real measure of political power for the freedmen. Sharecropping took shape during Reconstruction, and there was no going back afterward.

That there was no going back suggests a second reason why sharecropping prevailed: It was a good fit for cotton agriculture. We can see this in the experience of other countries that became major producers in response to the global cotton famine set off by the Civil War. In all these places — India, Egypt, Brazil, and West Africa — some variant of the sharecropping system emerged.

Most striking was the adoption everywhere of crop-lien laws, at the behest of the international merchants and bankers who put up the capital. Indian and Egyptian villagers got the advances they needed to shift from subsistence agriculture to cotton but at the price of being placed, as in America, permanently under the thumb of the furnishing merchants. Implicit in advancing that money, of course, was the realization that cotton, unlike sugar cane, could be raised efficiently by small farmers (provided they had the lash of indebtedness always on their backs). American planters resisted sharecropping because they started at a different place: not traditional, subsistence economies that had to be converted to cotton but a proven plantation system over which they had been absolute masters.

For America's ex-slaves, sharecropping was not the worst choice; it certainly beat laboring for their former owners. But for southern agriculture, the costs were devastating. Sharecropping committed the South inflexibly to cotton because, as a market crop, it generated the cash required by landlords and furnishing merchants. Neither soil depletion nor low prices ever enabled sharecroppers to shift away from cotton. With farms leased on a year-to-year basis, neither tenant nor owner had much incentive to improve the property. And the crop-lien system lined merchants' pockets with unearned profits that might otherwise have gone into agricultural improvement. The result was a stagnant farm economy, blighting the South's future and condemning it to economic backwardness — a kind of retribution for the fresh injustices being visited on the people it had once enslaved.

▶ Do you think it was predictable in 1865 that five years later, the ex-slaves would receive a constitutional right to vote? Was it predictable that, having gone that far, the nation would deny the vote to women? Why or why not?

▶ Why did the ex-slaves' struggle for land result in the sharecropping system?

The Undoing of Reconstruction

Ex-Confederates were blind to the achievements of radical Reconstruction. Indeed, no amount of success could have persuaded them that it was anything but an abomination, denying them their rightful place in southern society. Led by the planters, ex-Confederates staged a massive counterrevolution designed to "redeem" the South. But the Redeemers could not have succeeded on their own. They needed the complicity of the North. The undoing of Reconstruction is as much about northern acquiescence as about southern resistance.

Counterrevolution

Insofar as they could win at the ballot box, southern Democrats took that route. They got ex-Confederates restored to the voting rolls, they put forward tickets appealing to southern patriotism, and they campaigned against black rule. But force was equally acceptable. Throughout the Deep South, especially where black voters were heavily concentrated, ex-Confederates organized secretly and terrorized blacks and their white allies.

Nathan Bedford Forrest in Uniform, c. 1865
Before he became Grand Wizard of the Ku Klux Klan, Forrest had been a celebrated cavalry general in the Confederate army. This photograph shows him in uniform before he was mustered out. Library of Congress.

No one looms larger in this bloody story than Nathan Bedford Forrest, the Confederacy's most decorated cavalry general. Born in poverty in 1821, he had scrambled up the booming cotton economy and had become a big-time Memphis slave trader and Mississippi plantation owner. A man of fiery temper, he championed secession. When the war broke out, Forrest immediately formed a Tennessee cavalry regiment, fought bravely (and was badly wounded) at the battle of Shiloh, and won fame as a daring cavalry raider. On April 12, 1864, his troopers perpetrated one of the war's worst atrocities, the slaughter of black troops at Fort Pillow, Tennessee, acting on rumors that they had harassed local whites.

Although nominally in control since 1862, Union authorities never managed to subdue Tennessee's irreconcilable Confederate sympathizers. William G. Brownlow, the Republican who was elected governor in 1865, was a tough man, a former prisoner of the Confederates who was not shy about calling his enemies to account. They struck back with a campaign of terror, targeting especially Brownlow's black supporters. Amid this general mayhem, some among their number formed the first den of the Ku Klux Klan in late 1865 or early 1866.

As it proliferated across the state, the Klan turned to General Forrest, who had been trying, unsuccessfully, to rebuild his prewar fortunes. Late in 1866, at a secret meeting in Nashville, Forrest donned the robes of Grand Wizard. His activities are mostly cloaked in mystery, but there is no mystery about why Forrest gravitated to the Klan. For him, the Klan was politics by other means, the instrument by which disfranchised former Confederates like himself might strike a blow against the despised Republicans who ran Tennessee.

In many towns, the Klan became virtually identical to the Democratic Party. In fact, Klan members—including Forrest—dominated Tennessee's delegation to the Democratic national convention of 1868. On the ground, the Klan unleashed a murderous campaign of terror. Although Governor Brownlow responded resolutely, in the end it was the Republicans, not the Klan, who cracked. In March 1869, Brownlow retreated to the U.S. Senate. The Democrats were on their way back to power, and the Klan, having served its purpose, was officially disbanded in Tennessee.

Elsewhere, the Klan raged on, murdering Republican politicians, burning black schools and churches, and attacking Republican Party gatherings. By 1870, the Democrats had seized power in Georgia and North Carolina and were making headway across the South.

Congress responded by passing legislation designed to put down the Ku Klux Klan and enforce the rights of ex-slaves under the Fourteenth and Fifteenth Amendments. These so-called Enforcement Laws authorized federal prosecutions, military intervention, and martial law to suppress terrorist activities. In South Carolina, where the Klan became most deeply entrenched, federal troops occupied nine counties, made hundreds of arrests, and drove as many as 2,000 Klansmen from the state.

The Grant administration's assault on the Klan, while raising the spirits of southern Republicans, also revealed how dependent they were on Washington. The potency of the anti–Ku Klux Klan legislation, a Mississippi Republican wrote, "derived alone from its source" in the federal government. "No such law could be enforced by state authority, the local power being too weak." If they were to prevail over antiblack terrorism, Republicans needed what one carpetbagger described as "steady, unswerving power from without."

But northern Republicans grew weary of Reconstruction and the endless bloodshed it seemed to produce. Prosecuting Klansmen was an uphill battle against all-white juries and unsympathetic federal judges. After 1872, prosecutions began to drop off, and many Klansmen received hasty pardons. Then the constitutional underpinnings of the antiterrorist campaign came into question, culminating in the Supreme Court's decision in *U.S. v. Cruikshank* (1876) that the federal government had exceeded its authority. If the civil rights of the ex-slaves were being violated by individuals or private groups (such as the KKK), that was a state responsibility and beyond the federal jurisdiction.

In a kind of self-fulfilling prophecy, the reluctance of the Grant administration to shore up Reconstruction guaranteed that it would fail. One by one, Republican governments fell victim to the massive resistance of their ex-Confederate enemies: Texas in 1873, Alabama and Arkansas in 1874, Mississippi in 1875.

The Mississippi campaign showed all too clearly what the Republicans were up against. As elections neared in 1875, paramilitary groups such as the Rifle Clubs and Red Shirts operated openly. Mississippi's Republican governor, Adelbert Ames, a Congressional Medal of Honor winner from Maine, appealed to President Grant for federal troops, but Grant refused. Brandishing their guns and stuffing the ballot boxes, the Redeemers swept the 1875 elections and took control of Mississippi. Facing impeachment, Governor Ames resigned his office and returned to the North.

By 1876, Republican governments, backed by token U.S. military units, remained in only three southern states: Louisiana, South Carolina, and Florida. Elsewhere, the former Confederates were back in power.

The Acquiescent North

The faltering of Reconstruction stemmed from more than battle fatigue, however. Sympathy for the freedmen began to wane. The North was flooded with one-sided, often racist reports, such as James M. Pike's *The Prostrate State* (1873), describing South Carolina in the grip of "a mass of black barbarism." The impact of this propaganda could be seen in the fate of the ambitious civil rights bill that Charles Sumner introduced in 1870 to enforce, among other things, the rights of African Americans to equal access to public accommodation, schools, and jury service. By the time the bill passed in 1875, it had been stripped of its key provisions. The Supreme Court finished the demolition job when it declared the remnant Civil Rights Act unconstitutional in 1883.

The political cynicism that overtook Sumner's Civil Rights Act signaled the Republican Party's reversion to politics as usual. In many states, a second generation took over the party—men such as Roscoe Conkling of New York, who had little enthusiasm for Reconstruction except when it benefited the Republican Party. As the party lost headway in the South, they lost interest in the battle for black rights. In Washington, President Grant presided benignly over this transformation of his party, turning a blind eye to corruption even as it began to creep into the White House.

Even the high-minded antislavery Christian reformers turned against Reconstruction. The touchstone for them was "free labor," the idea of America as a land of self-reliant, industrious property owners. They had framed the Civil War as a battle between "free labor" and its antithesis, the plantation society of masters and slaves. Now, with the South defeated, the question became, Would the emancipated slaves embrace "free labor"? No, asserted propaganda such as Pike's *The Prostrate South*. Instead of choosing self-reliance, the freedmen were running riot, demanding patronage, becoming dependents of the corrupt Reconstruction regimes. With this tragic misreading of the former slaves—and of their uphill struggle for land and self-rule—Republican allies drifted away and turned against radical Reconstruction.

These advocates of "free labor," once zealous for black freedom, clambered to the safer ground of civil service reform. Henceforth, it was the evils of corrupt politics that would claim their attention. They repudiated the wartime expansion of federal power and refashioned themselves as **liberals**—believers in free trade, market competition, and limited government. And with unabashed elitism, they denounced universal suffrage, which "can only mean in plain English the government of ignorance and vice."

American reform had arrived at a dispiriting watershed. The grand impulse that had driven the antislavery struggle, insofar as it survived the trauma of Reconstruction, now took the form of pallid efforts at purifying American politics, with Grant as the first target.

As Grant's administration lapsed into cronyism, a revolt took shape inside the Republican Party, led by an influential collection of intellectuals, journalists, and reform-minded businessmen. Unable to deny Grant renomination in 1872, the dissidents broke away and formed a new party under the name Liberal Republican. Their candidate was Horace Greeley, longtime publisher of the *New York Tribune* and veteran of American reform in all its variety, including antislavery. The Democrats, still in disarray, also nominated Greeley, notwithstanding his editorial diatribes against them. A poor campaigner, Greeley was assailed so bitterly that, as he said, "I hardly knew whether I was running for the Presidency or the penitentiary."

Grant won overwhelmingly, capturing 56 percent of the popular vote and every electoral vote. Yet the Liberal Republicans had managed to shift the terms of political debate in the country. The agenda they had established—civil service reform, limited government, reconciliation with the South—was adopted by the Democrats, who were shedding their reputation for disloyalty and reclaiming their status as a legitimate national party.

Charges of Republican corruption, which had been mounting ever since Grant's reelection, came to a head in 1875. The scandal involved the Whiskey Ring, a network of liquor distillers and treasury agents who defrauded the government of millions of dollars of excise taxes on whiskey. The ringleader was a Grant appointee, and Grant's own private secretary, Orville Babcock, had a hand in the thievery. The others went to prison, but Grant stood by Babcock, possibly perjuring himself to save his secretary from jail. The stench of scandal, however, had engulfed the White House.

On top of this, the economy fell into a severe depression, triggered in 1873 by the bankruptcy of the Northern Pacific Railroad. Its main investor, Jay Cooke, had been the chief financier of the Civil War and was well connected in Washington, raising suspicions that Republican financial manipulation had caused the depression. Grant's administration responded ineffectually, rebuffing the pleas of debtors for relief by increasing the money supply (see Chapter 19).

Among the casualties of the bad economy was the Freedman's Savings and Trust Company, which held the small deposits of thousands of ex-slaves. When the bank failed in 1874, Congress refused to compensate the depositors, and many lost their life savings. In denying their pathetic pleas, Congress was signaling also that Reconstruction had lost its moral claim on the country. National politics had moved on. Concerns about the economy and political fraud, not the South, absorbed northern voters as another presidential election approached in 1876.

The Political Crisis of 1877

Abandoning Grant, the Republicans nominated Rutherford B. Hayes, governor of Ohio, a colorless figure but untainted by corruption—in other words, a safe man. His Democratic opponent was Samuel J. Tilden, governor of New York, a Wall Street lawyer with a reform reputation for cleaning up New York City politics. The Democrat Tilden, of course, favored **home rule** for the South; but so, more discreetly, did the Republican Hayes. Reconstruction actually did not figure prominently in the campaign and was mostly subsumed under broader Democratic charges of "corrupt centralism" and "incapacity, waste, and fraud." Little was said about the states still ruled by Reconstruction governments: Florida, South Carolina, and Louisiana.

Once the returns started coming in on election night, however, those three states began to loom very large indeed. Tilden led in the popular vote and seemed headed for victory until sleepless politicians at Republican headquarters realized that the electoral vote stood at 184 to 165, with the 20 votes from Florida, South Carolina, and Louisiana still uncertain. If Hayes took those votes, he would win by a margin of one. Republicans still controlled the election machinery in the three states; citing Democratic fraud and intimidation, they certified Republican victories. Newly elected Democratic officials also sent in electoral votes for Tilden, and when Congress met in early 1877, it faced two sets of electoral votes from those states.

The Constitution does not provide for this contingency. All it says is that the president of the Senate (in 1877, a Republican) opens the electoral certificates before the House (Democratic) and the Senate (Republican) and that "the Votes shall then be counted" (Article 2, Section 1). Suspense gripped the country. There was talk of inside deals, of a new election, even of a violent coup. Just in case, the commander of the army, General William T. Sherman, deployed four artillery companies in Washington. Finally, Congress appointed an electoral commission to settle the question. The commission included seven Republicans, seven Democrats, and, as the deciding member, David Davis, a Supreme Court justice not known to have fixed party loyalties. However Davis disqualified himself by accepting an Illinois seat in the Senate. He was replaced by Republican justice Joseph P. Bradley, and by a vote of 8 to 7, the commission awarded the disputed votes to Hayes.

Outraged Democrats had one more trick up their sleeves. They controlled the House of Representatives, and they stalled a final count of the electoral votes so as to prevent Hayes's inauguration on March 4. But a week before, secret Washington talks had begun between southern Democrats and Ohio Republicans representing Hayes. Exactly what deal was struck will probably never be known, but on March 1, the House Democrats suddenly ended their delaying tactics, the ceremonial counting of votes went forward, and Hayes was inaugurated on schedule. He soon ordered the Union troops back to their barracks, and the last Republican administrations in the South fell. Reconstruction had ended.

In 1877, political leaders on all sides seemed ready to say that what Lincoln had called "the work" was complete. But for the former slaves, the work had only begun. Reconstruction turned out to have been a magnificent aberration, a leap beyond what most white Americans actually felt was due their black fellow citizens. Still, something real had been achieved: three rights-defining amendments to the Constitution, some elbow room to advance economically, and, not least, a stubborn confidence among blacks that by their own efforts, they could lift themselves up. Things would, in fact, get worse before they got better, but the work of Reconstruction was imperishable and could never be erased.

▶ Why did the Redeemers resort to terror in their campaign to regain political control of the South?

▶ What changes in the North explain why the Republicans abandoned the battle for Reconstruction?

▶ Do you believe that the failure of Reconstruction was primarily a failure of leadership? Or, to put it more concretely, do you think that the outcome might have been different had Lincoln lived or had chosen a different vice president or had Andrew Johnson not been followed by Ulysses S. Grant? Explain your answer.

SUMMARY

By any measure — in lives, treasure, or national harmony — the Civil War was the most shattering event in American history. In this chapter, we describe how the nation picked up the pieces. Reconstruction confronted two great tasks: restoring the rebellious states to the Union and incorporating the emancipated slaves into the national citizenry. The two tasks were inseparably part of a single grand struggle.

Reconstruction went through three phases. In the presidential phase, Lincoln's successor Andrew Johnson unilaterally offered the South easy terms for reentering the Union. This might have succeeded had Southerners responded with restraint, but instead, they adopted oppressive Black Codes and welcomed ex-Confederates back into power. Infuriated by southern arrogance, congressional Republicans closed ranks behind the Radicals, embraced the freedmen's demand for full equality, placed the South under military rule in 1867, and inaugurated radical Reconstruction.

In this second phase, the new Republican state governments tried to transform the South's decrepit economic and social structures, while on the plantations, ex-slaves battled for economic independence. No amount of accomplishment, however, could reconcile the ex-Confederates to Republican rule, and they staged a violent counter-revolution in the name of white supremacy and "redemption."

Distracted by Republican scandals and economic problems, the Grant administration had little stomach for a protracted guerrilla war in the South. Left on their own, the Reconstruction governments fell one by one to Redeemer intimidation and violence. In this third phase, as Reconstruction wound down, the concluding event was the contested election of 1876, which the Republicans resolved by trading their last remaining southern strongholds — South Carolina and Louisiana — for retention of the White House. On that unsavory note, Reconstruction ended.

Connections: Sectionalism

In many ways, Reconstruction marked the final stage in a long-developing struggle between sections. As the essay that opened Part Three noted:

> The North developed into an urbanizing society based on free labor, whereas the South remained a rural agricultural society dependent on slavery.

In Chapter 13, we described how the sectional crisis that arose from these differences broke the Union apart in 1861. The Civil War (Chapter 14) tested the war-making capacities of the rival systems. At first, the advantage lay with the military prowess of the agrarian South, but in the end, the superior resources of the industrial North prevailed. Even in defeat, however, the South could not be forced into a national mold. That was the ultimate lesson of Reconstruction. In the aftermath, the South persisted on its own path, as we will see in Chapter 17, which discusses the South's distinctive low-wage labor system, and Chapter 19, which describes its one-party, whites-only politics. The gradual, if partial, dissolution of southern uniqueness in the twentieth century is a theme of later chapters of this book.

FOR FURTHER EXPLORATION

The best book on Reconstruction is Eric Foner's major synthesis, *Reconstruction: America's Unfinished Revolution, 1863–1877* (1988), available also in a shorter version. *Black Reconstruction in America* (1935), by the African American activist and scholar W. E. B. Du Bois, deserves attention as the first book on Reconstruction that stressed the role of blacks in their own emancipation. On the freedmen, Leon F. Litwack, *Been in the Storm So Long: The Aftermath of Slavery* (1979), provides a stirring account.

TIMELINE

1863 ▶ Lincoln announces his Ten Percent Plan

1864 ▶ Wade-Davis Bill passed by Congress

▶ Lincoln pocket vetoes Wade-Davis Bill

1865 ▶ Freedmen's Bureau established

▶ Lincoln assassinated; Andrew Johnson succeeds as president

▶ Johnson implements his restoration plan

1866 ▶ Civil Rights Act passes over Johnson's veto

▶ Memphis riots

▶ Johnson makes disastrous "swing around the circle"; Republicans carry congressional elections

1867 ▶ Reconstruction Act

1868 ▶ Impeachment crisis

▶ Fourteenth Amendment ratified

▶ Ulysses S. Grant elected president

1870 ▶ Ku Klux Klan at peak of power

▶ Fifteenth Amendment ratified

1872 ▶ Grant's reelection

1873 ▶ Panic of 1873 ushers in depression of 1873–1877

1875 ▶ Whiskey Ring scandal undermines Grant administration

1877 ▶ Compromise of 1877; Rutherford B. Hayes becomes president

▶ Reconstruction ends

More recent emancipation studies emphasize slavery as a labor system: Julie Saville, *The Work of Reconstruction: From Slave to Wage Laborer in South Carolina, 1860–1870* (1994), and Amy Dru Stanley, *From Bondage to Contract* (1999), which expands the discussion to show what the onset of wage labor meant for freedwomen. In *Gendered Strife & Confusion: The Political Culture of Reconstruction* (1997), Laura F. Edwards explores via a close-grained local study the impact of "peripheral" people—the ordinary folk of both races—on Reconstruction politics. Eric Foner, *Nothing But Freedom: Emancipation and Its Legacy* (1983), helpfully places emancipation in a comparative context. William S. McFeely, *Grant: A Biography* (1981), deftly explains the politics of Reconstruction. The emergence of the sharecropping system is explored in Gavin Wright, *Old South, New South* (1986), and Edward Royce, *The Origins of Southern Sharecropping* (1993). On the Compromise of 1877, see C. Vann Woodward's classic *Reunion and Reaction* (1956). A helpful Web site on Reconstruction, with documents and illustrations, can be found at **www.pbs.org/wgbh/amex/reconstruction/index .html**, which derives from the PBS documentary in the *American Experience* series.

TEST YOUR KNOWLEDGE

To assess your mastery of the material in this chapter and for Web sites, images, and documents related to this chapter, visit **bedfordstmartins.com/henrettaconcise**.

Documents

The Declaration of Independence

The Unanimous Declaration of the Thirteen United States of America

When in the Course of human events, it becomes necessary for one people to dissolve the political bands which have connected them with another, and to assume among the Powers of the earth, the separate and equal station to which the Laws of Nature and of Nature's God entitle them, a decent respect to the opinions of mankind requires that they should declare the causes which impel them to the separation.

We hold these truths to be self-evident, that all men are created equal, that they are endowed by their Creator with certain unalienable rights, that among these are Life, Liberty, and the pursuit of Happiness. That to secure these rights, Governments are instituted among Men, deriving their just powers from the consent of the governed. That whenever any Form of Government becomes destructive of these ends, it is the Right of the People to alter or to abolish it, and to institute new Government, laying its foundation on such principles and organizing its powers in such form, as to them shall seem most likely to effect their Safety and Happiness. Prudence, indeed, will dictate that Governments long established should not be changed for light and transient causes; and accordingly all experience hath shown, that mankind are more disposed to suffer, while evils are sufferable, than to right themselves by abolishing the forms to which they are accustomed. But when a long train of abuses and usurpations, pursuing invariably the same Object evinces a design to reduce them under absolute Despotism, it is their right, it is their duty, to throw off such Government, and to provide new Guards for their future security.— Such has been the patient sufferance of these Colonies; and such is now the necessity which constrains them to alter their former Systems of Government. The history of the present King of Great Britain is a history of repeated injuries and usurpations, all having in direct object the establishment of an absolute Tyranny over these States. To prove this, let Facts be submitted to a candid world.

He has refused his Assent to Laws, the most wholesome and necessary for the public good.

He has forbidden his Governors to pass Laws of immediate and pressing importance, unless suspended in their operation till his Assent should be obtained; and, when so suspended, he has utterly neglected to attend to them.

He has refused to pass other Laws for the accommodation of large districts of people, unless those people would relinquish the right of Representation in the Legislature, a right inestimable to them and formidable to tyrants only.

He has called together legislative bodies at places unusual, uncomfortable, and distant from the depository of their public Records, for the sole purpose of fatiguing them into compliance with his measures.

He has dissolved Representative Houses repeatedly, for opposing with manly firmness his invasions on the rights of the people.

He has refused for a long time, after such dissolutions, to cause others to be elected; whereby the Legislative powers, incapable of Annihilation, have returned to the People at large for their exercise; the State remaining in the mean time exposed to all the dangers of invasion from without and convulsions within.

He has endeavoured to prevent the population of these States; for that purpose obstructing the Laws of Naturalization of Foreigners; refusing to pass others to encourage their migrations hither, and raising the conditions of new Appropriations of Lands.

He has obstructed the Administration of Justice, by refusing his Assent to Laws for establishing Judiciary powers.

He has made Judges dependent on his Will alone, for the tenure of their offices, and the amount and payment of their salaries.

He has erected a multitude of New Offices, and sent hither swarms of Officers to harass our People, and eat out their substance.

He has kept among us, in times of peace, Standing Armies without the Consent of our legislature.

He has combined with others to subject us to a jurisdiction foreign to our constitution, and unacknowledged by our laws; giving his Assent to their Acts of pretended Legislation:

For quartering large bodies of armed troops among us:

For protecting them, by a mock Trial, from Punishment for any Murders which they should commit on the Inhabitants of these States:

For cutting off our Trade with all parts of the world:

For imposing taxes on us without our Consent:

For depriving us in many cases, of the benefits of Trial by jury:

For transporting us beyond Seas to be tried for pretended offences:

For abolishing the free System of English Laws in a neighbouring Province, establishing therein an Arbitrary government, and enlarging its Boundaries so as to render it at once an example and fit instrument for introducing the same absolute rule into these Colonies:

For taking away our Charters, abolishing our most valuable Laws, and altering fundamentally the Forms of our Governments:

For suspending our own Legislatures, and declaring themselves invested with Power to legislate for us in all cases whatsoever.

He has abdicated Government here, by declaring us out of his Protection and waging War against us.

He has plundered our seas, ravaged our Coasts, burnt our towns, and destroyed the lives of our people.

He is at this time transporting large armies of foreign mercenaries to compleat the works of death, desolation, and tyranny, already begun with circumstances of Cruelty & perfidy scarcely paralleled in the most barbarous ages, and totally unworthy the Head of a civilized nation.

He has constrained our fellow Citizens taken Captive on the high Seas to bear Arms against their Country, to become the executioners of their friends and Brethren, or to fall themselves by their Hands.

He has excited domestic insurrections amongst us, and has endeavoured to bring on the inhabitants of our frontiers, the merciless Indian Savages, whose known rule of warfare, is an undistinguished destruction of all ages, sexes, and conditions.

In every stage of these Oppressions We have Petitioned for Redress in the most humble terms: Our repeated petitions have been answered only by repeated injury. A Prince, whose character is thus marked by every act which may define a Tyrant, is unfit to be the ruler of a free people.

Nor have We been wanting in attention to our British brethren. We have warned them from time to time of attempts by their legislature to extend an unwarrantable jurisdiction over us. We have reminded them of the circumstances of our emigration and settlement here. We have appealed to their native justice and magnanimity, and we have conjured them by the ties of our common kindred to disavow these usurpations, which, would inevitably interrupt our connections and correspondence. They too have been deaf to the voice of justice and of consanguinity. We must, therefore, acquiesce in the necessity, which denounces our Separation, and hold them, as we hold the rest of mankind, Enemies in War, in Peace Friends.

We, therefore, the Representatives of the United States of America, in General Congress, Assembled, appealing to the Supreme Judge of the world for the rectitude of our intentions, do, in the Name, and by Authority of the good People of these Colonies, solemnly publish and declare, That these United Colonies are, and of Right ought to be FREE AND INDEPENDENT STATES; that they are Absolved from all Allegiance to the British Crown, and that all political connection between them and the State of Great Britain, is and ought to be totally dissolved; and that as Free and Independent States, they have full Power to levy War, conclude Peace, contract Alliances, establish Commerce, and to do all other Acts and Things which Independent States may of right do. And for the support of this Declaration, with a firm reliance on the Protection of Divine Providence, we mutually pledge to each other our Lives, our Fortunes, and our sacred Honor.

John Hancock

Button Gwinnett	George Wythe	James Wilson	Josiah Bartlett
Lyman Hall	Richard Henry Lee	Geo. Ross	Wm. Whipple
Geo. Walton	Th. Jefferson	Caesar Rodney	Saml. Adams
Wm. Hooper	Benja. Harrison	Geo. Read	John Adams
Joseph Hewes	Thos. Nelson, Jr.	Thos. M'Kean	Robt. Treat Paine
John Penn	Francis Lightfoot Lee	Wm. Floyd	Elbridge Gerry
Edward Rutledge	Carter Braxton	Phil. Livingston	Step. Hopkins
Thos. Heyward, Junr.	Robt. Morris	Frans. Lewis	William Ellery

Thomas Lynch, Junr.	Benjamin Rush	Lewis Morris	Roger Sherman
Arthur Middleton	Benja. Franklin	Richd. Stockton	Sam'el Huntington
Samuel Chase	John Morton	Jno. Witherspoon	Wm. Williams
Wm. Paca	Geo. Clymer	Fras. Hopkinson	Oliver Wolcott
Thos. Stone	Jas. Smith	John Hart	Matthew Thornton
Charles Carroll of Carrollton	Geo. Taylor	Abra. Clark	

The Articles of Confederation and Perpetual Union

Between the states of New Hampshire, Massachusetts Bay, Rhode Island and Providence Plantations, Connecticut, New York, New Jersey, Pennsylvania, Delaware, Maryland, Virginia, North Carolina, South Carolina, Georgia.*

Article 1

The stile of this confederacy shall be "The United States of America."

Article 2

Each State retains its sovereignty, freedom and independence, and every power, jurisdiction, and right, which is not by this confederation expressly delegated to the United States, in Congress assembled.

Article 3

The said states hereby severally enter into a firm league of friendship with each other for their common defence, the security of their liberties and their mutual and general welfare; binding themselves to assist each other against all force offered to, or attacks made upon them, or any of them, on account of religion, sovereignty, trade, or any other pretence whatever.

Article 4

The better to secure and perpetuate mutual friendship and intercourse among the people of the different states in this union, the free inhabitants of each of these states, paupers, vagabonds, and fugitives from justice excepted, shall be entitled to all privileges and immunities of free citizens in the several states; and the people of each State shall have free ingress and regress to and from any other State, and shall enjoy therein all the privileges of trade and commerce, subject to the same duties, impositions, and restrictions, as the inhabitants thereof respectively; provided, that such restrictions shall not extend so far as to prevent the removal of property, imported into any State, to any other State of which the owner is an inhabitant; provided also, that no imposition,

---

*This copy of the final draft of the Articles of Confederation is taken from the *Journals*, 9:907–25, November 15, 1777.

duties, or restriction, shall be laid by any State on the property of the United States, or either of them.

If any person guilty of, or charged with treason, felony, or other high misdemeanor in any State, shall flee from justice and be found in any of the United States, he shall, upon demand of the governor or executive power of the State from which he fled, be delivered up and removed to the State having jurisdiction of his offence.

Full faith and credit shall be given in each of these states to the records, acts, and judicial proceedings of the courts and magistrates of every other State.

Article 5

For the more convenient management of the general interests of the United States, delegates shall be annually appointed, in such manner as the legislature of each State shall direct, to meet in Congress, on the 1st Monday in November in every year, with a power reserved to each State to recall its delegates, or any of them, at any time within the year, and to send others in their stead for the remainder of the year.

No State shall be represented in Congress by less than two, nor by more than seven members; and no person shall be capable of being a delegate for more than three years in any term of six years; nor shall any person, being a delegate, be capable of holding any office under the United States, for which he, or any other for his benefit, receives any salary, fees, or emolument of any kind.

Each State shall maintain its own delegates in a meeting of the states, and while they act as members of the committee of the states.

In determining questions in the United States, in Congress assembled, each State shall have one vote.

Freedom of speech and debate in Congress shall not be impeached or questioned in any court or place out of Congress: and the members of Congress shall be protected in their persons from arrests and imprisonments, during the time of their going to and from, and attendance on Congress, except for treason, felony, or breach of the peace.

Article 6

No State, without the consent of the United States, in Congress assembled, shall send any embassy to, or receive any embassy from, or enter into any conference, agreement, alliance, or treaty with any king, prince, or state; nor shall any person, holding any office of profit or trust under the United States, or any of them, accept of any present, emolument, office or title, of any kind whatever, from any king, prince, or foreign state; nor shall the United States, in Congress assembled, or any of them, grant any title of nobility.

No two or more states shall enter into any treaty, confederation, or alliance, whatever, between them, without the consent of the United States, in Congress assembled, specifying accurately the purposes for which the same is to be entered into, and how long it shall continue.

No state shall lay any imposts or duties which may interfere with any stipulations in treaties entered into by the United States, in Congress assembled, with any king, prince, or state, in pursuance of any treaties already proposed by Congress to the courts of France and Spain.

No vessels of war shall be kept up in time of peace by any State, except such number only as shall be deemed necessary by the United States, in Congress assembled, for the defence of such State or its trade; nor shall any body of forces be kept up by any State, in time of peace, except such number only as, in the judgment of the United States, in Congress assembled, shall be deemed requisite to garrison the forts necessary for the defence of such State; but every State shall always keep up a well regulated and disciplined militia, sufficiently armed and accoutred, and shall provide, and constantly have ready for use, in public stores, a due number of field pieces and tents, and a proper quantity of arms, ammunition and camp equipage.

No State shall engage in any war without the consent of the United States, in Congress assembled, unless such State be actually invaded by enemies, or shall have received certain advice of a resolution being formed by some nation of Indians to invade such State, and the danger is so imminent as not to admit of a delay till the United States, in Congress assembled, can be consulted; nor shall any State grant commissions to any ships or vessels of war, nor letters of marque or reprisal, except it be after a declaration of war by the United States, in Congress assembled, and then only against the kingdom or state, and the subjects thereof, against which war has been so declared, and under such regulations as shall be established by the United States, in Congress assembled, unless such State be infested by pirates, in which case vessels of war may be fitted out for that occasion, and kept so long as the danger shall continue, or until the United States, in Congress assembled, shall determine otherwise.

Article 7

When land forces are raised by any State for the common defence, all officers of or under the rank of colonel, shall be appointed by the legislature of each State respectively, by whom such forces shall be raised, or in such manner as such State shall direct; and all vacancies shall be filled up by the State which first made the appointment.

Article 8

All charges of war and all other expences, that shall be incurred for the common defence or general welfare, and allowed by the United States, in Congress assembled, shall be defrayed out of a common treasury, which shall be supplied by the several states, in proportion to the value of all land within each State, granted to or surveyed for any person, as such land and the buildings and improvements thereon shall be estimated according to such mode as the United States, in Congress assembled, shall, from time to time, direct and appoint.

The taxes for paying that proportion shall be laid and levied by the authority and direction of the legislatures of the several states, within the time agreed upon by the United States, in Congress assembled.

Article 9

The United States, in Congress assembled, shall have the sole and exclusive right and power of determining on peace and war, except in the cases mentioned in the 6th article; of sending and receiving ambassadors; entering into treaties and alliances, provided that no treaty of commerce shall be made, whereby the legislative power of the respective states shall be restrained from imposing such imposts and duties on foreigners as their own people are subjected to, or from prohibiting the exportation or importation of any species of goods or commodities whatsoever; of establishing rules for deciding, in all cases, what captures on land or water shall be legal, and in what manner prizes, taken by land or naval forces in the service of the United States, shall be divided or appropriated; or granting letters of marque and reprisal in times of peace; appointing courts for the trial of piracies and felonies committed on the high seas, and establishing courts for receiving and determining, finally, appeals in all cases of captures; provided, that no member of Congress shall be appointed a judge of any of the said courts.

The United States, in Congress assembled, shall also be the last resort on appeal in all disputes and differences now subsisting, or that hereafter may arise between two or more states concerning boundary, jurisdiction or any other cause whatever; which authority shall always be exercised in the manner following: whenever the legislative or executive authority, or lawful agent of any State, in controversy with another, shall present a petition to Congress, stating the matter in question, and praying for a hearing, notice thereof shall be given, by order of Congress, to the legislative or executive authority of the other State in controversy, and a day assigned for the appearance of the parties by their lawful agents, who shall then be directed to appoint, by joint consent, commissioners or judges to constitute a court for hearing and determining the matter in question; but, if they cannot agree, Congress shall name three persons out of each of the United States, and from the list of such persons each party shall alternately strike out one, the petitioners beginning, until the number shall be reduced to thirteen; and from that number not less than seven, nor more than nine names, as Congress shall direct, shall, in the presence of Congress, be drawn out by lot; and the persons whose names shall be so drawn, or any five of them, shall be commissioners or judges to hear and finally determine the controversy, so always as a major part of the judges who shall hear the cause shall agree in the determination; and if either party shall neglect to attend at the day appointed, without shewing reasons which Congress shall judge sufficient, or, being present, shall refuse to strike, the Congress shall proceed to nominate three persons out of each State, and the secretary of Congress shall strike in behalf of such party absent or refusing; and the judgment and sentence of the court to be appointed, in the manner before prescribed, shall be final and conclusive; and if any of the parties shall refuse to submit to the authority of such court, or to appear or defend their claim or cause, the court shall nevertheless proceed to pronounce sentence or judgment, which shall, in like manner, be final and decisive, the judgment or sentence and other proceedings begin, in either case, transmitted to Congress, and lodged among the acts of Congress for the security of the parties concerned: provided, that every commissioner, before he sits in judgment, shall take an oath, to be administered by one of the judges of the supreme or superior court of the State where the cause shall be tried, "well and truly to hear and determine the matter in question, according to the best of his judgment, without favour, affection, or hope of reward:" provided, also, that no State shall be deprived of territory for the benefit of the United States.

All controversies concerning the private right of soil, claimed under different grants of two or more states, whose jurisdictions, as they may respect such lands and the states which passed such grants, are adjusted, the said grants, or either of them, being at the same time claimed to have originated antecedent to such settlement of jurisdiction, shall, on the petition of either party to the Congress of the United States, be finally determined, as near as may be, in the same manner as is before prescribed for deciding disputes respecting territorial jurisdiction between different states.

The United States, in Congress assembled, shall also have the sole and exclusive right and power of regulating the alloy and value of coin struck by their own authority, or by that of the respective states; fixing the standard of weights and measures throughout the United States; regulating the trade and managing all affairs with the Indians not members of any of the states; provided that the legislative right of any State within its own limits be not infringed or violated; establishing and regulating post offices from one State to another throughout all the United States, and exacting such postage on the papers passing through the same as may be requisite to defray the expences of the said office; appointing all officers of the land forces in the service of the United States, excepting regimental officers; appointing all the officers of the naval forces, and commissioning all officers whatever in the service of the United States; making rules for the government and regulation of the said land and naval forces, and directing their operations.

The United States, in Congress assembled, shall have authority to appoint a committee to sit in the recess of Congress, to be denominated "a Committee of the States," and to consist of one delegate from each State, and to appoint such other committees and civil officers as may be necessary for managing the general affairs of the United States, under their direction; to appoint one of their number to preside; provided that no person be allowed to serve in the office of president more than one year in any term of three years; to ascertain the necessary sums of money to be raised for the service of the United States, and to appropriate and apply the same for defraying the public expences; to borrow money or emit bills on the credit of the United States, transmitting, every half year, to the respective states, an account of the sums of money so borrowed or emitted; to build and equip a navy; to agree upon the number of land forces, and to make requisitions from each State for in quota, in proportion to the number of white inhabitants in such State; which requisitions shall be binding; and thereupon, the legislature of each State shall appoint the regimental officers, raise the men, and cloathe, arm, and equip them in a soldier-like manner, at the expence of the United States; and the officers and men so cloathed, armed, and equipped, shall march to the place appointed and within the time agreed on by the United States, in Congress assembled; but if the United States, in Congress assembled, shall, on consideration of circumstances, judge proper that any State should not raise men, or should raise a smaller number than its quota, and that any other State should raise a greater number of men than the quota thereof, such extra number shall be raised, officered, cloathed, armed, and equipped in the same manner as the quota of such State, unless the legislature of such State shall judge that such extra number cannot be safely spared out of the same, in which case they shall raise, officer, cloathe, arm, and equip as many of such extra number as they judge can be safely spared. And the officers and men so cloathed, armed, and equipped, shall march to the place appointed and within the time agreed on by the United States, in Congress assembled.

The United States, in Congress assembled, shall never engage in a war, nor grant letters of marque and reprisal in time of peace, nor enter into any treaties or alliances, nor coin money, nor regulate the value thereof, nor ascertain the sums and expences necessary for the defence and welfare of the United States, or any of them: nor emit bills, nor borrow money on the credit of the United States, nor appropriate money, nor agree upon the number of vessels of war to be built or purchased, or the number of land or sea forces to be raised, nor appoint a commander in chief of the army or navy, unless nine states assent to the same; nor shall a question on any other point, except for adjourning from day to day, be determined, unless by the votes of a majority of the United States, in Congress assembled.

The Congress of the United States shall have power to adjourn to any time within the year, and to any place within the United States, so that no period of adjournment be for a longer duration than the space of six months, and shall publish the journal of their proceedings monthly, except such parts thereof, relating to treaties, alliances or military operations, as, in their judgment, require secrecy; and the yeas and nays of the delegates of each State on any question shall be entered on the journal, when it is desired by any delegate; and the delegates of a State, or any of them, at his, or their request, shall be furnished with a transcript of the said journal, except such parts as are above excepted, to lay before the legislatures of the several states.

Article 10

The committee of the states, or any nine of them, shall be authorized to execute, in the recess of Congress, such of the powers of Congress as the United States, in Congress assembled, by the consent of nine states, shall, from time to time, think expedient to vest them with; provided, that no power be delegated to the said committee, for the exercise of which, by the articles of confederation, the voice of nine states, in the Congress of the United States assembled, is requisite.

Article 11

Canada acceding to this confederation, and joining in the measures of the United States, shall be admitted into and entitled to all the advantages of this union; but no other colony shall be admitted into the same, unless such admission be agreed to by nine states.

Article 12

All bills of credit emitted, monies borrowed and debts contracted by, or under the authority of Congress before the assembling of the United States, in pursuance of the present confederation, shall be deemed and considered as a charge against the United States, for payment and satisfaction whereof the said United States and the public faith are hereby solemnly pledged.

Article 13

Every State shall abide by the determinations of the United States, in Congress assembled, on all questions which, by this confederation, are submitted to them. And the articles of this confederation shall be inviolably observed by every State, and the union shall be perpetual; nor shall any alteration at any time hereafter be made in any of them, unless such alteration be agreed to in a Congress of the United States, and be afterwards confirmed by the legislatures of every State.

These articles shall be proposed to the legislatures of all the United States, to be considered, and if approved of by them, they are advised to authorize their delegates to ratify the same in the Congress of the United States; which being done, the same shall become conclusive.

The Constitution of the United States

We the People of the United States, in Order to form a more perfect Union, establish Justice, insure domestic Tranquility, provide for the common defence, promote the general Welfare, and secure the Blessings of Liberty to ourselves and our Posterity, do ordain and establish this Constitution for the United States of America.

Article I

Section 1. All legislative Powers herein granted shall be vested in a Congress of the United States, which shall consist of a Senate and a House of Representatives.

Section 2. The House of Representatives shall be composed of Members chosen every second Year by the People of the several States, and the Electors in each State shall have the Qualifications requisite for Electors of the most numerous Branch of the State Legislature.

No Person shall be a Representative who shall not have attained to the Age of twenty-five Years, and been seven Years a Citizen of the United States, and who shall not, when elected, be an Inhabitant of that State in which he shall be chosen.

Representatives and direct Taxes shall be apportioned among the several States which may be included within this Union, according to their respective Numbers, *which shall be determined by adding to the whole Number of free Persons, including those bound to Service for a Term of Years, and excluding Indians not taxed, three fifths of all other Persons** The actual Enumeration shall be made within three Years after the first Meeting of the Congress of the United States, and within every subsequent Term of ten Years, in such Manner as they shall by Law direct. The Number of Representatives shall not exceed one for every thirty Thousand, but each State shall have at Least one Representative; and *until such enumeration shall be made, the State of New Hampshire shall be entitled to chuse three, Massachusetts eight, Rhode Island and Providence Plantations one, Connecticut five, New-York six, New Jersey four, Pennsylvania eight, Delaware one, Maryland six, Virginia ten, North Carolina five, South Carolina five, and Georgia three.*

When vacancies happen in the Representation from any State, the Executive Authority thereof shall issue Writs of Election to fill such Vacancies.

The House of Representatives shall chuse their Speaker and other Officers; and shall have the sole Power of Impeachment.

Note: The Constitution became effective March 4,1789. Provisions in italics have been changed by constitutional amendment.

*Changed by Section 2 of the Fourteenth Amendment.

Section 3. The Senate of the United States shall be composed of two Senators from each State, *chosen by the Legislature thereof,** for six Years; and each Senator shall have one Vote.

Immediately after they shall be assembled in Consequence of the first Election, they shall be divided as equally as may be into three Classes. The Seats of the Senators of the first Class shall be vacated at the Expiration of the second Year, of the second Class at the Expiration of the fourth Year, and of the third Class at the Expiration of the sixth Year, so that one-third may be chosen every second Year; *and if Vacancies happen by Resignation, or otherwise, during the Recess of the Legislature of any State, the Executive thereof may make temporary Appointments until the next Meeting of the Legislature, which shall then fill such Vacancies.*†

No person shall be a Senator who shall not have attained to the Age of thirty Years, and been nine Years a Citizen of the United States, and who shall not, when elected, be an Inhabitant of that State for which he shall be chosen.

The Vice President of the United States shall be President of the Senate, but shall have no Vote, unless they be equally divided.

The Senate shall chuse their other Officers, and also a President pro tempore, in the absence of the Vice President, or when he shall exercise the Office of President of the United States.

The Senate shall have the sole Power to try all Impeachments. When sitting for that Purpose, they shall be on Oath or Affirmation. When the President of the United States is tried, the Chief Justice shall preside; And no Person shall be convicted without the Concurrence of two thirds of the Members present.

Judgment in Cases of Impeachment shall not extend further than to removal from Office, and disqualification to hold and enjoy any Office of honor, Trust or Profit under the United States: but the Party convicted shall nevertheless be liable and subject to Indictment, Trial, Judgment and Punishment, according to Law.

Section 4. The Times, Places and Manner of holding Elections for Senators and Representatives, shall be prescribed in each State by the Legislature thereof, but the Congress may at any time by Law make or alter such Regulations, except as to the Places of Chusing Senators.

The Congress shall assemble at least once in every Year, and such Meeting *shall be on the first Monday in December, unless they shall by Law appoint a different Day.*‡

Section 5. Each House shall be the Judge of the Elections, Returns and Qualifications of its own Members, and a Majority of each shall constitute a Quorum to do Business; but a smaller number may adjourn from day to day, and may be authorized to compel the Attendance of absent Members, in such Manner, and under such Penalties, as each House may provide.

Each House may determine the Rules of its Proceedings, punish its Members for disorderly Behavior, and, with the Concurrence of two thirds, expel a Member.

---

*Changed by Section 1 of the Seventeenth Amendment.
†Changed by Clause 2 of the Seventeenth Amendment.
‡Changed by Section 2 of the Twentieth Amendment.

Each House shall keep a Journal of its Proceedings, and from time to time publish the same, excepting such Parts as may in their Judgment require Secrecy; and the Yeas and Nays of the Members of either House on any question shall, at the Desire of one-fifth of those Present, be entered on the Journal.

Neither House, during the Session of Congress, shall, without the Consent of the other, adjourn for more than three days, nor to any other Place than that in which the two Houses shall be sitting.

Section 6.   The Senators and Representatives shall receive a Compensation for their Services, to be ascertained by Law, and paid out of the Treasury of the United States. They shall in all Cases, except Treason, Felony and Breach of the Peace, be privileged from Arrest during their Attendance at the Session of their respective Houses, and in going to and returning from the same; and for any Speech or Debate in either House, they shall not be questioned in any other Place.

No Senator or Representative shall, during the Time for which he was elected, be appointed to any civil Office under the Authority of the United States, which shall have been created, or the Emoluments whereof shall have been increased, during such time; and no Person holding any Office under the United States, shall be a Member of either House during his Continuance in Office.

Section 7.   All Bills for raising Revenue shall originate in the House of Representatives; but the Senate may propose or concur with Amendments as on other Bills.

Every Bill which shall have passed the House of Representatives and the Senate, shall, before it becomes a Law, be presented to the President of the United States; If he approve he shall sign it, but if not he shall return it, with his Objections to that House in which it shall have originated, who shall enter the Objections at large on their Journal, and proceed to reconsider it. If after such Reconsideration two thirds of that House shall agree to pass the Bill, it shall be sent, together with the Objections, to the other House, by which it shall likewise be reconsidered, and if approved by two thirds of that House, it shall become a Law. But in all such Cases the Votes of both Houses shall be determined by Yeas and Nays, and the Names of the Persons voting for and against the Bill shall be entered on the Journal of each House respectively. If any Bill shall not be returned by the President within ten Days (Sundays excepted) after it shall have been presented to him, the Same shall be a Law, in like Manner as if he had signed it, unless the Congress by their Adjournment prevent its Return, in which Case it shall not be a Law.

Every Order, Resolution, or Vote to which the Concurrence of the Senate and the House of Representatives may be necessary (except on a question of Adjournment) shall be presented to the President of the United States; and before the Same shall take Effect, shall be approved by him, or being disapproved by him, shall be repassed by two thirds of the Senate and House of Representatives, according to the Rules and Limitations prescribed in the Case of a Bill.

Section 8.   The Congress shall have Power To lay and collect Taxes, Duties, Imposts and Excises, to pay the Debts and provide for the common Defence and general Welfare of the United States; but all Duties, Imposts and Excises shall be uniform throughout the United States;

To borrow money on the credit of the United States;

To regulate Commerce with foreign Nations, and among the several States, and with the Indian Tribes;

To establish an uniform Rule of Naturalization, and uniform Laws on the subject of Bankruptcies throughout the United States;

To coin Money, regulate the Value thereof, and of foreign Coin, and fix the Standard of Weights and Measures;

To provide for the Punishment of counterfeiting the Securities and current Coin of the United States;

To establish Post Offices and post Roads;

To promote the Progress of Science and useful Arts, by securing for limited Times to Authors and Inventors the exclusive Right to their respective Writings and Discoveries;

To constitute Tribunals inferior to the supreme Court;

To define and punish Piracies and Felonies committed on the high Seas, and Offenses against the Law of Nations;

To declare War, grant Letters of Marque and Reprisal, and make Rules concerning Captures on Land and Water;

To raise and support Armies, but no Appropriation of Money to that Use shall be for a longer Term than two Years;

To provide and maintain a Navy;

To make Rules for the Government and Regulation of the land and naval Forces;

To provide for calling forth the Militia to execute the Laws of the Union, suppress Insurrections and repel Invasions;

To provide for organizing, arming, and disciplining the Militia, and for governing such Part of them as may be employed in the Service of the United States, reserving to the States respectively, the Appointment of the Officers, and the Authority of training the Militia according to the discipline prescribed by Congress;

To exercise exclusive Legislation in all Cases whatsoever, over such District (not exceeding ten Miles square) as may, by Cession of particular States, and the acceptance of Congress, become the Seat of Government of the United States, and to exercise like Authority over all Places purchased by the Consent of the Legislature of the State in which the Same shall be, for the Erection of Forts, Magazines, Arsenals, dock-Yards, and other needful Buildings;—And

To make all Laws which shall be necessary and proper for carrying into Execution the foregoing Powers, and all other Powers vested by this Constitution in the Government of the United States, or in any Department or Officer thereof.

Section 9. *The Migration or Importation of such Persons as any of the States now existing shall think proper to admit, shall not be prohibited by the Congress prior to the Year one thousand eight hundred and eight but a tax or duty may be imposed on such Importation, not exceeding ten dollars for each Person.*

The privilege of the Writ of Habeas Corpus shall not be suspended, unless when in Cases of Rebellion or Invasion the public Safety may require it.

No Bill of Attainder or ex post facto Law shall be passed.

No capitation, or other direct, Tax shall be laid, unless in Proportion to the Census or Enumeration herein before directed to be taken.*

No Tax or Duty shall be laid on Articles exported from any State.

No Preference shall be given by any Regulation of Commerce or Revenue to the Ports of one State over those of another: nor shall Vessels bound to, or from, one State, be obliged to enter, clear, or pay Duties in another.

No Money shall be drawn from the Treasury, but in Consequence of Appropriations made by law; and a regular Statement and Account of the Receipts and Expenditures of all public Money shall be published from time to time.

No Title of Nobility shall be granted by the United States: And no Person holding any Office of Profit or Trust under them, shall, without the Consent of the Congress, accept of any present, Emolument, Office, or Title, of any kind whatever, from any King, Prince, or foreign State.

Section 10.   No State shall enter into any Treaty, Alliance, or Confederation; grant Letters of Marque and Reprisal; coin Money; emit Bills of Credit; make any Thing but gold and silver Coin a Tender in Payment of Debts; pass any Bill of Attainder, ex post facto Law, or Law impairing the Obligation of Contracts, or grant any Title of Nobility.

No State shall, without the Consent of the Congress, lay any Imposts or Duties on Imports or Exports, except what may be absolutely necessary for executing its inspection Laws: and the net Produce of all Duties and Imposts, laid by any State on Imports or Exports, shall be for the Use of the Treasury of the United States; and all such Laws shall be subject to the Revision and Control of the Congress.

No State shall, without the Consent of the Congress, lay any duty of Tonnage, keep Troops, or Ships of War in time of Peace, enter into any Agreement or Compact with another State, or with a foreign Power, or engage in War, unless actually invaded, or in such imminent Danger as will not admit of delay.

Article II

Section 1.   The executive Power shall be vested in a President of the United States of America. He shall hold his Office during the Term of four Years, and, together with the Vice President, chosen for the same Term, be elected, as follows:

Each State shall appoint, in such Manner as the Legislature thereof may direct, a Number of Electors, equal to the whole Number of Senators and Representatives to which the State may be entitled in the Congress; but no Senator or Representative, or Person holding an Office of Trust or Profit under the United States, shall be appointed an Elector.

The Electors shall meet in their respective States, and vote by Ballot for two Persons, of whom one at least shall not be an Inhabitant of the same State with themselves. And they shall make a List of all the Persons voted for, and of the Number of Votes for each; which List they shall sign and certify, and transmit sealed to the Seat of the Government of the United States, directed to the President of the Senate. The President of the Senate shall,

---

*Changed by the Sixteenth Amendment

in the Presence of the Senate and House of Representatives, open all the Certificates, and the Votes shall then be counted. The Person having the greatest Number of Votes shall be the President, if such Number be a Majority of the whole Number of Electors appointed; and if there be more than one who have such Majority, and have an equal Number of Votes, then the House of Representatives shall immediately chuse by Ballot one of them for President; and if no Person have a Majority, then from the five highest on the List the said House shall in like Manner chuse the President. But in chusing the President, the Votes shall be taken by States, the Representation from each State having one Vote; a quorum for this Purpose shall consist of a Member or Members from two thirds of the States, and a Majority of all the States shall be necessary to a Choice. In every Case, after the Choice of the President, the Person having the greatest Number of Votes of the Electors shall be the Vice President. But if there should remain two or more who have equal Votes, the Senate shall chuse from them by Ballot the Vice President.

The Congress may determine the Time of chusing the Electors, and the Day on which they shall give their Votes; which Day shall be the same throughout the United States.

No Person except a natural born Citizen, or a Citizen of the United States, at the time of the Adoption of this Constitution, shall be eligible to the Office of President; neither shall any Person be eligible to that Office who shall not have attained to the Age of thirty five Years, and been fourteen years a Resident within the United States.

In Case of the Removal of the President from Office, or of his Death, Resignation, or Inability to discharge the Powers and Duties of the said Office, the same shall devolve on the Vice President, *and the Congress may by Law provide for the Case of Removal, Death, Resignation, or Inability, both of the President and Vice President, declaring what Officer shall then act as President, and such Officer shall act accordingly, until the Disability be removed, or a President shall be elected.*†

The President shall, at stated Times, receive for his Services a Compensation, which shall neither be increased nor diminished during the Period for which he shall have been elected, and he shall not receive within that Period any other Emolument from the United States, or any of them.

Before he enter on the Execution of his Office, he shall take the following Oath or Affirmation:—"I do solemnly swear (or affirm) that I will faithfully execute the Office of President of the United States, and will to the best of my Ability, preserve, protect and defend the Constitution of the United States."

Section 2. The President shall be Commander in Chief of the Army and Navy of the United States, and of the Militia of the several States, when called into the actual Service of the United States; he may require the Opinion, in writing, of the principal Officer in each of the executive Departments, upon any Subject relating to the Duties of their respective Offices, and he shall have Power to Grant Reprieves and pardons for Offences against the United States, except in Cases of Impeachment.

He shall have Power, by and with the Advice and Consent of the Senate, to make Treaties, provided two thirds of the Senators present concur; and he shall nominate,

---

*Superseded by the Twelfth Amendment.
†Modified by the Twenty-fifth Amendment.

and by and with the Advice and Consent of the Senate, shall appoint Ambassadors, other public Ministers and Consuls, Judges of the supreme Court, and all other Officers of the United States, whose Appointments are not herein otherwise provided for, and which shall be established by Law: but the Congress may by Law vest the Appointment of such inferior Officers, as they think proper, in the President alone, in the Courts of Law, or in the Heads of Departments.

The President shall have Power to fill up all Vacancies that may happen during the Recess of the Senate, by granting Commissions which shall expire at the End of their next Session.

Section 3.   He shall from time to time give to the Congress Information of the State of the Union, and recommend to their Consideration such Measures as he shall judge necessary and expedient; he may, on extraordinary Occasions, convene both Houses, or either of them, and in Case of Disagreement between them, with Respect to the Time of Adjournment, he may adjourn them to such Time as he shall think proper; he shall receive Ambassadors and other public Ministers; he shall take care that the Laws be faithfully executed, and shall Commission all the Officers of the United States.

Section 4.   The President, Vice President and all civil Officers of the United States, shall be removed from Office on Impeachment for, and Conviction of, Treason, Bribery, or other high Crimes and Misdemeanors.

Article III

Section 1.   The judicial Power of the United States, shall be vested in one supreme Court, and in such inferior Courts as the Congress may from time to time ordain and establish. The Judges, both of the supreme and inferior courts, shall hold their Offices during good Behaviour, and shall, at stated Times, receive for their Services a Compensation, which shall not be diminished during their Continuance in Office.

Section 2.   The judicial Power shall extend to all Cases, in Law and Equity, arising under this Constitution, the Laws of the United States, and Treaties made, or which shall be made, under their Authority;—to all Cases affecting Ambassadors, other public Ministers and Consuls;—to all Cases of admiralty and maritime Jurisdiction;—to Controversies to which the United States shall be a Party;—to Controversies between two or more States;—*between a State and Citizens of another State,**—between Citizens of different States;—between Citizens of the same State claiming Lands under Grants of different States, and between a State, or the Citizens thereof, and foreign States, Citizens or Subjects.

In all Cases affecting Ambassadors, other public Ministers and Consuls, and those in which a State shall be Party, the supreme Court shall have original Jurisdiction. In all the other Cases before mentioned, the supreme Court shall have appellate Jurisdiction, both as to Law and Fact, with such Exceptions, and under such Regulations as the Congress shall make.

---

*Restricted by the Eleventh Amendment.

The trial of all Crimes, except in Cases of Impeachment, shall be by Jury; and such Trial shall be held in the State where said Crimes shall have been committed; but when not committed within any State, the Trial shall be at such Place or Places as the Congress may by Law have directed.

Section 3.   Treason against the United States, shall consist only in levying War against them, or in adhering to their Enemies, giving them Aid and Comfort. No Person shall be convicted of Treason unless on the Testimony of two Witnesses to the same overt Act, or on Confession in open Court.

The Congress shall have Power to declare the Punishment of Treason, but no Attainder of Treason shall work Corruption of Blood, or Forefeiture except during the Life of the Person attainted.

Article IV

Section 1.   Full Faith and Credit shall be given in each State to the public Acts, Records, and judicial Proceedings of every other State. And the Congress may by general Laws prescribe the Manner in which such Acts, Records, and Proceedings shall be proved, and the Effect thereof.

Section 2.   The Citizens of each State shall be entitled to all Privileges and Immunities of Citizens in the several States.

A Person charged in any State with Treason, Felony, or other Crime, who shall flee from Justice, and be found in another State, shall on demand of the executive Authority of the State from which he fled, be delivered up, to be removed to the State having Jurisdiction of the Crime.

*No Person held to Service or Labour in one State, under the Laws thereof, escaping into another, shall, in Consequence of any Law or Regulation therein, be discharged from such Service or Labour, but shall be delivered up on Claim of the Party to whom such Service or Labour may be due.**

Section 3.   New States may be admitted by the Congress into this Union; but no new State shall be formed or erected within the Jurisdiction of any other State; nor any State be formed by the Junction of two or more States, or parts of States, without the Consent of the Legislatures of the States concerned as well as of the Congress.

The Congress shall have Power to dispose of and make all needful Rules and Regulations respecting the Territory or other Property belonging to the United States; and nothing in this Constitution shall be so construed as to Prejudice any Claims of the United States, or of any particular State.

Section 4.   The United States shall guarantee to every State in this Union a Republican Form of Government, and shall protect each of them against Invasion; and on Application of the Legislature, or of the Executive (when the Legislature cannot be convened) against domestic Violence.

---

*Superseded by the Thirteenth Amendment.

Article V

The Congress, whenever two thirds of both Houses shall deem it necessary, shall propose Amendments to this Constitution, or, on the Application of the Legislatures of two thirds of the several States, shall call a Convention for proposing Amendments, which, in either Case, shall be valid to all Intents and Purposes, as Part of this Constitution, when ratified by the Legislatures of three fourths of the several States, or by Conventions in three fourths thereof, as the one or the other Mode of Ratification may be proposed by the Congress; Provided that no Amendment which may be made prior to the Year One thousand eight hundred and eight shall in any Manner affect the first and fourth Clauses in the Ninth Section of the first Article; and that no State, without its Consent, shall be deprived of its equal Suffrage in the Senate.

Article VI

All Debts contracted and Engagements entered into, before the Adoption of this Constitution, shall be as valid against the United States under this Constitution, as under the Confederation.

This Constitution, and the Laws of the United States which shall be made in Pursuance thereof; and all Treaties made, or which shall be made, under the Authority of the United States, shall be the supreme Law of the Land; and the Judges in every State shall be bound thereby, any Thing in the Constitution or Laws of any State to the Contrary notwithstanding.

The Senators and Representatives before mentioned, and the Members of the several State Legislatures, and all executive and judicial Officers, both of the United States and of the several States, shall be bound by Oath or Affirmation, to support this Constitution; but no religious Test shall ever be required as a Qualification to any Office or public Trust under the United States.

Article VII

The Ratification of the Conventions of nine States shall be sufficient for the Establishment of this Constitution between the States so ratifying the Same.

Done in Convention by the Unanimous Consent of the States present the Seventeenth Day of September in the Year of our Lord one thousand seven hundred and Eighty seven and of the Independence of the United States of America the Twelfth. In Witness whereof We have hereunto subscribed our Names.

Go. Washington
President and deputy from Virginia

New *Hampshire*	*New Jersey*	*Delaware*	*North Carolina*
John Langdon	Wil. Livingston	Geo. Read	Wm. Blount
Nicholas Gilman	David Brearley	Gunning Bedford jun	Richd. Dobbs Spaight
	Wm. Paterson	John Dickenson	Hu Williamson
	Jona. Dayton	Richard Bassett	
		Jaco. Broom	

Massachusetts	*Pennsylvania*	*Maryland*	*South Carolina*
Nathaniel Gorham	B. Franklin	James McHenry	J. Rutledge
Rufus King	Thomas Mifflin	Dan. of St. Thos. Jenifer	Charles Cotesworth
	Robt. Morris	Danl. Carroll	Pickney
Connecticut	Geo. Clymer		Pierce Butler
Wm. Saml. Johnson	Thos. FitzSimons	*Virginia*	
Roger Sherman	Jared Ingersoll	John Blair	*Georgia*
	James Wilson	James Madison, Jr.	William Few
New York	Gouv. Morris		Abr. Baldwin
Alexander Hamilton			

Amendments to the Constitution

Amendment I [1791]*

Congress shall make no law respecting an establishment of religion, or prohibiting the free exercise thereof; or abridging the freedom of speech, or of the press; or the right of the people peaceably to assemble, and to petition the Government for a redress of grievances.

Amendment II [1791]

A well regulated Militia, being necessary to the security of a free State, the right of the people to keep and bear Arms shall not be infringed.

Amendment III [1791]

No Soldier shall, in time of peace, be quartered in any house, without the consent of the Owner, nor in time of war, but in a manner to be prescribed by law.

Amendment IV [1791]

The right of the people to be secure in their persons, houses, papers, and effects, against unreasonable searches and seizures, shall not be violated, and no Warrants shall issue, but upon probable cause, supported by Oath or affirmation, and particularly describing the place to be searched, and the persons or things to be seized.

Amendment V [1791]

No person shall be held to answer for a capital or otherwise infamous crime, unless on a presentment or indictment of a Grand Jury, except in cases arising in the land or naval forces, or in the Militia, when in actual service in time of War or public danger; nor shall any person be subject for the same offence to be twice put in jeopardy of life or limb; nor shall be compelled in any criminal case to be a witness against himself, nor be deprived of life, liberty, or property, without due process of law; nor shall private property be taken for public use, without just compensation.

---

*The dates in brackets indicate when the amendments were ratified.

Amendment VI [1791]

In all criminal prosecutions, the accused shall enjoy the right to a speedy and public trial, by an impartial jury of the State and district wherein the crime shall have been committed, which district shall have been previously ascertained by law, and to be informed of the nature and cause of the accusation; to be confronted with the witnesses against him; to have compulsory process for obtaining witnesses in his favor, and to have the Assistance of Counsel for his defence.

Amendment VII [1791]

In suits at common law, where the value in controversy shall exceed twenty dollars, the right of trial by jury shall be preserved, and no fact tried by a jury, shall be otherwise reexamined in any Court of the United States, than according to the Rules of the common law.

Amendment VIII [1791]

Excessive bail shall not be required, nor excessive fines imposed, nor cruel and unusual punishments inflicted.

Amendment IX [1791]

The enumeration in the Constitution, of certain rights, shall not be construed to deny or disparage others retained by the people.

Amendment X [1791]

The powers not delegated to the United States by the Constitution, nor prohibited by it to the States, are reserved to the States respectively, or to the people.

Amendment XI [1798]

The Judicial power of the United States shall not be construed to extend to any suit in law or equity, commenced or prosecuted against one of the United States by Citizens of another State, or by Citizens or subjects of any foreign state.

Amendment XII [1804]

The Electors shall meet in their respective States and vote by ballot for President and Vice-President, one of whom, at least, shall not be an inhabitant of the same State with themselves; they shall name in their ballots the person voted for as President, and in distinct ballots the person voted for as Vice-President, and they shall make distinct lists of all persons voted for as President, and of all persons voted for as Vice-President, and of the number of votes for each, which lists they shall sign and certify, and transmit sealed to the seat of the government of the United States, directed to the President of the Senate;—the President of the Senate shall, in the presence of the Senate and House of Representatives, open all the certificates and the votes shall then be counted;—The person having the greatest number of votes for President, shall be the President, if such number be a majority of the whole number of Electors appointed;

and if no person have such majority, then from the persons having the highest numbers not exceeding three on the list of those voted for as President, the House of Representatives shall choose immediately, by ballot, the President. But in choosing the President, the votes shall be taken by States, the representation from each State having one vote; a quorum for this purpose shall consist of a member or members from two-thirds of the States, and a majority of all the States shall be necessary to a choice. And if the House of Representatives shall not choose a President whenever the right of choice shall devolve upon them, before *the fourth day of March* next following, then the Vice-President shall act as President, as in the case of the death or other constitutional disability of the President.*—The person having the greatest number of votes as Vice-President, shall be the Vice-President, if such number be a majority of the whole number of Electors appointed, and if no person have a majority, then from the two highest numbers on the list, the Senate shall choose the Vice-President; a quorum for the purpose shall consist of two-thirds of the whole number of Senators, and a majority of the whole number shall be necessary to a choice. But no person constitutionally ineligible to the office of President shall be eligible to that of Vice-President of the United States.

Amendment XIII [1865]

Section 1.   Neither slavery nor involuntary servitude, except as a punishment for crime whereof the party shall have been duly convicted, shall exist within the United States, or any place subject to their jurisdiction.

Section 2.   Congress shall have power to enforce this article by appropriate legislation.

Amendment XIV [1868]

Section 1.   All persons born or naturalized in the United States, and subject to the jurisdiction thereof, are citizens of the United States and of the State wherein they reside. No State shall make or enforce any law which shall abridge the privileges or immunities of citizens of the United States; nor shall any State deprive any person of life, liberty, or property, without due process of law; nor deny to any person within its jurisdiction the equal protection of the laws.

Section 2.   Representatives shall be apportioned among the several States according to their respective numbers, counting the whole number of persons in each State, excluding Indians not taxed. But when the right to vote at any election for the choice of electors for President and Vice-President of the United States, Representatives in Congress, the Executive and Judicial officers of a State, or the members of the Legislature thereof, is denied to any of the male inhabitants of such State, being twenty-one years of age, and citizens of the United States, or in any way abridged, except for participation in rebellion, or other crime, the basis of representation therein shall be reduced in the proportion which the number of such male citizens shall bear to the whole number of male citizens twenty-one years of age in such State.

---

*Superseded by Section 3 of the Twentieth Amendment.

Section 3.   No person shall be a Senator or Representative in Congress, or elector of President and Vice-President, or hold any office, civil or military, under the United States, or under any State, who, having previously taken an oath, as a member of Congress, or as an officer of the United States, or as a member of any State legislature, or as an executive or judicial officer of any State, to support the Constitution of the United States, shall have engaged in insurrection or rebellion against the same, or given aid or comfort to the enemies thereof. Congress may by a vote of two-thirds of each house, remove such disability.

Section 4.   The validity of the public debt of the United States, authorized by law, including debts incurred for payment of pensions and bounties for services in suppressing insurrection or rebellion, shall not be questioned. But neither the United States nor any State shall assume or pay any debt or obligation incurred in aid of insurrection or rebellion against the United States, or any claim for the loss or emancipation of any slave; but all such debts, obligations and claims shall be held illegal and void.

Section 5.   The Congress shall have power to enforce, by appropriate legislation, the provisions of this article.

Amendment XV [1870]

Section 1.   The right of citizens of the United States to vote shall not be denied or abridged by the United States or by any State on account of race, color, or previous condition of servitude—

Section 2.   The Congress shall have power to enforce this article by appropriate legislation.

Amendment XVI [1913]

The Congress shall have power to lay and collect taxes on incomes, from whatever source derived, without apportionment among the several States, and without regard to any census or enumeration.

Amendment XVII [1913]

The Senate of the United States shall be composed of two Senators from each State, elected by the people thereof, for six years; and each Senator shall have one vote. The electors in each State shall have the qualifications requisite for electors of the most numerous branch of the State legislatures.

When vacancies happen in the representation of any State in the Senate, the executive authority of such State shall issue writs of election to fill such vacancies: *Provided,* That the legislature of any State may empower the executive thereof to make temporary appointments until the people fill the vacancies by election as the legislature may direct.

This amendment shall not be so construed as to affect the election or term of any Senator chosen before it becomes valid as part of the Constitution.

Amendment XVIII [1919]

Section 1.   After one year from the ratification of this article the manufacture, sale, or transportation of intoxicating liquors within, the importation thereof into, or the exportation thereof from the United States and all territory subject to the jurisdiction hereof for beverage purposes is hereby prohibited.

Section 2.   The Congress and the several States shall have concurrent power to enforce this article by appropriate legislation.

Section 3.   This article shall be inoperative unless it shall have been ratified as an amendment to the Constitution by the legislatures of the several States, as provided by the Constitution, within seven years from the date of submission hereof to the States by the Congress.*

Amendment XIX [1920]

The right of citizens of the United States to vote shall not be denied or abridged by the United States or by any State on account of sex.

Congress shall have power to enforce this article by appropriate legislation.

Amendment XX [1933]

Section 1.   The terms of the President and Vice-President shall end at noon on the 20th day of January, and the terms of Senators and Representatives at noon on the 3d day of January, of the years in which such terms would have ended if this article had not been ratified; and the terms of their successors shall then begin.

Section 2.   The Congress shall assemble at least once in every year, and such meeting shall begin at noon on the 3d day of January, unless they shall by law appoint a different day.

Section 3.   If, at the time fixed for the beginning of the term of the President, the President elect shall have died, the Vice-President elect shall become President. If a President shall not have been chosen before the time fixed for the beginning of his term, or if the President elect shall have failed to qualify, then the Vice-President elect shall act as President until a President shall have qualified; and the Congress may by law provide for the case wherein neither a President elect nor a Vice-President elect shall have qualified, declaring who shall then act as President, or the manner in which one who is to act shall be selected, and such person shall act accordingly until a President or Vice-President shall have qualified.

Section 4.   The Congress may by law provide for the case of the death of any of the persons from whom the House of Representatives may choose a President whenever the right of choice shall have devolved upon them, and for the case of the death of any of the persons from whom the Senate may choose a Vice-President whenever the right of choice shall have devolved upon them.

---

*Repealed by Section 1 of the Twenty-first Amendment.

Section 5 Sections 1 and 2 shall take effect on the 15th day of October following the ratification of this article.

Section 6. This article shall be inoperative unless it shall have been ratified as an amendment to the Constitution by the legislatures of three-fourths of the several States within seven years from the date of its submission.

Amendment XXI [1933]

Section 1. The eighteenth article of amendment to the Constitution of the United States is hereby repealed.

Section 2. The transportation or importation into any State, Territory, or possession of the United States for delivery or use therein of intoxicating liquors, in violation of the laws thereof, is hereby prohibited.

Section 3. This article shall be inoperative unless it shall have been ratified as an amendment to the Constitution by conventions in the several States, as provided in the Constitution, within seven years from the date of submission hereof to the States by the Congress.

Amendment XXII [1951]

Section 1. No person shall be elected to the office of President more than twice, and no person who has held the office of President, or acted as President, for more than two years of a term to which some other person was elected President shall be elected to the office of the President more than once. But this Article shall not apply to any person holding the office of President when this Article was proposed by the Congress, and shall not prevent any person who may be holding the office of President, or acting as President, during the term within which this Article becomes operative from holding the office of the President or acting as President during the remainder of such term.

Section 2. This article shall be inoperative unless it shall have been ratified as an amendment to the Constitution by the legislatures of three-fourths of the several States within seven years from the date of its submission to the States by the Congress.

Amendment XXIII [1961]

Section 1. The District constituting the seat of Government of the United States shall appoint in such manner as the Congress may direct:

A number of electors of President and Vice-President equal to the whole number of Senators and Representatives in Congress to which the District would be entitled if it were a State, but in no event more than the least populous State; they shall be in addition to those appointed by the States, but they shall be considered, for the purposes of the election of President and Vice-President, to be electors appointed by a State; and they shall meet in the District and perform such duties as provided by the twelfth article of amendment.

Section 2.   The Congress shall have power to enforce this article by appropriate legislation.

Amendment XXIV [1964]

Section 1.   The right of citizens of the United States to vote in any primary or other election for President or Vice-President, for electors for President or Vice-President, or for Senator or Representative in Congress, shall not be denied or abridged by the United States or any State by reason of failure to pay any poll tax or other tax.

Section 2.   The Congress shall have power to enforce this article by appropriate legislation.

Amendment XXV [1967]

Section 1.   In case of the removal of the President from office or of his death or res-ignation, the Vice-President shall become President.

Section 2.   Whenever there is a vacancy in the office of the Vice-President, the Presi-dent shall nominate a Vice-President who shall take office upon confirmation by a majority vote of both houses of Congress.

Section 3.   Whenever the President transmits to the President pro tempore of the Senate and the Speaker of the House of Representatives his written declaration that he is unable to discharge the powers and duties of his office, and until he transmits to them a written declaration to the contrary, such powers and duties shall be discharged by the Vice-President as Acting President.

Section 4.   Whenever the Vice-President and a majority of either the principal offi-cers of the executive departments or of such other body as Congress may by law pro-vide, transmit to the President pro tempore of the Senate and the Speaker of the House of Representatives their written declaration that the President is unable to discharge the powers and duties of his office, the Vice-President shall immediately assume the powers and duties of the office as Acting President.

Thereafter, when the President transmits to the President pro tempore of the Senate and the Speaker of the House of Representatives his written declaration that no inability exists, he shall resume the powers and duties of his office unless the Vice-President and a majority of either the principal officers of the executive department or of such other body as Congress may by law provide, transmit within four days to the President pro tempore of the Senate and the Speaker of the House of Represen-tatives their written declaration that the President is unable to discharge the pow-ers and duties of his office. Thereupon Congress shall decide the issue, assembling within forty-eight hours for that purpose if not in session. If the Congress, within twenty-one days after receipt of the latter written declaration, or, if Congress is not in session, within twenty-one days after Congress is required to assemble, determines by two-thirds vote of both Houses that the President is unable to discharge the pow-ers and duties of his office, the Vice-President shall continue to discharge the same as Acting President; otherwise, the President shall resume the powers and duties of his office.

Amendment XXVI [1971]

Section 1.   The right of citizens of the United States, who are eighteen years of age or older, to vote shall not be denied or abridged by the United States or by any State on account of age.

Section 2.   The Congress shall have power to enforce this article by appropriate legislation.

Amendment XXVII [1992]

No law varying the compensation for services of the Senators and Representatives, shall take effect, until an election of Representatives shall have intervened.

Appendix

TABLE 1   Territorial Expansion

Territory	Date Acquired	Square Miles	How Acquired
Original states and territories	1783	888,685	Treaty of Paris
Louisiana Purchase	1803	827,192	Purchased from France
Florida	1819	72,003	Adams-Onís Treaty
Texas	1845	390,143	Annexation of independent country
Oregon	1846	285,580	Oregon Boundary Treaty
Mexican cession	1848	529,017	Treaty of Guadalupe Hidalgo
Gadsden Purchase	1853	29,640	Purchased from Mexico
Midway Islands	1867	2	Annexation of uninhabited islands
Alaska	1867	589,757	Purchased from Russia
Hawaii	1898	6,450	Annexation of independent country
Wake Island	1898	3	Annexation of uninhabited island
Puerto Rico	1899	3,435	Treaty of Paris
Guam	1899	212	Treaty of Paris
The Philippines	1899–1946	115,600	Treaty of Paris; granted independence
American Samoa	1900	76	Treaty with Germany and Great Britain
Panama Canal Zone	1904–1978	553	Hay–Bunau-Varilla Treaty
U.S. Virgin Islands	1917	133	Purchased from Denmark
Trust Territory of the Pacific Islands*	1947	717	United Nations Trusteeship

*A number of these islands have since been granted independence: Federated States of Micronesia, 1990; Marshall Islands, 1991; Palau, 1994.

TABLE 2 The Labor Force (thousands of workers)

Year	Agriculture	Mining	Manufacturing	Construction	Trade	Other	Total
1810	1,950	11	75	—	—	294	2,330
1840	3,570	32	500	290	350	918	5,660
1850	4,520	102	1,200	410	530	1,488	8,250
1860	5,880	176	1,530	520	890	2,114	11,110
1870	6,790	180	2,470	780	1,310	1,400	12,930
1880	8,920	280	3,290	900	1,930	2,070	17,390
1890	9,960	440	4,390	1,510	2,960	4,060	23,320
1900	11,680	637	5,895	1,665	3,970	5,223	29,070
1910	11,770	1,068	8,332	1,949	5,320	9,041	37,480
1920	10,790	1,180	11,190	1,233	5,845	11,372	41,610
1930	10,560	1,009	9,884	1,988	8,122	17,267	48,830
1940	9,575	925	11,309	1,876	9,328	23,277	56,290
1950	7,870	901	15,648	3,029	12,152	25,870	65,470
1960	5,970	709	17,145	3,640	14,051	32,545	74,060
1970	3,463	516	20,746	4,818	15,008	34,127	78,678
1980	3,364	979	21,942	6,215	20,191	46,612	99,303
1990	3,186	730	21,184	7,696	24,269	60,849	118,793
2000	2,464	475	19,644	9,931	15,763	88,260	136,537

SOURCES: U.S. Bureau of the Census, *Historical Statistics of the United States, Colonial Times to 1970* (1975), 139; *Statistical Abstract of the United States, 1998,* table 675; *Statistical Abstract of the United States, 2006.*

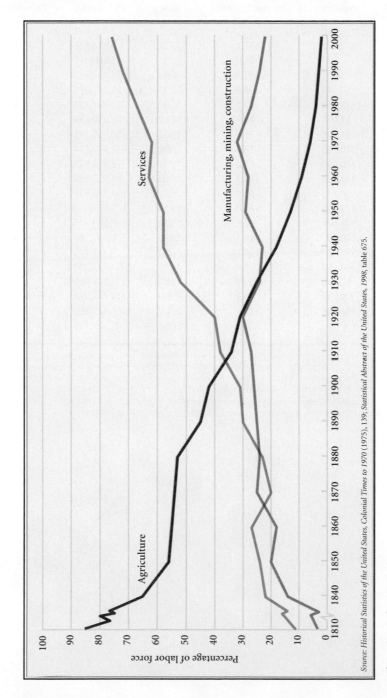

Source: Historical Statistics of the United States, Colonial Times to 1970 (1975), 139; Statistical Abstract of the United States, 1998, table 675.

Changing Labor Patterns

TABLE 3	American Population				
Year	Population	Percent Increase	Year	Population	Percent Increase
1610	350	—	1810	7,239,881	36.4
1620	2,300	557.1	1820	9,638,453	33.1
1630	4,600	100.0	1830	12,866,020	33.5
1640	26,600	478.3	1840	17,069,453	32.7
1650	50,400	90.8	1850	23,191,876	35.9
1660	75,100	49.0	1860	31,443,321	35.6
1670	111,900	49.0	1870	39,818,449	26.6
1680	151,500	35.4	1880	50,155,783	26.0
1690	210,400	38.9	1890	62,947,714	25.5
1700	250,900	19.2	1900	75,994,575	20.7
1710	331,700	32.2	1910	91,972,266	21.0
1720	466,200	40.5	1920	105,710,620	14.9
1730	629,400	35.0	1930	122,775,046	16.1
1740	905,600	43.9	1940	131,669,275	7.2
1750	1,170,800	29.3	1950	150,697,361	14.5
1760	1,593,600	36.1	1960	179,323,175	19.0
1770	2,148,100	34.8	1970	203,235,298	13.3
1780	2,780,400	29.4	1980	226,545,805	11.5
1790	3,929,214	41.3	1990	248,709,873	9.8
1800	5,308,483	35.1	2000	281,421,906	13.2
			2007	301,621,157	7.0

Note: These figures largely ignore the Native American population. Census takers never made any effort to count the Native American population that lived outside their reserved political areas and compiled only casual and incomplete enumerations of those living within their jurisdictions until 1890. In that year, the federal government attempted a full count of the Indian population: The Census found 125,719 Indians in 1890, compared with only 12,543 in 1870 and 33,985 in 1880.

SOURCES: U.S. Bureau of the Census, *Historical Statistics of the United States, Colonial Times to 1970* (1975); *Statistical Abstract of the United States, 2001;* U.S. Bureau of the Census, Population Finder, http://factfinder.census.gov.

| TABLE 4 | Presidential Elections | | | | |

Year	Candidates	Parties	Percentage of Popular Vote	Electoral Vote	Percentage of Voter Participation
1789	**George Washington**	No party designations	*	69	
	John Adams†			34	
	Other candidates			35	
1792	**George Washington**	No party designations		132	
	John Adams			77	
	George Clinton			50	
	Other candidates			5	
1796	**John Adams**	Federalist		71	
	Thomas Jefferson	Democratic-Republican		68	
	Thomas Pinckney	Federalist		59	
	Aaron Burr	Democratic-Republican		30	
	Other candidates			48	
1800	**Thomas Jefferson**	Democratic-Republican		73	
	Aaron Burr	Democratic-Republican		73	
	John Adams	Federalist		65	
	Charles C. Pinckney	Federalist		64	
	John Jay	Federalist		1	
1804	**Thomas Jefferson**	Democratic-Republican		162	
	Charles C. Pinckney	Federalist		14	
1808	**James Madison**	Democratic-Republican		122	
	Charles C. Pinckney	Federalist		47	
	George Clinton	Democratic-Republican		6	
1812	**James Madison**	Democratic-Republican		128	
	De Witt Clinton	Federalist		89	
1816	**James Monroe**	Democratic-Republican		183	
	Rufus King	Federalist		34	
1820	**James Monroe**	Democratic-Republican		231	
	John Quincy Adams	Independent Republican		1	
1824	**John Quincy Adams**	Democratic-Republican	30.5	84	26.9
	Andrew Jackson	Democratic-Republican	43.1	99	
	Henry Clay	Democratic-Republican	13.2	37	
	William H. Crawford	Democratic-Republican	13.1	41	
1828	**Andrew Jackson**	Democratic	56.0	178	57.6
	John Quincy Adams	National Republican	44.0	83	
1832	**Andrew Jackson**	Democratic	54.5	219	55.4
	Henry Clay	National Republican	37.5	49	
	William Wirt	Anti-Masonic	8.0	7	
	John Floyd	Democratic	‡	11	
1836	**Martin Van Buren**	Democratic	50.9	170	57.8
	William H. Harrison	Whig		73	
	Hugh L. White	Whig		26	
	Daniel Webster	Whig	49.1	14	
	W. P. Mangum	Whig		11	

(continued on next page)

*Prior to 1824, most presidential electors were chosen by state legislators rather than by popular vote.

†Before the Twelfth Amendment was passed in 1804, the Electoral College voted for two presidential candidates; the runner-up became vice president.

‡Percentages below 2.0 have been omitted. Hence the percentage of popular vote might not total 100 percent.

Year	Candidates	Parties	Percentage of Popular Vote	Electoral Vote	Percentage of Voter Participation
1840	**William H. Harrison**	Whig	53.1	234	80.2
	Martin Van Buren	Democratic	46.9	60	
1844	**James K. Polk**	Democratic	49.6	170	78.9
	Henry Clay	Whig	48.1	105	
	James G. Birney	Liberty	2.3	0	
1848	**Zachary Taylor**	Whig	47.4	163	72.7
	Lewis Cass	Democratic	42.5	127	
	Martin Van Buren	Free Soil	10.1	0	
1852	**Franklin Pierce**	Democratic	50.9	254	69.6
	Winfield Scott	Whig	44.1	42	
	John P. Hale	Free Soil	5.0	0	
1856	**James Buchanan**	Democratic	45.3	174	78.9
	John C. Frémont	Republican	33.1	114	
	Millard Fillmore	American	21.6	8	
1860	**Abraham Lincoln**	Republican	39.8	180	81.2
	Stephen A. Douglas	Democratic	29.5	12	
	John C. Breckinridge	Democratic	18.1	72	
	John Bell	Constitutional Union	12.6	39	
1864	**Abraham Lincoln**	Republican	55.0	212	73.8
	George B. McClellan	Democratic	45.0	21	
1868	**Ulysses S. Grant**	Republican	52.7	214	78.1
	Horatio Seymour	Democratic	47.3	80	
1872	**Ulysses S. Grant**	Republican	55.6	286	71.3
	Horace Greeley	Democratic	43.9	0	
1876	**Rutherford B. Hayes**	Republican	48.0	185	81.8
	Samuel J. Tilden	Democratic	51.0	184	
1880	**James A. Garfield**	Republican	48.5	214	79.4
	Winfield S. Hancock	Democratic	48.1	155	
	James B. Weaver	Greenback-Labor	3.4	0	
1884	**Grover Cleveland**	Democratic	48.5	219	77.5
	James G. Blaine	Republican	48.2	182	
1888	**Benjamin Harrison**	Republican	47.9	233	79.3
	Grover Cleveland	Democratic	48.6	168	
1892	**Grover Cleveland**	Democratic	46.1	277	74.7
	Benjamin Harrison	Republican	43.0	145	
	James B. Weaver	People's	8.5	22	
1896	**William McKinley**	Republican	51.1	271	79.3
	William J. Bryan	Democratic	47.7	176	
1900	**William McKinley**	Republican	51.7	292	73.2
	William J. Bryan	Democratic; Populist	45.5	155	
1904	**Theodore Roosevelt**	Republican	57.4	336	65.2
	Alton B. Parker	Democratic	37.6	140	
	Eugene V. Debs	Socialist	3.0	0	
1908	**William H. Taft**	Republican	51.6	321	65.4
	William J. Bryan	Democratic	43.1	162	
	Eugene V. Debs	Socialist	2.8	0	

Year	Candidates	Parties	Percentage of Popular Vote	Electoral Vote	Percentage of Voter Participation
1912	**Woodrow Wilson**	Democratic	41.9	435	58.8
	Theodore Roosevelt	Progressive	27.4	88	
	William H. Taft	Republican	23.2	8	
1916	**Woodrow Wilson**	Democratic	49.4	277	61.6
	Charles E. Hughes	Republican	46.2	254	
	A. L. Benson	Socialist	3.2	0	
1920	**Warren G. Harding**	Republican	60.4	404	49.2
	James M. Cox	Democratic	34.2	127	
	Eugene V. Debs	Socialist	3.4	0	
1924	**Calvin Coolidge**	Republican	54.0	382	48.9
	John W. Davis	Democratic	28.8	136	
	Robert M. La Follette	Progressive	16.6	13	
1928	**Herbert C. Hoover**	Republican	58.2	444	56.9
	Alfred E. Smith	Democratic	40.9	87	
1932	**Franklin D. Roosevelt**	Democratic	57.4	472	56.9
	Herbert C. Hoover	Republican	39.7	59	
1936	**Franklin D. Roosevelt**	Democratic	60.8	523	61.0
	Alfred M. Landon	Republican	36.5	8	
1940	**Franklin D. Roosevelt**	Democratic	54.8	449	62.5
	Wendell L. Willkie	Republican	44.8	82	
1944	**Franklin D. Roosevelt**	Democratic	53.5	432	55.9
	Thomas E. Dewey	Republican	46.0	99	
1948	**Harry S Truman**	Democratic	49.6	303	53.0
	Thomas E. Dewey	Republican	45.1	189	
1952	**Dwight D. Eisenhower**	Republican	55.1	442	63.3
	Adlai E. Stevenson	Democratic	44.4	89	
1956	**Dwight D. Eisenhower**	Republican	57.6	457	60.6
	Adlai E. Stevenson	Democratic	42.1	73	
1960	**John F. Kennedy**	Democratic	49.7	303	64.0
	Richard M. Nixon	Republican	49.5	219	
1964	**Lyndon B. Johnson**	Democratic	61.1	486	61.7
	Barry M. Goldwater	Republican	38.5	52	
1968	**Richard M. Nixon**	Republican	43.4	301	60.6
	Hubert H. Humphrey	Democratic	42.7	191	
	George C. Wallace	American Independent	13.5	46	
1972	**Richard M. Nixon**	Republican	60.7	520	55.5
	George S. McGovern	Democratic	37.5	17	
1976	**Jimmy Carter**	Democratic	50.1	297	54.3
	Gerald R. Ford	Republican	48.0	240	
1980	**Ronald W. Reagan**	Republican	50.7	489	53.0
	Jimmy Carter	Democratic	41.0	49	
	John B. Anderson	Independent	6.6	0	
1984	**Ronald W. Reagan**	Republican	58.4	525	52.9
	Walter F. Mondale	Democratic	41.6	13	

(continued on next page)

Year	Candidates	Parties	Percentage of Popular Vote	Electoral Vote	Percentage of Voter Participation
1988	**George H. W. Bush**	Republican	53.4	426	50.3
	Michael Dukakis	Democratic	45.6	111*	
1992	**William J. Clinton**	Democratic	43.7	370	55.1
	George H. W. Bush	Republican	38.0	168	
	H. Ross Perot	Independent	19.0	0	
1996	**William J. Clinton**	Democratic	49	379	49.0
	Robert J. Dole	Republican	41	159	
	H. Ross Perot	Reform	8	0	
2000	**George W. Bush**	Republican	47.9	271	51.3
	Albert A. Gore	Democratic	48.4	266†	
	Ralph Nader	Green Party	2.7	0	
2004	**George W. Bush**	Republican	51.0	286	59.0
	John F. Kerry	Democratic	48.0	252	
2008	**Barack Obama**	Democratic	53.0	364	61.2
	John McCain	Republican	46.0	174	

*One Dukakis elector cast a vote for Lloyd Bentsen.
†One Gore elector abstained.

Glossary

A Note to Students This list of terms will help you with the vocabulary of history. Many of these terms refer to broad, enduring concepts that appear not only in your textbook but also in the historical literature more generally and in discussions of current events. The terms appear in bold print at their first use in each volume. The glossary notes the pages on which the terms appear in bold print. For definitions and discussions of other unfamiliar words and concepts, consult the book's index or a dictionary.

American Renaissance A burst of American literature during the 1840s, highlighted by the novels of Herman Melville and Nathaniel Hawthorne; the essays of Ralph Waldo Emerson, Henry David Thoreau, and Margaret Fuller; and the poetry of Walt Whitman. (p. 238)

American System The mercantilist system of national economic development advocated by Henry Clay and adopted by John Quincy Adams. It had three interrelated parts: a national bank to manage the nation's financial system; protective tariffs to encourage American industry and provide revenue; and a nationally funded network of roads, canals, and railroads. (p. 293)

anarchism The advocacy of a stateless society achieved by revolutionary means. Feared for their views, anarchists became the scapegoats for the 1886 Haymarket Square bombing. (p. 516)

Anglo-Saxonism A theory widely held in the late nineteenth century that the English-speaking peoples were racially superior and, for that reason, justified in colonizing and dominating the peoples of less-developed areas of the world. Combined with Social Darwinism, Anglo-Saxonism fueled American expansionism in the late nineteenth century. (p. 615)

armistice A temporary cessation of military hostilities. World War I ended when the armistice signed in November 1918 led to the Versailles Treaty of 1919. (p. 647)

artisan republicanism An ideology that celebrated small-scale producers, men and women who owned their own shops (or farms), and defined the ideal republican society as one constituted by, and dedicated to the welfare of, independent workers and citizens. (p. 268)

Benevolent Empire A broad-ranging campaign of moral and institutional reforms inspired by Evangelical Christian ideals and endorsed by upper-middle-class men and women in the 1820s. Ministers who promoted benevolent reform insisted that people who had experienced saving grace should provide moral guidance and charity to the less fortunate. (p. 281)

bills of exchange Credit slips that British manufacturers, West Indian planters, and American merchants used in the eighteenth century in place of currency to settle transactions. (p. 86)

Black Codes Laws passed by southern states after the Civil War denying ex-slaves the civil rights enjoyed by whites and intended to force blacks back to the plantations. (p. 439)

blacklist A list of people to be excluded from an activity or organization. Throughout the nineteenth century, employers blacklisted workers affiliated with unions. In the 1950s, governments and private businesses blacklisted alleged Communists, denying them positions in government, motion pictures, and many industries and unions. (pp. 312, 783)

business cycle The periodic rise and fall of business activity characteristic of market-driven, capitalist economies. To increase profits, producers increase output; as supply exceeds demand, there is a cutback in production and an economic recession. In the United States, major periods of expansion (1802–1818, 1824–1836, 1846–1856, 1865–1873, 1896–1914, and 1922–1928) were followed either by relatively short financial panics (1819–1822 and 1857–1860) or by extended economic depressions (1837–1843, 1873–1896, and 1929–1939). Since 1945, government intervention has moderated the business cycle. (pp. 227, 692)

capitalism A system of economic production based on the private ownership of property and the contractual exchange for profit of goods, labor, and money (capital). In the United States before 1820, a full-scale capitalist economy — and society — emerged during the Market Revolution (1820–1850) and reached its pinnacle during the final decades of the century. See *Market Revolution*. (p. 225)

carpetbaggers A derisive name given by Southerners to Northerners who moved to the South during Reconstruction. Former Confederates despised these Northerners as transient exploiters. Carpetbaggers actually were a varied group, including Union veterans who had served in the South, reformers eager to help the ex-slaves, and others looking for business opportunities. (p. 450)

caste system A form of social organization that divides a society along relatively rigid lines of status based primarily on birth. (p. 27)

chattel slavery A system of bondage in which a slave has the legal status of property and so can be bought and sold like property. (p. 49)

civic humanism The belief that individuals owe a service to their community and its government. During the Italian Renaissance, political theorists argued that selfless service was crucial in a republic, a form of government in which authority lies in the hands of some or all of the citizenry. (p. 17)

civil religion A term used by historians to refer to a religious-like reverence for various political institutions and ideologies. An example is the belief in "republicanism" after the American Revolution. (p. 188)

clan A group of families that share a real or legendary common ancestor. Most native peoples north of the Rio Grande consisted of a group of clans, which combined to form a distinct people based on language and culture. (p. 9)

classical liberalism An ideology based on the economic principles of private property and competitive markets propounded by Adam Smith and the political ideas of individual liberty and limited government advanced by John Locke. Also see *laissez-faire*. (p. 307)

closed shop A workplace in which a job seeker had to be a union member to gain employment. In the nineteenth century, the closed shop was favored by craft unions as a method of keeping out incompetent and lower-wage workers and of strengthening the unions' bargaining position with employers. (p. 514)

closed-shop agreement A labor contract in which an employer agrees to hire only union members. Many employers strongly opposed these agreements and went to court to try to have them declared illegal. (p. 312)

collective bargaining A process of negotiation between labor unions and employers, particularly favored by the American Federation of Labor (AFL). Led by Samuel Gompers, the AFL accepted the new industrial order but fought for a bigger share of the profits for the workers. (p. 513)

Columbian Exchange The transfer in the sixteenth century of agricultural products, people, and diseases from the Western Hemisphere to other continents and from those other continents to the Western Hemisphere. (p. 27)

common law The centuries-old body of English law based on custom and judicial interpretation, not legislation, and evolving case by case on the basis of precedent. The common law was transmitted to America along with English settlement and became the foundation of American law at the state and local levels. In the United States, even more than in Britain, the common law gave the courts supremacy over the legislatures in many areas of law. (pp. 49, 589)

companionate marriage A marriage based on equality and mutual respect — both republican values. Although husbands in these marriages retained significant legal power, they increasingly came to see their wives as partners rather than as inferiors or dependents. (p. 234)

conscience Whigs Whig politicians who opposed the Mexican War (1846–1848) on moral grounds. They maintained that the purpose of the war was to expand and perpetuate slavery. They feared that the addition of more slave states would ensure the South's control of the national government and undermine a society of yeomen farmers and "free labor" in the North. (p. 386)

conservation Advocacy for the protection of the natural environment for sustained use. As applied by Theodore Roosevelt, conservation accepted development of public lands, provided that this was in the public interest and not wastefully destructive. In contrast, preservationists valued wilderness in its natural state and were more broadly opposed to development. (p. 598)

craft worker An artisan or other worker who has a specific craft or skill. For example, a mason, a cabinetmaker, a printer, or a weaver. (p. 267)

cultural pluralism A term coined in 1924 that posits that multiple levels of identity, including religious and ethnic diversity, can be a source of strength in a democratic nation and that such cultural differences should be respected and valued. (p. 720)

deficit spending Government spending in excess of tax revenues based on the ideas of British economist John Maynard Keynes. During the Great Depression, Keynes argued that governments should go into debt to stimulate a stagnant economy. (p. 714)

deflation The sustained decline of prices, generally accompanying an economic depression, but in the United States after the Civil War, the result of rapidly rising productivity, market competition, and a tight money supply. (p. 574)

deist, deism The Enlightenment-influenced belief that the Christian God created the universe and then left it to run according to natural laws. (p. 110)

deregulation Process of removing or limiting federal regulatory mechanisms, justified on the basis of promoting competition and streamlining government bureaucracy. President Carter began deregulation in the 1970s, starting with the airline, trucking, and communications industries. The process continued under subsequent administrations. (p. 876)

détente From the French word for "a relaxation of tension," this term was used to signify the new foreign policy of President Nixon, which sought a reduction of hostility between the United States and the Soviet Union and China in the early 1970s. (p. 856)

direct primary The selection of party candidates by a popular vote rather than by the party convention, this progressive reform was especially pressed by Robert La Follette, who viewed it as an instrument for breaking the grip of machines on the political parties. In the South, where it was limited to whites, the primary was a means of disfranchising blacks. (p. 591)

division of labor A system of manufacture that assigns specific — and repetitive — tasks to each worker. The system was first implemented between 1800 and 1830 in the shoe industry and soon became general practice throughout the manufacturing sector of the U.S. economy. Although it improved productivity, it eroded workers' control and sense of achievement. (p. 261)

dollar diplomacy Policy adopted by President Taft that emphasized the connection between America's economic and political interests overseas. The benefits would flow in both directions: Business would gain from diplomatic efforts in its behalf, while the strengthened American economic presence overseas would give added leverage to American diplomacy. (p. 630)

domino theory An American Cold War concept associated with the containment policy that posited that the loss of one country to Communism would lead to the toppling of other non-Communist regimes. The term was first used by President Eisenhower, who warned of "falling dominos" in Southeast Asia if Vietnam became Communist. (p. 790)

dower, dower right A legal right originating in Europe and carried to America that provided a widow with the use of one-third of the family's land and goods during her lifetime. (p. 16)

enclosure acts Laws passed in sixteenth-century England that allowed landowners to fence in the open fields that surrounded many villages and to use them for grazing sheep. This enclosure of the fields left peasants without land to cultivate, forcing them to work as wage laborers or as wool spinners and weavers. (p. 32)

encomiendas Land grants in America given by the Spanish kings to privileged landholders (*encomenderos*) in the sixteenth century. *Encomiendas* gave the landholders legal control over native peoples who lived on or near their estates. (p. 27)

entitlement programs The kind of government program that provides individuals with personal benefits to which potential beneficiaries have a legal right whenever they meet eligibility conditions specified by the law authorizing the program. Examples include Social Security, Medicare, unemployment compensation, and agricultural price supports. (p. 854)

established church A church that is given privileged legal status by the government. Before 1776, most of the American colonies had established churches that were supported by public taxes; often, they were the only legally permitted religious institutions. By 1830, no state had a legally established church, though most states gave legal and financial privileges to religious institutions. (p. 245)

ethnocultural Refers to the distinctive social characteristics of immigrants and religious groups, especially in determining their party loyalties and stance on political issues touching personal behavior and public morality. (p. 559)

ethnocultural politics The argument by historians that people's political allegiance and voting in the nineteenth and twentieth centuries was determined less by party policy than by their membership in a specific ethnic or religious group. (p. 316)

factory A structure first built by manufacturers in the early nineteenth century to concentrate all aspects of production — and the machinery needed to increase output — in one location. (p. 261)

Federalists Supporters of the Constitution of 1787, which created a strong central government, called themselves Federalists; those who feared that a strong central government would corrupt the nation's newly won liberty came to be known as Antifederalists. (p. 187)

feminists Women who subscribed to the doctrine advanced in the early twentieth century by women activists that women should be equal to men in all areas of life. Earlier women activists and suffragists had accepted the notion of separate spheres for men and women, but feminists sought to overcome all barriers to equality and full personal development. (p. 586)

fiscal policy The range of decisions involving the finances of the federal government. These decisions include how much to tax, how much to spend, and what level of resulting deficit or surplus is acceptable. Such decisions — fiscal policy — have a big effect on a nation's allocation of economic resources, the distribution of income, and the level of economic activity. (p. 781)

Fourteen Points President Wilson proposed these principles as a basis for the peace negotiations at Versailles in 1919. They included open diplomacy, freedom of the seas, free trade, territorial integrity, arms reduction, national self-determination, and establishment of the League of Nations. (p. 660)

franchise The right to vote. During the 1820s and 1830s, most states revised their constitutions to extend the vote to all adult white males. In 1870, the Fifteenth Amendment gave the vote to black men; in 1920, the Nineteenth Amendment extended the franchise to women. (p. 291)

freehold, freeholder Property owned in its entirety, without feudal dues or landlord obligations. The first settlers of New England instituted this landholding system because they repudiated exploitative leaseholds and feudal obligations. Freeholders have the legal right to improve, transfer, or sell their property. (p. 50)

free market A system of economic exchange in which prices are determined by supply and demand and no producer or consumer dominates the market. The term also refers to markets that are not subject to government regulation. (p. 184)

free-soil movement A political movement of the 1840s that opposed the expansion of slavery. Motivating its members—mostly white yeomen farmers—was their belief that slavery benefited "aristocratic men," who exploited slave labor. Free-soilers wanted farm families to settle the western territories and install democratic republican values and institutions there. The short-lived Free-Soil Party (1848–1854) stood for "free soil, free labor, free men," which subsequently became the program of the Republican Party. (p. 388)

fundamentalism, fundamentalist Any movement that pursues a "pure" and rigid belief system. In the United States, it usually refers to Evangelical Protestants who interpret the Bible literally. In the 1920s, fundamentalists opposed modernist Protestants, who reconciled Christianity with Darwin's theory of evolution and other scientific discoveries. Fundamentalists' promotion of antievolution laws for public schools led to the famous Scopes trial of 1925; in recent decades, fundamentalists have strongly supported legislation to prohibit abortions, gay marriages, and stem-cell research. (p. 687)

gang-labor system A collective system of work discipline used on southern cotton plantations in the mid-nineteenth century to enforce work norms and achieve greater productivity. Planters assigned tasks to gangs of enslaved workers which were constantly supervised by white overseers or black drivers. (pp. 361, 443)

general strike A strike that draws in all the workers in a society, with the intention of shutting the entire system down. Radical groups such as the Industrial Workers of the World (IWW) in the early twentieth century saw the general strike as the means for initiating a social revolution. (p. 520)

gentility A refined style of living and elaborate manners that came to be highly prized among well-to-do English families after 1600. (p. 85)

gentry A class of English men and women who were substantial landholders but lacked the social privileges and titles of nobility. During the Price Revolution of the sixteenth century, the relative wealth and status of the gentry rose while those of the aristocracy fell. (p. 32)

gerrymander The political strategy (named after the early nineteenth-century politician Elbridge Gerry) of changing the boundaries of voting districts to give the dominant party an advantage. (p. 566)

ghetto Term describing an urban neighborhood composed of the poor, and occasionally used to describe any tight-knit community containing a single ethnic or class group. Ghettos came into being in the nineteenth century, in tandem with the enormous influx of immigrants to American cities. (p. 536)

Great American Desert The name given to the drought-stricken Great Plains by Euro-Americans in the early nineteenth century. Believing the region to be unfit for cultivation or agriculture, Congress designated the Great Plains as permanent Indian country in 1834. (p. 471)

greenbacks Paper money issued by the U.S. Treasury during the Civil War to finance the war effort. Greenbacks had the status of legal tender in all public and private transactions. Because greenbacks were issued in large amounts, their value fell during the war to forty cents (as compared to a gold or silver dollar), but they gradually recovered their full value as the Union government won the war and subsequently reduced its war-related debt. (p. 421)

guild An organization of skilled workers in medieval and early modern Europe that regulated a craft. Guilds did not develop in colonial America because artisans generally were in short supply. (p. 18)

habeas corpus Latin for "bring forth the body," a legal writ forcing government authorities to justify their arrest and detention of an individual. Rooted in English common law, habeas corpus was made a formal privilege in the U.S. Constitution (Article 1, Section 9), which also allows its suspension in cases of invasion or insurrection. During the Civil War, Lincoln suspended habeas corpus to deter anti-Union activities. The USA PATRIOT Act (2001) likewise suspends this privilege in cases of suspected terrorism, but the constitutional legitimacy of this and other provisions of the act have not been definitively decided by the courts. (p. 418)

heresy A religious doctrine that is inconsistent with the teachings of a church. Some of the Crusades between 1096 and 1291 targeted groups of Christians whose beliefs the leaders of the Roman Catholic Church judged to be heretical. (p. 17)

home rule A rallying cry used by southern Democrats who portrayed Reconstruction governments as illegitimate—imposed on the South—and themselves as the only party capable of restoring the South to "home rule." By 1876, northern Republicans were inclined to accept this claim. (p. 460)

homespun Cloth spun and woven "at home" by American women and traditionally worn by poorer colonists. During the boycotts of British goods, wearing homespun clothes became a political act, and even people who could afford better made cloth wore homespun fabrics. Making homespun cloth allowed women to contribute directly to the Patriot movement. (p. 144)

ideology A systematic philosophy or political theory that prescribes a set of values or beliefs and/or purports to explain the character of the social world. (pp. 17, 556)

impeachment First step in the constitutional process for removing the president from office, in which the House of Representatives passes charges of wrongdoing (articles of impeachment). The Senate then conducts a trial to determine whether the impeached president is guilty of the charges. (p. 448)

indenture A contract that required service for a specified period. In the seventeenth century, thousands of workers came to North America as indentured servants. In exchange for agreeing to work for four or five years without wages, the workers received passage across the Atlantic, room and board, and status as a free person at the end of the contract period. (pp. 33, 489)

indulgence A certificate granted by the Catholic Church that claimed to pardon a sinner from punishment in the afterlife. In his *Ninety-five Theses*, written in 1517, Martin Luther condemned the sale of indulgences, a common practice among Catholic clergy. (p. 28)

Industrial Revolution The fabrication of goods, usually in well-organized factories, by machines powered by waterwheels, steam engines, or electrical engines. The Industrial Revolution began in the English textile industry in the 1750s and spread to the United States around 1800. The new machine technology vastly increased the output of goods, and the spread of the factory system split industrial society into a class of wealthy capitalist owners and a mass of propertyless wage-earning workers. (p. 260)

industrial union All workers in a single industry (for example, automobile, railroad, or mining) organized into a single association, regardless of skill, rather than into separate craft-based associations. The American Railway Union, formed in the 1880s, was one of the first industrial unions in the nation. (p. 518)

injunction A court order that immediately requires or prohibits an activity, either temporarily or permanently. Between the 1830s and the 1930s, probusiness judges often issued injunctions to stop workers from picketing or striking. (p. 313)

isolationism, isolationist A foreign-policy stance that favored limited American involvement with other nations, especially with respect to political agreements or diplomatic alliances. The common view of post–World War I U.S. foreign policy is that it was isolationist, but in fact, the United States played an active role in world trade and finance. (p. 662)

Jim Crow A term first heard in antebellum minstrel shows to designate black behavior and used in the age of segregation to designate facilities restricted to blacks, such as Jim Crow railway cars. (p. 568)

jingoism This term came to refer to the superpatriotism that took hold in the mid-1890s during the American dispute with Spain over Cuba. Jingoes were enthusiastic about a military solution as a way of showing the nation's mettle, and when diplomacy failed, they got their wish with the Spanish-American War of 1898. (p. 616)

joint-stock corporation A financial organization devised by English merchants around 1550 that subsequently facilitated the colonization of North America. In these corporations, a number of investors pooled their capital and, in return, received shares of stock in the enterprise in proportion to their share of the total investment. (p. 53)

Keynesian economics The theory, developed by British economist John Maynard Keynes in the 1930s, that purposeful government intervention into the economy (through lowering or raising taxes, interest rates, and government spending) can affect the level of overall economic activity and thereby prevent both severe depressions and runaway inflation. (p. 714)

"King Cotton" A term that describes the importance of raw cotton in the nineteenth-century international economy. More specifically, the Confederate belief during the Civil War that their cotton was so important to the British and French economies that those governments would recognize the South as an independent nation and supply it with loans and arms. (p. 420)

labor theory of value The belief that human labor produces value. Adherents argued that the price of a product should be determined not by the market (supply and demand) but by the amount of work required to make it and that most of the price should be paid to the person who produced it. The idea was popularized by the National Trades' Union and other labor leaders in the mid-nineteenth century. (p. 268)

laissez-faire French for "let do" or "leave alone." The principle that the less government does, the better, particularly in reference to the economy. This was the dominant philosophy of American government in the late nineteenth century and the guiding light of conservative politics in the twentieth. (pp. 307, 554)

land bank An institution, established by a colonial legislature, that printed paper money and lent it to farmers, taking a lien on their land to ensure repayment. (p. 93)

leasehold, leaseholder A piece of property rented out by means of a formal contract for a period of time. The contract specified the obligations of the owner and the lessee. Some leaseholds ran for "three lives"—those of the lessee, his son or heir, and his grandson. (p. 96)

liberal, liberalism Terms that in the nineteenth century referred to support for limited government and individual responsibility but that evolved in the twentieth century to mean support for an activist state and social welfare. In the nineteenth century, Mugwumps were liberals. In the twentieth century, New Dealers were liberals. (p. 459)

liberal consensus Refers to widespread agreement among Americans in the decades after World War II that the progovernment policies of the New Deal were desirable and should be continued. In politics, the liberal consensus was reflected in the relatively small differences on economic and social policies between Republicans and Democrats until the advent of Ronald Reagan. (p. 788)

lien (crop lien) A legal device that enables a creditor to take possession of the property of a borrower, including the right to have it sold in payment of the debt. Furnishing merchants took such liens on cotton crops as collateral for supplies advanced to sharecroppers during the growing season. This system trapped farmers in a cycle of debt and made them vulnerable to exploitation by the furnishing merchant. (p. 455)

literacy tests The requirement that an ability to read be demonstrated as a qualification for the right to vote. It was a device easily used by registrars to prevent blacks from voting, whether they could read or not, and was widely adopted across the South beginning with Mississippi in 1890. (p. 562)

machine tools Cutting, boring, and drilling machines used to produce standardized metal parts, which were then assembled into products like sewing machines. The rapid development of machine tools by American inventors throughout the nineteenth century was a factor in the rapid spread of industrialization. (pp. 266, 511)

Manifest Destiny A term coined by John L. O'Sullivan in 1845 to describe the idea that American citizens should settle the North American continent from the Atlantic to the Pacific Ocean. Adding geographical and secular dimensions to the Second Great Awakening, Manifest Destiny implied that the spread of American republican institutions and Protestant churches across the continent was part of God's plan for the world. In the late nineteenth century, the concept was broadened to include overseas expansion. (p. 378)

manorial system A quasi-feudal system of landholding. In the Hudson River valley of New York, wealthy landlords leased out farms to tenants, who paid rent and a quarter of value of all improvements (houses, barns, etc.) if they sold the lease; tenants also owed the landlord a number of days of personal service each year. (p. 67)

manumission From the Latin *manumittere*, "to release from the hand," the legal act of relinquishing property rights in slaves. In 1782, the Virginia assembly passed an act allowing manumission; within a decade, planters had freed 10,000 slaves. Worried that a large free black population would threaten the institution of slavery, the assembly repealed the law in 1792. (p. 239)

Market Revolution The dramatic increase between 1820 and 1850 in the exchange of goods and services in market transactions. The Market Revolution was the result of the increased output of farms and factories, the entrepreneurial activities of traders and merchants, and the development of a transportation network of roads, canals, and railroads. (p. 260)

mass production A system of factory production that often combines sophisticated machinery, a disciplined labor force, and assembly lines to turn out vast quantities of identical goods at low cost. In the nineteenth century, the textile and meatpacking industries pioneered mass production, which eventually became the standard mode for making consumer goods from cigarettes to automobiles to telephones, radios, televisions, and computers. (pp. 261, 511)

matrilineal A system of family organization in which social identity and property descend through the female line. Children are raised in their mother's household, which is headed by her brother (their uncle), who assumes many of the responsibilities assigned to a biological father in a patrilineal society. (p. 11)

mechanic A nineteenth-century term for a skilled craftsman who built, repaired, and improved machinery and machine tools for industry. Mechanics developed a professional identity and established institutes to spread their skills and knowledge. (p. 262)

mercantilism A set of governmental policies designed to enhance national wealth by active intervention into the economy. In different forms, mercantilism was practiced by Elizabeth I in the 1570s, by Parliament in the Navigation Acts (1650–1773), by American state governments (1790–1840), and by the Japanese government after World War II. In colonial America, the policies encouraged the production of agricultural goods and raw materials for export to Britain, where they were sold to other European nations or made into finished goods. (p. 32)

mestizo A person of mixed racial ancestry; specifically, the child of a European and a Native American. (p. 27)

middle class A term first used in England around 1800 to describe traders and propertied townspeople. In the early-nineteenth-century United States, it referred both to an economic group (of prosperous farmers, artisans, and traders) and to a cultural outlook (of self-discipline, hard work, and social mobility). In the twentieth century, the term embraced white-collar (office) workers, college-educated people, and propertied consumers. (p. 231)

Middle Passage The brutal sea voyage from Africa to the Americas in the eighteenth and nineteenth centuries that took the lives of nearly a million enslaved Africans. (p. 78)

military-industrial complex A term first used by President Eisenhower in his farewell address in 1961, it refers to the interlinkage of the military and the defense industry that emerged with the arms buildup of the Cold War. Eisenhower particularly warned against the "unwarranted influence" that the military-industrial complex might exert on public policy. (p. 792)

Minutemen Colonial militiamen who stood ready to mobilize on short notice during the imperial crisis of the 1770s. These volunteers formed the core of the citizens' army that met British troops at Lexington and Concord in April 1775. (p. 153)

muckrakers Journalists in the early twentieth century whose stock-in-trade was exposure of the corruption of big business and government. Theodore Roosevelt gave them the name as a term of reproach. The term comes from a character in *Pilgrim's Progress*, a religious allegory by John Bunyan. (p. 583)

national debt The financial obligations of the U.S. government for money borrowed from its citizens and foreign investors. Alexander Hamilton wanted wealthy Americans to invest in the national debt so that they would support the new national government. In recent decades, that same logic has led the American government to encourage crucial foreign nations — Saudi Arabia and Japan, for example — to invest billions in the U.S. national debt. (p. 195)

nationalize, nationalization Government seizure and ownership of a business or natural resource. In the 1890s, the Populist Party demanded nationalization of American railroads; in the 1950s, the seizure by Cuba of sugar plantations and gambling casinos owned by American citizens sparked a long-lasting diplomatic conflict. (p. 573)

national self-determination This concept, derived from European history, holds that language groups have the right to form sovereign states. A central component of Woodrow Wilson's Fourteen Points, it challenged the multinational empires of pre-1914 Europe (Ottoman, Austro-Hungarian, German, and Russian) and the colonial empires of Germany, France, and Britain. The right of national self-determination continues to be invoked by ethnic groups without independent states, such as the Basques in Spain, the Kurds in Turkey and Iraq, and the Palestinians in the Middle East. (p. 660)

nativist, nativism Antiforeign sentiment in the United States that fueled drives against the immigration of Irish and Germans in the 1840s and 1850s, the Chinese and Japanese in the 1880s and 1890s, migrants from eastern and southern Europe in the 1910s and 1920s, and Mexicans in the 1990s and 2000s. Nativism prompted the Chinese Exclusion Act of 1882, the Immigration Restriction Act of 1924, and the internment of Japanese Americans during World War II. (p. 685)

New Right A conservative political movement that began in the 1960s, with the Republican presidential campaign of Barry Goldwater, and assisted the election of Ronald Reagan in 1980. New Right activists generally support unilateral action in foreign affairs and governmental policies to limit abortions, same-sex relationships, and affirmative action. (p. 886)

nullification The constitutional argument that a state could void a law passed by Congress. The concept had its origins in the Kentucky and Virginia resolutions of 1798, which were drafted by Thomas Jefferson and James Madison, and was fully developed in John C. Calhoun's *South Carolina Exposition and Protest* (1828) and in the Ordinance of Nullification (1832). (p. 300)

oligopoly In economics, the situation in which a small number of large-scale companies dominates and sets prices in a given industry (steel making, automobile manufacturing). (p. 500)

outwork A system of manufacturing, also known as *putting out*, that was used extensively in the English woolen industry in the sixteenth and seventeenth centuries. Merchants bought wool and then hired landless peasants who lived in small cottages to spin and weave it into cloth, which the merchants would sell in English and foreign markets. (p. 31)

pagan A person whose spiritual beliefs center on the natural world. Pagans do not worship a supernatural God; instead, they pay homage to spirits and spiritual forces that dwell in the natural world. (p. 16)

party caucus A meeting held by a political party to choose candidates, make policies, and enforce party discipline. (p. 292)

patronage The power of elected officials to grant government jobs and favors to their supporters; also the jobs and favors themselves. Beginning around 1820, politicians systematically used — and abused — patronage to create and maintain strong party loyalties. After 1870, political reformers gradually introduced merit-based civil service systems in state and federal governments to reduce patronage abuses, but they have continued to the present and now cost taxpayers billions of dollars. (pp. 292, 553)

peasant The traditional term for a farm worker in Europe. Some peasants owned land, but many leased or rented small plots from landlords. In some regions, peasants lived in communities with strong collective institutions. (p. 14)

peonage (debt peonage) As cotton prices declined during the 1870s, many sharecroppers fell into permanent debt. Merchants often conspired with landowners to make the debt a pretext for forced labor, or peonage. (p. 455)

personal-liberty laws Laws enacted in many northern states to protect free blacks and fugitive slaves from southern slave catchers. Early laws required a formal hearing before a local court. When the Supreme Court declared these kinds of provisions unconstitutional in *Prigg v. Pennsylvania* (1842), new laws prohibited state officials from helping slave catchers. (p. 394)

pocket veto Presidential way to kill a piece of legislation without issuing a formal veto. When congressional Republicans passed the Wade-Davis Bill in 1864, a harsher alternative to President Lincoln's restoration plan, Lincoln used this method to kill it by simply not signing the bill and letting it expire after Congress adjourned. (p. 438)

political machine A highly organized group, often led by a "boss," that controls the policies of a political party. Political reformers believed that the machines were antidemocratic, and Robert La Follette and other Progressive-era leaders made them a special target. These reformers denied the machines their traditional patronage by creating a merit-based civil service, and they limited party bosses' power to nominate candidates by the primary election system. (pp. 292, 540)

poll taxes Taxes paid for the privilege of voting, used in the South beginning during Reconstruction to disfranchise freedmen. Nationally, the northern states used poll taxes to keep immigrants and others deemed unworthy from voting. (p. 449)

polygamy The practice of marriage of a man to multiple wives. Polygamy was customary among many African peoples and was practiced by many Mormons in the United States, particularly between 1840 and 1890. (p. 38)

popular sovereignty The democratic republican principle that ultimate power resides in the hands of a broad electorate. Popular sovereignty dictates that voters directly or indirectly (through their elected representatives) approve the laws that govern them and ratify the constitutions of their state and national governments. During the 1850s, the U.S. Congress applied the principle to western lands by enacting legislation giving territorial residents the authority to determine the status of slavery. (p. 158)

pragmatism A philosophical doctrine developed primarily by William James that denied the existence of absolute truths and argued that ideas should be judged by their practical consequences. Problem solving, not ultimate ends, was the proper concern of philosophy, in James's view. Pragmatism provided a key intellectual foundation for progressivism. (p. 583)

praying town A Native American settlement in seventeenth-century New England supervised by a Puritan minister. Puritans used these settlements to encourage Indians to adopt English culture and Protestant Christianity. (p. 59)

predestination The idea that God chooses certain people for salvation even before they are born. Sixteenth-century theologian John Calvin was the main proponent of this doctrine, which was a fundamental tenet of Puritan theology. (p. 29)

preservation, preservationist Early-twentieth-century activists, such as John Muir, who fought to protect the natural environment from commercial exploitation, particularly in the American West. (p. 598)

Price Revolution The impact of the high rate of inflation in Europe in the mid-1500s. American gold and silver, brought to Europe by Spain, doubled the money supply at a time when the population also was increasing. The increase in prices caused profound social changes, reducing the political power of the aristocracy and leaving many peasant families on the brink of poverty, thus setting the stage for substantial migration to America. (p. 32)

primogeniture The practice of passing family land, by will or custom, to the eldest son. Republican-minded Americans of the Revolutionary era disapproved of this practice but did not prohibit it. But most states enacted laws specifying that if a father dies without a will, all his children must receive an equal portion of his estate. (p. 16)

probate inventory An accounting of a person's property at the time of death, as recorded by court-appointed officials. Probate inventories provide detailed lists of personal property, household items, and financial assets and debts and tell historians a good deal about people's lives. (p. 88)

proprietors Groups of settlers who received land grants from the General Courts of Massachusetts Bay and Connecticut, mostly between 1630 and 1720. The proprietors distributed the land among themselves, usually on the basis of social status and family need. This system encouraged widespread ownership of land in New England. (p. 57)

protective tariff A tax on imports levied to protect domestic products from foreign competition. Protective tariffs were particularly controversial in the 1830s and again between 1880 and 1914, when protectionist Whigs or Republicans opposed free-trade Democrats over this issue. Recently, battles over NAFTA (the North American Free Trade Agreement) and globalization have revived this controversy, with free-trade Republicans opposed by protectionist Democrats. (p. 196)

pueblos Multistory and multiroom stone or mud-brick buildings that were built as residences by native peoples in the southwestern United States. (p. 10)

pump priming Term first used during the Great Depression of the 1930s to describe the practice of using increased government spending to stimulate a broad economic recovery. (p. 694)

Radical Whigs An eighteenth-century faction in Parliament that protested corruption in government, the growing cost of the British empire, and the rise of a wealthy class of government-related financiers. (p. 89)

reconquista The campaign by Spanish Catholics to drive North African Moors (Muslim Arabs) from the Spanish lands. After a centuries-long effort, the Spaniards defeated the Moors at Granada in 1492 and secured control of all of Spain. (p. 22)

republic A state without a monarch that has a representative system of government. In European city-states, elected representatives came from an elite of aristocrats and merchants; in the American states, they represented "the people," defined initially as property-owning male citizens and gradually expanded to include most adult inhabitants. (p. 17)

republicanism A political ideology that repudiates rule by kings and princes and celebrates a representative system of government. Historically, most republics limited active political participation to men of property. After 1800, the United States became a democratic republic, with widespread participation by white adult men of all social classes and, after 1920, by adult women. (p. 174)

republican motherhood The idea that the primary political role of American women was to instill a sense of patriotic duty and republican virtue in their children and mold the children into exemplary republican citizens. (p. 236)

residual powers The Constitutional principle that powers not explicitly granted to the federal government belong to the states. (p. 557)

restrictive covenants Clauses in real estate transactions intended to prevent the sale or rental of properties to classes of the population considered "undesirable," such as African Americans, Jews, or Asians. The Supreme Court decision in *Shelley v. Kraemer* (1948) declared such clauses unenforceable, but they continued to be instituted informally in spite of the ruling. (p. 802)

revenue tariff A tax on imports levied to pay the expenses of the national government. See *protective tariff.* (p. 196)

revival, revivalism An outburst of religious enthusiasm, often prompted by the preaching of a charismatic Baptist or Methodist minister. The Great Awakening of the 1740s was significant, but it was the revival that swept across the United States between the 1790s and 1850s that imparted a deep religiosity to the culture. Subsequent revivals in the 1880s and 1890s and in the late twentieth century helped to maintain a strong Evangelical Protestant culture in America. (p. 110)

rotten boroughs Tiny electoral districts for Parliament whose voters were controlled by wealthy aristocrats or merchants. In the 1760s, Radical Whig John Wilkes called for the elimination of rotten boroughs to make Parliament more representative of the property-owning classes. (p. 135)

rural ideal Concept advanced by the landscape architect Andrew Jackson Downing urging the benefits of rural life, it was especially influential among middle-class Americans making their livings in cities but attracted to the suburbs. (p. 528)

salutary neglect A term often used to describe British colonial policy during the reigns of George I (r. 1714–1727) and George II (r. 1727–1760). By relaxing their supervision of internal colonial affairs, royal bureaucrats inadvertently assisted in the rise of self-government in North America. (p. 89)

scalawags Southern whites who joined the Republicans during Reconstruction and were ridiculed by ex-Confederates as worthless traitors. They included ex-Whigs and yeomen farmers who had not supported the Confederacy and who believed that an alliance with the Republicans was the best way to attract northern capital and rebuild the South. (p. 450)

scientific management A system of organizing work, developed by Frederick W. Taylor in the late nineteenth century, designed to get the maximum output from the individual worker and reduce the cost of production, using methods such as the time-and-motion study to determine how factory work should be organized. The system was never applied in its totality in any industry, but it contributed to the rise of the "efficiency expert" and the field of industrial psychology. (p. 512)

secondary labor boycott A technique used by unions during a strike in which pressure is applied on a second party to bring pressure on the primary target and force it to accept demands. A secondary labor boycott was used in the Great Pullman Boycott of 1894 and failed when the government intervened. (p. 517)

secret ballot Before 1890, most Americans voted in "public." That is, voters either announced their vote to a clerk or handed in a ballot that had been printed by—and so was recognizable as the work of—a political party. Voting in "private" or in "secret" was first used on a wide scale in Australia. When the practice was adopted in the United States around 1890, it was known as the "Australian ballot." (p. 364)

self-made man A nineteenth-century ideal; an ideology that celebrated men who rose to wealth or social prominence from humble origins through self-discipline, hard work, and temperate habits. (pp. 280, 696)

sentimentalism A late-eighteenth-century European cultural movement that emphasized emotions. Sentimentalism came to the United States around 1800 and influenced literature (romantic novels), theater (melodrama), and religion (revivalism). It also encouraged marriages based on love rather than on financial considerations. (p. 233)

separate spheres Term used by contemporaries and historians to describe the nineteenth-century view that men and women have different gender-defined characteristics and, consequently, that the sexes should inhabit different social worlds. Men should control the public sphere of politics and economics, while women should manage the private sphere of home and family. In mid-nineteenth-century America, this cultural understanding was both sharply defined and hotly contested. (pp. 345, 563)

separation of powers The constitutional arrangement that gives the three governmental branches—executive, legislative, and judicial—independent standing, thereby diffusing the federal government's overall power and reducing the chances that it might turn tyrannical and threaten the liberties of the people. (p. 438)

severalty Individual ownership of land. The term applied to the Dawes Severalty Act of 1890, which undertook to end tribal ownership and grant Indians deeds to individual holdings, i.e., severalty. (p. 480)

sharecropping The labor system by which freedmen agreed to exchange a portion of their harvested crops with the landowner for use of the land, a house, and tools. A compromise between freedmen and white landowners, this system developed in the cash-strapped South because the freedmen wanted to work their own land but lacked the money to buy it, while white landowners needed agricultural laborers but did not have money to pay wages. (p. 453)

Social Darwinism The application of Charles Darwin's biological theory of evolution by natural selection to the development of society, this late-nineteenth-century principle encouraged the notion that societies progress as a result of competition and the "survival of the fittest." Intervention by the state in this process was thought to be counterproductive because it impeded healthy progress. Social Darwinists justified the increasing inequality of late-nineteenth-century industrial American society as natural. (p. 557)

socialism A theory of social and economic organization based on the common ownership of goods. Utopian socialists of the early nineteenth century envisioned small planned communities; later socialists campaigned for state ownership of railroads and large industries. (p. 326)

Sons of Liberty Colonists—primarily middling merchants and artisans—who banded together to protest the Stamp Act and other imperial reforms of the 1760s. The Sons first appeared in Boston in 1765 and were soon imitated in other colonies. (p. 138)

specie Gold and silver coin, the most trusted currency in the preindustrial world. (p. 69)

spoils system The widespread award of public jobs to political supporters after an electoral victory. In 1829, Andrew Jackson instituted the system on the national level, arguing that the rotation of officeholders was preferable to a permanent group of bureaucrats. The spoils system became a central—and corrupting—element in American political life. (pp. 292, 553)

states' rights An interpretation of the Constitution that exalts the sovereignty of the states and circumscribes the authority of the national government. Expressed first by Antifederalists in the debate over the Constitution and then in the Virginia and Kentucky resolutions of 1798, the ideology of states' rights informed white southerners' resistance to the high tariffs in the 1820s and 1830s, to legislation limiting the spread of slavery, and to attempts by the national government in the mid-twentieth century to end Jim Crow practices and promote racial equality. (p. 201)

subtreasury system A scheme deriving from the Texas Exchange, a cooperative in the 1880s, through which cotton farmers received cheap loans and marketed their crops. When the Texas Exchange failed in 1891, Populists proposed that the federal government take over these functions on a national basis through a "subtreasury," which would have had the added benefit of increasing the stock of money in the country and thus pushing up prices. (p. 571)

suburbanization The movement of the upper and middle classes beyond city limits to less crowded areas with larger homes that are connected to city centers by streetcar or subway lines. By 1910, 25 percent of the population lived in these new communities. The 1990 census revealed that the majority of Americans lived in the suburbs. (p. 531)

suffrage The right to vote. Classical republican ideology limited suffrage to property owners, who had "a stake in society." Between 1810 and 1860, state constitutions extended the vote to virtually all adult white men and some free black men. Since then, suffrage has expanded toward universality as barriers of race, gender, and age have fallen. In the late nineteenth and early twentieth centuries, women activists on behalf of the vote were known as "suffragists." (pp. 231, 447)

syndicalism A revolutionary movement that, like socialism, believed in the Marxist principle of class struggle, but advocated the organization of society on the basis of industrial unionism. This approach was advocated by the Industrial Workers of the World (IWW) at the start of the twentieth century. (p. 520)

tariff A tax on imports, which has two purposes: raising revenue for the government and protecting domestic products from foreign competition. A hot political issue throughout much of American history, the tariff became particularly controversial in the late nineteenth century as protection-minded Republicans and pro-free-trade Democrats made it the centerpiece of their political campaigns. (p. 553)

temperance movement A long-term effort by various reform groups to encourage individuals and governments to limit the consumption of alcoholic beverages. Leading temperance groups include the American Temperance Society of the 1830s, the Washingtonian Association of the 1840s, the Women's Christian Temperance Union of the late nineteenth century, and Alcoholics Anonymous, which was founded in the 1930s. (p. 284)

Third World This term came into use in the post–World War II era to describe developing nations and former colonies that were not aligned with either the West or the Soviet Union. Geographically, it referred to Asia, Africa, Latin America, and the Middle East. (p. 789)

total war A form of warfare, new to the nineteenth and twentieth centuries, that mobilized all of a society's resources and subjected the lives and property of enemy civilians to attack. Governments now mobilized massive armies of conscripted civilians and destroyed enemy industries and their civilian workers. American examples include Sherman's march through Georgia in the Civil War and the massive American bombing of Dresden, Hamburg, and Tokyo during World War II and of North Vietnam during the Vietnam War. (p. 417)

town meeting A system of local government in New England in which all male heads of households met regularly to elect selectmen, levy local taxes, and regulate markets, roads, and schools. (p. 57)

trade slaves Africans held in bondage who were not considered members of the society and were sold from one African kingdom to another or to foreign merchants. For centuries, Arab merchants carried trade slaves from sub-Saharan Africa to the Mediterranean region; around 1440, Portuguese ship captains joined in this trade. (p. 21)

transcendentalism A nineteenth-century American intellectual movement, inspired by European Romanticism, that posited the existence of an ideal world of mystical knowledge and harmony beyond the world of the senses. As articulated by Ralph Waldo Emerson and Henry David Thoreau, transcendentalism called for the critical examination of society and emphasized individuality, self-reliance, and nonconformity. (p. 320)

trusts A term that was originally applied to a specific form of business organization that enabled participating firms to assign the operation of their properties to a board of trustees but which, by the early twentieth century, was applied more generally to corporate mergers and business combinations that exerted monopoly power over an industry. It was in this latter sense that progressives referred to firms such as United States Steel and Standard Oil as trusts. (p. 596)

union shop The requirement that, after gaining employment, a worker must join a union, as distinct from the closed shop, which requires union membership before gaining employment. (p. 780)

vaudeville A professional stage show composed of singing, dancing, and comedy routines that changed live entertainment from its seedier predecessors such as minstrel shows to family entertainment for the urban masses. Vaudeville became popular in the 1880s and 1890s, the years just before the introduction of movies. (p. 543)

vice-admiralty court A tribunal presided over by a judge, with no jury. The Sugar Act of 1764 required that offenders be tried in a vice-admiralty court rather than in a common-law tribunal, where a jury decides guilt or innocence. This provision of the act provoked protests from merchant-smugglers, who were accustomed to acquittal by sympathetic local juries. (p. 136)

virtual representation The claim made by British politicians that the colonists were virtually (and thus adequately) represented in Parliament by those members who were merchants connected with the American trade and who were absentee sugar planters with estates in the West Indies. (p. 137)

voluntarism The view that citizens should themselves improve their lives rather than rely on the efforts of the state. Especially favored by Samuel Gompers, voluntarism was a key idea within the labor movement but one that it gradually abandoned in the course of the twentieth century. (p. 589)

war of attrition A military strategy of small-scale attacks used, usually by the weaker side, to sap the resources and morale of the stronger army. Examples include the attacks carried out by Patriot militias in the South during the War of Independence and the guerrilla tactics of the Vietcong and North Vietnamese during the Vietnam War. (pp. 172, 837)

welfare capitalism A system of labor relations that stresses management's responsibility for employees' well-being. Originating in the 1920s, welfare capitalism offered such benefits as stock plans, health care, and old-age pensions. Its goal was to maintain a stable workforce and undercut the growth of trade unions. (p. 676)

welfare state A nation that provides for the basic needs of its citizens, such as old-age pensions, unemployment compensation, child-care facilities, education, and health care. Industrialized countries in Europe began to provide such programs around 1900; the New Deal of the 1930s brought them to the United States. In the twenty-first century, aging populations and the emergence of a global economy (the transfer of jobs to low-wage countries) threaten the economic foundation of the European and American welfare systems. (p. 711)

Whigs An English political party that demanded a constitutional (rather than an absolutist) monarchy. The English Whigs rose to power following the Glorious Revolution of 1688 and governed Britain until the eve of the American Revolution. In the 1830s, an American political party headed by Henry Clay and Daniel Webster took the name *Whig* to protest the "monarchical" actions of Andrew Jackson, whom they dubbed "King Andrew I." (p. 308)

white-collar Middle-class professionals who are salaried workers rather than business owners or wage laborers; they first appeared in large numbers during the industrial expansion in the late nineteenth century. Their ranks were composed of lawyers, engineers, and chemists as well as salesmen, accountants, and advertising managers. (p. 503)

yellow-dog contract An agreement by a worker, as a condition of employment, not to join a union. Employers in the late nineteenth century used this along with the blacklist and violent strikebreaking to fight unionization of their workforces. (p. 516)

yellow journalism Term that refers to newspapers that specialize in sensationalistic reporting. The name came from the ink used in Hearst's *New York Journal* to print the first comic strip to appear in color in 1895 and is generally associated with the inflammatory reporting leading up to the Spanish-American War of 1898. (p. 546)

yeoman In England between 1500 and 1800, a farmer who owned enough land to support his family in reasonable comfort. In America, Thomas Jefferson envisioned a nation of yeomen, that is, of politically and financially independent farmers. (p. 14)

Credits

Chapter 2

"Magisterial Justice in Maryland." From John Demos, ed., *Remarkable Providence: Readings in Early American History* (Boston: Northeastern University Press, Copyright © 1972), pp. 135–137. Reprinted with permission of the University Press of New England.

Chapter 3

Alexander Spotswood, "Confronting the House of Burgesses." From R. A. Brock, ed., *The Official Letters of Alexander Spotswood* (Richmond: Virginia Historical Society, 1885). Reprinted with permission of the Virginia Historical Society.

Chapter 7

William Cobbett, "Peter Porcupine Attacks Pro-French Americans." Reprinted from David A. Wilson, ed., *Peter Porcupine in America: Pamphlets on Republicanism and Revolution.* Copyright © 1994 by Cornell University. Reprinted with permission of Cornell University Press.

Chapter 8

Caroline Howard Gilman, "Female Submission in Marriage." From Anya Jabour, ed., *Major Problems in the History of American Families and Children.* Copyright © 2005 Houghton Mifflin Co. Reprinted with permission.

Chapter 9

Ernst Stille, "German Immigrants in the Midwest." From Walter D. Kamphoefner, Wolfgang Helbid, and Ulrike Sommer, eds., *News from the Land of Freedom: German Immigrants Write Home.* Copyright © 1988 by C. H. Beck'sche Verlagsbuchhandlung. English trans. by Susan Carter Vogel, copyright © 1991 Cornell University Press. Reprinted with permission of Cornell University Press.

Chapter 10

Alexis de Tocqueville, "Parties in the United States." From *Democracy in America,* by Alexis de Tocqueville, trans. Henry Reeve. Copyright © 1945 and renewed 1973 by Alfred A. Knopf, a division of Random House, Inc. Used with permission of Alfred A. Knopf, a division of Random House, Inc.

Chapter 11

"The Mystical World of the Shakers." From Noel Rae, ed., *Witnessing America.* Copyright © by Noel Rae and the Stonesong Press LLC. Used with permission of the publisher.

Chapter 12

Figure 12.1: "The Surge in Cotton Production, 1835–1860." Adapted from Figure 25 in *Time on the Cross: The Economics of American Negro Slavery* by Robert William Fogel and Stanley L. Engerman. Copyright © 1974 by Robert William Fogel and Stanley L. Engerman. Used with permission of W. W. Norton & Company, Inc.

Bernhard, Duke of Saxe-Weimar-Eisenach, "The Racial Complexities of Southern Society." From C. J. Jeronimus, ed., *Travels by His Highness Duke Bernhard of Saxe-Weimar-Eisenach Through North America in the Years 1825 and 1826*, trans. William Jeronimus. Copyright © 2001, University Press of America. Used with permission of the publisher.

Mollie Dawson, "Memories of Slavery." From *Bullwhip Days* by James Mellon. Copyright © 1998 by James Mellon. Used by permission of Grove/Atlantic, Inc.

Chapter 13

Axalla John Hoole, "'Bleeding Kansas': A Southern View." From William Stanley Hoole, ed., "A Southerner's View of the Kansas Situation, 1856–1857," from *Kansas Historical Quarterly 3* (1934). Used with permission of the Kansas State Historical Society.

Salomon de Rothschild, "A French Banker Analyzes the Election of 1860 and the Threat of Secession." From Sigmund Diamond, ed. and trans., *A Casual View of America, 1859–1861: The Home Letters of Salomon de Rothschild*. Copyright © 1961 by the Board of Trustees of the Leland Stanford Jr. University, renewed by author 1985. All rights reserved. Used with permission of Stanford University Press, www.sup.org.

Chapter 14

Ernest Duvergier de Hauranne, "German Immigrants and the Civil War Within Missouri." From *A Frenchman in Lincoln's America* by Ernest de Hauranne. Copyright © 1974 R. R. Donnelley & Sons. Reprinted with permission. Lakeside.classic@lakesideclassicbooks.com.

Chapter 15

David Macrae, "The Devastated South." From Allan Nevins, ed., *America Through British Eyes* (Gloucester, MA: Peter Smith Publisher, Inc., 1968). Used with permission of the publisher.

Jourdon Anderson, "Relishing Freedom." From *Looking for America*, Second Edition, Volume 1, by Stanley I. Kutler. Copyright © 1979, 1976 by Stanley I. Kutler. Used with permission of W. W. Norton & Company, Inc.

Index

A note about the index: Names of individuals appear in boldface; biographical dates are included for major historical figures. Letters in parentheses following pages refer to: (*f*) figures, including charts and graphs; (*i*) illustrations, including photographs and artifacts; (*m*) maps; and (*t*) tables.

ARCTIC OCEAN

80°N

Greenland
(Den.)

Alaska

60°N

ICELAND

CANADA

UNITED
KINGDOM

IRELAND

BEL.
FRANCE
SWITZ.
SPAIN

40°N

UNITED STATES

PORTUGAL

Azores
(Port.)

ALGERIA

ATLANTIC
OCEAN

MOROCCO

Canary Is.
(Sp.)

Western Sahara
(Mor.)

BAHAMAS

20°N

DOMINICAN
HAITI REPUBLIC

MEXICO

CUBA

Puerto Rico (U.S.)

ST. KITTS AND NEVIS

MAURITANIA

JAMAICA

ANTIGUA AND BARBUDA

CAPE
VERDE

MALI

Hawaii

BELIZE

Guadeloupe (Fr.)

DOMINICA

SENEGAL

GUATEMALA

HONDURAS

Martinique (Fr.)

ST. VINCENT AND THE GRENADINES

GAMBIA

EL SALVADOR

NICARAGUA

ST. LUCIA

BARBADOS

GUINEA-BISSAU

COSTA RICA

GRENADA

TRINIDAD AND TOBAGO

GUINEA

PANAMA

VENEZUELA

GUYANA

SIERRA LEONE

SURINAME

LIBERIA

COLOMBIA

French Guiana (Fr.)

CÔTE D'IVOIRE

0°

Equator

Galápagos Is.
(Ec.)

ECUADOR

BURKINA FASO

GHANA

PACIFIC OCEAN

SAMOA

PERU

BRAZIL

N

W   E

S

TONGA

20°S

BOLIVIA

Easter I.
(Chile)

PARAGUAY

CHILE

ATLANTIC
OCEAN

0   1,500   3,000 miles

URUGUAY

0   1,500   3,000 kilometers

ARGENTINA

40°S

Falkland Is.
(U.K.)

60°S

80°S

160°W   140°W   120°W   100°W   80°W   60°W   40°W   20°W

ARCTIC OCEAN

NORWAY
SWEDEN
FINLAND
ESTONIA
LATVIA
LITHUANIA
DEN.
NETH.
GER. POLAND
LUX.
CZ. REP.
AUS. SLK.
SLN.HUNG.
ITALY   ROMANIA
MONT.   SER.
KOS.   BULGARIA
ALB.   MAC.
—MALTA   GREECE
TUNISIA

RUSSIAN FEDERATION

BELARUS
UKRAINE
MOLDOVA

KAZAKHSTAN

MONGOLIA

UZBEKISTAN
KYRGYZSTAN
TURKMENISTAN
TAJIKISTAN

GEORGIA
ARMENIA
TURKEY
AZERBAIJAN

AFGHANISTAN

CHINA

N. KOREA
S. KOREA

JAPAN

CYPRUS   SYRIA LEBANON
ISRAEL   IRAQ
JORDAN   IRAN
KUWAIT
BAHRAIN
SAUDI ARABIA
QATAR
UNITED ARAB
EMIRATES

PAKISTAN

NEPAL

BHUTAN

BANGLADESH

MYANMAR
(BURMA)

TAIWAN

PACIFIC OCEAN

LIBYA   EGYPT

OMAN

INDIA

VIETNAM
LAOS

THAILAND
CAMBODIA

PHILIPPINES

Mariana Is.
(U.S.)

Guam
(U.S.)

MARSHALL
IS.

NIGER

CHAD   SUDAN
ERITREA YEMEN
DJIBOUTI

MALDIVES

SRI
LANKA

BRUNEI

PALAU

FEDERATED STATES
OF MICRONESIA

NAURU

KIRIBATI

NIGERIA
BENIN
TOGO   CENTRAL
         AFRICAN REP.
CAMEROON
EQ.
GUINEA
GABON

ETHIOPIA

SOMALIA

MALAYSIA

TUVALU

SINGAPORE

SOLOMON
IS.

RWANDA   UGANDA
         KENYA
DEM. REP. OF
THE CONGO
SÃO TOME BURUNDI TANZANIA
& PRÍNCIPE

COMOROS
SEYCHELLES

INDIAN OCEAN

INDONESIA

PAPUA
NEW
GUINEA

VANUATU

FIJI

ANGOLA

ZAMBIA   MALAWI

EAST TIMOR

New Caledonia
(Fr.)

NAMIBIA   ZIMBABWE
BOTSWANA

MADAGASCAR

MAURITIUS

AUSTRALIA

NEW
ZEALAND

SOUTH
AFRICA
LESOTHO

MOZAMBIQUE
SWAZILAND

Tasmania
(Aust.)

ABBREVIATIONS	
ALB.	ALBANIA
AUS.	AUSTRIA
BEL.	BELGIUM
B.H.	BOSNIA AND HERZEGOVINA
CR.	CROATIA
CZ. REP.	CZECH REPUBLIC
DEN.	DENMARK
GER.	GERMANY
HUNG.	HUNGARY
KOS.	KOSOVO
LUX.	LUXEMBOURG
MAC.	MACEDONIA
MONT.	MONTENEGRO
NETH.	NETHERLANDS
SER.	SERBIA
SLK.	SLOVAKIA
SLN.	SLOVENIA
SWITZ.	SWITZERLAND

ANTARCTICA

20°E   40°E   60°E   80°E   100°E   120°E   140°E   160°E

Get customized feedback with the Online Study Guide.

The popular Online Study Guide for *America: A Concise History* is a free, personalized learning tool designed to help students master themes, concepts, and information in the text.

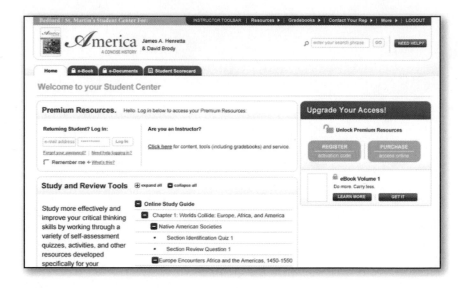

- **Diagnostic Quizzes** enable students to determine where they need more help.

- **Chapter Summaries** provide a useful review of major concepts.

- **Defining Terms** activities allow students to review key terms and test themselves with an interactive flashcard exercise.

- **Visual Activities** facilitate analysis of visual evidence by providing an image and a series of in-depth questions.

- **Map Activities** improve geographic literacy through drag-and-drop exercises and questions.

- **Timeline Activities** promote mastery of critical events through an interactive chronology.

- A **Quiz Gradebook** lets instructors easily monitor students' progress.

Available at **bedfordstmartins/henrettaconcise**.